STRATEGIES FOR TEACHING LEARNERS WITH SPECIAL NEEDS

Fourth Edition

Edward A. Polloway
Lynchburg College

James R. Patton
University of Hawaii

James S. Payne
University of Mississippi

Ruth Ann Payne
Department of Rehabilitation Services, Oxford, Mississippi

Merrill Publishing Company
A Bell & Howell Information Company
Columbus Toronto London Melbourne

Cover Art: Design by Cathy Watterson; computer-generated art by ICOM, Inc., Columbus, Ohio

Published by
Merrill Publishing Company
A Bell & Howell Information Company
Columbus, Ohio 43216

This book was set in Korinna.

Administrative Editor: Vicki Knight
Production Coordinator: Constantina Geldis
Art Coordinator: Vincent A. Smith
Cover Designer: Brian Deep

This book was previously published under the title *Strategies for Teaching Retarded and Special Needs Learners.*

Photo credits: pp. 1, 95, 125, 167, and 255 by Gale Zucker; pp. 3 and 13 by Andy Brunk/Merrill Publishing; p. 37 by Celia Drake; pp. 39, 287, 361, and 411 by Lloyd Lemmerman/Merrill Publishing; p. 61 by Paul Conklin; pp. 147, 207, and 463 by Bruce Johnson/Merrill Publishing; and p. 185 by Kevin Fitzsimons.

Library of Congress Catalog Card Number: 88-61554
International Standard Book Number: 0-675-20994-3
Printed in the United States of America
1 2 3 4 5 6 7 8 9—92 91 90 89

We dedicate Strategies for Teaching Learners with Special Needs *to James E. Smith, Jr., our friend and colleague. Our lives are all much richer for having known Smitty. His influence on the lives of countless professionals and persons with handicaps continues.*

PREFACE

Revising a textbook always represents a challenge of balancing the old with the new, retaining the positive features of earlier editions while incorporating the burgeoning new information within the profession. As we have approached the fourth edition of this text, we have been particularly committed to changes that reflect the realities of special education in the late 1980s and 1990s.

Our title, *Strategies for Teaching Learners with Special Needs,* reflects the more generic focus adopted in the third and fourth editions of the text. This broadened scope reflects the idea that appropriate teaching methods are rarely category-specific but primarily represent good teaching. Many individuals who in the past were placed in classes designated for the mentally retarded, for example, may now be identified as slow learners or more specifically labeled as learning disabled or emotionally and behaviorally disordered. As the title of the book acknowledges, methods that are effective for such students are selected from the broad domain of effective instructional practices.

Although our text is designed for the realities of cross-categorical programs, we are nevertheless committed in our belief that learners with handicaps need a comprehensive curriculum. Therefore, the discussion of curricular design, the clarifications within content chapters, and the further attention to transitional and career concerns emphasize that there are significant differences among subgroups of special students that must be reflected in programming.

This fourth edition is intended to provide teachers with a useful resource for specialized instruction in the 1990s, whether it is provided in self-contained settings, regular classes, or resource programs. The text is a major revision of previous editions; but, like its predecessors, it reflects our commitment to equipping educators with appropriate and practical methods for teaching. Our assumption is that learning can be considered a direct result of the quality of instruction. Effective education must be based on a systematic program that has been organized and structured to maximize the progress of individual students. The goal of the book is thus to present a selection of proven approaches to foster educational success.

Numerous major changes have been made in this edition. New chapters include consideration of study skills and consultation. Previous discussions on the arrangement of the temporal and physical environment have been consolidated within one chapter. Attention to the relationship between teaching and learning, previously spread over several chapters, has been extended and consolidated within Chapter 2; it is accompanied by a review of key learning characteristics of students with special needs. The increasing influence of technology on teaching is reflected in the thoroughly revised chapter on microcomputers. Our increased awareness of teachers' responsibilities beyond the core curriculum of reading, writing, and arithmetic has prompted significantly more attention to science, social studies, arts, music, and creative dramatics. We have broadened our focus on vocational preparation to include career development and the acquisition of life skills as well as the transitional process. Finally, all chapters have been updated to reflect current research, recent curricular developments, and additional suggestions for teaching activities for children and adolescents with handicaps.

As we have tried to integrate the old and the new, we have continued to be inspired by the memory of James E. Smith, Jr., to whom the book is dedicated. Smitty was an individual who enriched the lives of all who knew him. Those who count themselves among his friends know that when he died, they lost a significant piece of themselves. We hope that, through this text, we can help in a small way to communicate Smitty's commitment to students who are handicapped.

Along with the text revisions has come an increased need to acknowledge the support of colleagues. The assistance of James Tawney, Lisa Takemoto, Monica Ondrusko, Sandra L. Bailey, Eric Jones, Annette Shuck, W. N. Creekmore, Pat Cegelka, Reuben Altman, John Langone, Charles Kokaska, Donna Krick, Florence Harrison, Sharon Sams, Mike Boryan, Kathy Dowdy, Ann Archambeault, Paula Mills, and Linda Wilberger continues to enhance this fourth edition, as it did the first three editions. The additional help of Ken West and Fred Conner has been much appreciated. Material written by Ginger Blalock (Chapter 6), Ted Hasselbring and Laura Goin (Chapter 7), Dawn Libby Clary and Sherry Edwards (Chapter 9), Rosel Schewel (Chapter 10), and John Hoover (Chapter 15) represents a major contribution to this edition. We also acknowledge the continuing support of Vicki Knight, our administrative editor, and Connie Geldis, our production editor at Merrill. In addition, we would be remiss if we failed to thank Mary Benis, our copyeditor and "fifth author," for her commitment and diligence in making this a far better volume. Special thanks go also to reviewers Mary Lynne Calhoun, University of North Carolina; Flora Foltz, Illinois State University; Amelia Blyden, Trenton State College; Walter Cegelka, University of Missouri at St. Louis; and William E. Morrison, Stephen F. Austin State University, all of whom provided substantial guidance in framing the final product. Finally, we would like to thank Betty Shelton, Phyllis Lane, Martha Averett, Kathy Byers, Cathy Webb, Ginger Tindall, Gayle Tsukada, Tammy Kaneshiro, Sheryl Nakashima, and Lynda Murakami for their assistance in making our disjointed notes appear as readable manuscript.

Edward A. Polloway
James R. Patton
James S. Payne
Ruth Ann Payne

CONTENTS

PART ONE
TEACHING LEARNERS
WITH SPECIAL NEEDS

1
Teaching Learners with Special Needs

Few careers can promise the opportunities for service to others and for personal growth that teaching, in general, and special education, in particular, afford. Teaching can bring rewards and personal fulfillment to confident, well-trained, and organized teachers. Students learning from these teachers can develop the ability to apply what they have learned to new challenges of life.

As the title implies, *Strategies for Teaching Learners with Special Needs* provides strategies and methods to teach students with educational difficulties. The book emphasizes practical, relevant teaching approaches derived from learning theory, research, and experience. The straightforward teaching approaches and suggestions presented are intended to enable beginning teachers to achieve initial classroom success and to provide experienced teachers with an opportunity to extend and refine their repertoire of skills.

The primary focus of this text is on strategies for teaching students who have been identified as mildly or moderately handicapped. Included within this generic category are subgroups of pupils who may have been categorized in a variety of ways, such as mentally retarded, learning disabled, educationally handicapped, emotionally disturbed, or behaviorally disordered. However, these labels or conditions dictate little about the adoption of a particular curriculum or the use of specific teaching strategies. Rather they indicate primarily that students so classified have had difficulty learning through traditional means or within traditionally structured environments and thus are likely to require more directive, intensive, and highly individualized instruction to reach their learning potential. The book's title, therefore, reflects the equivalent merit of the strategies highlighted for individuals with a variety of learning problems, regardless of whether they have been labeled as handicapped (e.g., learning disabled) or have been merely set apart informally from others in the classroom (e.g., slow learners). Ultimately, analysis of an individual's learning needs determines the relevance of any instructional strategy.

One overriding concern across categories of exceptionality and programs in special education is especially worthy of discussion at this point. We can no longer allow ourselves to focus on individual children only in terms of their needs at the present time. Rather we must adopt an attitude typified by concurrent concern for students' success in the future. Regardless of the population being served or the setting in which services are being delivered, all teachers must be cognizant of how their programmatic efforts will affect students' transitions into subsequent environments, which should be at the core of educational efforts. Professional attention has been increasingly directed toward certain significant transitions: those from preschool to kindergarten, from elementary to secondary school, and through different stages of adult development.

The specific transition receiving the most attention has been that from school to work. Over the years teachers and researchers have devoted much time and energy to the task of preparing students with handicaps for life after high school (Patton, 1985). However, to date we still find that persons who are handicapped are proportionately underrepresented in the nation's workforce as well as in many education, training, and employment programs. In fact, the employment and training data are shocking. The process of transition is complex, involving the efforts of local school personnel, vocational rehabilitation counselors, postsecondary educators, adult services providers, and various community agency staff. Heretofore, too little cooperation among these important groups has been evident, and too few efforts to systematically study the entire transition process have been attempted. Because we have guaranteed students the right to an appropriate education, we should also assist them in benefiting from it (Patton, 1985).

Given the importance of focusing on both the current and subsequent environments of students, this text has two broad objectives. The first is to direct attention to the necessity of effective teaching methods that will result in the learning of specific skills. Second, the text presents appropriate curricula to ensure that learning proves to be relevant beyond the moment.

This chapter includes a preliminary discussion of the legislation in the United States that provides the framework for the delivery of educational services to students who are handicapped—the Education for All Handicapped Children Act (EAHCA). Although other governmental units both inside and outside the United States are bound by additional or different statutes, the EAHCA is perhaps the most influential civil rights and regulatory legislation of its type ever approved. Following this brief discussion, a consideration of teachers' roles and effective teaching introduces the strategies discussed throughout the text. Finally, the last section of the chapter provides an overview of the book.

EDUCATION FOR ALL HANDICAPPED CHILDREN

It has been well over a decade since the passage of the Education for All Handicapped Children Act (Public Law 94–142). In spite of various political efforts to restrict its interpretation, its influence on special education delivery continues, bolstered by significant amendments that have strengthened and expanded various provisions and have extended coverage to a more broadly defined population. However, governmental policies change, and teachers must continue to monitor special education requirements.

PL 94–142 initially authorized funding to the states to assist in the development, expansion, and improvement of special education programs. The spirit of the law was to ensure the rights of all handicapped children, and access to the funds to address these rights was dependent on adherence to mandated provisions. Among the key provisions were the following:

☐ a free, appropriate public school education for all students
☐ eligibility and placement decisions based on evaluations and input from a student's parents
☐ programming in the least restrictive environment, as determined by the individual needs of each child
☐ an individualized education program geared to a child's needs
☐ periodic review of the educational program's appropriateness, again with parental input

These basic rights and provisions are briefly discussed here. They are elaborated on further as they relate to specific educational practices discussed within various later chapters.

Free, Appropriate Special Education

A free public school education provides the educational services to meet the needs of students with special learning requirements. If school programs cannot meet a child's specific needs, then other agencies must provide necessary services at public expense. The schools must also furnish transportation and related services (e.g., counseling, physical therapy) to ensure an appropriate education.

Consent of Parents

Parental consent must accompany every decision affecting a child who is handicapped. Specifically, parents must consent to the evaluation of a student's educational abilities and needs, the determination of necessary services, and the actual placement of a child in any type of special program. School officials must fully explain to parents in the parents' native language all proposals regarding diagnosis, testing, and placement.

Least Restrictive Environment

Schools must educate children with handicaps—to as great an extent as possible—in regular school settings with nonhandicapped children. The least restrictive environment provides an opportunity for students to attend school in the most normalized, integrated setting possible.

Individual Education Program

An individual education program (IEP) is a written document summarizing a student's learning program. The major purposes of an IEP are (1) to establish learning goals for an individual child, (2) to determine services the school district must provide to meet those learning goals, and (3) to enhance communication among parents and other professionals about a child's program. Both the stated goals and the services to be delivered should depend on an analysis of a student's strengths and weaknesses.

Periodic Review

Although parents may request a review or revision of the IEP at any time, at least once a year officials must meet with parents to review the appropriateness of the student's educational program. Placement, instruc-

tional goals, and objectives should be considered for modification at this time.

1983 Amendments

In 1983 and again in 1986, Congress reaffirmed the federal commitment to the education of all individuals who are handicapped. In 1983 PL 98–199 provided for a new program to stimulate and improve secondary education and transition to postsecondary settings, grant monies for parent training and for the education of preschool children with handicaps, and expansion of model demonstration programs at the postsecondary level.

1986 Amendments

In 1986 PL 99–457 further modified 94–142. Most significantly, it extended the provisions of EAHCA to children as young as 3 years of age (rather than 5) by the school year 1990–91. Other major initiatives included creation of a new voluntary state grant program to meet the needs of infants and toddlers (0–2), an expanded authority on technology, media and materials for children who are handicapped, and a national center on recruitment and employment in special education.

TEACHING AND TEACHERS

A book devoted to instructional methods should first address the nature of teaching and teachers' appropriate role in education. Describing what teaching is and precisely what role special educators should play is no easy task, however. Practicing teachers could provide endless descriptions; teaching is a real joy for some, a job for others, and a nightmare for a few. For most, teaching consists of both good and bad days, and it is everyone's continuing desire to ensure that the former far outnumber the latter.

Effective Teaching

On a fundamental level an **effective teacher** describes someone with requisite skills for teaching who successfully facilitates learning. Teacher effectiveness is basically a function of two dimensions: (1) the amount of learning the child masters and (2) the nature of the teaching behaviors associated with this learning (e.g., time and effort). Brophy and Good (1986) suggest that learning includes socialization, personal/affective development, as well as gains in the typical curricular areas. They also advise using the more neutral term *teacher effects* rather than the more commonly employed *teacher effectiveness.*

Obviously, the more a student learns, the more significant are the teacher effects. If students learn more quickly from one teacher than from another, then the more **efficient** teacher will also logically be judged as the more effective. In other words, the effective teacher not only helps children to learn more but also may accelerate learning. As Skinner (1968) states, "Teaching is the expediting of learning; a person who is taught learns more quickly than one who is not" (p. 5). Thus, teacher effectiveness depends on the amount learned and the time in which learning takes place.

Use of this concept leads to consideration of specific competencies that produce a specifiable degree of effectiveness. Oliva and Henson (1980, p. 117) draw from their work in this area in describing the effective teacher as one who

- [ ] has a broad general education
- [ ] understands the role of the school in our society
- [ ] holds an adequate self-concept
- [ ] understands basic principles of the learning process
- [ ] demonstrates effective techniques of instruction

- [ ] efficiently handles classroom management
- [ ] possesses personal characteristics conducive to classroom success
- [ ] is interested in students as individuals
- [ ] has patience and is willing to repeat
- [ ] displays fairness
- [ ] explains things thoroughly
- [ ] is humorous
- [ ] is open-minded
- [ ] is informal, does not feel superior
- [ ] is knowledgeable and interested in the subject to be taught

Although these characteristics provide a fuller picture of the effective teacher, they do not operationalize the competencies that teachers should possess. Bateman (1971) provides a functional extension of the concept of effectiveness by outlining the "essentials of teaching," based on some of Sowards' (1969) efforts. Bateman identifies five essentials for the effective teacher.

1. selection and formulation of learning objectives stated in measurable, observable terms
2. selection and organization of content consistent with the relevant concerns of the specific curricular areas and appropriate to the needs of the individual learner
3. selection of appropriate instructional methods to achieve the specified learning objectives
4. evaluation of the outcomes of instruction in terms of the learner's acquisition of skills
5. demonstration of the competence and commitment necessary to accept and discharge professional responsibilities

The first four competencies within this list focus attention on the responsibilities of assessment, planning, implementation, and evaluation. They outline the procedures that educators follow to ensure learning. This sense of responsibility for learning adds further specificity to the concept of the effective teacher.

Effectiveness can also be viewed from a more instructional orientation. A general model of effective instruction has been compiled from the literature, highlighting six major domains (Rosenshine & Stevens, 1986).

1. reviewing, checking previous day's work (and reteaching, if necessary)
2. presentation of new content/skills
3. guided student practice (with a check for understanding)
4. feedback and correctives (reteaching, if necessary)
5. independent student practice
6. weekly and monthly reviews

The model implies that effective teachers demonstrate these behaviors.

Such competencies coincide to a large degree with the nature of direct instructional teaching approaches. Carnine (1983) identifies the following aspects of direct instruction that also illustrate the effective teacher's activities: covering a substantial amount of academic material by structuring the day to spend the most time on core curricular areas; using highly structured materials that elicit repeated, accurate responses by students; conducting instruction in small-group settings; providing immediate, relevant feedback to students. Englert's (1983) review reinforces the significance of these attributes and indicates that four teacher behaviors are linked to student achievement: maintaining a high level of content coverage, providing successful practice activities for students, providing feedback to signal the beginning and the conclusion of individual learning trials, and maintaining a high level of student task involvement.

Effective teaching can thus be understood as the acceptance of responsibility for students' learning.[1] Subsequent chapters provide detailed discussions of the specific methodological activities that promote successful learning. One final point, however, concerns the distinction between the good teacher and the effective teacher. Good teaching subsumes effective teaching, but both can be extended to make learning an enjoyable activity. Several examples illustrate this point.

Grobman (1972) cites a classic study of the effects of extreme anxiety produced in junior- and senior-high math students. He suggests that students may have lacked the initiative to apply previously acquired math skills to new situations because the **effective** teacher caused animosity toward the content. Effective procedures for teaching various sports, such as tennis or swimming, have also caused problems. In many cases the well-trained, skillful athlete, once away from the coach's authority, refuses to participate or train because of a cultivated hatred for the sport or, in some cases, the coach. Most of us have at some time experienced aversive teaching from an overzealous or tactless teacher.

Effectiveness is thus important but is not the sole criterion of good teaching. Good teaching must, to a degree, consider a student's attitude toward instruction. There is little evidence to show that a student learns more or possesses greater transfer of learning when the learning is actually enjoyable. Common sense, though, says that if learning situations are distasteful, then teachers are probably doing a disservice to students,

---

[1]In endeavoring to accept responsibility for learning, teachers should keep in mind that they cannot realistically "do it all," that is, succeed in teaching all skills to all students. The authors acknowledge the input of a colleague, Jim Kauffman, in encouraging teachers to be realistic in evaluating their own performances.

the content, and themselves. Professionals must strive to be both **effective** and **affective** teachers.

The Teacher as Professional

The fifth competency identified by Bateman (1971) concerns the special educator's role as a professional. It extends beyond competence in instruction to focus on the broader issue of commitment. Bateman's basic premise is that effective special educators must be more than able to perform specific pedagogical tasks; they must also display a high degree of personal determination to positively influence the education, adjustment, and acceptance of persons with special needs.

Bateman (1971) identifies the teacher behaviors indicative of **professionalism**: having a personal philosophy of education, having a willingness to be an agent of social change, being accountable for services provided, possessing and continuing to develop personal competencies and knowledge base, and caring deeply about all human beings, including oneself. Although each of these aspects of professionalism is important, this book concerns itself particularly with the teacher's role as an agent of change. Teachers play two roles as change agents: providing direct instruction to students and interacting beyond the instructional setting. This latter role provides the opportunity for advocacy critical to the welfare of students who are handicapped. This role may also present special problems to the would-be professional.

Birch and Reynolds (1982) contend that special education has reached the status of only a semiprofession, based on the degree of training required, legal status, and autonomy of control. As Heller (1982) indicates, such status essentially means that, whereas professionals are accountable to their pro-

fession, members of a semiprofession are accountable to their employers. "Without the support of a profession behind them, they have the choice to comply, or to resist and thereby risk dismissal" (p. 85).

Although teachers, particularly beginning teachers, probably should not attempt to upset the structure of education, the role of special educators as change agents requires them to question whether their own and others' actions best benefit students. Accepting minimal levels of professional conduct or acquiescing to administrative practices contrary to students' and parents' basic interests threatens those aspects of special education that have attracted numerous committed individuals.

To illustrate potential dilemmas, Bateman (1982) discusses several situations in which teachers must decide between what is best for the child and what is consistent with local school board policy. She notes the following dilemmas that teachers face: **informing parents** of their legal rights, knowing that such information will give parents a basis for demanding more extensive services for their child; **testifying** at due process hearings when the employer is believed to be at fault; and **instruction in controversial topics,** such as sex education and birth control, which the teacher deems critical to the curriculum but which often conflict with parental concerns or administrative guidelines. Each of these examples presents an ethical dilemma for which no easy solution exists. Assuming a professional role requires the commitment of an advocate as much as it demands competence in instruction.

A Personal Perspective

Evaluating our personal views of teaching has reminded us of certain observations from our own teaching careers. These anecdotal observations suggest valuable lessons worthy of sharing.

Some graduates of teacher-preparation programs feel underprepared or inadequately trained. This feeling can occur to individuals completing excellent training programs staffed by competent faculties; these graduates may simply lack self-confidence or job readiness. Teachers completing their initial year of teaching often comment that the first year on the job has taught them more than an entire training program. Underprepared teachers may learn from other, more experienced teachers; from crash, noncredit, self-initiated courses in curriculum, methods, and management; from trial and error; and from untiring daily perseverance. As different people respond differently to teaching pressures, three identifiable teacher types emerge.

Survivors are so actively preparing and keeping up with the daily necessities that they don't have time to look up from their content and see children, not objects. Until such an awakening occurs, survivors may teach only isolated facts, rather than students. Curriculum may consist primarily of semirelated seatwork designed to keep students busy. The central point to be learned from this period of development is that teachers **must first teach students rather than content.**

Happiness specialists feel sorry for their students, who may be disabled, and want to make them well-adjusted and content. This attitude may lead to an overemphasis on affective, inappropriately operationalized concerns or a focus on arts and crafts, field trips, parties, and other diversions. However, a curriculum exclusively designed to produce happiness may result in discontent and will hinder students' emotional and academic growth. The teacher **must place a priority on practical, beneficial, and functional content.**

Missionaries view themselves as managers, modifiers of behavior, and, in extreme cases, practitioners whose calling is to cure those with problems. Such individuals may be skillful and talented and may set out to teach effectively in the true sense of the word. They do, in fact, teach the students, who **do** learn (in some cases whether they want to or not). The efforts of these teachers may inadvertently be devoid, however, of affective concerns. Occasionally these overdiligent taskmasters unintentionally alienate their students or co-workers and consequently create some unfortunate situations. Teachers **must remember that all individuals have feelings and need to maintain a sense of self-worth.**

The stereotypes outlined here represent possible responses to the realities of instructional demands and pose a significant challenge to professionals. The goal of this book is to provide positive assistance to the teacher in focusing on students, effectively teaching important content, and providing instruction within a supportive environment.

ORGANIZATION OF THE BOOK

This text is divided into three parts that deal with the broad range of methodology and curriculum associated with teaching. Part One, "Teaching Learners with Special Needs," provides an overview of successful educational efforts. Part Two, "Strategies for Teaching," focuses on specific methodologies for managing instructional caseloads. Part Three, "Curriculum," discusses instructional strategies within specific content areas. A brief overview of the chapters is provided here.

Chapter 2 discusses learning in the general sense and ways that teachers can positively influence it. The chapter outlines a model for teaching, specific stages of learning, and effective techniques for each of the stages. Based on the assumption that successful teaching must begin with a recognition of the learner's specific traits, the chapter also includes a discussion of key educational characteristics of learners with special needs.

Chapter 3 begins Part Two and encourages the reader to move beyond knowledge of group characteristics to the specific learning needs of individual students. Principles of educational assessment, setting of objectives, and educational planning are discussed.

The organization and management of a classroom is discussed in chapter 4. Topics include various classroom arrangements, grouping, scheduling, and record keeping.

Chapter 5 includes strategies to facilitate behavior change. General goals, prerequisites to successful management, and specific techniques for promoting appropriate and discouraging inappropriate behavior are discussed.

Concern for the other persons involved in the educative process is the focus of chapter 6. Attention is given to collaborative efforts with paraprofessionals, regular education teachers, and parents.

Chapter 7 focuses on the role of microcomputers in education. Types of computer software programs are highlighted, along with specific suggestions on how technology can make a significant contribution to instruction.

Part Three begins with an overview of curriculum development and program design in chapter 8. Attention to the nature of curriculum precedes an analysis of alternative curricular models and discussion of program design and materials acquisition.

The remaining chapters in the book (9–18) present strategies for instruction within the various curricular areas. Each chapter includes information on assessing learners within a particular curricular area, general and specific approaches to instruction, suggested teaching activities, resources for professional development, and student materials.

This text provides concepts and information with which to develop good teaching techniques. Good teachers are, above all, effective; they direct learning, are confident, constantly evaluate their teaching programs, and make learning enjoyable. Most teachers gain additional skill with experience; in time they accumulate a variety of motivating methods and materials. Although it seems that nothing takes the place of experience, enthusiasm can prove to be a productive substitute. A teacher who remains enthusiastic, continues to work hard, masters good teaching competencies, and develops a broad repertoire of skills, ideas, and instructional activities can begin to achieve teaching excellence.

2
Foundations for Effective Instruction: Instructional Models and Learner Characteristics

In designing appropriate programs for students with special learning needs two essential considerations are the nature of the learning environment and the specific characteristics of the students to be taught. This chapter first presents a general conceptualization of learning, including major tenets on which instruction can be based. A model is then presented that relates these principles of learning to the various components of effective instruction identified in the literature and provides a framework for subsequent discussions of this important topic. The chapter also gives an overview of the more common characteristics of students with mild handicaps. Many of the special needs identified can be addressed through careful consideration of instructional design and implementation.

We believe that an understanding of the basic concepts presented in this chapter is critical for a true appreciation of much of the material presented in the remainder of this book. This chapter encapsulates a large body of literature on learning, effective instruction, and learner characteristics. Further discussion of various topics occurs in other chapters of this text or in other relevant resources that are cited.

A CONCEPTUALIZATION OF LEARNING

Recent educational research has focused on important relationships between teaching and learning, particularly the influence of environment on learning. Learning is extremely complex, yet the teacher can isolate and control many events that occur before and after specific types of learning take place. Unfortunately, many teachers overlook the importance of some of these events.

Antecedents, the conditions or events preceding learning, include environmental arrangements, classroom climate, and scheduling. All such events and conditions can affect learning. Competently applied subsequent or consequent events can also greatly facilitate learning. Examples include the appropriate use of reinforcement and corrective feedback. Teachers must use reinforcement strategies contingent upon demonstration of appropriately predetermined behaviors.

Figure 2.1 illustrates the interrelationship of antecedents, consequences, and learning. Most skillfull teachers can use strategies to maximize learning probability. Proper management of both antecedent conditions and consequent contingencies can enhance instructional effectiveness. Understanding the relationship of teaching to learning is critical to designing learning environments in which students can succeed academically, socially, and emotionally.

Learning has been defined in various ways: "the acquisition of knowledge of skills," "the development of awareness and insight," "observable changes in behavior resulting from interactions with the environment." It is clearly a broad concept and can occur in a variety of settings and conditions, including independent activity, one-to-one tutoring sessions, small groups, classes of 30 or 40 diverse students, or lecture sections of several hundred students. If learn-

FIGURE 2.1
Paradigm of teaching
and learning

ing is the acquisition of knowledge and skills, it can apply to many different special populations and can be evaluated in observable, measurable ways.

Basic Propositions About Learning

Because this book emphasizes teaching that maximizes learning probability, the following premises of learning need more specific explanation. These closely related propositions provide a useful way for teachers to view learning.*

1. *Complex forms of human functioning are learned.* Children are products of their environmental experiences, and the directive teacher can manipulate the school-based dimension of the environment to ensure effective teaching. A teacher who asks, "Why can't Johnny learn?" and answers, "Because there is something wrong with him, that's why," conveys a parsimonious and fatalistic view of Johnny's future. This perspective, implying a predetermination of skill and knowledge attainment, results in a nonproductive situation. In sharp contrast is this view of learned behavior: "Why can't Johnny learn? Because the most appropriate teaching strategies have not been implemented yet; several options are still open to us." A belief in the assumption that behavior is learned can help the teacher establish a plan of action.

2. *Learning is reflected in and inferred from a change in behavior.* As Stephens (1970) notes,

   Something must happen for learning to occur. In other words, without some type of behaviors little learning will take place in schools. Behavior in some form is required of learners, and if teachers are engaged in activities for which they were employed,

teacher behavior should serve to expedite learning. (p. 43)

Most learning behaviors can be observed. A child who can subtract can work a problem in a workbook. One who can spell can recite the letters aloud or write them down. Of course, some aspects of cognition cannot be observed directly. But for teachers to receive feedback on whether they have taught and whether a child has learned, the learner must respond by writing, speaking, gesturing, and so on.

3. *Because behavior is learned, it can be changed.* If antecedent events and consequences result in learned behavior, then antecedent events and consequences can be manipulated to change behavior. Children who learn that being late to school means getting special attention can also learn that being on time may bring special attention. Intervention specialist, change agent, and effective teacher—the terms are closely interrelated.

4. *Acquisition of certain skills depends upon acquisition of other prerequisite skills.* The idea that learning involves the cumulative acquisition of knowledge and skills is neither a new nor a major discovery; it merely represents common sense. For instance, determining a cube's volume ($v = s^3$) requires multiplication skills. Staats (1971, 1975) delineates the concept of cumulative-hierarchical learning.

The hierarchical conception of learning suggests that learning to be human is a long-term affair. It involves a process in which a repertoire of behavioral skills is learned that is the basis for the learning of additional, more advanced behavioral skills. The acquisition of the new skills, in combination with others already acquired, then enables the acquisition of even more advanced behavioral skills. The acquisition of complex repertoires of great skill can only be understood in

*Items 1–3 were adapted from Stephens (1970, p. 43).

terms of the basic skills upon which the advanced learning is founded. (1975, p. 282)

From an instructional perspective the concept that certain skills are prerequisite to other more complex skills suggests sensitivity to skill development. Too much sensitivity, however, can make one reluctant to move students ahead in their programs; thus, balance is required.

5. *Interactions within the learning environment significantly influence learning.* Certain qualitative aspects of the learning environment can have demonstrable effects on students. The pedagogical qualities of the teacher are as essential as a healthy atmosphere or "classroom climate" (Moos, 1976). Although many of us may have learned in repressive, anxiety-provoking environments, this type of setting can devastate some students. The relationship of stress in classroom situations to learning problems is receiving more attention (cf. Elkind, 1983). How children deal with stress in their lives is not fully understood. Nonetheless, educators should realize that it may pose a significant difficulty for some exceptional children.

A MODEL FOR EFFECTIVE INSTRUCTION

Much time is spent discussing the effectiveness of programs, materials, and people. But what does *effective* mean? In an article concerning the effectiveness of special classes for students with educable mental retardation, Stanton and Cassidy (1964) poignantly suggest that "in order to decide effectiveness . . . we must first answer the critical question—effective for what?" (p. 12). Any evaluation must outline clearly recognizable objectives and criteria.

On a general level, responding to the query "What is effective instruction?" is relatively easy. An answer to the question would probably imply that some type of learning takes place. However, reflection makes this question difficult to answer. To what specific skills are we referring: academic, social, or other? Does time come into play here; is rate of learning important? Effective instruction implies the most facile acquisition of a wide range of knowledge or skills in a psychologically healthy, appropriately structured learning environment.

There is a growing amount of information, much of it data-based, indicating what constitutes effective instruction. As depicted graphically in Figure 2.2, the model of effective instruction is predicated on a division of the total instructional process into three major time-related areas: (1) activities, events, and variables that precede teaching; (2) various behaviors performed during actual instruction; and (3) actions that teachers must perform subsequent to instruction.

Precursors to Teaching

Physical Dimension This dimension emphasizes the importance of the physical features of the learning environment. The critical goal is to develop what Lindsley (1964) originally referred to as a "prosthetic environment" (i.e., one specifically designed to facilitate successful student learning). A classroom's structure and organization play a major role in constructing such an environment by creating a setting in which good teaching behaviors can occur and certain unwanted behaviors are prevented. Some of the more noteworthy issues are highlighted here and are addressed in chapter 4 in more detail.

Classroom arrangements can be particularly important. Hewett's (1968) "engineered classroom" exemplifies systematic planning and careful structure. Designating areas of the classroom for certain activities may provide advantages. Some of the most orga-

Precursors to Teaching	Teaching Behaviors	Follow-ups to Teaching

Physical dimension
  Classroom arrangements
  Environmental factors

Psychosocial dimension
  Teacher variables
  Student variables
  Classroom/school variables
  Parent variables
  Peer variables

Management dimension
  Classroom rules and procedures
  Scheduling
  Record-keeping
  Grouping
  Behavior management
  Time management

Instructional dimension
  Selection of curricular orientation
  Interpretation of diagnostic
   information
  Program planning
  Acquisition of materials
  Modification of materials

Effective instructional practices
  Appropriate for learning stage
  Individualized
  Teacher-directed
  Demonstration-guided practice-
   independent practice paradigm
  Clear communication

Active engagement of students

Appropriate utilization of specialized
  techniques
  Equipment
  Materials
  Methodologies

Self-regulated instruction

Consistent curricular-based monitoring
  of progress

Feedback to students
  Motivational
  Informational

Data management and
  decision making
  Data entry
  Data analysis
  Future planning

Grading

Communication to profes-
  sionals and parents

Analysis of instructional
  environment

FIGURE 2.2
Components of effective instruction

nized classrooms are preschool classes containing distinctly identified areas, such as those used for storytime, exploration, and playing with toys.

Anyone who has worked with people in an instructional setting realizes that some seating arrangements are preferable to others. Although knowledge about students' interpersonal skills may not be available until school begins, beneficial arrangements usually become evident early in the school year. Carelessly planned seating arrangements may precipitate disruptive, nonproductive behavior (Axelrod, Hall, & Tams, 1979). Teachers must also take into account the need for sufficient work space.

In folklore, and sometimes in reality, spe-

cial education classes have been located in what was previously a closet or storage room, and special education teachers usually "inherit" the classroom furnishings that everyone else has rejected. Naturally, certain types of furnishings are desirable, and special education teachers should seek them. Students should have individual desks suitable for their right- or left-handedness. In addition, tables of varying shapes and sizes, sufficient chalkboard space, carpeting in the majority of the room, running water, and storage space are important. This is only a partial list; other furnishings may be very useful as well.

Environmental factors (e.g., noise, lighting, and temperature) must also be examined in terms of their possible impact on learning. These factors can significantly inhibit learning either by distracting students or by creating an uncomfortable situation. Although environmental problems and their seemingly straightforward solutions are obvious, teachers sometimes overlook them.

Psychosocial Dimension   The overall feel of a certain school is very much determined by the principal, whereas the psychological atmosphere of the classroom is largely a function of the teacher's disposition and actions. Social dimensions of a classroom are closely related to Moos's (1976) concept of social climate, or the "personality" of the environment. Moos's conceptualization embodies the following important dimensions: relationships (e.g., involvement, affiliation, teacher support); personal development (e.g., task orientation, competition); and systems maintenance and change (e.g., order and organization, rule clarity, teacher control, innovation). These dimensions differentiate one classroom from another.

Similarly, other factors that precede learning can significantly influence the dynamics of classrooms and affect the actual teaching process. Key variables include

☐ *teacher variables:* attitudes (e.g., about learners with special needs), characteristics (e.g., organized versus disorganized), philosophies (e.g., toward teaching, classroom management, curricular content), and expectations

☐ *student variables:* attitudes (e.g., about school, authority figures, classmates), previous educational experiences, self-concept, and perceptions of schooling (Weinstein, 1983)

☐ *classroom/school variables:* attitudes of school personnel toward students, general ambiance of the school, location of classrooms, and student accessibility to school functions, events, and facilities

☐ *parent variables:* attitudes toward education, amount of personal support, and degree of pressure put on children

☐ *peer variables:* values and behaviors and pressures

Even though this list is not exhaustive, it does suggest areas that may deserve more careful analysis. Considering certain dimensions may assist in appropriately matching a student with a particular teacher or classroom setting.

Management Dimension   This particular area may be one of the most neglected aspects in teacher preparation programs. Yet for many teachers it is one of the most critical in terms of effective instruction. First-year teachers consistently cite difficulties in classroom management as their most significant problem. The major issues related to classroom management involve logistical concerns that teachers must address before beginning instruction.

Scheduling can cause many resource teachers headaches. Scheduling students into special settings and structuring their academic and social programs once they arrive require considerable time and effort. Good rapport with regular education teachers and other involved individuals is essential. As Wiederholt, Hammill, and Brown (1983) state, "Careful consideration and deliberate planning are necessary for developing a schedule that will work agreeably in a given school" (p. 92).

The process of keeping track of student performance is implemented subsequent to teaching; however, teachers must develop record-keeping systems prior to instruction. Teachers should locate a system with which they are comfortable and then refine, personally adapt, and practice using it.

The constraints of providing successful learning experiences to multiple students with learning problems usually force special education teachers to teach small groups of students. Grouping students appropriately for instruction before instruction begins requires careful analysis of the students, their skill levels, their needs, and the curricular objectives.

It is also extremely important that rules and procedures be firmly established early in the school year. Effective teachers spend a great deal of time presenting and practicing these rules with their students; the rules must be taught directly. Identifying all situations that require systematic procedures (e.g., sharpening pencils or using the restroom) and developing ways to deal with these situations before students ever arrive in the classroom are beneficial in the long run. This topic is covered more thoroughly in chapter 5.

Knowledge of the basic principles of behavior management enhances the effectiveness of most teachers. Knowing how to increase desired behaviors, decrease unwanted behaviors, and encourage new behaviors that presently do not exist is often useful. Learning about the subtleties of certain techniques and innovative ways to apply them can be rewarding. Much of chapter 5 is devoted to this topic.

We include the topic of time management within this dimension because it is often overlooked. Teachers must learn how to manage their time so that they prepare adequately for teaching but still have time left for themselves, their families, and their friends. Beginning teachers often find themselves swamped by the demands of lesson planning and all of the other duties that befall professional educators. Gerlach and Patton (1988) have identified eight goals of time management.

☐ getting more done in less time
☐ delegating more effectively
☐ successfully planning and prioritizing each day

☐ handling paper work more effectively
☐ reducing interruptions from co-workers
☐ increasing quality time
☐ nipping time wasters in the bud
☐ reducing stress

We suggest that all teachers evaluate their performance in this area. If assistance is needed, various print sources (e.g., Turla & Hawkins, 1983) or workshops on the topic are available.

Instructional Dimension A principal concern in this area is to match students with appropriate curricula, instructional materials, methodologies, and assignments. Teachers must be cognizant of students' strengths and weaknesses and plan programs accordingly. Teacher preparation programs typically stress these competencies; however, successful execution in the classroom depends on the teacher's commitment to implementing them.

Curricular orientation must be determined early; it is important that students' programs be developed in line with their present and future needs. Although various curricular orientations are available, certain options (e.g., remedial) tend to dominate programmatic efforts. These options are examined in chapter 8.

Before designing individual student programs, teachers must accurately interpret the diagnostic information pertaining to their students. This task, often taken for granted, demands training and experience. Teachers need to be able to understand the data obtained from formal measures as well as information collected through curriculum-based techniques. It is important that teachers refrain from focusing solely on the weaknesses and problem areas of their students and consider their strengths and individual interests. Interest inventories can be helpful in detecting topics and activities that students like and are apt to handle successfully.

Teachers must be able to move from testing to planning and ultimately to teaching. Program planning implies that teachers are able to design instructional formats to meet diverse student needs. Such planning requires a knowledge of what individual education programs (IEPS) are and how they should be developed. At the secondary level it must also address transitional needs. These issues are explored in greater depth in chapters 8 and 16.

Acquiring instructional materials is an involved process for most teachers. It requires knowledge of usefulness, appropriateness, and value. In addition, it demands information about ordering and familiarity with a current price list. Clearly, ordering and acquisition of materials must precede instruction by many months. Teachers should try to keep up to date by requesting current brochures and catalogs from various publishers and securing literature from conferences.

Once materials are acquired, it is frequently necessary to modify them for students' particular learning needs. Modification of instructional materials usually involves changing the way they look or the way in which they are used. Sometimes materials must be augmented by other resources. Suggestions along these lines are provided in the chapters devoted to specific subject areas.

Teaching Behaviors

Basically, good teaching is the same whether it occurs in a regular, bilingual, Chapter 1, or special education classroom. The precursors and follow-ups to teaching are the same for any teaching situation. What happens during teaching may differ across various settings, but often there are obvious commonalities as well. As outlined by Tikunoff (1982), "active teaching behaviors" include clear communication of instructional demands, active engagement of students, continual monitoring of progress, and regular provisions for immediate feedback. Learning environments that provide students with much instructional and interactive teacher contact have been found to promote significant learning gains (Brophy, 1979).

This section addresses key considerations in teaching students who display characteristics that may hamper their performance. Many of the topics covered are relevant for all teachers; however, they are extremely important for teachers of students with special needs.

Effective Instructional Practices Even though many factors can be associated with quality instruction, only a few of the most prominent are discussed here. The literature on effective practices regularly identifies certain facets of the teaching process as particularly noteworthy; these are presented in Figure 2.2. An analysis of the learning process also differentiates a distinct sequence of stages. It is important to understand each stage and recognize how the properties of each relate to appropriate teaching practices.

Acquisition learning refers to the initial development of a skill or block of knowledge. Once a skill has been introduced and acquired, it must be developed to a level of **proficiency** or **fluency.** At this point the student becomes more masterful and adept at successfully demonstrating the newly acquired skill and may demonstrate increases in rate or accuracy.

When a student can perform a skill or behavior at an acceptable level of success, the next step is to perform the skill in novel contexts or situations. **Generalization** of the learned skill in response to novel stimuli then becomes the focus of instruction. Research suggests that this stage of learning presents a problem for learners with special needs; therefore, systematic generalization efforts must be programmed into the students' instructional regimens (Deshler, Alley, Warner, & Schumaker, 1981).

The last stage in the learning sequence, **maintenance learning,** involves the ability to retain what has been learned over time. Maintenance implies more than recall and cannot be equated with memory. It takes learners from acquisition/proficiency to solid establishment of a fact, concept, or skill in their response repertoires. Maintenance may best be viewed as a combination of remembering and refining the learned material.

Students progress when their programs and instructional regimens are individualized to accommodate the students' needs. This means that instruction may be provided differently to certain students at various times. Individualized instruction does not imply routine one-to-one instruction, which would be very difficult to accomplish with large numbers of students. Nonetheless, this format may be needed at times.

Teacher-directed instruction implies that the teacher plays an active role during the teaching process. This role varies, depending on the objectives of the lesson or subject area. For instance, spelling instruction typically differs from laboratory activities in science. Blosser (1986) affirms the importance of this component: "Instructional techniques which help students focus on learning (preinstructional strategies, increased structure in the verbal content of materials, use of concrete objects or realism) are effective in promoting student achievement" (p. 169). Good (1983) argues persuasively that teachers engaged in active instruction do make a difference in student learning. Students with mild learning problems often receive attention because they are not dealing well with traditional methods and materials. It is essential that these students be provided with lessons in which teachers pace instruction briskly, question students appropriately, and involve them actively. Directive instruction should always be an integral part of acquisition learning.

In a demonstration–guided practice–independent model, the teacher demonstrates the behavior or skill to be taught. At the next stage the student performs the behavior with guidance. The student eventually practices the behavior without assistance of guidance, still receiving feedback from the teacher as necessary. Because prompts are an integral component of such a system, teachers should understand what they are and how to use them instructionally. Prompts are stimuli that the learner receives along with the task being taught. Prompts occur before the student responds, to increase the chances of a correct response. Prompting generally consists of a variety of techniques (e.g., physical prompts, verbal cues, highlighting or accenting, and modeling).

Becker, Engelmann, and Thomas (1971) suggest several guidelines for increasing prompting effectiveness. All prompts (1) should be implemented after the instructional task stimuli but prior to student response; (2) should not distract attention from the stimuli to be learned; (3) should be the weakest possible (i.e., least noticeable) to facilitate fading; and (4) should be withdrawn gradually through fading procedures until the prompts are no longer required. Some of the most frequently used prompts are described here.

- ☐ *physical prompts:* physical assistance/ guidance given to students (e.g., pencil grips)
- ☐ *verbal prompts:* verbal cues that help students complete a task (e.g., voice inflections)

☐ *gestural prompts:* gestures made to help students (e.g., hand signals to indicate when it is appropriate to respond)

☐ *visual prompts:* cues that students see (e.g., highlighting of materials, or making materials bigger)

Classroom communication needs to be lucid and conceptually understandable. Instruction suffers from the use of complex language, concepts not previously presented to students, or unclear statements. Consequently, teachers should adequately prepare for lessons to be presented to students, identifying illustrative examples beforehand and incorporating both positive and negative examples of a concept being taught (Becker & Carnine, 1981). In addition, teachers should be prepared to alter their original lesson format if necessary. A thorough list of considerations for clear lessons has been developed by Rosenshine and Stevens (1986) and is presented in Table 2.1.

Active Engagement of Students   Much attention has been given to this topic recently. Graden and colleagues (1982) note that researchers have found a strong positive relationship between the amount of time that students are actively engaged in learning and their achievement. The temporal components of a school day are shown in Figure 2.3. Although these elements are self-explanatory, it is important to note the distinc-

---

TABLE 2.1
Aspects of clear presentations

1. Clarity of goals and main points
   a. State the goals or objectives of the presentation.
   b. Focus on one thought (point, direction) at a time.
   c. Avoid digressions.
   d. Avoid ambiguous phrases and pronouns.
2. Step-by-step presentations
   a. Present the material in small steps.
   b. Organize and present the material so that one point is mastered before the next point is given.
   c. Give explicit, step-by-step directions (when possible).
   d. Present an outline when the material is complex.
3. Specific and concrete procedures
   a. Model the skill or process (when appropriate).
   b. Give detailed and redundant explanations for difficult points.
   c. Provide students with concrete and varied examples.
4. Checking for students' understanding
   a. Be sure that students understand one point before proceeding to the next point.
   b. Ask the students questions to monitor their comprehension of what has been presented.
   c. Have students summarize the main points in their own words.
   d. Reteach the parts of the presentation that the students have difficulty comprehending, either by further teacher explanation or by students tutoring other students.

Source. From "Teaching Functions" by B. Rosenshine and R. Stevens. Reprinted with permission of Macmillan Publishing Company from HANDBOOK OF RESEARCH ON TEACHING, 3rd Edition, M. C. Wittrock, Editor. Copyright, © 1985 by American Educational Research Association.

FIGURE 2.3
Breakdown of time spent in learning (From *Academic Engaged Time and Its Relationship to Learning: A Review of the Literature* by J. Graden, M. L. Thurlow, & J. E. Ysseldyke, 1982, Minneapolis: University of Minnesota, Institute for Research on Learning Disabilities. Copyright 1982 by the University of Minnesota. Adapted by permission.)

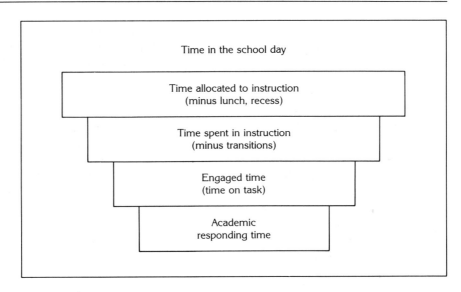

tion between the last two. "Engaged time" implies that a student is paying attention (i.e., on-task), but it differs from "academic responding time," which refers to active behaviors that students perform while attending. In their review of the literature on this topic, Graden and associates report that "engaged time is related positively to achievement, that relatively little absolute time in the school day is spent engaged in academics, and that the percentage of time engaged varies considerably across classrooms and across individual students within classroom" (pp. 22–23).

Mindful of these findings, teachers should strive to maximize the amount of time that students are actively engaged in learning situations. Two factors contribute significantly to the alarming low rates: instructional design and classroom management. Instructional lessons must be designed so that students are required to be actively involved; effective practice is important. Lack of attention to certain aspects of classroom organization is also critical. Las-

ley and Walker (1986) have identified particular areas of concern: starting class on time, managing transitions effectively, developing routines, limiting and controlling classroom interruptions, circulating around the room, and minimizing disruptions.

Appropriate Utilization of Specialized Techniques In addition to the many elements of effective teaching that can be found in all types of classrooms, certain specialized and adaptive strategies find more frequent use in special education settings. Such strategies and techniques can be organized within three broad areas: equipment, materials, and methodologies. Specific suggestions and ideas are found throughout this text; however, a few examples are provided here.

- [ ] *equipment:* microcomputers (e.g., with voice input), tape players
- [ ] *materials:* high interest/low vocabulary programs designed for special populations (e.g., *Me Now*)
- [ ] *methodologies:* mnemonic illustrations, advanced organizers, peer tutoring

Self-Regulated Instruction Ultimately, students should become independent learners, able to monitor their own behavior in ways that assist in maximizing the amount of time engaged in learning. Many students with special needs have significant difficulty in this area, which limits their chances of successful integration into regular education classes where self-regulation is expected. Cohen and deBettencourt (1983) suggest that it is the teacher's responsibility to train students to become independent learners and to structure the classroom environment to help them achieve this goal.

One self-regulatory technique that has received considerable attention is self-monitoring, which teaches students to monitor their on- and off-task behavior. The underlying assumption is that students will pay attention for longer periods of time (engaged time), thus increasing their academic responding time and leading to achievement gains. Evidence shows that this methodology enables students whose primary problem is attention-to-task to attend for longer periods of time. Any resultant gains in achievement remain to be documented. An excellent resource for teaching students how to monitor their own behavior is a manual written for teachers (Hallahan, Lloyd, & Stoller, 1982).

Consistent Curricular-Based Monitoring of Progress Good teachers know how their students are progressing toward predetermined goals. Well-organized teachers collect data to help them make determinations about the instructional programs being delivered. It is a good idea to collect information on student performance as an ongoing part of the instructional routine. Data should be gathered frequently and systematically, using a student's present curriculum as the information source. One technique that has been used for some time and that follows this model is precision teaching. Other methodologies for collecting data are also available and are discussed in other chapters of this book. Teachers are encouraged to consult other resource materials to see examples of how this type of assessment can be conducted (i.e., Howell & Morehead, 1987; Idol, Nevin, & Paolucci-Whitcomb, 1986).

Follow-Ups to Teaching

Feedback to Students After students complete a task, it is essential that they receive feedback of two types. First, they need motivational feedback—typically positive statements relative to the desirable behaviors they displayed. Second, although they may not request it, students often need informational feedback about the nature of their performance; if they erred or did not follow directions, they may require instructional information to help them modify their responses so as to produce correct answers (Cohen, Perkins, & Newmark, 1985). Too often, teachers' feedback to students includes only quantitative statements about accuracy. Teachers must be sensitive to students' needs and be willing to provide corrective feedback to help them do better next time.

Some suggestions for using corrective feedback are warranted. Teachers working directly with students should try to provide corrective information without being punitive or negative. For instance, a teacher might say, "Naomi, you sure gave it a good shot, but your answer is just not quite right. Let's go back and . . ." or "Scott, I'm glad to see you finished your assignment. I'd like you to tell me how you arrived at a couple of your answers. . . ." In both situations the teacher starts on a positive note and moves into the corrective component in a nonthreatening manner.

Data Management and Decision Making This particular component of effective instructional practice relates closely to the curricular-based data collection suggested previously. Without useful records of student progress, teachers will find it difficult to determine what to do next with certain students. Furthermore, teachers who fail to evaluate the effectiveness of their instruction by way of student learning risk educational stagnation. Data entry involves taking collected data and entering them into some system that organizes them in a meaningful way. This can be done by hand or machine. Microcomputers can greatly assist in this process, minimizing the amount of time needed to perform such activities. One piece of software available for this purpose is *AIMSTAR* (Hasselbring & Hamlett, 1984a). Data analysis implies that something is done with the data that are collected. Analysis should lead to decision making about students' present and future instructional programs.

Grading   Another concern that must be addressed is the grading of student performance, both on individual assignments and as an overall assessment reported at the end of a grading period. Carpenter (1985) suggests that specific decisions regarding grading be made in response to the following questions: On what criteria should grades be based? What type of medium (e.g., pass-fail) should be used? Who should participate in the grading process? How frequently should grades be given? Specific recommendations for grading students are provided in chapter 4.

Communication to Professionals and Parents   Special education teachers must be able to communicate knowledgeably and effectively with other professionals, such as psychologists, counselors, various types of therapists, medical personnel (doctors, nurses), and administrators. This requirement demands competence in oral and written communication as well as some un-

derstanding of the professional perspective from which others come.

In addition, effective teachers recognize the importance of working with parents in ways that enhance what teachers do in the classroom as well as what students do at home. Establishing open relationships with parents early in the school year can pave the way for smooth interactions throughout the course of the year. Working with other individuals is so important that chapter 6 is devoted to that topic.

Analysis of the Instructional Environment
The last element in this model of effective instruction requires evaluation of the major components of the process. Ysseldyke and Christenson (1986, 1987) suggest that information be gathered in the following 12 areas:

- ☐   instructional presentation
- ☐   classroom environment
- ☐   teacher expectations
- ☐   cognitive emphasis
- ☐   motivational strategies
- ☐   relevant practice
- ☐   academic engaged time
- ☐   informed feedback
- ☐   adaptive instruction
- ☐   progress evaluation
- ☐   instructional planning
- ☐   student understanding

We include the evaluation of learning environments as a follow-up activity to review effective teaching. However, it is equally viable as a precursor to teaching to identify potential problems in a proactive, preventative fashion.

Brophy and Good (1986) point out that effective classroom managers are characterized more by their ability to prevent problems than by their skills in responding to them. We believe that this statement holds for effective teachers in general; they pay close attention to many of those facets of teaching that occur before a lesson is ever presented. We also agree with Kounin's (1970) thesis that effective teachers have two other characteristics, which he calls "withitness" and "overlapping." The former feature implies a complete control of the classroom; the teacher is aware of all that is occurring, and the students know it. The latter characteristic refers to the teacher's ability to do more than one thing at a time—for instance, working with one student individually while monitoring the rest of the class. Although some would argue that these qualities are innate, we would argue that they can be learned. However, it is clear that some teachers become more proficient at these skills than others.

LEARNER CHARACTERISTICS

The preceding discussion of an instructional model emphasizes the importance of a deliberate and careful analysis of the teaching/learning process as a basis for planning intervention. Central to this activity is the idea that achievement and development are directly related to the effectiveness of the instruction provided. The validity of this concept has been confirmed in numerous research studies of typical learners (see Brophy & Good, 1986; Rosenshine & Stevens, 1986). Our conclusion is that this relationship is even more valid for students with identified special needs, regardless of categorical label or educational placement.

This section outlines information on the learning characteristics of students with special needs that can be integrated with the preceding model for effective instruction to provide a strong foundation for teaching. Researchers have scrutinized learning processes for such students for decades. This discussion attempts to translate research findings into practical instructional principles and thus provide an understanding of the role of research in developing educa-

tional procedures. The discussion outlines the nature of each particular learning domain, the abilities and/or deficits commonly found in learners with special needs, and specific suggestions for translating research into practice. General limitations to learning cannot be casually associated with students who are handicapped. Rather, specific aspects of learning must become primary topics of inquiry, not only for researchers but also for practitioners, leading to a better understanding of ways to emphasize student strengths and overcome weaknesses.

Several cautionary notes must precede this review. First, policy decisions and related developments in the field of special education in the 1970s and 1980s have gradually altered the nature of the population being served within various disability programs as well as that of students who remain unidentified and in regular classes (Algozzine & Korinek, 1985; Forness, 1985; Gerber, 1985; Polloway & Smith, in press). Second, the discussion here represents an orientation to the types of problems reported in groups of students either identified as handicapped or described as having remedial needs. References are made, as applicable, to characteristics found commonly in groups of students classified as learning disabled, mentally retarded, emotionally disturbed, or behavior disordered. Nevertheless, in numerous instances intragroup variance supercedes intergroup variance (Hallahan & Kauffman, 1977). Group descriptors should be recongized for what they are: at best, a collective basis for investigating the nature of individual traits.

The third caution concerns the nature of the research reported in the professional literature. As MacMillan (1982) notes, the practitioner needs to consider that much of the published empirical work relative to exceptional individuals has been performed in laboratories or other somewhat contrived settings and must be applied carefully to the classroom setting. The principles discussed here should benefit such applications.

Attentional Variables

Attention, the prerequisite for each individual learning act, is a complex phenomenon that has been a major focus of research efforts in special education for over 20 years, particularly in the fields of learning disabilities and mental retardation. Although the mentalistic nature of attention was responsible for its initial rejection by behaviorally oriented psychologists (Stevenson, 1972; Hagen & Kail, 1975), a resurgence in interest has increased the importance of attention in psychological formulations. Alabiso (1972) notes that the generic term *attention* can be broken down into three distinct components: attention span, focus, and selective attention. He defined *attention span* as the length of time on task, *focus* as the inhibition of distracting or incidental stimuli, and *selective attention* as the discrimination of important stimulus characteristics. Clearly, the latter two components are closely related. Hagen and Kail (1975) attest to this interrelationship in their description of attentional processes as "how the individual selects the important information and ignores the unimportant from the vast amount of input that is available to the individual at any given time" (p. 165).

Mercer and Snell (1977) identify four aspects of an instructional task's attentional demands: maintaining the level of arousal necessary to attend, scanning the field of possible stimuli to select those relevant to the task at hand, shifting attention rapidly to accommodate changes in the relevant stimuli, and maintaining attention over time. A particular concern that crosses these aspects is what Krupski (1981) refers to as voluntary attention. She states that children within varied categories of exceptionality have more difficulty than do their nonhandi-capped peers with learning tasks that demand high degrees of voluntary attention.

Zeaman and House (1963) first identified the importance of attention in the discrimination learning of persons with mental retardation. They posited a two-stage model of learning with the first stage being attention and the second, learning. Their experimental discrimination-learning task required individuals to choose one of two stimuli that varied in certain dimensions (e.g., color and shape). The experimenter presented pairs of stimuli over a period of time, then consistently reinforced the subject for responding to a particular dimension (e.g., blue or square). Thomas and Patton (1986) graphically illustrate this experiment.

Support for the two-stage learning theory of Zeaman and House came from observation of their subjects' backward learning curves. The researchers found that the first stage represented their subjects' ability to attend to task, that is, to orient themselves to the relevant stimuli being rewarded. The graph showed this stage as a chance segment (i.e., with 50% accuracy) in which the individuals were attending to irrelevant dimensions and only accidentally chose the correct stimuli. In the second stage the subjects identified the relevant dimension and learned the discrimination. The graph showed a steep rise, similar to that of other learners. The researchers concluded that the problems of these individuals stemmed from their inability to attend to the relevant stimuli; however, they were capable of learning once they mastered this initial stage.

Researchers have used numerous other methodologies to investigate attentional processes. For example, Hagen (see Maccoby & Hagen, 1965) devised a simple task to study selective attention; it required a child to attend to the specific features of a series of animal picture cards. In general, research in this area shows that students who are mentally retarded do not consistently display significant selective attention deficits when compared with children of the same mental age (e.g., Fisher, 1970; Hagen & Huntsman, 1971; Hallahan, Stainback, Ball, & Kauffman, 1973). Although these findings on selective attention are not consistent with those of Zeaman and House (1963), it is accepted that persons who are retarded can benefit from efforts to enhance their attentional skills.

Researchers in other fields, including learning disabilities and behavior disorders, have further examined the role of this key variable in the learning process. As a consequence, a substantial research base has developed to guide intervention with students who have attentional problems (e.g., Dunlap, Koegel, & Burke, 1981; Kauffman, 1986; Krupski, 1981; Tarver, 1981). The research has yielded specific implications for teaching. Mercer and his colleagues (Mercer & Payne, 1975; Mercer & Snell, 1977) present a number of suggestions. Stimuli should vary in only a few distinct dimensions relevant to the student. More obvious stimuli differences should be used to facilitate successful initial discrimination. Teachers should enhance children's responses by drawing their attention to relevant procedures and associations. Removing extraneous stimuli and rewarding adherence to the task can foster attention; however, teachers should not let such rewards interfere with the learning process.

Teachers who wish to increase student attention to facilitate learning have many methods available. To cut down on extraneous stimuli and to reinforce attention, one effective procedure is to darken the classroom and present instructional material on an overhead projector. By highlighting what the child should concentrate on while at the same time removing distractions, the teacher can increase on-task performance and can then provide reinforcement while moving around the room. Spotlights and electronic pointers can be used in much the same way. Cubicles have also been commonly used to reduce extraneous stimuli for students with short attention spans.

In addition, the use of visual cues and prompts can enhance a child's ability to discriminate between various stimuli. Westling and Koorland (1979), for example, report on a signal procedure for teaching sight words that uses superimposed picture cues to promote error-free learning. Polloway and Polloway (1980) report on a fading technique that enables primary school children with learning disabilities to discriminate between the commonly reversed b and d.

Using novel and varied stimuli properties in instructional materials and increasing motivation through reinforcement are two other logical and effective ways to increase attention and thus capitalize on students' learning abilities. In either case the goal is to heighten a child's incentive to actively seek the salient properties of the stimuli that will facilitate accurate response.

Self-monitoring of attention, another promising approach developed for children with learning disabilities, also has merit for students with other handicapping conditions. This method increases individuals' awareness of their own attention. Research has illustrated that a simple recorded tone can cue self-recording of on-task behavior and thus significantly increase attention (see Hallahan, Lloyd & Stoller, 1982; Kneedler & Hallahan, 1981; Rooney, Hallahan, & Lloyd, 1984). Several researchers (Connis, 1979; Howell, Rueda, & Rutherford, 1983) have suggested training modifications for instructing lower-functioning students in self-monitoring (e.g., pictorial cues, back-up reinforcers). McLaughlin, Krappman, and Welsh (1985) have used other procedures successfully with students with behavior disorders. A detailed description of self-monitoring is provided in chapter 5.

Two notes of caution should be given concerning efforts to enhance attention. Attention should be considered in terms of the characteristics of the child, the nature of the task to be learned, and the demands of the instructional setting (Krupski, 1981; Pelham, 1981), as well as the incentive conditions that may apply. As Krupski (1981) notes, deficits in attention—"episodes of inattention"—occur most often when the demands of the task reflect the need for high degrees of voluntary attention and when the setting is highly structured, as opposed to little demand for voluntary attention and an informal setting.

A second concern is that attention needs to be seen as a vehicle for content to be learned—most often, academic in nature. Attention deficits will be most functionally conceptualized in relation to the tasks to be accomplished. Specific interventions, such as self-monitoring, may have substantially greater proven effectiveness in increasing attention than in improving academic productivity (Rooney, Polloway, & Hallahan, 1985; Snider, 1987). Thus, it would be a mistake to allow the focus on attention to be isolated from the more important concern, which is learning.

Mediational Strategies

Students find many learning tasks simpler when mental processes are activated to assist in problem solving, retention, or recall. These processes can be collectively described as mediational strategies because they involve the use of specific techniques as intermediaries between task stimuli and required responses. Mature learners commonly use mediational strategies, such as verbal rehearsal and repetition, labeling, classification, association, and imagery. Figure 2.4 illustrates how this process operates: an individual can process an incoming stimulus (S) through verbal mediation (R_{vm}) and

transform it into a mediated stimulus (S_{vm}) before making a response (R). Because most mediational strategies require at least rudimentary verbal skills, teachers should consider students' language development prior to instituting training procedures.

Educators have used various poetic or rhythmic mediation techniques for years. Some of the most common include "When two vowels go walking, the first one does the talking"; "Thirty days hath September . . ."; and "*I* before *e*, except after *c*. . . ." In each case the simple rhyme-song facilitates recall of a given bit of information.

The critical question underlying mediational strategies is the ability of students with disabilities to produce and use them. Flavell, Beach, and Chinsky (1966) define two terms that provide a conceptual base for understanding this question: a *mediation deficiency* is an inability to mediate effectively, regardless of whether guidance and assistance are provided; a *production deficiency* is an inability to create mediators, even though an individual may be able to use them if they are provided by others. Clearly, the former difficulty has more serious consequences. Available research generally indicates that a production deficiency best characterizes the learning processes of student who are retarded (e.g., Bray, 1979;

FIGURE 2.4
Process of verbal mediation (From *Children's Learning* [p. 58] by H. W. Stevenson, 1972, Englewood Cliffs, NJ: Prentice-Hall. Copyright 1972 by Prentice-Hall. Adapted by permission.)

Robinson & Robinson, 1976) or learning disabled (e.g., Hallahan, Tarver, Kauffman, & Graybeal, 1978). Thus, it seems safe to postulate that students with learning handicaps do not spontaneously develop and use mediational strategies (Wallace & Kauffman, 1986).

Teaching such strategies to students with handicaps is a logical addition to their instructional programming and is effective in modifying their performance (McLoone, Scruggs, Mastropieri, & Zucker, 1986). However, it is important to note that strategy training is most appropriate and effective when it is tied to the content to be learned. As Swanson (1982) notes, this linkage can "provide an integrative program of instruction so needed by these children" (p. 81). Instructional efforts should therefore focus on functional mediators related to important specific skills. For example, strategies tied to phonetic analysis in reading can serve as mediators to assist in word recognition; similarly, a sequential strategy approach to problem solving can be helpful in mathematics learning. Mediational strategies can also be used effectively in various learning tasks including memory.

Memory

Memory is the ability to store information and retrieve it on demand. It has been the subject of a plethora of research efforts and many elegant as well as quaint models. For example, Kolstoe (1972) describes two early theories popularly used to explain memory deficiencies. According to the "leaky bucket" hypothesis, information leaks out of a child's memory in equal amounts, regardless of the kind of information being taught. The "peanut brittle" theory advances the notion that a memory storage system retains some blocks of information while forgetting other blocks. Empiri-

cal research has advanced well beyond these early conceptualizations of memory deficits.

Theorists now understand memory processes as including short-term memory (STM) and long-term memory (LTM) stores. Theories of recall focus on the ways that information is successfully attended to, stored, and retrieved for later usage while preventing decay (e.g., Atkinson & Shiffrin, 1968). Spitz (1980) likens human memory to a refrigerator with the bins, or temporary storage areas, representing STM and the freezer, LTM. In both cases systematic storage facilitates ease in retrieval.

Research efforts have investigated the variables thought to be involved in storage and retrieval. For example, Ellis (1963) identified STM as an area of difficulty for persons with mental retardation. He postulated that they have difficulty with STM because of a deficiency in stimulus trace (S_t) processes. The S_t concept can be simply described as the trace that an environmental stimulus leaves on the central nervous system; it is followed by a behavioral event. Ellis saw intelligence as a limiting function of the S_t and thus a contributor to the deficit.

Although further research has failed to verify the existence of stimulus trace processes, STM deficits have been commonly reported. Ellis's (1970) later research on the topic presents an alternative, multiprocess memory formulation. Ellis restates his belief that STM varies directly with intelligence and may be a central factor in intellectual inadequacy. Although research has not consistently supported this causal theory, it remains one of several interesting hypotheses concerning memory processes. Robinson and Robinson (1976) review several other models of memory.

Memory deficits resist simple empirical resolution. As Schonebaum and Zinobar (1977) note, memory performance is influenced by the manner in which items are learned and maintained in memory, the rate of loss from memory (or forgetting), and the manner in which items that have been learned and retained are located and retrieved from memory. Accurate short term recall reflects the combined efficiency of all these processes. (p. 262)

As these researchers indicate, the complexity of memory requires that a model for deficits include "an inefficient acquisition process, storage system, or retrieval strategy, or combination of these" (p. 262).

Memory research has traditionally indicated that students with handicaps exhibit deficits in some aspect of STM (e.g., Baumeister, Smith, & Rose, 1965; Ellis, 1963, 1970; Hermelin & O'Connor, 1964; Scott & Scott, 1968; Torgesen & Greenstein, 1982; Wallace & Kauffman, 1986). Long-term memory, however, continues to be an area in which learners with retardation and nonhandicapped children exhibit comparable skills—that is, no significant differences have been consistently found in their rates of forgetting comparable material (Belmont, 1966; Klausmeier, Feldhusen, & Check, 1959).

The focus of more recent research has shifted from structural features to control processes related to mediation and, specifically, to rehearsal strategies. As Atkinson and Shiffrin (1968) report, "Rehearsal serves the purpose of increasing the strength [of material to be recalled] built up in long-term store, both by increasing the length of stay in [short-term store] . . . and by giving coding and other storage processes time to operate" (p. 111). Rehearsal thus bridges the gap between STM and LTM and also facilitates later retrieval. Because capacity deficits in students with handicaps are difficult to verify and educators cannot biologically change students anyhow, a focus on strategies for recall seems particularly apt (Kirk &

Chalfant, 1984; Lerner, 1985). As noted earlier, students who are handicapped do not spontaneously produce rehearsal strategies and do not approach tasks in an organized, planful fashion but have improved significantly when shown how to do so (Baumeister & Brooks, 1981; Borkowski & Cavanaugh, 1979; Houck, 1984). In addition, these students can maintain the use of learned strategies over time (Kramer, Nagle, & Engle, 1980). The major difficulty to be faced is in generalization—transferring this ability to new tasks (Kramer et al., 1980) or in developing new strategies (Borkowski & Cavanaugh, 1979). As an example of the generalization problem, trained individuals may learn a strategy for recalling phone numbers and may retain it for this task. However, they may not be able to use this rehearsal ability to facilitate remembering other factual information; that is, they cannot generalize the strategy to another task.

The transition from basic research to application has lagged as significantly in this area as in any other area of learning research. Consequently, teachers need to remain aware of current developments that can affect methodology. Recent inquiries include some preliminary findings that students now considered to be in the higher-functioning, or borderline, region of mild retardation can maintain and generalize strategies when they receive prolonged, in-depth training and feedback on the purpose of strategies (Borkowski & Cavanaugh, 1979). The development of memory awareness (meta-memorial training) certainly holds promise for the future. Eventually, the absolute limit in rehearsal ability may be determinable, as well as whether such a limit depends on structural processes, developmental level, intellectual status (Baumeister & Brooks, 1981; Spitz, 1973), and/or the presence or absence of specific learning dysfunctions.

A set of implications can be drawn from the basic and applied research on memory processes in students with various handicapping conditions. The key strategies that follow have been culled from a variety of research reviews in this area (e.g., Baumeister & Brooks, 1981; Ellis, 1970; Estes, 1970; Ingalls, 1978; Mercer & Snell, 1977; Smith, 1974; Torgesen & Greenstein, 1982; Wallace & Kauffman, 1986).

☐ Instruction should focus on rehearsal strategies and related mediation tools, such as labeling and verbal associations.

☐ Students should receive information in manageable units and should be given assistance in grouping or clustering items.

☐ Information to be learned and retained should be meaningful and relevant.

☐ Students should be given mnemonics for specific content and should be assisted in using them.

☐ When learning memory strategies, students must be given opportunity to practice and apply them.

☐ Direct instruction should be provided to demonstrate to students how to group information.

☐ Visual imagery can be used to provide a picture into which verbal information can be placed.

☐ Paraphrasing information—putting it into one's own words—facilitates storage and recall.

☐ Incentives should be provided as needed, with a subsequent shift to self-regulation.

☐ Overlearning, repetition, and constant use and application of learned material and strategies should be ensured.

Again, it is important to emphasize that memory should not be seen as a training goal apart from the content to be recalled. Memory is not the goal of instruction but rather a vehicle to facilitate learning (Reid & Hresko, 1981).

One example of memory learning involves a simple mathematics equation, such as $5 \times 6 = 30$. Numerous ways might be used to teach this fact to aid its retention. Initially, manipulative objects and pictorial representations can be used to present the problem. These enactive (concrete) and iconic (semiconcrete) means promote understanding of the process and the symbols involved. Next, overlearning, repetition, and application can help commit the fact to memory through games, flash cards, worksheets, oral recitations, and story problems. Repetition is most effective in a variety of contexts. For example, to facilitate the formation of rehearsal strategies, a teacher might use musical rhythm to accompany a given multiplication table sequence. Repetition should not be limited to repetitive drills; rather, it should stress overlearning in varied contexts. The diversity of presentations enables the learner to transfer the information to long-term memory, store it, and later recall and successfully retrieve it.

Motivation

When performance is not consistent with projections, one explanation of the variance may be the motivational variables within the performer's environment. Unfortunately, as Baumeister and Brooks (1981) note, there has typically been little regard for such factors.

> . . . it is one of our most commonly shared human experiences that the desire and motivation to perform may be the most critical ingredient of all. Perhaps how we approach a task strategically matters less than the intensity and purpose with which we engage in intellectual activity. As one reads through the voluminous research on information processing, one finds concentration on such attributes as memory, language, semantic struc-

tures, visual and auditory patterns, and the like. Yet, little is said about values, purposes, and the consequences of the activity.

It is reasonable to assume that individuals whose efforts to apply solutions to problems consistently meet with failure will become distrustful of their own strategies and, in effect, learn to be helpless, to expect to fail or do poorly. . . . These, too, are cognitive styles—not adaptive ones, to be sure, but ones which surely affect performance. We assert that factors other than purely cognitive or intellective ones determine performance in every meaningful human encounter with the environment. (p. 105)

The research efforts of Zigler and his colleagues have been particularly significant in focusing professional attention in the field of mental retardation on motivational concerns. Zigler's research conceptualizes the functional disparity between the learning of students who are handicapped and those who are nonhandicapped and thus provides a framework for exploring a host of motivational variables. Several studies have elucidated the nature of key classroom factors.

History of failure in school is an important motivational concern to be considered. In many cases persons with disabilities may be motivated more to avoid failure than to achieve success (Zigler, 1973). They also tend to settle for less success (Stevenson & Zigler, 1958; Kier & Zigler, 1969, in Zigler, 1973). To overcome "failure set," students who are handicapped must have the opportunity to experience and feel success. Many teachers do an excellent job of telling students that they are successful, but the students must believe in the basis for this praise to experience the effect of success. Otherwise, the praise is ineffective, and the teachers' credibility with the students is lessened (Bryan, 1983). Research on failure set, summarized by MacMillan (1982) and Logan and Rose (1982), provides numerous recommendations: (1) focusing attention on task cues that result in successful task completion; (2) adapting instructional presentations to the student's ability by avoiding too difficult/too easy tasks; (3) providing support when failure is unavoidable; (4) maintaining a positive attitude and communicating it to the student; and (5) altering methods to facilitate an understanding of task requirements. During a reading period, for example, the activity should be one in which the child has previously performed successfully. This initial success increases motivation to attempt more difficult tasks throughout the period. In math, the teacher might cut up a worksheet and have the child complete one line, rather than a full page, of problems. The child develops a sense of accomplishment and can then complete the remaining portions of the assignment.

Closely related to a failure set is the use of outer-directed problem-solving strategies. Balla and Zigler (1979) identify three determinants of this motivational style: (1) a low level of cognitive development, prompting imitative behavior; (2) attachment to adults, resulting in strong dependence; and (3) past failure, leading to external orientation. Not surprisingly, children who are handicapped often tend to be oversensitive to models (Turnure & Zigler, 1964) and rely significantly on external cues (Achenbach & Zigler, 1968). These tendencies inhibit internal judgment and decision making.

An outer-directed style is clearly linked to attribution theory and the locus of control concept (Lawrence & Winschel, 1975). Persons who have experienced failure develop an external locus, sense limited control over events, and can exhibit learned helplessness (see Seligman, 1975). Learners with external attributions may avoid accepting responsibility for personal failures and successes, seeing both as determined by events that are beyond their control (Pearl, Bryan, & Donahue, 1980). Students with both learn-

ing and behavior disorders have been reported to have the lowest scores on
measures of internal locus of control when
compared to students identified as only
learning disabled or behaviorally disordered
(Morgan, 1986). Bryan and her colleagues
(Bryan, Pearl, Donahue, Bryan, & Pflaum,
1983) accurately summarize the problem of
external attributions for children with learning disabilities.

> [They] assumed that failures were the result of
> their inadequacies and that success in the fu-
> ture was doubtful . . . [leading them] to avoid
> new challenges and to engage in maladaptive
> behavior rather than to risk failure or public
> disclosure. (p. 17)

Teachers should make provisions for students to succeed and thus trust in their own
abilities. For example, if a teacher gives similar worksheets to two children—one who
can complete the task successfully and one
who cannot—the less able child quickly realizes that the path of least resistance is to
copy information from a peer's paper. Constant teacher supervision of students' work,
denying independent activities, can also inadvertently reinforce outer-directedness and
an external locus of control.

The various findings in this broadly defined area consistently treat observed differences between functioning level and
expected performance as possible reflections of motivational differences, not as specific handicaps per se. One can conclude,
therefore, that much can be done to assist
handicapped persons to maximize their
skills and thus enhance adjustment and independence. Finding ways to develop children's positive mind-set toward learning will
enhance their learning progress. Providing
success experiences will promote learning
based on self-reliance and a desire to exceed

the minimum. A variety of experiences accompanied by reinforcement (e.g., attractive
bulletin boards highlighting work accomplishment) can help reach this goal (Glazzard, 1978).

A particularly appropriate anecdote by
Zigler (1973) tells of a classroom he studied,
in which he found that results on his outer-
direction experiment contradicted his hypothesis. After closer examination of the
classroom, he reported the following:

> [The teacher] showered new pupils with suc-
> cess experiences and attempted to increase
> their self-esteem. Thereafter he specifically
> reinforced what he called "figuring things out
> for yourself," rewarding independent thought
> more highly than correct responses. We exam-
> ined the performance of these 16 retarded
> subjects on our learning tasks and discovered
> not only that they relied on cues significantly
> less than our other retarded children but that
> they relied on them less, albeit not signifi-
> cantly so, than did the children of normal in-
> tellect. Again, we see that it is not the
> retardation per se that produces the behavior,
> but rather the particular experiences to which
> retarded children are subjected. (p. 292)

The research reviewed here has highlighted significant deficiencies common to
individuals with handicapping conditions
yet has supported optimism concerning the
learning potentials of these individuals. Frequently, the nature of their problems can be
traced to an inability to develop effective
strategies for monitoring performance; the
central difficulty, thus, is one of awareness
of how to learn, recall, or solve problems
rather than an inherent structural limitation.
This presumption suggests that many of the
critical aspects of learning deficits are
within the control of effective teachers.

The following recommendations briefly
summarize the implications of learning re-

search, thus providing a blueprint for teaching learners with special needs.

1. Emphasize concrete, meaningful content in initial instruction.
2. Ensure mastery of new material through overlearning and repetition.
3. Provide learners with methods of verbal mediation and strategies for learning, recalling, and problem solving.
4. Increase attention initially by highlighting relevant dimensions and minimizing extraneous stimuli. As attending skills develop, gradually increase the extraneous stimuli to facilitate improvement in attending skills.
5. Promote an atmosphere of success on which to base future learning tasks.
6. Incorporate incentives into learning arrangements as needed. Shift to natural consequences and self-regulation as soon as possible.
7. Sequence instruction from easy to difficult.
8. Use a variety of methods to present material and reinforce learning.

SUMMARY

This chapter provides three general foundations for teaching: a conceptualization of learning, a model for instruction, and characteristics of learners with special needs. Early discussion reflects the biases of the authors concerning the nature and process of learning and the key components of effective practice within the teaching/learning process. These components are reflected throughout the remainder of the text.

This chapter also provides an overview of research and implications relative to learning and learner characteristics. Particular attention is given to attention, mediational strategies, memory, and motivation. With a limited number of exceptions, recent research efforts in special education have consistently reinforced an optimistic view of the possibility of modifying learning deficits. Sound educational principles should be incorporated into daily instructional practices and should be continuously reevaluated.

PART TWO
STRATEGIES FOR
TEACHING

3
Strategies to Develop Individualized Programs

Chapter 2 highlights important components of the teaching process on a general level. This chapter focuses on the individual student, emphasizing diagnosis as it leads from initial concern for students at risk for having school problems to more thorough examination of their problems and on to appropriate educational programming.

Regular education classrooms contain substantial numbers of students with diverse learning needs. Many of these students display characteristics that can significantly interfere with successful learning, resulting from factors such as language, intellectual and cognitive abilities, behavior, or culture. All of these at-risk students require special attention; however, only some of them require special services. For those who do, it is important to investigate their needs diagnostically.

Various professional disciplines define the term *diagnosis* differently. The *American College Dictionary* defines *diagnosis* as "the process of determining by examination the nature and circumstances of a diseased condition." For educational purposes diagnosis generally refers to the full evaluative process, from initial **identification** of an individual as potentially handicapped to the ongoing assessment-based instruction. This chapter discusses major diagnostic and instructional considerations critical to teachers and consistent with the Education for All Handicapped Children Act. Figure 3.1 outlines the major components of the diagnostic process as it relates to federal legislation and common educational practice. The specific elements represent the general organization of the chapter.

IDENTIFICATION

Identification refers to locating and verifying the needs of children who appear to have difficulties associated with various handicapping conditions. Although haphazard

FIGURE 3.1
The diagnostic process

efforts and arbitrary, often-discriminatory decisions once characterized this process, the legal impetus supplied by the Education for All Handicapped Children Act and related litigation has increased fairness and consistency within the procedures. Application of the due process clause of the Constitution has been a particularly important aspect of this trend.

Due process seeks to ensure that no citizen is deprived of legal rights or privileges. Special education has operationalized due process in the following procedures and general considerations:

1. Parents must receive written notification before evaluative efforts can begin.
2. Notification must be in the parents' native language.
3. Special education placement must be reviewed at least annually.
4. Parents have a right to question placement decisions in an impartial hearing.
5. A child has the right to be granted a surrogate parent if necessary.

Individual state and federal regulations elaborate on these aspects of due process.

All teachers must therefore become aware of the specific regulations that govern administrative aspects of special education. Of great importance is the spirit of an open and fair process for determining whether to provide services to a child and what form they will take. Ultimately, it is the best interest of the student that should guide decisions and practice.

"Child find" is the initial step in identification. It attempts to develop an awareness of handicapping conditions and the services children can use within the community and the schools. Community awareness is particularly important in identifying preschool children with handicaps. Posters, circulars, and the media should be used to inform parents about developmental delays and to tell them how to have their children assessed. A variety of individuals and agencies must be involved to ensure a successful community child-find program. Pediatricians, parents' groups, social service agencies, religious groups, and fraternal organizations should all participate.

Nonetheless, many children who are mildly handicapped and some who are moderately handicapped will not be identified during their preschool years, either because an effective service system is lacking or because the problem has not yet manifested itself. When these children enter school, the regular class teacher assumes the responsibility for identifying students with possible learning handicaps and for referring them for further observation and testing. Referrals are the initial step in screening and may be initiated by parents, teachers, or other school personnel. Figure 3.2 presents a sample form for classroom referrals.

Screening attempts to make preliminary judgments about children who may need special services. The specific goal is to decide which students need further, more extensive and intensive evaluation. The primary concern is to use procedures that are both effective (i.e., able to identify all children whose problems warrant further assessment) and efficient (i.e., requiring minimal time and effort). Screening is generally based on the results of classroom observation of the student as well as on reasonably short tests, either formal or informal. Using these preliminary data, a screening committee or child-study team at the school can decide whether further assessment is necessary. If the decision is not to proceed, the committee should make specific suggestions to assist the regular teacher in modifying instruction for the student within the regular class program. An excellent example of attending to student needs in the regular classroom is the concept of teacher assistance teams (Chalfant, Pysh & Moultrie, 1979). If the decision is to proceed, further assessment will ensue, and the question of eligibility will need to be addressed.

ASSESSMENT

Educational assessment data can be used in the multidisciplinary evaluation that precedes eligibility determination; in the formative, ongoing assessment that should be a major part of the instructional program; in the summative evaluation of student progress; and in the more general systematic analysis of program effectiveness. Assessment data are critical to all instructional decisions; hence, we use the term *assessment-based instruction* to stress the idea that sound instruction should be preceded by an appropriate analysis of learning-related behaviors. The information discussed here is pertinent to data gathered throughout the diagnostic process.

Collecting Assessment Data

Teachers can use a variety of assessment sources to profile students' learning needs and will probably need to analyze academic,

School _____ Date _____

Student's name _____

Grade _____ Referred by _____

Reason for referral (behavioral description):

_____

_____

_____

Check areas of concern:

    Self-help _____   Reading _____   Spelling _____

    Oral language _____   Behavior _____   Handwriting _____

    Written language _____   Social _____   Arithmetic _____

                        Other _____

Comments:

_____

_____

Can the pupil be observed in your room? _____

Suggested day/time: _____

Preliminary estimate of services needed:

    Resource teacher _____   Special class _____   Social work _____

    Speech therapy _____   Psychological _____   Other _____

FIGURE 3.2
Classroom referral form

behavioral, social, and often psychomotor domains to develop a comprehensive intervention program. The key is that educational assessment results should clearly indicate how to teach individual students; otherwise the assessment represents wasted time and resources (Wallace & Larsen, 1978).

Diagnostic concerns can relate to various academic domains. In math this might mean determining whether a child can carry, borrow, and use zeros. In reading, diagnostic information might be obtained on a child's phonetic analysis skills, comprehension abilities, and relative strength of sight vocabulary. The information should indicate to the teacher where to begin instruction and what to teach initially. Knowledge of the scope and sequence of the particular skill area then determines the teaching direction and the long-term goals most appropriate for the learner.

Diagnostic information regarding a student's behavior, especially target behaviors, also needs to be obtained. A target behavior is observable, measurable, specific, and repeatable. Complex behaviors such as aggressiveness, hyperactivity, and withdrawal actually consist of a cluster of specific behaviors. For instance, aggressive children may push in line, punch the children sitting behind them, or kick individuals walking by. Most teachers find dealing with a complex behavior difficult. However, knowing that a child punches someone every 5 minutes allows the teacher to zero in on a target behavior. Specificity helps facilitate change, which of course is one purpose of teaching.

Accurate assessment requires varied teacher competencies. McNutt and Mandlebaum (1980) identify the following:

☐ ability to select the appropriate test, based on its reliability, validity, and standardization sample as well as on the expected results

☐ ability to construct informal tests and understand the construction of formal instruments

☐ competency to personally administer tests and evaluate the results of tests given by others to determine whether they were appropriately administered

☐ proficiency in interpreting test results and applying them to program planning

Case Histories Students' case histories contain a great amount of information. Permanent records, for example, can provide information about teaching approaches that have proved successful or unsuccessful with a child, motivational and attitudinal data, health reports, and previous test results. Parents can provide information about specific interests, emotional factors, physical and sensory disabilities, and the general tenor of the child's life. Past teachers can indicate how they taught the child, that is, which particular strategies and methods they used and what the child's interests and reinforcement preferences were. Of course, much of this information does not provide specific data for programming. Other limitations to the use of historical assessment information include (1) absence of control over what data were previously collected, (2) difficulty verifying the information, (3) inability to verify the conditions under which the information was collected, and (4) lack of reliability of remembered observations (Salvia & Ysseldyke, 1985).

For these reasons teachers should evaluate the efforts needed to develop an indepth case history analysis against the benefits likely to accrue. In most cases a clear picture of a student's prior learning history as well as ecological factors, such as home background and out-of-school environment, will suffice.

Formal Assessment

Formal assessment instruments are generally available commercially and typically contain statistical data regarding validity, reliability, and standardization procedures. Many formal tests are **norm-referenced—** that is, they are based on a standardized sample of students—and can thus allow comparison between one individual's score and a sample. Formal tests can be divided into two types, **survey** and **diagnostic.** Survey tests are usually administered to obtain a global score or level of functioning. Diagnostic tests attempt to obtain more specific information about a student's strengths and weaknesses. Formal tests provide quantitative and sometimes qualitative data based on student performance in the testing situation. It is important to remember that these tests attempt to obtain a measure of a student's best performance in a contrived situation as opposed to a student's typical performance under natural conditions.

Formal test results typically include raw data as well as derived scores. Raw scores are not very useful, in and of themselves. More helpful information comes from the derived scores, determined by comparing a student's performance to that of a comparable group. The usual types of derived scores include age or grade equivalents, percentiles, standard scores, and sometimes stanines. Because these scores are regularly used, it is essential that teachers understand them and are able to explain them to parents. For information on the specific meanings of the terms, the reader is referred to any one of several texts on educational assessment (e.g., McLoughlin & Lewis, 1986; Salvia & Ysseldyke, 1985; Swanson & Watson, 1982).

Formal tests have numerous uses and advantages.

☐ They are research based; therefore, validity, reliability, and standardization information should be available.
☐ They can provide a screening instrument for individual or group administration.
☐ They can be valuable for those unfamiliar with informal tests who need a model for assessment.
☐ They are ready-made and convenient.

☐ They are often given by someone else and therefore can save a teacher's time.
☐ Some are available in parallel forms for test-retest purposes.
☐ They might provide information that can be used for instructional planning.
☐ They fulfill the legal administrative requirements for determining eligibility and placement.

Despite these positive features of formal tests, they also have potential disadvantages. Many tests have neither proven reliability nor demonstrated relevance to school tasks (Hammill & Bartel, 1982). They may lack instructional validity, providing little or no information about where or how to start teaching. They may indicate what a pupil knows, but not how this knowledge was gained, stressing the learning product to the exclusion of the learning process. If administered by someone other than the teacher, the information obtained may not be translated into educational recommendations. And both false positives and false negatives can occur in the results (Hammill, 1971). Other factors that should be evaluated include purpose, because formal tests are often given to obtain only a global score; form, which can hinder the exploration of specific subskills if it is too rigid; ignorance of behavioral observation in favor of procedural matters; administrative time requirement; and use with pupils not represented by the standardized sample, possibly creating biased results.

Bias is a major concern with formal testing. Teachers must be sure that neither tests nor testing circumstances lessen the chances for minority or ethnic students to succeed. Gonzales (1982) offers the following checklist to ensure unbiased assessment (p. 389):

1. Have all medical, visual, auditory, and emotional variables been eliminated as possible deterrents to test success?

2. Has language dominance been measured to accommodate receptive and expressive strengths and weaknesses?
3. Has the child's sociocultural background been taken into account?
4. Has the child had exposure to the educational and environmental opportunities necessary to learn the material and skills being measured?
5. Is the child adequately motivated to do well on the test?
6. Is the child's self-concept adequate?
7. Is the child aware of the purpose of the test?
8. Does the child have adequate test-taking experience to understand the concepts, directions, and skills necessary to do well?
9. Has the child been completely familiarized with the testing procedures?
10. Has the test selection been carefully planned to ensure that the purpose of the test matches the purpose of the evaluation?
11. Does test administration allow for evaluation in a bilingual setting if appropriate?
12. Will final decisions be based on systematic, pluralistic assessment, taking all necessary information into account?

For additional information on bias in assessment, Oakland (1980) provides an excellent review of possible sources of bias prior to, during, and after collection of assessment data.

Teachers should carefully weigh the advantages and disadvantages of formal tests for their specific diagnostic purpose. Formal tests do fulfill legal requirements and administrative regulations for classification purposes. Careful student evaluation, however, requires more than just reaffirming that a child has learning problems. As Smith and Neisworth (1969) point out, true **assessment** for teaching requires more than **testing.** It involves looking beyond test results to analyze a student's functioning. Although formal tests provide one approach to this objective, most critical information surfaces through informal means.

Informal Assessment

Informal techniques include a variety of methods of data collection—seat-work assignments, timed quizzes, informal reading inventories, check sheets, rating scales, verbalizations, teacher observations. Informal assessment procedures enable teachers to study a host of areas, including specific skills, level of academic functioning, approach to problems, learning process, reaction to stimuli, motivational factors, social interactions, and desirable and undesirable behaviors.

Two systematic approaches to informal assessment are particularly noteworthy. The first is the use of **curriculum-based measures** (CBM), or **curriculum-based assessment** (CBA). Unlike norm-referenced tests, such tools are teacher-constructed and criterion-referenced, using the actual curriculum as the standard. This type of assessment can serve many purposes: identification, eligibility, program planning, progress monitoring, and program evaluation (Marston & Magnusson, 1985). Consistent with the principles of applied behavior analysis, curriculum-based assessment can assist in focusing attention on changes in academic behavior within the context of the curriculum being used, thus enhancing the relationship between testing and teaching (Deno & Fuchs, 1987). Because it encourages reliance on methods keyed to the curriculum and administered by classroom teachers, curriculum-based assessment is more ecologically valid (Fuchs & Fuchs, 1986) than norm-referenced testing.

The inherent attractiveness of direct, frequently collected measures in curriculum-based assessment has contributed to their widespread endorsement in special education (Deno, 1985; Gickling & Thompson, 1985). However, unlike many norm-referenced tests, which have been subjected to validity studies and reliability evaluations, curriculum-based measures have received relatively little attention to such concerns. One recent study (Epstein, Polloway, & Patton, 1987) of curriculum-based measures in spelling and arithmetic did find them to be reliable techniques for analyzing student performance.

Curriculum-based measures can be developed through systematic analysis of a given curriculum, selection of specific items, and construction of assessment formats (e.g., questions, cloze activities, worksheets). Idol, Nevin, and Paolucci-Whitcomb (1986) suggest that three different forms of the same test be developed to be used on alternate days of testing. Although resources for developing curriculum-based instruments exist (e.g., Deno & Fuchs, 1987; Idol et al., 1986), they can serve only as guides because the instruments must reflect the different curricula being assessed.

A second important tool for informal assessment is the analysis of instructional tasks. Wallace and Kauffman (1978) define **task analysis** as "a sequence of evaluation activities which pinpoint the child's learning problem and guide the teacher in planning an effective remedial sequence of instructional tasks" (p. 85). Task analysis involves determining specific and important educational tasks, the sequential steps involved in learning the tasks, and the specific behaviors needed to perform each step (Lerner, 1985). Lloyd (1980) has reconceptualized this idea as **academic strategy training** and has demonstrated its usefulness for instructional planning (Lloyd & deBettencourt, 1982).

An example can illustrate the applicability of task analysis to the diagnostic process. In arithmetic an assessment reveals that Reggie cannot carry in two-digit addition; he must master the task of regrouping. The steps involved are adding the digits in the units column; regrouping this subtotal into units and 10s; recording the units and carrying the 10s to the 10s column; adding the digits in the 10s column and recording that sum. Prerequisite skills include recognizing and writing numbers, adding single-digit numbers, regrouping numbers, and understanding place value. After analyzing this addition task, the teacher can assess and compare Reggie's skills with the abilities needed to complete the task.

Curriculum-based assessment and task analysis, together with the variety of other regular evaluative activities classified as informal tools, have numerous uses and advantages.

- ☐ They are closely tied to the formulation of learning objectives (i.e., they have good curricular validity).
- ☐ They produce practical, relevant information.
- ☐ They allow easy pinpointing of weaknesses and quick intervention with specific teaching strategies.
- ☐ They can complement and check the validity of formal tests.
- ☐ They are inexpensive.
- ☐ They do not require a significant amount of time to administer.
- ☐ The individual who administers these measures also sees the student in a wide variety of curricular situations.
- ☐ Informal measures can fulfill the requirement of ongoing assessment of short-term objectives and annual goals in an IEP.
- ☐ They can and should be administered frequently.
- ☐ They can provide informative data for making educationally sound decisions.

Nonetheless, informal assessment is not a panacea for all assessment needs. There are several potential disadvantages.

☐ The development of informal measures may be time-consuming.

☐ A teacher may overlook additional sources of diagnostic information.

☐ Informal tests demand knowledge of the sequences of skills and/or curriculum being taught.

☐ These measures can result in the teaching of isolated skills rather than a hierarchy of tasks.

Informal tools also share some of the problems of formal instruments. Both are subject to measurement errors and thus may produce data that are neither reliable nor valid.

Teachers who are skilled in the use of informal assessment techniques should be able to use them to obtain most of the specific information they need for identification, eligibility, planning, instruction, and evaluation. However, teachers should draw from all relevant sources of assessment data, using formal tests as well as informal tools.

ELIGIBILITY

After referral and screening, the process of determining eligibility for special services begins. The essential question is whether an individual student should be classified within a specific category of exceptionality, thus to be appropriately placed in a particular special education program. Under current regulations governing education, classification serves a necessary and generally useful function. However, given the fact that labels designating handicapping conditions can represent powerful statements about individuals, teachers must realize that classification is a descriptive rather than a explanatory process. This hypothetical conversation between a teacher and a school psychologist illustrates the potential for misuse.

Teacher: Were you able to find out why Johnny can't read?

Psychologist: Yes, I've found that he's retarded. And retarded children often have reading problems.

Teacher: But what is the basis of the reading problem?

Psychologist: Johnny has been slow to develop academic skills.

Teacher: Why has he been slow to develop skills?

Psychologist: Because he's retarded.

Teacher: But how can you be certain that he's retarded?

Psychologist: Because he's having great problems learning to read.

This type of circular reasoning indicates the danger inherent in any system of classification and labeling.

Legally, eligibility assessment requires multidisciplinary input. Generally, this requires, at a minimum, the following components:

1. a **psychological** evaluation including, but not limited to, an individually administered intelligence test, such as the Wechsler Intelligence Scale for Children, Revised (WISC- R), the Stanford-Binet Intelligence Scale, or the recently developed Kaufman Assessment Battery for Children (K-ABC).

2. a **medical** evaluation including a physical exam and an investigation of any significant health factors that might affect the learning process

3. a **sociological** evaluation of the student's home environment, family history, and any significant aspects of social development

4. an **educational** evaluation, including a summary of test results and an analysis

of the student's general strengths and weaknesses, particularly in academic, behavioral, and personal/social areas
5. a **speech/language** evaluation, when indicated, to provide data on possible receptive and expressive problems as well as specific speech disorders

The particular data necessary to justify eligibility obviously differ among categories of exceptionality. Classifying a student as mentally retarded, for example, requires by definition (Grossman, 1983) the presence of subaverage general intellectual functioning, accompanied by deficits in adaptive behavior. Professional debate and local practice in operationalizing these standards have had a significant impact, particularly on the concept of mild retardation and thus on eligibility decisions. Similar debates rage over the identification criteria for other areas of exceptionality, especially over the determination of discrepancy between ability and achievement in the field of learning disabilities (Cone & Wilson, 1981; Mercer, Hughes, & Mercer, 1985; Polloway & Patton, in press) and the validity of data generated from rating scales, behavioral measures, and projective instruments in the field of emotional disturbance (Kauffman, 1985).

An eligibility committee considers all available evaluation information to determine whether a student needs special services and to provide some direction for appropriate placement. Prior to the advent of federal regulations, parents were frequently uninformed about the process, but they now have the right to be involved and should be encouraged to participate actively in the decision-making process.

The affirmation of parental rights of involvement has resulted in more consistency in the operation of eligibility conferences. First, the school must inform parents of any intention to review their child's status and must elicit their input in selecting the optimum program. Figure 3.3 shows a sample form inviting parents to participate in the meeting of an eligibility committee. Second, if parents do not participate in the eligibility meeting, they must be informed of the committee's decision. Figure 3.4 shows a sample form advising parents of a committee decision. Third, parents are entitled to a hearing, with support from legal counsel, to contest a proposed placement. In this way, parents and the due process officer or hearing board members can review the rationale for the placement decision. These procedural changes imply that the parents' position has changed from one of passive receipt of accomplished decisions to one of potential influence in placement decisions affecting their child. Established procedures also enable parents to seek special services that they believe their child needs but is not receiving.

After completing all phases of the eligibility process, the multidisciplinary team decides whether special services are warranted and, if so, which to provide. For the student found ineligible for special services, the committee suggests ways that the student can be more successful in the regular classroom. Program adaptations or modifications may be particularly appropriate. For the student found eligible, the assessment information that has been collected should provide the basis for developing the child's individual education program (IEP).

INDIVIDUAL EDUCATION PROGRAMS

The passage of PL 94–142 incorporated the IEP into routine pedagogical practice. Data gathered in the classification process and further information collected by multidisciplinary specialists and by both special and regular teachers determine the IEP, which outlines specific plans for placement and instruction of a student.

FIGURE 3.3
Invitation to parents
to attend an eligibility
committee meeting

Date _____

Dear _____,

    The process of gathering assessment information on _____

_____ has been completed. To best determine how to use this information and develop a realistic and adequate program, we request your attendance at an Eligibility Committee

meeting to be held at _____ School on

_____, 19 _____, at _____ A.M./P.M. We invite your attendance so that we can share our findings with you and receive your suggestions and concerns. If you have any questions, please feel

free to call me at _____.

    Please return the enclosed form indicating your intention to attend or not to attend the meeting.

Sincerely yours,

Director of Special Education
(or teacher)

IEPs represent many previously used teaching practices. They clearly emphasize the individual: rather than relying on traditional clinical categories, IEPs acknowledge each student's need for a specifically designed program. As Harvey (1978) states, "... with the IEP, the child drives the program rather than the program driving the child."

Although IEPs can be used for a number of purposes, three stand out from the rest. First, IEPs can provide instructional direction. Conscious, written goal setting can help to remedy the "cookbook approach" (i.e., pulling together isolated or marginally

related instructional exercises in the name of good teaching). Second, IEPs function as the basis for evaluation. Formally established learning objectives for children help determine teacher effectiveness and efficiency, although this form of accountability is not intended to become the basis for evaluating teachers for tenure. A third use of IEPs is improved communication. Individual education programs can facilitate contact among staff members, teachers, and parents and to some extent, between teachers and students. Parental involvement, in particular, has resulted in increased mutual support and cooperation be-

FIGURE 3.4

Notification of eligibility for special program

Date _____

Dear _____,

    After careful consideration the recommendation of the Special Education Eligibility Committee is that _____(student)_____ be placed in _____(program)_____. This placement is being made pursuant to _____ and specifically under Rule _____ of the Special Education Program Services Rules issued by the Department of Education, State Board of Education.

_____ is recommended for this program because the committee believes that it will most effectively meet the educational needs of your child. The evaluation data on which the decision was based are included in the meeting report of the eligibility committee. You may request a copy.

    By law you are allowed a hearing on this educational placement, if you so desire. The hearing procedure is outlined on the attached form.

If you wish to appeal this decision, you must do so within _____ days of the receipt of this notice. Should you decide to request a hearing, please complete the form and mail to

_____

If you disagree with the local hearing decision, you have the right to appeal the decision to _____. You may wish to consult with someone from the enclosed list to assist you in determining whether you should accept this placement or request a hearing.

    If you are satisfied with the placement indicated, please return the enclosed self-addressed envelope and indicate your approval. We will contact you regarding your child's individual education program within

_____ days of receiving your approval.

    We look forward to working with you in the future to meet your child's educational needs.

Sincerely yours,

_____

Director of Special Education

tween home and school. The implications of these shifts in practice are further delineated in the discussions in chapter 6 relative to working with regular class teachers and parents.

IEP Components

Individual education programs are intended to function as an integral part of the diagnostic process; thus, the development of the IEP follows initial identification and collection of assessment data. The individual education program then details the least restrictive, most appropriate placement and outlines the instructional program. The IEP must be evaluated and then rewritten annually as long as services are still necessary.

PL 94–142 outlines eight major components of the IEP: statement of current level of performance, annual instructional goals, short-term objectives, statements detailing the special services to be provided and the degree of integration into the regular classroom, schedules for institution and evaluation of services, and provision for signed consent. This section focuses on the first three components, and Figure 3.5 shows them in relationship. As the figure illustrates, annual goals and short-term objectives emanate from a child's present level of performance. Although the law does not specify the exact form of these components, the following information should serve as a general guide for writing IEPs.

FIGURE 3.5
Interrelationship of three IEP components

Performance Levels   A summary of a student's current functioning provides a basis for subsequent goal setting. Performance levels should be assessed in all areas needing special instruction. Depending on the individual, areas of concern might include cognitive, personal/social, or psychomotor domains. Relevant information could be related to academic skills, behavioral patterns, self-help skills, vocational talents, or communication abilities.

Performance levels should be viewed as summaries of an individual's strengths and weaknesses. These statements can take a variety of forms, including formal test scores, informal test results, behavioral descriptions, a listing of specific abilities relative to a sequence of skills in a given area, and self-report data obtained from the student.

Appropriate written statements of performance levels should meet two major criteria: they must provide specific data sufficient for later goal setting, and they must emphasize positive aspects of the student.

Annual Goals   The second key component of an IEP is the listing of annual goals. As the name implies, these goals predict long-term gains during the school year. The annual goals should reflect the educator's (and the parents') best guess of the student's possible accomplishments and achievements. The following concerns can help determine realistic expectations: (1) chronological age, (2) past learning profile, and (3) recent learning history and response to instruction. Merbler (1978) provides an estimation formula that assists in specifying expected instructional time for a given goal. Essentially, it encourages the teacher to stipulate goals with a range of likely outcomes from the most optimistic to the most pessimistic.

The following examples illustrate the close relationship that should exist between annual goals and performance levels.

1. Current level: Imitates with one-word labels for objects
   Possible goals: Two-word phrases
   Three-word phrases
   Use of interrogative forms
2. Current level: Identifies three letters of the alphabet
   Possible goals: Letters of own name
   All letters of the alphabet
   All letters and consonant sounds
3. Current level: Adds without regrouping
   Possible goals: Adding with regrouping
   Subtracting without regrouping
   Subtracting with regrouping

Annual goals should consider four major criteria: they should be measurable, positive, student-oriented, and relevant. **Measurable** goals provide a basis for evaluation. Statements should use precise, behavioral terms that denote action and can therefore be operationally defined (e.g., **pronounce, write,** or **identify motorically**) rather than vague, general language that confounds evaluation and observer agreement (e.g., **know, understand,** or **appreciate**). "Will correctly identify all initial consonant sounds" is more appropriate than the unmeasurable "will learn to read." Although goals continue to be commonly written in general fashion, such as "To improve _____ skills" (Epstein, Polloway, Patton, & Foley, in press; Weisenfeld, 1986), such a format provides little information related to yearly expectations.

Positive goals provide an appropriate direction for instruction. Avoiding negative goals creates an atmosphere that is helpful in communication with parents as well as in charting student progress. The goal "will learn to respond at appropriate times" gives the student something to strive for, as opposed to "will learn to keep mouth closed," which negatively emphasizes something to avoid.

Goals should also be **oriented to the student.** Developing students' skills is the intent, and the only measure of effectiveness should be what is learned, not what is taught. Thus, "will verbally respond to questions with two-word phrases" is preferable to "will be given oral language readiness materials."

Finally, goals must be **relevant** to the individual student's actual needs. Unfortunately, research indicates that IEPs frequently do not meet this criterion. For example, goals for students with mild handicaps have often been found to be academically focused, to the relative exclusion of social-emotional and communication skills at the elementary level (Epstein et al., 1987) and career-vocational or socio-behavioral domains at the middle school level (McBride & Forgnone, 1985).

Short-Term Objectives Instructional objectives (IEP-type) are intended to serve as major stepping-stones toward annual goals. The objectives should therefore illustrate the path that the teacher will follow to reach the goals. Generally, short-term objectives (STOs) have been conceptualized and developed as more specific representations of the skills to be learned. Although legal requirements do not stipulate the use of strict behavioral objectives (as in Mager, 1975), STOs should be specific, observable, measurable, student-oriented, and positive. They should also include a stated criterion of task success, a consideration that annual goals may not necessarily have addressed explicitly. Mager (1975) and Thompson (1977) contain further information and guided practice in writing behavioral objectives.

One of the most important tasks in developing individual education programs is establishing objectives that are consistent with the student's annual goals. Because the objectives are viewed as sequential steps to those goals, the STOs should reflect major instructional achievements between the current performance level and the ultimate goal. Typically, three to eight objectives per goal are sufficient, with each objective representing a skill that might reasonably be acquired in 1 to 3 months. This understanding of objectives should set them apart from the process of daily or weekly lesson planning (to be discussed in chapter 4).

The evolution of objectives from goals reflects an adaptation of task-analysis procedures. It consists of breaking down a more general goal into its major components. This approach can enable the teacher to develop consistent objectives. Table 3.1 provides some sample goal-objective clusters. Development of a functional sequence of skills for each curricular area can facilitate establishment of these clusters. Many commercial materials such as the Brigance Diagnostic Inventory (Brigance, 1980, 1983) and the Instructional Based Appraisal System (Meyen, 1976), attempt to assist in accomplishing this purpose. In addition, numerous software packages containing sequenced goal-objective clusters have been marketed in recent years. Although the benefit of reduced paperwork may be significant, there remains the issue of whether a student's curriculum is truly consistent with individual needs.

PLACEMENT

The initial consequence of implementing an individual education program is the designation of a specific educational placement for a student. The central concern is to ensure that placement decisions are based on the individual's specific needs. The effects of federal law are particularly apparent in the area of placement. One specific legal requirement has relevance to all placement alternatives: all children who are handicapped must be educated in the least restrictive environment (LRE).

Alternatives

Special education options are often represented as a **cascade of services,** or a continuum of placements (Deno, 1970; Gallagher, 1969, in Rothstein, 1971; Mercer & Payne, 1975). Two assumptions underlie the cascade. First, a child should be moved away from the normal situation only as far as is needed to provide an appropriate education. Second, the student should be returned to the normal situation as soon as possible. The LRE mandated by federal law and implicit in many state regulations is based on these two assumptions.

Public schools have traditionally made four general provisions for students who are handicapped: regular class–based programs, special class–based programs, special schools, and non-school-based programs. This discussion briefly describes the first two of these options, which represent the most widely used placements for individuals who are mildly and moderately handicapped.

Regular Classes The ultimate goal of educational placement is to provide the most beneficial services to students with the least segregation from their nonhandicapped peers. The term **mainstreaming** has been used to refer to the practice of integrating learners with special needs into regular classrooms. Multiple uses and definitions of the term, however, have produced undue concern and confusion among teachers and parents.

The educational needs of some children who are mildly handicapped can be met

TABLE 3.1
Sample goal-objective clusters

Goal 1: Identify and write numerals 0–100 with 95% accuracy as measured by teacher-made test.

1. Recognize the numerals 0–100 with 95% accuracy.
2. Write and say in sequence the numerals from 0–100 with 95% accuracy.
3. Write and say in isolation the numerals 0–100 with 95% accuracy.
4. Write from memory the numerals 0–100 with 95% accuracy.

Goal 2: Divide shapes and sets into halves, quarters, and thirds with 95% accuracy.

1. Divide shapes into halves with 95% accuracy.
2. Divide sets into halves with 95% accuracy.
3. Divide shapes into fourths with 95% accuracy.
4. Divide sets into fourths with 95% accuracy.
5. Divide shapes into thirds with 95% accuracy.
6. Divide sets into thirds with 95% accuracy.

Goal 3: Multiply a three-digit number by another three-digit number using regrouping.

1. Give the answer to each fact with 95% accuracy when multiplication facts with a multiplier of 12 or less are presented, one at a time, visually and auditorily.
2. Multiply a two-digit number by another two-digit number without regrouping with 95% accuracy.
3. Multiply a two-digit number by another two-digit number with regrouping with 95% accuracy.
4. Multiply a three-digit number by another three-digit number without regrouping with 95% accuracy.

without direct special instructional services. The **consultation model** enlists the services of a support teacher or educational strategist whose knowledge about curriculum, materials, and teaching methodology can assist in planning and implementing programs for individuals or entire classes. This arrangement can also provide diagnostic services. In this case a diagnostician would work with individual children to assess their academic and social skills and would then prescribe an educational program for the regular teacher to implement.

Another approach provides a variety of services through a **resource teacher.** Most often, the resource teacher deals directly with students having difficulty with a specific problem or a general subject area. Although resource programs vary as much as the teachers who develop them, the basic concept involves a resource room where an individual or small group regularly receives special services for a given time period. Figure 3.6 presents 10 service arrangements that are possible using a resource program. Proceeding clockwise from the upper right, the options represent gradual movement away from total integration in the regular class and toward an increase in the intensity of services provided to the child. In the final option the resource teacher facilitates the student's transition into the more restrictive setting of a special class.

Special Classes Special classes provide a self-contained instructional environment for students unable to fully profit from the regular class programs just discussed. A special class is usually restricted to approximately 10 to 15 students and is often staffed with a

TABLE 3.1
continued

5. Multiply a three-digit number by another three-digit number with regrouping with 95% accuracy.

Goal 4: Correctly identify the first 176 words of the 220 words on the basic sight word list.
1. Correctly identify all 88 words on the preprimer and primer basic sight word list.
2. Correctly identify all 44 words on the first grade basic sight word list.
3. Correctly identify 90% of the 44 words on the second grade basic sight word list.

Goal 5: Correctly identify all consonant and vowel sounds.
1. Correctly pronounce all consonant blends when presented with a 20-word recognition list.
2. Correctly pronounce all consonant digraphs when presented with a 20-word recognition list.
3. Correctly pronounce all vowel diphthongs when presented with a 20-word recognition list.
4. Correctly pronounce all phonetically regular one-syllable words on a 20-word recognition list.

Goal 6: Cursively write the letters of the alphabet (in isolation) with 95% accuracy.*
1. Cursively write the letters *a, c, d, g, o* with 95% accuracy.
2. Cursively write the letters *b, h, f, k, l, e* with 95% accuracy.
3. Cursively write the letters *i, j, p, r, s, t, u, w* with 95% accuracy.
4. Cursively write the letters *m, n, v, x, y, z* with 95% accuracy.

*These letters have been grouped by the similarity of strokes necessary for formation.

teacher and an aide. Full-time special class programs give the teacher complete curricular responsibility for the students. Traditionally, the full-time special class has operated autonomously and with minimal integration of students into the regular program. This autonomy, or perhaps **benign neglect,** is a negative condition and is one of several factors that contributed to the mainstreaming movement, which began in earnest in the early 1970s. Today, full-time special class placement can be justified for only a small number of students who are handicapped.

With the growing emphasis on integrative programs, part-time or modified special class programs have become more popular. These arrangements can include integration with nonhandicapped peers during nonacademic periods (e.g., physical education, re-

cess, and lunch) as well as during academic periods in which a student can benefit from regular class instruction. This alternative is discussed in the section that follows.

Selecting the Best Alternative

Perhaps no other special education issue has been debated as long as the selection of the most appropriate placement has been. A recent review by Polloway (1984) highlights the issue's evolution over 50 years of research, conjecture, and bias and its ability to continue attracting attention. This review identifies five historical stages: the origins of special schools and classes in the early 1900s, the tremendous growth in the numbers of these classes at midcentury, the call for abolition of special class placement in

FIGURE 3.6
Service arrangements involving a resource teacher. (From *Mental Retardation: Introduction and Personal Perspectives* [p. 131] by J. M. Kauffman and J. S. Payne, 1975, Columbus, OH: Merrill. Copyright 1975 by Merrill Publishing Company. Adapted by permission.)

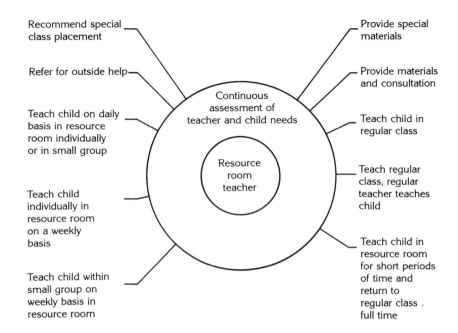

Recommend special class placement

Refer for outside help

Teach child on daily basis in resource room individually or in small group

Teach child individually in resource room on a weekly basis

Teach child within small group on weekly basis in resource room

Continuous assessment of teacher and child needs

Resource room teacher

Provide special materials

Provide materials and consultation

Teach child in regular class

Teach regular class, regular teacher teaches child

Teach child in resource room for short periods of time and return to regular class full time

the late 1960s to early 1970s, the move to regular class alternatives (i.e., resource programs) in the 1970s, and finally the evaluation of alternatives for the 1980s in light of the learning needs of students currently being served.

The challenge of matching an individual student with the most appropriate placement prohibits considering the options outlined earlier as discrete choices. Instead, placement selection requires investigating modifications of both special class and regular class programs. Polloway and Smith (1980) summarize this perspective.

Much emphasis has been placed on the development of individual educational plans in accordance with the law. There has been less obvious emphasis, however, on the assurance that each school system will provide a full range of educational placement alternatives. Although the law calls for the least restrictive environment possible for each child, there has not been the obvious insistence on the most educative environment possible for each child. It would seem of greatest impor-

tance . . . to create a vehicle for ensuring appropriate educational provisions for each individual child. There is a need to adopt specific individual placement alternatives on the same basis that individual instructional plans are adopted. (p. 10)

Polloway and Smith (1980) further discuss how a full range of services would most benefit students. Administratively, such a continuum dictates the need for a flexible system whereby children have the opportunity to move progressively toward the most appropriate and least restrictive learning environment. Philosophically, a continuum of services approaches the ideal of attending to each child's individual needs. Practically, it ensures that children will be placed only into situations where a reasonable degree of success can be expected. Consideration of service alternatives on such a continuum would enable placement decisions to fall in line with the specifically tailored instructional programs mandated by law. The key implication is that students must be placed according to their ability to profit from a given program rather than as a matter of regular administrative practice or as a reflection of any trend in the professional literature.

Consideration of four criteria should help determine the best educational program.

1. *Severity of the problem.* The student's specific academic, linguistic, and personal/social characteristics must be weighed initially. Behavioral patterns and work and study skills must also be considered.
2. *Regular class situation.* Competencies and attitudes of the teacher, the availability of an aide, and the number of students enrolled are crucial factors in the regular class.
3. *Availability of supportive school personnel.* Placement decisions can be greatly affected by the resource people who can support the regular teacher when mainstream options are selected.
4. *Outside resources.* Tutorial assistance by volunteers from the community can also significantly contribute to the prospects for successful placement in a regular class.

In the past, decisions have most often revolved around administrative variables and less often around the individual student. Recently, considerations of learner characteristics have received more attention as the primary focus of placement decisions. A flexible placement system should be based on the need to specify the degree of integration that is truly most appropriate and least restrictive for the student. Inherent in such a system is a rejection of the special class/regular class dichotomy.

Specific curricular needs of exceptional children fall along a continuum ranging from full-time special to full-time regular classes. Few children identified as handicapped belong in either extreme. All students can profit to some specifiable extent from contact with nonhandicapped peers. Students with more serious handicaps might interact through bus travel, recess, lunch, and physical education classes. Other children with varied levels of handicaps might also profit from integration into nonacademic settings such as art, music, and drama. For those students with less significant problems, educators should investigate regular class programs supplemented by consultative or supportive services in specific content areas.

Implementing Integrative Programs

The adoption of a placement continuum for individuals with handicaps ensures that most students will be actively involved in both special and regular programs throughout the instructional day. The student, therefore, must become the joint responsibility of all involved teachers, and special educators must work closely with regular instructors to ensure the student's success. A variety of considerations relate to successful implementation of integrative programs.

☐ *Assessing situational variables in the regular classroom.* The special teacher should assess what will be expected of a student after placement; that is, how the regular teacher presents material, groups students, tests, and assigns homework. In addition, specific academic and social expectations should be evaluated. Preparation of students before placement should be based on these factors.

☐ *Modifying the student's work and study skills.* Based on assessment of the regular class situation, the special teacher may need to change the student's behavior to conform to the expectations of the mainstream teacher.

☐ *Considering locus of control.* With a low student-teacher ratio in the special class, students may develop an external locus of control—that is, they may come to expect frequent praise and/or rewards for work and behavior. The special teacher often needs to train students to accept personal responsibility for their actions, thus developing an internal locus of control.

☐ *Identifying probable areas of difficulty.* Prior identification of potential problems may help to prevent initial failure in the regular classroom.

☐ *Preparing the regular teachers.* A discussion of a student's specific strengths and weaknesses and of successful methods and materials enhances the chances for a smooth transition. Appropriately designed in-service activities can play a major role in achieving this objective.

Several key elements characterize successful integrative programs. A primary concern for the development of cooperative relationships between special education and regular class teachers is critical. Suggestions for establishing this collaborative role are provided in chapter 6. Implementation of specific regular education instructional practices to facilitate mainstreaming efforts is also important. Stainback, Stainback, Courtnage, & Jaben (1985) provide a summary of three such practices.

Diagnosis can be defined as the collection of information that delineates a child's learning needs. **Prescription,** then, involves determining which teaching strategies, methods, and materials will be most effective for instructing the child or modifying behavior. **Remediation** is the consequence of these two processes; it is geared toward eliminating problems—even though that goal often cannot be realistically achieved. In a broad sense good educational practice follows the scientific or medical model (Kauffman & Hallahan, 1974). For instance, if one diagnoses poison ivy, based on observing the skin, one will probably prescribe calamine or cortisone treatment. Remediation should eliminate discomfort, itching, and discoloration. Similarly, if class worksheets indicate that a child cannot recognize the numeral 5, the prescription will suggest ways to teach the student to recognize that number. Remediation will be complete when the child learns to identify the numeral 5.

The assessment-based instructional model does not stress an in-depth initial diagnosis followed by long-term planning of a prescriptive program. Rather, it is a cyclical, repeated process of assessment and teaching (Lerner, 1985), as illustrated in Figure 3.7, which is adapted from Lerner's concept.

ASSESSMENT-BASED INSTRUCTION

Special education's increasing stress on the diagnosis of learning problems, spurred to some extent by regulation and statute, must be evaluated for any detrimental effect on the time and attention given to instruction. Within this text we encourage use of the term *assessment-based instruction* (ABI) to indicate that the primary value of diagnostic activity lies in its contributions to actual programming.

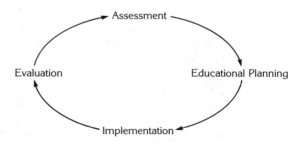

FIGURE 3.7
The assessment-based instructional cycle

This prescriptive process can be used informally, although it works most efficiently when tied to systematic record keeping (see chapter 4). **Diagnosis** is based on the initial collection of data about the child, enabling the teacher to pinpoint abilities and disabilities. The key is that the information gathered is accurate. Otherwise, any plan will be built on invalid assumptions.

After diagnosis available teaching options are surveyed, and the most appropriate for the individual child are selected. Various antecedent and subsequent factors can shape this educational recommendation, or **planning.** Important considerations include how to present relevant stimuli in a variety of ways, such as prompting, cuing, and modeling, and which mode of presentation to choose. Other antecedent considerations concern the environmental arrangement and the daily schedule. Consequent factors include appropriate reinforcement and attention to the use of positive versus negative reinforcers.

After developing the educational prescription for a determined period of time, the next step is to **implement** it. Basically, implementing a program should involve direct, intensive teaching—following instructional recommendations concerning antecedent and consequent factors and staying constantly alert to any need for change in content or method. Such **evaluation** may lead to alterations in both diagnosis and subsequent educational planning.

This structured view of assessment-based instruction belies the fact that much learning can also take place at unstructured or unplanned times. Hammill and Bartel (1982) caution against assuming that all learning occurs with scheduled events and that all tasks can be reduced to easily planned, executed, and evaluated pencil-and-paper activities. They encourage teachers to be ready to capitalize on unplanned interactions. In several curricular areas, most notably oral language development, such an orientation is particularly important.

Instructional Principles

Assessment-based instruction is essentially an attitude that suggests that teaching practices should be derived from an evaluation of the learner. The following list of principles identifies some basic tenets of effective teaching.

1. *Flexibility.* Not all children can learn by the same method, nor does any individual learn solely through one method. In order to meet individual needs, teachers must try different teaching approaches and materials and must determine the most effective ones.
2. *Variety.* Within individual teaching periods, instruction must reflect a variety of teaching methods. Change is often necessary to maintain interest.
3. *Motivation.* Children who are handicapped, like most nonhandicapped children, must have a reason to learn. Often, intrinsic reinforcers, such as the value of knowledge, do not supply sufficient motivation, and other reinforcers must be found.
4. *Structure.* The teacher of students with handicaps must teach, not just guide or facilitate, if students are to learn. Adherence to routines and structure is an essential feature of their instructional program.
5. *Success.* Providing each child with an opportunity to succeed is one of the most valuable ingredients in any effective intervention program.

No approach, material, gadget, game, or technological invention alone will determine the success or failure of the instructional process. The most important element in teaching is the teacher, and in the end the teacher's effectiveness is the most critical factor in determining what a student learns, maintains, and generalizes.

EVALUATION AND REVIEW

Evaluation and review focus on the individual student as well as on the overall program (as defined by the classroom, school division, or state agency). Student evaluation can best be viewed chronologically, with three levels of review. Long-term evaluation calls for regularly scheduled complete diagnostic analyses, usually every 3 years (hence the term *triennial* review). This review considers the student's eligibility for services, based on assessment of psychological, educational, medical, and sociological components.

The second level of review is the annual evaluation of a student's individual education program. This review is the time to reconsider both placement decisions and instructional goals from the previous year and to devise a new IEP if a continuation of service delivery is warranted.

Finally, instructional lessons should include planned evaluative activities that provide ongoing information on student progress. To be effective, teachers should continuously evaluate instruction and make changes as indicated.

Program evaluation is devoted to overall assessment and improvement of an entire educational program. Such periodic evaluative efforts can provide educators with a broader perspective on program goals. Evaluation of this type may be particularly significant when multiple staff members or disciplines are involved in implementation.

SUMMARY

The development of strategies to promote individual instruction requires a determination of students' educational needs in order to tailor instruction to their individual strengths and weaknesses. The full diagnostic process includes identification of children having difficulties at home and at school, multidisciplinary assessment of their current level of functioning, and establishment of their eligibility for special services. Individual education programs then specify the most appropriate, least restrictive placement alternative as well as the instructional goals and objectives for the next year of instruction.

4
Strategies for Classroom Organization and Management

This chapter focuses on instructionally related dimensions that are intricately associated with effective teaching: organization and management of the classroom. This topic includes those noninstructional activities that teachers need to perform to operate their classrooms efficiently—functions like the physical design and arrangement of the classroom, student grouping, instructional planning, record keeping, and grading.

The importance of classroom organization and management has been documented in two different literature bases: (1) initial problems of first-year teachers and (2) research on teaching. However, as Doyle (1986) highlights, the significance of these areas was largely overlooked until relatively recently.

PHYSICAL DIMENSIONS OF THE CLASSROOM

The classroom environment is a critical determinant of successful teaching and learning, yet discussions of teacher competencies frequently overlook it. Lindsley (1964) coined the term *prosthetic environment* to describe effective classrooms designed to facilitate learning. Associated approaches might include seating arrangements that stimulate responding and discourage distractibility, audiovisual equipment that assists in highlighting and emphasizing important points, charts that provide consistent reminders of specific rules, and classroom areas that encourage companionship and sharing. Although physically a prosthetic environment is separate from the teacher-student dyad, conceptually it is an extension of the teaching-learning paradigm. Antecedent events and consequences emerge from any environment. The effectiveness and efficiency with which they are managed are particularly enhanced in a well-planned environment.

Unfortunately, many teachers give little consideration to alternatives for arranging and manipulating the classroom environment. Often they model their own classroom after that of their cooperating teacher during student teaching, even though their students' ages and abilities and the two teachers' personalities, competencies, interests, and educational goals may differ significantly. This discussion of various environmental aspects should assist teachers in planning an effective environment and should provoke some thinking about environmental options. However, a teacher can plan a prosthetic environment only after knowing and understanding the needs of the students to be taught.

Environmental Design

Historically, U.S. education has recorded dramatic changes, often extreme, regarding what the school environment should be and how it should appear. The one-room school of the turn of the century eventually led to graded, self-contained classes. Later, the emphasis shifted back to the open classroom, with some similarities to the one-room school in the form of educational pods, which were aesthetically pleasing with their carpeted floors, low ceilings, nondistracting illumination, brightly colored walls and furnishings, and lots of space in which to create. (See Knoblock, 1975, for a discussion of the use of open classrooms in special education.) Subsequently, however, many schools became disenchanted with this concept and returned to more traditional, structured situations.

What we know now is that not all students benefit from the same type of educational setting. In an open setting some children learn well, whereas others find it difficult, if not actually distracting. Some students function well in a self-contained classroom with a structured program, whereas others feel stifled and may be educationally harmed in such an environment. In addition, teachers' preferences must be considered; certain instructional styles are better matched to open or structured environments.

Students who are handicapped generally need more structure and guidance than do their nonhandicapped peers. However, one of a teacher's major goals must be to help students learn how to handle and control themselves in less structured situations. Therefore, classroom arrangements should provide structure, organization, and regimentation when needed as well as freedom, exploration, and permissiveness when it can be handled. To achieve these seemingly conflicting goals, teachers should conceptualize the degree of structure along a continuum from highly structured to permissive arrangements and determine which best suits the needs of a particular learning task. Educational environments must be flexible and adaptable to individual needs, and they must change as pupils grow. Zentall (1983) includes a cogent theoretical argument on the need for accommodating individual differences within learning environments. Gray (1975) lists several considerations in designing and organizing such an educational environment (p. 75).

☐ *Human scale.* Physical settings must satisfy the need for a sense of identity. If the chairs, tables, and desks are too large or too small, the student will at first experience discomfort and, later, psychological discontent.

☐ *Personal territory.* Students and teachers alike need a sense of their own turf. This may include a place to keep personal possessions as well as a place to be alone to think and to be separate from group pressures.

☐ *Spatial variation.* A building should provide options in the sizes and shapes of subspaces so that people can gather in twos, fours, or larger groups.

☐ *Manipulability and flexibility.* Patterns of use need not be fixed or predetermined. The environment must allow itself to be manipulated by its users so that spaces can be changed. A manipulatable environment gives its users a sense of possession.

☐ *Environmental feedback.* A school facility must allow its occupants to stamp their presence on it. It must be ready to accept the graphic presentation of student activities and interests so that the building reflects who the students are and how they are doing. Displays of student work help build a sense of identity and also make the surroundings more lively and relevant.

☐ *Optional seating and work surfaces.* The facility must acknowledge that people work in a variety of natural postures: sitting up straight, lounging, leaning, perching, and standing. It should offer a variety of seating and work-surface heights (including the floor) to accommodate students.

☐ *Graceful wear and renewal.* Furniture should be able to be used, worn out, and renewed.

☐ *Work esthetic.* The look of learning in action is a busy one, with things out and in use. Some adults may view this as a violation of some cultural sense of order, but administrators, teachers, and custodians need to realize that a useful, interesting, and relevant environment becomes attractive to its users.

Classroom Arrangement

Not long ago many special education classes were small, underequipped, and located in peculiar areas of the school building. Even today, a substantial number of classrooms continue to fit this description. In addition, at some schools the principal evaluates a good teacher by how clean the floor is, how even the window shades are, how empty the wastebaskets are, and how effectively the children are contained in the room. It is easy to criticize these fastidious administrators, but to some extent their concerns may be important and worth heeding. Many students with handicaps come from environments lacking order. School should be a pleasant place to be; it should look and smell good. It is not too much to expect students, regardless of age or ability, to clean up after themselves and exercise reasonable control. Teachers must distinguish between providing an opportunity to enjoy school and express oneself and allowing students to behave inappropriately within a chaotic environment. A logical assumption is that students can learn (and can profit from learning) to maintain their environment: picking up paper from the floor, washing chalkboards, straightening shades, and putting things away where they can be found and used another day.

Each classroom teacher must operate within certain administrative guidelines. Although all schools have physical limitations, the teacher must provide for large and small group instruction, individual work, and a nonseated area where students can become involved in interesting independent activities. Whether the existing room is small and self-contained or more open, these dimensions are essential for developing a prosthetic, effective environment.

The starting point for environmental design is the same as that for all other instructional strategies: the assessment of students' specific strengths and weaknesses in core curricular areas and in their response to various environmental arrangements. After this initial assessment, teachers may begin to develop a prosthetic environment but must realize that as more is learned about the students and as they learn and develop, the classroom should change to incorporate this newly acquired data. This does not mean that the classroom should be changed

radically on a weekly basis, but it does mean that the room is adaptable and flexible.

In determining possible alternatives for classroom arrangement, the teacher can begin by drawing a rough sketch of the floor plan of the room. Basic equipment, such as desks, chairs, tables, is then added, possibly through cutouts or three-dimensional representatives. Space should be allotted for areas for large and small group instruction, seat work, time out, carrels, and places where learners can work away from their desks, such as interest centers.

One valuable concept to consider is the division of the classroom into high- and low-probability areas. Based loosely on the Premack principle explained in chapter 5, this concept suggests that the academic areas (or low-probability areas) should be separated from the interest and activity centers (high-probability areas). Students earn time in the favored high-probability area through successful work completion in the low-probability area. Figure 4.1 reflects this concept. Classroom design based on the Premack principle offers an opportunity to combine primary instructional areas with sections devoted to reinforcement activities. Although the classroom in Figure 4.1 is based on access to two connected rooms, the concept can be easily utilized within one room. The reader is referred to Haring (1974) and Polloway and Smith (1982) for further information on this concept.

Regardless of the chosen classroom arrangement, every teacher should periodically review why the room is arranged as it is. There is no one best way to arrange a classroom, but some ways are clearly better than others.

Adjuncts to the Instructional Environment

Several common adjuncts can assist the teacher in designing an effective environ-

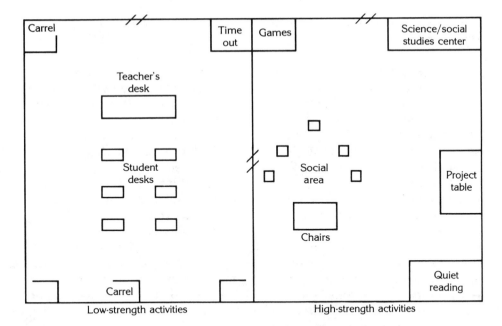

FIGURE 4.1
Classroom design showing application of the Premack principle (From
Teaching Language Skills to Exceptional Learners [p. 379] by E. A. Polloway
and J. E. Smith, 1982, Denver: Love. Copyright 1981 by Love Publishing
Company. Reprinted by permission.)

ment, especially bulletin boards, study carrels, and interest centers. Additionally, the microcomputer has unquestioned potential for making significant contributions to instructional technology. Because of its increasing availability for classroom use, chapter 7 discusses the microcomputer in detail.

Bulletin Boards   Bulletin boards can facilitate development of a prosthetic environment by making the classroom attractive and by promoting both incidental and directed learning. Regardless of the goal, bulletin boards should be integrated into the curriculum and thus planned for and prepared accordingly.

One of the most appropriate uses of boards is to display students' work. In addi-

tion to featuring arts and crafts projects, the displays can also include students' academic work samples and thus provide social recognition for successful achievement.

Bulletin boards also foster creativity by giving students an opportunity to choose topics and plan a related message. Monthly features for primary-aged students might include the following: September, autumn leaves; October, witches; November, turkeys; December, seasonal celebrations; January, snowpersons; February, valentines, cherry trees; March, clover; April, flowers; May, baseball, mothers; and June, flags. Local customs and special events can provide further ideas for themes. Teachers should also be sensitive to the value of bulletin boards with junior and senior high students. Allowing students to design, create, and produce their own displays is simultaneously an excellent learning tool, motivational device, and management technique.

Study Carrels Virtually every classroom can benefit from having at least one study carrel for students who are handicapped. A study carrel is essentially a place for independent, individual work. Carrels, or cubicles, have two main purposes: (1) to limit outside stimuli and (2) to provide a specific place for concentrated study.

A study carrel should be designed to minimize the distraction of various classroom activities. Consequently, it should be placed in a quiet area. Cubicles come in many shapes and forms. Some have elaborate, commercially made wooden frames; others are cardboard refrigerator cartons; still others are little more than a small table and chair placed in the back corner of the classroom, where the child sits facing the corner. As long as it substantially decreases outside stimuli, the study carrel's appearance is not of great significance.

The carrel becomes a work area for the teacher who uses it as a special place for concentrated study. The teacher may suggest that students go to their "office" to study, or students may ask for permission to do so. Use of carrels should emphasize the positive features of cubicles rather than their association with punishment for inappropriate behavior.

Interest Centers Interest centers are basically an outgrowth of independent, seatwork activities, and thus some teachers have uncharitably referred to them as "laminated seat work." Although this description may sometimes be accurate, interest centers are an attempt to take the monotony out of seat work and put more variety into classroom instruction. Interest centers can be used for (1) instruction in which a student works at the center to review something previously learned, (2) promotion of social interaction for two or three students who are working together, and (3) development of independent work skills and self-direction.

Teachers should consider several key components of interest centers: (1) the user, (2) objectives, (3) rules for use, (4) directions, and (5) materials or equipment needed. Because interest centers are intended for students, the user is the most important element. In developing ideas for effective interest centers, teachers should keep in mind the user's characteristics. In effect, an interest center becomes a well-planned lesson presented primarily without the teacher's direct assistance.

Another important step is to determine the objectives of the particular center. Without clear objectives the results of the center will always be in question. Did the student learn something beneficial? The implication here is that an interest center can be an attractive creation, but without clear objectives it may be of dubious value.

Rules and directions go hand-in-hand in promoting effective use of an interest center. They provide students with parameters, or boundaries, so that they will understand what is expected of them and how they can accomplish the objectives of the interest center. Rules tell pupils what they can and cannot do in the center; directions tell them how they can learn something.

The last concern in developing an interest center is securing the materials and equipment. The best advice to follow is to keep it simple. Making centers complicated or intricate increases the probability that students will not be able to use them effectively without the teacher's help, thus defeating one of the teacher's purposes in developing the center (i.e., providing independent study material). Keeping component parts of an interest center to the bare minimum increases the probability of the students' working alone efficiently and preserves the center's function. Figure 4.2 gives sample

FIGURE 4.2
Filmstrip viewing
center

Directions:
1. Get a filmstrip.
2. Put it in the viewer.
3. Watch the filmstrip.
4. Choose one of the next three activities:
   (a) Go to the easel and paint something from the filmstrip.
   (b) Go to the writing center and write a description of the filmstrip.
   (c) Go to the tape recorder and record your feelings about the filmstrip.

directions for an audiovisual center; Figure 4.3 describes a center activity that could be used at the secondary level. The format illustrated in Figure 4.3 could be adapted for elementary use simply by making the items easier.

Teaching a child to work in an interest center is important; therefore, it must be done directly and precisely. In the same way that students can be taught how to study independently, how to take turns in a game, or how to stay on task in a working situation,

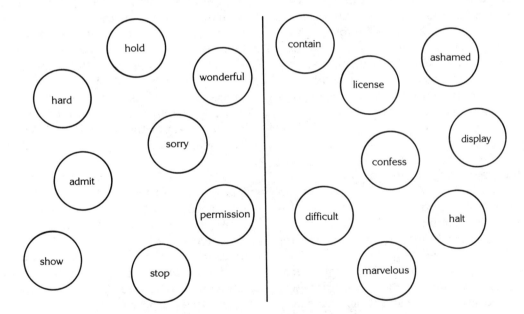

By using checkers to cover all the words, two people can play this game. Each player removes two checkers (one from each side), then replaces the checkers if the revealed words are not synonyms. When a player uncovers two words that are synonyms, that player can keep the two checkers. The player with the most checkers when all have been removed from the board is the winner. (As reinforcement, the answers should be available with the game.)

Answers: hold—contain; permission—license; sorry—ashamed; admit—confess; show—display; stop—halt; wonderful—marvelous; hard—difficult

FIGURE 4.3
Interest center activity on synonyms

they can also be taught how to appropriately use a center.

Because several pupils may want to go to the same center, traffic-control measures are necessary. One way to limit the number of children per center is to design tickets for each center and issue them to students at the teacher's discretion. If the teacher wants all children to enter all the centers over a period of time, the ticket method can guide students into particular centers as well as limit the number of students per center.

Some easy centers to make are a magazine corner where children can lounge, looking at or cutting out pictures; a numbers center for matching numerals with pictures containing the correct number of objects; a listening center equipped with headphones so that students can listen to records; and an area with a Language Master accessible for reviewing previously learned materials. Computer centers are another important option; the principles for microcomputer usage discussed in chapter 7 are helpful in this regard.

GROUPING

Another major organizational concern is instructional grouping[1] and its relationship to instruction with maximum benefit to students. A discussion of how best to group for instruction must first address a concern for individualization. Among the foremost principles on which the field of special education was founded is the importance of individualization in instruction. In many cases the primary justification for the provision of special services has been the assumption that instruction must be geared to

---

[1]Portions of this discussion are from "The Efficacy of Group Instruction v. One-to-One Instruction: A Review" by E. A. Polloway, M. E. Cronin, and J. R. Patton, 1986, *Remedial and Special Education, 7* (1), 22–30. Copyright 1986 by Pro-Ed. Adapted by permission.

the individual's specific needs. The requirement for individual educational programs (IEPs) in PL 94–142 further underscores this emphasis. The literature in the field also reflects the importance of individualization; textbooks are replete with references to its importance.

Nonetheless, a distinction should be made between the concepts of individualization and one-to-one instruction. Individualization refers to instruction **appropriate** to the individual, whether or not it is accomplished on a one-to-one basis. In fact, individualization can be accomplished through one-to-one or one-to-two ratios, in small groups, or even occasionally in large groups. In elaborating on this concept, Stevens and Rosenshine (1981) state that "individualization is considered a characteristic of effective instruction if the term implies helping each student to succeed, to achieve a high percentage of correct responses, and to become confident of his or her competence" (p. 3). Thus, even though individualization presumes that instruction is geared to the needs of the individual child, it does not mean that it is provided on a one-to-one basis.

In considering the issue of one-to-one versus group instruction, there are three predominant concerns—instructional effectiveness, efficiency, and social benefits—all of which are discussed here. Although the focus of this text is on individuals with mild/moderate handicaps, this brief review includes a broader range of populations for illustrative purposes.

Effectiveness

Effectiveness is a measure of whether the skills taught have been learned by students. Research on effectiveness has been equivocal. In several studies advantages for one-to-one instruction have been reported (Jenkins, Mayhall, Peschka, & Jenkins, 1974; Matson, DiLorenzo, & Esveldt-Dawson, 1981; Westling, Ferrell, & Swenson, 1982); in other instances group procedures have been found more effective (Biberdorf & Pear, 1977; Oliver, 1983; Orelove, 1982; Rincover & Koegel, 1977; Smith & Meyers, 1979). More commonly, comparable results have been reported (e.g., Favell, Favell, & McGimsey, 1978; Handleman & Harris, 1983; Ranieri, Ford, Vincent, & Brown, 1984).

Although most research on effectiveness has been primarily concerned with the acquisition of new skills, several studies also considered maintenance and generalization. In these cases some interesting results were reported. For example, generalization advantages were reported for group instructional efforts by Koegel and Rincover (1974), Fink and Sandall (1980), and Oliver and Scott (1981). Elium and McCarver (1980) reported that group training and one-to-one instruction produced comparable response maintenance when evaluated after a 1-year follow-up.

Although there are few data directly comparing group and one-to-one training models with children with mild handicaps, nevertheless there has been substantial support for instructional strategies in which group arrangements are an essential element. In particular, direct instruction programs, characterized by group work, have demonstrated effectiveness for students identified as mildly handicapped, disadvantaged, and slow learners (e.g., Becker, 1977; Becker & Carnine, 1980; Gregory, Hackney, & Gregory, 1982; Stevens & Rosenshine, 1981).

Efficiency

Efficiency refers to the amount of time required for something to be learned. Most research in this area has favored the use of group instruction (e.g., Elium & McCarver, 1980; Kazdin & Erickson, 1975; Orelove, 1982; Rincover & Koegel, 1977), thus reaffirming what many professionals in the field of special education have stated for years.

> The economics of public schools obviously requires the development of techniques that will allow children to be handled in a group situation . . . even if the techniques of behavior remediation should prove to be very highly effective when applied on an individual basis, they are nevertheless likely to remain economically unfeasible unless they can be adapted for use in group settings such as the classroom. (Quay, 1966, p. 46)

An undeniable benefit of group instruction is an increase in the number of students who can be served. Because one-to-one instruction is clearly expensive, it could lead to a lack of services for children who might otherwise be eligible (Jenkins et al., 1974).

Social Benefits

A third consideration relative to the efficacy of group or one-to-one instruction is that of social outcomes—whether there are benefits or detriments. Several research studies have cited the potential of group instruction for gains in this domain, which can be achieved through a variety of means. One social benefit of group instruction is simply the opportunity for learning to participate with others. Fink and Sandall (1980) posit that the introduction of small group work with preschoolers results in an increased ability to function in common school situations. Handleman and Harris (1983) state that group work provides more normalizing experiences, which can eventually lead to integration. Brown and his colleagues (Brown, Hermanson, Klemme, Hanbrich, & Ora, 1970) indicate that group training results in the spontaneous development of social reinforcers as well as group enthusiasm.

The obverse of this situation may occur through an overemphasis on a one-to-one instructional model. Bryan (1983) stresses this point in discussing the social implications of the traditional resource model used with students with learning disabilities. She notes that a predominant focus on one-to-one instruction can result in greater difficulty for students in the regular classroom.

A potential solution to the problem of isolation or rejection has been presented by Slavin and his colleagues (Slavin, 1983; Slavin, Madden, & Leavey, 1984). They emphasize the value of cooperative learning approaches that structure goals and tasks for groups of students, both handicapped and nonhandicapped, to facilitate successful learning and socialization. Cooperative learning can be defined simply as classroom techniques that involve students in group learning activities with recognition and reinforcement based on group performance (Slavin, 1980).

Schniedewind and Salend (1987) have identified three basic formats that can be used to implement cooperative learning. These include peer teaching, group projects, and the "jigsaw." The reader is referred to their article for further information. Group projects are intended to provide an opportunity for students to pool their knowledge and skills to complete an assignment. The jigsaw format involves giving all students in a group individual tasks that must be completed before the group can reach its goal. Slavin (1983) summarizes the potential for cooperative learning.

All too often mainstreaming involves putting academically handicapped students in regular classrooms where their learning problems cause them to be resegregated. If the use of cooperative learning strategies in the mainstreamed classroom can make it possible for academically handicapped students to be integrated with their normal-progress classmates, this would represent an important step forward. (p. 101)

Social skills training has often been identified as a prerequisite to the successful integration of students with handicaps (e.g., Gottlieb & Leyser, 1981; Gresham, 1982). Efforts to provide structured group interactions can afford excellent opportunities for the development of positive social behaviors (Semmel & Cheney, 1979).

Implications

Research on grouping arrangements thus encourages the consideration of group training with students who are handicapped. A variety of positive benefits can accrue from the use of group methodology, including the promotion of observational learning, facilitation of overlearning and generalization, the teaching of turn-taking, increased and better use of instructional time, more efficient student management, and increased peer interaction (Borus, Greenfield, Spiegel, & Daniels, 1973; Johnson, Flanagan, Burge, Kaufman-Debriere, & Spellman, 1980; Kohl, Wilcox & Karlan, 1978; Oliver & Scott, 1981). What seems to be the most critical variable favoring group instruction is increased contact with the teacher. In Stevens and Rosenshine's (1981) review of best practices, the importance of "academic engaged time" and its relationship to higher achievement levels was clearly demonstrated and has been consistently supported by other research (e.g., Algozzine, Mirkin, Thurlow, & Graden, 1981; Denham & Lieberman, 1980; Thurlow, Ysseldyke, Graden, & Algozzine, 1983). The opportunities for teacher demonstration and corrective feedback are strong arguments in favor of group instruction.

Grouping for Acquisition

Meeting student's diverse needs across different stages of learning requires instructional organization. The teacher's goal is to maximize directive teaching to ensure optimal acquisition of skills and abilities. If the teacher appropriately chooses to work daily with each child on a direct basis, the problem becomes one of ensuring the greatest classroom learning efficiency.

The initial option is to work with each student on a one-to-one basis. This approach has the advantage of providing the learners with instruction specifically tailored to their needs and abilities. Individual teaching appears to be ideal for the acquisition stage of learning. However, as noted earlier, a strict one-to-one arrangement has a number of drawbacks.

Teaching lessons to the entire class at one time provides another alternative, which can increase both teacher control and instructional time for each child. Teachers can thus supervise each child throughout entire periods (i.e., all children are visible at all times), can provide constant instruction (of a large group nature), and can manage students by exercising direct control. However, because large groups do not properly accommodate individual needs, such instruction may drastically reduce the acquisition of skills, knowledge, and concepts. Experience has shown that when the size of the instructional group increases beyond about six, diminishing results are obtained.

The obvious alternative to one-to-one and large group models is to provide instruction in small groups. Unfortunately, grouping evokes images of educational or recreational rank-ordering (e.g., reading groups of sparrows, redbirds, and crows; or swimming groups of minnows, porpoises, and whales. Use of grouping, however, does not (and should not) dictate rigid adherence to standard groups for all subjects. To assist students in acquisition learning, the group can organize around a specific skill the members need to acquire. Groups should be flexible; they should neither restrict a child's improvement beyond the group mean nor force the child to work at too fast a pace.

How do large group and one-to-one models fit into this grouping picture? Large group instruction never quite accommodates the acquisition stage of learning, but on rare occasions it can provide the class with general introductions, serve as a forum for classwide discussions, and allow more advanced students a chance to review what other students are seeing for the first time. On the other hand, individual attention will continue to demand some class time. It may be essential for students who are unable to learn in the small group setting, who are working on a skill different from the focus of the rest of the class, or who are receiving assistance with specific aspects of work assignments.

Ideally, then, grouping can afford the teacher some organizational flexibility while providing a vehicle to give individuals what they need. For example, a class divided into three groups during a 1-hour academic period could provide several advantages: each child would receive 15 or 20 minutes of teacher-directed, small group instruction; the teacher would need to plan for only a limited number of children outside the group at any one time; and the teacher could still supervise individual students occasionally and briefly. Thus, this flexible system would allow maximum efficiency at each learning stage.

If acquisition of a skill or concept is important, then its learning cannot be left to chance. Direct instruction through flexible grouping arrangements is essential to sound teaching that maximizes learning probability.

Enhancing Proficiency and Maintenance

A system for ensuring proficiency and maintenance must accompany acquisition learning strategies. Commonly associated with this stage are terms such as *repetition* and *overlearning.* Although acquisition is the primary thrust of directive teaching, daily instruction should also include techniques to ensure proficiency and maintenance. Small group instruction provides a regular opportunity for students who are not working directly with the teacher to pursue educational activities that further develop and maintain what was acquired through direct instruction. Some simple techniques and activities to assist in repetition and overlearning of skills previously taught include

☐ tutoring by a peer
☐ board work
☐ group projects
☐ individual seat work folders
☐ instructional games
☐ interest centers
☐ programmed materials
☐ working with partners
☐ short composition on a current topic
☐ silent reading assignments
☐ tutoring other students
☐ viewing filmstrips
☐ using a microcomputer

In addition, several guidelines may help teachers keep these activities going smoothly.

1. Assess and ensure that students display acceptable independent working and interpersonal relationship skills.
2. Choose assignments that can be realistically accomplished independently to avoid constant interruptions by students.
3. Be sure directions for completing each task are clear.
4. Build in self-correction methods so that students will receive immediate feedback.
5. Closely coordinate tasks with the direct instruction.
6. Vary the activities, allowing each student to work on several assignments during a period.

7. Allow students some freedom to choose their activities.
8. Refrain from initially requiring students to do extremely complex activities.
9. Allow time to provide feedback or reinforcement for independent work.
10. If possible, have teacher aides, peer tutors, or volunteers assist in supervising independent work. (See Cooke, Heron, and Heward, 1983, for an excellent discussion of peer-tutoring programs.)

INSTRUCTIONAL PLANNING

A third major aspect of classroom organization and management concerns the development of instructional plans and daily schedules. The importance of a carefully planned schedule within the context of an organized classroom cannot be overemphasized. Instructional tempo and pace are dramatically affected by the schedule of daily events. By planning interesting, creative, and exciting activities throughout the day, the teacher can develop an enjoyable, educationally profitable program.

Scheduling involves general temporal arrangement for each day, supplemented with a series of specific lesson plans. The daily schedule ensures sufficient activities for the day and, conversely, sufficient time to complete them. A carefully planned schedule intersperses more enjoyable learning activities with those less appealing to students.

Lesson Planning

Lesson plans focus directly on the teaching objectives derived from the students' IEPs. Thus, plans should be consistent with prior assessment of students' specific learning needs. Lesson plans force teachers to state exactly what they will teach and how. Prescriptive teaching lessons sometimes replace those plans with educational profiles and/or learning graphs or charts of instructional alternatives. The important aspect for the teacher is not the format of the lesson plan, but rather the careful consideration of what will be taught and how.

Figure 4.4 illustrates a typical lesson plan format. Because teachers present varied types of material to many children, few experienced teachers regularly write such detailed lesson plans. Lesson plans are extremely important, but elaborate ones are often unnecessary. However, for the beginning teacher constructing detailed lesson plans is an excellent exercise that assists in focusing precisely on the instructional process.

Regardless of format and specificity, all lesson plans should attend to the questions of why, what, and how. An assessment of needs determines why. The what is expressed as behavioral objectives stated in terms of observable student performance, which can be evaluated to determine whether the student has attained the objective. The teacher measures attainment by some predetermined level or criterion of competence, usually expressed in percentages or in terms of successful trials (e.g., able to correctly identify the color red in four of five trials). For Geno (Figure 4.4) the criterion was set at 90%. The **how** of the lesson plan is the method of presentation; it describes the teaching process and any instructional materials or programs to be used. All lesson plans should also provide for evaluation of teaching efficiency and effectiveness.

FIGURE 4.4
Lesson plan format

Student: Geno Taylor

Objectives: Long-range—Student will verbally name all primary and secondary colors on command (e.g., "What color is this?") Specific lesson—Student will be able to point to the correct colored object (red and yellow) upon verbal command 90% of the time (e.g., "Point to the red cup").

Materials: Red cup, yellow cup, shield (blotter), popcorn

Method of presentation: Place the red and yellow cups upside down in front of the student. Shield the cups from the student's view with the blotter. While the cups are shielded, place a piece of popcorn under one of the cups (e.g., yellow), take the shield away, and say, "Pick up the yellow cup." When the child picks up the yellow cup, let the child have the popcorn. If an incorrect choice is made, say, "No, this is yellow," take the popcorn, and repeat the process. Be sure to alter the placement of the cups so that the student does not learn position placement rather than color. Use alternative objects to vary the presentation.

Evaluation of lesson:
Criterion attained: _____%
Projected needs:
Student's reaction to instruction:

Daily Scheduling

The daily schedule provides the foundation for all classroom learning. A number of guidelines should be considered in the development of students' schedules. Gallagher (1979) highlights 11 specific suggestions for planning effective daily schedules, pointing out that these suggestions may be more necessary early in the school year or early in the student's program.

1. Provide each student with a daily schedule.
2. Alternate high probability tasks with low probability tasks.
3. Schedule work that can be finished by the end of the school day.
4. Plan for leeway time.
5. Require students to complete one task before beginning another.
6. Provide time reminders.
7. Don't assign additional work if tasks are completed ahead of schedule.
8. Plan ahead and anticipate student needs.
9. Establish expectations in advance and do not introduce unexpected activities.
10. Include feedback and evaluative marks with a student's daily schedule.
11. Provide positive feedback. (pp. 244–250)

The first step in developing a daily schedule is to analyze how much time students are under the teacher's direction. In an average daily schedule for a self-contained special education class at the elementary level, the children may be at school for 6 hours. However, lunch may be 30 minutes, and an additional 30 minutes may be required for physical education. Thus, the actual time the children are in the teacher's room is 5 hours. This time block requires further analysis to determine reasonable events and activities.

Opening Exercises The day might begin with an exercise of approximately 15 to 20 minutes that includes any number of activities—for example, collection of lunch money, recognition of birthdays, discussion of planned events for the day. Opening exercises that are omitted or are haphazardly conducted can result in devastating days. Openings should be conducted to establish a learning set for beginning the day's activities. Although the activities described here are most appropriate for elementary students, they can be easily adapted for adolescents.

Collecting lunch money is not exciting; however, for most children with learning problems, counting is an important skill to be acquired. For students just learning to count, money might be exchanged for pennies and counted aloud. If public funds provide lunches and no actual coin exchange takes place, an alternative can be explored. Even with minimal planning, collection of lunch money can be educational and somewhat individualized. One might ask simple questions for more limited students, complex questions for more advanced students.

The flag salute is another basic opening activity, but for students who are younger or lower functioning, the concepts in the pledge may be meaningless. To make it more meaningful, the teacher might print the pledge, illustrated with rebuses, on a transparency or large piece of cardboard. While the class recites the pledge in choral fashion, a child might direct the activity by pointing to the words or rebuses.

The discussion of the day, month, and year is commonly conducted using a large calendar on a chalkboard or bulletin board. Students can place or write numerals indicating the day, the month, and perhaps the year. Every effort should be made to ensure success and decrease the probability of guessing, which can hamper rather than facilitate learning. One approach allows a student to choose the correct number from a pair of numbers instead of having to select from a large number of possibilities. Another procedure for assisting students in arriving at the correct date is to have the teacher count in rote fashion with them.

One of the most important activities conducted during openings is a discussion of the plan of events for the school day. Preparing students for daily activities brings together the classroom routine and student expectations. Discussion usually focuses first on what has already taken place. The teacher might write student responses on the chalkboard and make corrections when necessary. For more limited students pictures might be drawn; for more advanced individuals words depicting the activity might be written, or the responses could be written in phrases or complete sentences. Children functioning at different levels can be accommodated by the more experienced teacher during the same activity. For example, the teacher might ask the more limited students

with what sound *bus* begins, then quickly turn to a more advanced child and ask what the beginning letter is and how it is written, and finally ask a third student how to spell *bus*. After completing discussion of what has already happened, the teacher may focus on what activities will follow. The board may eventually look similar to one or more of the columns presented in Figure 4.5.

Closing Exercises The closing exercises should review daily occurrences, end the school day, and set the stage for orderly dismissal. First, the teacher might review the daily activities by going over the schedule discussed in the opening exercises. This is a good time for the teacher to ask various students what they enjoyed most and least.

Next, the teacher may get the students involved in activities by giving specific assignments. For a successful exercise each student must have one cleanup assignment (although some assignments may need to be paired, depending on children's abilities). Typical assignments involve emptying the wastebasket, sweeping the floor, cleaning

FIGURE 4.5
A sample plan of events that might be placed on a chalkboard

	bus	rode bus
	money—lunch	collected lunch money
	flag	said flag salute
	reading	reading groups
	recess	go out to recess
$1 + 1 = 2$	math	math groups
	phys ed.	go to physical education
	story	story time
	lunch	go to lunch

the chalkboard, straightening the desks, closing windows, and adjusting the shades. Early in the school year the teacher may have to teach students how to perform these tasks, but as students become more skillful, they can be rotated from task to task (see Figure 4.6). Cleanup will probably last approximately 10 minutes. Toward the end of this period, the teacher may wish to play a record appropriate to the students' ages and tastes.

Another closing activity popular with younger students is finger plays, which are songs or poems that require the use of the fingers, hands, and body. A few of the more common finger plays used at the primary level include "Eeency Weency Spider," "Wheels on the Bus," "This Old Man," and "Open Them, Shut Them." Older children may prefer the "Hokey Pokey" or songs like "Row, Row, Row Your Boat," which can be sung in an alternating fashion by different sets of children.

A series of finger plays, a collection of records of high appeal, and a cleanup chart and name tags provide the substance for closing activities that can be fun and educationally beneficial throughout the year with minimal further planning.

Curricular Planning

After opening and closing activities are accounted for, approximately 4½ hours remain in the school day. The teacher's primary concern should now be scheduling the content areas deemed most important within the overall curriculum. Reading and math are two curricular areas requiring direct, intensive, individualized instruction. The following discussion gives examples of ways to schedule a 60- or 70-minute period of instruction in each of those areas.

FIGURE 4.6
Assignment of possible cleanup activities (emptying wastebasket, sweeping floors, cleaning chalkboards, straightening desks, closing windows, and straightening shades)

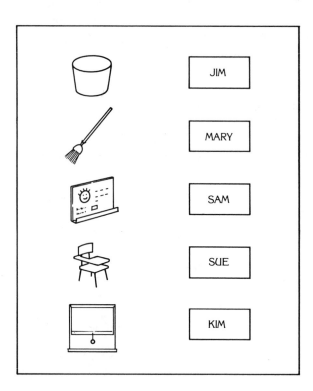

Reading In this example a class of 12 students is used for illustration; grouping is the basic instructional format. The class is broken into three groups of four students each, labeled Groups A, B, and C. Each group meets with the teacher for 20 minutes of direct instruction during the 70-minute period. Group A illustrates the components of a typical reading session.

During the initial 20-minute block Group A meets with the teacher for phonetic analysis instruction on initial consonants. A series of activities allows presentation of the concepts involved in a variety of ways. Phonovisual charts are used to help students associate sounds and symbols with the beginnings of familiar words. Next, the teacher reads a group of words aloud, with the students noting what sound or letter is heard at the beginning of each word. Students are then asked to complete riddles using words beginning with prescribed consonants (e.g., "I bounced the ball, as I walked down the h_____"). Twenty minutes of direct instruction are thus presented with three related activities sandwiched between brief introductory and closing exercises.

For the next 40 minutes the teacher provides proficiency and maintenance activities to complement the direct teaching activity. Interesting and diverse activities can ensure attention—for example, worksheets with pictures to be labeled by the initial consonant sound of the item portrayed; silent reading of a story appropriate for these specific skills and for the child's independent reading level; pegboard work pairing pictures of items with the letters with which they begin; a visit to an interest center that develops skills in writing consonants. Each of these assignments should reflect previously acquired skills.

The remaining 10 minutes in the reading period are kept flexible for a variety of instructional purposes, including individual minilessons for children experiencing difficulties with specific skills, time to check over seat work, an opportunity to reinforce appropriate behavior exhibited during the period, and time to gather evaluative information for future planning. With Group A's maintenance activities the teacher would likely be involved in correction of the consonant worksheets, brief discussions of the silent reading assignments, checking over students' work at the interest center, and specific help with problems.

Arithmetic The second intensive period of instruction that is illustrated involves arithmetic. Grouping again lends itself well to direct instruction, with individual assignments providing proficiency and maintenance activities. Based on the same class size used in the previous example, three groups have been established for direct teaching periods. Obviously, the groups must be reorganized around specific skills that particular children need. They must also be flexible enough to allow a student to move out of a group after mastery.

Generally, one can use either of two convenient approaches to planning the period. The first parallels the organization of the reading instruction, with the period divided into four blocks, each 15 minutes long in this case. The second, discussed here, reduces the group teaching lesson to 10 minutes per group, thus increasing the time that the teacher spends in individual instruction and assistance.

During the initial 10-minute period Group A receives seat work to help maintain arithmetic skills previously acquired—a short worksheet covering two-digit subtraction without regrouping. This activity is of a review nature, containing familiar knowledge or skills. At the end of the 10 minutes, the teacher circulates throughout the class for 5 minutes, checking the work of Group A and the other group with seat work and helping the students in the third group (who have just left the direct-teaching experience) begin their assignments.

During the next 10 minutes Group A meets with the teacher for a lesson in regrouping. The time is divided between the teacher's illustrating the process and the students' practicing either at the board or on paper. At the end of their 10 minutes, the students in Group A have an opportunity to work independently on problems they have mastered during the group instruction. Individual work folders are useful in organizing assignments for each student. Approximately 15 minutes of exercises are provided for Group A students at this time. For the initial 5 minutes when they are beginning their work and again after the next group's 10-minute instructional period, the teacher is available for consultation and assistance.

During the final 15 minutes of the daily math period, no groups are meeting with the teacher, and a variety of additional maintenance activities can be made available to students who have completed their seat work. For Group A these could include bingo subtraction, an interest center on initial borrowing concepts, and math records to play. In this final period of time, the teacher is able to check work, teach specific skills to individual students, and evaluate the day's lessons for future plans.

The two content areas of reading and math have been selected only for illustration. Depending on students' educational needs, self-help skills, vocational skills, or oral language development may be the most critical curricular components. Primary areas of concern, whichever they may be, are often scheduled in the morning to maximize learning. Thus, the daily schedule might now reflect a reading period from 9:20 to 10:30 and a math period from 10:45 to 11:45 with a brief recess in between the two. The teacher's remaining task is to complete the schedule with interesting, enjoyable, and educationally beneficial activities. Although overall curricular design should dictate choices for a specific student or group of students, the following discussion shows how other periods can complement the existing schedule.

Story Reading The period from 11:45 to 12:00, which follows math and precedes lunch, is an ideal time for reading a story. Material selection is extremely important, and librarians can be important resources. When selecting stories, the teacher must consider both interest and comprehension levels. The story selected need not be completed in the 15-minute period; it can continue in serial form. Longer stories such as *Tom Sawyer* and *Charlotte's Web* appeal to intermediate students, who can follow the story from day to day. Initial questions—"What happened yesterday?"—may help promote memory skills.

Teachers at the middle school level often fail to include reading time for adolescents, yet exciting material may be of benefit. Reading materials related to values are appropriate, as are high-interest, low-vocabulary books, which may be accompanied by filmstrips or tapes. Although some adolescents may not be able to read these materials for themselves, such books are often exciting and interesting and may be easily within the students' listening comprehension.

Teachers who are creative storytellers may wish to substitute telling stories for reading books. Many older students can help develop such stories. Local resources can also be tapped; for example, in one school near an Indian reservation, a native American volunteered to come to school two times a week to tell folk tales.

Language Development An appropriate focus for the period following lunch (from 12:30 to 1:30) might be separate or integrated oral and written language-training programs, again dependent on students' learning needs. Spoken language instruction is clearly one of the most critical instructional areas for many students who are handicapped. Chapter 9 provides a variety of suggestions for oral language programming. Written language training can focus on any of three areas: handwriting, spelling, and written expression. These three areas form the core of the written language curriculum and are discussed extensively in chapter 11.

Physical Education The period from 1:30 to 2:00 might be designated for physical education. This curricular domain presents an opportunity for teachers to develop students' gross motor skills and physical and health fitness. In addition, it provides an effective break from afternoon academic activities. Chapter 18 describes a variety of training programs and suggested activities for this area.

Completing the Schedule The time period from 2:00 to 2:45 may include any number of activities—for example, social skills training, creative arts, career education, science, social studies, or contingent free time. The discussion of curricular design in chapter 8 should assist in the selection of content areas and activities most appropriate for this period. Subsequent chapters on science and social studies, social skills, career education, and creative arts provide suggestions for program development and selection of specific instructional activities. Depending on the students and the nature of the instructional tasks, a teacher might schedule one or two areas for this time frame and alternate them over a series of days.

The basic format for the daily schedule is now complete. The content areas suggested for inclusion are presented merely as ex-

amples. Individual teachers must select actual areas according to a diverse set of criteria, such as students' ages, achievement levels, and educational needs; available resources; and teacher skills and interests. The final schedule will probably resemble this sample.

8:00	Planning and set up
9:00	Opening exercises
9:20	Reading instruction
10:30	Recess
10:45	Math instruction
11:45	Story reading (by teacher)
12:00	Lunch
12:30	Oral and/or written language instruction
1:30	Physical education
2:00	Curricular options
2:45	Closing exercises
3:00	Dismissal

Such a schedule has several purposes: to meet prescribed individual learning goals and objectives, to facilitate the planning process for the teacher, to assure varied teaching activities, and to provide a well-ordered day of learning. A well-designed schedule is valuable because it assists the teacher in planning a series of different activities and events that make coming to school interesting and stimulating enough for children and structured enough for efficient teaching.

Secondary School Programs[2]

The majority of high school self-contained programs encourage students who are handicapped to participate in regular classes in which they can succeed. The most common areas of integration are art, music, physical education, industrial arts, and

[2]A portion of this discussion is from *Teaching Exceptional Adolescents* (pp. 145–148) by J. E. Smith and J. S. Payne, 1980, Columbus, OH: Merrill. Copyright 1980 by Merrill Publishing Company. Adapted by permission.

home economics; however, each student should be carefully evaluated and prepared for further integration. Special educators most often focus on instruction in reading, math, English (writing and spelling), daily living skills, career education, and vocational training, as well as on social skills training, learning strategies, and study skills.

The more subjects taught in the secondary special education class, the more structurally similar the daily schedule becomes to the elementary schedule, just discussed. Secondary schools generally use a daily schedule composed of six to eight time periods. These periods are usually 40 to 50 minutes in duration with a short time between periods to change classes. Typically, about three-fourths of each student's daily schedule consists of academic classes, with the remaining portion devoted to band, athletics, school clubs, and other activities as well as lunch or study halls. Often, students in special programs, such as a vocational preparation program, follow a general schedule slightly different from that of the majority of students. Students in special programs may attend school for a half-day session in which they do academic work and may spend the other half day away from the school receiving other types of training.

Individual Periods In the overall secondary school schedule the individual period is the pivotal unit during which most daily instruction and other activities take place. An individual period may contain several components, such as daily activities, weekly activities, and activities requiring more than 1 or 2 weeks to accomplish.

It may appear that high school teachers have little need to develop a daily schedule, because they all have a fixed schedule. However, because the events must fit neatly into approximately 50-minute blocks of time and activities often are interrupted by bells and

other extraneous stimuli, effective planning at the high school level may actually be more difficult. The teacher must develop a series of minischedules—one for each class—which should contain brief opening and closure exercises. Depending on the teacher's particular objectives, daily instructional activities usually begin by introducing daily, weekly, or unit concerns to be addressed on that specific day. Activities aimed at fostering various stages of learning follow the introduction. For example, new activities are probably aimed at acquisition learning, whereas review activities might be geared to maintenance or generalization learning. Closure activities then represent an attempt to relate the different things that have taken place during the period.

Often, a specific objective cannot be accomplished in a single day or period. Thus, weekly activities focus on coordinating several ongoing daily activities. Also, because the goals and objectives of weekly activities are somewhat broader than those associated with daily endeavors, the weekly goals and objectives can be integrated more easily with similar concerns elsewhere in the school. Of course, even 1 or 2 weeks are not enough time to cover certain objectives or material.

Alternative Presentation Modes The individual or daily class schedule needs further examination to ascertain how a teacher might make maximum use of each period. The key element is teacher flexibility. A teacher who seldom deviates from a fixed schedule invites student boredom, apathy, and resistance. On the other hand, a variable schedule can renew student interest and active participation. Flexibility in the daily schedule can be enhanced in a variety of ways. One way is to vary the schedule from day to day, perhaps using teacher lectures, class discussions (led by the teacher or by the students), and individual or group projects during several individual periods. If varied activities are used, the teacher must organize each individual period differently.

A teacher who uses a lecture method might set up a daily schedule similar to Schedule 1.

Class lecture: History
Topic: The causes of the Civil War
Activities: Introduction   9:00
               Lecture   9:10
               Conclusion   9:45
               Dismissal   9:55

During this particular class session the most time would be spent acquainting students with various Civil War facts. In this situation instructor output is high, and student output is relatively low.

For class discussion, led by either the teacher or the students, a typical schedule might resemble Schedule 2.

Class discussion: History
Topic: The causes of the Civil War
Activity: Introduction   9:00
          Discussion—Topic I   9:05
          Discussion—Topic II   9:25
          Summary of discussion   9:45
          Dismissal   9:55

This type of arrangement allows much more input/output by class members.

A period devoted to student projects might resemble Schedule 3.

Class: History
Topic: The causes of the Civil War
Activity: Introduction   9:00
          Presentation of Project I   9:05
          Presentation of Project II   9:20
          Presentation of Project III 9:35
          General discussion   9:50
          Dismissal   9:55

Of the three scheduling arrangements mentioned, this last one obviously allows the greatest amount of student participation.

Another way to achieve flexibility is to include a variety of presentation modes within one period. This approach is appropriate if adolescents with handicaps (or adolescents in general) have difficulty learning when they are expected to listen to a lecture, read from a text, or discuss a topic for the entire class session. One 50-minute period focusing on law and order might be scheduled as follows:

8:35   Opening exercises
8:40   Brief introductory lecture
8:50   Reading from "Law and Order"
9:00   Discussion of what happens when a person is arrested
9:20   Closure
9:25   Class dismissal

Set induction might be achieved through an opening statement about what is to be covered (e.g., "Today we are going to look at what law and order means to us. We will be interested in answering questions such as What is law? Why should we have laws? Who enforces the law?"). The teacher might then read from Elder's *Making Value Judgments* (1972, Chapter 9). The discussion session might probe what happens when a high school–aged student, as opposed to an adult, is arrested. Closure might involve a forward look (e.g.,"Tomorrow we are going to discuss where we get our attitudes toward law and determine differences between shoplifting, income tax evasion, and other offenses. What other issues do you think we need to be concerned with?")

One final scheduling arrangement is based on total individualization of activities. Some classes are structured so that students entering the room pick up work folders or packets. The teacher moves about the room to check their work and to reinforce students who are working. In this case the teacher omits opening exercises and handles all questions individually. Teachers considering such an arrangement should evaluate the benefits of individual assignments as opposed to direct instruction by the teacher.

Resource Teaching

Certain principles should be considered in setting up resource programs in general. These concerns are briefly outlined here as an adjunct to the general principles of scheduling discussed earlier. For further information, the reader is encouraged to review Wiederholt, Hammill, and Brown (1983).

☐ Regular, frequent instruction in the resource room (four to five periods per week) is preferable to only one or two instructional periods per week.

☐ To the maximum degree possible, students should be grouped with same-age peers for instruction.

☐ Instructional periods should be set up to allow for consistency across curricular needs for a given group of students, with attention given concurrently to individual differences.

☐ Resource teachers should determine the extent of their responsibilities for schoolwide assessment activities and committee work (e.g., child study committees) and should allow sufficient planning time.

☐ Resource teachers' schedules should avoid any appearance of preferential treatment (e.g., no bus duty or lunch duty).

☐ Individual determination should be made as to whether students will be best served by having their resource instruction in a particular area (e.g., reading) scheduled in lieu of or in addition to regular class instruction in that area.

☐ When scheduling results in a child's completely missing instruction in a given curricular area, resource teachers should investigate ways to help the student compensate for this curricular gap.

☐ Individual periods should provide students with an appropriate sequence of instructional activities that incorporates previously mentioned principles of opening exercises, acquisition instruction, review, proficiency/maintenance and generalization activities (as appropriate), and closure.

☐ Program management often dictates the development of appropriate contingencies for students in terms of moving directly to and from the regular classroom and adhering to scheduled times for instruction.

☐ Resource teachers should serve as advocates in helping to avoid the instructional abuses that stem from incorrect administrative practices relative to the resource model (e.g., haphazard blending of resource and self-contained models, significant variance in groups within a given period in terms of curricular needs and age levels, assignment of groups of more than four or five students per period).

Although these principles may reflect the ideal rather than the real, they are intended to serve as a direction toward which programs should move. These scheduling principles can provide a basis for improved effectiveness and accountability.

Unit Teaching

Scheduling need not focus entirely on multiple curricular areas such as math, spelling, reading, or self-help skills. Rather, a teacher can incorporate specific instructional content subjects into units. For instance, a capable teacher might spend a significant portion of a school day on a specific project (e.g., a class play or mock TV show) and in so doing integrate writing (preparing the script), reading (reading the script for try outs and rehearsal), and math (selling tickets, anticipating the number in the audience). Other curricular areas, such as science and social studies, can also be integrated into the play. Skilled teachers who are familiar with their pupils can individualize such a project by assigning responsibilities according to each pupil's needs and abilities. Other opportunities are also available; for example, a cooking/baking project provides opportunities for reading skills (e.g., reading recipes) and math skills (e.g., determining proportions of ingredients, counting ingredients, monitoring baking time).

By definition unit teaching involves integrating material from several content areas focusing on one theme. The instructional objectives, incorporated from the multiple content areas, should be stated in clear, concise, observable terms as in any lesson plan. Unit teaching presents material in an interesting, relevant format that can enhance transfer of learning. In general, unit teaching is most appropriate for maintenance and generalization learning. The following list outlines the specific aspects to consider in constructing an instructional unit.

1. Unit theme and general objectives
   a. Clearly identify the theme.
   b. State the rationale as related to students' needs.
   c. Establish relevant general objectives.
2. Specific learning objectives
   a. Establish specific objectives for thematic factors.
   b. Establish specific objectives for skills acquisition, maintenance/proficiency, and generalization.
3. Integrated content areas
   a. Identify curricular areas included.
   b. Outline how each area will be incorporated.
4. Unit activities outline
   a. Identify daily sequence of activities (for approximately 10 to 20 sessions).
   b. Ensure that activities relate to unit objectives.
5. Evaluation
   a. Outline overall plan for evaluation of unit.
   b. Specify in terms of learner performance and instructional effectiveness.
6. Resources and References
   a. Identify resources available for student use and instructor preparation.
   b. Consider books, articles, audiovisual materials, and speakers.

A general overview and specific daily activities follow for a career education unit dealing with vocational vocabulary words.[3]

Title of the unit: Words to Help You on the Job

Type of students: Secondary students in an applied academics or vocational class.

Notes to the teacher: This unit is based on the 100 most essential career vocational words (See Schilit & Caldwell, 1980). Its purpose is to enable the adolescent to recognize on sight and use in context a sample of words from this list. Word choices may vary for an individual class, depending on the types of jobs in which students may be interested. This unit is designed for a 2-week period, but one could extend it to incorporate a more substantial list of vocabulary words.

Monday: Write words (e.g., *boss, supervisor, manager, employee*) on the board. Read each word and divide it into syllables, sounding each one out. Discuss each word and print a simple meaning by it. Talk about the responsibilities of each position. Show how words relate vocationally. Have students copy words and meanings in career notebooks. Read each word again with students. Have volunteers talk about the definitions and responsibilities of each job title. Provide magazines and find pictures of persons

---

[3]This unit was initially developed by Ann Cerillo, Campbell County Schools, Rustburg, VA, 1980. Reprinted by permission.

filling each role. Label each and paste them in a notebook. Write the proper job title by each picture. As students complete the project, have each individual read the words to you.

Tuesday: Have a student write words on the board for the class to read aloud. Have students make up sentences and recite them, while you copy one sentence for each word on the board. Have students copy the sentences in their notebooks, noting the particular word from the list in each sentence. Read the words again. Present new words and phrases (e.g., *job, help wanted, workers, work, signature, punch in*), reading them aloud as you write them on the board. Distribute a word list and go over new words. Have students complete a decoding sheet, using a numerical code for the alphabet (e.g., 10–15–2 = *job*). As students finish, read their work over with them individually.

Wednesday: Read together all words from the first 2 days. Have students write Tuesday's words in notebooks. Discuss meanings and have students copy the teacher's meanings from the board into their notebooks. Do a hunt-the-word exercise for all 10 words and phrases. Review the sheets in class. Have students read all words into a microphone and record them as they complete work. Quiz them on all words (true/false).

Thursday: Have students do a worksheet with fill-in blanks for a story (all 10 words and phrases). Go over in class. Role-play positions and situations using words. Have students copy new words from the board into notebooks (e.g., *hired, fired, overtime, part-time, full-time*). Discuss meanings; include 8-hour workday and 40-hour workweek, who hires and fires and for what kinds of reasons. Talk about people who work overtime, part-time and full-time—where and when. Read over the words again.

Friday: Read over all words. Write simple definitions and have students copy. Have students who have been hired for a job talk

about how the process worked. Have a part-time worker tell about the job, pay, hours, working conditions, and so forth. Have full-time and overtime persons tell about their jobs, the pros and cons, and the things that are involved. Read over all words together. Have students do a crossword puzzle using all words.

Monday: Plan a short written and oral test on all words (students should be able to recognize words, know meanings, use words properly in context). Read and write new words (e.g., *paycheck, deduction, gross income, net income, take-home pay*) on the board to be copied in notebooks. Discuss and write meanings. Show relationship of words—on the board, work several simple problems with paychecks, showing gross income, deductions, net income, and take-home pay. Look at check stubs and locate these items. Give out demonstration sheets with problems worked and labeled. Have volunteers work a problem on the board. Read over all words.

Tuesday: Use yesterday's words in sentences and copy them in notebooks. Work a sample problem on the board to find take-home pay. Give each student two problems to work and label. Check individually as each finishes and discuss them. Make sure each student reads the words. Review all words.

Wednesday: Present new words (e.g., *danger, dangerous, hazardous, emergency, first aid, hospital*). Copy them in a notebook and talk about how these words apply to work. Have students discuss possible accidents on the job. Have a school nurse talk to the class about possible accidents and appropriate responses. Role-play accident situations, with the nurse giving directions. Relate situations when patients may need to go to the hospital (consider what to do, etc.). Read all words aloud.

Thursday: Review all words. Have each student choose two words (perhaps pick them from a hat) to read, discuss, and use in a sentence recorded on the tape recorder. Play sentences back. Read over words together. Provide worksheets for all words (puzzles, decoding, matching, likenesses and differences, problems, accident situations, true/false). Correct and discuss.

Friday: Role-play job situations requiring words learned, trying to use as many of the new words as possible. Have each student choose a job from the job box (a collection of occupational words) with which to explore using words just learned. Test on all words.

Unit teaching can be an excellent organizational teaching strategy for adding instructional variety while promoting skills acquisition, maintenance, and generalization. Units provide meaningful contexts for instruction and opportunities to include functional life skills as well as direct, concrete experiences. Teachers should select unit themes based on students' interests and ability levels. Table 4.1 lists possible topics for instructional units within four broad curricular areas.

RECORD KEEPING

Record keeping consists of collecting, maintaining, and utilizing data for instructional purposes. Many teachers find the thought of managing a data/information system frightening, and the pressures of an already-demanding amount of paperwork discourage some from establishing record-keeping systems. Although initiating such a system requires effort, it need not continue to consume inordinate amounts of time. A properly designed, effective record-keeping system should reduce the time needed to prepare for teaching.

Two types of record-keeping systems are discussed here. The first type involves evaluating student progress; the second assists

TABLE 4.1
Sample instructional units

Science	Social Studies
solar energy	family history
neighborhood fauna	ethnic studies
pond life	map and globe skills
magnetism	backyard history
appliances	local geography
kitchen physics/chemistry	supply and demand
electricity	community resources
grocery store science	voting and elections
rocketry	citizen rights
weather	forms of transportation
Career Development	*Health and Safety*
career clusters	dental care
job searching	foreign travel
interviewing techniques	treatment of maladies
résumé writing	first aid
occupational interest	smoking
hobbies and leisure activities	diet and health
postsecondary options	AIDS
using community transportation	exercise
community helpers	household hazards
occupations of family members	medical insurance

the teacher in the daily management of the instructional program.

Evaluation of Student Progress

Obtaining information about a student's progress in a given program or about an instructional technique's effectiveness is essential to effective teaching and has been strongly advocated by proponents of curriculum-based assessment, which regularly requires instructionally related decisions. Although a certain amount of "clinical" judgment, acquired with experience, can be quite accurate, most evaluation specialists suggest collecting observable, measurable data. A system that effectively monitors student progress "enables the teacher to make necessary midcourse program corrections . . . responsive to each individual's unique needs" (Lund, Schnaps, & Bijou, 1983, p. 155). Lund and her colleagues stress how important record keeping becomes, especially when teachers and school systems are subject to accountability measures.

A variety of specific techniques for keeping track of data have been developed (see Howell, Kaplan, and O'Connell, 1979, for a thorough discussion of various evaluation systems). Sometimes referred to as **formative evaluation**, recording techniques may include narrative/anecdotal logs, charts, or matrices. All of these forms involve recording quantifiable data, usually in terms of a correct number or percentage. Another useful procedure is precision teaching, which focuses on accuracy as well as rate and can predict a student's progress based on previously collected data. Table 4.2 provides examples of these techniques. Above all, as Wang (1980) points out, the system chosen should provide important information about student learning without being burdensome to the teacher.

Keeping records of student progress emphasizes the accurate, systematic collection of data. It assumes that one can observe and measure the student performance being monitored. If developed prior to the beginning of a school year, such a system can be implemented immediately. A number of suggestions developed by Guerin and Maier (1983) may help in designing a record-keeping system.

1. Use recording procedures that are as simple and efficient as possible.
2. Have students or aides, when appropriate, participate in the recording process.
3. Record information so that it accurately represents the critical elements of the event.
4. Use a recording format that does not require transfer of the raw data to another form. (pp. 57–58)

Another suggestion is to graph the data collected. Although this idea is recommended because of the ease in interpreting the data contained in a graphic representation, this practice can have one notable drawback. Often, teachers post performance statistics (e.g., students' performance charts) on the wall for all to see. This display reinforces students who **are** progressing but does not motivate students who are not. If these students become frustrated, educators should consider graphing student performance in folders that students can inspect privately.

Daily Assignment Sheets

Teachers face two problems in the smooth delivery of instruction: (1) keeping track of assignments and activities that students are to do and (2) informing students of what they are to do, especially seat work activities. Once again, developing appropriate systems requires some effort but can eliminate two classroom administrative hassles.

TABLE 4.2
Systems for evaluating student progress

Technique	Data	Possible Interpretation
Narrative log	Marie did better today in math and reading. Her acting-out behavior was under more control.	Marie actually 1. did better, or 2. did more work The teacher was 1. less hassled, or 2. in a better mood
Arithmetic chart	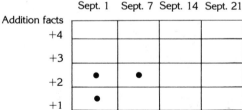	Child's percentage correct has increased.
Learning matrices		Child has mastered first and second tasks but not third or fourth.
Precision teaching	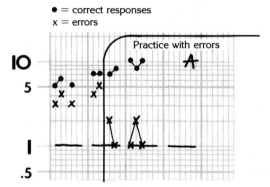	Child initially had many errors. Errors were isolated and worked on separately. Learning is now occurring. Child should master task within 3 to 4 days.

Source. From *Evaluating Exceptional Children: A Task Analysis Approach* (p. 139) by K. W. Howell, J. S. Kaplan, and C. Y. O'Connell, 1979, Columbus, OH: Merrill. Copyright 1979 by Merrill Publishing Company. Adapted by permission.

Figures 4.7 through 4.10 are examples of assignment sheets. These samples are provided as guides only; the best method for any given teacher is custom-made. Regardless of the system chosen, however, students must understand how it works; it should be demonstrated and practiced. Figure 4.7 is a simple daily activity sheet for one subject area. It contains the date of the assigned activity, a description of the assignment, some

Name _____

Subject _____

Date	Assignment	Evaluation	Comments

FIGURE 4.7
Basic assignment sheet

DAILY SHEET

Subject *Allen Sheppy*

English

Year *88-89*   Period ___5th___

DATE	ACTIVITY	COMMENTS	FINAL POINTS	CONTRACT POINTS	+/-/o
Monday Sept. 12	As the Year Passes Card 6	fin ———— 12/14			+
Tuesday Sept. 13	Card 7	Inc. — refused to work — upset about girl			—
Wednesday Sept. 14	Card 7 absent	ey			O

FIGURE 4.8
Daily assignment sheet (From *Record Keeping for Individualized Junior-Senior High Special Education Programs* [p. 28] by Ellen McPeek Glisan, 1984, Freeport, IL: Peekan Publications. Copyright 1984 by Peekan Publications, Inc. Reprinted by permission.)

FIGURE 4.9
Student's assignment sheet

	Monday 3/10	Tuesday 3/11	Wednesday 3/12	Thursday 3/13	Friday 3/14
Phonics Workbook A	21	22		23	24
Phonics Cards	6		7		

Code: Each cell with a number = specific page in the instructional material.

Date above the column = date assigned.

Diagonal line (/) = student indication that assignment has been completed.

Diagonal line (\) = teacher indication that work has been corrected.

Assignment Sheet for __Subject /__

	Week of _4/6_			Week of ___		Week of ___
Phonics Wkbk. A	76 ⑦ ⑦) 78 79) 80 81)					
Vocabulary	㉑ ★㉒) 23					
Spelling Fun	14 ⑮)					
Sound Foundation II	★⑦ ★⑧) 9 10) 11 12)					
Capitalization/Punctuation	★32 ㉝) 34 35) 36					
Phonics Cards	④ ⑤) 6					
Points	Ⓜ Bonus +5 Ⓣ +5 W Th F			M T W Th F		M T W Th F

Code: A different color ink is used for each day (e.g., 76 and 77 are assigned on Monday and are written in red ink).

) separates daily assignments.   ◯ means the assignment needs to be rechecked.

☆ means the assignment is correct.   / means the assignment is correct after revision.

Points can be given, based on performance, and can be tied into a token system.

FIGURE 4.10
Sample assignment sheet (From E. Nishida, n.d., unpublished classroom tool. Adapted by permission.)

type of evaluative information (e.g., points, checkmarks), and any necessary comments. Glisan (1984) has developed a daily sheet that is a variation of the one presented in Figure 4.7. She includes columns for the points earned for the assignment, the points applied to a contract system, and a subjective evaluation of behavior indicated by one of three symbols. A sample sheet following this format is given in Figure 4.8. Figures 4.9 and 4.10 illustrate other samples of daily assignment sheets. The procedures for using those particular forms are provided in the figures. Even though Figure 4.10 represents a more complicated system, elementary-aged students are capable of learning and using it efficiently.

If designed and introduced properly, systems like the four presented here should enable students to pick up their individual folders, turn to the assignment sheet, and begin seat work without any teacher direction. Some teacher assistance may still be needed (e.g., for the reluctant student), but a well-established system generally releases a teacher from the task of directing students to assignments. The primary reason for implementing a management system is efficiency. Nonetheless, such a system requires the teacher to first develop it and clearly explain it to students. Moreover, it demands daily use and maintenance.

Grading

Grading is a required form of student evaluation and record keeping. As Carpenter (1985) emphasizes, giving grades to special learners is a difficult task: "Educators are challenged to devise grading methods which are clear, accurate, and supportive of the education mission" (p. 54). The issue of grading needs to be examined from the different perspectives of those students who are in special settings and those who are mainstreamed.

Okada (1987) studied the grading practices of special education teachers at 12 public schools in Hawaii. She found that most teachers base grades on individual progress (98%) and IEP objectives (90%) and issue grades on a very frequent basis (81% on a daily basis). These are good practices; however, a few other guidelines are important as well (Carpenter, 1985).

☐ Use a multicategory grading system, that is, letter grades rather than pass/fail.

☐ Use more than one grade if more than one message needs to be conveyed (e.g., progress versus effort).

☐ Involve students in their own grading when possible (e.g., use of contracting).

☐ Supplement the symbolic grades with oral and written information.

For students placed in integrated settings, other concerns arise. The success of these students in the resource or modified self-contained setting is in juxtaposition to their grades earned within the regular class. In the resource room, students may have successfully acquired new skills; at the same time they may have obtained a collection of low grades in the various subjects taught in regular classrooms. The solution to the problem of grading probably can be found through student advocacy and tactful interpersonal relationships. The special teacher generally needs to provide a clear description of an individual student's strengths, weaknesses, capabilities, and needs, thus giving the classroom teacher additional data on which to base a letter-grade evaluation. The solution that emphasizes cooperative efforts is the one most likely to succeed.

Although no simple solutions to grading questions exist, the following suggestions may prove helpful to special education teachers:

☐ Keep the lines of communication open at all times, meeting with classroom teachers on a regular basis to discuss student progress.

☐ Ensure that classroom teachers are aware of a student's level of functioning by sharing assessment data and including the teachers in IEP meetings and decisions.

☐ Stress effort as a basic criterion central to grade assignment.

☐ Emphasize the acquisition of new skills as a basis for grades assigned, thus providing a perspective on the student's relative gains. Charting progress may help illustrate these gains.

☐ Investigate alternative procedures for evaluating content taught (e.g., evaluation via oral examinations for poor readers in a science class).

☐ Whenever possible, engage in cooperative grading agreements (e.g., grades for language arts might reflect both regular classroom as well as reading resource performance).

☐ Serve as a resource for teachers by helping them balance fair grades and student efforts.

☐ Lobby for schoolwide use of narrative reports either in toto or as a major portion of the report card, especially for younger children. These reports can then be complemented by data on specific target behaviors related to a student's IEP.

☐ Ensure that grading systems are consistent with diploma requirements for all students in a diploma-track program.

SUMMARY

The implementation of successful strategies for classroom organization and management can clearly differentiate between effective and ineffective educational programs. The various topics addressed within this chapter represent important concerns that should be addressed as precursors or follow-ups to the process of teaching.

An effective environment facilitates student learning. To be aesthetically pleasant, a classroom should look lived-in, show graceful wear, and contain signs of renewal. One way that teachers can plan the classroom environment is to develop a floor plan of the room and add necessary equipment to it. Environmental designs should include areas for conducting a variety of instructional activities as well as a place for social interaction and reinforcement. Common instructional adjuncts that can be useful program additions include bulletin boards, study carrels, and interest centers. Ultimately, the classroom environment should assist the teacher in instruction.

An important consideration for teachers is the grouping of students. Particular concerns relate to the effectiveness and efficiency of small group, large group, and one-to-one arrangements. Effective practices for acquisition and proficiency/maintenance learning also have implications for grouping.

Planning a daily schedule can be deceptively simple, yet very important in setting the stage for each instructional day. Lesson plans are an integral part of scheduling and should attend to the why, what, and how of teaching. A daily schedule may begin with opening exercises and end with closing exercises, with varied activities occurring throughout the day. To begin planning the schedule, the teacher determines the time parameters for the day and fixed times for given activities (e.g., lunch and recess). The rest of the time slots are then filled with curricular content areas deemed most important to the students. Teaching approaches should maximize direct instruction. Although a high school schedule differs significantly from an elementary schedule, both follow the same principles and procedures. Resource programs require other specific considerations vis-à-vis scheduling. An alternative to daily lessons is unit plans, which have the advantage of placing the material to be learned in a relevant context to facilitate transfer of learning.

Record keeping must be an integral part of all educational programs. Data collection on student progress and teaching activities provides the basis for evaluating student performance and program effectiveness and thus determining needed modifications.

5
Behavior Change
Strategies

A major factor in successful teaching is the instructor's ability to implement educational strategies that increase a student's motivation to perform while assisting in the development of appropriate classroom behavior. All elements of good teaching—including the various aspects of methodology and curriculum discussed in this chapter and the next—contribute to motivation and management. Although discussions of methodology and curriculum focus primarily on antecedent events, this chapter emphasizes the role of both antecedent and consequent strategies. As Worell and Nelson (1974) indicate, the teacher's role is basically that of a **change agent** whose primary goal is educational intervention. Therefore, the discussion in this chapter focuses on strategies for changing behavior with an emphasis on those approaches that have been found effective with students who have special needs.

In considering the various techniques to assist in behavior change, the teacher should reflect on two key concerns. The first is the need to be **systematic.** Haphazard modification is, at best, misleading in the interpretation of results. It can also be confusing and possibly detrimental to the student who needs structure and predictability within the daily instructional routine. The need for a systematic policy of record-keeping to accompany precise teaching techniques cannot be overstated, particularly for children with more serious learning difficulties.[1]

The second important concern is **creativity.** Countless approaches may be effective for a given instructional problem. A teacher should be creative in devising alternatives and should become both proficient in the

appropriate use of these alternatives and experienced in deciding when a given technique should be applied. Payne (1972) reiterates the importance of these two principles, noting the unlikely but nevertheless valid similarities between **teaching** and **mind reading.**

> We know that in a night club mind reading act it is highly probable that the types of questions asked at the 6 P.M. performance will differ from those asked at 8 P.M., 10 P.M. or midnight. In education we know that it is highly probable that when children play on a playground of gravel, someone someday is going to throw rocks. We know this as experienced educators, but what teacher has ever been instructed to anticipate this situation, let alone know the alternatives in handling it? The lessons we can learn from the mind reading profession is the value of keeping records of children's behavior; the next step is to develop creative and effective alternatives for dealing with specific behavior. (p. 51)

This chapter is divided into four major sections. The initial section focuses on prerequisites to successful classroom management and pays particular attention to antecedent variables. The succeeding two sections deal with consequent control, under the assumption that consequences are frequently the chief determinants of successful learning, maintenance, proficiency, and generalization. Two goals of consequent control are discussed: increasing appropriate behavior and reducing inappropriate behavior. The chapter concludes with a discussion of several special considerations in programming. Throughout the chapter a variety of specific strategies for behavior change are presented. The key to effectiveness is to use these strategies within a comprehensive management plan responsive to the needs of the individual student.

---

[1]More detailed information can be found in the excellent discussions on data collection in Kerr and Nelson (1983), Alberto and Troutman (1986), and Cooper, Heron, and Heward (1987).

PREREQUISITES TO SUCCESSFUL MANAGEMENT

Despite the abundance of alternative methods for behavior management, some discrepancy remains between a teacher's acquisition of a repertoire of empirically validated, specific behavioral tools and subsequent success in managing the class. This discrepancy is particularly problematic because it is difficult to tease from research the precise variables that ensure subsequent success in classroom management. The authors believe that successful management is frequently not due merely to learning and exercising a series of high-powered strategies but rather to employing effective procedures in the classroom. Certainly a teacher's ability to structure the environment and to present organized instruction is critical to overall management success. Thus, the key prerequisites to successful classroom management discussed here are, in large part, outgrowths of the information presented in chapter 4. Establishing a prosthetic learning environment is an effective way to prevent problems.

Classroom Procedures

Antecedents to learning can be traced back to teachers' initial planning in setting up their instructional days. In addition to concern for the physical and temporal environment, a number of procedural aspects of teaching are important. Evertson, Emmer, Clements, Sanford, and Worsham (1984) have focused on the specific elements involved in planning classroom procedures. Although "some of the items may appear trivial," Evertson and her colleagues stress the "complexity and detail" involved in such planning, indicating that these efforts "form the mosaic of the management system" (p. 24). Table 5.1 illustrates the five major areas

that Evertson et al. (1984) have identified as keys to procedural planning at the elementary level. For each major area specific concerns are listed. The column to the right then provides space for identification of particular procedures to be followed or expectations to be held.

A similar format to that of Evertson et al. (1984), a procedural planning sheet for secondary level classes, is presented in Table 5.2. Four major areas of concern are noted.

Classroom Rules

Most children and adolescents function best in situations in which they know what is expected of them. Students need to be aware of what a teacher expects and will accept. Explaining classroom rules and then posting them are sound practices to aid in the prevention of problem behaviors; students should not have to test the limits if the teacher has already clearly explained the distinction between acceptable and unacceptable behaviors. Classroom rules should be few in number, clearly defined, and linked to specific consequences when violated. Teachers should encourage students to discuss the rules and assist in their formulation and development. Later, students can also assist in the addition, deletion, or modification of the rules. Students frequently benefit from learning the give-and-take process of developing and modifying classroom rules. The following example illustrates how rules can help problem children learn self-control. A teacher and students initially agreed on these rules:

1. Students must receive permission for a hall pass.
2. Students are not allowed to swear while in the classroom.
3. Students are not to talk while in the blue areas.

TABLE 5.1

Planning classroom procedures at the elementary level

Subject	Procedures or Expectations
I. Room use	
A. Teacher's desk and storage areas	
B. Student desks and storage areas	
C. Storage for common materials	
D. Drinking fountains, sink, pencil sharpener	
E. Bathrooms	
F. Center, station, or equipment areas	
II. Seat work and teacher-led instruction	
A. Student attention during presentations	
B. Student participation	
C. Talk among students	
D. Obtaining help	
E. Out-of-seat procedures during seat work	
F. When seat work has been completed	
III. Transitions into and out of the room	
A. Beginning the school day	
B. Leaving the room	
C. Returning to the room	
D. Ending the day	
IV. Procedures during reading or other groups	
A. Getting the class ready	
B. Student movement	
C. Expected behavior in the group	
D. Expected behavior of students out of group	
V. General procedures	
A. Distributing materials	
B. Interruptions	
C. Bathrooms	
D. Library, resource room, school office	
E. Cafeteria	
F. Playground	
G. Fire and disaster drills	
H. Classroom helpers	

Source. From *Classroom Management for Elementary Teachers* (p. 32) by C. M. Evertson, E. T. Emmer, B. S. Clements, J. P. Sanford, and M. E. Worsham, 1984, Englewood Cliffs, NJ: Prentice-Hall. Copyright 1984 by Prentice-Hall, Inc. Adapted by permission.

TABLE 5.2
Planning classroom procedures on the secondary level

Subject	Procedures or Expectations
I. **General** procedures	
A. Beginning-of-period procedures	
1. Attendance check	
2. Students absent the previous day	
3. Tardy students	
4. Behavior expected of all students	
5. Leaving the room	
B. Use of materials and equipment	
1. Equipment and materials for students	
2. Teacher materials and equipment	
C. Ending the period	
1. Readiness for leaving	
2. Dismissal	
II. Procedures during **seat work** and **teacher-led instruction**	
A. Student attention during presentations	
B. Student participation	
C. Procedures for seat work	
1. Talk among students	
2. Obtaining help	
3. Out-of-seat procedures	
4. When seat work has been completed	
III. Procedures for **student group work**	
A. Use of materials and supplies	
B. Assignment of students to groups	
C. Student goals and participation	
IV. **Miscellaneous** procedures	
A. Signals	
B. Public address (PA) announcements and other interruptions	
C. Special equipment and materials	
D. Fire and disaster drills	
E. Split lunch period	

Source. From *Classroom Management for Secondary Teachers* (p. 34) by E. T. Emmer, C. M. Evertson, J. P. Sanford, B. S. Clements, and M. E. Worsham, 1984, Englewood Cliffs, NJ: Prentice-Hall. Copyright 1984 by Prentice-Hall, Inc. Adapted by permission.

They discussed the rules on the first day of school; the teacher then printed them on a poster board and fastened it to the wall at the front of the room. During the hall pass discussion the teacher displayed the pass. The profanity rule was introduced with children telling what they considered inappropriate words. Despite initial reluctance some interesting words were suggested and were listed under Rule 2. The blue areas were designated by blue tape attached to the floor. If a student situated in the blue study area talked during a study period, the teacher merely turned and pointed to the individual violating the rule and declared "3." If a child used profanity, the teacher turned to the child in question and said "2." After the first week the students knew the rules and seldom violated them. Success was achieved because the class did not want to violate reasonable rules and responded appropriately when rules were consistently applied.

Establishing rules is a good approach to the prevention of specific management problems. Thereafter, regular review, immediate notification of infractions, and frequent praise for compliance facilitate adherence to the rules and, hence, classroom management.

Kounin's Group Management

Kounin's (1970) research on management focused on finding which teacher variables predicted compliance and appropriate behavior in students. As Kounin reports, previous efforts to determine the efficacy of "desists"—that is, traditional statements that teachers make so that students will desist from inappropriate behaviors—had proven less than fruitful. According to Kounin, the following variables are among those related to successful classroom management:

1. **With-it-ness,** essentially awareness, refers to the teacher's ability to follow classroom action, be aware of possible deviance, communicate awareness to the class, and intervene at the initiation of the problem.
2. **Overlapping** indicates an ability to deal with two events simultaneously and thus to respond to target behaviors promptly.
3. **Movement management** refers to smooth transition between activities. When the teacher can maintain momentum between instructional periods, the degree of behavioral compliance is likely to increase.
4. **Group alerting** consists of specific skills for maintaining attention throughout various teaching lessons, as with a specific signal or procedure that involves all students.
5. **Accountability and format** include the methods that teachers develop to ensure a group focus by actively involving all students in appropriate activities.
6. **Avoiding satiation** on instructional activities refers to the ability to perceive when continuing tasks would end students' interest and then to vary activities to prevent inappropriate behaviors.

Kounin (1970) assumes that mastering these basic group concerns will minimize the time needed for problem management, thus leading to an increase in the time available for individualized instruction.

INCREASING APPROPRIATE BEHAVIOR

The majority of intervention efforts undertaken to produce change in behavior are oriented toward the increasing of appropriate, desirable behaviors. For students with special needs, this orientation includes a host of adaptive behaviors, most notably academic, social, and daily living skills. The most socially acceptable and pedagogically sound method of providing consequences to increase appropriate behavior is through positive reinforcement.

Principles of Positive Reinforcement

Reduced to simplest terms, positive reinforcement refers to the supplying of a desirable consequence after appropriate behavior. In more precise terms it refers to those consequent environmental events that increase a specific desired behavior by presenting a reinforcer. Positive reinforcement can be simply a smile or a wave extended to a courteous driver, a weekly paycheck, applause for the winning basket, or a thank you from someone receiving a gift. The classroom presents constant opportunities for the use of positive reinforcers.

Positive tools can be used in three basic ways. First, and most common, reinforcement can be made contingent on appropriate target responses selected to be increased. This approach provides motivation for building new skills. Second, positive events can be used to reinforce a behavior incompatible with one to be decreased. An example might be reinforcing on-task time to decrease out-of-seat behavior. Third, teachers can positively reinforce proximate peers to demonstrate to a given student that certain actions will receive reinforcement. For example, the teacher might praise several students for raising their hands in class as an alternative to reprimanding another pupil for talking out of turn.

Successful use of positive reinforcement initially involves determining reinforcer preferences. With a wide variety of alternatives available, a teacher should establish a reinforcement "menu" most appropriate for the individual student. The following techniques can be used:

1. direct questioning of the child
2. indirect questioning of parents, friends, or past teachers
3. observation of the child within the natural environment
4. structured observation, as in arranging specific reinforcement alternatives from which the child may select
5. trial and error of a variety of reinforcers

Generally, teachers select from a pool of three types of reinforcers: social, tangible, or activity reinforcers.

Social Reinforcers Praise is the positive reinforcer most readily available to teachers. Praise, and for that matter all reinforcement, is most effective if used appropriately—that is, if it is meaningful, specific, and immediate. The following examples illustrate the importance of these three attributes.

Maria has just completed her arithmetic assignment. If her teacher checks the work and then informs her that she is a wonderful girl with good posture, praise has been provided, but it is not **meaningful** to Maria's efforts. If, instead, Maria's teacher tells her that she is doing well in her work, some meaning is involved in the praise, but **specificity** is lacking. The best manner of praising is to state exactly how well Maria has done (for example, "I like the way you arranged the problems on your paper. You have numbers 1, 2, 4, and 5 correct"). For an older student the teacher might say, "Tom, the quality of your work has improved dramatically—you made no errors on today's spelling assignment. Would you like to post it on the bulletin board?"

The third criterion of appropriate reinforcement is **immediacy.** During the acquisition stage of learning, praise needs to follow each desired response immediately. For example, if intensive efforts to teach Carly to go directly to her seat after entering the room are to succeed, then she should receive praise as soon as she does so. The immediate, systematic application of praise is used to assist Carly in learning this behavior. After acquiring the behavior, she may be placed on a maintenance schedule of intermittent praise. Even during maintenance, however, the praise should come immediately after Carly displays the desired response.

A second social reinforcer that can be used in combination with praise is **physical contact.** Characteristics of the teacher and the student must determine how much touching is used and how effective it is. Careful consideration of its appropriateness is particularly important with adolescents. Physical contact can take several forms. Shaking hands, a pat on the back, and a hug can all serve as positive consequences depending on the teacher, the student, and the situation. Certainly, some combinations are not as acceptable as others (e.g., it would generally be better for a female senior high teacher to shake a male student's hand rather than hug him), but the teacher usually has some options to use contact in supplementing praise. Successful physical reinforcement must come through experience and familiarity with individual children.

Tangibles Tangible reinforcers may evoke images of the M&M syndrome sometimes associated with the illogical concept of behavior modification as **bribery.** However, just as consequent events are not limited to the use of tangibles, tangibles are not limited to M&Ms. The addition of tangible reinforcements to an instructional program may enhance the value of the social reinforcers with which they should be paired. Research on the motivational aspects of learning shows that tangible reinforcers can be a particularly powerful component of the reinforcer hierarchy for many students who are mildly handicapped.

The tangible item with primary reinforcing value is usually food because it is desired instinctively. For students who are younger or lower functioning, food often is very effective. However, because highly desirable edible items, such as sweets, are often nutritionally unsound, the volume of food intake should be considered. One efficient method of making food available as a consequence is to break it down into small

pieces that can be earned for specific steps in an instructional task. A good example is the use of a soft drink, which can be dispensed in small quantities in several ways, such as by sips through a straw and by refills of a tiny creamer or soufflé cup. Each sip can be awarded on correct completion of an academic task or performance of a specific desired behavior. Other effective and frequently used food items include ice cream and applesauce. For adolescents, obtaining a soft drink at the end of the day can become the focus of points earned throughout earlier instructional periods.

Other paired reinforcers might be considered for children who have learned to delay gratification. This ability allows certain items to serve as symbols of reinforcers and to be exchanged later for such things as food or toys. In our society money serves this purpose; in the classroom this same principle can be applied through the use of tokens. **Tokens** represent items that learners desire; they will work to earn those tokens because they have learned that they are paired with the actual reinforcers. On a very basic level tokens can be used in an individual instructional session to reinforce appropriate behavior and then can be exchanged immediately upon task completion. On a grander scale tokens or artificial currency can become the exchange medium for a classroom-based economy, which is discussed in more detail later.

Activities Activities can also be highly reinforcing positive consequences. As an incentive an activity should be an event in which a child earns the right to participate specifically because of appropriate behavior. The teacher must distinguish between positive activities that the child normally has been accustomed to, such as lunch and recess, and those that are contingent on certain behavior. To be used as reinforcers, activities must represent a **positive plus** to the student (Payne, Mercer, Payne, & Davison, 1973). This concept requires that the activity be desirable for the student as well as extra. The following example illustrates the concept of a positive plus.

Joan has completed her math worksheet and is allowed to go to recess. If this period is the regular recess traditionally available to her, it is not a reward and, thus, may not serve as an effective consequence. If she does not complete her worksheet and still gets recess, she has not earned anything special by doing her work. And if she does not complete her math and consequently does not get to go, then recess actually has been taken away, and a form of punishment has been applied. To make recess a positive reinforcer requires that it be made extra. This can be accomplished by allowing more time for recess or by providing an additional period. In this way Joan can earn extra time as a positive plus rather than earning time that is rightfully hers anyway. If recess is used contingently, Joan is not punished if she fails to complete her math assignment; she simply does not earn extra time.

In addition to activities like recess, many other alternatives are available to the teacher. Depending on the student, free time, being first in line, or even taking the lunch money to the school office can become positive consequences. For adolescents, assisting with school maintenance or serving as a hall monitor might be deemed desirable. Table 5.3 contains other activities that might be reinforcing to individual students.

Reinforcement Schedules An important consideration after the selection of a particular consequence is the contingency schedule according to which it is presented to the learner. In general, schedules can be defined as either continuous or intermittent. A **continuous** schedule indicates that reinforcement is given with each occurrence of a given behavior; it is most useful for teaching and learning at the acquisition stage.

Intermittent schedules provide reinforcement less frequently and are more advantageous for maintenance/proficiency and generalization learning. Six intermittent schedules are fixed ratio, fixed interval, fixed response duration, variable ratio, variable interval, and variable response duration. A **fixed ratio** schedule specifies a particular relationship between occurrences and reinforcement (e.g., 5:1) and can be illustrated by piecework (e.g., stacking bricks) or rewards given according to the number of worksheets completed (e.g., a token given for every worksheet completed with 90% accuracy). **Fixed interval** reinforcement specifies the amount of time that will elapse before reinforcement—for example, using classroom timers and awarding points to all students working when the buzzer sounds at regular 5-minute intervals. A **fixed duration** schedule differs from a fixed interval schedule in that the target behavior must have occurred for the duration of the entire interval in order for the individual to earn the reinforcement. **Variable ratio, variable interval, and variable duration** schedules allow alterations in the frequency, elapsed time, or duration time between reinforcers.

Reinforcement schedules should be selected according to the class's specific instructional objectives. For certain goals, such as completing math worksheets or establishing quiet time during a reading period, fixed schedules may be most appropriate. In many situations, however, variable schedules are more effective, because students are unable to predict receipt of reinforcement as precisely; thus, programming tends to produce behaviors most resistant to extinction. The variable schedules inherent in slot machines illustrate how effective these contingencies can be in maintaining desired responses.

TABLE 5.3
Activity reinforcers

Selecting topic for group discussion	Helping the secretaries
Selecting game or activity for recess	Getting an extra recess
Reading to a friend	Passing out milk at lunch
Tutoring a classmate	Cleaning the lunchroom
Going to the office	Sitting in the front row
Erasing chalkboards	Sitting in the back row
Emptying trash or pencil sharpener	Reading comics, magazines
Cleaning, waxing, painting desks	Working with another teacher
Using the tape recorder	Having a class break for soft drinks
Listening to the radio with earplugs	Making visual aids
Running the projector	Playing games of all kinds
Doing homework in class	Doing arts and crafts
Having extra time in favorite subject	Keeping behavioral point records
Enjoying privacy	Acting as "bank" teller
Doing community projects	Shopping for supplies and materials
Going out first to recess	Checking the parking lot for cars
Taking attendance	with lights on
Collecting lunch money	Being an usher
Handing out papers	Taking guests' coats
Helping to correct papers	Getting guests' chairs
Opening/closing windows	Sitting next to the window
Being team captain	Sitting next to the door
Passing out books	Passing the wastebasket after an art
Passing out scissors or crayons	activity
Collecting scissors or crayons	Cleaning erasers
Helping put up a bulletin board	Cleaning outside grounds
Talking during free-time	Displaying a bulletin board
Helping the custodian	Taking down a bulletin board
Helping the principal	

Source. From *Living in the Classroom: The Currency-Token Economy* (pp. 39–41) by J. S. Payne, E. A. Polloway, J. M. Kauffman, and T. R. Scranton, 1975, New York: Human Sciences Press. Copyright 1975 by Human Sciences Press. Adapted by permission.

Gradual Change Processes The basic principles of positive reinforcement can create a false picture that learning, as defined by behavior change, is simply a matter of selecting the correct reinforcer and scheduling it effectively. For most educational objectives, learning is best characterized as a gradual process of behavior change. Shaping and chaining represent two such processes. The purpose of shaping is to reach an academic or behavioral goal through the gradual achievement and mastery of subgoals. The process involves establishing a shifting performance criterion to reinforce gradual increments in performance. As it is

most precisely defined, it refers to the gradual change in performance that is tied to a single behavior, to distinguish it from chaining (see Martin & Pear, 1983, for an extensive discussion of the relationship between shaping and chaining).

A shaping program includes four component steps (Martin & Pear, 1983): specification of a final desired behavior, selection of the starting behavior, choosing of the specific shaping steps, and movement through the steps at an appropriate pace, with reinforcement provided accordingly. Because shaping is based on a series of small, more easily achieved subgoals, it provides the teacher with a valuable strategy for building responses that are well beyond a child's present functioning.

Becker, Englemann, and Thomas (1971) provided one of the earliest illustrations of the use of shaping. The target behavior was the completion of 20 addition problems in 20 minutes. Initially, the student could complete only one problem in 2 minutes, with teacher assistance. The reinforcer was points marked on a card, with 25 points being worth an opportunity to play a special game at recess. A set of problems (of maintenance level difficulty) was chosen for the child to do. Several steps of subskills were established, from first giving the student a paper with only one problem printed on it—to be completed with the teacher's help—to the final step of presenting a paper with 20 problems to be completed independently within 20 minutes.

Shaping behavior through successive approximations to the desired goal is one of the basic uses of consequent events. When combined with both task analysis and prompting, it can be the basis for teaching precise, manageable skills to students. Systematic application of these techniques is critical for students who are young or severely handicapped. Such an approach provides the foundation for **chaining,** the linking of skills to complete a complex behavioral task. Forward chaining can be used to teach sequential steps in consecutive order, as with self-help skills such as shaving; backward chaining can effectively teach skills such as dressing by beginning just short of the completed task and gradually requiring the student to complete more steps within the task hierarchy.

Positive Reinforcement Programs

Effective teaching often requires the instructor to utilize systems for implementing reinforcement strategies. This section describes several reinforcement programs that have been successfully used in classroom situations, as well as the Premack principle, which conceptually underlies the various programs.

Premack Principle The most basic concept for dealing with consequences is the **Premack principle** (Premack, 1959). It is often called "grandma's law" because it is reminiscent of the traditional dinner table remark, "If you eat your vegetables, then you can have your dessert." The Premack principle asserts that a low-probability activity can be increased in frequency when paired with a high-probability activity. For example, a student who finishes a spelling lesson (a low-probability behavior) will be allowed to go out and play tetherball for 5 minutes (a high-probability behavior). Because tetherball is a desirable activity, the student has increased incentive to finish the spelling lesson.

The Premack principle provides the basis for the use of management **contingencies.** Teachers can make activities, food, or tokens contingent on completion of an academic task or performance of a specific appropriate behavior. Like the Premack principle, contingencies have been used for centuries to pair rewards with designated tasks.

Contingency Contracting Contracting represents an effective, versatile management system. The technique is most often associated with the work of Lloyd Homme, whose book *How to Use Contingency Contracting in the Classroom* (1969) clearly explains procedures for employing this system. Contracts can be oral or written; they state the work assignment the learner has contracted to complete and the consequences that the instructor will provide on completion. Contracts should be perceived as a binding agreement between student and teacher;

signatures on written contracts emphasize this perception. Homme (1969) identifies 10 fundamental rules of contracting.

1. The contract payoff (reward) should be immediate.
2. Initial contracts should call for and reward small approximations.
3. Small rewards should be given frequently.
4. The contract should call for and reward accomplishment rather than obedience.
5. The performance should be rewarded after it occurs.
6. The contract must be fair.
7. The terms of the contract must be clear.
8. The contract must be honest.
9. The contract must be positive.
10. Contracting as a method must be used systematically.

Contracting has been used extensively in a variety of situations and has been tied to a variety of instructional objectives. The following example illustrates a creative use of the technique. A middle school class of boys identified as high risk for dropping out of school lacked motivation to complete academic assignments. Their major concern seemed to revolve around when they could smoke their next cigarettes. To make use of this habit without condoning smoking, the teacher informed the boys that what they did in the bathroom adjoining the classroom was their own decision; translated, that meant "Smoke if you so choose." To reach the bathroom, however, required a pass entitling them to 5 minutes out of the room. Making receipt of the pass contingent on performance ensured that the boys would work especially hard on their assignments. Contracts stated that students could leave the room for 5 minutes after completing 10 problems or a short story.

Within a large class setting contingency contracting can also be handled efficiently and effectively. A teacher responsible for a

1-hour arithmetic period can make assignments that a student will need approximately 50 minutes to complete. The remaining 10 minutes can then be given to students to play games, read comics, or work at an interest center, contingent on the completion of specific academic tasks. Although the instructional time has been decreased by one-sixth, the students' motivation to complete their work and gain their free-choice time will probably compensate for the reduced time.

Figure 5.1 illustrates a simple form for a contingency contract. Changes and elaborations depend on the instructional goals of the specific situation. Contracts can be an extremely useful technique in a classroom situation. They can be age-appropriate, can provide initial training in understanding formal contracts, can facilitate home-school coordination, and can serve as an appropriate step toward self-management.

Token Economies Another systematic method for programming reinforcement is through establishment of a **token economy.** In general, a token system is based on items symbolizing actual reinforcers, much like the monetary reward system of free enterprise. Just as adults receive money or other tangible rewards for their performance, students can earn tokens for appropriate behavior and completion of tasks. Just as adults can exchange their money for food, clothes, shelter, and entertainment, students can redeem their tokens for items they want. Token systems can assist with both motivation and management within the instructional setting.

Token systems afford the teacher a number of distinct advantages over other forms of contingency management. Tokens can help bridge the gap between a specific behavior and the actual reinforcer with a minimal disruption in instruction. In addition, the interest generated by obtaining tokens

FIGURE 5.1
Sample contract

Contract

I Will do twenty multiplication problems every day during my math period.

Jerry Jeff Walker
(signed)

After successfully doing this, I may play basketball outside for fifteen minutes.

Date signed January 6, 1988   M. L. Brooks
(signed)

Date completed January 7, 1988

may actually increase the reinforcing value of the reinforcer for which they are exchanged. Tokens can be constructed to ensure portability and availability and can allow for a flexible reinforcement menu without incorporating a variety of reinforcers into the instructional class activities. Finally, token economies can have positive effects on teachers by emphasizing the need to reinforce students frequently and consistently.

A further benefit of token economies is that, through their use in modifying behavior, they can promote the smooth running of the classroom. For example, one typical activity that can cause disruption is lining students up for an activity out of the room. With tokens the teacher has a convenient alternative to the pleading, yelling, conning, and coercing that often accompany the verbal request to line up. Those who respond as requested are rewarded; those who fail to respond fail to receive a token.

Tokens can also be extremely beneficial in enhancing skill training and academic learning. Amounts to be paid when work is completed can be established for specific assignments. For example, a math sheet might be worth 10 tokens when completed

with 90% accuracy. With this added incentive for work completion, teachers frequently find that a student's quantity of work and rate of learning undergo dramatic changes.

Token systems can be used in a variety of ways. Outgrowths may include banking and checking, stores, and classroom governments. Tokens can also become integral parts of mainstreaming efforts, home-school relations, and interdisciplinary arrangements in residential facilities. Data on the efficacy of token systems have been collected from nonhandicapped students and students identified as mildly handicapped, as well as from numerous other populations (see Kazdin, 1972; Kazdin, 1977; Kazdin & Bootzin, 1972; O'Leary & Drabman, 1971). Mansdorf (1977) documents efforts to use such systems with severely handicapped individuals. When working with this population, however, teachers may need to plan more intensive procedural training for the learners before implementing the system.

Token economies can have direct educational benefits beyond providing an organized program of consequences. Currency-based economies are particularly helpful in meeting career education goals. In addition, as Payne, Polloway, Kauffman, and Scranton (1975) indicate, such a system's ultimate goal of reducing a learner's reliance on external reinforcers has direct implications for the possible success of self-regulatory forms of behavioral intervention (discussed later in this chapter). Stainback, Payne, Stainback, and Payne (1973) and Payne et al. (1975) provide further information on the establishment of token economies.

Extensions of Token Systems Although token economies have been criticized for stifling the spontaneity and creativity of both the teacher and the instructional program, in practice such programs can be tailored to facilitate a creative atmosphere. The currency system just discussed represents one way to accomplish this. Two other techniques that can assist in increasing the interest and excitement of existing token economies are auctions and lotteries.

Auctions can enhance the functioning of a token economy in several ways: (1) by helping to maintain student motivation at a high level through the addition of variety to the token economy; (2) by giving students an opportunity to deal with money and thereby learn to appreciate the intricacies of saving and spending currency; and (3) by broadening the scope and utility of an instructor's available reinforcers (Polloway & Polloway, 1979). Auctions can be conveniently built into an ongoing token or currency-based program. Their function is to supplement the classroom store, which is often established as the redemption center for tokens or currency. In lieu of, or as an adjunct to, a visit to the store, an auction can occur on a weekly or biweekly basis. Consistent with the traditional conception of this type of arrangement, students should bring their earnings and receive a chance to bid on specific items on the auction block.

Successful auctions can use unique and different items with particular appeal to a specific age group. Some particularly successful items include used athletic equipment, old texts and library books, jewelry, perfume and cologne, used wallets, old trophies, and a variety of games. Abandoned or recycled items may be as attractive as new ones. The key to item selection should, of course, be their value to students, not the teacher (Polloway & Polloway, 1979).

Schilling and Cuvo (1983) report on another alternative system for use with points or tokens. For adolescents with handicaps, these researchers set up a classroom **lottery** in which points earned were redeemable for lottery tickets at the end of the week; the tickets represented chances for a variety of material reinforcers. The program increased the time students remained in work areas, resulted in better student preparation for class, and decreased the amount of talking without permission.

Negative Reinforcement

As an approach to behavior management, negative reinforcement threatens an individual with aversive consequences in order to increase the occurrence of alternative behavior. Thus, even though negative reinforcement is philosophically inconsistent with the positive reinforcement strategies just discussed, it is an approach to increasing behavior. There are numerous examples of negative reinforcement in our environment: stopping at a traffic light to avoid an accident or a ticket, dressing conservatively to avoid stares from strangers, putting on a seat belt to silence the noxious buzzer. In the classroom, children commonly encounter a situation in which they are told that they can avoid certain negative stimuli by performing a desired behavior, such as sitting in their seats and remaining quiet.

Negative reinforcement is often confused with punishment. However, whereas punishment involves withdrawing a positive reinforcer or presenting an aversive stimulus to **decrease** behavior, negative reinforcement by definition **increases** the frequency of an escape or avoidance behavior under threat of aversive consequences. In an instructional environment dominated by the frequent use of punishment, student behavior may be largely based on the desire to avoid such consequences. It is estimated that a large number of teachers run their classes on principles of negative reinforcement tied to reminders of prior punishment. Because of some known or unknown threat (e.g., a trip to the principal's office, a paddle hanging on the wall, detention), students learn that academic productivity and controlled behavior will allow them to avoid noxious consequences. Although such an arrangement may effectively reduce undesirable behavior, it creates an atmosphere counterproductive to the acquisition of adaptive skills. Such procedures are cited here only to acknowledge their common presence in education. Every teacher relies on negative reinforcement to a degree; the key is to keep it from dominating the classroom environment.

BEHAVIOR REDUCTION TECHNIQUES

Successful teaching in the majority of special education settings requires the ability to manage a classroom (or caseload), which in turn requires the successful resolution of problem behaviors. Repp (1983) groups into three types the techniques that have proven effective for reducing disruptive and other inappropriate behaviors: reinforcement-related procedures, such as the differential reinforcement of incompatible behavior; aversive procedures, including punishment in different forms; and drug-based procedures. This section focuses on the first two types.

The use of reductive strategies requires an initial consideration of the techniques most natural to the classroom and school environment. Teachers should select approaches according to a hierarchy beginning with the least restrictive alternative strategies. Nelson and Rutherford (1983) suggest the following sequence (pp. 61–62):

1. differential reinforcement of other behavior—for example, increasing social reinforcement of seat work and cooperative play behaviors to reduce a pupil's aggressive behavior
2. extinction—for example, not responding to students who call out answers without first raising their hands
3. verbal aversive—for example, saying "No!" to a preschooler who takes another child's toy
4. response cost—for example, fining a student 10 points for cursing or taking away 5 minutes of recess time for failing to complete an assignment
5. time out from positive reinforcement
6. overcorrection
7. school exclusion—for example, giving a 3-day suspension for fighting in school

Natural and Logical Consequences

Before teachers consider exotic or high-powered consequences for inappropriate behavior—and before specific punishment strategies are implemented—attention should be given to specific consequent events that are natural and/or logical relative to the specific behavior. Although in some instances, these may be behaviorally defined as punishment, their cognitive relationship to the behavior itself makes them more attractive alternatives. As West (1986) notes, the use of natural and logical consequences can result in the learning of responsibility by children and adolescents.

Natural consequences occur when a parent or a teacher "does not intervene in a situation but allows the situation to teach the child. The technique is based on the adage that 'Every generation must learn that the stove is hot' " (West, 1986, p. 121). Several examples illustrate how this process can operate in a classroom setting. A student may refuse to do classwork or homework. The natural consequences are that he receives no credit for the work. The teacher need not say or do anything. In another situation a child may habitually forget her permission slip to attend a class function away from school. The natural consequences are that she has to stay behind when the class goes on a trip. The student's frustration may assist in teaching her to accept responsibility for the permission slip in the future.

With certain behaviors natural consequences could result in severe eventualities, such as injury to the learner. For example, depending on the natural consequences of walking into the street without looking would clearly be inappropriate. In these instances consideration should be given to alternatives that are **logical consequences** of the behavior. West (1986) aptly describes the role of logical consequences.

> The secret of good consequences is the logic between the misbehavior and the consequences. For example, it is not logical for a parent to drive consistently to school to give a child a forgotten lunch box. In this instance, the parent takes the consequence for the child. What is logical is that the child goes without lunch or borrows money from the principal. In this way, the child learns from the error. Often it is difficult to think of perfect consequences, but with practice, such techniques become easy to master. (p. 123)

Several examples of logical consequences in the classroom can be taken from Dreikurs, Grunwald, and Pepper (1982, pp. 121–122). **When a child pushes on the stairway,** the teacher may give the child a choice of not pushing or of going back to the classroom, waiting until the group has reached its destination, and then starting

out alone. **A child who is late from recess** might be given the choice of returning with the others or standing by the teacher during recess until it is time to return to class. Dreikurs et al. (1982) provide the following summation of logical consequences:

> There is no pat formula for applying **logical consequences.** What will work in one situation may not work in another. The child who likes to go outdoors, for example, will be differently affected by being kept in during recess than a child who hates to go out. Therefore, by treating these two children in different ways, similar results can be obtained. And since they have participated in setting up the logical consequences, they do not feel that they are punished by the teacher. It must be remembered that the use of logical consequences requires an understanding of the child and of the situation. **When** to do **what** and to **whom** requires judgment about many imponderables because every situation is unique. (p. 127)

In considering the use of behavior reduction strategies, the teacher is encouraged to continuously evaluate how natural and logical consequences can enhance a management program. For further information on these techniques, West's (1986) excellent text on parenting should be consulted, as well as the classic texts by Dreikurs (e.g., Dreikurs et al., 1982).

Differential Reinforcement Strategies

A number of strategies reduce inappropriate behaviors through positive reinforcement strategies. As outlined by Dietz and Repp (1983), these include differential reinforcement of a low rate of responding (DRL), differential reinforcement of the omission of behavior (DRO), and differential reinforcement of incompatible (DRI) or alternative behaviors (DRA).

A DRL strategy employs reinforcement based on the successive reduction of behavioral occurrences; it can thus be used, for example, to gradually decrease talking out of turn during an instructional period. DRL is an underused, yet potentially effective tool for changing classroom behavior. In Figure 5.2 the concept is clearly illustrated by the graphing of the reduction in disruptive responses among a group of 14 students identified as educable mentally retarded. The average number of disruptions per minute, approximately 3.5 prior to program implementation, dropped off on 12 of the 20 days of treatment to below the standard of 1.3 disruptions per minute.

DRO procedures call for reinforcement based on the omission of a given behavior for a specified time. For example, reinforcement could be tied to a student's remaining seated for a progressive period from 5 minutes to the entire instructional period; the inappropriate behavior is effectively **omitted** during these successively longer periods. Konczak and Johnson (1983) provide an interesting example of DRO procedures used

in a nonclassroom setting. In their research a DRO procedure effected significant decreases in the inappropriate verbalization of a client in a sheltered workshop.

DRI/DRA approaches can be used to strengthen behaviors that are not compatible with or that represent an alternative to the targeted inappropriate behavior. Thus, the reinforcement of hand raising could be used to decrease the occurrence of calling out in class. The following example underscores the importance of the latter approach.

Van frequently leaves his seat during work periods. Dealing directly with this behavior would involve negative alternatives: a reprimand from the teacher, a trip to the principal, or 5 minutes in the time-out room. Each of these methods illustrates the use of punishment to decrease the disruptive behavior, and each might be effective. But in the interest of promoting a positive atmosphere in the classroom, another option is to positively reinforce a target behavior that is **incompatible** with Van's being out

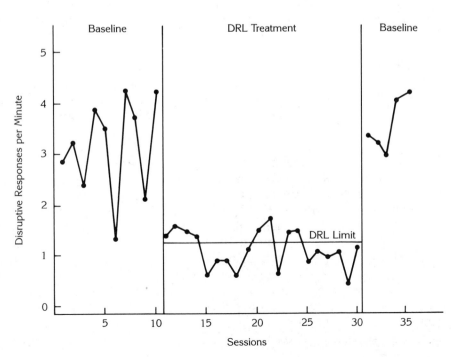

FIGURE 5.2
Example of DRL intervention (From "Reducing Inappropriate Classroom Behavior of Retarded Students Through Three Procedures of Differential Reinforcement" by S. M. Deitz, A. C. Repp, and D. E. D. Deitz, 1976, *Journal of Mental Deficiency Research, 20,* 155–170. Copyright 1976 by the *Journal of Mental Deficiency Research.* Reprinted by permission.)

of his seat. Staying seated would be a likely choice, although more stringent requirements, such as being on task, would also be appropriate. With this plan Van would receive positive consequences in the form of praise, a pat on the back, food, or tokens whenever he stayed in his seat. Ignoring him if he got out of his seat would prevent his obtaining any positive teacher response to his disruptiveness. Positive methods, in this case via differential reinforcement, are not the panacea for all behavior problems, but they do represent a valuable initial effort and should be considered before more restrictive means are selected. Dietz and Repp (1983) and Repp (1983) are excellent sources for further information.

Good-Behavior Game   One example of the use of differential reinforcement (especially DRL) is the good-behavior game. This technique—originally reported by Barrish, Saunders, and Wolf (1969)—divides a class into teams or groups. Each person has specific standards for meriting free time. Teams that remain below the maximum number of occurrences of inappropriate behavior receive the designated reinforcement. The technique is easy to implement and has been used successfully in regular classrooms (e.g., Medland & Stachnik, 1972) as well as in special education settings.

Although group contingencies such as those in the good-behavior game may seem unfair to individual students who are penalized for the actions of others, teachers may want to use them if, in the long run, all students will profit. Axelrod (1983) aptly points out that well-behaved students already suffer in a disruptive environment; therefore, any technique that effectively brings about classroom control serves their best interests. Naturally, the teacher must modify the structure of the game if one student consistently misbehaves for attention-seeking purposes and penalizes the team.

Extinction Procedures

As behaviorally defined, *extinction* refers to the withholding of reinforcement that previously maintained a specific behavior or behavior cluster. Analysis of antecedents, behaviors, and consequences relative to a particular situation may indicate that change can be effected by removing the reinforcer maintaining the behavior, thus extinguishing the response. The most typical example of extinction use in the classroom occurs when teacher attention has inadvertently been tied to students' inappropriate behavior (e.g., the teacher speaks to or walks over to the children only when they are out of their seats or are disruptive). Extinction then involves withholding attention at these times. For other behaviors peers may need to be involved in the intervention plan if their attention has been maintaining the inappropriate behavior (e.g., a child uses infantile language to receive others' attention, in the form of laughter).

Several cautions are needed concerning the use of extinction. First, extinction should be used only for a behavior for which it is appropriate and for which it is apt to be effective. Second, the initial withholding of attention or other forms of reinforcement may prompt a dramatic rise in the target behavior as students increase their efforts to receive attention. The efficacy of the procedure, thus, cannot be truly evaluated until several hours or perhaps days have passed. Third, extinction occasionally produces an aggressive response—not unlike that of the person who fails to receive a soft drink as reinforcement for inserting coins in a drink machine (Repp, 1983). A fourth concern is consistency of application. Without a commitment to consistency, the teacher may accidentally reinforce the undesirable behavior on an irregular basis and, thus, inadvertently maintain it at a higher rate of occurrence. Finally, other students may begin to imitate the behavior being ignored, thus exacerbating the situation. Alberto and Troutman (1982) aptly comment on the use of extinction.

> "Just ignore it and it will go away. He's only doing it for attention." This statement is one of the most common suggestions given to teachers. In truth, extinction is much easier to discuss than to implement. It *will* go away, all right, but not necessarily rapidly or smoothly. (p. 213)

Punishment

Although positive consequences should underlie both motivation and management efforts, circumstances may require occasional use of some form of punishment. In considering such procedures, the teacher should again make selections based on the least restrictive option; that is, programs chosen should curtail an individual's freedom no more than necessary to yield the desired behavior change (Barton, Brulle, & Repp, 1983). The use of various forms of punishment necessitates data collection to demonstrate that specific techniques are effective for a particular target behavior.

The generic term *punishment,* as typically defined, refers to two types of consequent arrangements. Most commonly, it is the presentation of an aversive or noxious event, such as corporal punishment or a verbal reprimand. Its second form is the removal or withdrawal of positive reinforcement, for example, restricting privileges or instituting a system of fines. Two examples of the second form, time out and response cost, are discussed initially, followed by a look at the presentation of aversive events.

Time Out   Punishment through withdrawal of positive reinforcement is best typified by **time-out** procedures. Although techniques may differ, the concept generally entails preventing a student from receiving the positive reinforcement that otherwise would be available. Time out includes planned ignoring, contingent observation (i.e., the student is removed from but can still observe the group), exclusion from the time-in environment, and seclusion in an isolated room or cubicle (Harris, 1985; Nelson & Rutherford, 1983). The discussion here focuses primarily on the last of these forms.

Teachers should observe several cautions in using time out. First, the effectiveness of time out depends on the presence of positive reinforcement in the classroom and its absence in the time-out area. Without both of these elements, the procedure can be of only limited assistance to the teacher. For example, if Susan dislikes the classroom situation (e.g., there is a substantial amount of yelling by the teacher, as well as difficult work assignments) and she is sent to the hall for time out, where friends wander by and chat, then she has been **rewarded** for her deviant behavior, not punished. This approach in the long run could increase Susan's misbehavior.

A second warning about time out pertains to the other end of the spectrum. Making the time-out area a dark, uncomfortable room to which a child is "sentenced" is neither necessary nor acceptable. A teacher's efforts should be directed toward changing behavior, not frightening students. The time-out area should be bland and unstimulating, but it need not be a dungeon. Time out may occur in a corner of the room, a small room adjacent to the classroom, a coat closet, or even a large box. It should be used sparingly for short periods and only in extreme cases. If it needs to be used frequently, the teacher should carefully consider alternative forms of consequent events.

Use of time out naturally varies according to the space available, the type of students, and the teacher. Regardless of the circumstances, however, Gast and Nelson (1977) suggest that time out should be

1. preceded by an explicit statement about when it will be used
2. selected only after trying other alternatives
3. accompanied by a brief explanation of why it is being used in each case
4. kept brief (e.g., usually a 5-minute maximum)
5. documented through record-keeping procedures (see Figure 5.3)
6. terminated contingent on appropriate behavior
7. combined with reinforcement for incompatible behavior
8. consistent with local laws and administrative policies

Consistency in structure helps time out to proceed more smoothly. For example, a timer, such as the ones filled with sand, can be given to students when they go to time out so that they know when they can return. The time-out room or space should be removed from the rest of the classroom and should never be used for academic purposes. For younger and more sensitive children, gradual introduction of time out may be wise, perhaps progressing from their sitting next to the time-out room, to being placed inside it with the door open, and eventually to being placed inside it with the door closed if the deviant behavior continues. Even with these steps, time out may not be appropriate for all children. Bereiter and Engelmann (1966) suggest that time out may have detrimental effects for more sensitive, noncalculating students.

When appropriate, time out must be used carefully. The student must know in advance that the teacher will not accept a particular behavior. Classroom rules must clearly indicate which specific behaviors merit time out, and the teacher must enforce the rules

consistently. The teacher should also consider any legal aspects that may apply in a given school district.

Response Cost   A second example of punishment based on withdrawing positive reinforcement is the use of response cost (RC). Such procedures include, in particular, subtracting points or tokens within established reinforcement systems. Response cost procedures can be used concurrently with positive reinforcement in the classroom, producing a reasonably rapid decrease in behavior; and they can be easily combined with other procedures to yield a comprehensive behavior program (Heron, 1987b).

Walker (1983) also supports the potential benefits of RC but identifies some cautions. Response cost is apt to have maximum effect when the teacher has clearly explained the system to the students, has closely tied it to a reinforcement system, and has developed an appropriate feedback and delivery system. In addition, Walker suggests seven rules for implementation.

☐ RC should be implemented immediately after the target response or behavior occurs.
☐ RC should be applied each time a target behavior occurs.
☐ The child should never be allowed to accumulate negative points.
☐ The ratio of points earned to those lost should be controlled.
☐ The teacher should never be intimidated by the target child using RC.
☐ Subtraction of points should never be punitive or personalized.
☐ A child's positive, appropriate behavior should be praised as frequently as opportunities permit. (p. 52)

Aversive Stimuli   A substantial amount of controversy has surrounded the use of aversive tools, or negative reinforcers, as conse-

FIGURE 5.3
Record of time out

Student name: _____ Teacher name: _____

School: _____ Inclusive dates: _____

Policy and procedures for use of time out in this classroom: _____

_____

_____

Date Used	Precipitating Behavior	Time Placed	Time Removed	Response to Time Out

quences for behavior. Basically, these tools range from soft reprimands in the classroom to shock treatments in laboratory settings, which have been used with children who are severely handicapped and self-abusive (see Lovaas, Schreibman, & Koegel, 1974). One possible advantage of aversive measures is that they can rapidly suppress behavior while allowing children to appreciate the seriousness of their behavior; for example, individual reprimands can clearly show a child why certain behavior was judged inappropriate. Nevertheless, punishment has been appropriately denigrated, particularly because it lacks generalizability and because it elicits emotional responses (e.g., crying, tantrums) as a by-product of its use.

Corporal Punishment For years one of the most pervasive forms of school discipline has been corporal punishment. Despite voluminous research on motivation and alternative forms of classroom management, this approach continues to be the treatment of choice for many teachers and principals confronted with behavioral deviations. It has been used relatively frequently with students identified as mentally retarded, learning disabled, or emotionally disturbed (Rose, 1983).

Bolmeier (1976) indicates that the legal right to use corporal punishment originally stemmed from the concept of in loco parentis, whereby parents ceded their rights to the school as a condition for the education of their children. Although compulsory attendance apparently renders this idea moot, belief in the principle and, hence, the practice continues. Smith, Polloway, and West (1979) summarize the rationales for corporal punishment: (1) a legal basis ranging from the 18th and 19th centuries to the Supreme Court's decision in *Ingraham v. Wright* (1977); (2) apparent biblical support for the measure; and (3) alleged practical

benefits of quickness and effectiveness, combined with ready availability. A recent review (Rose, 1983) indicates that corporal punishment is applied most frequently in response to fighting, classroom disruptions, disrespect, disobedience, and truancy. Despite its common usage and assumed benefits, virtually no empirical evidence proves its effectiveness. Rose (1983) suggests that professional and public opinions are more often shaped by folklore and conjecture.

Opposition to corporal punishment has included arguments on moral, physical, and psychological grounds (Smith et al., 1979). Morally, critics link corporal punishment to a more brutal era when the absolute dictate "might makes right" often dominated. Physically, it has been represented as a serious threat to health and well-being when carried to unreasonable excess. Psychologically, corporal punishment has been recognized as a causative factor in anxiety, hostility, lack of self-direction, immaturity, attacks on teachers, and vandalism against schools. In addition, it has become a convenient crutch at times for ineffective or incompetent teaching; it provides a ready solution to problems that might have been prevented by good teaching.

A further critical concern is the effect of corporal punishment on the learning process. Although proponents point to it as a way of learning social expectations for behavior, it functions primarily as a suppressor and thus represents a direct challenge to the active learning process critical for child development. By emphasizing what to avoid rather than what to strive for, corporal punishment stifles growth and blocks an opportunity for teachers to model skills that would promote adaptation both within and outside the school environment.

Punishment in Perspective Punishment continues to be a commonly used technique in the classroom, and new teachers would be naive to assume that they will never rely on such techniques as part of a management program. It is illustrative and instructive to consider the frequency with which various reductive strategies are used in classrooms. Table 5.4 provides a data summary of 15 such strategies and their reported prevalence in regular and special education. Respondents were asked to rate whether they used a technique very often, occasionally, or never, using a Likert scale of 1 to 3. Mean ratings are provided under the column heading $\overline{X}$.

If punishment in some form must be used, the following guidelines should be considered (MacMillan, Forness, & Trumbull, 1973):

☐ Time the punishment so that it is presented early in the occurrence of the problem behavior.
☐ Make it intense enough to result in suppression of the behavior while avoiding embarrassment in front of peers.
☐ Combine it with a clear explanation of the rationale for punishing.
☐ Be consistent.

These additional guidelines may also be helpful.

☐ Do not rely on punishment as a basic means of management—use it sparingly.
☐ Reinforce behavior that is incompatible with the inappropriate behavior.

TABLE 5.4
Frequency of use of aversive contingencies for decreasing inappropriate social behavior

Nature of Item	T.S.		R.E.		S.E.		R.E. vs. S.E.
	$\overline{X}$	SD	$\overline{X}$	SD	$\overline{X}$	SD	P<
Teacher/student conference regarding inappropriate behavior	1.48	.54	1.52	.52	1.40	.57	.146
Withholding a desirable activity	1.62	.54	1.68	.51	1.50	.58	.033
Teacher/parent conference regarding inappropriate behavior	1.76	.51	1.75	.48	1.77	.57	.840
Raising voice	1.92	.45	1.88	.47	1.97	.43	.186
Time out in the classroom	1.93	.58	2.01	.51	1.78	.67	.011
Quiet time	1.99	.56	1.99	.51	1.96	.64	.939
Send to parents a note reprimanding the student	2.01	.59	1.91	.52	2.22	.67	.001
Ignoring	2.07	.57	2.17	.48	1.86	.66	.000
Removal from the classroom	2.17	.58	2.26	.50	2.00	.67	.033
Poor grades on report card	2.25	.76	2.27	.76	2.19	.76	.495
Send student to principal's office	2.32	.52	2.28	.47	2.36	.61	.332
After-school detention	2.41	.64	2.31	.58	2.57	.72	.009
Turning off lights	2.47	.66	2.37	.69	2.67	.53	.001
Repeated copying of lines	2.55	.54	2.45	.57	2.74	.44	.000
Physical punishment	2.88	.36	2.90	.30	2.85	.46	.412

T.S. = total sample; R.E. = regular educators; S.E. = special educators; $\overline{X}$ = mean scores; SD = standard deviation; P = probability.

Source. From "Regular and Special Education Teachers' Estimates of Use of Aversive Consequences" by S. J. Salend, L. Esquirel, and P. B. Pine, 1984, *Behavioral Disorders, 9,* p. 9. Copyright 1984 by Behavioral Disorders. Reprinted by permission.

☐ Evaluate spillover effects—changes in the behavior of nontarget children as a function of the punishment of target children (Heron, 1978).

☐ Avoid physical forms of punishment.

Overcorrection

The development of overcorrection procedures during the past 2 decades has provided some additional alternatives for reducing a variety of inappropriate, undesirable behaviors. Much of the research on these techniques stems from the initial efforts of Foxx and Azrin (1972, 1973). Although overcorrection has been used most frequently with persons who are severely handicapped, the techniques can also be employed with other populations.

Gardner (1977) describes two forms of overcorrection—restitutional and positive practice. **Restitutional** overcorrection involves improving an environmental situation as a consequence of inappropriate behavior. An example might be making restitution for stealing by returning not only the stolen property but also an additional specified amount (e.g., Azrin & Wesolowski, 1974). **Positive practice** involves the repetition of appropriate responses in situations in which the specific inappropriate behavior has occurred. For example, students breaking conduct rules might be required to recite the rule, describe the appropriate behavior, and then practice the desired behavior several times (e.g., Azrin & Powers, 1975). Positive practice has also been used in the teaching of spelling words to students who are moderately handicapped (Stewart & Sirgh, 1986).

Overcorrection, according to its advocates, is an attempt to avoid using aversive techniques as consequences for specific behaviors and to be **educative,** that is, more positive or at least neutral in its presentation to the individual (Repp, 1983). However,

the flavor of punishment remains in many instances. Teachers are encouraged to consider these tools carefully, become familiar with applicable research (e.g., Repp, 1983), and then consider **experimental** use with close attention to evaluation of efficacy. For overcorrection to be most successfully and appropriately used, Heron (1987a) identifies the following guidelines (p. 437): relate overcorrection procedures to specific offenses; ensure that the individual is calm before instituting procedures; use prompts only as they are required; when prompts are used, stress a businesslike tone and avoid debates; complement overcorrection with the reinforcement of incompatible behaviors; keep records of overcorrection use and use the data to make program decisions; do not provide reinforcement during overcorrection; and plan for generalization and maintenance of the effects of treatment.

SPECIAL CONSIDERATIONS

Considerations for Adolescents

Although each of the tools discussed in this chapter has been used effectively with older students, special circumstances must be considered in selecting a strategy to implement with adolescents with special needs. In light of the inherent difficulties in motivating students with long histories of school failure and in managing individuals with chronic patterns of inappropriate behavior, intervention programs must be carefully evaluated to determine their likely outcome. Kerr and Nelson (1983) suggest a number of considerations. First, consequences that are natural to the outcome of the behavior should be emphasized (e.g., being late results in detention). Second, careful attention should be given to the reinforcers controlled by a student's peer group so that management programs are designed to make these reinforcers as consistent as possible with the teacher's objectives. In addition, reinforcers that can be used with a minimum of teacher intervention should be sought; this concern is particularly important with response cost procedures. A point system, for instance, would be easier to use than a token system if something must be removed from a student's total. Furthermore, backup reinforcers for any systematic positive reinforcement program must reflect students' interests and must be varied.

Finally, and most importantly, teachers must carefully choose strategies based on their anticipated reception by adolescents. In the case of positive reinforcement programs, the system must be designed in an age-appropriate fashion; for example, token programs using Daffy Dollars or the like are high-risk approaches at the secondary level. For behavior reduction strategies teachers should obviously avoid interventions with potential for exacerbating current situations. Any strategy that encourages a confrontational interaction has an inherent risk of escalating a particular problem.

Self-Regulation

Perhaps the most important element of any behavior change program is its relationship to the maintenance of acquired skills over time and ultimately to their generalization to other settings and behaviors. The goal of all change programs should be the development of **self-regulation** in its students. Wallace and Kauffman (1978) recommend the following techniques: (1) gradually reduce the frequency and amount of reinforcement, (2) gradually delay reinforcement through the use of feedback to students, (3) gradually fade from artificial reinforcers to natural events, and (4) teach self-control behaviors through an emphasis on the cognitive aspects of modification.

Gardner (1977) notes four aspects of self-regulation to consider when helping a child

to move away from external behavior control: self-assessment, self-instruction, self-determination of reinforcement, and self-administered reinforcers. In **self-assessment** the individual determines the need for change and subsequently monitors or charts personal behavior. **Self-instruction** may include a cognitive approach to management, using self-cuing to inhibit certain inappropriate behaviors and to direct appropriate ones. **Self-determination of reinforcement** places on the student the primary responsibility for selecting reinforcers so that they can be **self-administered,** contingent on performance of the specified appropriate behavior.

Teachers can provide instruction in a number of ways that will promote a shift to self-regulation. In particular, the burgeoning field of cognitive behavior modification (CBM) has inspired the development of numerous techniques to promote behavior change through self-regulation. The work of Meichenbaum (e.g., Meichenbaum, 1980, 1983) is particularly noteworthy.

> [CBM] generally refers to the use of behavior modification methods (frequent direct measurement of behavior and manipulation of antecedents and consequences) to alter cognitions (thoughts and feeling states) as well as overt behavior. The idea behind CBM is that cognitions partially control behavior and that altering thought processes might therefore be an effective way of modifying overt behavior. Moreover, cognitions are accessible (to others through language and to oneself through conscious awareness and introspection) and can be modified in much the same ways that overt behavior can be controlled. Thus, CBM includes cognitive strategy training—teaching skills in thinking and self-control. (Wallace & Kauffman, 1986, p. 100)

The full scope of the research on CBM and its specific derivatives is beyond the scope of this chapter. (An entire issue of *Exceptional Education Quarterly* documented successful efforts in CBM and raised key questions related to the efficacy of the techniques.[2]) Attention is given here to one particular technique—**self-monitoring,** or recording, of behavior—which has been suc- cessfully used with students with learning disabilities, mental retardation, behavior disorders, and remedial needs; it illustrates how self-regulatory processes can be implemented in the classroom.

Self-monitoring, particularly of on-task behavior, is a relatively simple technique

[2]*Exceptional Education Quarterly,* 1980, *1*(1).

[front] **DAILY REPORT CARD**

Name: _____   Date: _____

Period/Time	Behavior				Schoolwork				Homework				Teacher
1.	1	2	3	4	1	2	3	4	1	2	3	4	
2.	1	2	3	4	1	2	3	4	1	2	3	4	
3.	1	2	3	4	1	2	3	4	1	2	3	4	
4.	1	2	3	4	1	2	3	4	1	2	3	4	
5.	1	2	3	4	1	2	3	4	1	2	3	4	
6.	1	2	3	4	1	2	3	4	1	2	3	4	
7.	1	2	3	4	1	2	3	4	1	2	3	4	

Note: Behavior, Schoolwork, and Homework ratings indicate—(1) Poor; (2) Fair; (3) Good; (4) Excellent. Student and teacher should discuss the meaning of these ratings.

[back]

Behavior Definitions: **Schoolwork Definitions:**   **Homework Definitions:**

(1) _____   (1) _____   (1) _____

(2) _____   (2) _____   (2) _____

(3) _____   (3) _____   (3) _____

(4) _____   (4) _____   (4) _____

(a)

FIGURE 5.4
A daily report card (From "The Daily Report Card: A Simplified and Flexible Package for Classroom Behavior Management" by E. H. Dougherty and A. Dougherty, 1977, *Psychology in the Schools, 14,* pp. 192, 194–195. Copyright 1977 by *Psychology in the Schools.* Reprinted by permission.)

that has been validated with children of average ability who have learning disabilities (e.g., Hallahan, Lloyd, Kosiewicz, Kauffman, & Graves, 1979; Hallahan, Marshall, & Lloyd, 1981; Lloyd, Hallahan, Kosiewicz, & Kneedler, 1982) as well as with children of borderline intellectual levels (Rooney, Pollo-

way & Hallahan, 1985) and students with mental retardation (Connis, 1979; Nelson, Lipinski, & Boykin, 1978) and behavior disorders (McLaughlin, Krappman, & Welsh, 1985). The subsequent effect of increased attention, achieved through self-monitoring, on academic achievement has also been re-

---

HOW TO USE THE DAILY REPORT CARD

The Daily Report Card is a tool designed to increase communication between teachers, students, and parents. By providing daily feedback regarding a student's behavior and performance, the card provides information about progress not usually available to parents. Moreover, students' successes as well as problem areas are pointed out for recognition or further remediation.

Instructions for students:

1. Put your name, date, and classes on the card before going to school.

2. Give the card to the teacher at the *end* of each class and request that the teacher rate your behavior and work by circling a number in each of the three columns titled, "Behavior," "Schoolwork," and "Homework." Make sure that the teacher crosses out the columns which might not apply for that class on that day. Also, the teacher *must* write his or her name in the last column.

3. If you have any questions about your ratings, they should be discussed with the teacher. If you feel that you deserved a different rating, ask the teacher why you were given a particular number and what you could do differently next time.

4. Give the completed card to your parents each evening. Any missing ratings will be regarded as "Poor" (Number One) ratings. This means that a missing card will be regarded as a card with all "Poor" ratings.

Instructions for teachers:

1. Your are to rate the child *only* when he or she remembers to give you the Daily Report Card at the end of your class.

2. Cross out all the numbers in a column which may not apply to your class on a particular day. For example, you may not have assigned any homework, or you may have a class with no schoolwork. Schoolwork and homework need not apply only to written assignments, but to class participation or other related performances.

3. Remember to sign your name in the last column.

4. Please discuss with the child why he or she received a particular rating, and what he or she could do to improve behavior or work.

5. Rating and discussion should take no longer than one minute on most days, and should not interfere with regular classroom functioning. Additional discussion should be scheduled at the teacher's convenience.

Instructions for Parents:

1. Please read your child's Daily Report Card every evening. Pay attention to and discuss the good ratings first, however small or few. The discussion should be positive and constructive, and aimed at helping your child find ways of doing better. This is *not* a system to emphasize faults or weak points.

2. Save the cards to indicate progress. Use them to communicate more meaningfully with your child as well as teachers and other school personnel.

(b)

FIGURE 5.4
(continued)

ported in studies by Hallahan and his colleagues (Hallahan et al., 1979; Heins, 1980; Lloyd et al., 1982; Rooney et al., 1985), although the nature of the relationship has been questioned (Rossmiller, cited in Arnold, 1983).

As designed by Hallahan and his colleagues (e.g., Hallahan et al., 1979; Hallahan, Lloyd, & Stoller, 1982), self-monitoring involves an easily implemented series of techniques that can be used in both regular and special education classrooms. It consists of the use of a tape-recorded tone that sounds at random intervals, averaging every 45 seconds, and a self-recording sheet. Children are instructed to ask themselves, each time the tone sounds, whether they were paying attention and then to mark the yes or no box on the self-recording sheet. Although this strategy has been used with accompanying reinforcement for correct use of the self-recording sheet (see Rooney, Hallahan, & Lloyd, 1984), in most instances it has been successful simply with appropriate training in the use of the techniques. The manual on self-monitoring developed by Hallahan et al. (1982) provides more detailed information on the techniques.

The mechanisms described here have been effectively utilized, primarily with students who are in the 8- to 11-year-old age bracket and whose IQs range from 85 to 125. Modifications may be needed for other students—for example, more intensive training for LD students with lower IQs (Rooney et al., 1985). Self-monitoring studies with students identified as mentally retarded have included such elaborative aids as pictorial cues and videotape practice, as well as backup reinforcers to improve self-recording ability (e.g., Connis, 1979; Howell, Rueda, & Rutherford, 1983; Nelson, Lipinski, & Boykin, 1978). Given the varied populations with which self-monitoring or self-

recording procedures have worked effectively, they are certainly worthy of consideration.

Home-School Coordination

Another special consideration in an ongoing management program is the coordination of home and school. Principles and procedures to facilitate home-school programming are developed in chapter 7. However, several specific techniques are discussed here to assist in the process of coordination.

A daily report card and a passport are two similar concepts that can be operationalized to enhance communication and consistency within a home-school management program. **Daily report cards** provide a system for home-based reinforcement tied to feedback on classroom performance. According to Dougherty and Dougherty (1977), such a package can be used for feedback on schoolwork, homework, and behavior; can range in complexity from simple rating-scale responses to precise behavioral definitions; can be tied to nonspecific consequences or to specific short- and long-term reinforcement; and can be individually designed. Figure 5.4a provides an example of a daily report card; Figure 5.4b gives instructions for its use (see pp. 120–121).

The **passport** is another communication tool between home and school. It can take the form of a notebook brought to each class and then taken home on a daily basis. Teachers and parents and, possibly, bus drivers and administrators can make regular notations. Reinforcement is based on having the passport as well as on the specific behaviors indicated in it (Runge, Walker, & Shea, 1975; Walker & Shea, 1984). Passports provide an opportunity for parents and teachers that is similar to that of daily report cards and other home-note systems

(Wielkiewicz, 1986). These aids can help ensure consistency in behavioral standards and management procedures and can assist in the generalization of specific target behaviors.

SUMMARY

Behavior change strategies afford teachers a wide variety of options for motivating and managing students who are handicapped. The techniques discussed in this chapter focus in particular on the importance of antecedent and consequent events in successful teaching and learning. Systematic use of positive reinforcement can increase appropriate behavior. Teachers can program positive consequences to shape desired behaviors through contingency contracting and token economies, both of which are based on the Premack principle. Behavior reduction strategies can also include the use of reinforcement, although teachers may need to select techniques from among the various forms of punishment to successfully decrease targeted inappropriate behaviors. Ultimately, behavior change programs should have the goal of shifting to self-regulation. The techniques discussed in this chapter can be powerful tools. Teachers should use them carefully, constantly evaluating whether changes are in the students' best interests.

6
Strategies for Working with Significant Others

GINGER BLALOCK
University of New Mexico

EDWARD POLLOWAY
Lynchburg College

JAMES PATTON
University of Hawaii

Special education in the post–PL 94–142 era has witnessed numerous significant changes. Perhaps the most profound change for special education teachers has come in the shifting and redefining of professional roles in the wake of federal, state, and local legislative and regulatory attention. Gone are the days when teachers could view their classrooms as isolated sanctuaries, unaffected by external forces.

Special education today is a far more open arena, making different demands on the individual professional. Teachers are now expected to be effective not only in their instruction but also in their interaction with other adults. This chapter focuses on three groups of "significant others" for special educators: within the classroom, paraprofessionals; within the school, regular class teachers; and beyond the school, parents.

PARAPROFESSIONALS

Even model programs are impaired occasionally because of interpersonal conflicts among professionals and paraprofessionals (e.g., teacher aides, therapy assistants, residential workers). These problems typically result from inadequate communication practices, a common problem stemming from a lack of systematic training in working closely with other adults. This section provides suggestions for improving and monitoring collaboration among co-workers in a special education or related service program. The ideas offered are based on the assumption that effective teamwork is the desired outcome, with the ultimate goal being quality services for persons with special needs. Teamwork in the classroom or center involves distinct, complementary roles that sometimes overlap but that serve separate, unique purposes (Semrau, LeMay, Tucker, Woods, & Hurtado, 1979).

The supervisor wanting to utilize fully the paraprofessional's potential contributions is encouraged to use a democratic style of leadership, with most responsibilities shared. The only real justification for hiring paraprofessionals is to improve instruction and service delivery. Thus, they should actively participate in almost every aspect of the teaching process, with the distribution of tasks dependent on who can best perform each in the most helpful way (Leone, Moore, Kalan, & Diaz, 1980). The ideas that follow are geared to fully integrating a second adult into the classroom or center.

Employment of Paraprofessionals

The New Careers Movement, a major force in the employment of paraprofessionals in education and social services, emerged in the late 1960s in response to teacher shortages, the War on Poverty, and cries for social and educational reform. One of its outstanding characteristics was the enlistment of local neighborhood residents for training and employment as paraprofessionals. The advantages of such staffing patterns have been repeatedly documented (Blalock, 1984; Gartner, Jackson, & Riessman, 1977; Pickett, 1986). Primary benefits include an understanding of the backgrounds and languages of target students, familiarity with community expectations and resources, ability to communicate with families and agency or business personnel, and easier access to the rapport essential to effect change in learners. In many communities paraprofessionals serve as the major translators in communicating with parents whose dominant language is other than English. Local adults who are unemployed, underemployed, or eager for career change are the optimal recruitment pool for the paraprofessional labor force. Many of these individuals move on as the best possible recruits for teaching positions.

Current paraprofessionals can be a primary resource for publicity about job openings and should be encouraged to inform likely candidates about job opportunities. Each applicant will present a different profile of experiences, abilities, interests, educational philosophies, and goals. The task for the teacher or other supervisor is to develop a specific job description for the paraprofessional and to match applicants to the particular job (Frith & Mims, 1985). Administrators desiring quality team collaboration should require professionals to help interview their own prospective assistants so that the most appropriate matches are made. Conversely, veteran paraprofessionals (with training, if needed) should participate in interviewing applicants who may become their supervisors.

Defining Roles and Responsibilities of Team Members

According to Leone et al. (1980), the instructional team model begins with a definition of roles and responsibilities for each team member. The largest single area of frustration between professionals and paraprofessionals appears to be their expectations about respective roles and duties. Professionals have ultimate responsibility for their students' educational programs and therefore are closely involved with preparation of IEPs. Development and implementation of a worthwhile individualized program, however, necessarily involves personnel other than the team leader. The paraprofessional role is one of assistance and flexibility, whether in mainstreaming situations, supervising small groups, tutoring individuals, enhancing affective adjustment, assisting with supportive services, or coordinating with other teachers or parents (Leone et al., 1980; Semrau et al., 1979). Table 6.1 suggests a breakdown of some

major responsibilities delegated to both the teacher and the paraprofessional, as a way of ensuring that no questions remain about who should do what.

Teachers need to list exactly what they want their assistants to do (if not already included in the job description) or develop lists jointly with employed paraprofessionals. The list of duties should be reviewed at the beginning of each year or at the start of the working relationship; the paraprofessional should be given an opportunity to respond to each item. This collaborative analysis of the job allows team members to pinpoint potential sources of problems, such as training needs, philosophical preferences, or cultural practices or prohibitions. Figure 6.1 is a compilation of responsibilities within a special education program, derived from several sources. As indicated, the supervisor checks expectations in the left column, and the paraprofessional responds to each selected item.

Identifying Strengths, Weaknesses, and Work Styles

During the interview and/or initial employment, the supervising professional has the opportunity to assess the paraprofessional's experiences, abilities, interests, educational philosophy, and goals in an effort to achieve a good match between paraprofessional and position. Brizzi (1982) suggests a variety of questions that can provide insights into the division of academic and general classroom responsibilities (p. 4).

☐ Why do you want to work with students?
☐ Tell me what you think makes the best learning environment.
☐ What do you think you can offer the students in this class?
☐ What are your talents? skills? What do you do in your leisure time?

TABLE 6.1
Designation of
complementary duties

Teacher	Paraprofessional
Classroom Management	
Plans weekly schedule	Helps with planning and carrying out of lessons/activities
Plans lessons/activities for class and individuals	Makes teaching aids
Plans learning centers	Helps gather or copy teaching materials
Is responsible for all students at all times	Provides classroom supervision in emergency situations
Participates in teachers' duty schedule at school	Participates in aides' duty schedule at school
Arranges schedules for each student's related services	Accompanies individuals or small groups to other locations in the school
Assessment	
Assesses all students as needed on an ongoing basis	Assists with giving, monitoring, and scoring tests
Administers tests	Helps with observing/charting student behaviors/progress
Is responsible for collection and recording of student data	Assists in grading assignments or tests and recording grades
Teaching	
Introduces new material	Assists with follow-up instruction for small groups or individuals
Teaches entire class, small groups or individuals	Helps support large group instruction as needed
Behavior Management	
Plans strategies for behavior management for entire class or individuals	Assists in implementing the teacher's behavior management strategies, using the same emphasis and techniques
Parents	
Meets with parents	Helps with parent contacts, such as phone calls or notes
Initiates conferences	Accompanies teacher to parent conferences when appropriate and possible
Schedules IEP meetings	

□ Do you type? speak another language? participate in sports, recreation, games? like math? do artistic activities?

□ Are you comfortable communicating with students? staff? parents?

□ What work have you done before? What did you like and dislike about your previous job(s)?

□ What is your goal after this job?

□ What subjects did you like and dislike in school?

□ Who was your favorite teacher and why? What kind of teacher did you dislike and why?

□ What could students learn from you that would help them develop independence? What do you think an independent person is?

The supervising professional can enhance the paraprofessional's willingness to respond by sharing some personal characteristics or experiences in the areas mentioned.

Individual work styles are also important to understand for a teamwork relationship; they are best explored when team members first begin to work together to avoid or minimize mistaken assumptions and disappointments. Figure 6.2 (a and b), based on Houk and McKenzie's (1985) scale, delineates a limited number of work-style behaviors for both supervisors and paraprofessionals. The parallel structure of the two forms aids discussion about areas in which the pair's expectations might conflict so that solutions can be planned before problems arise.

For those who prefer more informal assessment of work-style differences, Brizzi (1982) proposes several questions similar in content to the scales (p. 4).

□ How do you like to work? Do you prefer to initiate activities or be directed toward most tasks?

□ How do you want to be corrected if a mistake occurs?

□ Are you likely to ask for help or let your supervisor know when something is unpleasant, or are you likely to avoid talking about it?

These questions can be modified so that both parties describe their favored work styles.

It is important that teachers and paraprofessionals seek mutually satisfying ways to accommodate work-style differences so that optimal classroom operations result. For example, if a supervisor values a paraprofessional's instructional and management abilities but resents the para's lack of punctuality, numerous alternatives are possible: (1) the paraprofessional might stay longer in the afternoon to help prepare for the following day; (2) the teacher and paraprofessional might plan constructive, independent activities for the students for the first period each morning; (3) the paraprofessional might come in fairly early or stay fairly late once or twice a week; and/or (4) the paraprofessional might assume responsibility for arranging field trips or making home visits after school hours. Creativity and humor in problem solving can go far toward generating positive outcomes in potentially negative situations.

Team Planning Strategies

Numerous sources advise that the most critical step toward facilitating communication is to set aside a regular daily or biweekly time for cooperative planning, coordination of efforts, and feedback (Boomer, 1981; Leone et al., 1980; Semrau et al., 1979). In addition, frequent impromptu discussions may have to be arranged because of changes in schedules, student needs, or policy (Boomer, 1981). Table 6.2, based on Krueger and Fox (1984), illustrates a format for combining regularly scheduled feedback and planning sessions with specific assignment of duties for both team members.

Supervisors can significantly enhance the confidence and sense of belonging of paraprofessionals by consistently including them in decision making regarding students' programs, unit plans, activities, and collaboration with other teachers and parents. IEP and annual review meetings are another important arena, in which paraprofessionals can contribute critical information about students with whom they work

DIRECTIONS: Listed below are a number of tasks that you may want your para to perform. Please review this list with your para, checking in the column on the left those duties that you would like assistance with. At the same time have your para tell you which tasks s/he feels capable of doing and which tasks s/he feels untrained to do.

INSTRUCTIONAL SUPPORT		OK	NOT OK
1. _____	Help students practice reading, math, and/or spelling to reinforce what is being taught.	_____	_____
2. _____	Watch and record students' daily progress in academic skills.	_____	_____
3. _____	Teach all content areas as needed, under guidance.	_____	_____
4. _____	Correct assigned activities.	_____	_____
5. _____	Help students with workbooks and commercial kits.	_____	_____
6. _____	Help non-English-speaking students and students weak in language skills with vocabulary.	_____	_____
7. _____	Listen to a student or small group of students read.	_____	_____
8. _____	Help with listening activities.	_____	_____
9. _____	Help students select library books.	_____	_____
10. _____	Change or modify written materials with teacher's supervision or approval.	_____	_____
11. _____	Help in managing small groups when scheduled activities create conflicts for the teacher.	_____	_____
12. _____	Read to students.	_____	_____
13. _____	Help with students who have unique physical needs.	_____	_____
14. _____	Tape-record stories, lessons, and assignments when needed.	_____	_____
15. _____	Help students work on projects assigned in the regular classroom.	_____	_____
16. _____	Help contact parents, perhaps sending notes and progress reports home if appropriate.	_____	_____
17. _____	Talk with students about hobbies, interests, and possible careers.	_____	_____
18. _____	Take initiative in helping teacher or students when not busy with other tasks.	_____	_____
19. _____	Assist in testing student (if para is trained).	_____	_____
20. _____	Assist students with self-help skills (grooming, bathrooming, dressing, feeding).	_____	_____
21. _____	Help in developing behavioral objectives and planning daily activities for students.	_____	_____

CLASSROOM ORGANIZATIONAL SUPPORT		OK	NOT OK
1. _____	Help to find relevant materials needed for teaching.	_____	_____
2. _____	Help to develop learning centers (develop, if experienced).	_____	_____
3. _____	Help to manage learning centers (manage, if experienced).	_____	_____
4. _____	Prepare classroom displays.	_____	_____
5. _____	Make bulletin board displays.	_____	_____
6. _____	Make instructional games, with teacher's assistance or guidance.	_____	_____
7. _____	Work with regular education teachers to help students succeed in other classrooms.	_____	_____
8. _____	Supervise students on arrival or departure.	_____	_____
9. _____	Supervise students during lunch and/or recess.	_____	_____

FIGURE 6.1
Checklist of paraprofessional duties

10. _____	Help in ordering materials and supplies.		_____	_____
11. _____	Mix paints, prepare clay, and get other materials ready for activities.		_____	_____
12. _____	Help prepare and clean up snacks and lunch.		_____	_____
13. _____	Help students clean up after activities.		_____	_____
14. _____	Distribute supplies, books, etc., to students and collect completed work.		_____	_____
15. _____	Organize supplies in the classroom.		_____	_____
16. _____	Put lessons on the chalkboard.		_____	_____
17. _____	Check for effective seating arrangements to facilitate learning.		_____	_____
18. _____	Set up and run filmstrip, film, overhead and opaque projectors.		_____	_____
19. _____	Operate tape recorders, record players, and videotape machines.		_____	_____
20. _____	Make visual aids (transparencies, posters, etc.).		_____	_____
21. _____	Escort students to the bathroom, library, assemblies, etc.		_____	_____
22. _____	Accompany students to other programs at school, such as physical therapy, library, swimming, etc.		_____	_____
23. _____	Schedule guest speakers, in coordination with teacher.		_____	_____
24. _____	Handle routine interruptions in the classroom (tours, individual therapies, etc.).		_____	_____

BEHAVIOR MANAGEMENT SUPPORT		OK	NOT OK
1. _____	Assist in classroom management, such as supervising time-out, giving positive reinforcement and support, making sure class and school rules are followed.	_____	_____
2. _____	Observe and record (chart) student behavior.	_____	_____
3. _____	Help students develop organizational skills to complete tasks and meet deadlines.	_____	_____
4. _____	Manage conflicts between students.	_____	_____
5. _____	Enhance students' self-concepts by giving positive feedback.	_____	_____
6. _____	Provide close supervision for a student with behavior problems in the classroom, supporting the teacher's management system.	_____	_____
7. _____	Translate or interpret behavior and nonverbal communication for the teacher, who may not be familiar with the local community.	_____	_____
8. _____	Circulate in the classroom to see whether students are working and to supply help where needed.	_____	_____

CLERICAL SUPPORT		OK	NOT OK
1. _____	Take attendance.	_____	_____
2. _____	Type reports, tests, seat work, book lists, and other teaching materials.	_____	_____
3. _____	Operate copier, Thermofax, and ditto machines.	_____	_____
4. _____	Sort and file student papers, teaching materials, etc.	_____	_____
5. _____	Record grades.	_____	_____
6. _____	Collect book, milk, activity, and other fees.	_____	_____
7. _____	Grade and record objective tests, with training or supervision.	_____	_____
8. _____	Help with paperwork to facilitate parent-teacher appointments.	_____	_____
9. _____	Inventory materials and fill out necessary forms.	_____	_____
10. _____	Arrange all scheduled field trips.	_____	_____

FIGURE 6.1
continued

FIGURE 6.2
Inventory of
work styles

(a)

> ### SUPERVISOR'S WORK STYLE
>
> Please indicate the manner in which you tend to manage your work
> site by placing a check mark on each continuum wherever you believe
> your style is represented. Your answers will help you and your
> paraprofessional(s) decide how best to work together.
>
> 1. Will you identify specific materials and methods to be used, or
>   will the paraprofessional have freedom to choose?
>   Structured / . . . . / . . . . / . . . . / . . . . / Unstructured
>
> 2. Will specific duties be assigned for exact periods of time, or will
>   the para have a flexible schedule?
>   Firm / . . . . / . . . . / . . . . / . . . . / Flexible
>
> 3. Will the para's job require specific training and / or abilities, or
>   will the duties be fairly simple or easy?
>   Complex / . . . . / . . . . / . . . . / . . . . / Simple
>
> 4. Will you provide close supervision, or will you expect the
>   paraprofessional to work independently?
>   Supervision / . . . . / . . . . / . . . . / . . . . / Independence
>
> 5. I like to be very punctual.
>   Most like me / . . . . / . . . . / . . . . / . . . . / Least like me
>
> 6. I am a very flexible person.
>   Most like me / . . . . / . . . . / . . . . / . . . . / Least like me
>
> 7. I have some very firm beliefs about educational interventions.
>   Most like me / . . . . / . . . . / . . . . / . . . . / Least like me
>
> 8. I like to take on challenging tasks.
>   Most like me / . . . . / . . . . / . . . . / . . . . / Least like me
>
> 9. I like to let the para know exactly what I expect.
>   Most like me / . . . . / . . . . / . . . . / . . . . / Least like me
>
> 10. I like to give frequent feedback about the para's work.
>   Most like me / . . . . / . . . . / . . . . / . . . . / Least like me
>
> 11. I encourage others to think for themselves.
>   Most like me / . . . . / . . . . / . . . . / . . . . / Least like me
>
> 12. I regularly let the para know how s/he can improve.
>   Most like me / . . . . / . . . . / . . . . / . . . . / Least like me
>
> 13. I like taking care of details.
>   Most like me / . . . . / . . . . / . . . . / . . . . / Least like me
>
> 14. I like to bring problems at work out in the open.
>   Most like me / . . . . / . . . . / . . . . / . . . . / Least like me
>
> 15. I try to ensure the para's inclusion as a team member.
>   Most like me / . . . . / . . . . / . . . . / . . . . / Least like me

FIGURE 6.2
continued

(b)

PARAPROFESSIONAL'S WORK STYLE

Please place a check mark on each continuum to indicate which job features you believe bring out your best efforts. Your answers will help you and your supervisor decide how best to work together.

1. Should the materials and methods you use with students be specifically identified, or do you prefer choosing them?

    Structured / . . . . / . . . . / . . . . / . . . . / Unstructured

2. Do you like to know exactly when to start and stop a task, or do you like to have a flexible schedule at work?

    Firm / . . . . / . . . . / . . . . / . . . . / Flexible

3. Would you prefer duties that require specific training and / or skills or tasks that are fairly simple or easy?

    Complex / . . . . / . . . . / . . . . / . . . . / Simple

4. Do you prefer close supervision, or do you like to work independently?

    Supervision / . . . . / . . . . / . . . . / . . . . / Independence

5. I like to be very punctual.

    Most like me / . . . . / . . . . / . . . . / . . . . / Least like me

6. I am a flexible person.

    Most like me / . . . . / . . . . / . . . . / . . . . / Least like me

7. I have some very firm beliefs about educational interventions.

    Most like me / . . . . / . . . . / . . . . / . . . . / Least like me

8. I like to take on challenging tasks.

    Most like me / . . . . / . . . . / . . . . / . . . . / Least like me

9. I like to know exactly what is expected of me.

    Most like me / . . . . / . . . . / . . . . / . . . . / Least like me

10. I need to have frequent feedback about my performance.

    Most like me / . . . . / . . . . / . . . . / . . . . / Least like me

11. I like to be encouraged to think for myself.

    Most like me / . . . . / . . . . / . . . . / . . . . / Least like me

12. I need to know how I can improve, on a regular basis.

    Most like me / . . . . / . . . . / . . . . / . . . . / Least like me

13. I like taking care of details.

    Most like me / . . . . / . . . . / . . . . / . . . . / Least like me

14. I like to bring problems at work out in the open.

    Most like me / . . . . / . . . . / . . . . / . . . . / Least like me

15. I want to be included as part of the instructional team.

    Most like me / . . . . / . . . . / . . . . / . . . . / Least like me

TABLE 6.2
Sample schedule
of responsibilities
and interaction

Time	Teacher Activity	Paraprofessional Activity

8:00		Open windows, adjust blinds
		Check work box and find
		   spelling words
		Grade, record, make list
		   of common spelling errors

8:30	Conference with para: change approach to managing two
	   children's behavior; select new strategy and plan how to
	   evaluate success	

9:00	Welcome children	Assist teacher
9:03	Opening	Take attendance

	Begin reading, working with
	   groups or using selective
	   reading
		Work with two groups in
		   reading, using flash cards
		   and word games

10:00	Spelling: present new
	   lesson
		Prepare spelling tape for
		   two students to use at
		   listening center

10:20	Recess	Recess

10:30	Math: present lesson to
	   group 1 (group 2 finishing
	   assignment from previous
	   day)
		Listen to lesson presentation
		Help individuals as needed
		   in group 2

	Present lesson to group 2	Give individual help to students in group 1
	Give individual help	Give individual help and correct math papers
11:30	Students to lunch	
	Evaluation with paraprofessional	
11:35	Lunch	Finish math papers

closely. Even if they do not attend, paraprofessionals should be familiar with each student's IEP, as well as with all school correspondence (Boomer, 1981). In addition, instructional assistants are often valuable participants in parent conferences, offering observational data, language translation, or clarification of school policies or cultural practices. Such meetings provide professionals with good opportunities to inform parents and other school personnel about important contributions of the paraprofessionals. Administrators and supervising teachers often have to set the stage for recognition of the role of paraprofessionals in instructional programs. Their advocacy

efforts are important in demonstrating to paraprofessionals that teamwork is truly desired.

Paraprofessional Training Activities

Inadequate attention to training needs is reported as a significant factor in burnout among special education paraprofessionals (Frith & Mims, 1985). Initial requirements are typically no more than a high school diploma, and the supervising professional necessarily becomes the primary trainer (or training arranger) for the paraprofessional. Initial discussions of expected duties are an important means of identifying training needs. Several instruments (e.g., Vasa, Steckelberg, & Ronning, 1983) have been prepared to aid in this identification. The topics of most formal training programs match the competency areas listed in job descriptions and evaluation tools. The most common topics are listed here.

- ☐ human growth and development
- ☐ overview of exceptionalities and their effects on normal development
- ☐ basic special education principles and approaches
- ☐ paraprofessional roles/interactions
- ☐ behavior management
- ☐ health and safety
- ☐ specialty core (e.g., severe/profound handicaps, behavior disorders)
- ☐ supervised field experience

After areas of needed training are determined, the most feasible scheduling and mechanisms to achieve such training must be explored and secured. For classroom-based or school-based training activities, the teacher and the paraprofessional should schedule topics and procedures when they are most feasible and relevant.

Options for securing specific training vary from location to location. Within the school building, specialists usually abound. Involving various clerical, administrative, and content area personnel in short training activities greatly enriches the paraprofessional's competence and strengthens the position of the special education program within the school. Staff in resource positions within the district should also be available for specific instruction in a few areas. Community individuals, such as medical or business personnel, should be sought as needed. Formal training programs for paraprofessionals in special education, rehabilitation, human services, or child development are the richest sources of appropriate, relevant educational experiences. Community colleges are the primary source for cer-

tificate or associate degree programs in these areas; a few 4-year colleges and universities also carry such offerings.

Several important considerations relate to the training of adults in general. First of all, adult learners differ from youthful learners. Because their needs to learn are based on actual life demands, adult learning activities should target tasks perceived as part of real life. Adults are also more task-oriented than theory-based, preferring to do rather than to listen. Thus, the importance of role-playing various situations cannot be overly stressed. In addition, training personnel need to validate the adults' life and work experiences and use them as foundations on which to build new learning. Adults must be involved in any decisions about desired learning outcomes (i.e., goal setting), as well as the means for achieving those goals.

Development of a learning program for paraprofessional staff should follow the same good teaching principles incorporated into students' programs: preassessment, rationale, clear statement of task or skill to be learned, modeling, practice, and feedback. Private enterprise has confirmed the efficacy of many of these strategies in motivating adults and has restated some old insights (e.g., "People who feel good about themselves produce good results"). Understanding people's needs (e.g., for affiliation, achievement, power) also helps supervisors and paraprofessionals generate more effective collaboration strategies.

Evaluation Techniques

Regularly scheduled meetings provide a forum for supervisors to give ongoing feedback about paraprofessionals' performance. The 1-minute praisings and 1-minute reprimands proposed by Blanchard and Johnson (1982) have proven to be quick, powerful management tools that leave no room for doubt or surprises. Another feedback device for teachers and paraprofessionals was produced by Krueger and Fox (1984) and is easily modified or used in oral rather than written form (see Figure 6.3 for a modified written version of their device). Its focus could also be shifted to a more self-evaluative emphasis if desired.

Many performance rating instruments have been developed for paraprofessionals in special education and related fields (Blalock, 1984). However, the most important guideline is that evaluations should be based directly on the current job description(s) provided to the paraprofessional. To carry meaning, performance feedback should also be related to future goals for both student and paraprofessional growth. A sequence of three to four skill levels, each quite distinct from the other in terms of required competencies and salary level, would comprise the basis for a career ladder in an agency, district, or state education department (Frith & Mims, 1985). Career ladders provide the long-term incentive for improving competency and exhibiting professionalism that short-term support offerings (e.g., time off for classes, payment for training) cannot sustain for very long. Professionals who extend themselves to improve paraprofessionals' working conditions and expertise will experience enhanced teamwork and will watch their students reap the rewards many times over.[1]

REGULAR CLASS TEACHERS

The relationship between teachers in special and regular education settings is a critical one in determining the success of any integration efforts for individual students. (Although the emphasis here is on special/regular education collaboration, this discussion also has applicability to interactions between any groups of professionals.) It is useful to place the process of integration within the context of transition, in this case from a special to a regular program setting. The transitioning of students from special to regular classes is far more complex than the mere physical relocation of the child. Successful mainstreaming is predicated on systematic preparation of both the classroom teacher and the child about to be integrated. The key questions become these: How best can special education teachers contribute to successful integration? What role should they serve in developing cooperative relationships with regular class teachers?

At the heart of these questions are concerns relative to the concepts of consultation and collaboration. Although the terms are similar within the context of educational cooperation, *consultation* can imply expertise, which may inadvertently result in unequal status—perhaps projecting the special educator as the authority on a variety of learning, behavioral, and administrative matters. This expert status can create the absurd expectation that beginning special teachers will provide authoritative advice to veteran regular class educators (Dunn, 1980). *Collaboration* better suggests the cooperative role essential to successful integration. It implies that the special and regular education teachers are in parallel positions to share ideas, talents, and training. Although both terms are used in this

[1]Project ASSIST of Western Kentucky University, Project LEEP of North Carolina A & T State University, the Department of Community Development within the Los Angeles County Schools, the Bilingual Exceptional Student Education Demonstration Project of the Broward County (Florida) School Board, Project PARA of the University of Nebraska-Lincoln, and the Paraprofessional Facilitator Program of the Kansas State Department of Education have prepared materials to help paraprofessionals and professionals work together effectively. Information about these materials and others dealing with training and utilization of paraprofessionals is available from Anna Lou Pickett, Director, National Resource Center for Paraprofessionals, CASE/NCTL, Graduate School, City University of New York, 33 West 42nd Street, New York, NY 10036.

FIGURE 6.3
Paraprofessional
feedback form

In order for us to work more effectively with students, it is important that we assess our activities on a regular basis. Please complete this form and return it to your supervising teacher.

1. List the activities that you most enjoyed this week.

   _____

   _____

   _____

2. List the activities that you least enjoyed this week.

   _____

   _____

   _____

3. Comment on activities that you might like to do next week.

   _____

   _____

   _____

4. How can we work together more effectively?

   _____

   _____

   _____

chapter, the assumption here is that the collaborative concept is most apt for school settings.

Regardless of terminology, a consultative or collaborative role represents a shift toward at least partial reliance on an instructional model requiring special educators to provide indirect support for handicapped children. This shift is graphically illustrated in Figure 6.4. This change from providing only direct instruction to providing both direct and indirect support will be seen increasingly in the job responsibilities of special education teachers in the 1990s. The provision of consultative services can be conceptualized within the same framework as that of the prescriptive, or clinical, teaching cycle discussed in chapter 3. According to that model, effective programs are derived from assessment efforts, program planning and implementation, and evaluation.

Determining Needs

In most consultative undertakings an initial concern is the identification of needs. Duncan, Schofer, and Veberle (1982) provide the following useful perspective on the process of needs assessment:

> It is essential to differentiate between what is needed and what is wanted. Topics that personnel may identify as what they would like to have addressed at an inservice activity may not relate to a need. Personnel may request a topic that is currently of high interest or may be a popular "fad" or may be related to a real issue in education; however, the topic may or may not be related to real or immediate needs. We like to think of an inservice need as something which, if corrected, would improve delivery of educational services. (p. 11)

Needs assessment is the collecting and analyzing of information that will assist in decision making. In the process it is important

FIGURE 6.4
Instructional and
collaborative models

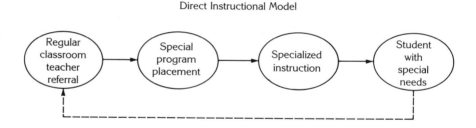

Direct Instructional Model

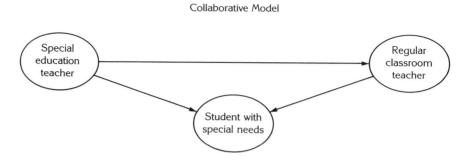

Collaborative Model

not to overlook the needed and not to develop plans to improve the unneeded.

Although a variety of approaches can be used to determine needs, a primary concern is that appropriate means are used to collect data from those persons who will be the recipients of the services or support. Depending on the size of a school or the nature of the consultative services to be offered, appropriate formats may be more or less formal.

Implementing Collaborative Services

The planning and implementation of collaborative services within the school setting are the obvious outcome of successful assessment activities. Although the scope of this chapter does not permit a full discussion of the logistics of planning, this constraint should not imply its lack of importance. Research provides guidance for the development of a program of consultation. For example, Idol-Maestas (1983) summarizes

research findings on a number of key features (pp. 295–296).

☐ School-based programs in which teachers participate as helpers and planners of activities tend to be successful more frequently than programs planned and conducted without teachers' assistance.

☐ Programs that have different or individualized training experiences for different teachers are successful more frequently than programs that have common activities for all.

☐ Programs that require teachers to generate and define ideas, materials, and target behaviors are successful more frequently than programs in which teachers accept ideas and behaviors from an instructional agent.

☐ Programs that emphasize demonstration, supervised trials, and feedback are successful more frequently than programs in which teachers are expected to make unsupervised applications at some future time.

☐ Teachers are more likely to benefit from programs that are part of a long-term, systematic staff development plan than from one-shot, short-term programs.

☐ Teachers are more likely to benefit from programs in which they choose their own goals and activities than from programs in which goals and activities are preplanned.

In-service Training Three broad focuses can be identified for in-service workshops and related training activities: awareness, instructional or procedural information, and hands-on training. Awareness workshops simply seek to provide exposure to a given topic or body of information or to foster a particular attitude. This format is probably the most common for in-school workshops, readily exemplified by the presentations made during orientation at the beginning of the school year. Sample topics include

☐ breadth and scope of special education services
☐ characteristics of children with specific handicapping conditions
☐ simulations of handicapping conditions
☐ roles of the resource teacher

Awareness formats can be effective in increasing the knowledge base of participants and in improving their attitudes toward a given topic or group of persons.

The instructional or procedural information format has as its general goal the sharing of information that can be useful in developing an instructional program. Even though the presentation may be similar to that of an awareness workshop (i.e., lecture-type, large group arrangement), the goal is quite different. Specific topics include

☐ procedures relative to referral forms or IEPs
☐ sequence of steps in eligibility decisions

☐ description of formal tests typically used in the assessment process
☐ discussion of appropriate techniques of behavior management
☐ discussion of appropriate instructional techniques

Both of these types of in-service activities have the disadvantage of being typically a one-shot format without opportunity for active involvement. They call into question the likelihood of transfer to the teaching situation. An alternative is the training format, which emphasizes a more active involvement of participants. Examples of training formats include

☐ administering, scoring, and interpreting a formal test
☐ viewing specific behaviors in a videotape and taking data
☐ reviewing student strengths and weaknesses and cooperatively writing IEPs
☐ listening to an audiotape of a language sample and developing a tentative instructional plan
☐ writing behavioral contracts

Ongoing Collaboration In most instances ongoing collaborative activities serve as the core of successful schoolwide and individual programs of student integration. Although workshops can serve a large number of persons, they are not a panacea for identified needs within the school setting.

Like the in-service activities just discussed, ongoing consultation can serve three purposes—influencing attitudes, supporting instructional programs, and providing demonstration/training in specific areas. A number of specific principles can provide assistance in implementing a program of ongoing collaboration.

☐ Advice is better received when requested than when imposed.
☐ The role of listener is more important initially than the role of advisor; it is

necessary to determine what really is needed before providing assistance.

☐ Collaborative relationships should be designed to ensure that they are shared efforts.

☐ The sanctity of a teacher's classroom must not be violated without an invitation to observe or interact with the students; the classroom is the teacher's kingdom (Idol et al., 1986).

☐ The fix-it and I've-got-a-secret type mentalities should be avoided (Montgomery, 1978).

☐ The special educator should be perceived as a fully functioning member of the staff without special privileges.

☐ Follow-up to suggestions and plans not only serves the needs of evaluation but also demonstrates interest and commitment.

Ongoing collaboration can take the form of instructional advice and assistance as well as training related to a particular instructional method or technique. Advising includes suggestions for management strategies, approaches to assessment, curricular development, and specific methodological ideas. It may take the form of problem-centered consultation, an attempt to develop a mental plan for solving an isolated problem, or it may involve developmental consultation, a long-range process of sequenced objectives (Heron & Harris, 1982). The former might include issues related to scheduling concerns for a resource student (e.g., missing science or recess to go to the resource room for reading); the latter might include issues related to schoolwide grading practices.

Six steps, taken from Project RETOOL of the Council for Exceptional Children, can assist in the problem-solving process and can provide a framework for providing collaborative assistance. The steps include definition of the problem, generation of potential solutions, evaluation of the solutions generated, selection of an acceptable solution, implementation of the solution, and evaluation of the selected solution. The most important of these steps for the consulting teacher is the ability to generate possible solutions with a colleague. One helpful system for achieving this objective is the behavioral learning paradigm developed by Lindsley (1964) and subsequently modified by Payne (see Polloway & Smith, 1982).

$$A \text{————} S \text{————} B \text{————} C$$

general   instructional   student   contingent
arrangement   stimuli   behavioral   consequent
                             response   event

This model identifies the various elements that can be manipulated to bring about learning. Consulting teachers can theoretically modify the events labeled A, S, and C in order to bring about an increase in learning (B).

The general arrangement (A) can be viewed as the stage set for teaching. Variables that can be modified include the curriculum and skills sequence, the classroom environment, the daily schedule, and the manner of grouping for instruction. Instructional stimuli (S) include the specific modes of presenting a learning task: lectures, audiovisual presentations, use of concrete objects, modeling, flashcards, and questioning strategies. These stimuli can also be accompanied by specific prompts or cues to simplify the stimulus and/or to facilitate a student's response. Consequences (C) refer to both the schedule for providing feedback reinforcement and the reinforcement itself. To increase motivation to learn, a variety of alternatives are available. The amount or the frequency of reinforcement can be increased, or the power of the reinforcers can be adjusted (e.g., food rather than praise). Behavioral paradigms are often associated with an emphasis on reinforcement and other consequent events, but this system gives greater attention to antecedent events (A + S). As Lindsley (1964) notes, there is merit in not trying to "jack up a dull curriculum" with a rich reinforcement schedule.

In some specialized instances the vehicle of choice for ongoing consultation may be a more active involvement of participants through demonstration and training. Although a full discussion of training procedures is beyond the scope of this chapter, it is instructive to consider the value of one particular program for training. The Active-Response In-Service Training Method developed by Snell and colleagues (Snell, undated; Snell, Thompson, & Taylor, 1979) can be adapted for either broad in-service training goals or for direct training of an individual teacher. The following steps have been adapted from Snell (undated).

1. *Identification.* The identification of the problem or area of interest for in-service training is generally a cooperative effort of the trainer and the staff. Informal discussions coupled with classroom observation can aid the process. Identified concerns are then stated behaviorally so that training can proceed.

2. *Assessment.* Assessment of the student(s) identified as part of the problem seeks to further define the problem or identify the instructional levels of the student(s) concerned. Such assessment may be formal or informal and may be conducted by the in-service trainer or the staff. At times the trainer may also instruct staff in using a new assessment procedure.

3. *Assessment-based training.* The training program is designed to remediate the identified problem. Besides the reading and thinking needed at this step, the trainer and staff may need to locate or construct training materials, arrange a training area in the classroom, pilot test

the procedures, determine appropriate reinforcers for the students involved, and describe acceptable approximations of the behavior being trained.

4. *Demonstration.* The trainer demonstrates the training procedures to the staff in the classroom with the student(s) assessed in Step 2. Demonstration serves two purposes: it allows staff to become familiar with the training procedures through observation of their use, and it permits the trainer to adjust the procedures to better fit the student(s), the learning goals, and the actual situation. At each step an inability to obtain success results in a return to the prior step. Therefore, if the demonstration reveals that adjustments must be made in the training procedures, then the trainer makes the adjustments and repeats the demonstration.

5. *Skill development.* The staff member is now given the opportunity to use the training procedures with the student(s). The trainer observes and provides cues and prompts as needed while reinforcing approximate and correct usage of the procedures. This process is generally completed immediately after the demonstration by the trainer. If necessary, additional demonstrations can be given by the trainer, and more complex procedures can be demonstrated to guarantee success for the staff member. Written guides describing the training procedures in a step-by-step manner can be left with the staff to reinforce skills in the absence of the trainer.

6. *Follow-up.* The trainer monitors continuing use of the new skills and procedures and provides any needed adjustments, reassessment of students, or additional instruction of staff.

Evaluating Collaboration

Evaluation serves as the final component of a collaborative program so that feedback on current efforts can influence future activities. Within an individual school setting, evaluation may be appropriately handled in an informal fashion; however, there are instances when a more structured approach is beneficial. The most commonly used formats are open-ended responses and rating scales. The reader is referred to Polloway and Smith (1982) and Idol-Maestas (1983) for specific examples.

PARENTS

If establishing good working relationships with parents enhances the school experience of their children, then it is important to achieve and maintain such relationships. Most professionals acknowledge the importance of parent involvement in the schooling of their children. Winton (1986) notes that the value of this involvement has been documented extensively by the early childhood programs of the 1970s. She cautions, however, that much of what we have done with parents has been related to their children's goals (i.e., student progress), with little attention given to parental outcomes (i.e., their particular needs). Both can be critical elements of parent involvement efforts.

As Patton and colleagues (1986) suggest, "Interchange of information is extremely important to maintain a productive treatment program, as both parties need to be aware of the child's progress in each setting [school and home]" (p. 255). The type of information that needs to be exchanged depends on the particular circumstances of a given situation; however, both teachers and parents gain from cooperative relationships.

It is also important to recognize that parents have been guaranteed certain rights under current federal mandate. For the most part these rights relate to procedural matters that safeguard the interests of the child and family in several major areas.

☐ records—availability and confidentiality

☐ notice—appropriate information about actions taken

☐ consent—decision-making powers

☐ evaluation—availability

☐ independent evaluation—outside services

☐ least restrictive environment—maximum participation with students who are not handicapped

☐ hearings—due process guarantees

Recently, professional attention has been extended beyond parent orientation to family orientation. Turnbull (1988) suggests that all members of the family must be considered and that family needs do not vanish upon completion of formal schooling. Although we agree with Turnbull's perspective wholeheartedly and underscore the idea that families have lifelong needs, the scope of this chapter has necessitated our limiting the focus here to school-related issues typically involving parents.

Parent-Professional Relationships

Teachers perceive their working with parents in many different ways. Some disdain the idea and prefer to minimize their contact with parents. Others believe that this partnership is extremely important and do everything they can to establish good working relationships. Most professionals gravitate toward this latter position and in so doing realize that it is necessary to understand two factors: parental roles and family backgrounds.

Parents of children with special needs are not only faced with the typical challenges of child rearing but also must deal with additional demands. Teachers can benefit from being aware of these responsibilities, as Heward, Dardig, and Rossett (1979) point out.

Such an understanding cannot help increasing your respect for the knowledge and experience most parents have of their child. And this respect can become the basis for developing a healthy and productive parent-professional partnership. (p. 5)

Heward and colleagues identify seven different roles commonly undertaken by parents of students with special needs: teacher, counselor, manager of behavior, parent of children who are not disabled, maintainer of family and marital harmony, educator of significant others, and advocate for appropriate services.

Another important dimension about which teachers must be aware is family background, including culture and values. Although there is little need to become private investigators, there is reason to understand various family situations. The extent of parent involvement in their child's program may depend on events affecting the family at a given time. Very concerned parents may, at times, be unable to participate as they would like. Furthermore, it may be helpful to learn about the cultural background of a family, particularly as it relates to attitudes toward schooling and child-rearing.

Assessment of family preferences may also be important. An instrument developed by Turnbull and Turnbull (1986) and illustrated in Figure 6.5 focuses on the communication process to give the teacher a wealth of information about what a particular family desires. It would be advisable to have parents complete such an instrument early in the school year so that effective procedures could be established in the beginning.

Parent-Professional Interactions

Conferences At some time during the course of the school year, teachers are involved in parent conferences and need to demonstrate understanding of family situations and good communication skills. Turnbull and Turnbull (1986) stress that teachers need to be able to reinforce parental comments, paraphrase what has been said, respond appropriately to parental affect and feelings, question effectively, and summarize the major points brought up. Teachers must be good listeners and clear speakers.

Parent-teacher conferences are of three types. Procedural conferences are those that relate to student assessment and program planning and review. IEP meetings are one example. Crisis conferences are those that arise in response to a current problem. They can be initiated by either the parent or the teacher and are characterized by a need for immediate action. Routine conferences are those that occur throughout the year on a scheduled or unscheduled basis. They may be formal or informal.

Some general guidelines can be helpful with any type of conference.

☐ Be honest and direct with parents.
☐ Avoid technical terms and concepts that parents may not understand. For example, use percentiles rather than standard scores when discussing test results.
☐ Be clear and concise.
☐ Do not speculate about issues for which you have no information. Discuss only what you know and what you can document.
☐ Prepare for the conference by notifying parents well in advance, organizing your notes, reviewing pertinent information, planning an agenda (for more formal meetings), and creating a pleasant environment for the conference.
☐ During the conference itself create a positive atmosphere, set the purpose of the meeting, employ good communication skills, have actual student work with you and have it organized so that it

To ensure that your child is receiving the best possible educational program, it is important that there be ongoing communication between your family and school professionals. It is our experience that families have different preferences for what kinds of information will be shared. In addition, families have different preferences regarding how and how often such information will be transmitted. The purpose of this inventory is to determine your individual preferences for communicating with the professionals in our program.

Listed below are a number of different examples of types of information that can be shared. There are also a number of different examples of strategies or methods that can be used to share this information.

In the box immediately to the right of each item, please rate your level of interest:

put "0" if it has no interest to you at all
put "1" if the information has a *low* priority for you
put "2" if the information has a *medium* priority for you
put "3" if the information has a *high* priority for you

Next, please tell us how often you would like to share information:

put a (√) under *never* if you are not interested at all
put a (√) under *occasionally* if you would like to share the information 3–5 times per year
put a (√) under *regularly* if you would like to share the information 2–3 times per month
put a (√) in the appropriate box under *frequently* to indicate whether you would like to share the information weekly or daily

For example, Mr. Christopher filled out the first item this way:

	Priority	Never	Occasionally	Regularly	Frequently Weekly	Daily
Special accomplishments	3	☐	☐	☐	√	☐

Mr. Christopher's answer tells us that it is very important for school professionals and his family to share his son's special accomplishments and that he would like to communicate on a weekly basis about such accomplishments.

Please indicate your preferences on the following chart.

FIGURE 6.5

Home-school communication preference inventory (From *Families, Professionals, and Exceptionality* [pp. 142–143] by A. P. Turnbull and H. R. Turnbull, 1986, Columbus, OH: Merrill. Copyright 1986 by Merrill Publishing Company. Reprinted by permission.)

can be retrieved quickly, take notes of what is being discussed (prepared sheets are helpful), and end the meeting by saying something positive and thanking the parents for coming.

☐ After the conference organize your notes for future reference, initiate action on any items requiring attention, and determine when a follow-up meeting is necessary.

☐ If you think that the conference will be a hostile one, have someone else from your school sit in with you to help verify what transpires.

TYPE OF INFORMATION I WOULD LIKE SHARED BETWEEN HOME AND SCHOOL

	Priority	Never	Occasionally	Regularly	Frequently Weekly	Daily
Special accomplishments	☐	☐	☐	☐	☐	☐
Special activities (e.g., going to the park, going swimming, visiting grandma)	☐	☐	☐	☐	☐	☐
Progress toward educational goals/grades	☐	☐	☐	☐	☐	☐
Toileting habits	☐	☐	☐	☐	☐	☐
Eating habits	☐	☐	☐	☐	☐	☐
Sleeping/napping habits	☐	☐	☐	☐	☐	☐
Behaviors	☐	☐	☐	☐	☐	☐
Other (please specify)	☐	☐	☐	☐	☐	☐
_____	☐	☐	☐	☐	☐	☐
_____	☐	☐	☐	☐	☐	☐
_____	☐	☐	☐	☐	☐	☐
_____	☐	☐	☐	☐	☐	☐

HOME-SCHOOL COMMUNICATION STRATEGIES

Home visits	☐	☐	☐	☐	☐	☐
Informal school visits	☐	☐	☐	☐	☐	☐
Individual conferences	☐	☐	☐	☐	☐	☐
Group conferences	☐	☐	☐	☐	☐	☐
Telephone calls	☐	☐	☐	☐	☐	☐
Log books, notes	☐	☐	☐	☐	☐	☐
Newsletters	☐	☐	☐	☐	☐	☐
Audio tapes	☐	☐	☐	☐	☐	☐
Report cards	☐	☐	☐	☐	☐	☐
Other (please specify)	☐	☐	☐	☐	☐	☐
_____	☐	☐	☐	☐	☐	☐
_____	☐	☐	☐	☐	☐	☐
_____	☐	☐	☐	☐	☐	☐
_____	☐	☐	☐	☐	☐	☐

FIGURE 6.5
continued

Written Communication Teachers often send information home to parents in written form. The most common form of written communication is the note, which is intended to convey information in a variety of formats. It can be typed or handwritten. Teachers for whom spelling and/or expression is troublesome should have someone else check their notes for spelling and grammatical errors. Progress reports to parents are also common. Often, they occur only at the end of a grading period; however, we suggest more regular correspondence about progress. For some students this communication should be daily; for others it can oc-cur less frequently. Whatever the schedule, teachers are encouraged to develop systems for sharing progress information with par-ents. One approach uses student assign-ment books with space for homework assignments and for teacher and parent comments as well. This type of interchange can easily occur on a daily basis.

Some teachers find newsletters an inter-esting and attractive way to convey to par-ents what is going on in their classrooms. Obviously, the technique does not address individual student concerns; however, it is effective for sharing overall program infor-mation, upcoming events, and general top-ics. Even though the quality of newsletters varies greatly, according to the equipment available, we believe that newsletters should look attractive and be error-free. Teachers who want to produce newsletters should be alert to what may be the most difficult ob-stacle—keeping to a schedule.

Telephone Conversations The telephone is used by teachers and parents alike for sharing information, usually of a more im-mediate nature. Some teachers encourage parents to call them at home; other teachers discourage this practice. We believe that a teacher's job can be enriched by open lines of communication with parents, which sometimes require availability beyond the school day. We also suggest that teachers take notes of every telephone conversation with parents that pertains to a student/school/home issue.

Parent Groups Many teachers who have developed parent groups have found them to be beneficial. Such groups can provide information on certain topics (e.g., AIDS) or can expose parents to training (e.g., how to communicate openly with adolescents). This type of parent involvement requires thor-ough planning and preparation, effective and efficient execution of the meeting itself, and punctual follow-up. Parents must feel that these groups are meaningful, or partici-pation declines rapidly. We like this concept but advise teachers not to establish parent groups haphazardly.

SUMMARY

This chapter discusses three key groups of significant others within the instructional programs of special educators: paraprofes-sionals, regular educators, and parents. The discussion of paraprofessionals highlights the importance of communication in the classroom and suggests effective ways to in-volve teacher assistants in the instructional process. The discussion of regular class teachers focuses on the nature of the con-sultative/collaborative role and presents techniques for determining and meeting ex-pressed needs and for evaluating this form of support. Finally, the role of parents is highlighted, and suggestions are made for enhancing home-school coordination. In-structional programs are most successful when all persons involved are working to-gether as a team.

7
Enhancing Learning Through Microcomputer Technology

TED S. HASSELBRING
LAURA I. GOIN
Peabody College of Vanderbilt University

Microcomputers are by no means new to the field of special education, and from every indication the number of microcomputers being placed in special education classrooms is on the rise.[1] Thus, teachers of students with special needs will most likely be expected to use computers for instruction and management purposes. In fact, because many schools have invested large amounts of money in computer equipment, teachers with computer skills are often hired before teachers without those skills, and teachers lacking computer skills are often expected to acquire them promptly. The effective use of computers is becoming an important part of teaching.

Since microcomputers were first introduced into special education classes, there have been significant advances in the sophistication of the equipment. Today, computers that easily fit atop a student's desk are as powerful as computers that filled entire rooms in the not-too-distant past. It is important to note, however, that advances in computer technology have not led uniformly to improvements in the lives of all students in special education. For people with physical and sensory handicaps, the use of the computer as a prosthetic device has been extremely successful and is well documented (Budoff, Thormann, & Gras, 1984; Goldenberg, 1979); computer technology has led to more normalized lives for these individuals. However, for the large number of individuals with learning handicaps, many of the promises of enhanced learning have not yet been fully realized.

Recently, some people have questioned the value of using computers with children with learning handicaps because gains in student learning have fallen short of expectations. However, the best research to date suggests that a student's failure to learn on the computer probably has very little to do with the technology itself. In most cases failure to learn is a result of poor instruction delivered by poorly designed software or inappropriate use of computer-based instruction. Too often educators have been led to believe that instruction delivered on a computer is better than instruction delivered in a more traditional manner. Nothing could be further from the truth. The effectiveness of computer-based instruction depends on the quality of the instruction and not on the medium. Richard Clark (1983) states that instructional technologies are "mere vehicles that deliver instruction but do not influence student achievement any more than the truck that delivers our groceries causes changes in our nutrition" (p. 445). Clark adds that "bad instruction" will not result in student learning, whether or not it is delivered by a computer; but good instruction will result in learning, regardless of the medium in which it is presented.

This chapter introduces the microcomputer as an educational tool and provides examples of how microcomputers and other related technology can be used appropriately and effectively to teach students with mild handicaps. A simple discussion of hardware and software commonly found in special education classrooms today is followed by a discussion of the role of the computer in learning and the use of the computer as a tool for enhancing productivity.

UNDERSTANDING HARDWARE AND SOFTWARE

Essentially, all computers are composed of the same universal components. No matter what make or model, microcomputer sys-

---

[1]An excellent source listing microcomputer resources for special education is *Connections: A Guide to Computer Resources for Disabled Children and Adults*, which can be obtained from Apple Computer, Inc., Office of Special Education, 20525 Mariani Avenue, Cupertino, CA 95014.

FIGURE 7.1
Hardware components
of a microcomputer

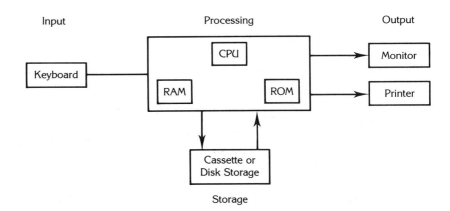

tems must have both hardware and software to operate. The hardware components of a microcomputer are the visible, touchable parts. Software, on the other hand, refers to the instructions used by the hardware that allow the computer to carry out a specific task, such as providing a student with practice on a set of math facts. These instruction sets are called programs. Thus, for a microcomputer to work as an effective instructional tool, both the hardware and the software must work interactively.

Hardware

The hardware components of a microcomputer system are designed to carry out four basic functions: input, processing, storage,

and output of information. As Figure 7.1 shows, the hardware components are interconnected and work interactively.

Input For any microcomputer system to be useful, one must be able to communicate with it. Today, the most common method of communicating with the computer is entering information through a keyboard (see Figure 7.2). Virtually every microcomputer on the market has a keyboard that resembles the keyboard on a standard typewriter. The user enters letters, numbers, and symbols into the computer by pressing the appropriate key.

In addition to the standard typewriter keys, some computer keyboards have a numeric keypad that resembles the key con-

FIGURE 7.2
Typical microcomputer keyboard

figuration of a touch-tone telephone. A numeric keypad is quite useful for entering large amounts of numeric data (e.g., when practicing math facts.) Some keyboards also have a special set of keys called function keys. Many software programs take advantage of the function keys to carry out specific and frequently used operations. For example, within some word processing programs, the user can delete a word, sentence, or paragraph by striking just one of several different function keys.

As technology improves, so do the methods of entering information into a computer.[2] In addition to the keyboard, there are alternate input devices that are extremely useful for individuals whose motor problems preclude the use of a keyboard. Alternate input devices serve as a substitute for the keyboard. Some examples include voice-entry terminals (the user talks information to the computer), braille writers (the user enters information in braille), and expanded keyboards (oversized touch-sensitive keyboards for individuals with poor motor control). In addition, several devices such as the Adaptive Firmware Card and the PC A.I.D. allow the user to press a single switch to select multiple letters and symbols to enter into the computer.

Other alternate input devices are designed to simplify the process of entering information and are especially useful with young children with handicaps and individuals with severe disabilities. These devices include touch-sensitive screens (the computer screen presents choices and recognizes which choice the user touches), touch-sensitive pads (overlays of pictures or words are placed on an electronic "tablet" for the user to touch), and simplified keyboards like the Muppet Learning Keys, which arranges the letters in alphabetical order to make them easier for a young child to find (see Figure 7.3).

Processing After information is entered into the microcomputer, it is processed in what we will call the system unit. The system unit consists of a central processing unit (CPU); read only memory (ROM), or permanent memory; and random access memory (RAM), or temporary memory. Essentially, the CPU serves as the brain of the microcomputer, because it controls every other part of the computer and processes information. Read only memory (ROM) is a type of preprogrammed memory containing the programs and information vital to the computer. For example, all computers use ROM to hold programs that start the computer when it is turned on. ROM is also where the computer stores facts, such as pi = 3.14159 or the letter *A* precedes *B*. ROM contents are built into the computer at the factory and remain in the computer when the power is turned off. Random access memory (RAM) can be thought of as a temporary work space that stores programs and information that the user enters into the computer. RAM is temporary, because information in RAM is erased when the computer is turned off. The user must reenter this information into the computer the next time it is needed.

In referring to the amount of RAM, or work space, that a computer has, people often use the term *K*; they may say, for example, that a computer has 128*K*. *K* comes from the Greek word *kilo*, meaning "1000," and refers to the number of characters (in

---

[2]The Center for Special Education Technology, a national exchange on the use of technology in the education of handicapped children, is operated by the Council for Exceptional Children, 1920 Association Drive, Reston, VA 22091–1589. The center provides a service called Tech-Tapes, a series of informational messages about technology, which can be heard by calling 1–800–345–TECH. The center also provides a hotline for answering questions; that number is 1–800–873–TALK.

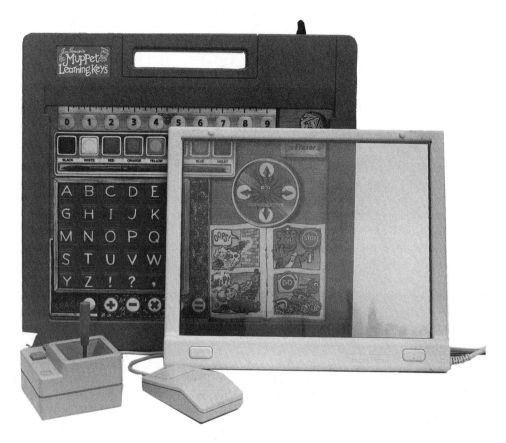

FIGURE 7.3
Alternate input devices

thousands) that a computer's memory can hold (actually, in the computer world $1K = 1024$ characters). Thus, a computer with $128K$ of memory is capable of storing approximately 128,000 characters (letters, numbers, and symbols) in the temporary work space at any one time. The larger the K, the greater the amount of information that can be stored. It is important to know that some programs need more memory space than others. Software catalogs often advertise that a particular program requires $128K$ or $256K$. Thus, in order to use these programs, the computer must be equipped with at least equivalent random access memory.

External Storage   Although RAM is an efficient means of storing and retrieving information, it lacks the permanence that most applications need. External storage devices allow one to take information from the temporary work space in RAM and store it permanently. Three basic types of external storage devices are currently used with microcomputers: the $3\frac{1}{2}$ inch floppy disk, $5\frac{1}{4}$ inch floppy disk, and hard disk. All three devices store information magnetically and vary only in the type of medium on which the information is stored (see Figure 7.4).

The advantage of external storage devices should be obvious. The management

FIGURE 7.4
External storage devices

of IEP information provides a good example. Teachers who want to keep a list of different IEP goals and objectives for each of their students first enter the information through the keyboard and then save it on disk. Each time they want to review, change, or print out IEP information, they simply load it back into the computer through the external storage device. Information stored on a disk does not need to be reentered manually through the keyboard.

Output After information has been entered into the microcomputer and processed by the CPU, the computer must have some means to give out the results. The microcomputer generally outputs information in one of two forms, through either a monitor or a printer. A monitor resembles a TV; most computers today can use either a monochromatic or a color monitor. The monitor allows the computer to **display** text and graphics for the user to view. The monitor is the primary device through which the computer communicates with the user.

One problem with a monitor is that its screen does not display information permanently. If the screen is cleared, the information cannot be recalled without having the computer process it again and print it back on the screen. To overcome this problem, most microcomputers can be attached to a printer that provides a paper copy of the information appearing on the screen. The user can then save the paper printout and refer to it without reprocessing the information. Print quality varies widely, depending on the type of printer used.

Although monitors and printers are the most common devices for information output, other types of output devices are available. For example, microcomputers can use speech synthesizers to convert text into an artificial voice that actually talks to the user, or braille printers can print out information in braille characters.

In summary, most microcomputer systems have similar hardware components. Generally, a keyboard is used to enter information into the computer, a system unit processes the information, and a monitor outputs text and graphics to the user. Disks are used as external storage devices that permanently store programs and data for future use, and printers make permanent copies of output. Other special devices allow microcomputers to carry out many useful tasks, such as responding to human speech or printing output in braille. These special devices, however, are not necessary for day-to-day instructional use.

Software

As mentioned earlier, microcomputer hardware is controlled by a set of specific instructions called programs, or software.[3] Operating system software, as the name implies, controls the hardware's actual physical operation; it is required to make the computer work. These systems are usually provided by the computer manufacturer at the time of purchase and are machine specific (i.e., operating system software for an IBM microcomputer will not work on an Apple microcomputer). Although some attempts have been made to remedy this situation, none appear to have solved the problem completely.

Applications software differs from operating system software in that it is designed and written to carry out specific tasks. For example, applications programs for the special education teacher include word processing, IEP management, record-keeping, and academic instruction and remediation. Applications programs are also machine specific.

---

[3]Software for use in special education can be obtained from numerous educational software companies. One source that distributes software from a variety of publishers is the Cambridge Development Laboratory, Inc., P.O. Box 605, Newton Lower Falls, MA 02162. Their catalog features numerous software titles appropriate for use with mildly handicapped students.

COMPUTER-BASED INSTRUCTION

The use of computer-based instruction (CBI) has been an integral part of special education for the past 5 to 7 years. During this time the influx of CBI software has been accompanied by enormous claims and promises of enhanced learning for children with mild handicaps. Unfortunately, for a large number of these students, many of the promises of more efficient learning have not yet been realized. Although some empirical studies have been able to demonstrate learning advantages resulting from instructional use of computers, others have not. Thus, many teachers, parents, and administrators are left confused and uncertain about the benefits of CBI. In cases where computer-based instruction has been successful, the research suggests that it is most often the result of using the computer to deliver well-designed and well-managed instruction. Conversely, in cases where equivocal results have been attained, more often than not the findings have had little to do with computer technology per se. From our review of existing research, we believe that the equivocal findings are more directly related to the use of the computer to deliver ineffective instruction.

Traditionally, computer-based instruction has been subdivided into six different categories: drill-and-practice; tutorials; simulations; gaming; problem solving; and tool applications. Over the years these classifications have become less and less functional because much of the existing CBI software now incorporates several of these categories into a single program. It is not uncommon to find tutorial, drill-and-practice, and gaming activities all in one program. We believe that a more functional classification scheme for CBI is based on the four stages of learning: **acquisition, fluency or proficiency, maintenance,** and **generalization.** Unfortunately, to date, the relationship between computer-based instruction and different stages of learning has been largely misunderstood. For example, even though it is inappropriate to use proficiency- or fluency-type teaching strategies during the acquisition phase of learning, it appears that this is common practice when computers are used for instruction. It is important to understand how CBI fits into each distinct learning stage.

Acquisition

Direct instruction is the teaching method of choice for initial learning, or acquisition, of a skill. Direct instruction provides the student with clear models of the desired skill or behavior along with frequent corrective feedback and reinforcement. When a teacher enlists a computer to assist in teaching a new skill, the same teaching strategies should be incorporated into the software selected.

Traditionally, teachers have selected two types of software to assist in the acquisition of a skill—drill-and-practice and tutorial. Although drill-and-practice software is ideal for providing endless practice in almost any curricular area, it is inappropriate when a student is in an acquisition phase of learning. Computer-based drill-and-practice is designed to reinforce previously learned information rather than provide direct instruction on new skills. Perhaps Alan Hofmeister (1983) says it best: "Drill and practice activities that are used as a substitute for the necessary teaching of the underlying concepts, and drill that is not followed by meaningful applications of the skills are inappropriate uses of drill and practice, regardless of whether a computer is used or not" (p. 4-2).

If a computer is to be used during the acquisition phase of a new skill or concept, the computer-based tutorial is the most appropriate type of program. The computer-based tutorial differs from drill-and-practice software in that tutorial programs attempt to play the role of a teacher and provide direct instruction on a new skill or concept. The tutorial presents the student with new or previously unlearned material in an individualized manner, providing frequent corrective feedback and reinforcement. We currently know much more about how to develop good tutorial software than is evidenced in many of the commercial software packages on the market today. For example, we know that effective tutorial software should

1. require a response that resembles the skill being taught
2. limit the amount of new information presented at one time
3. provide review of recently learned information
4. provide corrective feedback
5. provide a management component that monitors student progress through the learning stages

Over the years much of the appeal of computer software has come from the variety of graphics and game formats that have been available. One reason for this emphasis is that it keeps the attention of the child. We now know, however, that simply keeping the child's attention on the computer screen does not guarantee learning. When selecting tutorial software, teachers should carefully analyze the nature of the response required of students. Flashy graphics or games do not necessarily add to the instructional value of the software. Well-designed tutorial software should present a skill in such a way that the student response approximates the terminal skill being taught. For example, in a spelling tutorial a student should be required to type the correct sequence of letters from memory, rather than simply selecting the correct spelling from a list of choices or rearranging letters to spell a word.

Torgesen (1986) notes that interference in learning new skills is avoided by carefully limiting the size of the information set to be learned and gradually increasing it as material is acquired. A good math tutorial might present a few facts at a time rather than, for example, all the number facts with sums up to 10. Additionally, students should receive instruction that is spaced over a number of days rather than concentrated in one or two. As new material is acquired, a well-designed tutorial should also provide for appropriately spaced review, and the software should provide students with specific corrective feedback when incorrect responses are given. Corrective feedback prevents the learning of an incorrect strategy or information set that must be unlearned at a later time, a common problem with many paper-and-pencil materials. Finally, a good tutorial should include a management component that tracks student performance and, at the very least, signals when the student is ready for fluency training on a skill. Good tutorial software must incorporate the principles of effective instruction.

Fluency

Most researchers today believe that fluency in basic skills is a prerequisite for proficient performance on higher-order learning tasks. Fluency in basic skills reduces the attention demand required to carry out those skills, thereby freeing up more of an individual's information processing capacity for higher-level concepts. Thus, it appears that the ability to succeed in higher-level skills is directly related to the efficiency with which lower-level processes are executed. For example, both Lesgold (1983) and Torgesen (1984) believe that fluency in decoding is a necessary prerequisite to higher-level functioning in reading. If excessive attention is

required for decoding words, then a student can devote only a reduced amount of attention to higher-order skills, such as comprehension and synthesis of the material. This point becomes clear with children who cannot recognize words by sight. As they read along, they must devote excessive attention to the decoding task, sounding out each word that is encountered. Because this tedious process leaves few mental resources available for thinking about the meaning of the passage, by the time these children reach the end of the passage, there is virtually no understanding of what has just been read. Similar problems are also encountered in other academic areas, such as math and language arts.

Students must develop fluency in any skill that is to become functional. The goal of fluency training is to increase the rate at which a student performs a skill; therefore, activities should emphasize speed of performance. Well-designed software for developing fluency should

1. provide practice on acquired skills only
2. provide practice on the desired terminal skill
3. provide ample opportunities for practice
4. emphasize speed of responding
5. provide a management component that monitors student progress

Generally, drill-and-practice programs lend themselves well to developing fluency in a skill. Current research suggests that the use of drill-and-practice software results in positive student gains for students in the fluency stage of learning (Hasselbring, Goin, & Bransford, 1987; Torgesen, 1986). However, each program must be examined for inclusion of the features previously listed before it can be assumed to be effective for developing fluency. Perhaps the importance of these features can best be seen in the area of mathematics.

Many teachers who have used drill-and-practice software to develop student fluency in basic math facts have been unsuccessful. We believe that there are several reasons for this failure. First, a student is usually placed on drill-and-practice before the terminal skill is acquired, leading to practice on a nonterminal skill. For example, math facts such as 7 + 5 and 12 – 7 can be solved in two ways: the student can retrieve the answer from memory, or the student can reconstruct the answer using a counting method. The preferred terminal skill is to retrieve the fact from memory, yet most teachers place students on drill-and-practice programs before students are able to retrieve correct answers. Consequently, students end up practicing counting strategies. Our research shows that in this situation the only behavior that becomes more fluent is counting. And there is no indication that students using counting strategies to solve basic math facts will begin recalling the answers from memory as a result of using drill-and-practice (Hasselbring, Goin, & Bransford, 1987).

A second problem of many drill-and-practice programs in math is that they do not emphasize rapid responding. Too often, students are given an unlimited amount of time to respond, which again encourages students to use counting strategies to solve problems rather than retrieving answers from memory. For fluency to be developed, students must be encouraged to respond as quickly as possible, and software should be designed accordingly.

Finally, much of the existing drill-and-practice software does not have a management system to monitor student progress. In math a computer without a management system has no way of knowing which problems to give students to practice, thereby leading again to inappropriate practice sets and the practicing of nonterminal skills.

Maintenance

Maintenance of academic skills, in many respects, requires simply that students be given the opportunity to practice previously learned skills on a regular basis in order to maintain high levels of fluency. The microcomputer provides a perfect environment for the maintenance of many basic skills. Computer-based maintenance software should exhibit all of the characteristics important to fluency software. In fact, the software that is used for developing fluency is ideal for maintenance activities. Teachers can choose the drill-and-practice software that was used to develop fluency initially or can find other drill-and-practice programs that emphasize the same skill and allow students to select the software of their choice. What is most important is the regular opportunity to maintain the skill at a high level of fluency.

Generalization

The ultimate goal of all teachers is to develop generalization skills in their students. We want students to take the skills they have learned in school and apply them to real-life problems and experiences. Unfortunately, the generalization of skills may be the most significant obstacle for children with learning problems. Unless students are able to use their knowledge in everyday problem solving, the knowledge becomes useless. To overcome this problem, many educators have suggested that the computer be used for the development of thinking and problem solving in youngsters with learning handicaps (Maddux, 1984; Russell, 1986; Schiffman, Tobin, & Buchanan, 1982). The two ways most often suggested to develop problem-solving skills via the computer have been interactive programming languages, such as Logo, and simulations.

Logo   Logo was originally developed as a computer-based learning environment in which children could learn computer programming, problem solving, and mathematical thinking. The Logo learning environment is based on the developmental psychology of Jean Piaget. Although Logo is generally thought of as a language for nonhandicapped children, the philosophy of Logo developers has been "no threshold, no ceiling." Thus, any student, including one with learning handicaps, should be able to learn Logo.

Much has been written concerning the use of Logo with various handicapping conditions.

> The Logo experience is often the first in which disabled students tackle problems which require them to initiate solutions, try them out, respond to feedback, and decide whether to change track or to persist—all those things that tend not to happen in the dependent situations that typify their lives and most of their schooling. (Weir, Russell, & Valente, 1982, p. 347)

One feature of the Logo language that seems to be especially adventitious for students with learning handicaps is turtle graphics, with which students program a "turtle" (a small triangular object) to move around the screen and construct geometric and graphic designs. Weir and Watt (1981) believe that this use of the computer has specific positive outcomes for students.

1. Fine motor skills are improved (through typing).
2. Short-term memory is developed (as students learn to use a typewriter keyboard and the various logging in and programming procedures).
3. Students learn to spell the commands.
4. Students develop direction-giving and direction-following skills.

5. Students can move from concrete to more abstract levels of thinking.

Although much has been written about the virtues of using Logo with handicapped populations, we have far too little empirical data to make any conclusive statements about the advantages or disadvantages of that application. As Torgesen (1986) points out, thus far all of the evidence on the use of Logo with children who are handicapped is anecdotal, and even the evaluation of Logo with nonhandicapped youngsters is ambiguous. Thus, the role of Logo in developing problem-solving skills has yet to be substantiated.

Simulations   Computer-based simulations have also been recommended for teaching problem solving to students with learning handicaps (Goldenberg, Russell, & Carter, 1984). A number of explanations have been offered as to why simulations are useful for developing thinking and problem solving. In a simulation the computer can model or re-create a real-life event that cannot be carried out easily in a traditional teaching environment. Thus, simulations allow students to experience vicariously such real-life events as traveling in space, homesteading in the 1800s, conducting a science experiment, or living as prey or predator in a food chain. Simulations can introduce a sense of realism into what are often frustratingly abstract subjects for learners with handicaps. Furthermore, computer simulations provide for active participation rather than the passive observation that is more commonly expected of learners with handicaps.

Guidelines for the appropriate use of computer simulations identify instances when simulations are most appropriate substitutes for real-life experiences.

1. when learning objectives are complex and students are unlikely to be able to

develop the needed skills in a real-life environment (e.g., work skills)

2. when the time scale of the real-life event is too long or too short to allow efficient learning (e.g., money management)
3. when the real-life experience involves danger and/or high cost (e.g., driver training)
4. when the real-life event cannot be carried out in a normal teaching environment (e.g., voting)

Many simulations are described as programs for developing decision making, which is unquestionably an important aspect of thinking and problem solving. For example, in one of the most popular simulations, Oregon Trail, students must make numerous decisions as they interact with the simulation.

> Oregon Trail simulates a settler family's journey by covered wagon, from Missouri to Oregon. Budget allotments must be made before the journey; the settlers' survival hinges on the judicious allocation of funds for clothing, medicine, supplies, ammunition, food, and emergency cash. Settlers can periodically choose between hunting for food, stopping at a fort (purchasing expensive supplies), or moving on. Hunting is simulated with the space bar on the keyboard (rifle) which fires bullets at a deer running across the screen. The settler may select the degree of perception and eye-hand coordination required to kill the running deer, or attacking bandits. Hailstorms, breakdowns, illnesses, injuries, and bandit attacks take their toll on the settlers and their resources. And, if their marksmanship or planning is inadequate, the family will not survive. (Joiner, Silverstein, & Ross, 1980, p. 36)

Although Oregon trail is enjoyed by students and teachers alike, several noted authorities on thinking and problem solving believe that students can solve and master a simulation such as Oregon Trail without developing effective problem-solving skills (Bransford, Stein, Delclos, & Littlefield, 1986). Bransford and his colleagues argue that decisions made in many simulations can be based on trial-and-error guessing rather than on systematic analysis of available information. The danger that simulations will encourage trial-and-error responding is increased by the fact that, initially, students have very little information about the simulations and hence are reduced to guessing. Bransford et al. argue that a more effective procedure would be to teach information-gathering skills, first helping students consult external sources of information that might assist them in making more rational decisions during the simulations. Woodward, Carnine, and Collins (1986) used the approach advocated by Bransford et al. in a series of simulation activities in health-related areas. In their study students were assigned to either a simulation or a conventional instruction group. The results of the study indicate that the simulation group was superior to the conventional group on measures of problem solving in diagnosing health problems, prioritizing their effects on longevity, and prescribing appropriate remedies.

Thus, it appears that computer simulation can be used to extend the boundaries of the traditional teaching environment in a safe and effective manner. However, some caution must be observed. As Bransford et al. point out, individuals often fail to use appropriate concepts and strategies because they do not realize that this information is relevant. They need to be taught to link relevant pieces of information. Although simulations may produce improved problem solving, this is likely to occur only when prior information is provided and can be used as part of the simulation.

Word Processors and Writing   A third way of promoting generalization is to encourage students to be producers of information, not simply consumers of information. Perhaps the most obvious way for students to produce information is through the writing process. Much has been written about the use of word processors to improve the writing skills of children with learning handicaps. Many authors have lauded the positive effects that word processors have on the writing process of learners who are handicapped (Goldenberg, Russell, & Carter, 1984; Hagen, 1984). The ease of text revision, production of a clean and readable text, and a sense of authorship are mentioned most often as attributes of word processors that lead to improved writing. However, until recently, little empirical evidence supported the effectiveness of using word processors with children with handicaps. Recent research has provided some insight into this area of microcomputer-based instruction.

As stated previously, good instruction has a positive effect on student achievement. Writing instruction follows this principle, also. Helpful guidelines for teaching writing with a word processor can be drawn from a 2-year study by Morocco and Newman (1987) on this topic.

1. Teach keyboarding skills before students use a word processor to write.
2. Teach the mechanics of the word processor before students use it to write.
3. Select teaching strategies that reflect a student's current stage of writing.
4. Teach strategies for generating ideas.
5. Have students compose directly on the word processor.
6. Save editing until the text is fully composed.

The issue of keyboarding and word processor mechanics is often overlooked as an important prerequisite to word processing. However, if students are preoccupied with finding the right keys or figuring out how to delete or insert text, little attention is left for the writing process. Thus, students should be able to type as fast as they write and should be able to use a word processor fluently before they use it for writing.

In all writing instruction teachers must focus on students' writing stages and adjust teaching strategies accordingly. Even though word processors make student text (and errors) highly visible, teachers should resist the tendency to provide direct instruction on the mechanics of writing, such as spelling and punctuation, while students are still in the composing stage of writing. A shift in student attention from composing to editing results in fewer written ideas. During the composition stage teachers must also resist the temptation to collaborate with students. Although initially helpful, this approach leaves students dependent on teacher coaching. Instead, teachers should give students strategies for generating ideas and let students retain control.

As students are taught to compose on a word processor, they should be cautioned against excessive revision. The ease of revision prompts some students to erase more than they keep. MacArthur, Graham, and Skarvold (1986); Neuman and Morocco (1986); and Vacc (1987) all found that when using word processors, students focused more on revisions that made their writing "technically correct" than on revisions that enhanced the quality of their writing. Students must learn that editing follows composition.

PRODUCTIVITY SOFTWARE

The microcomputer is often overlooked as a device that can help teachers with time-consuming record keeping and generation of materials. However, with productivity software the computer can ease the job of teaching children with learning problems and can save time in the process. Although this software has the potential to increase efficiency, one must be cautioned that some applications require a large amount of preliminary learning and set-up time. Thus, unless the task is something that is done on a repetitive basis, there may be no advantage in trying to use a computer.

Word Processing

Word processing software is particularly well suited to the types of record management required by teachers. Although there is no shortage of single-purpose software—such as grade-book programs, worksheet generators, and IEP programs—a good word processing program can also perform many of these tasks and requires mastery of only one piece of software.

A word processing program allows the user to quickly enter information that can be stored as a permanent record or file on a disk. Once stored, this information can be easily recalled and revised each time a change is required. Some of the files that might be maintained on disk include student information and class lists, student schedules, classroom schedules, skill lists, behavioral objectives, and documentation of contacts with parents.

The word processor is particularly useful for documents that are used frequently but require alterations for each use. For example, a teacher might need a form letter regarding field trips. A master letter could be created with blanks for the information that would change for each trip, such as the date and location. This template could be stored and later recalled, updated, printed, and distributed. Other templates that teachers have found useful include form letters for parent conferences or meetings, behavior contracts, accident reports, progress reports, and especially IEP forms.

Computer-Generated IEPs

All teachers of special needs students are required to write an individualized education plan for each student. Few teaching tasks require more time or effort on the part of the classroom teacher than writing IEPs correctly. The time and cost of developing IEPs are a particularly serious concern for local school districts. Price and Goodman (1980) report that teachers spend an average of $6^1/2$ hours developing each IEP, with the majority of that time invested in the mechanical process of writing the document. The time-consuming and costly nature of IEP development has prompted many school districts to use computer technology to assist in the process.

Basically, there are two ways that the computer can be used to assist in the IEP process. The first is by using word processing software. With a word processor two files are created—one that is a template of the IEP form and another that contains lists of appropriate behavioral objectives. To write an IEP a teacher would begin with the IEP template, insert a student's identifying information, and then transfer selected goals from the objectives file. Once written in this manner, an IEP can be easily revised as a student progresses.

The second way that a computer can be used to produce IEPs is through the use of previously developed IEP programs. Generally, with these programs a teacher can select an objective from a large bank of objectives or can create an objective by selecting from a set of **condition, behavior,** and **criterion** stems. This latter procedure allows the teacher to create a variety of unique objective statements.

Several advantages exist for using the computer to develop IEPs. The major benefit is the reduction in development time. Lillie (1980) estimates that IEP development time can be reduced by 60% with a computer, allowing a teacher to devote more time to direct instruction. The quality of the IEP can also be enhanced by a computer. Lillie reports that a nationwide survey conducted by the Research Triangle Institute found that a majority of the IEPs used in public schools lacked internal consistency and were poorly developed. Caccamo and Watkins (1982) report that their computerized IEP program has produced valuable byproducts: IEPs are consistent districtwide, and all instructional objectives are teachable and measurable. Furthermore, with automated printing each IEP can be neat and clear, making the document easily readable by teachers and parents alike.

Although computers allow for the automation of the IEP process, care must be taken not to misuse the technology. A student's individual needs must be the primary consideration in the development of any IEP, and the use of a computer does not guarantee that that student's needs are being met. It is the teacher's responsibility to assure the student a quality individualized education plan.

Data-Based Instruction

The successful planning and management of instruction for children with mild handicaps requires sound decision making— knowing when an instructional plan should be changed and what kind of change should be made. Unfortunately, most teachers have not been trained adequately in the decision-making process. As a result, the act of making decisions is often unconscious and arbitrary (Shavelson, 1973, 1976). In recent years the technology of decision making has been improved through the use of data-based instruction (DBI). DBI procedures use regular monitoring of students' performance under different instructional procedures to provide a data base from which individualized instruction programs can be developed empirically. With DBI procedures teachers select long-term goals, design measurement systems that correspond to those goals, use those measurement systems to routinely monitor student progress, use that data base to evaluate the effectiveness of the educational program, and modify instruction as needed to ensure goal attainment (Fuchs, Fuchs, Hamlett, & Hasselbring, 1987).

Research on the effectiveness of data-based instruction indicates that this methodology is quite promising for improving student achievement. For example, Fuchs and Fuchs (1986) analyzed 21 research studies that evaluated DBI procedures. The results of their analysis indicate that the teachers' use of DBI procedures significantly increased their students' academic achievement. Fuchs and Fuchs confirmed this effect within special education and conclude that the greatest gains can be expected when teachers use specific data-based rules to make instructional decisions and display data graphically. Despite the apparent effectiveness of DBI procedures, however, teachers seem reluctant to employ them. In a national survey of LD teachers, Wesson, King, and Deno (1984) found that teachers do not use the methodology because it is too time-consuming, even though they believe that DBI procedures are effective.

Computer-based Monitoring In an attempt to make data-based instruction less time-consuming and easier for teachers to implement, a number of developers have proposed the use of microcomputers in implementing DBI procedures (Fuchs, Deno, & Mirkin, 1984; Hasselbring & Hamlett, 1984b; Walton, 1986; West, Young, & Johnson, 1984). Basically, these monitoring programs have been designed to assist teachers in storing, graphing, and analyzing student performance data.

One such computer program that has been used successfully in special education is AIMSTAR. AIMSTAR is an integrated set of computer programs designed to assist teachers in storing, graphing, and analyzing student performance data. To use AIMSTAR, the teacher creates a student data file, including descriptive information about the student's instructional program, the program objectives, and teaching procedures. After each teaching session the teacher enters student performance data into the computer—for example, the number of correct and incorrect responses exhibited by the student and the amount of time required for the student to complete the trials. AIMSTAR then stores this information, allows the teacher to graph the student's data (see Figure 7.5), applies data-based decision rules, and produces a printout giving the status of the student's instructional program, with recommended changes when appropriate.

Monitoring programs, such as AIMSTAR, do not eliminate the need for teacher intuition and judgment in planning instruction. Rather, these programs supplement teacher judgment by providing additional empirical data and analytical procedures. Special edu-

cation teachers using this technology are able to respond more flexibly and effectively to changing student needs and promote greater student growth through this use of technology.

Computer-Based Diagnosis and Assessment

PL 94–142 specifically states that all handicapped children have the right to a full individual evaluation prior to being placed in a special class. Thus, the need to diagnose and assess specific disabilities in learners with handicaps constitutes a major part of the special educator's teaching responsibilities; it provides teachers and other school personnel with the information for sound educational decisions. A comprehensive assessment assists teachers in deciding what instruction and remediation best meet each student's needs (Zigmond, Vallecorsa, & Silverman, 1983). However, the diagnosis and assessment of students with special needs is a labor-intensive process requiring a significant amount of time and effort. Recent developments in the use of computers for diagnosis and assessment show promise as

FIGURE 7.5
AIMSTAR graph of
student performance

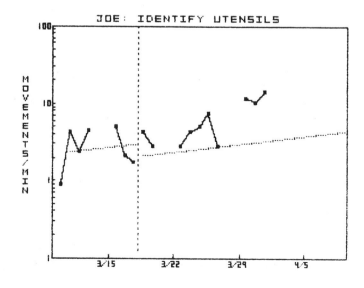

an alternative to traditional procedures. Microcomputers are being used to alleviate some of the tedium associated with the assessment process.

Computer-based diagnosis and assessment instruments generally take either an interactive or a noninteractive form. Noninteractive programs are used by an examiner for scoring, analyzing, and sometimes writing reports on commonly used standardized tests, such as the WISC-R, WAIS-R, PIAT, Stanford-Binet, and Woodcock-Johnson Psycho-Educational Battery. With this type of program, the examiner simply enters a student's test scores; the computer summarizes and prints out the results in report form. The primary advantage of this type of program is the time saved in performing repetitive and tedious tasks, such as adding raw scores and reading norm tables, together with the decrease in likelihood of error (Bennett, 1982). With these programs the assessment instrument is administered in its traditional form, and the student does not interact with the computer.

In interactive programs the student does interact directly with the computer. The assessment instrument is encoded into a computer program, and the computer is responsible for carrying out the complete assessment. Research indicates certain advantages with this type of assessment. First, a significant savings in examiner time can be accrued, an important consideration if the classroom teacher is responsible for administering, scoring, and interpreting assessments for a large number of students. Research has shown that student learning problems can be reliably diagnosed by a computer, thus freeing the teacher to carry out other teaching activities. In addition, examiner bias, administration inconsistencies, scoring errors, and invalid interpretations can be more tightly controlled and often eliminated in interactive computer assessment (Hasselbring & Crossland, 1982;

Owens, Fox, & Hasselbring, 1983).

Several different types of interactive assessment instruments have been or are being developed for use with special needs students. Early attempts to use interactive computer-based assessment with students with mild handicaps have been quite encouraging. With computerized reading, spelling, and math assessments, sound educational diagnosis can now be made by teachers who have had neither the time nor the training to analyze the specific learning problems of a special needs student. When programmed appropriately, microcomputers can play the full role of the assessor, presenting a student with assessment items, monitoring student responses, scoring, interpreting, and summarizing the student's performance. Although computers are not apt to eliminate all of the problems we face in the assessment of students with special needs, existing research suggests that the assessment process can be enhanced through the continued development and responsible use of computer-based assessment systems (Hasselbring, 1986).

Teaching Materials

A number of special applications programs that allow for the generation of classroom materials and learning aids are available for the microcomputer. Computer generation of materials can save teachers many hours. Graphics programs, like the Print Shop, can assist in the development of materials such as banners for classroom displays, notices, invitations, and awards. Other programs simplify the process of creating newsletters, certificates, and even crossword puzzles and word games.

Authoring Systems

Teachers who want to develop their own computer-assisted instruction (CAI) but have no experience with a programming language can now use software programs known as authoring systems. Authoring systems attempt to overcome the need to learn a computer programming language by separating the logical control of the computer from the instructional content of the CAI lesson. For example, with some authoring systems the author simply enters the text for presentation frames, question frames, correct answers, incorrect answers, and feedback messages for each alternate answer. The authoring system provides a template in which the author places the content to be presented and prompts the author to enter each piece of information. The sequence and instructional logic are automatically controlled by the system. Thus, this type of authoring system makes it easy for a teacher to develop material in which the computer prompts a student for a response, evaluates it, and then either reinforces the correct response or provides feedback on why the response was incorrect (Merrill, 1982).

Even though authoring systems provide an inexperienced programmer with the ability to develop simple CAI lessons, the development of an educationally sound CAI lesson is a time-consuming process. Blackhurst (1983) estimates that the development of a CAI lesson requires approximately 1 hour of planning and programming for each minute of instruction. Clearly, there is a high cost in terms of human effort in developing CAI materials, even with the use of an authoring system.

An alternate and possibly less time-consuming solution for creating customized lessons is the use of **editors** frequently included within existing CAI software. Many CAI programs include an option for teachers to alter the items presented in the program. With this option teachers might customize spelling word lists or select a range of math problems. They might also decrease the difficulty level of the software by reducing the number of items presented at one time. Such options make additional programs appropriate for students.

SUMMARY

This chapter presents an overview of microcomputer systems and a sampling of the instructional uses of the microcomputer with students who are handicapped. The applications described here have the potential to enhance the delivery of services in special education classrooms. It must be remembered, however, that the use of microcomputers contributes to special education only when the strengths of the technology are maximized and inappropriate applications are minimized. The computer is not magical; it is simply a tool of education. In the hands of a skilled craftsman, the results can be quite spectacular; in the hands of a novice, the results can be quite discouraging. This chapter emphasizes appropriate and effective uses of the computer. It is the teacher's job to take this information and apply it skillfully. Teachers of children with learning handicaps must learn to use computers as skilled artisans; our students deserve nothing less.

PART THREE
CURRICULUM

8
Curriculum Development, Program Design, and Material Selection

The most critical programming component in classes for individuals with mild and moderate handicaps is the curriculum. Ultimately, regardless of teaching effectiveness and efficiency, questions of value address the issue of what has been taught. This chapter presents an overview of the content of educational programs of learners with special needs. It also introduces part three, providing the framework for the specific curricular domains discussed in chapters 9 through 18.

Although there is little reason to arrive at a precise definition of *curriculum,* it is helpful to begin by considering the various applications of the term. Ragan and Shepherd (1971) identify three distinct uses of the term: (1) *curriculum* **as "courses offered"** represents a narrow concept that simply lists specific content areas in which a student receives instruction; (2) *curriculum* **as "a document"** refers to a design that others have developed and that a teacher implements in the classroom; and (3) *curriculum* **as "an experience"** suggests a broad, dynamic perspective encompassing all of the educative experiences for which teachers and schools accept responsibility. Discussion within this chapter is based on the assumption that curriculum develops from basic considerations of program design and gains its value from the ways in which staff members apply these considerations.

This chapter discusses several major curricular concerns. General curricular models are identified and evaluated for benefit to students with handicaps. Selection of specific curricular content is discussed to introduce the specific chapters that follow and to further delineate elements of program design. The chapter concludes with a discussion of the process of selection and use of curricular materials.

CURRICULAR ORIENTATIONS

Programs for individuals with mild or mod-

erate handicaps must be **comprehensive;** the preeminent goal is to meet the diverse needs of students within these populations. In order to accomplish this general goal, curriculum should be

- ☐ responsive to the needs of the individual student at the current point in time
- ☐ reflective of the need for balance between maximum interaction with nonhandicapped peers and attention to critical curricular needs
- ☐ integrally related to placement so that program content can be delivered efficiently within a specific service delivery model
- ☐ consistent with the transitional needs of students across the lifespan (i.e., providing a foundation to meet future needs)
- ☐ derived from a realistic appraisal of potential adult outcomes (a top-down perspective)
- ☐ sensitive to diploma track goals for students at the secondary level

Although curricular orientations are defined differently by various professionals (e.g., Alley & Deshler, 1979; Meyen, Vergason & Whelan, 1983; Vergason, 1983), our discussion identifies three general orientations, each of which includes two or three specific curricular models: remedial, focusing on basic academic skills and social adjustment; maintenance, including tutorial and compensatory approaches and training in the use of learning strategies; and functional, emphasizing vocational training and an adult outcomes orientation. Educators must assume that students with special needs require a varied, flexible curriculum that can be adjusted to meet individual needs.

Remedial Model: Basic Skills

Unquestionably, the most common model

for special education curricula has been and continues to be the remedial, basic skills orientation. Such a model presumes that the major attention of instruction should focus on developing academic skills. Therefore, intensive programming in reading, mathematics, and language provides the core of the instructional program. Clearly, a basic skills orientation addresses academic deficits and emphasizes apparent student needs. A basic skills model is typically the focus of most elementary special education curricula. It has a long-term orientation, based on the assumption that direct instruction of academic skills will ultimately increase academic achievement.

Few doubt that an academic focus is a necessary component of the curriculum for students who are mildly and moderately handicapped or who have remedial needs; therefore, there is little reason to debate the merit of this orientation in the simple sense. The particular advantages of a remedial model are that it focuses on students' specific deficits, offers an intensive option to regular class programs, and can assist in increasing literacy, thus potentially benefiting the individual in both school and extra-school learning tasks (Alley & Deshler, 1979; Wiederholt & McNutt, 1979).

However, there are several notable difficulties associated with a basic skills approach. First, such an orientation may neglect the specific strengths of students and may reinforce their sense of failure by continuing to focus on areas of difficulty. In addition, such an approach may fail to address issues of transfer, whether to the regular class setting or to postsecondary environments. Finally, there has been a relative lack of curricular programs appropriate for use with students at the secondary level. Therefore, continued reliance on a basic skills model with adolescent learners has been questioned (e.g., Alley & Deshler, 1979; Deshler, Schumaker, Lenz, & Ellis, 1984).

Despite these difficulties, however, teachers should consider the proven effectiveness of individual programs. For example, the Corrective Reading Program (CRP) (Engelmann, Becker, Hanner, & Johnson, 1980) was specifically designed for older students who continue to experience difficulties in basic reading recognition and comprehension skills. CRP is based on the same principles and methodology of direct instruction that have been demonstrated to be effective with younger students (see Stebbins, St. Pierre, Proper, Anderson, & Cerva, 1977). A growing body of research (e.g., Campbell, 1983, cited in Becker, 1984; Gregory, Hackney, & Gregory, 1982; Polloway, Epstein, Polloway, Patton, & Ball, 1986; Thorne, 1978) offers support for the fact that this program can be effective with older students. Further information on the Corrective Reading Program is provided in Chapter 10.

Positive findings of the effectiveness of CRP with adolescents reinforce the observation made by Meyen and Lehr (1980) that a large number of adolescents can profit from academic remediation if exposed to intensive programs. Meyen and Lehr characterized **intensive instruction** as possessing these attributes:

1. consistency and duration of time on task
2. timing, frequency, and nature of feedback based on the student's immediate performance and cumulative progress
3. regular and frequent communication by the teacher to the student of his or her expectancy that this student will master the task and demonstrate continuous progress
4. pattern of pupil-teacher interaction in which the teacher responds to student initiatives and uses consequences appropriate to the responses of the student. (p. 23)

Careful consideration of the possible benefits and limitations of the basic skills model is important as the program design proceeds. Certainly, adoption of the remedial model alone requires caution. Because the underlying premise of remediation is cure, this model is unlikely to succeed totally with most students who are handicapped. At some point educators must shift the curriculum to achieve maximum independent functioning beyond the school setting.

Remedial Model: Social Adjustment

The second model is characterized by an emphasis on social skills acquisition and behavior change. It has been classified as a remedial model simply to indicate that it also represents a deficit view of the characteristics of individual students. A social adjustment orientation is rarely used as the sole focus of curricular efforts except for students identified as emotionally disturbed or behaviorally disordered. Three general, interrelated approaches are associated with this model: social skills acquisition, behavior change, and an affective emphasis. Specific behavior training strategies are discussed in chapter 5; both social skills acquisition and the affective emphasis are included in chapter 15.

One significant benefit of training in social adjustment is the potential contribution to the successful mainstreaming of students who are handicapped. Gresham's (1982) review of efforts in this area clearly highlights the misguided attempts at mainstreaming that he attributes to reliance on three faulty assumptions: that placement alone ensures increased interaction between handicapped and nonhandicapped peers; that such placement increases the social acceptance of students with handicaps; and that mainstreamed children model the behavior of nonhandicapped peers solely through exposure. Gresham's review presents a strong case for requiring systematic social skills training prior to integration efforts.

In terms of effectiveness, there are two major considerations. First, any program claiming a social adjustment orientation as a primary focus should be accountable for meaningful change. Too often, special education, especially in the form of affective education, has been neither special nor educational, showing little evidence of documented change in skills and/or behavior. A second area of concern is the generalizability of the programs selected. To justify its use, a program must be able to demonstrate that it can contribute to a student's success in subsequent environments. One interesting and useful program in this regard is the School Survival Skills Curriculum, developed by the Learning Research and Development Center at the University of Pittsburgh (Zigmond & Sansone, 1986; Zigmond & Brownlee, 1980). This program focuses on teacher-pleasing behavior, study skills, and behavior control.

A fruitful approach to the issue of generalization is the use of cognitive approaches to behavior change and social skills acquisition. To the degree that such programs can demonstrate internalization, they offer a good deal of promise for future programming efforts within this curriculum model. The issue of self-regulation within the context of cognitive behavior modification is discussed in chapter 5.

Emphasis on social facets of curriculum cuts across all functioning levels and age ranges. Teachers can safely assume that most children and adolescents who are mildly or moderately handicapped need some instruction in this area. Chapter 15 discusses specific instructional approaches.

Maintenance Model: Tutorial Assistance

Traditionally, one of the most common models in special education, especially in programs for adolescents with learning disabilities, has been tutorial assistance. Most commonly used within a resource model, such a program seeks to maintain the student within the regular class curriculum.

There are several apparent reasons that tutorial models have been and continue to be popular in some schools and school divisions. Foremost is the motivational aspect tied to such an approach. Quite simply, students are interested in the supportive services that come with this model and that enable them to be more successful in the regular classroom. Perhaps as a by-product regular class teachers and parents are also frequent supporters of such an orientation. To the extent that such an orientation is effective, tutoring may have positive implications for classroom letter grades and for diploma requirements.

In spite of the possible benefits of such an approach and cognizant of the fact that **all** special education teachers engage in some tutoring, such an orientation nevertheless has a short-term emphasis that may offer little lasting value. Among the main disadvantages of such an orientation are the following:

☐ valid concerns about whether the material taught and learned is relevant to the needs of the students

☐ concern about whether the instruction is responsive to an individual student's long-term needs

☐ possible undertraining of special education teachers, who are asked to provide tutorial assistance across a wide range of subjects

☐ possible overtraining because tutoring frequently requires little advanced training and can often be handled by a paraprofessional

The tutorial orientation's heavy emphasis on short-term outcomes is responsible for both its major advantages and its numerous disadvantages. Teachers working with students who require some tutorial support should investigate the possibilities of involving peers, paraprofessionals, and classroom volunteers in the process.

Maintenance Model: Compensatory Efforts

A compensatory orientation represents a limited approach to curriculum. Basically, this model seeks to circumvent some of the key problems that students face in school and, to a lesser extent, out of school. This approach is used most frequently at the secondary level to complement one of the other core models. The ultimate goal is often to provide a student with an alternative route to a high school diploma (Wiederholt & McNutt, 1979).

The various forms of such a model are best illustrated by examples of compensatory strategies, which include recording classroom lectures, taking written tests in oral form, and using talking books. Additional strategies are listed here.

☐ For the child who has difficulty reading, the teacher aide or a student in the class may tape the lesson in advance. The poor reader may, with the use of earphones, listen to the lesson while reading it and thus receive auditory as well as visual input.

☐ The student who learns well from environmental stimuli with a minimum amount of printed symbols can use many good film strips on almost any subject and on almost every grade level. These film strips are for use with individual viewers.

☐ A student having difficulty spelling words for a written assignment may use a stack of small cards or pieces of paper. Another student or the teacher can write the words needed as the student asks. For a long-range project, the student should place the cards in alphabetical order in a cheese box or on a large notebook ring for ready access.

☐ For the student having trouble remembering mathematical facts but who understands the computation process, a table of math facts should be provided for easy reference.

☐ A small battery-operated calculator may help the student who understands the steps necessary for mathematical problem solving but cannot correctly compute. The student can check it out at the beginning of each class and return it at the end of the period.

☐ The student who finds writing difficult can dictate answers or written lessons to a cassette tape recorder. When cassettes are not available, a buddy or student secretary may be assigned to help.

☐ The student who suffers from severe inability to write or form letters legibly may be permitted to use a typewriter. The student should also be encouraged to type homework assignments. If the student does not know the touch method, hunt and peck may be permitted. (Bailey, 1975, pp. 34–35)

Further extensions of a compensatory model can include efforts to assist students to function independently in the community—for example, a reading curriculum focusing on protection words (see Chapter 10 for a list of possible words to teach). In all cases, however, teachers should use compensatory strategies primarily as an addition to the basic curriculum.

Maintenance Model: Learning Strategies

A learning strategies approach presents an opportunity for students to learn **how to learn** rather than learning **specific skills.** It utilizes a cognitive orientation, stressing ways that students can use their abilities and knowledge to acquire new information. As defined by Weinstein and Mayer (1986), learning strategies are "behaviors and thoughts that a learner engages in during learning and that are intended to influence the learner's encoding process" (p. 315). The learning strategies approach points beyond the special education environment and stresses maximum successful progress in the regular classroom.

Much of the work on the development of learning strategies for learners with special needs was initiated by Gordon Alley and Donald Deshler and was subsequently refined at the University of Kansas Institute for Research on Learning Disabilities. As presented by Alley and Deshler (1979), a learning strategies approach is most appropriately used in resource programs where the major objective is generalization of skills to the regular classroom. A major focus of the approach is the importance of cooperation between special and regular education teachers. Alley and Deshler (1979) identify the characteristics of students who appear to benefit most from a learning strategies approach.

☐ reading achievement above a third-grade level

☐ ability to deal with symbolic as well as concrete learning tasks

☐ demonstration of at least average intellectual ability

However, they also note that "these conditions are not all necessary, nor are they necessarily exhaustive" (Alley & Deshler, 1979, p. 22). Clearly, components of the approach can be effective for individuals beyond this defined population.

A full discussion of the learning strategies approach is beyond the scope of this chapter. Numerous resources exist for readers interested in further exploring the use of such an approach; for example, Ellis, Lenz, and Sabornie (1987a, 1987b) provide an excellent discussion of research and practice.

A methodology for teaching learning strategies has been developed for this curricular model. As described by Ellis and Sabornie (1986), the process includes eight steps.

1. Pretest the strategy to be taught and obtain a commitment from the student to learn.
2. Describe the particular strategy to be taught.
3. Model the use of the strategy.
4. Engage the student in the verbal rehearsal of the strategy.
5. Provide practice in the application of the strategy in controlled materials (e.g., reading materials at the instructional level of the student).
6. Provide practice in the application of the strategy in content materials (e.g., the regular science textbook).
7. Obtain the student's commitment to generalize the strategy.
8. Achieve generalization through three phases:
   a. Orientation as to where it can be applied
   b. Activation of the strategy by moving from explicit to less explicit instructions and assignment
   c. Strategy maintenance over time

A number of specific strategies have been developed by Deshler and his colleagues at the University of Kansas (see Deshler & Schumaker, 1986). Included are specific strategies for note taking, proofreading written work, listening to lecture material, skimming reading assignments, responding to objective tests, and studying texts from content areas, such as social studies and science. A good example is the strategy for skimming assignments, called the Multipass program (Schumaker, Deshler, Alley, & Denton, 1982). It includes the following components:

☐ **Survey:** main ideas, chapter organization (title, introductory paragraph(s), subtitles, summary paragraph(s), etc.)

☐ **Size up:** gain specific information (read questions, look for textual cues, self-question, skim, paraphrase, review)
☐ **Sort out:** answer all chapter questions

Additional information on strategies and related cognitive interventions has been developed and/or summarized by Hoover (1986), Rooney (1987), and Williams and Rooney (1986). Figures 8.1 and 8.2 illustrate other strategies, and strategies relevant to study skills are further discussed in chapter 14.

The learning strategies approach represents an encouraging development in programming, especially for students at the middle school and high school level. However, there are certain considerations to attend to when evaluating the possible adoption of such an approach as a major part of the curriculum. First, if such a model is used exclusively, it can result in limited attention to other curricular needs, such as areas of functional skills. Second, careful attention should be given to the salability or appeal of the particular strategy being taught. For some students motivation to learn a strategy that affords long-term benefits may be a difficult hurdle. Finally, efficacy data are relatively limited on this approach, particularly as it relates to strategy generalization.

The learning strategies model, when used comprehensively, has clear merit for use with older students possessing basic skills. Its emphasis on transfer of learning, self-instruction, and independence recommends its use with students beyond the specific target population. For example, the model's basic orientation is consistent with the curricular objectives identified by Winschel and Ensher (1978) as being critical to students who are mildly and moderately retarded. These authors encourage teachers to focus their attention on cognitive processes that

FIGURE 8.1
A strategy for
attacking word
problems (SOLVES IT)

S	SAY the problem to yourself (repeat)
O	OMIT any unnecessary information from the problem
L	LISTEN for key vocabulary indicators
V	VOCABULARY Change vocabulary to math concepts
E	EQUATION Translate problem into a math equation
S	SOLVE the math sentence
I	INDICATE the answer
T	TRANSLATE the answer back into the context of the word problem

FIGURE 8.2
A strategy for teaching
older readers to
analyze words in
independent reading
assignments
(CURSSED)

C	CONTEXT: Use contextual analysis to anticipate words
U	UNIMPORTANT: Skip over words that are unimportant to meaning
R	RAPID: Quickly analyze the word (i.e., initial consonant) in conjunction with context
S	STRUCTURAL: Analyze specific structural attributes (i.e., prefixes, suffixes, compound words)
S	SYLLABICATE: Apply syllabication strategy and phonetically analyze
E	EXTERNAL: Ask for external help (i.e., teacher, aide)
D	DICTIONARY: Look up the word

encourage learning to learn, such as development of short-term memory, hypothesis testing, listening and attending behavior, and problem solving.

Functional Model: Vocational Training

The two functional models are interrelated but have been separated out because certain of their features are discrete. Both models are discussed briefly here and in greater detail in chapter 16.

Vocational training has traditionally been associated with secondary programming for students with mild/moderate retardation. The classic work on this orientation is Kolstoe and Frey's (1965) work-study program for students identified as educable mentally retarded. More recently, a vocational emphasis has been considered for students identified as learning disabled or behavior disordered, as an alternative to the regular core curriculum at the high school level. The obvious advantage of vocational training programs is that they are clearly related to transitional efforts undertaken to prepare adolescents for postsecondary environments. This relevance to adult settings is a major factor in the area of motivation. Enrollment in a vocational program may keep many students from dropping out of school—an important consideration, given the recent media estimates that 39% of all students who are handicapped **do** drop out.

Two key trends are worthy of note. First, there is a significant need for community-based learning opportunities as an alternative or at least a complement to simulated vocational opportunities within a school setting. The implications for generalization and realistic job training are obvious. Second, an encouraging trend in vocational training is the supported employment program developed by Wehman and others in recent years (see Wehman, Renzaglia, & Bates, 1985). Basically a job-coaching approach, supported employment places individuals on the job and provides them with assistance that is gradually faded out over time.

The advantages of a vocational orientation are apparent. It provides specific training in skills for life beyond the school setting, adds relevance and motivation to the curriculum, and shifts the focus away from past failure in academic domains. The model emphasizes training in functional skills. On the other hand, such programs are difficult to initiate without broad support from the school administration, they can restrict options for students, and the generalizability of the skills taught must be carefully evaluated. In addition, vocational training may be difficult to implement for special educators with limited vocational training and/or vocational educators with limited experience teaching students who are handicapped. A high degree of cooperative planning is a prerequisite to success in most school situations.

Functional Model: Adult Outcomes

As noted, a curriculum with an adult outcomes emphasis reflects a degree of overlap with a vocational training orientation. It is separated here because such an approach emphasizes life skills relative to postsecondary adjustment. Adult outcomes curricula tend to be less intensively focused on vocational training and more comprehensive in their response to the numerous concerns of adult adjustment (Cronin & Gerber, 1982).

An adult outcomes emphasis implies a top-down orientation to curricular development, that is, a focus looking back, or down, from the demands of adulthood. Common components include the development of consumer skills, home management and budgeting, civic and social responsibilities, and leisure skills. Such a program is intended to be indexed against the realities of the community into which an individual will be moving.

One example of an adult outcomes curriculum is the Adult Performance Level (APL), adapted for secondary students in special education. Used in a number of school divisions in Texas and Louisiana, the APL serves as a core curriculum blending practical academic development with applications to the various demands of adulthood. Further information on this program is provided in chapter 16. Another excellent program is Fundamental Life Skills, developed by the Montgomery County (MD) Public Schools.

Students who have been experiencing chronic difficulty in school may be inherently interested in a curriculum that radically shifts attention away from academic deficits and toward future learning and skill needs. Thus, an approach emphasizing adult outcomes is frequently more attractive to adolescents and may have positive motivational consequences. A major caution relates to the nature of the program itself. Haphazard attention to adult outcomes may provide little content of either immediate or long-term value. In addition, what constitutes community survival skills is subject to interpretation.

Both the vocational and adult outcomes orientations are consistent with the need to provide career education to students who are handicapped. To appreciate the way that career education can be implemented across age levels, the reader is referred to the comprehensive career development curriculum developed by Brolin and Kokaska (1984). Their model includes **career awareness,** beginning in the primary grades and exposing children to a variety of life experiences; **career exploration,** initiated in the late elementary years and concerned with the functioning of society and children's specific interests in the world of work; **career preparation** at the secondary level, which includes training for specific vocational competencies; and **career placement** at the culmination of formal schooling.

CURRICULAR DECISION MAKING

The alternative curricular models presented here do not represent mutually exclusive approaches. Rather, they reflect the most common models, from which teachers may wish to choose a combination of approaches. Three general considerations should affect the selection of a curricular model(s).

One initial concern is the correlation of curricular model and service delivery alternative. Some models (e.g., the learning strategies approach) work particularly well in resource programs; others (e.g., vocational training) demand more extensive curricular modification than would generally be associated with special class programs. Placement, however, should not be viewed as a **fait accompli,** which dictates curricular choice. Instead, initial decisions should be based on curricular needs, and then the appropriate service delivery model should be selected. For example, if a group of adolescents with learning disabilities will have their needs best met by a learning strategies approach, then a resource model will probably be most appropriate. On the other hand, if a group of elementary students identified as mildly retarded have significant basic skill deficits, social skill difficulties, and definite need for career education, a strong argument can be made for a modified self-contained model.

The changing population of students served in mild retardation programs in many states aptly illustrates the need for curricular decisions to precede placement decisions. Mainstream classes typically emphasize academic skills; however, the learning needs of many students who are mildly retarded dictate a broader base than a remedial-academic model can provide (Edgar, 1987; Epstein, Polloway, Patton, & Foley, in press; McBride & Forgnone, 1985; Polloway & Smith, in press). The relatively recent back-to-the-basics movement in regular education offers another example; such an emphasis might exclude the comprehensive curriculum needed by most students identified as mildly retarded (Smith & Dexter, 1980).

A second factor in curricular decision making is level of schooling. Few question spending the majority of time in elementary programs on basic skills and remedial training to maximize students' academic achievement. At this point social adjustment and early career preparation efforts, for example, can complement the academic core of the curriculum. As students reach middle- and high-school years, however, teachers must carefully evaluate continuation of such a focus. Academic instruction for those not bound for postsecondary education must be functional and, thus, must shift to a more practical, applied orientation. Halpern and Benz (1987) report that secondary teachers have the greatest need for low-level, age-appropriate curricula in basic skills and for functional curricula in independent living and vocational areas. A shift in curricular focus is clearly important in light of the discouraging data on school dropouts and employment rates among students with disabilities (Edgar, 1987).

A third concern is the question of diploma status at graduation for exceptional learners. Particularly in states with minimum competency tests (MCT), curriculum may need to be restricted to provide students with the training necessary to succeed on competency tests and thus receive their diplomas. Student incentive to receive a diploma and employers' positive response to it often make efforts to obtain it appear more important than acquisition of skills with more direct relevance to postschool adjustment (Cohen, Safran, & Polloway, 1980). Cohen and her colleagues (1980) provide a detailed analysis of the merits, demerits, and implications of the MCT movement, which the reader may wish to consult.

In addition to these three general concerns, numerous, more specific factors should be considered during the curricular decision-making process. Based on the initial work of Dangel (1981), as expanded upon by Vergason (1983), the key variables listed in Table 8.1 should be considered in determining the correct curricular approach for an individual student or group of students. Clearly, program design is a complex process, and the common matching of curricular model to group label is a potentially dangerous practice. For example, the assumption that students with mild retardation cannot profit from a remedial model at certain age levels may be just as fallacious as the assumption that students with learning disabilities require a remedial orientation across age levels. Programs must be appropriate for the individual students for whom they are intended.

CURRICULAR ORGANIZATION

Selection of specific curricular content areas follows adoption of a particular curricular model(s). Klein, Pasch, and Frew (1979), summarizing the work of Tyler (1950), note that curricular content should be generated from three sources: the needs of individual students, both expressed and implicit; useful content from traditional curricular areas; and specific societal needs, such as employment and citizenship. Figure 8.3, based on a design originally developed by Dunn (1973), illustrates the changing importance of vari-

ous content areas across different educational levels. Naturally, emphasis should vary according to the individual student, variance within the group, and the curricular model being followed. This particular distribution of time would probably be most appropriate for students identified as mildly retarded and served in a special class program.

Integrated Curriculum

An alternative that has been growing in popularity is the integrated curriculum. The principal idea of this type of programming is a closer relationship among different subject and skill areas. Much work is being done with gifted students to create differentiated, integrated programs, and it is crucial to realize that not all of the features of such programming can be adapted to students with learning problems. However, as Oyama (1986) points out, "Curricular integration appears appropriate for special learners since it provides numerous opportunities through related activities for basic skill reinforcement and extension" (p. 15).

Although it is possible to design an entire curriculum around a broad-based theme, most integrative efforts with special learners are less extensive. Oyama (1986) provides an excellent example of how various selections from a basal reading series can be integrated (see Table 8.2). Cawley (1984) provides numerous examples of ways to integrate mathematics into a general curriculum. One suggestion is to adapt reading passages to include various quantifying statements, which can then be used to generate math-related sets of questions. The advantage of this technique is that it capitalizes on material that the student has already read.

Curriculum Guides

Curriculum guides provide a detailed set of

TABLE 8.1
Factors affecting
curricular decision
making

Student Variables	Mainstream Environmental Variables
cognitive-intellectual level	teacher and nonhandicapped
academic achievement	student acceptance of diversity
grade placement	(classroom climate)
motivation and responsibility (in	administrative support
general)	acceptability of variance in
motivation	curriculum
behavioral patterns	accommodative capacity of the
social skills	classroom
	flexibility and schedules
Parent Variables	options for vocational education
expectations	
degree of support provided (e.g.,	*Special Education Variables*
financial, academic)	size of caseload
parental values	access to curricular materials
possible cultural influences	focus of teacher's training
	support available to teacher
	Community Variables
	access to postsecondary programs
	economic climate
	unemployment rates
	evaluation of ecology of community
	relative to living climate
	access to transitional services

objectives matched to specific instructional suggestions. Although previously developed guides can generate ideas for teaching, the process of developing a curriculum guide may have value in outlining a particular program. Such an effort, although time-consuming, can result in consistent instruction at various levels of schooling and a more appropriate program for students.

The following recommendations, derived from Cegelka (1977), provide a general outline of the process of developing curriculum guides.

☐ Curriculum guides should be based on at least one sound learning theory, with the ultimate goal being attainment of increasingly complex behavior, personal control over the environment, and behavioral characteristics culturally designated as normal.

☐ Individual learning objectives should specify the skill area, instructional method, performance criterion, and evaluation methodology. General performance objectives should be further broken down or subdivided into specific process objectives representing steps toward attaining the desired skill.

☐ All objectives, both performance and process, should require monitoring and evaluation of teacher as well as student behavior.

☐ If the unit approach is used, its structure should include objectives and subobjectives.

☐ In all cases the appropriate and meaningful sequencing of activities should receive careful consideration.

☐ All curriculum guides should include a table of contents as well as an index to aid in information retrieval.

FIGURE 8.3
Changing curricular
emphases

Level of schooling

| | Primary | Elementary | Middle | Secondary |

Approximate
Percentage
of
Instructional
Time

Academic/
Remedial
training

Language
development

Social skills

Career
education/
Vocational
training

90

80

70

60

50

40

30

20

10

□ Suggestions concerning commercial materials should be referenced appropriately and their cost specified.

□ Because modification or revision of information is to be expected, the guide should be constructed so that its pages can be replaced or additional materials can be added with ease, for example, in notebook fashion.

□ All guides should conspicuously state the title, sponsors, or contributors to the guide and should tell where the guide can be purchased and for what price.

MATERIAL SELECTION AND USAGE

Instructional materials are a useful adjunct to the teaching process. Their actual impor-

tance has been debated and is most often subject to teacher variables. Gall (1981) points out that their role "differs with each teaching situation, varying with the learning outcomes desired, the teacher, the students, and the situational context" (p. 7). Although there is little documentation as to how teachers select instructional materials, it is likely that many do not thoroughly investigate what they are acquiring. In some cases, as with major program adoptions, teachers may actually have little or no input into the final decision of a selection committee. Nevertheless, there is a sequence of stages that should guide the selection and use of instructional materials.

Need

Teachers regularly find it important to obtain new instructional materials. New teach-

TABLE 8.2
An integrated curriculum based on a unit theme of friendship (focusing on relationships between people and animals)

Reading Topic	Language Arts	Math	Science
Robin and the Sled Dog Race (pp. 50–59) (A girl overcomes her desire to win an Alaskan dog race because of her concern for another racer.)	Discussion on value of friendship versus importance of winning Research on Alaska: various sources; note taking; factual reporting	Read and record daily temperatures (graph) Compare and convert Fahrenheit to Celsius	Study weather components and weather patterns Set up a weather station: use various weather instruments; interpret and record data; make predictions
About Dogs (pp. 60–65) (Probable history of the domestication of dogs)	Essay on dogs as helpers and/or friends	Bar graph of types and numbers of pets owned Graph of food intake and growth measurements of class pet	Collect data and report on history of breeding dogs for specific purposes Record observations of class pet
Arion (pp. 70–76) (Greek folktale of a poet/singer who was saved by dolphins)	Creative writing: poems about dolphins		Identify endangered marine species (e.g., pink dolphin) List ways we can help that species

ers may find it helpful to leave their training programs with a prepared "wish list" of materials (categorized by subject area), which they would like to have in their classrooms. Their new classrooms may be well stocked or new materials may have to be selected and obtained quickly—a difficult task. Continuing teachers should also keep an updated wish list. The need to obtain materials may arise for any number of reasons: a new area/topic/unit may need to be presented; the particular needs of students may require specialized intervention; or a program may need variety. Gallagher (1979, p. 31) suggests going through various catalogs regularly, identifying materials of interest, and

marking them with a code: A (need to have), B (nice to have), C (can be teacher-made). This system keeps a teacher ready to order.

Availability

Staying aware of what is available can be accomplished by consulting catalogs, attending conferences and in-service activities, taking courses, and visiting other classrooms. To order any desired material, it is essential that a **current** catalog be consulted, because an outdated price list will significantly delay final acquisition. Teachers may want to get their names on the mailing lists of major publishers (see Appendix).

TABLE 8.2
continued

Social Studies	Creative Arts	Health	Career and Life Skills
Research Alaskan culture: people, climate, housing, food, employment Geography: map skills	Snowflake cutouts Paste on a friendship card	Discuss the effects of weather on health and safety	Consideration of weather forecasts for outings or travel Related careers: meteorologists, plotters, forecasters, TV weather announcers
Identify ways that dogs help us (e.g., guard, hunt, police, guide, herd, rescue) Visit or listen to a person from the humane society	Listen to stories (e.g., *Old Yeller, Sounder*)	Discuss and demonstrate responsibility in caring for class pet	Develop responsibility for caring for others Related careers: veterinarian, breeder, trainer
Obtain info on Save the Whales and Greenpeace organizations Research Greek culture	Listen to *Island of the Blue Dolphins* Dramatize dolphin movements Replicate a dolphin wall mural	Discuss water safety: safety rules, drownproofing	Environmental awareness Water safety Related careers: oceanographer, marine biologist, animal trainer, veterinarian, poet, writer

Source: From *Curricular Integration Through a Basal Reading Series* by E. Oyama, 1986, Honolulu: University of Hawaii. Adapted by permission.

Evaluation

The most important stage in selecting materials is a thorough and systematic examination. Gall (1981) suggests three major strategies: examine the actual materials, read any evaluative data that are available, and field test the materials with the targeted student groups. Checklists, rating scales, and inventories can provide a framework for inspection of materials. Gall (1981) has developed a comprehensive set of criteria to help with the process (pp. 118–120).

Publication and Cost

1. Is the cost of the materials reasonable relative to other comparable materials?
2. Were the materials adequately field tested and revised prior to publication?
3. Is this edition to be in publication for several years, or is a new edition to be released shortly?
4. Were these materials published within the last 2 years?
5. Does the publisher of these materials have a good reputation among educators?
6. Are there likely to be difficulties in obtaining sufficient quantities of the materials for each student who will be using them?

7. Are there special resources required to use the materials?

8. Does use of the materials require special skills or training?

Physical Properties

9. Are the materials likely to appeal to the user's aesthetic sense?

10. Do the materials contain so many components that teachers will have difficulty keeping tack of and using them?

11. Does the product make unnecessary use of consumable materials?

12. Do the materials have components that are especially vulnerable to wear?

13. Did the publisher use high-quality materials in the production process?

14. Are there possible hazards to students or teachers using the materials?

Content

15. Does the developer use an approach consistent with the curriculum being followed?

16. Are the objectives of the materials compatible with the curriculum?

17. Are the materials free of biases that are misleading or unacceptable to teachers, students, and the community?

18. Do the materials reflect the contributions and perspectives of various ethnic and cultural groups?

19. Are the scope and sequence of the materials compatible with the curriculum?

20. Is the content of the materials free of sex stereotypes?

21. Does the content of the materials reflect current knowledge and culture?

Instructional Properties

22. Do the materials contain helpful assessment devices?

23. Are the materials compatible with other materials currently being used?

24. Does the design of the materials allow teachers to use them differently, according to student needs?

25. Does the publisher provide any data on the effectiveness of the materials in actual use?

26. Are the materials appropriate for the students who will be using them?

27. Are the materials an appropriate length so that they can fit conveniently into the teacher's instructional schedule?

28. Is use of the materials easily managed by the teacher?

29. Are the materials likely to excite the interest of students and teachers?

30. Are students likely to have the prerequisite knowledge or skills necessary for learning the content of the materials?

31. Are the materials written at an appropriate reading level for the students who will be using them?

32. Do the materials include activities that students are capable of doing and that they will enjoy doing?

33. Do the materials include activities that teachers will find interesting and rewarding?

It is also advisable to obtain evaluative information about the instructional materials being considered. Of particular interest are critical reviews that have appeared in journals or other periodicals and technical reports that accompany the materials. In addition, a publisher is often able to provide evaluative data on a particular item.

To conduct a field test, one must obtain the desired materials for a set amount of time, either by requesting an examination copy from the publisher or by borrowing the materials. Publishers may be reluctant to send major programs on an examination basis; however, such materials may sometimes be available at a school district's resource/materials center.

In reality, most teachers may be unable to accomplish all of these suggestions because of logistical limitations. Nevertheless, such an approach is strongly recommended. The ultimate goal is acquisition of instructional materials that are appropriate and useful.

Ordering Materials

When it comes time to actually order materials, a few ideas are worth considering. In addition to current pricing information, teachers should be aware of budget, time line, and procedures.

In general, teachers need to be aware of how much money they can spend on acquisition of materials and whether the available funds are restricted to certain types of purchases (e.g., textbooks, equipment, consumable items). They also need to know what materials are regularly supplied by the school district (e.g., art supplies, workbooks, and so on), recognizing that this policy varies among school districts and sometimes from school to school. Additional funds for instructional materials acquisition are sometimes available within school districts and possibly through the state/province federation of the Council for Exceptional Children (CEC). These monies may be distributed as small grants to support innovative projects, for example, and may require a proposal. Interested teachers should ask their principals, district level personnel, other teachers, or CEC federation officers for information.

Actual procedures for ordering materials must also be clearly understood. Teachers must know whether there is a time line or, more precisely, a deadline for ordering instructional materials. In many situations orders for the coming school year must be submitted well in advance (typically in the spring). Individual requests usually require a sequence of approvals (department chairperson, principal, district supervisor) before final authorization is granted. The value of being organized, current, and prepared is obvious.

Material Usage

Although many curricular materials can be used in the form in which they are provided by the publisher, it is important to evaluate whether they might be more effective with modification. The diverse learning needs of students with handicaps suggest that specific materials may require individualization. This concern is particularly apt with materials designed primarily for use in the regular classroom with nonhandicapped students.

Lambie (1980) identifies a series of questions that can be posed to determine a basis for modification. Areas of concern include the number of items on a page, speed of the program, sufficiency of repetition, presence/absence of feedback, presentation of directions, language level of the material, inherent interest of the material, durability of the material, and sequence of skills or concepts. The reader is encouraged to consult Lambie (1980) or Burnette (1987) for suggestions to remedy these problems.

Lambie (1980) also provides some basic guidelines to assist with planning and implementing changes in materials as well as in instruction and assignments. In particular, teachers need to become familiar with the strengths and weaknesses of the material and the characteristics of the learner(s), to determine whether a mismatch is likely to occur; they should consider changes only when a mismatch has been established; they should focus on the simplest changes possible that will enhance the effectiveness of the material; they should evaluate the effectiveness of the changes; and they should be sure that any supplements are compatible with the material being used (e.g., requiring similar reading skills).

SUMMARY

Nearly half a century ago, Richard Hungerford, an influential special educator, provided an apt perspective on programming for students who are handicapped. He proposed the **three Rs of a special education curriculum:** relatedness, reality, and responsibility (Blatt, 1987). Each of these concepts has merit in our efforts to evaluate the needs of students, compare and contrast the curricular alternatives, and design an appropriate program that will prepare exceptional students for success in subsequent environments. The discussions in this chapter have focused on defining a comprehensive curriculum for students who are handicapped, identifying alternative curricular models, selecting the appropriate model, organizing the curriculum, and selecting and using curricular materials.

9
Spoken Language

DAWN LIBBY CLARY
*Columbia County, Georgia,
Public Schools*

SHERRY EDWARDS
*Halifax-South Boston,
Virginia, Schools*

Children's language skills develop through a hierarchical sequence of listening, comprehending, speaking, reading, and writing. Successive skills build on firm acquisition of preceding abilities. This chapter addresses listening and speaking; chapters 10 and 11 cover reading and writing, respectively.

The ability to attach a symbol to an object or a concept enables one to learn about it. Without some symbol for the referent, there is no ability to communicate about it and thus to learn more about it. Language is at the core of learning (Finch-Williams, 1984). Communication can be defined as meaningful interaction between two or more individuals, whether it be verbal, gestural, or paralinguistic (i.e., use of body movement, facial animation). Language is a form of communication; it is also a set of symbolic relationships mutually agreed upon by a user community to facilitate communication. Speech is a verbal code developed as a manner of expressing language. Speech, however, need not be used as communication, as in the case of echolalia, in which phrases are repeated without the intent of conveying meaning, or in self-stimulation, in which words or phrases are used as a litany, purely for the speaker's benefit.

Children who are learning disabled or mildly/moderately mentally handicapped often develop language in a delayed or disordered manner. When language is delayed, various components of receptive and expressive language indicate fairly equal levels of development. Disordered language, which is more frequent in students who are disabled, is characterized by inconsistent abilities. Weinrich, Glaser, and Johnston (1986) indicate that children with delayed or disordered language do not outgrow their language problems; instead, other problems are added as they grow older. Reading, writing, and spelling problems emerge and are compounded as greater demands are made in these areas.

Teachers cannot overlook the area of language as solely the domain of speech/language clinicians; language and learning are not easily divided. The younger the child or the lower the functioning level, the more inseparable language and learning become. Language and learning, thus, are effectively taught concurrently with the development of basic cognitive skills. Once prelanguage skills (e.g., attending and responding) have been observed in a student, instruction in language and cognitive areas is the next step for language instruction.

Most teachers enter the classroom setting already acknowledging the importance of language; fewer are actually ready to implement a program in this area, for a number of reasons. First of all, inter- and intrafield disagreements exist over the origin, development, and remediation of language. There is also a good deal of difficulty breaking down language into manageable presentations (Morley, 1972) and for many years language instruction has been perceived as the sole domain of speech/language specialists. In addition, most children come to school with their individual language patterns and uses already established.

Classroom teachers and speech/language clinicians need to work together as closely as possible, each group reinforcing the work of the other and ultimately seeking to maximize students' linguistic abilities. To facilitate this effort, this chapter focuses on language development, curriculum development, and assessment and instruction in receptive and expressive communication. The discussion refers to the five components of our language system: phonology, the study of speech sounds (phonemes); morphology, the study of units of meaning (morphemes) within words; syntax, the study of grammatical structure; semantics, the study of the analysis of meaning in discourse; and pragmatics, the study of language usage. A comprehensive intervention program must attend to all five of these areas. Activities are suggested at the end of the chapter for use with students who have language deficits.

LANGUAGE PROGRAMMING WITHIN THE CURRICULUM

Oral language instruction should play a major role in the curriculum of virtually all students who are mildly or moderately handicapped. Difficulties in this area are not only significant in their own right but also must be considered probable precursors to specific problems in other academic areas, such as reading and writing. The classroom teacher should not be reluctant to implement speech/language activities within the classroom. Although problems like stuttering or cleft palate speech are appropriate targets for a qualified professional, the classroom teacher should at least attempt to spur language use in general. A speech/language clinician within the school system would probably be eager to work cooperatively and to help provide direction. Whereas a clinician within the public school system can rarely spend more than 1 or $1\frac{1}{2}$ hours a week in direct therapy with a student, the teacher has many more opportunities for instruction on a daily basis. By increasing students' receptive vocabularies and encouraging their use of expressive skills, a teacher can make a positive difference for children and adolescents with special needs.

In recent years speech therapists have begun working with students within the regular classroom setting. This practice has increased the possibility of working with students on subjects of significance, while eliminating the need for generalization from the isolated therapy setting to the natural environment of the classroom. It also increases the interaction between the speech therapist and the classroom teacher and provides the teacher with tools for continued language training.

Although students with mild or moderate handicaps have acquired some language skills before entering school, these skills are frequently inadequate. In planning a curriculum, teachers should consider three points. First, many individuals who are moderately handicapped have a great need for structured programming if they are to develop beyond a level of limited and perhaps repetitive usage. Second, many students from culturally different backgrounds need assistance in acquiring the standard English required in school. Finally, language instruction cannot be forsaken at the middle or secondary school levels; even though students may have developed basic skills, they still need instruction to refine these skills and to learn to apply them in community settings.

ASSESSMENT

The purpose of assessment is to determine a student's area(s) of strength and weakness in language and to relate that information directly to the creation of a program of remediation that is relevant to the child's home, school, and community interactions. Assessment efforts should be undertaken in a way that is consistent with typical milestones in language development. As a reference point Table 9.1 outlines the general developmental stages. Teachers should also be familiar with the common signs of delayed or disordered speech/language, which should signal the need for referral to a speech/language therapist.

1. A student's articulation of sounds in conversation is different enough to call attention to itself.
2. A student enters kindergarten with speech not easily intelligible.
3. A student aged 7 or older has misarticulated sounds in conversation, other than those related to a cultural dialect.

4. A student is regularly observed to hesitate before uttering a phrase or to prolong or repeat sounds, parts of words, whole words, or phrases in conversation.
5. A student uses primarily stereotypical phrases in answering questions (e.g., "Huh?" or "I don't know") or frequently echoes questions or phrases.
6. A student's language is obviously less well developed than that of other students of that age. Words may be consistently omitted, or incorrect grammatical structure may be observed. Difficulty with description or word recall may be noted.
7. A student's attention span appears inordinately short during learning or listening activities.
8. A student frequently fails to follow a series of three commands.
9. A student's voice quality appears to be unusually nasal, hyponasal, high or low in pitch or rough and raspy.

10. A student appears not to hear when the teacher or another student speaks to him or her.
11. A student's language (e.g., choice of words, intonation, inflection) frequently appears to be inappropriate to the situation.

Before discussing specific assessment approaches, it is important to consider several aspects of formal and informal assessment. Formal instruments are typically designed to assess a general population and may not provide a true test of any particular child's ability. Such tests may have strengths in one area and weaknesses in another. In addition, they are generally conducted in clinical settings, away from a child's natural classroom environment. To circumvent these biases, more than one formal assessment tool should be used, and results should be compared with those of informal assessment, such as a language sample or observation (Wallace, Cohen, & Polloway, 1987).

TABLE 9.1
Stages of language development

Age	Accomplishment
Birth	Crying and physiological sounds; some visual imitation
1–2 months	Cooing, responsive sounds
6 months	Babbling
9–14 months	Receptive: language developing rapidly, able to respond to complex utterances
	Expressive: recognizable words beginning (usually nouns)
$1\frac{1}{2}$–2 years	Receptive: may have vocabulary of 300 words
	Expressive: two- to three-word sentences (noun-verb sentence structure typically)
$2\frac{1}{2}$ years	Saying nursery rhymes, singing songs, remembering most of the words
3 years	Correct use of pronouns, use of plurals, color recognition not unusual
4 years	Receptive: understanding of verb tenses
	Expressive: complex sentence structures
5 years	1500 to 1800 words in use; fully intelligible speech with the exception of some age-appropriate articulation errors

Source. From *Communication Skills for Exceptional Learners* (pp. 95–96) by M. Webber, 1981, Rockville, MD: Aspen. Copyright 1981. Reprinted with permission of Aspen Publishers, Inc.

One of the most valuable procedures for informally assessing language is observation. Natural observation of language skills often provides information unobtainable in any other way (Spekman & Roth, 1984; Spradlin, 1967). Long-term, daily interactions provide ample opportunities to observe and assess all facets of a student's language development in many different natural settings, such as the classroom, playground, and cafeteria. Because fewer natural occasions for observing language skills exist at the secondary school level, teachers may need to build in structured opportunities such as class reports, student debates, and verbal instructions for complex assignments.

Receptive Language

Receptive language deals with the skills of attending, listening, and comprehending. Problems can occur when children display an inability to attend, retain what they have heard, hear what has been said (i.e., a hearing loss), or understand what has been spoken. Listening assessments indicate the extent to which a student can attend to relevant stimuli, tune out unimportant stimuli, gain meaning from what is heard, and sustain these abilities over a significant period of time. If a student has a listening span of 5 minutes or less and is easily distracted by environmental noises, such as people talking, plans must be made to remediate the difficulty.

Table 9.2 lists some of the available assessments that are concerned with receptive language. Some aspects of formal assessment are typically the domain of a speech/language clinician. However, a number of formal tests are appropriate for teacher administration.

A teacher can informally assess listening skills simply by consciously observing a stu-

dent's behavior. The following questions can be used to guide observation:

- ☐ Does the student establish and maintain eye contact with the person speaking?
- ☐ Is the student restless in a group activity of varying duration (5, 10, 15 minutes)?
- ☐ Is the student's attention easily diverted during a group activity?
- ☐ Can the student complete a simple task below the student's ability level? at ability level?
- ☐ Can the student repeat simple and complex statements? follow simple and complex commands?

Specific approaches to informal assessment of receptive subskills are also discussed here.

Auditory Discrimination A preliminary check should determine whether the student understands the words *same* and *different* because screening relies on these basic concepts. The initial step in this area then is to test discrimination of grossly different environmental sounds. If the student misses several items, is generally inattentive, has trouble following simple directions, and shows poor understanding of basic concepts, testing for a hearing disorder is recommended. If hearing is found to be within normal limits, the teacher can make a more refined assessment of auditory discrimination.

Testing continues with an evaluation of the ability to discriminate between significantly different words. For example, the student might be told to raise a hand every time the word *soap* is spoken. The teacher might then say, "Soap, soap, bird, show, soap, car, soap. . . ." The next assessment area would be discrimination of similar words and then of different isolated speech sounds or phonemes.

TABLE 9.2
Selected measures of receptive language

Test Name	Publisher	Appropriate Ages	Domain(s) Assessed
Auditory Discrimination Test (Wepman, 1973)	Language Research Associates	5 to 8 years	Auditory discrimination
Boehm Test of Basic Concepts (Boehm, 1980)	Psychological Corporation		Receptive vocabulary
Clinical Evaluation of Language Functions (CELF) (Wiig & Semel, 1980)	Psychological Corporation	Kindergarten	Processing oral directions; processing spoken paragraphs
Detroit Tests of Learning Aptitude (DTLA-2) (Hammill, 1985)	Pro-Ed	5 to 10 years; 5 to 16 years	Auditory attention span for unrelated words; oral directions
Goldman-Fristoe-Woodcock Test of Auditory Discrimination (Goldman, Fristoe, & Woodcock, 1970)	American Guidance Service	6-3 to 19-0 years	Auditory discrimination
Peabody Picture Vocabulary Test (Dunn, 1965, 1980)	American Guidance Service	4 years to adult	Receptive vocabulary
Vocabulary Comprehension Scale (Bangs, 1975)	Teaching Resources	1-6 to 18 years; Kindergarten and first grade	Receptive vocabulary

Auditory Memory Assessing a child's auditory recall inevitably examines short-term memory. A quick, informal evaluation involves saying two unrelated words and asking the student to repeat them. After two correct responses the number of words presented can be increased by one, until two consecutive trials are missed. Another means of evaluation is to provide sentences of varying length and complexity for the child to imitate: "I smell smoke," "The balloon is yellow," "The nurse said I was sick," "Is this my thumb?"

Occasionally, number sequences of expanding length and complexity can also be used for repetition, although this method is limited because numbers are less relevant in everyday communication. Nevertheless, digit span is a common part of many formal assessment tools and does measure length of recall for this message form.

Comprehension Assessment in this area seeks to measure a student's ability to understand the spoken word. It can include following basic directions, receptive vocabulary, and knowledge of basic concepts.

An informal check of a student's ability to follow directions can be easily devised. The student is first given simple one-step commands, such as "Sit down," "Raise your hand," "Stand up." After succeeding at those commands, the student is given two-, three-, and four-step commands as warranted. Appropriate use of morphological and syntactical structures is basic to success in this area.

Receptive vocabulary can be informally assessed by asking a student to point to different items in a simple picture or on a book page. With this technique the teacher can assess semantic variables, such as an understanding of nouns, verbs, and adjectives. For example, a student might be shown a page with someone running and someone sitting and might be asked to point to the runner. Words for initial evaluation might include these: nouns—*dog, cat, boy, girl, fish, house;* verbs—*running, walking, jumping, sitting, working, typing;* adjectives—*tall, big, round, soft.* For older students vocabulary can be altered to reflect interests and ability levels.

Informal assessment of basic concepts might involve surveying a student's comprehension in a variety of different areas.

- ☐ simple opposites
- ☐ knowledge of colors
- ☐ counting to ten
- ☐ knowledge of body parts
- ☐ discriminating between shapes
- ☐ general time concepts (days of week, months, seasons)
- ☐ spatial relationships (in, under, outside, first, last, middle)
- ☐ comparatives and superlatives (big, bigger, biggest)
- ☐ personal information (boy, girl, personal name)

Expressive Language

Expressive language includes spoken words, vocalized sounds, and gesturing. Although verbal language is not the only acceptable form of communication, it is the goal. Assessment techniques for the various components of expressive language are discussed here.

Gestures Gestures are among the simplest forms of communication and are used to enhance the message conveyed by the spoken word. For a student whose speech mechanism does not function properly, this communication form should be expanded and encouraged. For others, however, gestures should not be a substitute for verbalization. Teachers should be aware of the amount of gesturing students utilize in communicating and the proportion to informative verbalization. Excessive gesturing to relay a message frequently indicates a poor lexicon of words from which to draw.

Verbal Expression In the assessment of verbal expression five specific areas need to be monitored—amount of verbal expression, utilization of descriptive terms, sentence structure, speech disorders, and language usage within a given social context.

The amount and type of a student's verbal expression determine how a teacher judges the student's language strengths, limitations, and interactions within the environment. Does the student talk all the time uncommunicatively? Does the student ever initiate an expression, or are all verbalizations in response to someone's questions? Does the student talk only with peers and never with an adult? These questions represent important areas of concern that should be assessed.

Use of descriptive terms can be assessed by having a student describe things in the environment, such as home, classroom, or a favorite person. Illustrated books can also provide a structured occasion to describe specific items in particular pictures. The teacher tries to determine whether the student uses color, action, or size words or other cogent descriptors. Older students may respond when asked about their favorite rock singer, a recent film, or their opinion of the previous school year.

Of primary importance in informally assessing expressive language, particularly language structure, is the use of a language sample (Tunn & Van Kleeck, 1986). This is achieved by recording verbal interchanges and gestures during conversation between the student in question and another person(s). A tape recorder can prove very helpful in this assessment. The teacher objectively records the antecedents and the behaviors and verbalizations of the student (see the sample recording form in Figure 9.1). Generally, at least 50 conversational utterances, or sentences, are collected and analyzed for syntax, semantics, articulation, fluency, and pragmatic content.

For children whose sentence length is usually four words or less, the mean length of utterance (MLU) is an important measure of structural language. MLU is calculated by adding the total number of words spoken during the sample and dividing that sum by the total number of utterances spoken. For utterances that generally exceed four words,

FIGURE 9.1

Example of a recorded language sample

Student: Q   Date: October 11, 1988

Others: H and B

Setting: Classroom during free time. Student seated at reading
          center.

Others' Remarks and Behaviors	Student's Remarks and Behaviors
H: Walks up to Q, taps him on shoulder, says "Hi."	
	Q: Looks down at his book, says "Hi."
H: Looks toward Q's book, says "What are you reading?"	
	Q: Shrugs shoulders, continues to look down.
B: Walks up to H and Q, says "Hey, guys."	
H: Says "Hi."	
	Q: Glances at B, looks back at book.
H: Looks back at Q, says "What's your book about?"	
	Q: Looks at H, looks quickly back at book, says "Dinosaurs."

the following aspects should be considered in evaluating the effectiveness of the communication:

1. sentence complexity (one-word responses, simple sentences, complex sentences)
2. correctly used negatives
3. interrogatives used (why, where, what, when)
4. arrangement of phrases and sentences
5. immature grammatical patterns (e.g., "me can go" rather than "I can go")
6. appropriateness to the social situation

Conant and Budoff (1986) present a strong argument for using a variety of measures in analyzing data gleaned from language samples. Although one child may show a marked increase in action words and pronouns without significant increase in MLU over a specific time period, another may have a significantly increased MLU. The tester must also be aware of slight gains that indicate trends in a child's language development. Some of the possible categories for analysis include number and percent of one-, two-, and three-word turns; turns greater than three words; longest turn; number of action words used; number of pronouns; number of negations; and number of requests (Conant & Budoff, 1986).

Of interest in the collection of a language sample is a finding by Tunn and Van Kleeck (1986). Their research indicates that when the language sample involved the tester and the child, significantly more spontaneous utterances were recorded when the tester utilized fewer questions and made more comments on actions by expanding on the child's utterances.

When assessing syntactical and morphological elements, the teacher must take care to differentiate between language deficits and dialectal differences that are common in many students identified as mildly handicapped. An understanding of, and appreciation for, the integrity of dialectal variances is critical to accurate assessment and programming.

If sentence analysis reveals student difficulty with language structure, the teacher should consider referral for more in-depth evaluation. Most formal instruments intended for this area are designed for interpretation by a language specialist. On the basis of both classroom and clinical evaluation, the teacher and the specialist may then develop a specific intervention strategy to assist the student in overcoming verbal expressive problems.

Speech disorders can be assessed by monitoring a student in a natural environment, perhaps using a tape recording. The teacher should try to develop a critical ear to determine the specific type(s) of speech errors.

☐ *Articulation.* Listen for individual sounds that are consistently mispronounced; for example, the *r* sound might be replaced by a *w* in words like *red* or *rabbit, barrel* or *carrot.* The *r* sound might be distorted whenever it is associated with a vowel, as in *car, first,* or *Thursday.* The *r* blends might deviate in words like *brush, fruit, grape, tree,* or *drink.* In immature speech the final sounds or syllables may be omitted in many words. Thus, *cat* becomes "ca," and *water* becomes "wa."

☐ *Voice.* Components of a pleasant voice include volume, pitch, and quality. The volume should be loud enough to be heard without calling undue attention to itself. The pitch should be appropriate to age and sex with a variety of ranges from high to low. Quality should be clear and resonant without nasality, stuffiness, or hoarseness.

☐ *Fluency.* Attention should be given to the number and kinds of dysfluencies, as well as the precipitating factors. Teachers need to be sure *not* to call attention to problems, students should not be told to stop and begin again, for example. The interactive aspects of dysfluencies make a therapist's involvement especially critical; a speech therapist has strategies that are appropriate for the classroom and can assist the teacher in employing them. A data sheet may be an important part of the intervention and can be designed by both the clinician and the teacher.

Pragmatics, or language usage in a specific social context, is another important area of concern for teachers. According to Johnston, Weinrich, and Johnson (1984), children who are pragmatically disordered are likely to be very frustrated. They cannot make language do what they want it to, and their intentions are frequently misinterpreted. They therefore begin to perceive themselves as social misfits and are often unable to adapt to new school situations. The subtle forms of humor and sarcasm that older children enjoy are often beyond the pragmatically disordered child, further widening the gap of real and perceived differences. Reading and writing experiences, which require students to be flexible in creating and recreating and to interpret in many contexts, are also difficult for students with language usage problems (Dudley-Marling & Rhodes, 1987).

Weinrich et al. (1986) postulate that effective communication requires individuals to:

1. use appropriate words
2. be relevant to the topic of conversation
3. give an appropriate amount of information
4. be polite to listeners
5. be truthful in their accounts

Informal assessment of pragmatic skills can be done within the classroom. Some possible techniques are listed here.

☐ *Requesting.* Ask the child to draw a "mumsel" and see whether he asks what one is.
☐ *Denying.* Ask the child to draw but don't provide a crayon, or make a mistake in your observation of a picture.
☐ *Commenting.* Present an interesting object without comment, or drop an object on the floor. Wait for the child's response.
☐ *Expressing reason.* Ask why a particular occurrence took place.
☐ *Turn-taking.* Engage in conversation, the topic of which is known to the child. Note the manner and number of turns taken.
☐ *Accepting silence.* Remain silent for several seconds; observe the student's comfort or discomfort with the situation.
☐ *Informing.* Give the child a choice of pictures from which to choose. Ask her to describe the selected picture without showing it.

Prutting and Kirchner (1983) present a protocol designed for the assessment of pragmatic skills, which Duncan and Perozzi (1987) investigated and found to be a reliable and valid tool in determining pragmatic abilities.

Table 9.3 lists instruments that can be used to assess expressive skills. Additional information is available in Compton (1984).

INSTRUCTIONAL APPROACHES

In implementing a program of language development and remediation, teachers must balance structure and organization while accommodating the natural spontaneity of communication. Specific instructional targets must be supplemented by attention to students' personal use of language to control their social environment. Finding the approach, curriculum, or activities that best suit the needs of particular students is a dif-

TABLE 9.3
Instruments to assess expressive language

Test Name	Publisher	Appropriate Ages	Domain(s) Assessed
Environmental Language Inventory (MacDonald & Horstmeier, 1978)	Psychological Corporation		Expressive language
Preschool Language Scale (Zimmerman, Steiner, & Evatt, 1979)	Psychological Corporation	1-6 to 8 years	Expressive skills (also auditory comprehension)
Test of Adolescent Language—2 (TOAL-2) (Hammill, Brown, Larsen, & Wiederholt, 1987)	Pro-Ed	11-0 to 18-5 years	Expressive language (also receptive components)
Test of Language Development—Intermediate (TOLD-I) (Hammill & Newcomer, 1982)	Pro-Ed	8-6 to 12-11 years	Expressive language (also receptive components)
Test of Language Development—Primary (TOLD-P) (Hammill & Newcomer, 1982)	Pro-Ed	4 to 8-11 years	Phonology, syntax, semantics, and pragmatics

ficult task. Based on the students' strengths and weaknesses, teachers must determine whether and how to address receptive or expressive skills or both.

General Considerations

Two general approaches to programming are operant, or behavioral, training and environmental intervention. Behavioral approaches have long been an integral part of instructional programming for students with handicaps. Language teaching can be facilitated by behavioral techniques that stress the manipulation of instructional stimuli and consequences to effect improvements in verbal behavior.

Jens, Belmore, and Belmore (1976) list minimum antecedent and subsequent skill techniques for teachers interested in teaching language skills. At the top of their list is positive reinforcement, using both primary (e.g., food, drink) and secondary (e.g.,

praise, toy) reinforcers. Modeling and imitation apply to students who do not have the desired behavior in their repertoire but who do have the skills necessary to perform the behavior or some approximation of it. As introduced in chapter 5, shaping is the reinforcement of partial completion of a desired response, gradually requiring closer approximation to the behavior for reinforcement; it is suggested for students who do not have the skills to perform the desired behavior. Prompting (the physical movement of a student through a desired response) is used with students needing additional cues; fading, or gradual lessening of physical prompts, is incorporated when prompts are no longer necessary. Generalization must be programmed to ensure transition to other situations. All techniques should complement language learning in the natural environment.

Environmental language intervention (ELI) techniques are those in which intervention is undertaken in the natural setting (Cavallaro, 1983). As opposed to operant conditioning approaches, which provide reinforcers for responses elicited under contrived circumstances, ELI endeavors to teach desired skills within the natural environment. Within this intervention model language training is conducted throughout the day in all situations, rather than in a separate block of time set aside for language. A speech therapist can be instrumental in facilitating this approach. The child's ability to imitate the modeling of the teacher seems to be a key factor in the success of this program (Cavallaro & Poulson, 1987).

Standards of learning (SOL) for each student can be incorporated into either behavioral or environmental language remediation programs and can aid both the speech/language clinician and the classroom teacher. As an example, Virginia's SOL 5.1 states:

> The student will use oral communication skills in a variety of situations. *Descriptive Statement:* Emphasis is on individual oral presentation, which may include reports, readings, plays and role-playing. Effective use of pitch, rate, stress, tone, and volume is to be demonstrated.

Using this SOL as a guideline, the clinician and the teacher could then outline various times within a typical school day during which this problem area might be addressed.

By coming into the classroom to conduct language therapy, a clinician can assist individual students as they carry out oral assignments, such as answering questions and role-playing. The therapist can be beside individual students as their turns come to participate and can provide words, phrases, and questions to enable the students to interact appropriately (Cluver, 1987).

Receptive Language

A major focus of instructional programming is the remediation of receptive deficits. As Wallace, Cohen, and Polloway (1987) point out, to help learners with special needs, teachers need to (1) be sure directions are short and clear; (2) pair spoken messages with visual stimuli; (3) get children involved in doing an activity; and (4) use variety in the ways learning is presented. Among the activities Wallace et al. recommend for these purposes are role-playing, mime, and charades.

Poor listening skills are frequently cited as a deficit in learners who are handicapped. Wallace and colleagues (1987) state that these students demonstrate poor comprehension and memory skills and often do not seek clarification. As the children grow older and the complexities of language to which they are exposed increase, the deficits become more marked. Therefore, a segment of auditory training or listening activities should be included in the daily classroom curriculum so that listening skills are not left to incidental learning. This is an area of concern for all students, not just children with special needs.

Teachers may be instructing children with poor listening skills who come from overcrowded homes. These children may "have learned at an early age to 'tune out' or disregard sounds around them. Instruction for such children must begin with basic sound awareness in which the child learns to focus attention on particular sounds . . ." (Wallace et al., 1987, p. 73).

Another area of receptive language deficits is comprehension. To help children with comprehension deficits, teachers must first aid them in identifying when comprehension has not occurred; after that students can focus on asking questions for clarification. Dollaghan and Kaston (1986) used a four-part training system in their work with children who have learning impairments. They taught the students to identify and label, detect, react to, and eventually correct their own comprehension errors. Teaching students the "correct way to do it" was less effective than making them responsible for their own comprehension.

Expressive Language

Several general considerations are worthy of attention in developing expressive language skills. One concern in oral language instruction is the creation of an appropriate psychological environment in the classroom. According to Shafer, Staab, and Smith (1983), "Children need to feel good about themselves and about being in school. . . . Only as these good feelings are fostered will children be likely to express themselves freely in talk and desire to engage in group activities which facilitate this talk" (pp. 30–31). Wood (1969) provides a list of suggestions for promoting oral language development that continues to be relevant. She emphasizes language as a natural communicative act rather than an artificial instructional goal.

1. Work with students at their own level of speech and language rather than use suggested words from methods and word lists.
2. Allow students to say what they are attempting to say by not being too specific or demanding.
3. Translate gestures into simple, concrete words.
4. Allow students to show you what they mean if they are unable to express their ideas verbally.
5. Always make students feel you are interested in what they are attempting to say.
6. Attempt to eliminate gestures that substitute for understanding verbal commands.
7. Work from the concrete to the abstract.
8. Capitalize on students' strengths.

9. Use manipulative objects initially to work with a child having limited speech.
10. Use stimuli natural to the students' individual environments.
11. Keep careful records of students' progress. (pp. 51–52)

The use of gestures as an aid in developing language skills is also worthy of special attention. Acredalo and Goodwyn (1985) found gestures to be a part of the language development of infants and of normal language training by parents. Gestures should therefore be seen as a tool for conveying meanings of words to children who are developmentally delayed. Because these children are often found to respond primarily to visual stimuli, the addition of gestures in teaching the meaning of a word(s) can be seen as an enrichment or expansion in the teaching process, one that occurs spontaneously within the natural learning environment of a young child. Gestures or signs can add precision to a statement as well as convey meaning.

Studies show that language develops more rapidly with the use of signing. In addition, once oral terms are learned and generalized, signs disappear spontaneously (Abrahamsen, Cavallo, & McCluer, 1985; Acredalo & Goodwyn, 1985). Signing has also been shown to have a significant influence on the development of language in children who are already verbal but who, because of developmental delay, have difficulty with specific areas of language development. Musselwhite (1986) lists several areas in which the use of gestures has proven to be of significance.

1. inclusion of inflectional markers (e.g., *-ing*)
2. appropriate use of personal pronouns (e.g., *me* for *I*)
3. understanding of basic concepts (e.g., *over*)
4. initiating of requests
5. generalizing of these and other language structures (p. 32)

Musselwhite (1986) also notes that self-cuing (i.e., gesturing as a reminder to one-self of the referent) is seen as a learning aid. Once the cue is learned, a child can use it as a self-reminder until the concept is sufficiently learned. Once the concept is learned, the gesture typically fades naturally.

Another specific area of concern is that of pragmatics. To help children with pragmatic disorders, specific intervention strategies must be planned. Hurvitz, Pickert, and Rilla (1987) designed an instructional approach in which teachers set up activities that "use language to promote and regulate social interaction" (Hurvitz et al., 1987, p. 12). Correction of grammatical and articulation errors is not a primary emphasis here. The teacher must develop situations that allow students to experience the effects of language usage on the world around them. Leadership experiences, which give children enough responsibility so that others must respond to their requests, are a good place to begin. Hurvitz et al. (1987) suggest allowing individual children to lead the entire group in a movement activity (calling out commands) and to assign jobs for the day.

Another area to concentrate on is the structuring of social interactions. The teacher can focus on providing appropriate models or suggesting ways to help or begin an interaction (Hurvitz et al., 1987). Dramatic play can encourage verbalization, too. Students not only need to establish and regulate roles, but they must also express the imagined situation. In a dramatic play situation a teacher might supply props (e.g., a doll, a diaper, and a bottle) and then tell the participants to care for the baby. Familiar settings or stories are used initially; as children gain confidence and experience, the

teacher can provide situations that stretch their ability and imagination further.

Various instructional techniques lend themselves well to pragmatic instruction. Younger students, who have not yet learned metapragmatics (the ability to talk about pragmatics), can benefit from modeling and role-play. By engaging in pretend activities, the teacher can model appropriate initiating, questioning, requesting, topic changing, and closing. Parallel talking and sentence expansion are also important techniques with the younger child. By providing the words for which the child is searching and by rephrasing the child's question or comment in expanded form, the teacher is modeling within the appropriate social context. Creating situations involving verbal turn-taking is also important. And forcing verbalization is helpful when it is appropriately utilized—for example, "John, tell Sabrina how to make the sandwich the way you want it." Another technique is pretending not to understand, thus requiring the child to use more varied skills to communicate. The teacher is promoting regular and natural interaction (Hurvitz, Pickert, & Rilla, 1987).

Older students who can understand the concept of pragmatics can respond through group discussion and role-play of specific situations, such as how to talk to a girl (or boy), how to respond to rejection, and how to talk on the telephone. In addition, high school students are facing adult situations and should discuss and role-play job interviews and on-the-job social behaviors. Verbalizing and acting out possible situations help students to visualize them and have appropriate remarks and behaviors ready.

Older students can also be encouraged to talk about subjects of interest, such as hobbies or sports. Emphasis should be on content and social skills rather than on syntax and semantics. Teachers can rephrase to emphasize or encourage students to continue, thus modeling appropriate phrasing without interrupting or correcting. Older students can also keep a daily journal in which they write about feelings or topics of interest. Teachers can ask students to share with the group if they wish to, but journal entries should not be graded, to encourage the development of expressive skills.

Culturally Different Students

Special considerations are necessary in working with students from culturally variant backgrounds. Special education programs in general and classes for students who are mildly retarded and behavior disordered in particular have traditionally enrolled a significant number of students from minority groups. Thus, teachers must devise strategies to give standard English instruction to students from culturally different backgrounds without violating the integrity of the various dialects. The following list (Polloway & Smith, 1982) highlights a number of specific guidelines and methods for instruction in this area.

1. Avoid negative statements about the child's language, exercising particular caution in front of large groups. Rather than saying, "I don't understand you" or "You are not saying that right" several times, the teacher should use a statement such as, "Could you say that in a different way to help me understand?"
2. Reinforce oral and written language production. A first goal in working with language-different pupils is to maintain and subsequently increase the language output. Reinforcing desired productions will ensure that this goal is reached.
3. Set aside at least a short period during the day to stress language development.

4. During the language instruction period, work with five pupils or fewer so that each pupil has several chances to make an oral response. Working with a small group will make it possible for group members to see each other and the teacher to physically prompt and reinforce each student.
5. Set definite goals and objectives for language development just as you would for other instructional areas.
6. Reduce tension during the language development period by moving to a less formal part of the room. Strive to arrange as relaxed an environment as possible so that pupils feel free to make oral and written contributions in the new language they are learning.
7. One goal of language training is to produce longer and more complex utterances. To reach this goal, develop and maintain systematic records comparing each pupil's performance at different times.
8. During the language development period, encourage standard and nonstandard English speakers to talk about language differences and to compare different language forms.
9. Involve persons from the linguistically different community in the total school program as much as possible so that these persons, as well as "native" speakers, can share language experiences.
10. The teacher should model standard English usage. For example, when a student says, "Dese car look good," you could say, "Yes, these cars do look good." (pp. 83–84)

Curricular Programs

Numerous commercial materials have been developed to offer sequential instructional programs to students with special needs. Table 9.4 provides a brief summary of a representative sample of broadly focused programs.

TABLE 9.4
General language programs

Program/Publisher	Appropriate Ages	Domain(s) Addressed
Developing Understanding of Self and Others (DUSO) (Dinkmeyer, 1972)/American Guidance Service	Kindergarten to Grade 4	Program is designed to increase verbal language skills and social interaction. The activities are intended to be an enrichment program with enough lessons for a full year. The program has no screening or evaluation measures but does contain all required materials. The activities are adaptable for language development or remediation.
Direct Instruction for Teaching and Remediation (DISTAR) (Engelmann & Osborn, 1971, 1972, 1976)/Science Research Associates	Preschool to Grade 4	Program includes three sequential levels: DISTAR I—language used in classroom instruction; DISTAR II—skills needed to analyze language; and DISTAR III—basic understanding of sentence form and content as well as skills to aid in upper elementary work. Skills are sequentially presented; presentations are fast-paced for active involvement; modeling techniques, positive reinforcement, and immediate feedback are important components.
Game Oriented Activities for Learning Language Development (GOAL) (Karr, 1972)/Milton Bradley Company	Mental ages 3 to 5 years	Program is designed to remediate language delays and develop social skills and problem-solving abilities. In addition to the lessons, GOAL includes picture cards, situation pictures, templates, and puzzles and games needed to follow the lessons. Checklists of guidelines to determine a child's language deficits are included to aid in placement and to use as an ongoing assessment of needs. The lessons are to be followed daily.
Peabody Language Development Kits (PLDK) (Dunn, Horton, & Smith, 1967; revised 1982)/American Guidance Service	Preschool to Grade 3 (can be adapted for use with upper elementary children with special needs)	Kits are designed as a supplement to a regular language arts program. Fast-moving and game-oriented activities encourage and build oral language skills. The kits have no evaluations other than teacher observations and contain all the necessary pictures, tapes, and other materials. Activities are as informal as possible, requiring no reading, writing, or seat work.

ACTIVITIES

Specific activities appropriate for oral language programming are included in this section. Language development activities in the first two sections focus on receptive and expressive language, respectively; the third section includes mixed activities appropriate for older students. Teachers need to extend language instruction into middle and secondary schools to further develop and refine the receptive and expressive abilities of adolescents with handicaps.

Receptive Language

1. Go for a nature walk, naming trees, flowers, and so forth. Back in the classroom show pictures of things named outside. Say the name of one, and ask whether that is what the picture is. Require a yes or no answer.
2. Ask one student to find three rough items in the room and bring them to you. Send another student to find three soft items. Use other concepts that you know the children have studied.
3. Play a tape of various sounds, having students raise their hands each time they hear an animal.
4. Read a short story, instructing students to stand up each time they hear a certain word.
5. Play recordings of different sounds in the environment. Have several students identify the particular sounds.
6. Say two words that differ only in the initial consonant sound—for instance, *hat, mat* or *fun, run.* Have a pupil say whether the words were the same or different in beginning sounds. Occasionally say the same word twice so that the pupil cannot always correctly respond that the words were different. As students become more familiar with this task, have them name initial consonants for each word that you say. A similar activity requiring finer discriminations is to say several words with the same beginning consonant sound. Include a word with a different initial sound and ask pupils to repeat the word (e.g., fun, fan, four, ball; dad, do, man, doll).
7. Beginning with one simple direction and lengthening the list of directions, have a child perform a simple task in the classroom (e.g., stand up, turn around, close the door).
8. Play a game with students—"Teacher, may I?" The students stand at the back of the room. The teacher gives an instruction (e.g., "Sam, take three giant steps"), to which the child replies, "Teacher, may I?" The teacher then says yes or no. A child who forgets to say "Teacher, may I?" must go back to the beginning. The first child to reach the front of the room wins. Many kinds of steps may be used—for example, baby steps, leaps, bunny hops, and so on.
9. Place two students at a table separated by a screen. Place identical objects in front of both students. Have one describe an object; the other must pick the object being described. Later they can tell how the object works or can describe its uses.
10. Orally present a list of three words. Two should be related in some way. Ask a student to tell which are related and why (e.g., horse, tree, dog).

11. Divide a sheet of paper into four sections. Label each with a color. Have a student draw or cut out objects that are a particular color and attach them to the appropriate section.

12. Tape-record a 5-minute segment of information—part of a story, weather report, or a morning news broadcast. Play the tape while you take care of beginning-of-the-day details. Have students respond to prepared questions about the recording (Leverentz & Garman, 1987).

13. Read the description of a physical scene to the class. Encourage students to draw pictures related to what they heard.

14. Label a box "Treasure Chest" and fill it with familiar objects. Designate one student as king or queen. The royal person begins by saying, "Bring me my _____ , my _____ , and my _____ ." A "subject" is then chosen to follow the directions. If the directions are followed correctly, the subject becomes the king or queen (Glazzard, 1982).

Expressive Language

1. Tell a flannelboard story and ask a student to retell it. Allow the child to use the flannelboard pieces also and to receive help from classmates if necessary. For older students use cassette tapes of old radio shows, such as "The Shadow" or "The Green Hornet." After listening to most of a tape, ask a student to repeat the plot and guess "who done it."

2. The day after a field trip, encourage students to recount their feelings and experiences.

3. Create a group nonsense story. The teacher supplies the first sentence. Each student then adds a sentence to embellish the tale until everyone has had a turn.

4. Read an action story and assign a student or group to play a specific part by acting like that object (e.g., dog, rifle). Each time that particular part is named, the students should respond by saying a related word or sound (e.g., bowwow, bang).

5. An oral language activity that many students seem to enjoy is show and tell. Encourage students with speech problems to share their happy experiences with others. This should be a time for little or no pressure regarding speech.

6. Place an object in the center of a small group of students. Have each tell one thing about the object. Encourage different observations about color, size, shape, function, and so on.

7. Write simple sentences on the board, or read simple sentences to students. Instruct them to pick out descriptive or action words. Vary the activity by having students change the words so that the meaning of the sentence changes.

8. Many singing activities promote use of the same articulators that speech does, but singing has the added advantage of increasing fluency. Use singing activities to help promote oral language skills.

9. Borrow a set of telephones from the local phone company. Instruct the students on how to answer properly and how to take and give messages.

10. Many students enjoy playing tongue-twister games, in which the initial sounds are very similar in all words of a sentence or paragraph (e.g.,

"Surely Sharon shall sail shortly;" "Betty bought a batter of bitter butter; why was the batter of butter Betty bought bitter?") Tongue twisters can help a pupil work with initial and final consonant sounds or blends. Dr. Seuss books can be a useful resource.

11. Have students act out a sentence or a simple story. Let the others guess what the actor is "saying."

12. Use a Language Master with cards of familiar faces, objects, and places to encourage vocalization.

13. Place several objects (e.g., ball, pencil, book) before a pupil. Make up a sentence describing one of the objects. Have the pupil say the name of the described object.

14. Use unnarrated films as a springboard for discussion on plot, characters, and environment to enhance receptive and expressive language. May (1979) presents titles and discussions of several such films.

15. Choral speaking allows practice of rhythmic speech patterns and speech sounds. The shy student remains anonymous, and it can be fun for all. Poems and song lyrics are excellent sources.

16. Klein (1979) suggests serious as well as light-hearted content in language activities. A time set aside for jokes and storytelling may enhance receptive as well as expressive language. Content of jokes must be monitored.

17. Gearheart (1985) recommends using puppetry in a variety of activities—acting out stories created by students, stories from books, or stories initiated by the teacher. Designing and making puppets may also elicit opportunities for discussion, and the puppets may help children participate in these discussions.

18. Karnes (1968) recommends asking questions, such as "Tell me how . . . ," "Why do we . . . ," or "Tell me where. . . ." For example, "Tell me how . . . you tie your shoes [play kickball, wash a car]."

19. Introduce a "Word of the Day," and encourage students to use it throughout the day.

20. Involve students in "interrupted readings." Select a story to read aloud. Tell students that you will stop as you read and will call on them to give a word that they think the author might use (Barhydt, 1987).

21. Vary the previous activity by reading a poem or short story to the students and then rereading it, leaving out key words for the students to fill in. This activity also aids in the development of auditory memory skills.

Activities for Adolescents

1. Some tape recorders or record players are equipped with a public address system that can be used to create a mock radio station. Let students describe their concepts of different jobs at a radio station, and then choose jobs on a rotating basis to put a class radio station into operation.

2. To help a student develop vocational interview skills, have students play either the interviewer or interviewee. Stress the process the interviewee goes through in being questioned about job qualifications.

3. The Adult Puzzle draws on life situations that adults encounter, such as

renting an apartment, cashing a check, or buying on credit. The life situation is divided into its component parts. Have each member of the class take one part, and ask three adults for their opinions on how best to solve or meet the requirements of that one step. Within a number of days the class members should assemble the individual steps in the solution of the larger puzzle. The game requires students to gather and exchange information using spoken language. Written information can then reinforce class discussions.

4. Students can rotate as a special events reporter. At a specific time during the day the designated student reports to the class on school or community events.

5. Tiedt and Tiedt (1978) list 150 topics for impromptu or planned speaking activities. Categories of topics include amusement, education, customs, friends, hobbies, manners, home, sports, nature, occupations, organization, pets, morals, reading, and travel.

6. Try brainstorming activities that follow Osborn's (1963) guidelines for creative group collaboration.
   a. Criticism is disallowed.
   b. Encourage ideas: "It's easier to tame down than to think up."
   c. Quantity is desired; the more ideas, the more likely it is that useful ones will be suggested.
   d. Combination and improvement are prized.
   e. Problems should be simple and specific (e.g., What should we do on the final day of school?).
   f. Discuss each idea's value according to its appropriateness, feasibility, and efficiency.

7. Some students may be able to memorize parts of poems and recite them to the class. This activity can work well with middle- and secondary-school students who are studying poets and poems that are of interest to them.

8. Some secondary students may be ready for developing skills related to the analysis and judgment of propaganda. Have students listen to political and religious speeches and TV commercials, looking for such things as name calling, generalities, testimonials, card stacking, bandwagoning, sex exploitation, and side-tracking (Lamb, 1967).

9. Cohen and Plaskon (1980) suggest setting aside a time daily or weekly for role-playing activities. They suggest such topics as asking for a favor, following procedures during an emergency, handling an embarrassing moment, dealing with an angry person, and extending an invitation.

10. Simply reading plays orally from teen magazines gives pleasure to many older students. "Reader's theatre," a formal dramatic presentation of a script by a group of readers, is a similar activity highly recommended by Busching (1981). She suggests it to develop expressive language in students with disabilities because the script is practiced, not memorized. Students need not worry about their bodies; they merely concentrate on their voices. Teachers can assign parts of varying difficulty according to academic and linguistic ability. Children's books offer a treasure chest of scripts.

11. Haley-James and Hobson (1980) encourage interviewing to increase

expressive and receptive language. They offer the following suggestions: (a) conduct a practice interview; (b) tell students they will receive only as much information as they ask for, so if they ask yes/no questions, they will get yes/no answers; (c) discuss the information gained and the kinds of questions that produced the greatest amounts of information. Once students learn the process, interviews can be scheduled with people from the school or community.

12. Peck and Schultz (1969) suggest keeping a chart to record amelioration of speaking errors over time. Start by identifying a few errors (e.g., *done* for *did*, "this here"). Place marks next to errors when they occur, and show students their performance. Suggestions for improvement should be given with consideration and sensitivity.

13. Older students also enjoy a sharing time (i.e., a modified show and tell). This sort of activity usually works best in the morning, before academics. Structure and content are important. Topics may include the activities of the previous afternoon meals, television viewing, weekend activities, or special events. Limits need to be set on individual sharing. Try to draw out students who are not actively involved. Criticism is not allowed.

14. For language development to result in significant gains, Edelsky (1978) suggests that students need to be involved in project planning, problem solving, and decision making. She suggests that older students record stories for younger students. As students decide on stories and try out voices for the tape, they will improve their expressive and receptive language.

15. Give students opportunities to practice impersonations. Encourage them to imitate each other's voice qualities and word patterns.

16. Open-ended problems may be presented to enhance thinking skills as well as spoken language. Questions might include "What are some things you might do if you have a flat tire?" "What would you take with you if you were going to spend 2 weeks on an island?" "What might you do if you saw a $5 bill on the ground?" (Gearheart, 1985).

17. Verriour (1984) suggests that the use of drama in the classroom offers many benefits. Different dramatic situations help children learn about the world around them through different language modes, increasing their awareness of the power of symbolic thought. Reflective thought, problem solving, and decision making are often a part of drama. Dramatic situations may provide incentive for students who are reluctant to express themselves.

18. Older students may be encouraged to create and perform "rap" songs for younger children. Topics can include good advice about health and nutrition, bike and traffic safety, ways to say no to drugs and alcohol, and the importance of school.

10
Reading

ROSEL SCHEWEL
Lynchburg College

The ability to read is essential for living in today's world; personal independence requires at least functional literacy. Failure to read restricts academic progress because proficiency in math, English, or social studies depends on an ability to read. Most jobs in our technologically advanced society also require at least minimal reading skills. Reading may even be the key to personal/social adjustment and to successful involvement in community activities.

In his book *Illiterate America,* Kozol (1986) states that millions of American adults cannot read well enough to function in today's world. Filling in job applications and reading restaurant menus and grocery store ads are beyond their reading level. *The Reading Report Card,* a publication of the United States Department of Education (1986), documents that many school children are also unable to read well enough to understand and complete grade-appropriate reading assignments. The report states that 40% of 13-year-olds and 16% of 17-year-olds attending high school are unable to read intermediate level reading materials and are unable to search for specific information or to make generalizations from information in their social studies, science, or literature textbooks. Unfortunately, many students who cannot read drop out of school, thus removing themselves from an opportunity to improve their reading skills (Brody, 1986).

Reading, reading failure, and ways to teach reading remain dominant issues today, as they have been since the initiation of public school education. Recent federal and state legislation requires all school systems to provide reading instruction for children with handicaps and, when possible, place exceptional children into regular classrooms. Because these students' special problems require modification of reading approaches and special teaching techniques, educators are now approaching

reading instruction in innovative ways (Savage & Mooney, 1979). It is estimated that 10% to 15% of the general school population have reading disabilities but that 85% of the population labeled learning disabled have reading disabilities (Hallahan, Kauffman, & Lloyd, 1985).

Kirk, Kliebhan, and Lerner (1978) describe three correlates of reading failure—environmental, psychological, and physical. Savage and Mooney (1979) list cognitive deficits, psychological problems, and motor problems as the major contributors to reading failure. These researchers' theories indicate the variety of ways to view this problem. Although specific causes of reading failure have not yet been validated, researchers generally agree that correctly designed, individualized instruction can minimize the influence of most factors.

Selecting the correct teaching approach is another debated issue in the reading field; few agree that any single method is the most effective with all slow learners. The responsibility for teaching reading can thus seem awesome, particularly because more than 100 approaches have been identified for teaching beginning reading (Aukerman, 1971). Often an eclectic approach is necessary to meet exceptional students' individual needs. In fact, a major study of 1828 elementary school students, conducted by the Federal Reserve Bank of Philadelphia and the Philadelphia Public Schools (Kean, Summers, Raivetz, & Farber, 1979), indicates that teachers' consistent, direct, personal involvement in reading instruction is the single most important influence in achievement.

Although recognizing the importance of the correct methods and materials in reading instruction, Leinhardt, Zigmond, and Cooley (1980, cited in Zigmond, Vallecorsa, & Leinhardt, 1980) determined that the amount of time actually spent reading is the major factor in reading progress. Their study of the classroom routines of 105 learning disabled students between the ages of 6 and 12 years indicated that only 27 minutes out of the 287 minutes in an average school day are spent reading. An analysis of the students' reading progress established a direct correlation between time spent reading and reading achievement. Leinhardt et al. conclude, therefore, that teachers must reorganize the daily classroom schedule to increase the time students are actively engaged in reading if students with learning disabilities are to improve their reading skills.

In their classic book on teaching reading to slow learners, Kirk and Monroe (1940) outline three goals that help provide a framework for instruction of readers who are handicapped. A minimal goal for all students who are mildly and moderately handicapped is the ability to read for protection. Implicit in this goal is the concept of survival. Recently, Polloway and Polloway (1981) conducted a survey of teachers working with adolescent students. The survey resulted in identification of 54 words and 50 phrases most necessary in developing daily living skills. Those lists, presented in Tables 10.1 and 10.2, can help teachers select the words or phrases most appropriate to their

TABLE 10.1
Fifty most essential survival vocabulary words

Word	N*	X̄**	Word	N*	X̄**
1. poison	52	4.90	26. ambulance	54	4.02
2. danger	53	4.87	27. girls	54	4.00
3. police	52	4.79	28. open	53	3.98
4. emergency	54	4.70	29. out	53	3.98
5. stop	53	4.66	30. combustible	54	3.94
6. hot	53	4.53	31. closed	54	3.90
7. walk	53	4.49	32. condemned	54	3.90
8. caution	54	4.46	33. up	53	3.89
9. exit	53	4.40	34. blasting	54	3.87
10. men	54	4.39	35. gentlemen	52	3.86
11. women	53	4.32	36. pull	53	3.73
12. warning	53	4.32	37. down	53	3.72
13. entrance	53	4.30	38. detour	53	3.71
14. help	54	4.26	39. gasoline	54	3.70
15. off	52	4.23	40. inflammable	53	3.70
16. on	53	4.21	41. in	54	3.68
17. explosives	52	4.21	42. push	53	3.68
18. flammable	53	4.21	43. nurse	52	3.58
19. doctor	54	4.15	44. information	54	3.57
20. go	53	4.13	45. lifeguard	52	3.52
21. telephone	53	4.11	46. listen	54	3.52
22. boys	54	4.11	47. private	53	3.51
23. contaminated	54	4.09	48. quiet	53	3.51
24. ladies	53	4.06	49. look	53	3.49
25. dynamite	52	4.04	50. wanted	54	3.46

Source: From "Validation of a Survival Vocabulary List" by E. A. Polloway and C. H. Polloway, March 1981, *Academic Therapy, 16,* p. 446. Copyright 1981 by Academic Therapy Publications. Reprinted by permission.

*The number of participants varies because of omissions or errors by raters.

**Maximum rating of an item was 5; minimum was 1.

TABLE 10.2
Fifty most essential survival vocabulary phrases

Phrase	N	$\overline{X}$	Phrase	N	$\overline{X}$
1. Don't walk	53	4.70	26. Wrong way	53	3.96
2. Fire escape	54	4.68	27. No fires	54	3.96
3. Fire extinguisher	54	4.59	28. No swimming	53	3.92
4. Do not enter	53	4.51	29. Watch your step	52	3.92
5. First aid	54	4.46	30. Watch for children	54	3.91
6. Deep water	50	4.38	31. No diving	54	3.91
7. External use only	53	4.38	32. Stop for pedestrians	54	3.89
8. High voltage	54	4.35	33. Post office	52	3.85
9. No trespassing	52	4.35	34. Slippery when wet	53	3.85
10. Railroad crossing	52	4.35	35. Help wanted	54	3.85
11. Rest rooms	52	4.35	36. Slow down	53	3.81
12. Do not touch	52	4.33	37. Smoking prohibited	54	3.80
13. Do not use near open flame	53	4.24	38. No admittance	54	3.78
14. Do not inhale fumes	53	4.24	39. Proceed at your own risk	53	3.77
15. One way	53	4.24	40. Step down	52	3.77
16. Do not cross	53	4.17	41. No parking	52	3.75
17. Do not use near heat	53	4.11	42. Keep closed	54	3.74
18. Keep out	53	4.09	43. No turns	53	3.73
19. Keep off	54	4.07	44. Beware of dog	54	3.72
20. Exit only	53	4.07	45. School zone	53	3.72
21. No right turn	52	4.04	46. Dangerous curve	53	3.71
22. Keep away	52	4.00	47. Hospital zone	54	3.70
23. Thin ice	53	3.98	48. Out of order	53	3.66
24. Bus stop	54	3.98	49. No smoking	53	3.66
25. No passing	52	3.98	50. Go slow	52	3.65

Source. From "Validation of a Survival Vocabulary List" by E. A. Polloway and C. H. Polloway, March 1981, *Academic Therapy, 16,* p. 447. Copyright 1981 by Academic Therapy Publication. Reprinted by permission.

students' life-styles and the community.

A second goal, reading for information and instruction, is realistic for many students who are mildly and moderately handicapped. Implied in this goal is functional reading that allows the individual to deal with job applications, newspaper advertisements, job instruction manuals, telephone books, and countless other sources of information and assistance. The third goal is reading for pleasure. For some adolescents with disabilities this may also be a realistic goal and should be the long-range objective of teachers working with all children.

READING IN THE CURRICULUM

The importance of reading within the curriculum of virtually all students who are mildly and moderately handicapped is universally accepted. The reading class must be a significant part of the school day, and teachers should seek ways to integrate reading instruction into other areas of the curriculum. Given the frequency of significant reading difficulties among these students, additional practice to maintain and refine basic skills is warranted. In addition such opportunities provide a place for students to generalize their reading ability. Thus, adolescents can improve their comprehension skills while acquiring basic vocational competencies from trade books; younger students can practice word recognition skills while learning basic science concepts.

This chapter examines the assessment and instruction of reading skills. The approaches discussed here provide a sound foundation for a reading program. Specific topics include assessment of reading skills, programs and approaches to teaching reading, implementation of a reading program, and reading activities and resources.

ASSESSMENT

Reading consists of many essential subskills. The teacher must understand these skills and know how to determine which skills each student does or does not possess. It is also important for the teacher to determine each student's specific reading level before implementing any skills program. Reading instruction will fail if the material is too difficult. Thus, the primary purpose of reading assessment is instructional planning.

Reading Competencies

Assessing a student's reading according to the sequential development of specific skills is complicated by the diverse order in which various individuals acquire these skills. A number of reading competencies can be identified, and Table 10.3 provides a general guide for teachers to use in organizing systematic instruction. However, two important points must be noted: (1) many reading-readiness skills and competencies are not listed, because they can be extrapolated from the discussion of language development in chapter 9; and (2) many of the competencies listed develop simultaneously in

children, such as the ability to verbalize sounds, blend sounds, and recognize high-frequency sight vocabulary words.

Two types of assessment instruments—informal and formal—can assist the teacher in determining an individual's level of reading competency. Instruments of both types can be designed to determine an approximate grade-level equivalent for reading and to analyze specific skill strengths and weaknesses. In general, most reading-assessment devices derive reading levels using similar criteria and comparisons to norm groups or graded materials. Likewise, most tests assess skill deficits similarly; the major differences are in precision and specificity.

Informal Assessment

Informal Reading Inventories Informal reading inventories (IRIs) are a common informal instrument to assess reading skills. Several IRIs, most notably those developed by Ekwall (1986) and Silvaroli (1986), are commercially available. Most IRIs contain four parts: a word-recognition inventory, oral reading passages, silent reading passages, and comprehension questions to accompany the passages.

Word-recognition inventories are lists compiled from the vocabularies used in instructional materials. The student receives the master copy, and responses are checked on the teacher's score sheet. Administration of the test continues with increasingly more difficult word lists until the student misses 25% of the words. The number of words per grade list usually ranges from 20 to 30.

Three classifications of reading ability can be determined from these inventories. The independent reading level refers to vocabulary that a student can read without teacher assistance, identifying approximately 95% of the words correctly. Library books and seat work instructions should be

TABLE 10.3
Reading competencies

Word-Analysis Competencies

1. Recognizes upper- and lowercase letters of alphabet
2. Verbalizes phonetic sounds when shown graphic symbols:
   a. Consonant sounds
   b. Short vowel sounds
   c. Long vowel sounds
   d. Consonant blends (e.g., *st, spr, nk, nd*)
   e. Consonant digraphs (e.g., *ch, th*)
   f. Regular vowel combinations (e.g., *ee, ay*)
   g. *R*-controlled vowel combinations (e.g., *er, ar, ir*)
   h. Hard and soft sounds of *g* and *c*
   i. Vowel diphthongs (e.g., *oy, oi*)
3. Blends sounds to form words
4. Recognizes common, irregular words on sight (e.g., *was, to, come*)
5. Can rhyme words
6. Recognizes words through context clues
7. Makes use of structural analysis for identification
   a. Compound words
   b. Common word endings—noun, verb, and adjective forms
   c. Common prefixes (e.g., *un-, re-, dis-*)
   d. Common suffixes (e.g., *-ly, -ful, -less*)
   e. Syllables within a word

Comprehension Competencies

1. Recalls main idea of written material
2. Recalls sequence of events and/or ideas
3. Locates and/or recalls answers to detail questions from written material
4. Follows written directions
5. Follows simple cause-and-effect relationships
6. Makes inferences based on materials read
7. Recognizes absurdities
8. Recognizes factual versus fictional material
9. Uses book's table of contents and index
10. Uses charts, graphs, and maps
11. Applies multiple meanings to words

at the student's independent level. The instructional reading level refers to vocabulary that the student can read with some outside assistance. Students should be 85% to 95% accurate at this level. The frustration reading level is that at which the student cannot read with any degree of independence, accurately identifying fewer than 80% of the words. The material at this level is too difficult.

Listening level can also be obtained, indicating to the teacher the level at which a

student can comprehend material that is read aloud by someone else. Thus, this section of the IRI gives the teacher a basis for deciding the level at which instruction and comprehension testing should begin. An analysis of errors can give added information on specific word-attack deficits; for this reason mispronounced words should be recorded phonetically. The errors can be classified in common areas, such as incorrect sounds, full reversals, partial reversals, or incorrect beginning, medial, or final consonants.

The oral reading inventory samples a student's oral reading and comprehension capabilities at various levels. The format, administrative procedures, and scoring practices may vary. However, it may be advantageous to record the student's reading so that the teacher can listen critically and analyze errors later. As with the word-recognition inventory, three levels of reading proficiency can be determined, as well as a listening level for instructional purposes.

IRIs can also assess silent reading. Achievement and skill deficits in reading rate and comprehension can be determined by students' responses to comprehension questions.

Reading Classroom Inventory The commercially prepared Classroom Reading Inventory (CRI) (Silvaroli, 1986) is a diagnostic tool designed for teachers who have had no prior experience with informal reading inventories. It assesses silent and oral reading, listening, and sight-word knowledge. Comprehension is measured by a total of five factual, inferential, and vocabulary questions that follow the oral or silent reading of graded paragraphs. Forms A and B are used to assess elementary school students' word recognition and comprehension skills. Forms C and D differ in that they include high interest stories for students of high school age or low-functioning adults.

Inventory of Elementary Reading Skills The informal Inventory of Elementary Reading Skills (IERS) (Pope, 1970) is another alternative that provides information on primary reading skills. It measures phonetic analysis and can guide those teaching basic reading skills. Parts of the IERS can be given to a group and used in conjunction with an IRI. The IERS assesses varied skills.

1. *Auditory recognition of initial consonants.* The student listens to a word pronounced by the teacher, then writes the sound heard at the beginning of the word. If 10 sounds are missed, the student is asked to repeat each sound to see whether it was heard correctly.

2. *Auditory recognition of final consonants.* The same procedure is followed as in the initial consonant section. The main sounds to assess are *d, g, s, m, f, z, c* or *k, l, n, t, b,* and *p*.

3. *Visual recognition of consonants.* The consonants are printed on individual cards that are presented to the student with instructions to give the letter sound orally.

4. *Visual recognition of short vowel sounds.* Three-letter words (consonant-vowel-consonant) are printed on cards, and each vowel sound is used twice. Sample words include *pad, jam, pet, Jim, mop*.

5. *Auditory recognition of consonant blends and digraphs.* This follows the same procedure as the auditory recognition of initial consonants. Sounds include *sm, dr, th, gr, pl,* and *gl*.

6. *Visual recognition of consonant blends and digraphs.* This section follows the same procedure as visual recognition of consonants.

7. *Reading knowledge of vowel combinations, including vowels followed by r.* This follows the procedure used in short vowel sounds. Words with vowel combinations such as *oa, aw, ee, ea, oi,* and *oo* are used.

Observation and Checklists Checklists developed from a summary of reading competencies are also an effective informal diagnostic procedure. The teacher selects a particular area to assess and, during a classroom lesson, observes and records a student's skills on the checklist. To observe comprehension skills during a small group reading lesson, the teacher might ask questions of the types noted on the chart in Figure 10.1.

Intervention Assessment   Intervention assessment (Paratore & Indrisano, 1987) is a procedure for measuring a student's reading comprehension, first with traditional questions and answers after the student has independently read a selection and then again after the student has been taught some intervention strategies. The purpose of this approach is to assist the teacher in selecting strategies to improve the student's comprehension. This model of assessment is designed specifically for readers who are disabled; it is based on research emphasizing the importance of the knowledge that the reader brings to the printed page (Garner, 1987).

A process approach to reading comprehension assessment, intervention assessment attempts to answer the following questions:

1. Does the student have relevant prior knowledge?
2. Does the student use that knowledge to make logical predictions about the selection?
3. Is the student able to set purposes for reading by formulating appropriate questions in preparation for reading?
4. When prior knowledge related to specific content is lacking, is the student able to use knowledge about the ways authors

organize information to make logical predictions about passage content?

Specific intervention strategies are described by the model's authors. The results obtained after these strategies are taught indicate to the teacher the instructional procedures that are most helpful to the student.

Formal Instruments

Formal tests are recommended for teachers who need specific guidelines or tools for screening and other administrative purposes, such as eligibility. The instruments discussed in this chapter provide teachers with grade-level information as well as assessment data on specific skills. However, teachers must realize that a grade-level score of 4.2 on a formal test may be misleading; it does not necessarily mean that the student should be placed in a fourth-grade reading program. No formal test can guarantee a student's exact reading level, because publishers use different methods to determine reading levels. Nevertheless the score does supply a starting point. Students should start with material $\frac{1}{2}$ year below the tested reading level. If problems become apparent, the teacher can modify materials until the proper level of difficulty is determined.

Formal instruments can be used to analyze skills much as the informal inventories were used. If word lists or paragraphs are read orally by a student, the teacher phonetically records the errors at the time of the

Student names	Main idea	Factual	Inferential	Cause and effect	Comments
Martha	X	X			
Raul		X			
Lucinda	X	X	X		
Harry		X			

FIGURE 10.1
Checklist of comprehension skills

reading or later from a tape recording. Once categorized, the errors provide a picture of the student's needs.

The purposes of formal instruments form a continuum ranging from a survey of global reading performances to a pinpointing of specific strengths and weaknesses. Global tests are frequently used as pre- and postmeasures to assess reading improvement. They also have been used to determine class placement. Diagnostic tests are used primarily to identify specific problems and to highlight skills needing remediation.

Global Tests

☐ Metropolitan Achievement Test (Durost, Bixler, Wrightstone, Prescott, & Balow, 1978) is a group test available in various levels and forms, thus facilitating its use as a pre- and postmeasure. It is designed for use at the end of kindergarten or the beginning of first grade, to measure skills needed for success in first grade. Applicable subtests cover word meaning, listening, matching, and alphabet. The primary-one level is designed for Grades 1.5 through 2.4, primary-two for 2.5 through 3.4, and elementary for 3.5 through 9.9. Each is available in three forms. Reading subtests include word knowledge, word analysis, reading sentences, and reading stories.

☐ The Wide Range Achievement Test (WRAT) (Jastak & Jastak, 1965, 1978) is an individual achievement test that covers arithmetic, spelling, and reading. The student's test performance determines a grade level, standard score, and percentile rank. The test has two levels: Level 1 is designed for ages 5 to 12 years and Level 2 for 12 years to adulthood. The reading subtest measures word recognition and can be given in approximately 10 to 15 min-

utes. It is composed of a group of words that the student reads orally. Words pronounced incorrectly are marked phonetically to aid in determining the need for remedial instruction. Because the WRAT assesses only word recognition, no judgments can be made about total reading ability.

☐ The Peabody Individualized Achievement Test (PIAT) (Dunn & Markwardt, 1970) tests mathematics, reading recognition, reading comprehension, spelling, and general knowledge. The reading-recognition subtest measures word-attack skills. As with the WRAT, errors can be analyzed to determine skills that need to be taught. The comprehension subtest presents paragraphs to be read silently, after which the student is shown four pictures and is instructed to pick the one that best fits the paragraph. The PIAT yields grade and age equivalents, percentiles, and a standard score.

☐ The Slossan Oral Reading Test (SORT) (Slosson, 1975) is an individualized test of a student's reading level using lists of sight words. Word lists progress in difficulty from primer to high school levels, and the test can be repeated to measure the student's achievement annually. It consists of one page of word lists and is easy to administer and score. Results must be used with caution, because the total assessment is derived from isolated sight words.

Diagnostic Tests

☐ The Gray Oral Reading Test—Revised (Wiederholt & Bryant, 1986) measures oral reading fluency and diagnoses oral reading problems. The test is available in two forms; each contains 13 reading passages ranging in difficulty from pre-primer to college. Each passage is accompanied by questions that orally measure literal comprehension. Error analysis gives performance levels for meaning similarity, function similarity, and graphic/phonemic similarity.

☐ The Woodcock Reading Mastery Test: Revised (Woodcock, 1986) is appropriate for students from Grades 1 through 12. It is an individual test that measures reading achievement as well as specific diagnostic information. The test is available in two forms with subtests for letter and word identification, word attack, word comprehension, and passage comprehension. The test takes approximately 30 minutes to administer.

☐ The Gates-McKillop Reading Diagnostic Test (Gates & McKillop, 1962) is an individual reading test designed for students reading at second- through seventh-grade levels. It provides an extensive evaluation of reading skills with subtests covering oral reading; word and phrase recognition; recognition of word parts; letter sounds and names; initial, final, and vowel sounds; auditory blending; spelling; and other specific reading skills. The test requires approximately 1 hour to administer if all subtests are used. The test has two forms, and each subtest has its own norms. Thus, the test can be administered in toto or in any combination.

☐ The Durrell Analysis of Reading Difficulty (Durrell & Catterson, 1980) can measure an individual's reading level as well as give diagnostic information on oral and silent reading, word recognition and analysis, listening comprehension, and several other skill areas. It is appropriate for nonreaders as well as for those reading up to an eighth-grade reading level. Twelve subtests are included in the Durrell, which takes 30 to 60 minutes to administer, depending on how many of the subtests are used.

Criterion-Referenced Tests Criterion-referenced tests measure specific mastery of individual skills. They do not assess a student's performance in relation to a standardized sample but focus on the ability to perform the specific skill stated in the accompanying behavioral objective. An example of such a test is the Brigance Diagnostic Inventory of Basic Skills (Brigance, 1983). The Brigance is available for students at three levels: preschool, kindergarten through 6th grade, and 4th through 12th grades. It assesses basic readiness and academic skills in key subjects, including reading, language arts, and mathematics. Specific areas measured in the reading section are word recognition, comprehension, word analysis, and vocabulary. Information obtained from this test indicates a student's specific skills and deficits. The Inventory of Essential Skills is a section for Grades 4 through 12 that assesses minimal competencies and skills commonly identified as necessary for successful life experiences. It is especially useful in assessing students with handicaps.

Use of Assessment Data

Efficient assessment should begin with survey tests that identify major areas of difficulty. Diagnostic tests then pinpoint specific strengths and weaknesses, which are described as precise tasks through informal tests and task analysis (Polloway & Smith, 1982). Goals and objectives for IEPs are derived from this test information. Teachers then prepare instructional lessons to teach the specific skills indicated by the diagnosis, using teaching approaches that capitalize on students' strengths. The teachers evaluate the lessons when they are completed and try alternative methods if necessary.

Assessment should always be considered a continuous process, and the initial appraisal process should take no more than 2 weeks. Students do not learn to read through assessment and appraisal but through good, sound teaching practices. Teachers should remember that the best evaluation is ineffective if the findings are not used in planning the instructional program, if the evaluation process becomes so complicated and tedious that it leaves no room for instruction, or if the evaluation process itself becomes a substitute for ac-tual teaching and learning.

Information from diagnosis is used to individualize reading instruction. Tailoring reading lessons to meet each student's needs may appear to be an overwhelming task to the teacher unfamiliar with management systems. However, efficient, yet simple record-keeping procedures like those in Figures 10.2 and 10.3 can lead to success. Fig-

FIGURE 10.2
Reading diagnosis form for an individual student

Student's name: _____ Age: _____
Class placement: _____ Teacher: _____

Key: N = Not acquired   P = Needs practice   M = Mastered

Reading levels: Independent _____   Tests used: IRI _____
                Instructional _____   Survey _____
                Frustration _____   Diagnostic _____
                                                Other _____

Sight word vocabulary: SORT _____   Dolch list _____   Other _____

Phonics:
  Consonants

b	c	d	f	g	h	j	k	l	m	n	p	q	r	s	t	v	w	x	y	z

Vowels:

	a	e	i	o	u	y
Long sound						
Short sound						

Digraphs

ch	sh	th	wh

Variant vowels

ar	er	ir	or	ur	au	al	on	ow	oi	oy

Blends

bl	cl	fl	gl	pl	sl	br	cr	dr	fr	gr	pr	tr	wn	ap	st

Comprehension: Factual questions _____   Main idea _____
                Inferential questions _____   Sequence of events _____
                Application questions _____   Cause and effect _____

Reading interests: _____
Comments: _____
_____

FIGURE 10.3
Class profile of
phonics skills

Skills		Students								
		Lyndsay P.	Karen C.	Mike E.	Sharon G.	Jason T.	Marcus W.	Tony S.	Alison B.	
Reading levels	Independent									
	Instructional									
Consonants	Initial consonants									
	Final consonants									
	Consonant blends									
Vowels	Long sound									
	Short sound									
	Variant									
	Prefixes									
	Suffixes									
Comments:										

Key: N = Not acquired
         P = Needs practice
         M = Mastered

ure 10.2 represents an analysis of student's strengths and weaknesses in various reading areas; Figure 10.3 is a sample class profile of phonics skills in a format that is appropriate for other reading skill areas as well. Figure 10.4 presents some specific questions that teachers can then use to translate diagnostic information into individualized teaching plans.

Once information about each student is organized and easily accessible, a teacher can individualize group instruction. Within a reading group, for example, a few students might be assigned a literal-level purpose in reading a selection whereas other students might be required to make inferences. The group can discuss the story together with teacher guidance.

1. What are the student's specific strengths?
   a. What specific phonic knowledge is mastered: letter names? letter sounds? blending?
   b. What specific knowledge of structural analysis is mastered: plural endings? prefixes? suffixes? compound words?
   c. What sight word categories are mastered: Dolch list? content area words?
   d. What specific comprehension skills are mastered: vocabulary? getting the main idea? summarizing? making inferences? recognizing cause and effect?
   e. Does student comprehend best when reading orally or silently?
   f. What is the student's reading level?
2. What skills are priority concerns (based on the school's curriculum guide, skills checklist, or a basal reader's scope and sequence chart)?
3. What is the next needed skill in each area that can be taught to the student at this time?
4. What is the student's attitude toward reading and reading instruction?
5. What organizational arrangement that is possible for this classroom setting best meets the needs of the student? (Can the student fit into a small group of students in need of instruction on word endings? Does the whole class need instruction in making inferences? Can the student's sight word knowledge be developed by using the computer program designed for that purpose?)
6. What reading program is most appropriate for the student?
7. What independent practice and reinforcement activities can the student engage in successfully (e.g., follow-up worksheets, computer program use, group projects, learning center activities, silent reading and reporting, creative activities like illustrating, dramatizing, constructing, manipulating materials?
8. What serves as a reinforcer for the student (e.g., progress checklists, gold stars for daily progress, frequent verbal praise, grades, progress notes sent home to parents)?

FIGURE 10.4
Diagnostic considerations in instructional planning in reading

TEACHING READING SKILLS

Direct Instruction

In general, students with reading disabilities require precise, direct instruction to facilitate acquisition of reading skills. The directive teacher specifically teaches the target skill. Direct instruction can be provided by modeling, demonstration, and explanation. Practice and reinforcement activities in workbooks, games, and other independent activities are introduced after the word or strategy has been directly taught and the student has learned it. Follow-up tasks provide maintenance activities for mastery and retention but not actual instruction for skill acquisition. Two direct teaching strategies appropriate for reading instruction are described here.

Merlin and Rogers (1981) suggest four steps in direct teaching (pp. 292–297).

1. Identify and set specific objectives.

2. Direct the student's attention to what is to be learned: "Today you will learn. . . ."

3. Engage in direct teaching by modeling the process: (a) show the student the process, (b) demonstrate how the student will perform the skill, (c) ask the student to imitate what you do, (d) provide op-

portunities for frequent response and reinforcement, and (e) reduce the cues as the student responds correctly.

4. Provide opportunities for practice, application, and generalization. For example, (a) ask students a question about the main idea of a story, then demonstrate that the reasons for the answers are actually the supporting details; (b) highlight paragraphs in which the main idea is the first or last sentence, pointing out that this is frequently the way paragraphs are designed; and (c) give students continued and varied opportunities to apply this skill in other classroom work by asking them to select major details in a content-area selection.

Direct teaching requires opportunities for student response and manipulation of the item or strategy to be learned. McNinch (1981) developed the following strategy, which includes demonstration, interaction, clarification, application, and practice applied to teaching sight words.

1. Select a word for students to learn that has meaning and usefulness to them. Present the word orally in context, making certain that they learn or know the word's meaning and use.

2. Write the word on the board (or on cards) in a sentence in which all other words are recognizable. Read the sentence to the students, emphasizing and highlighting the new word (e.g., tracing for configuration, underlining, or using different colors).

3. Write the word in isolation on the board. Ask questions such as, Which is its first letter? What does it mean? Which are its tall letters?

4. Present the word in simple sentences for students to read aloud. Learning and retention require a minimum of two sentences read with 100% accuracy.

5. Have students read the word silently in context and answer related questions requiring them to use the new word.

6. Continue practice activities that use the new word, and give the student opportunities for application and generalization.

Steps 1 through 5 are quickly paced, emphasizing and reinforcing success. Activities for the final step may be selected from commercial workbooks and other available materials.

The most complete book written on the direct teaching of reading is *Direct Instruction Reading* (Carnine & Silbert, 1979). Teachers interested in learning more about this topic should study this text. Without question, the two best-selling and most comprehensive commercial reading series advocating the direct teaching of reading are DISTAR and SRA Corrective Reading, which are discussed later in the chapter.

Sight Word Vocabulary

For learners who are handicapped, reading usually begins with learning sight words. Through a whole-word approach students learn to recognize words without analysis and must then receive decoding instruction. The teacher can use acquired sight words to introduce and teach decoding skills. Students must achieve automaticity with the sight words they have learned—they must recognize them immediately and automatically—to allow for continuous movement through a written passage (Polloway & Smith, 1982). Fluent readers use their sight vocabulary consistently, applying phonetic analysis only to new words or names.

To be remembered, sight words must already be in the learner's speaking and comprehension vocabulary. Sight words can be selected from a variety of sources. Language experience stories include words important to the student and are therefore an excellent source of initial words. Survival words, such as *exit* and *poison,* are also important. If a basal series is used, then words from the particular program become a focus of sight word instruction.

With all students, but especially with those experiencing reading difficulty, a variety of strategies must be used to teach sight words. Recent attention has been focused on the imagery level of the word to be learned (Hargis, 1982). Imagery level refers to the ease with which a word evokes a concrete picture. High-imagery words include *ear, house,* and *bird* in contrast to low-imagery words such as *democracy, idea, believe,* and *have.* High imagery immediately increases the speed at which students who are non-handicapped or handicapped can learn. In some instances, high imagery can be provided for a word by the context in which it is presented. For example, the word *see* in "I see a big lion" becomes more concrete and memorable. A rich experiential background enhances a student's wealth of high-imagery words, including traffic signs, restaurant names, store names, and names of tools, cars, and flowers.

Students with handicaps require many repetitions to learn a sight word. Hargis (1982) has adapted the estimates of Goates (1931) to arrive at the number of repetitions necessary for students according to their IQ levels. Those estimations appear in Table 10.4.

A reading selection should present a minimum number of new words to a student. Because basal series and high-interest, low-readability books introduce new words at a higher frequency rate and with fewer repetitions, teachers must provide activities that increase the number of repetitions. Sight word diagnosis, then, must document the words known as well as those unknown. The teacher should be using the words students can read, no matter how few, to teach new words (Hargis, 1982). This process is difficult when a student has learned only five words, but using these as the contextual setting for high-imagery words and providing numerous repetitions will enable students to steadily increase their vocabulary. A variety of strategies are appropriate to teach sight words.

Fernald Method (Fernald, 1943) The Fernald method is a multisensory remedial approach combining language experience with visual, kinesthetic, and tactile (VAKT) instructional techniques. The program consists of four basic steps: eliciting a word from the student; writing it large enough for the student to trace; saying the sound as the student traces the word; and having the student write the word from memory. Words learned by this procedure can then be alphabetically filed in a word bank. When several words have been learned, the student uses them to dictate a story to the teacher. As the student progresses, the procedure can be modified in various ways. Tracing can be done with letters made of sandpaper, smooth paper laid on sandpaper, or sand sprinkled on glue. Modifications of the Fernald technique are frequently necessary for disabled readers. Variations suggested by Miccinati (1979) include adding the haptic dimension by writing the word on the student's back while saying it.

Word Banks Words to be learned through this strategy are written on index cards and placed in each student's "bank," a box decorated for that purpose. Students prepare cards for their bank by writing the word,

TABLE 10.4
Mean number of word repetitions required by varying IQ levels

Repetitions	IQ Range
20	120–129
30	110–119
35	90–109
40	80–89
45	70–79
55	60–69

Source: From "Word Recognition Development" by C. H. Hargis, 1982, *Focus on Exceptional Children, 14,* p. 3. Copyright 1982 by Love Publishing Company. Reprinted by permission.

drawing the picture, and dictating a sentence for the teacher to write.

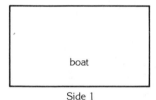

Side 1

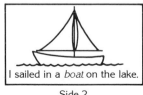

Side 2

These cards are continuously used to practice the words, but they also need to be used in context, because repeated practice of words in isolation is the least efficient method of learning sight words. Strategies for repeated use of the words in context are described in the activities section of this chapter. Collecting words in a bank gives students a sense of ownership that may motivate them. It also makes the words easily available for informal practice and reference.

Errorless Discrimination The errorless discrimination strategy is especially appro-

priate for students with moderate/severe handicaps and others who have failed to learn by conventional methods. In this approach the teacher presents the word in isolation, reads it aloud, and says, "Point to the word _____." In the four to six trials that follow, the target word appears among three or four other words. At first the words differ significantly from the target word but converge in appearance as the exercise continues. After the students begin pointing to the word with 100% accuracy, the teacher directs them to "read this word" (Walsh & Lamberts, 1979).

Paired Associates This strategy pairs the word to be learned and a picture depicting its meaning. The picture is gradually faded out, and the student learns to transfer the meaning from the picture to the written word, focusing on specific characteristics of the target word as the picture is faded out (Dorry & Zeaman, 1975; Polloway & Smith, 1982).

Word Imprinting Word imprinting, like the Fernald method, is a multisensory approach. Students learn sight words in six steps, using tactile and kinesthetic reinforcement (Carbo, 1978).

1. The teacher says the word; the student repeats it.
2. The meaning of the word is discussed and taught.
3. The word's configuration is drawn.
4. The actual word is traced.
5. The student says the word while tracing it.
6. With eyes closed the student tries to visualize the word and write it in the air.

This procedure is repeated daily; words can be taped for continued practice at home or independent practice at school. The availability of the words on tape gives students a sense of control over their own learning while providing an opportunity for repetition and drill.

Functional Reading

A sight word approach is recommended for initiating functional reading, a level of literacy necessary for information and protection. An understanding of this concept is particularly important for teachers of high school-age students who must decide how to teach reading.

The case of Mario is not unusual. Mario is 14 years old. His WISC-R score is 65; for the past 4 years he has been placed in an EMR self-contained class. Previous teachers have attempted to teach Mario to read, using a variety of strategies and programs. In spite of these efforts, Mario's reading level is only Grade 2. He has lost interest in learning to read and plans to drop out of school in 18 months, on his 16th birthday. Which reading program should the current teacher select? Is it best in the limited time remaining to teach him functional reading so that he will know some words for his own protection and safety? Or is there still time to teach him decoding strategies, aiming toward an acceptable level of literacy?

Teachers of adolescent students continually encounter this dilemma. Choosing the most appropriate approach for each student must depend on a number of critical factors.

1. the student's attitude, energy, and motivation for learning to read
2. the teacher's assessment of the previously used instructional approaches
3. diagnostic information related to causes of an inability to read
4. the teacher's knowledge of strategies essential to reading progress for the student
5. identifying the type of program that will provide a successful experience for the student

After weighing these factors, the teacher can decide to concentrate efforts on functional reading, exert a final effort toward teaching remedial skills, or focus primarily on one option but include the other in a less intensive form. This decision is most effective if made in conjunction with high school-aged students. They need to understand clearly what the goal is and how it will be measured at specific intervals. When goals are organized into small steps, adolescent students are motivated by their progress, which suggests that the problem they have faced unsuccessfully throughout their school careers may have a solution.

Reading for protection requires minimal but practical competence. Generally, this is the level of reading achievement that enables survival in today's word-dependent world. Survival words should be taught as sight words, using the strategies described earlier. Comprehension of these words must also be specifically taught. The teacher may need to provide an actual experience that demonstrates the word's meaning, produce a concrete object, or identify a special characteristic of the concept.

Vocational Application of Functional Reading With few exceptions students with mild handicaps learn to read beyond the level of survival words. The next stage of functional reading addresses what the world of work requires and thus focuses on sufficient skill to fill out applications and related forms, pass a driver's test, follow simple factory check-in directions, order from a restaurant menu, and handle other similar life tasks.

Teachers can use a combination of strategies to teach this level of functional reading. Using the whole-word approach, the specific vocabulary of applications and forms can be taught, and then decoding clues can be introduced. The most important step is teaching students to generalize this knowledge by providing practice with a variety of formats and situations they are likely to encounter. Many workbooks contain samples of forms and applications.

Word Analysis Skills

Phonetic analysis teaches a student to "attack" an unfamiliar word. Although it does not teach the total range of reading skills, it does teach the essential skills of decoding. In addition, pictorial, contextual, and syntactic clues can help decode unknown words, as can configurational and structural analysis. Children can use all of these methods to unlock new words at one time or another, and beginning readers use this variety of strategies most frequently.

In phonics, students are taught the sounds for consonants and vowels and the ways to blend these sounds. Key words are usually presented to reinforce the memory of each letter sound; for instance, *sun* suggests the *s* sound. Phonics instruction is divided into two basic, complementary methods. The synthetic method teaches letter sounds and blends and then progresses to words, such as *c-a-t → cat*. The analytic method begins with the teacher dictating words to students, who then break the words into their component sounds: *cat → c-a-t*.

Phonetic analysis can be used with students at all educational levels, although it is most appropriate in elementary school. It can be used with young students just beginning to learn to read as an initial step in a developmental program, or it can be used as a remedial technique with students who have developed a strong sight vocabulary but lack the skills needed to analyze unfamiliar words. It can be adapted for learners being taught with a basal series or with a language-experience approach using simple drills and games to reinforce basic rules. In each case the teacher's goal is to produce fluent readers with the necessary skills to decode unknown words. Once decoded, the word should become part of the students' sight word vocabularies so that they can be read without analysis when next encountered.

Prerequisites for learning phonics include skill in auditory and visual discrimination. Students must be able to recognize the difference in the sounds that begin words such as *tent* and *boat* and the difference in the configuration of the letters. Students must also recognize that the sounds that begin *tent* and *toe* sound and look alike. In addition, a sight vocabulary of 25 to 50 words is recommended before phonetic instruction begins.

The sequence for teaching phonetic and structural analysis that is described here is adapted from Orton (1964).

1. *b, s, f, m, t* in initial and final positions
2. short *a*
3. all consonants except the five already learned
4. short *o, i*
5. digraphs (*sh, ch, th, wh*)
6. initial consonant blends (*bl, br, st*)
7. short *u*
8. final consonant blends (*nd, nk*)
9. short *e*
10. long vowels (final *e,* double vowels)
11. syllabication
12. *r*-influenced vowels (*er, ir, ur, ar*)
13. suffixes (*-s, -ing, -ed*)
14. vowel teams (*ai, ea, ow, ea*)
15. diphthongs (*oy, au*)
16. prefixes (*re-, pre-, un-*)

This sequence introduces five consonants, then short *a*. It allows the formation of short words quickly (e.g., *bat, fat, tab*) to provide immediate decoding experience. Carnine and Silbert (1979) suggest a similar sequence for sound/symbol introduction (p. 76).

a m t s i f d r o g l h u c b n T L M F
k v e p D I N A R H G B w j y x q z J E Q

Teaching Phonics The strategy for teaching phonics that is presented here is based on six steps identified by Kaluger and Kolson (1969). It begins with known sight words, using these as a basis for introducing key phonetic generalizations. The six steps included in this approach are to introduce, identify, visually cue, synthesize, reinforce, and review.

1. Introduce
   a. Write the letter *t* on the chalkboard.
   b. Explain that the object of the lesson is to learn the sound of the consonant *t*.
   c. Write on the chalkboard three or four words beginning with *t* that are in the students' sight vocabulary (e.g., *take, tent, toe*).
   d. Read the words aloud, emphasizing *t*.
   e. Ask students for additional words that begin with the same sound.
   f. Write these in another list on the chalkboard, underlining the letter *t*.
2. Identify
   a. Instruct students to look at all the words on the chalkboard and identify how they are alike.
   b. Ask a student to say the sound of the letter *t* as heard in the word *tent*.
   c. Read the list of words again, pointing to the *t* in each one, saying its sound, and reading the word.
3. Visually cue
   a. Give each student a 3-inch square tagboard card.
   b. Instruct students to draw a picture of a tent and write the letter *t* on the card, just like the one drawn on the chalkboard.
4. Synthesize
   a. Introduce activities requiring students to use and manipulate the phonic generalization just learned. (In the initial stages of learning, when only two or three letters are known, it is difficult to design these activities, but once four or five consonants and a vowel are learned, the possibilities are numerous.)
5. Reinforce
   a. Assign and supervise practice activities.
   b. Dictate words and syllables that use the newly learned letters and have students write them.
6. Review
   a. Remind students that this letter has the sound of the *t* in *tent*.
   b. Ask students for additional words that begin with *t*.

Writing from dictation and using cue cards are major components of this instructional sequence; both actively involve students in the learning process. All six steps apply to the teaching of consonant sounds and vowel generalizations, as well as to structural analysis.

Structural analysis skills enable students to use larger segments of words for decoding cues. Recognition of root words, compound words, prefixes, suffixes, contractions, and plurals allows students to use clusters of letters to assist in reading a new word. Structural analysis is an essential word-recognition strategy that directly influences reading fluency; continued letter-by-letter phonetic analysis slows the reading process and often inhibits comprehension (Robech & Wilson, 1974). The strategies suggested for teaching phonics also apply to teaching structural analysis.

Guidelines for Word Analysis Instruction

1. Be certain that students have the necessary skills for reading before beginning phonics training. Primary skills include oral language development, visual and auditory discrimination, and memory.
2. Emphasize blending sounds when initiating the phonics program.
3. Before teaching students who have had school experience, diagnose specific needs.

4. If lessons are scheduled separately from actual reading, provide an opportunity for students to apply newly learned skills to actual reading material.

5. Teach phonics skills from a base of sight words so that students recognize generalizations in application instead of memorizing isolated rules.

6. Sounds should generally be taught in word contexts and not in isolation. However, some students may fail to learn sounds when presented in words and must be taught them in relative isolation.

7. Phonics should be taught as only one part of the total reading program.

8. Use directive teaching for phonics instruction. Worksheets should be used only for follow-up reinforcement.

9. Provide a variety of reinforcement activities so that students overlearn specific skills.

10. First, teach grapheme/phoneme correspondence and phonetic generalizations that follow the rules. Teach exceptions only after students have learned and can apply these generalizations.

11. Instruct students to use context plus the initial consonant as the first strategy for attacking an unknown word.

12. Teach students a series of sequential steps for decoding an unknown word (Spache & Spache, 1973).

    a. Look at the sound of the initial consonant.

    b. Does a word that begins with that sound also fit this context?

    c. According to the placement of the vowel, does it have a long or short sound?

    d. Is there a silent vowel or consonant?

    e. Say the word and read the remainder of the sentence. Does it fit? If not, try it with the opposite vowel sound (long or short).

    f. If the word still is not decoded, ask for assistance.

Teacher's guides accompanying basal reading series also include instructions and a sequence for teaching phonics and structural analysis. In addition, a selection of programs specifically designed to teach word analysis skills is available.

Word Analysis Instructional Programs

☐ The phonovisual method (Schoolfield & Timberlake, 1974) is an organized system of instruction based on phonetically arranged pictorial charts. The program teaches initial consonants, final consonants, vowels, and blends and uses workbooks, word lists, and games to supplement the program. Phonovisual can be used as a developmental program for beginning readers as well as a remedial program for older students. Because it is intended to be taught daily as a separate subject, the crucial consideration for its effectiveness lies in the teacher's ability to ensure transfer to other reading instruction. The program can be used successfully with students identified as learning disabled or mildly retarded.

☐ The Glass analysis for decoding (Glass & Glass, 1978) is a technique to teach letter clusters; it uses packs of cards organized into 119 clusters, ranging from the most common to the most difficult. Students learn a sound cluster and, through a rapid series of steps, add letters that change and extend the cluster. They are taught both to see and hear sounds as letter clusters in whole words. This is a unique technique that can also motivate adolescent students still in need of phonics practice and is particularly recommended for students with learning disabilities.

☐ The Cove school reading program (Rogan, Dadouche, & Wennberg, 1980) is designed especially for primary aged children experiencing problems in learning to read. It consists of five workbooks that a teacher uses for phonics instruction. Large lettering, repetition, frequent review, and manipulative practice activities characterize the program.

☐ The syllabication method was developed to teach advanced structural analysis skills to disabled readers while minimizing their need to learn the many complex rules and exceptions of the English language. Two syllabication rules form the basis for a systematic approach to analyzing polysyllabic words. Using this program, students learn to recognize and count syllables, to apply the two rules to words with two or more syllables, to use context clues, and to rely on vocabulary to correct any distortions in pronunciations. Without a multitude of rules to memorize, students can learn to read larger words using the generalizations learned previously.

The first rule, dividing syllables between two consonants, can be illustrated by the word *rabbit.* Instruction would emphasize that *rabbit* should have two syllables (two sounded vowels), should be divided between *b* and *b* (two consonants together), and then read as two small words and blended. The word *between,* an exception to this rule, would first be pronounced *between* and then read correctly after the student notes the distortion.

The second rule, dividing syllables between a vowel and a consonant, can be illustrated by the word *favor.* Division would fall between *a* and *v* (because of the vowel-consonant-vowel combination), and the word would be read and blended. These two rules can extend to words with more syllables (e.g., *discussion* and *tomato,* respectively) and with both combinations present (e.g., *envelope, remainder*). Polloway and Polloway (1978) discuss the full 11-step program, which can provide

a method of improving word-attack skills for students who have reached approximately third- or fourth-grade reading levels.

☐ The phonic remedial reading lessons, developed by Kirk and his colleagues (Kird, Kirk, & Minskoff, 1986), are a revision of the remedial reading drills (Hegge, Kirk, & Kirk, 1955) originally published more than 40 years ago. The revised program is designed to teach phonics to students who have been unable to learn decoding skills in a conventional school program. The 77 phonic lessons are divided into six parts, ranging from the presentation of single-letter solid single-sound associations to sound units that are exceptions to the usual patterns and finally to the use of plurals, possessives, affixes, compound words, and syllabication. Strategies for repeated practice in blending sounds and writing the sounds from memory are included in this structured and sequential phonics program.

☐ The Brody method (Brody, 1986) is designed for use with at-risk students in Grades 2 through 12 and for students with learning disabilities. The method first teaches the six basic syllable patterns (VC, VR, V, VV, VCe, CLe) as the major tool for decoding and then reinforces the use of this strategy by providing application in content material. In *Patterning: Reading Becomes Easy* (Brody, 1984) the syllabication patterns are taught by their application to words, not by isolated rule memorization. After the initial stage students are taught self-questioning strategies as an aid to comprehension. Because the Brody method emphasizes the integration of writing and reading, students immediately begin writing syllable patterns from dictation, ultimately writing the words that fit the syllabication patterns being studied. These patterns provide a structure for identifying the sounds within words and focus students' attention on letter groupings that appear repeatedly within words.

Comprehension Skills

Word recognition, although clearly an important basic skill, is not the final goal. The goal of reading is comprehension—obtaining meaning from printed material. Students' difficulty in understanding abstract concepts and generalizing information often adversely affects their ability to comprehend written material. Therefore, their reading programs must emphasize comprehension skills.

Durkin (1978–1979) reports from her observation of elementary schools that the teachers spent almost no time on comprehension skills. However, a minimum of three to four lessons per week for 10 to 15 weeks would have been necessary for improvement to occur over the long term. Durkin's research focused on students in the regular classroom; one can assume that students experiencing difficulty in understanding language concepts are likely to require additional training beyond that required by nonhandicapped children to become comprehending readers.

New knowledge is acquired from reading that is internalized and processed to make it useful (Rupley & Blair, 1979). Processing involves categorizing the new information, associating it with previously learned material, and questioning its content to allow comprehension. Traditionally, most teachers have taught comprehension by asking students questions after they have read a specific passage. This approach continually tests students' comprehension without directing or instructing them in comprehension strategies.

Prediction Strategies In recent years research has changed our knowledge and understanding of reading comprehension. As Smith (1979) states, "Prediction is asking questions—and comprehension is getting these questions answered" (p. 85). Smith emphasizes that as people read, listen to speakers, and study, they constantly ask questions. Comprehension occurs when people perceive answers to their own questions or find their predictions validated or refuted. Knowledge and experience directly influence predictions and thus comprehension. According to Smith (1979), students need not learn to predict because it is a natural process that begins in infancy.

Reading comprehension requires connecting what is read with prior knowledge of the topic (Wilson, 1983). The printed material provides new information; to understand it, readers use various information sources within their own memories. Thus, each reader's background of concepts directly influences the comprehension of passages read. Most comprehension instruction, therefore, should take place prior to a reading of the material. The teacher must stimulate students' thinking about the topic before oral or silent reading ever begins (Wilson, 1983).

A variety of teaching strategies make use of the role of prediction as an aid to comprehension. General strategies emphasizing prediction, or instruction before reading, include (1) setting the purpose for reading to arouse students' prior knowledge, (2) the cloze procedure, (3) anticipation guides, (4) directed reading/thinking activity, and (5) self-generated questioning.

Setting the Purpose Setting the purpose in advance of reading is one way to stimulate students' prior knowledge. A teacher can introduce a reading selection by saying, "As you read, think about what you would do if you were caught in a flood as Van is in this story." Immediately, students' prior knowledge (or lack of it) concerning floods comes to mind and thus helps prepare them for the passage to be read. Wilson (1983) also stresses the importance of teaching students to assume responsibility for their own comprehension. She advocates instructing children to self-monitor by asking themselves periodically, "Is this making sense to me?" Students who realize that they are not comprehending can try a variety of strategies: rereading the material, trying to rephrase it, reading ahead, or, if necessary, asking for help.

Cloze Procedure The cloze procedure is useful as a testing method and as a strategy for teaching comprehension. Its most common use has been to indicate students' instructional reading level. The cloze procedure deletes words from a selected passage; students then predict the deleted words and fill them in, using context clues, prior knowledge of the topic, their vocabulary background, and the passage's message to aid in word recognition. When students complete the passage, they experience closure—thus, the term *cloze* (Culhane, 1970).

To develop a cloze exercise, a teacher selects a reading passage from material at the students' independent or instructional reading level. The first and last sentences of the selection are left intact. Every fifth word is then deleted, and students are instructed to read the passage and fill in each blank with an appropriate word. A discussion of the completed passage should follow to encourage students to explain and defend their word choices. This technique fosters vocabulary development, as well as comprehension, beyond the literal level (Culhane, 1970).

Reading material that has been personalized for an individual student—by including name and school, for example—also increases comprehension. Neville and Hoffman (1981), reporting on the use of the cloze procedure, tested a group of seventh-grade retarded readers with personalized

and nonpersonalized passages. Results of their study indicate that personalizing material positively affected comprehension.

Anticipation Guide An anticipation guide (Bean & Peterson, 1981), another prediction strategy, introduces the important ideas of a selection before students read it. Statements are presented by the teacher, who then solicits students' opinions. The statements are discussed again after students have read the selection, and they are encouraged to defend their newly formed opinions and reactions. In developing an anticipation guide, the teacher must follow several steps (Wood & Mateja, 1983).

1. Decide the major concepts and details in the selection.
2. Present students with four or five false statements about the topic.
3. Encourage students to comment on the statements by giving their opinions, agreeing, or disagreeing.
4. Have students read the selection and justify or change their opinions.

Directed Reading/Thinking Activity One of the most useful questioning techniques to teach comprehension of content or expository material is the directed reading/thinking activity (DRTA). In this activity students are taught to make predictions about what they are going to read before they begin reading the text (VanJura, 1982). While reading, the students test and refine the predictions they made in advance. These predictions generate divergent questions and stimulate expanded thinking. DRTA teaches students to verify and defend their predictions and gives guidelines for reading to learn. The following procedures comprise the DRTA technique:

1. Students examine the story title, pictures, and subheadings.
2. Students individually or in a group list information they anticipate finding in the selection.

3. Students read the selection.
4. Students then look at each prediction on their list and decide whether it was correct or incorrect.
5. When uncertainty or disagreement occurs, students defend their positions by locating validating information in the text.

DRTA stimulates students to generate their own questions. Their predictions become questions when they search the text for supportive information.

Self-Generated Questions Cognitive psychology has fostered the use of self-generated questions. That field introduced the concept that to learn to read, children must actively participate in the learning process and take responsibility for their own learning (Reid & Hresko, 1981). Empirical work has indicated that one major influence on students' inability to read is that they do not take an active role in their own learning (Brown & Palinscar, 1982; Torgesen, 1982). The lack of metacognitive skills (e.g., self-monitoring, predicting, and controlling one's own attempts to study and learn) limits students' success in learning to read (Wong, 1982). Self-questioning is one way to stimulate development of the poor reader's metacognitive skills and improve comprehension (Cohen, 1983; Modolfsky, 1983).

With this strategy students are first trained in question writing. This orientation includes identification of good and poor questions, discrimination between questions and statements, and awareness of question words. Students are then instructed to read the story, describe what it is about, and generate two questions. Finally, students answer their own questions or exchange questions with a peer. This technique may subsequently be introduced as a study skill to be used with science, social studies, or other content material (Cohen, 1983).

Teachers can develop students' meta-cognitive skills by directly teaching and modeling comprehension processing (Schewel & Waddell, 1986). Another approach to self-questioning skills instructs students to perform the following tasks (Schewel & Waddell, 1986):

1. identify the main idea of a paragraph and underline it
2. develop questions related to the main idea and write them where they can be referred to easily
3. check those questions with the teacher's models to be certain that they are correctly stated
4. read the passage, answer the questions, and learn the answers
5. continually look back over the questions and answers to note the accumulation of information

Graphic-Aid Strategies These strategies use visual formats or structures to assist students in organizing information for better comprehension. Several graphic aids apply to teaching students who are handicapped.

Central Story Problem This strategy leads students to determine the central problem of a story and the various characters' reactions. As students read, they make notes that address specific questions about or elements within that particular selection (see Figure 10.5).

Story Frames Story frames constructed by the teacher also help students organize and summarize information. This strategy guides comprehension by helping students sort out the important concepts and ideas of the material. Fowler (1982; Fowler & Davis, 1986) describes the five steps necessary for constructing a story frame.

1. Identify the problem of the story on which you want students to focus.
2. Write a paragraph about that problem.

FIGURE 10.5
Sample chart for a central story problem approach
(From "Teaching Students to Determine the Central Story Problem: A Practical Application of Schema Theory" by P. B. Modolfsky, 1982, *The Reading Teacher, 36,* p. 743. Copyright 1983 by the International Reading Association. Reprinted with permission of the International Reading Association and P. B. Modolfsky.)

Story	Central Problem of This Story	Ways of Acting That Were Part of the Story	Solution	Ways of Acting That Were Part of the Solution

3. Delete words, phrases, and sentences that are not necessary to guide one through the paragraph.
4. Under selected spaces place a clue to ensure that students can follow the frame.
5. Modify the frame for subsequent selections.

Story frames can focus attention on character comparison or analysis, plot, or setting. Figure 10.6 is an example of a story frame focused on plot. When first introducing story frames, the teacher should read a story to the students, and together they should discuss and fill in the blanks on the frame. Following this direct instruction, students should be able to successfully complete story frames with minimal assistance. They can then begin working through frames independently.

Semantic Mapping Semantic mapping, a strategy to aid in reading comprehension, is based on the concept of schema theory. Schema theory postulates that new information is learned and understood when it is integrated with prior knowledge. The theory is based on the concept that information is stored in the brain in categories known as schemata. When a student is introduced to new information through reading or other experiences, the new knowledge is learned as it is stored in the brain with similar schemata.

In relation to schema theory, the reading teacher's role is twofold: to continually work on building students' knowledge background through experiences, discussion, and literature and to teach students to stimulate their own schemata about a topic before beginning to read a passage. The teacher might instruct students in the use of self-questioning (e.g., "What do I already know about the Civil War?") or prediction strategies. Children with handicaps often have more limited experiential backgrounds and need additional guidance in gaining knowledge from the experiences they encounter.

Semantic mapping is a method of teaching reading comprehension that stimulates a student's prior knowledge of the topic. Semantic maps are diagrams developed by students and teacher before students read an assigned selection. The maps can be reused after reading to further stimulate

FIGURE 10.6
Story frame focused on plot (From "Developing Comprehension Skills in Primary Students Through the Use of Story Frames" by G. L. Fowler, 1982, *The Reading Teacher,* 36 [2], p. 176. Copyright 1982 by the International Reading Association. Reprinted by permission.)

In this story the problem starts when _____ .

After that _____ . Next, _____

_____ . Then, _____

_____ . The problem is finally

solved when _____ . The story ends _____

_____ .

comprehension. The semantic mapping procedure is as follows:

☐ The teacher presents a stimulus word or a core question related to the story to be read.
☐ Students generate words related to the stimulus word or predict answers to the question, all of which the teacher lists on the board.
☐ Students, with the teacher, then put related words or answers in groups, drawing connecting lines between the topics to form a semantic map.
☐ After reading the selection, students and the teacher discuss the categories and rearrange or add to the map.

Semantic mapping can appear in various forms. Figure 10.7 presents one possible semantic map for this section of this particular chapter.

When using semantic mapping, students are actively engaged in a strategy that stimulates retrieval and organization of prior knowledge. It is also useful both as a postreading exercise to enhance comprehension

and as a study skill technique (Heimlich & Pittelman, 1986).

Paragraph Structure Teaching students paragraph structure is another approach to better comprehension, and one way to teach this understanding is by graphic illustration (Ekwall & Shanker, 1983). With this technique students are shown a vertical series of rectangles in which the top rectangle is the widest. The teacher explains that the main idea of a paragraph, represented here by the widest rectangle, is supported by the paragraph's details (the more narrow rectangles). To illustrate the process, the teacher reads a paragraph to the students, filling in the series of rectangles with the main idea and the details. Then students and teacher together work through another paragraph orally. Finally, students repeat the exercise alone, with guidance as needed. Once students understand this paragraph format, the teacher modifies the graphic illustration for paragraphs in which the main idea is the final sentence and repeats the process.

Graphic illustrations provide the clarity and specificity often necessary for slower learners. The concept is also adaptable to teaching cause-and-effect relationships and drawing conclusions.

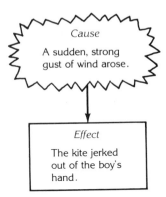

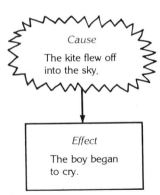

Sentence Combining This approach was originally introduced as a method to strengthen writing skills (Strong, 1973), but research has also indicated its value as an aid in developing reading comprehension skill, as well as its instructional value to reluctant readers (Combs, 1975). Strong suggests teaching students to combine short, kernel sentences to make them more interesting and meaningful. After successful experiences, students can attempt to combine longer sentences. The following is an example of a kernel sentence series:

1. The cars come cruising up Broadway.
2. The cars are glittering.
3. The paint is harsh.
4. The paint is metallic.
5. The paint is highly waxed.
6. There is a rumble of exhaust.
7. The rumble is great. (Strong, 1973, p. 19)

Teachers can design sentence-combining exercises in a variety of ways. One procedure that Combs (1975) recommends uses a sequence of sentences taken from the story line of a high-interest/low-vocabulary. book. The teacher writes a sentence about the story, ending it with *because,* and follows this with additional choices from which students select correct combinations. Sentence combining is discussed further in Chapter 11.

Fluency Strategies Reading through passages continuously and smoothly enhances comprehension. The techniques described here help students become more fluent readers and are applicable to a variety of students identified as mildly handicapped.

Neurological Impress Method (NIM) With this technique the student and the teacher read aloud in unison. The instructor sits behind the student and reads slightly faster and louder, pointing to the words as they are read (Ekwall & Shanker, 1983). As reading improves, students may begin the finger movements themselves. This method is recommended for use 10 to 15 minutes daily up to a maximum of 8 to 12 hours. Because progress usually occurs quickly, this strategy should be terminated if no improvement is noted in a reasonable period of time. NIM does not use questioning or discussion to encourage comprehension. Research on the technique has been equivocal (Lorenz & Yockell, 1979); therefore, teachers should evaluate its effectiveness when using it.

Repeated Readings With repeated readings students receive a selection approximately 200 words in length with instructions to

FIGURE 10.7
An example of
semantic mapping

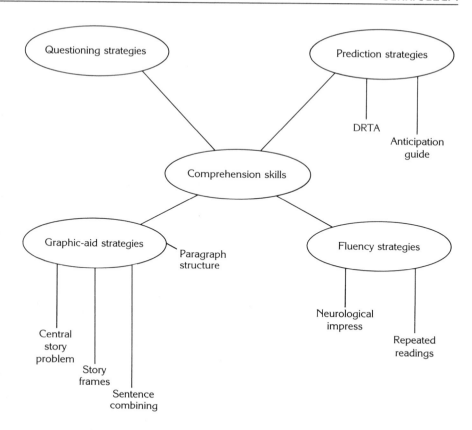

practice reading it orally while listening to a tape of the same material. When students decide they are ready, their time and errors are recorded. After further oral practice, another time/error check is made. This procedure continues until the student reads 85 words per minute, at which time the process begins again with new material.

Samuels (1979) reports that after practice with this technique, students required fewer readings with each new selection and comprehension continuously improved. He concludes that comprehension improved because the attention required for decoding was minimized. A full review of the advantages of repeated readings for speed and accuracy appears in Moyer (1982).

Bos (1982) found that a combination of repeated readings and the neurological im-

press method resulted in improved word recognition and comprehension skills for intermediate and junior high-aged students reading at the primary level. Bos used the following procedure:

☐ The teacher begins by reading to the student the first 15 to 30 words in the story.

☐ The teacher and the student reread the passage together, with the teacher pointing to the words, until the student is ready to read the passage aloud without assistance.

☐ As the student reads orally, the teacher notes the words the student does not recognize.

☐ Student and teacher discuss the message of the selection. The teacher teaches and reviews unknown words from the story, using a variety of activities.

By increasing fluency, this combination of two techniques allows the student to focus attention on comprehension (Bos, 1982).

Imitative Reading Imitative reading is a procedure for improving the fluency of students with severe reading difficulties. The teacher reads very simple, short segments aloud as the student follows silently. The student then tries to read the same phrase or sentence aloud. The procedure is repeated until the student reads the material with fluency. Gradually the teacher increases the length of the sections being read to the student (Henk, Helfeldt, & Platt, 1986).

Paired Reading In the paired reading technique two students who work well together and who have similar instructional reading levels read aloud in unison (Henk et al., 1986). Material familiar to both students is used in the initial stages of paired reading. After the two develop a sense of trust and cooperation, less familiar text can be introduced. As they work together, one student can assist when the other hesitates or makes an error. Tape recordings of these oral reading sessions can help both students evaluate their reading fluency.

Questioning Strategies Questioning is the instructional strategy used most often in teaching reading comprehension. Factual, inferential, and analytical questions are all essential for comprehension development. However, frequently the majority of questions that teachers ask are factual, and the answers are directly stated in the text, requiring no higher-level thinking by students. Teachers can stimulate students to begin inferential and critical thinking through higher-level questioning. Students who can

decode the material adequately can, with guidance and practice, become critical readers. If properly guided and questioned, slow learners as well as gifted students can learn to make inferences from the material they have read. Caskey (1970) reports that teachers' questions have more influence on higher-level comprehension than do students' intellectual levels. Questions that stimulate thought and motivate students to higher levels of comprehension can be asked on material at any readability level. Evaluative and interpretive questions also apply to every level of readability.

GENERAL APPROACHES TO READING INSTRUCTION

A variety of general approaches have been developed for teaching reading, and many have been used successfully with students who are handicapped. Generally, reading approaches can be divided into two types, developmental and remedial, although the words are often not specifically defined. Developmental approaches emphasize daily sequential instruction. They assume successful progress and minimal problems by the student. Basal reading programs are generally developmental. Remedial approaches consist of various teaching techniques and programs that have been designed to focus on learning deficits. The phonics drills of Kirk, Kirk, and Minskoff (1985) discussed earlier are a classic example of this type of approach.

In practice, few approaches to reading instruction are purely developmental or remedial. Most incorporate aspects of both approaches and thus are better represented along a continuum between the two extremes. For children with disabilities a variety of modified quasi-remedial or -developmental approaches can help build a systematic program of reading instruction. Otto, Mc-

Menemy, and Smith (1973) suggest the term *adaptive reading* to describe such an approach because this type of teaching involves adapting various techniques and materials to meet individuals' needs.

Regardless of the particular approach to reading, teachers should remember that special considerations are pertinent to the reading instruction of older students. The adolescent who is handicapped is likely to have experienced considerable frustration and failure in past efforts to learn or improve reading skills. The teacher, thus, must overcome not only skill deficits, but also problems in attitude, motivation, and fear related to failure expectancy. A positive, reinforcing manner with realistic expectations should underlie any approach to reading instruction with older students. Materials such as high-interest, controlled-vocabulary readers are particularly suitable for junior- and senior-high readers who are disabled.

Basal Reading Approach

Basal reading programs are used in the vast majority of elementary schools; consequently, such materials are readily available. Special educators should familiarize themselves with various basals. Basals usually contain a series of books or stories written at different difficulty levels, with most beginning at preprimer and primer levels and progressing through upper elementary levels. Most readers also have workbooks that allow students to practice specific skills.

Most basal programs are accompanied by comprehensive, highly structured teacher manuals that completely outline each lesson. They provide skill objectives, new vocabulary, suggested motivational activities, verbatim questions to check comprehension on each page of text, and lesson activities. The lessons follow a hierarchy of specific reading skills. Although some teachers think basal manuals limit creativ-

ity, others find value in their structure and guidance. Every beginning teacher should find the manuals informative and beneficial.

A basal program exposes students to a basic vocabulary that provides for repetition. Although structured in format, basals can be modified to meet individual needs while still following a sequential developmental pattern of skill building. They have often been used to assess a student's reading level and subsequent placement in an appropriate reading group. As long as the basal meets students' needs and falls within their interests and abilities, such placement may be temporarily adequate. The basal will not meet all needs, however, so the teacher must be prepared to revise and supplement the program.

Several methods can supplement basals when students begin to have difficulty with the vocabulary or cognitive processes demanded at increasingly higher levels. Teachers should avoid recycling students through the same stories, which can lower students' motivation to read. One alternative is to place students in another basal series at approximately the same level, thus giving them different reading experiences at approximately the same level and allowing for overlearning, which is important to students who are handicapped.

A second option is to follow the series outline of skills as the manual presents them, supplementing them with other commercial reading materials. Many low-vocabulary supplemental materials cover interesting topics. A third option is to require students to write their own stories, as in a language experience approach (to be discussed later). Such an experience can provide practice on reading skills that need reinforcement, and the students' stories can provide reading material. A final option is to discontinue basals in favor of an alternative approach. Teachers should realize that many children cannot learn effectively through basals and should not force students to fit into an inappropriate program.

Because basals provide a sequential, detailed, developmental program, they are valuable tools and should be considered one potential avenue for teaching reading to children with special needs. Only in very rare instances, however, can they be expected to furnish the entire program for children with reading difficulties. The developmental series that follow are designed especially for students with handicaps.

Stanwix House Reading Series Although the Stanwix House series resembles conventional basals, it introduces skills and vocabulary at a slower pace. It teaches phonics and other word-analysis skills in a series of highly motivating books and workbooks with both fictional and informational stories. A unique feature is the parallel material written at three different levels, allowing teachers to individualize reading assignments while still bringing students together for group discussions of material containing similar content. The Stanwix House series was written especially for children who are retarded with a mental age of 5 years or more.

Open Court Open Court's Headway Program is designed for direct teaching of basic reading skills. Through multisensory techniques students are taught 43 English sounds and 95 spellings. It is a highly structured, developmental approach in which students learn to write while learning to read. Selections in the readers cover a wide range of subjects, including nature, history, art, and fantasy. Components of this program are eight hardcover readers ranging from Grades 1 to 6, response cards, student storybooks, and readiness materials. The multisensory reinforcement, specific structure, dictation activities, use of matrix sentences, and comprehension strategies can make this reading program effective with learners with special needs.

Caught Reading (Quercus Publishing) This developmental series, designed for teenagers reading below the third-grade level, uses a format and story topics appropriate for adolescents. Five paperback student books and a teacher's manual comprise the program, which teaches word attack, comprehension, and study skills. Each story, complete on one page, is current and written to motivate reluctant teenagers.

Language Experience Approach (LEA)

LEA has been mentioned briefly as an alternative to be used in conjunction with a basal series, but it should not be used only in conjunction with other approaches. Even though one of the real strengths of LEA is its versatility as a complement to other techniques, many reading specialists advocate and use LEA as a total, initial reading program. Allen and Halvorsen (1961) describe the basis for LEA simply:

> What I can think about, I can talk about
> What I can say, I can write
> What I can write, I can read. (p. 33)

LEA encourages students to verbalize their thoughts and experiences, which are then written down by the teacher or the student and can be read. These stories are reread by the student and by other students as the program progresses. Word lists are made from the words used in the stories to develop word-recognition skills. Phonetic and structural analysis skills are taught when the teacher observes the student's readiness for such instruction. LEA lacks the developmental structure of the basal approach. Therefore, beginning teachers may need to follow the outline of a basal or another sequential program to guide students successfully through an LEA program.

Beginning readers may be introduced to LEA as a class group. The teacher should establish a common interest, such as a class animal, field trip, or television program. As students tell about their experience, the teacher needs to assist them in transcribing the words on paper. Students then receive copies of the stories for their books. Word lists and seat-work activities are made from the stories. Independent reading books are also made available and should be encouraged. The transition from student-written material must be made at some point. Commercial material should be presented early in the program, but it must be well within the student's independent level to ensure success.

The LEA program can be used in remedial fashion with adolescents who have met repeated defeat with printed material. The use of the student's own language and handwriting is a strong motivating tool. With older students the teacher should write the stories as students dictate. Then students can copy the stories for their books, thus reducing the use of incorrectly spelled words. Because of LEA's versatility and valuable motivational qualities, this approach is recommended as a supplementary program for any age student. It is most appropriately used in special programs when it accompanies systematic instruction in word-attack skills.

Programmed Instruction

Programmed approaches to reading instruction vary from teaching machines and computer programs to books and workbooks. The various programs are designed for levels ranging from beginning letter recognition through eighth-grade reading and have been successful as both developmental and remedial programs. Programmed instruction allows students to progress at their own rates using carefully sequenced learning steps with feedback and reinforcement from immediate correction. This approach can be extremely effective for students needing limited interaction with authority figures.

Sullivan Programmed Readers (Sullivan Associates) This relatively inexpensive programmed approach is especially suitable for use with young students. It is available in five different ability levels, each with placement tests, progress tests, programmed textbooks, correlated readers with worksheets, and teacher's manuals. The program can be adapted to remedial teaching with placement tests and the multitude of programmed textbooks based on acquisition of specific skills.

Computer-Assisted Instruction Chapter 7 discusses the general use of microcomputers in special education. Computers can be applied to reading instruction in several specific ways. Copying lists from printouts is a strategy for improving reading accuracy. Students discover that they have made an error in the list they typed into the computer when the program will not run; they must then proofread to find the error. Programs that require students to ask the computer questions improve comprehension, and solving computerized word-search puzzles provides repetition and practice of sight words (Mason, 1983). Knowledge of programming is not required of the teacher because of the increasing availability of software programs. Currently on the market are programs designed to provide drill and practice with basic reading skills, to diagnose students' weaknesses, and to specify proper remediation and motivate students to read more fluently.

Direct Instruction

Several direct instruction programs can provide comprehensive approaches to reading.

The Direct Instructional System for Teaching and Remediation (DISTAR) (Engelmann & Bruner, 1974, 1975) is based on the instructional procedures developed by Carl Bereiter and Siegfried Engelmann in the late 1960s for use with young, culturally disadvantaged children. DISTAR is a highly structured program that sequences each step of learning and contains criterion objectives for each learning task. DISTAR has been revised and restructured into six levels. DISTAR Reading I and II are appropriate as a developmental program in beginning reading instruction for any student and can be followed by the upper levels, Reading Mastery III through VI. Also, a Fast Cycle DISTAR program is appropriate for students who have completed DISTAR I but are not ready for DISTAR II. It is appropriate for students who are reading at a 1.5 through 2.5 grade level but who need remedial instruction on letter sounds and sound blending.

The Corrective Reading Program (CRP) (Englemann, Becker, Hanner, & Johnson, 1980), another direct instruction program of Science Research Associates, is a remedial program for upper elementary, middle, and high school students who have not mastered decoding and/or comprehension skills. The program is divided into two strands, decoding and comprehension, each with three levels of skill development. The decoding strand follows the traditional DISTAR approach in presenting decoding strategies; the comprehension strand presents a variety of formats involving real-life survival situations that are excellent for the adolescent learner. Because CRP uses the direct instruction approach, it provides a specific "script" for teachers to follow. Special motivation for adolescent students is provided in a group reinforcement component, with each student receiving additional points based on the group's performance.

Recent research (Polloway, Epstein, Polloway, Patton, & Ball, 1986) indicates that both students who were learning disabled and those who were mildly retarded increased decoding and comprehension skills after participating in the Corrective Reading Program for an academic year. This study also notes that, although CRP was effective with both groups, those students identified as learning disabled showed overall greater gains.

Other Reading Programs

Edmark Program The Edmark program (Edmark Associates) was developed to teach a 150-word sight vocabulary to students with retardation. It is appropriate for children who have some verbal skills (i.e., can repeat, can point, and have sufficient receptive language to understand and respond to a teacher). The program comes in kit form with more than 200 lessons consisting of word recognition, storybooks, picture/phrase matching, and a direction book.

Because Edmark's goal is to promote acquisition of sight vocabulary, the program can serve as a good beginning approach to reading. Successful completion of the program should provide students with a solid reading foundation that can then be supplemented with phonics instruction. It has been used effectively with students who are mildly, moderately, and severely retarded.

Predictable Books Predictable books are children's books or stories that use repetition, as in *Brown Bear, Brown Bear, What Do You See?* (Martin, 1983); a cumulative pattern, as demonstrated in the familiar Gingerbread Man story; or familiar day, month, or time sequences, as found in Maurice Sendak's (1962) *Chicken Soup with Rice.* These three types of predictable stories—through the use of rhythm, rhyme, and redundancy—give semantic and syntactic language cues that stimulate fluent reading for children with disabilities.

To use predictable books as a strategy for teaching reading, the teacher first reads the story aloud to the children, using an enlarged version or distributing multiple copies of the material so that children can read along for most of the story. After this, group and individual activities are developed by the teacher to teach and reinforce the sight words and phonics generalizations that are used in the predictable book (McClure, 1985).

Writing to Read Writing to Read is a computer-based teaching system recommended for beginning readers. It begins with the vocabulary that students already know and goes on to introduce 42 sound/symbol relationships that the author believes children need to learn before writing is introduced. The message conveyed to students is that they make the sounds that form letters and words, which can be seen, read, and written.

Students begin by working with the computer, then move to audiotapes, and then to electric typewriters. Some writing is also done on the chalkboard and in personal journals. The development of this unique approach to the teaching of reading was funded by International Business Machines (IBM), which has also created Writing to Read Centers in 100 schools located in eight states.

IMPLEMENTING THE READING PROGRAM

Although a variety of reading programs have been presented, teachers should realize that no one program or technique works for all students. A successful reading program matches a particular approach to individual needs. Only a sound process of assessment and familiarity with a variety of programs and methods can produce this combination.

Grouping

Successfully matching individual readers to appropriate reading materials requires that students be divided into small groups for reading instruction. Traditionally, these groups have remained static; reading-achievement level has been the primary determinant of group placement. Instead, teachers should consider options that introduce change and flexibility into grouping procedures. Interest and skill groups, as well as pupil pairs, should be incorporated into the program at regular intervals.

Interest groups can be formed around a common theme (e.g., snakes, spaceships, baseball) regardless of reading-achievement level. The teacher can assign trade book material at levels appropriate for each student, with questions and activities suitable for the group. In skill groups students periodically meet with the teacher to work on a specific skill deficit. Here again, students of varying levels of reading achievement work together on a common problem. A stronger student assisting a weaker one constitutes a pupil pair. With planning assistance from the teacher, this peer-tutoring approach can be as motivating and instructional for the tutor as it is for the tutee.

Flexible grouping provides models and motivation for weaker students by making them feel less "stuck" in the poorest reading group. They meet with peers focusing attention on a similar interest or skill need (Spache & Spache, 1973).

The Role of Oral Reading

Oral reading is an important component of a total reading program. It is particularly necessary in the early stages of reading instruction, because it gives the teacher insight into the beginning reader's knowledge of sight words and decoding skills. With most children oral reading has three major purposes: diagnosis, conveying directions or instruction, and personal pleasure. For slow learners oral reading has four additional purposes: articulation and vocabulary practice, memory reinforcement, rereading for better comprehension, and group participation.

Oral reading can assist development of correct word pronunciation by providing the disabled reader who seldom verbalizes with a structured opportunity to speak. When reading aloud, the student takes in information both auditorily and visually, adding an additional pathway to learning that is often necessary for memory. Rereading a passage orally after it has been read silently assists comprehension, particularly when the teacher designates a purpose for each reading.

Many slow learners have few opportunities to participate in group activity or performance. Oral reading experiences such as choral reading provide this occasion. Many oral reading activities also provide experiences to enhance students' self-concepts. Examples include reading a teacher-written advertisement over a simulated microphone, a sports announcement on a cut-outbox TV screen, or simple instructions to classmates for making a paper object.

Continuing oral reading for students with special needs longer than for average children is often beneficial. However, the students will eventually need practice and guidance in the transition from oral to silent reading (directed and encouraged by the teacher), because silent reading is ultimately the critical skill to develop.

Instructional Procedures

As teachers develop individualized reading programs, the following suggestions should help ensure success.

1. *Reduce tension.* For the student who has experienced some failure in learning to read, tension must be reduced before beginning any reading program or assessment. This may be accomplished by playing student/teacher games, counseling, or just talking and listening to one another. A recent issue of *Topics in Learning and Learning Disabilities*[1] contains a full discussion of the relationship between stress and learning.

2. *Help the student feel successful.* Although it is important to be positive and to praise the student frequently, it is equally important to present activities and materials with which the student can genuinely succeed.

3. *Assess continually.* The prescriptive process of test-teach-test is the keystone of any reading program. Through this process the teacher pinpoints specifically what has been learned.

4. *Start with a review.* Begin each session with some type of maintenance activity. Because success is important, it is advisable to begin and end each reading session with activities that the student knows and enjoys.

5. *Establish a purpose for reading.* To encourage comprehension, it is important to arouse students' prior knowledge of the subject of the reading material. One way to do this is to give students a specific or a general purpose for reading.

6. *Select appropriate materials.* A common reason that many students dislike reading is that the material is too difficult for them. When selecting material, carefully consider both difficulty and interest level.

7. *Ensure motivation*
   a. Establish rapport with students
   b. Provide success experiences

---

[1] *Topics in Learning and Learning Disabilities* (1983), *3* (9).

c. Illustrate progress (e.g., share progress charts and teach students to keep their own records and make their own graphs)

d. Consider social recognition—for example, provide reading material that may be related to other class work, thus enhancing the child's chance of contributing to other work and projects

e. Avoid monotony—provide varied instructional activities (at least three per reading session)

8. *Provide opportunity for silent reading.* Students must have frequent opportunities to read silently. After each short silent reading period, allow time for questioning to determine comprehension.

9. *Include writing activities related to reading tasks.* Writing reinforces many types of reading skills and should therefore be encouraged.

10. *Instill cooperation and trust.* Explain why certain activities were selected and share short-term plans with students.

11. *Use time efficiently.* Approach each session confidently and be well-organized. Routines need not be rigid, but the session should move rapidly through an organized plan.

12. *Involve parents.* Share reading plans with parents. Be objective and talk in terms of specific goals. Discourage parental pressure. For parents who want to help, encourage involvement with maintenance activities.

ACTIVITIES

Although the activities listed here are far from exhaustive, they are representative, and it is hoped that they will stimulate additional ideas. The activities are grouped according to four topics: readiness, word-attack skills, sight vocabulary, and comprehension.

Readiness

1. Make two identical sets of index cards using varied but similar designs. Turn one set of cards face up, spread on a flat surface. The second group remains face down in a stack. The child draws one card from the pile and places it on its mate. The game can be varied by replacing the designs with pictures, letters, and, for more advanced students, simple two-, three-, or four-letter words.

2. Give students a symbol (e.g., flower, boat, animal, shape) representing their place and belongings in the room. The symbol can be placed on a chart by their name and on all their possessions, desk, papers, and so forth.

3. Give students objects (e.g., pencils, finger puppets, crayons, or cards) of three or four colors. When you hold up a colored card, each child should raise the object that is the same color.

4. Letter recognition can become a daily activity by attaching library pockets to the children's desks and placing a tagboard card printed with a letter of the alphabet in each pocket. Each time that the class lines up, the teacher calls a letter of the alphabet, and the person with that letter gives it to the teacher and gets into line (Lake, 1987).

5. Have children sort small cardboard tiles with letters or small words on them into small milk cartons or egg-carton sections with a similar letter or word on the outside.

6. Make dominoes out of index cards, using colored shapes. Have children follow the basic game rules of dominoes.

7. Find two identical coloring books with large, simple drawings of familiar objects. Mount two similar pictures on two sheets of oaktag; laminate or cover with clear contact paper. Make a puzzle of one picture by cutting it into pieces, but keep the mate as a model. Begin by making only a three- or four-piece puzzle and then increase the number of pieces by one or two. These can easily be stored in manila envelopes.

8. Make jigsaw puzzles of index cards by cutting them in half, using different zigzags. Have the uppercase letter on one side of each puzzle and the lowercase letter on the other side.

9. Worksheets can be made of primary lined paper with a green margin drawn on the left for go and a red margin drawn on the right for stop. Each line has a series of geometric figures running across the page. Students put a mark in each figure, starting on the green and stopping on the red, to practice directionality.

10. Show students four objects, discuss them, and then remove one. Have students tell which object was removed.

11. Select one student to come to the front. Have the other students study the child, who then leaves the room. List all things that the other students can remember about the chosen child.

12. Cut strips of construction paper in sizes suitable for making paper chains. Draw paper chains on index cards, using the colors in different sequences on each card. Instruct the students to make their chains in the same sequence shown on the cards. The activity can be varied by using beads or macaroni of different shapes or colors.

13. Use cardboard tiles with letters on them. Arrange two or three tiles in a sequence. Allow students to match the sequence. For more advanced students, cover the model and have them reproduce it from memory.

Word Attack

1. Initial consonant sounds can be practiced by gluing pictures of simple objects on small cards. Have students place the cards on a grid on which each square has a consonant letter corresponding to the beginning sound of an object on the cards. Consonant blends and final consonant sounds can be drilled in the same manner.

2. Make word wheels of word families, changing only the initial consonants. These devices not only give practice in consonant sounds but also are excellent for sound blending. Word wheels are two circles made of oaktag, one smaller than the other and fastened together in the center with a brass fastener so that they can rotate. The different word bases (e.g., -ag, -ad, -at) are written on the exposed edge of the larger circle, and the different initial consonants are written on the edge of the smaller circle. As students rotate the top circle, different words are formed, which students can pronounce to a friend.

3. Make a tape recording of 20 to 25 words. Instruct students to listen to each word and write the sounds they hear at the beginning of each word. The answers can be given at the end of the tape or in an envelope to be opened at the end of the tape. Time can be saved and confusion avoided by providing a sheet for students to write their responses on that has been numbered to correspond with the tape. This activity can also be used with vowel sounds and ending sounds.

4. Make two-part puzzles with an initial sound on one part and a word family on the other. Have students put the puzzles together and pronounce the words. Animal shapes are popular and can be cut between the head and body or body and tail. Use the same idea for contractions, compound words, and root words with endings. Designs can be found in coloring books. Character combinations are popular also: Snoopy and his dog house, Woodstock and his nest, Batman and his cape, or Raggedy Ann with Raggedy Andy. Three-part puzzles can be made to accommodate adding prefixes and suffixes to root words (e.g., *unfolded*).

5. Class bookmaking and rhyming phrases can be combined to spark interest and creativity. On the first day read aloud a book that uses repeated phrases or rhymes (e.g., *Brown Bear, Brown Bear, What Do You See?* Martin, 1983) and have students draw a picture of themselves. On the next day have them complete the picture by adding details and activity to it to make it illustrate the repetitive phrase. They should write the phrase and their explanation of the picture below the illustration. Assemble all the pictures for a class version of the story (Hamilton, Miller, & Wood, 1987).

6. Have students make notebooks for their sounds. As sounds are presented, students can cut out pictures of objects that begin with each specific sound and glue them into the book. Later, students can write words that they have learned to recognize or spell that begin with each specific sound.

7. List on the board the letters for the vowels, blends, or consonants that have been studied. Have students stand in a large circle with one student in the center. The center student tosses a ball to a student in the circle and calls out one of the letters from the board. The student catching the ball has to say a word that contains the sound that was called. That student then goes to the center and throws the ball.

8. Compound words and contractions can be practiced by dividing the group into two teams. Give each member of each team part of a compound word or a contraction. Place a balance beam in the middle of the room. Call out part of a compound word or two words that can be made into a contraction. The student with the other half of the compound word or the appropriate contraction walks across the beam. The first team to get all members across the beam wins.

9. Recognition of prefixes and suffixes can be practiced by listing words on the chalkboard or on a worksheet and having students underline the prefix, suffix, or both. You may also call out words while students write the prefix or suffix they hear in the word, or they may find and write different words containing the same prefix or suffix.

10. Write multisyllabic words on small cards, one word per card. Place the cards in an envelope, and clip it to a manila folder. Inside the folder

draw several columns, numbered 2, 3, 4, and so on as room permits. The student counts the number of syllables in the word on the card and writes it in the proper column. The cards have the correct number of syllables written on the back, or an answer sheet can be provided for immediate feedback.

11. Draw several worms on a worksheet, and write a root word on their heads. Have students cut out circular worm sections containing a suffix and add appropriate sections to each worm. This can be varied using a train or octopus or by drawing the object on the board and letting students take turns adding the suffixes.

12. Give each student a set of index cards with one number on each card. When you say a word, students should hold up index cards with the number that corresponds to the syllables they hear.

13. Make sound wheels. Place a consonant in the center of each wheel. Have students write or draw words beginning with that sound on the spokes of the wheel.

14. Use a game board and a tape player to help students develop syllabication skills. Make a tape by first recording a new word and then pausing. During the pause students should determine the number of syllables in the word. After the pause record the correct number of syllables so that students can self-check. Using the on/off switch, students can listen to the tape and move pieces on a game board according to the number of syllables in the words. However, students can move their pieces only if they accurately determine the number of syllables. The first student to the end of the board wins (Aullis, 1978).

Sight Vocabulary

1. List words on the chalkboard. Have two students stand with their backs to the lists. As you call out a word, the students turn; the first to find the word receives a point.

2. Make a gameboard of oaktag with a path of squares. Mark start and finish squares and various outer squares with directions like "move ahead three squares," "move back three squares," or "short cut" with a path to another square. Laminate the board or cover it with clear contact paper. Write words that are to become sight vocabulary words in the open squares with a grease pencil. Students then throw dice to determine how far they are to move. They must pronounce the word they land on to remain in the game. The game can be varied by changing the words, and several boards can be made to fit the season of the year (e.g., in December each section might show a different toy; in the spring, a race track with small metal cars as markers, and so on).

3. Make a ladder or rocket ship blast-off pad, and place a sight word on each level. Have students pronounce words to see how far up they can get.

4. Give students cards with sight words on them. Call out the words, and have students hold the appropriate card up in front of them.

5. Put pictures of sight words like *ball, cake, truck,* or *car* on one side of a card, and write the word on the other side. Make a game board similar to a bingo card, with each sight word written on it for each child. Place

cards with the word side up in a pile. Students take turns drawing cards. They must be able to say the word correctly before placing it on their boards. The picture on the back makes the game self-correcting. If the student cannot recognize the word, the card is placed at the bottom of the pile. The first student to get four words in a row in any direction wins the game.

6. Make two sets of cards, one with pictures of sight words and the other with the words written out. Spread the word cards face up on a flat surface. Place the picture cards face up in a pile in the middle. The first student to point to the word matching each picture card takes the picture card, thus exposing the picture of the next word to be identified. The student with the most picture cards at the end of the game wins.

7. Put sight words on index cards, with each word appearing on four different cards. Then play a rummy-type game of "Go Fish," calling for various words.

8. A form of concentration can be played by making two sets of identical cards with sight words. Begin with five pairs of cards. Place the cards spread out in two areas, face down on a flat surface. The child turns up a card in one set and then tries to find the card that matches in the other set. When a match is made, the student pronounces the word and gets to keep the cards.

9. Use a chart-size pegboard and attach hooks on which index cards can be hung. Write vocabulary words on index cards, punch a hole in each card, and hang the cards from the hooks on the peg board. Give students a rubber jar-ring to toss at a hook on the board. When a ring lands on a hook, that card is removed from the hook, and the student pronounces the word to earn a point. The one with the most points wins. The game can be varied by using bean bags to throw at a card on a board or at cards hung from a miniature clothesline with pins.

10. Make word billfolds with manila envelopes. Students can decorate them with pictures from magazines. They then write difficult or new words on index cards and put them in their billfolds. Sentences and definitions can also be written on the index cards. Set up a vocabulary time to review the cards (Karlin & Berger, 1969).

11. Place four to six word cards in front of the student.

| boat | house | where | run |

Then read aloud a variety of sentences and questions: (a) "Point to the word you hear in this sentence: I live in a red brick house"; (b) "Read the word that rhymes with *sun*"; (c) "Hand me the word that completes this sentence: I went sailing in a _____"; (d) "Read the word that tells what we live in"; (e) "Read the word that names something used in the water"; (f) "Which word has almost the same meaning as the word *jog*?"

12. Encourage students to make comparisons by describing different objects. For example, list both the qualities of chalk and objects that are similar to chalk. Then direct students to write similes, such as "white as snow" or "round as a pencil" (Taylor et al., 1972).

13. Vocabulary words that depict their meaning when heard can be illustrated by students. Secretly assign a vocabulary word to each student,

who then illustrates the word and writes on a separate piece of paper a sentence using the word. Then write all of the vocabulary words on the board, and collect the illustrations. Give children paper to record their choices, and hold up the pictures one at a time while students choose the word they think each illustration depicts. Refer to the artist if a question arises. Permit discussion (Baroni, 1987).

14. To assist adolescents with vocabulary development, establish a word retirement area on a bulletin board. During the week have students list words that are overused by themselves and their peers. Once a week have the class review the words and choose one or two to focus on. Have students look the word(s) up and agree on the intended meaning(s). Then have them use a thesaurus to find synonyms for the overused word(s). Students should then keep a record of their use of the chosen synonym(s) for the next week. At the end of the time period the student using the new vocabulary word(s) the most becomes the manager of the word retirement "home" and is in charge of recording the next week's words (Pearson, 1987).

Comprehension

1. Make worksheets with several lists of words on them. Put several directions at the bottom of the sheet for students to follow (e.g., "Circle two animal names with red," "Draw a blue line under two things to wear," or "Put a green box around two things to eat").

2. Make worksheets containing sentences and groups of words. Have students put yes behind those that are sentences and no behind those that are not sentences. This activity can be varied by adding questions to the items and having students put a question mark behind items that are questions.

3. Have students read to remember instead of reading to find out and answer questions. Tell them to read to remember something they can share with their peers. When they finish, have them volunteer information to the class and write their statements on the board. At first begin with three pieces of information from each student. Write these statements on the board, and have the students place them in the sequence in which they occurred in the story. As students improve, more statements can be required and/or the remembered information can be written (Harden, 1987).

4. Make a reading kit for adolescents by gathering interesting reading materials that correspond to students' reading ability levels. Record identifying information on cards, which you number and laminate, and prepare discussion questions separately. Place the laminated cards in a file box. Have students obtain a card, read for recreation, and then set up a private student-teacher conference to discuss the material with you (Machart, 1987).

5. To encourage the use of the library and promote independent reading, have students help rate books. With the librarian's assistance, ask students to help the teachers and the rest of the students at the school by reading the books in the library that fall within their reading ability. As a group, have them establish a system for evaluating and recommend-

ing books to others. One system might be to place a color-coded dot on the book's binding, indicating the reading level required (Jamison & Shevitz, 1985).

6. Make worksheets with simple drawings of several different objects. Have students cut out the objects and glue them on a sheet of extra paper according to written directions that contain prepositional phrases (e.g., "Put the cat under the tree," "Put the apple on the tree," or "Put the ball on the table").

7. Write short paragraphs for which students will choose titles.

8. Have the children read a story and then tell what happened in the story in one breath.

9. Have a treasure hunt around the school. Write out directions for the children to follow that lead them from one clue to another (e.g., "Go to the flag pole to find your next clue," "Face the school building and walk straight ahead to the window").

10. An activity that includes reading for information, survival, and amusement uses menus from the community's restaurants, fast-food chains, or food counters. The more menus used, the better the exercise. Give students specific assignments to compare prices, develop lists of meals, or identify the top 10 places to go on a special date. Students might also construct a composite menu to be printed in the graphics department and used for personal review. This menu can provide a basis for a variety of exercises to develop vocabulary, attack skills, and word recognition.

11. Read mystery stories to encourage students to make inferences and draw conclusions. Students like who-done-it stories and usually enjoy figuring out the final outcome of an unclear chain of events. Brainstorming as part of the activity might assist them in drawing conclusions (Cole & Cole, 1980).

12. Have students report on books they have read by acting out a phone conversation about the book, using visual aids to illustrate an episode in the book, making comic strips depicting scenes in the book, drawing a mural, selecting friends to act out scenes, or developing advertisements for the book (Bailey, 1975).

13. Collect money from class members, parents, and the PTA to create a classroom library of high-interest/low-readability books. Encourage students to use the library for recreational reading (Karlin & Berger, 1969).

14. Newspaper articles from different sections of the paper can help students get the main idea of a story. Separate headlines from stories and place in random order. Have students match titles to stories (Taylor et al., 1972).

15. Show the words to a popular song on the overhead projector. Without naming the song, choose someone to read the lyrics orally. As soon as others recognize the words, they can elect to sing it together. Words can be memorized as they are sung and visually tracked (Bailey, 1975).

16. Have students complete some follow-up activities without teacher guidance.
    a. Write a letter to a main character in the book suggesting other ways the character might have solved the problem or acted in the situation.

b. Write sentences from the story that show that someone was excited, sad, happy, or ashamed.

c. Draw a picture of something in the story that indicates the setting is past, present, or future.

d. Find three pictures in magazines that remind you of the main characters in the story. Under each picture write your reasons for selecting it.

e. Draw a picture of one of the memorable scenes from the story, showing as many details as possible.

f. Make a poster advertising your book.

g. Make a list of 10 birthday presents your favorite characters might ask for and explain your choices.

17. Students can motivate others to read by sharing a book they have enjoyed. Some creative ways for them to share are listed here.

a. Publish a book review column for the school paper or a monthly book review sheet with short book reviews and reactions to books read.

b. After reading a biography or book of fiction, describe the main characters and their common problems. Tell how these problems were or were not solved.

c. Prepare a collection of something the class has read about (e.g., rocks, coins, stamps) with appropriate information for an exhibit.

d. Make a poster (either flat or three-dimensional) showing a scene or stimulating interest in a book.

e. Make and decorate a book jacket, writing an advertisement to accompany the book.

f. Write a letter to a friend or a librarian recommending a book you especially liked.

g. Dress as one of the characters in a book and tell about yourself.

h. Make a model with clay, soap, or wood to represent something or someone in the book.

i. Prepare a book fair to share books with other classes.

18. Students of all ages and abilities comprehend and retain information better if they are active readers.

a. Always give students a purpose for reading and gradually train them to set their own purposes.

b. Teach them to make predictions about content before beginning to read.

c. After reading, have students defend or reject their predictions.

d. Encourage students to ask themselves after each paragraph, "What is the main idea?"

RESOURCES

Professional

Aukerman, R. C. & Aukerman, L. R. (1981). *How do I teach reading?* New York: John Wiley & Sons. A truly comprehensive how-to-do-it book on the teaching of reading. A practical guide for teacher training and beginning teachers.

Buckley, L. A. & Cullum, A. (1975). *Picnic of sounds: A playful approach to reading.* New York: Citation Press. A resource book for teaching a beginning sound program. Includes approaches, word lists, and activities.

Burnmeister, L. E. (1978). *Reading strategies for middle and secondary school teachers.* Reading, MA: Addison-Wesley. A resource book for teaching the older, but not advanced, student. Includes techniques, lists of materials, and activities.

Carnine, D., & Silbert, J. (1979). *Direct instruction reading.* Columbus, OH: Merrill. Probably one of the most complete books ever written on reading instruction. Leaves no questions unanswered; outlines procedures and alternatives clearly.

Duffy, G. G., & Sherman, G. B. (1972). *Systematic reading instruction.* New York: Harper & Row. A highly structured approach to reading. Extremely involved sequencing but excellent for readers with serious disabilities.

Ekwall, E. E., & Shanker, J. L. (1983). *Diagnosis and remediation of the disabled reader* (2nd ed.). Boston: Allyn & Bacon. Outstanding chapters on informal diagnosis interpretation of test information, and remediation of comprehension skills. A useful resource for teaching students with special needs to read.

Farnette, C., Forte, I., & Loss, B. (1969). *Kid's stuff: Reading and writing readiness.* Nashville, TN: Incentive Publications. Book of teaching strategies, simple management systems, teacher resources, activities, and pupil pages ready to reproduce. Suitable for teaching on the primary and intermediate level.

Forgun, H. W., & Mangrum, V. C. T. (1981). *Teaching content area reading skills.* Columbus, OH: Merrill. An excellent book in a modular format with specific ideas for teaching students to read content area material more effectively.

Garner, R. (1987). *Metacognition and reading comprehension.* Norwood, NJ: Ablex. Targets professionals interested in the relationship of cognitive processes to reading achievement. Includes chapters on theories of metacognition and schemata, as well as classroom applications of metacognitive research.

Goodman, K. S. (Ed.). (1973). *Miscue analysis.* Urbana, IL: ERIC Clearinghouse on Reading and Communication Skills. Several informative chapters on the use of miscue analysis in diagnosis.

Goodman, Y. M., & Burke, C. (1980). *Reading strategies: Focus on comprehension.* New York: Holt, Rinehart & Winston. A practical book with specific comprehension lesson plans based on psycholinguistic concepts.

Hafner, L. E. (1977). *Developmental reading in middle and secondary schools.* New York: Macmillan. Outstanding chapters on reading-acquisition skills and applying learning principles to the teaching of reading. Not a beginning text but a well-concentrated study.

Heilman, A. W. (1981). *Phonics in proper perspective* (4th ed.). Columbus, OH: Merrill. An excellent handbook on the mechanics and sequential progression of phonics.

Heilman, A. W., & Holmes, E. A. (1972). *Smuggling language into the teaching of reading.* Columbus, OH: Merrill. Based on the premise that language is fascinating to youngsters. Presents dozens of ways to expand vocabulary and to develop critical reading.

Heimlich, J. E., & Pittleman, S. D. (1986). *Semantic mapping: Classroom application.* Newark, DE: International Reading Association. A valuable resource for teachers interested in classroom applications of semantic mapping procedures.

McNeil, J. D. (1987). *Reading comprehension.* Glenview, IL: Scott, Foresman. Contains many strategies for teaching comprehension, based on schema theory and metacognition.

Orton, J. L. (1964, 1975). *A guide to teaching phonics.* Cambridge, MA: Educators Publishing Service. Handbook on the Orton approach to phonics. Sequential lessons with complete word lists and activities.

Savage, J. F., & Mooney, J. F. (1979) *Teaching reading to children with special needs.* Boston: Allyn & Bacon. Contains excellent chapters on management and organization of reading programs. Provides a rationale for a variety of reading approaches appropriate for use with students who are handicapped.

Smith, C. B., & Elliott, P. G. (1979). *Reading activities for middle and secondary schools.* New York: Holt, Rinehart & Winston. Contains samples and models of activities suitable for adolescent students.

Smith, J. A. (1975). *Creative teaching of reading in the elementary school* (2nd ed.). Boston: Allyn & Bacon. Written for teachers in training and classroom teachers. Stimulates creative ways to teach reading. Includes many practical ideas.

Spache, E. B. (1976). *Reading activities for child involvement.* Boston: Allyn & Bacon. Collection of 472 activities covering all areas of reading. Organization and cross-referencing of activities by skill areas.

Stauffer, R. S. (1970). *The language experience approach to the teaching of reading.* New York: Harper & Row. Provides theoretical foundations and practical assistance for teachers interested in using the LEA approach. Includes discussion of LEA's usage in special education classes.

Reading Programs

Chandler Reading Program, Noble and Noble. An LEA series designed for culturally different urban children. Uses actual photographs and bold type to make reading materials as real as possible.

Diagnostic Reading for Your Classroom (Swalm, J. E.), Dreier. A guide to organizing and scheduling individual students and a classroom. Well-presented in easy-to-follow, step-by-step sequence.

The Emergency Reading Teacher's Manual (Fry), Dreier. Basic manual of practice methods for dealing with individual students. An alternative approach that can be of value to special educators.

Mott Semi-Programmed Series, Allied Education Council. Series of workbook texts programmed for self-pacing with immediate feedback. Clearly stated behavioral objectives for each unit. Covers beginning phonics, elementary comprehension, word-attack skills. Also includes cursive writing. Excellent for intermediate- through high school-level students.

Palo Alto Reading Program: Sequential Steps in Reading (Glim), Harcourt Brace Jovanovich. Linguistic-slanted reading program for readiness level through third grade. Materials and interest levels appropriate for use with primary- and intermediate-aged students.

Programmed Reading for Adults, McGraw-Hill. A program to bring older students up to a 6.0 reading level. The linguistic approach in a series of eight programmed workbooks. Claims that by the end of the program, students will be able to read for meaning any material written at grade levels 5 through 6 and have a vocabulary of 1500 words. Begins with letters of the alphabet and ranges up to content analysis and functional reading.

Reader's Digest Skill Builders, Reader's Digest Services. Short, interesting stories followed by activities on word-attack and comprehension skills. Available on all levels—from first grade to adult-level remediation.

Reading Incentive Program, Bowmar. Twenty high-interest subjects combined into a motivating program for intermediate- through high school-aged students. A book, filmstrip, and excellent skill-development sheets for each title. Covers motorcycles, horses, surfing, dogs, and hot-air balloons.

Recipe for Reading, Educators Publishing Service. Describes specific techniques to teach reading, based on earlier work by Orton and Gillingham. Includes sequence charts and spirit duplicating masters.

Specific Skills Series, Barnell Loft. Individual books covering comprehension skills, including getting the main idea, drawing conclusions, following directions, using the context, locating the answer, getting the facts, and working with sounds. Covers reading levels 1 through 8.

High-Interest/Low-Vocabulary Materials

Several of the materials listed are excellent sources for instruction in independent living skills. Information on additional series is available from most of the publishers cited.

Alley Alligator Series, Benefic Press. Stories centering around three rangers and a baby alligator. Appropriate series for primary youngsters.

Breakthrough Series, Allyn & Bacon. Covers reading levels 2 through 6, with interest level appropriate for junior and senior high school. Well-written stories.

Checkered Flag Series, Field Education Publications. Exciting stories appropriate for high school students and written on grade levels 2 through 5.

Choose Your Own Adventure Series, Bantam Books. Appropriate for interest level of Grade 4 and up. Teaches students to make their own decisions, use their imaginations, develop rapid silent reading skills, and become the main character by choosing a variety of plot options.

Crisis Series, Fearon. Six books focusing on personal crises that teenagers recognize. Serious teenagers experiencing difficult situations. Designed for adolescents reading at 3.0–4.0 level. Includes a teacher's guide and follow-up activity sheets.

Deep-Sea Adventure Series, Harr Wagner. High-interest/low vocabulary series with a controlled vocabulary and the same characters throughout the series. Grade level 2.5 through 6.

Four Seasons at Lakeview, EMC Corporation. A series of high-interest/low-vocabulary books that are primarily male-oriented. Titles in the series: *Pro Fever, The Sixth Man, The Unlikely Hero,* and *Rip's Ups and Downs.*

Galaxy 5, Fearon Pitman. Series of six books featuring the crew of the spaceship *Voyager* on a mission to establish a human colony on Planet 1, Star 84, Galaxy 5. Reading level approximately third grade.

Good Literature for Slow Readers, Frank E. Richards. Ten volumes. A literature series designed for those who will never be able to read the classics
in their original form. Stories stripped of long passages, difficult words,
and lengthy chapters. No reading level available. Includes *Heidi, Swiss
Family Robinson, Ivanhoe, The Prince and the Pauper,* and *Treasure Island.*

High Interest–Low Vocabulary Reading Center, McGraw-Hill. Designed to
promote better reading and to develop reading skills on an individual
basis. Contains five copies of title magazine (including story and accompanying activities), one tape cassette, four ditto masters, storage bag, and
a teaching guide. Includes Comprehension; Word Attack; S Blends, R
Blends, and L Blends; Vowel Combinations; Digraphs; Main Idea; and
Details.

Janus Books, Janus Books. Survival books that teach students about life
situations. Nine books in the series. Includes *Using Want Ads, First Aid,*
and *Using a Phone Book.*

Jim Hunter Books, Fearon. From the jungles of Africa to the mountains of
Canada, traveling by submarine, electric transmitter and jet backpacks. A
series of 16 books, reading level 1.0 to 3.0 written for teenagers reading
far below their grade level. Plot summaries, comprehension questions,
and language-skill activities in teacher's guide.

The Job Ahead, Science Research Associates. A career reading series for
potential dropouts. Contains three readers, four resource books, and an
instructor's guide.

Laura Brewster Books, Fearon. A high-interest/low-vocabulary mystery series
featuring a young woman investigator. Reading level approximately third
grade.

Life Skills—Driving, Educational Design. Techniques in driving, traffic signs,
safety, hazardous driving, and basic information concerning driving (driver's license, registering a car, and insurance). A review quiz with each
section and three final tests at the end of the book.

The Monster Books, Bowmar. Series of beginning reading books using natural language patterns of young children. Pictures and stories appealing to
primary- and intermediate-aged youngers.

Mystery Adventure Series, Benefic Press. Mystery stories involving a teenage
boy and girl, appropriate for Grades 5 through 12 with second through
sixth grade reading levels.

New Practice Readers, McGraw-Hill. Short, factual stories in each book followed by comprehension questions. Answer key and teacher's guide for
each level. Reading levels ranging from 2.5 to 6.8 across seven books (A
through G). Good for supplemental materials.

Pacemaker Series, Fearon Pitman. Appropriate for high school students
reading on grade levels 2 through 3.

Pal Paperbacks. Xerox Education Publications. Highly entertaining and exciting stories in paperback format. Truly high-interest/low vocabulary. Appropriate for middle school and higher.

Play the Game, Bowmar. A high-interest/low-vocabulary series appropriate
for high school level. Controlled vocabulary stories featuring the lives of
famous athletes.

Reading Shelf, McGraw-Hill. Reading levels Grades 4 to 6. High-interest/low-
vocabulary series. Each book containing adaptations of popular short

stories/novels. Includes *Requiem for a Heavyweight, Call of the Wild,* and *The Year the Yankees Lost the Pennant.* Could be used to furnish a reading corner in a secondary classroom. Seventeen books in the series.

Really Me Series, EMC Corporation. Included in this series: *Everyone's Watching Tammy, Will the Real Jeannie Murphy Please Stand Up; A Candle, A Feather, A Wooden Spoon;* and *Checkmate Julie.* Focusing on the problems and lives of several girls and young women.

Scope Skills Books, Scholastic Magazine and Book Services. Thirteen books designed to help the learner master and build skills in the areas of reading, word skills, language, and career/study skills. A different theme in each book (e.g., Driving, Fantastic Facts). Includes following directions and finding the main idea. Reading levels Grades 4 through 6. Suitable for persons in Grades 8 to 12.

Scoring High in Survival Reading, Random House. A series that focuses on daily living needs including *Getting Around* and *Earning and Spending.* Appropriate for middle school and secondary students.

Space Police, Fearon Pitman. A space-age cops and robbers series written on a third-grade reading level. Imaginative plots for classroom discussion.

Specter, Fearon Pitman. Eight storybooks written in Hitchcock style with themes of love, greed, intrigue, and ambition. Exciting stories on a third-grade reading level.

Sportellers, Fearon. Compelling stories at reading level 3.0, focusing on different sports, with subplots that explore conflicts confronting today's athletes. A teacher's guide with plot summaries, profiles of people in sports to generate discussion, and comprehension questions.

Sports Mystery Series, Benefic Press. Fast-paced adventure stories for children in Grades 4 through 12, with second- through fourth-grade reading levels.

Sprint Books, Scholastic Book Services. Books written for disabled readers. Cover a variety of interests and include sports, adventure, detective, suspense, and humor stories. Interest level Grades 4 to 6; reading levels grades 1 to 2.

The Time is Now, With It, Winner's Circle, Allyn & Bacon. Written at second-, third-, and fourth-grade reading levels about people of interest to teenage students. Suggestions for writing and follow-up activities included in the teacher's manual.

The Venture Series, Follett Educational Corporation. A reading incentive program for seventh- to twelfth-grade students written on a 4.0 to 6.5 reading level. Two levels, each with six separate books with a certain sport as the central theme of each. Approximately six related stories within each book. Many short biographies of famous athletes. Titles like "On the Boards" (basketball); "Racing to Indy" (Indy Racing); "Inside Track" (track); "Match Point" (tennis); "Slap Shot" (hockey); "Split Decision" (boxing); and "Line Drive" (baseball). Many full-color pictures. Student "Inquiry" books focusing mainly on the human aspect of sports to accompany the series.

11
Written Language

The development of written language skills represents the summit of the language hierarchy. Built on listening, speaking, and reading, writing is a critical component and an important goal within programs of language development.

Written language subsumes the areas of handwriting, spelling, and written expression and thus demands that the communicator have a host of mechanical, memory, conceptual, and organizational skills. Not surprisingly, therefore, writing can present a variety of significant challenges to students with special needs, who may have existing linguistic deficits in oral language and/or reading, low societal expectations for success, and limited encouragement and reinforcement for appropriate usage. The importance of writing to such students, however, should be apparent because it opens another avenue for communication and normalization of life. At minimal levels students must develop the capability to write their names and other personally identifying information. At more advanced levels they may want to complete job applications, take notes, respond to test questions, write letters of inquiry, and be creative.

Traditionally, written language has been relatively ignored in both regular and special education. In part, this lack of attention has reflected the fact that the domain has also been somewhat ignored in research. However, in recent years written language has received more attention. Significant increases in research activities and programming emphasis and the related development of practical instructional techniques have enhanced the status of the domain (Polloway & Decker, 1988).

These advances in research and programming come at an opportune time. For example, a 1986 media report from the federal government indicates that 80% of all high school students in the general population write inadequately, more than 50% do not like the process of writing, and approximately 80% cannot write well enough to ensure that they will convey their meaning. These problems are found to an even greater extent in special education. However, it is important to keep in mind that the writing difficulties of children and adolescents who have handicaps are also experienced by large numbers of other students.

WRITTEN LANGUAGE IN THE CURRICULUM

The role of handwriting, spelling, and written expression within the total curriculum is determined by the functioning levels of the individuals for whom the curriculum is designed. For the young child, handwriting and spelling instruction need to stress letters and then words having the most relevance for that individual (e.g., name, address, common lexicon). As students progress, these skill areas become tool subjects supporting the ability to communicate through writing. Table 11.1 lists a sequence of competencies in written language.

A comprehensive program provides for the development of both creative and functional uses of written language. The creative emphasis stresses individual expression and can promote personal and social adjustment. The functional emphasis serves a more utilitarian purpose, stressing skills with direct applicability to successful independent living. Teachers, particularly at the secondary level, should carefully evaluate both current performance levels in writing and expected future needs to determine which skills will benefit each student most. Written language development should occupy a key position in the curriculum of most students who are mildly or moderately handicapped.

HANDWRITING

Acquiring handwriting proficiency requires orderly, sequential development of skills. In

TABLE 11.1
General competencies in written language

Prerequisite Skills for Handwriting	*Spelling Skills*
Is able to touch, reach, grasp, and release objects	Recognizes letters of the alphabet
Is able to distinguish similarities and differences in objects and designs	Recognizes words
Has established handedness	Says words that can be recognized
Handwriting Skills	Recognizes similarities and differences in words
Grasps writing utensil	Differentiates between different sounds in words
Moves writing utensil up/down	Associates certain sounds (phonemes) with symbols or letters
Moves writing utensil left to right	Spells phonetically regular words
Moves writing utensil in a circular manner	Spells phonetically irregular words
Copies letters	Generates rules for spelling various words and word problems
Copies own name in manuscript form	Uses correctly spelled words in written compositions
Writes own name in manuscript form	*Written Expression Skills*
Copies words and sentences in manuscript form	Writes phrases and sentences
Copies manuscript from far-point	Begins sentences with a capital letter
Copies letters and words in cursive writing	Ends sentences with correct punctuation
Copies sentences in cursive writing	Uses proper punctuation
Copies cursive from far-point	Demonstrates simple rules for sentence structure
	Writes complete paragraphs
	Writes notes and letters
	Expresses creative ideas in writing
	Uses writing functionally to communicate

instructing learners with special needs, especially those with difficulties in recalling or forming specific strokes and letters, teachers should remember the ultimate goal of legibility. Efforts to achieve perfect reproduction are most often doomed to fail; even when successful, they are frequently short-lived triumphs because most students develop a personalized style.

The question of manuscript versus cursive handwriting has been discussed by numerous authors (e.g., Barbe, Milone, & Wasylyk, 1983; Early et al., 1976; Graham & Miller, 1980; Polloway & Smith, 1982). Rationales for teaching only manuscript traditionally include its similarity to book print, the relative ease of letter formation, and its benefit in not confusing students with a second writing form later. Rationales for cursive include its natural rhythm, amelioration of problems with spacing and reversals, social status, and speed.

Despite the various claims and disclaimers about the merits of these forms, the question is often moot: most students have already been taught according to the traditional sequence (i.e., manuscript followed by cursive at about the third grade) before referral for special services, and many students with more serious disabilities need to be taught first in manuscript because it makes fewer motoric demands. If most students ultimately are capable of learning both forms, they can then use the form of handwriting with which they feel most comfortable and are most proficient. No empirical data establish that one form of handwriting is clearly and inherently better than the other for a given population of students. Because most adults write cursively, some support can be generated for having persons who are handicapped write in this way to extend normalization of their development. However, only in personal signatures does cursive writing take clear precedence over manuscript.

Teachers should consider the possible benefits of scripts that combine features of both manuscript and cursive writing, thus eliminating or simplifying the transitional period between the two forms. The mixed script developed by Mullins and colleagues (Mullins, Joseph, Turner, Zawadski, & Saltzman, 1972) and the D'Nealian handwriting program (Thurber & Jordan, 1978) are recommended for this purpose. Consideration should also be given to typing, not only as an alternative for poor writers but as a basis for later instruction in computer keyboarding.

Assessment of Handwriting Skills

If a student has not formally started to write or is experiencing difficulty in acquiring a certain writing skill, the teacher must be able to assess the pupil's potential to develop this skill. Probably the easiest and best method of assessment is through visual inspection; the teacher watches the student forming letters and determines which particular actions in the formation process are causing problems. Teachers can also refer to a commercial writing workbook that contains examples of general and specific handwriting errors and lists steps to correct them.

Many screening devices, such as the Wide Range Achievement Test (Jastak & Jastak, 1965, 1978) and the Slingerland (Slingerland, 1962), have sections that require students to demonstrate mechanical handwriting skills. These tests, however, provide little diagnostic information per se. Another alternative is the Test of Written Language (Hammill & Larsen, 1983), which evaluates handwriting according to graded scales and is further discussed later in this chapter. Once screening has been accomplished, a close visual examination should give the teacher sufficient information to help a pupil develop or remediate specific handwriting skills. The reader is referred to Graham (1983) for a comprehensive review of approaches to assessment.

Prerequisite Skills

The development of prewriting skills demands adequate visual acuity and its coordination with motoric movements. Therefore, it is essential that when students who are handicapped enter formal schooling, they engage in the same type of visual and motoric activities that average children have probably mastered by the time of school entrance. Two objectives—developing visual/motor integration and establishing handedness—are central concerns at this stage. To achieve these goals, numerous activities are typically suggested for handwriting readiness: manipulation of objects, tracing of objects with the index finger in sand, manipulation of scissors for cutting paper, crayon and finger painting, placing forms in proper holes in form boxes, and connecting dots and completing figures. Readiness activities adjusted for differences in chronological age may also be helpful for older students. For example, fine motor skills can be developed in shop classes and in vocational training. Visual/motor integration can be fostered through dart board games and pantomime exercises, including popular games like charades. The activities section at the conclusion of the chapter provides other suggestions.

Several observations need to be made about readiness activities. First, some are clearly important for their own worth (e.g., cutting with scissors) and are thus of merit, regardless of their relationship to writing. However, there is no empirical support for the idea that these exercises assist in refining existing writing skills. It can be argued, instead, that the focus on nonwriting fine motor readiness activities simply takes time away from direct instruction in writing. Another caution concerns the use of readiness activities with children with limited skills; again, an overemphasis on fine motor skills may not be the most beneficial. The handwriting process itself provides fine motor practice and thus can accomplish both linguistically relevant goals and motoric goals (Polloway & Decker, 1988; Wallace et al., 1987). As Hammill (1986) notes, so-called prerequisites can be naturally developed by directing students to write letters and words rather than giving extensive readiness instruction.

Manuscript Writing

Given manuscript writing as the initial in-

o a d g q / b p / c e /
t l i k / r n m h / v w
x y / f j / u / z / s

FIGURE 11.1
A sequential grouping of lowercase manuscript letters according to common features

structional focus for most students, the teacher's first planning tasks are to determine an instructional sequence of letters and to select instructional methodology. There is no correct letter to start with in teaching manuscript writing; however, certain letters lend themselves to that function. For example, the letters of a child's first name have high utility value and motivate learning.

To ensure an appropriate instructional sequence, the teacher can group different letters by their shapes (see Figure 11.1) or can follow the letter sequence in one of many commercial manuscript workbooks available. Another alternative is to follow the order in which letters are introduced for reading. Attention should be given to the relative similarity of strokes required for the letters.

For students who experience difficulty at the beginning stages of writing, modifications of the writing implement should be considered; the greatest problem often encountered is the correct grip on the utensil. A variety of aids have been used to facilitate appropriate grip, including the larger primary-sized pencils, tape wrapped around the pencil, use of a multisided large pencil, and the adaptation of a standard pencil with a Hoyle gripper (a three-sided, plastic device that requires the child to place two fingers and the thumb in the proper position). Although research on handwriting instruction has not demonstrated the necessity of modifying writing utensils (Graham & Miller, 1980), the data base has not been generated from problem learners. Thus, it seems prudent to assess the grip of individual students who are experiencing difficulties in order to determine whether an adaptation is warranted (Polloway & Decker, 1988). Norton's (1980) suggestion that students be allowed to select the size of utensil most comfortable for them seems particularly apt.

The beginning stages of writing can be made less confusing by connecting a colored guideline to the lines on the paper that students can touch when they form letters. This guideline, similar to the lines on ordinary writing paper, would also indicate where to start writing. A broken guideline instead of a continuous one would help students focus even more on which lines to touch.

Another point of confusion is inconsistent descriptions of the letters of the alphabet. For example, referring to a "tall letter" or a "big letter" may leave students wondering whether the reference is to an uppercase letter or a large-sized lowercase letter. Use of the terms capital and small may also be confusing. Consistent use of the terms *uppercase* and *lowercase* is recommended when referring to different sizes or functions of a particular letter. Lowercase letters are introduced before most uppercase letters because students use them more often in daily exercises. Even though no hard and fast rules exist about when to introduce uppercase letters, some consistent sequence should be followed, such as that in Figure 11.2.

The most effective approach to teaching specific letters and words is one in which teacher presentation is consistent. Most pro-

LHTEFI / JU /
PRBDK/AMN
VWXYZ/S/
OQCG

FIGURE 11.2
A sequential grouping of uppercase manuscript letters according to common features

grams assume that these forms are best taught in isolation but that opportunities must be provided for their use in actual writing exercises. Graham and Miller (1980) provide an excellent review of effective instructional techniques and sequence to facilitate letter formation. The paragraph that follows is based on the specific steps they outline for instruction.

The first step is teacher demonstration of the formation of specific letters with students observing the specific strokes involved in the formation of the letter in question. Students' attention should be directed to the distinctive features of specific letters and their comparison with letters previously learned. As the children begin to transcribe letters, the teacher should use prompting (e.g., manual guidance during writing, directional arrows) and tracing to facilitate the task. When there is no longer a need for intrusive prompting, instruction becomes a function of copying—typically, from near-point (i.e., from a paper on the student's desk) and then from far-point (i.e., from the chalkboard). While copying and when writing from memory, students should be encouraged to engage in self-instruction by verbalizing to themselves the writing procedures being followed. After a letter can be written from memory, continued repetition of the form is needed to ensure learning and enhance proficiency. Finally, corrective feedback from the teacher, extrinsic reinforcement, and/or self-correction can be used so that the letter will be retained and increased legibility will be achieved.

As students master the formation of additional letters, they should be encouraged to write more about events occurring in the environment. Many teachers make good use of natural events by writing about them in the daily "class news." At this point, teachers should watch for opportunities to record dictated thoughts on paper so that students can associate speaking, reading, and writing. One of the best uses of language experience charts is to help students perceive that what they say can be written down and read later. To prepare secondary-level students for the world of work and for the forms and applications that so frequently specify "Please print," teachers should provide practical opportunities for improving manuscript writing.

During the same time that manuscript letters are being taught, work with the numerals 0 through 9 should be started. Because students will be dealing with number concepts in arithmetic and related areas, symbols including written numerals are needed to represent the abstractions that students will be making with these concepts.

Cursive Writing

The set of skills acquired while learning manuscript writing is of assistance to students when they begin to learn how to write in cursive form. The movement to cursive writing should stress the key features of that style: paper positioning, the pencil remaining on the paper throughout the writing of individual words, all letters starting at the baseline, a left-to-right rhythm, an appropriate slant to the right, connection of letters, and spacing between words. Students should be encouraged to begin with manuscript let-

ters that directly evolve into cursive forms.

Generally, instruction in cursive writing should follow the same format used with manuscript form: (1) start with letters that students are presently working with while following a predetermined sequence (see Figures 11.3 and 11.4) or follow the sequence found in a commercial cursive writing workbook; (2) consistently use *uppercase* and *lowercase* to describe a letter; and (3) work with previously written words at the beginning of students' cursive writing experiences to promote transfer and overlearning. In addition, teachers must always tell students whether they should be writing in cursive or manuscript. When students begin to use cursive writing, they will also be using more complex verbalizations and will be able to record them in sentence and paragraph form. Teachers should give students appropriate writing opportunities.

With both manuscript and cursive writing, there is a need for instructional procedures that promote proficiency and maintenance. A useful technique originally reported by Lovitt (1975) is selective checking. To use this technique, a teacher selects a specific letter to be evaluated at the end of a given daily assignment. A model is provided for the student with an established criterion for acceptable legibility. After reviewing the specific examples of the

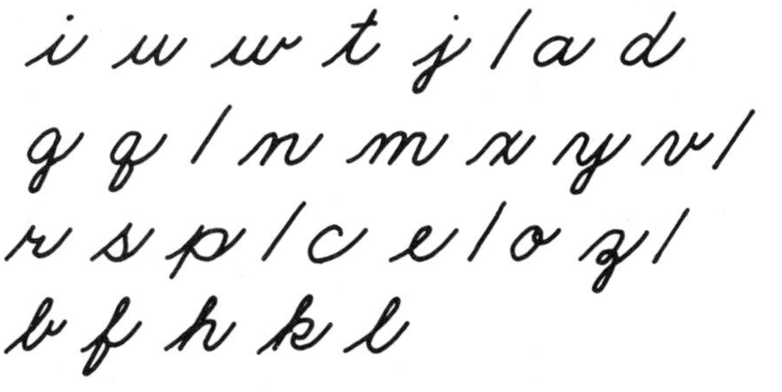

FIGURE 11.3
A sequential grouping of lowercase cursive letters according to common features

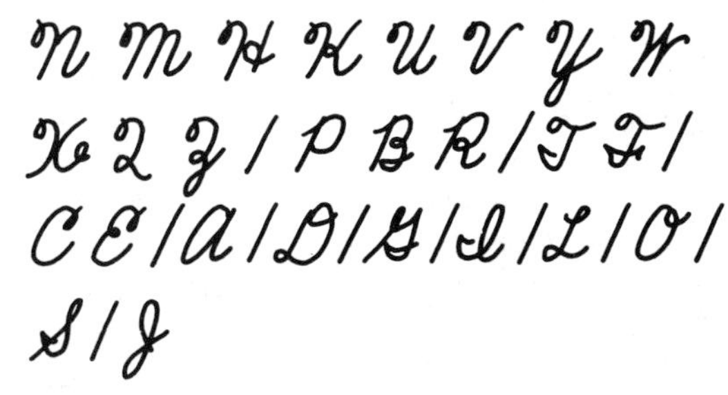

FIGURE 11.4
A sequential grouping of uppercase cursive letters according to common features

letter-of-the-day within the particular task, the teacher uses illegibility as the basis for assigning additional practice exercises and correct letter formation as the basis for reinforcement.

The success of any proficiency/maintenance program is ultimately based on the active involvement of the student. Therefore, teachers should emphasize self-regulation as the most effective long-term procedure to follow. In the case of writing, appropriate procedures include self-monitoring of letter or word formation, self-evaluation of the individual letter or word in comparison to the established criterion, and self-reinforcement for successful performance (for specific examples see Kosiewicz, Hallahan, Lloyd, & Graves, 1982; Graham, 1983).

Left-Handedness

Left-handed students often encounter special problems in writing, which may accentuate the other problems already present in students with learning difficulties. Left-handed students cannot see letters adequately as they form them because the left hand blocks out a letter shortly after it is written. One simple strategy is for these students to grasp the writing utensil further away from the tip while maintaining the same grip on the pencil or pen (Monroe, 1973). Left-handed students should not be encouraged to hook their hand to see better; this practice is tiring and may cause more problems. However, students who are already successfully writing in a hooked fashion should not be reeducated. The left-handed student's paper should also be slightly angled to the right side of the desk. If possible, students should be provided with a model for writing; cooperative grouping efforts in schools with a left-handed teacher are a possible way to provide such a model. Graham and Miller (1980) provide beneficial diagrams indicating alternative positioning for left-handed persons.

SPELLING

Because of the many potential rules for correct spelling and because many teachers do not consider themselves proficient spellers, teaching spelling is often viewed as a tedious, boring process. However, rather than viewing it as an isolated act, teachers should consider the strong relationship between spelling, handwriting, and reading and take advantage of that relationship to help students elevate performance in all three areas. This task can be accomplished by having students write about familiar situations and events; using familiar words in numerous contexts more easily motivates students to learn to spell.

In general, students can learn to spell in two complementary ways: by rote memory and by learning spelling rules. Even though rote learning does not always apply in other areas, Smith (1974) states that "as is true in no other area, rote instruction in spelling rather than emphasizing conceptual development and understanding is necessary" (p. 200). Lerner (1985) echoes these sentiments: "Spelling is one curriculum area in which neither creativity nor divergent thinking is encouraged. Only one pattern or arrangement of letters can be accepted as correct; there is no compromise or leeway" (p. 406). This implication cannot be overstated: since precise revisualization of words is necessary for success in spelling, rote learning is probably the most efficient way for handicapped students to learn. As they learn to spell a greater number of words, teachers can explain some beneficial spelling rules to help them learn to spell additional words. When developing a comprehensive instructional program, teachers should also be mindful of the role that phonetic and structural analysis, handwriting, and interest and motivation play in the process.

Assessment

Although many achievement tests contain

sections devoted to spelling, these tools generally do little more than give a gross estimate of a student's achievement. Even with a specific device, such as the traditional Gates-Russell Spelling Diagnostic Test (Gates & Russell, 1940), the teacher is left with a grade score for each of the subtests and the student's responses. The teacher must then analyze and evaluate the responses to determine exactly what the problem is. Another available instrument is the Test of Written Spelling (TWS) (Larsen & Hammill, 1976), which has been validated by research. The TWS measures a student's ability to spell both phonetically regular and irregular words. A modified form of the TWS is included in the Test of Written Language (Hammill & Larsen, 1983).

Informal approaches to assessment are of greater value to the teacher in planning instructional programs. Error analysis can provide the type of specific information to complement the data derived from standardized tests. Error analysis should be based on careful scrutiny of specific patterns in a student's misspellings. Edgington (1968) and Polloway and Smith (1982) suggest the following:

- ☐ additions of unneeded letters
- ☐ omissions of needed letters
- ☐ reflections of mispronunciation
- ☐ reflections of dialectal patterns
- ☐ reversals of letters
- ☐ reversals of syllables
- ☐ reversals of whole words
- ☐ phonetic overgeneralizations
- ☐ letter-order confusion
- ☐ final consonant changes

Another approach is to develop a simple diagnostic survey of words containing some of the most common spelling errors and administer it to students as an informal test. For example, the test could emphasize letter changes at the end of words.

1. *y* to *i* when a suf-   *happiness*
   fix is added

2. *y* to *i* in plurals   *flies*
   and tense
3. final *e* that makes   *rate, cane*
   preceding vowel
   long
4. final *e* dropped   *liking, using*
   when suffix
   is added
5. final consonant   *stopped, trapping,*
   doubled when   *planning*
   suffix is added

Instruction

Spelling instruction should begin soon after students have started to learn to read because they will be attempting to write certain words that they can read. Once again, the close ties between spelling, reading, and writing should lead to integrated instruction in these areas.

The first words that students write are very meaningful to them, not just because they are new, but because they are usually the names of people, places, and things with which the students are familiar. Teachers should make other new words as meaningful as possible, perhaps by using new words to make up stories about students' immediate environment, thus facilitating an easy passage from the old to the new, or by placing new words in colorful sequence on a bulletin board, thereby causing students to be interested in finding out what the words are and how to spell them.

Word selection can be made from a variety of sources. Based on a student's ability and interest level, a teacher can select from frequency-of-use lists such as Dolch words, linguistic word families (e.g., *fan/tan/pan*), words used regularly within a student's oral expressive vocabulary, lists promulgated by specific remedial programs, words taken from the student's list of mastered reading words, and functional words.

Students with special needs should have as many functional words in their spelling vocabularies as possible. Functional words help young students communicate more effectively and older individuals gain and maintain employment, adjust to environmental and social demands, and thus achieve social independence. Teachers are in the best position to draw up a list of functional words for students to learn (e.g., a word such as *subway* that has significance in the New York borough of Manhattan does not have the same meaning for a child in Manhattan, Kansas). Functional word lists can be integrated into the reading program and can help students develop skills not only for spelling, but for life in general. Additionally, special symbols and print forms important in vocational and/or social situations may require attention, particularly with adolescents: common abbreviations (e.g., *RSVP, Ms., Dr.*), technical symbols (e.g., + and − on battery terminals, *p.m., FM*), and common acronyms (e.g., *VCR, JV*).

A host of instructional strategies can assist students having difficulty with spelling. Teachers should plan a program allowing for regular, systematic instruction while drawing from a variety of word-study techniques that are effective for particular students. The most successful use multisensory approaches, promote revisualization of words, or assist students in formulating specific rules for accurate spelling. Some selected techniques outlined by Graham and Miller (1979, p. 14) and Polloway and Smith (1982) are presented in Table 11.2.

An emphasis on spelling rules can also be beneficial within a spelling program. Because the English language can provide "productive relationships" (Hodges, 1966, p. 332) between sounds and symbols, such an emphasis can be important as a mediating influence. The sequence provided by Brueckner and Bond (1967, p. 374) can be helpful in teaching generalizations.

1. Select a particular rule to be taught. Teach a single rule at a time.

2. Secure a list of words exemplifying the rule. Develop an understanding of the rule through a study of the words that it covers.

3. Lead pupils to discover the underlying generalization by discussing with them the characteristics of the words in the list. If possible, have pupils actually formulate the rule; help them to sharpen and clarify it.

4. Have pupils use and apply the rule immediately.

5. If necessary, show that the rule does not apply in some cases, but stress its positive value.

6. Review the rule systematically on succeeding days. Emphasize its use, but do not require pupils to memorize a formalized statement.

Another word study approach is the corrected-test method. In their review of research, Graham and Miller (1979) report this approach as the most effective in producing spelling improvement. Under a teacher's direction students correct specific spelling errors immediately after being tested. As Graham and Miller (1979) note, this strategy enables students to observe which words are particularly difficult, identify the part of the words creating the difficulty, and correct the errors under supervision.

Regardless of the word list selected or the approach utilized, spelling instruction can be effective only if students have opportunities to use the target words in written assignments and to proofread their work for possible errors. Although learning words in isolation facilitates acquisition, maintenance and generalization are achieved only when students are encouraged to make regular use of the words they have learned. However, because students risk a conceptual break in their expressive efforts as they ponder the correct form of a difficult word (see Personkee & Yee, 1966, 1968), they can be encouraged to write an approximation of

TABLE 11.2
Selected techniques for spelling instruction

Fitzgerald Method (Fitzgerald, 1951)

1. Look at the word carefully.
2. Say the word.
3. With eyes closed, visualize the word.
4. Cover the word and then write it.
5. Check the spelling.
6. If the word is misspelled, repeat Steps 1 through 5.

Horn Method (Horn, 1954)

1. Pronounce each word carefully.
2. Look carefully at each part of the word as you pronounce it.
3. Say the letters in sequence.
4. Attempt to recall how the word looks; then spell it.
5. Check this attempt to recall.
6. Write the word.
7. Check this spelling attempt.
8. Repeat the above steps if necessary.

Simultaneous Oral Spelling (Gillingham & Stillman, 1960)

1. Select a regular word and pronounce it.
2. Repeat the word after the teacher.
3. Say the sounds in the words.
4. Name the letters used to represent the sounds.
5. Write the word, naming the letters while writing them.

Fernald Method (1943) (Modified)

1. Make a model of the word with a crayon, grease pencil, or magic marker, saying the word as you write it.
2. Check the accuracy of the model.
3. Trace over the model with your index finger, saying the word at the same time.
4. Repeat Step 3 five times.
5. Copy the word three times correctly.
6. Copy the word three times from memory correctly.

Cover-and-Write Method

1. Look at the word; say it.
2. Write the word two times.
3. Cover and write it one time.
4. Check work.
5. Write the word two times.
6. Cover and write it one time.
7. Check work.
8. Write the word three times.
9. Cover and write it one time.
10. Check work.

the word initially and then review it and correct it as necessary during the postwriting phase.

WRITTEN EXPRESSION

The technical skills of handwriting and spelling warrant attention for particular benefits of their own, but their primary purpose is to serve as tools in written communication and expression. As the final step in the linguistic hierarchy, written expression builds on all of the skills acquired in other language domains. The process of writing can best be conceptualized as a multicom-

ponent model (Hall, 1981), a series of three or four sequential stages that not only define the process but also guide the necessary instruction. Writing models typically divide the process into the three stages of prewriting, or planning; writing, or drafting; and postwriting, or revision and editing (see, for example, Polloway, Patton, & Cohen, 1981, 1983).

Prewriting consists of what the would-be writer considers prior to the act itself. Input includes the various forms of stimulation that assist in forming a basic intent to write. Examples include environmental experience, reading, listening, and media exposure. Motivation includes the efforts of various stimulating activities, as well as the external factors that reinforce writing. Given the failure that older students in particular may have experienced in communicating, motivation remediation may be as critical as direct skill instruction (see Phelps-Gunn & Phelps-Terasaki, 1982). In addition, purpose must be established to assist in organization. Expressive writing is primarily concerned with creative, personal communication, whereas functional writing focuses on more utilitarian aspects (e.g., letters of inquiry, applications).

The writing stage encompasses primarily the handwriting and spelling previously discussed as well as the other craft aspects of written language. These mechanics include vocabulary, meaning and description, sentence form, paragraph sense, and the overall sequence of ideas, consistency, clarity, and relevance. The postwriting stage focuses on the importance of proofreading and general editing of these elements to improve the expression of the written product.

Viewing these three stages of writing as distinct and significant in their own rights enables instruction to focus on the specific tasks facing the would-be writer. However, it is important to realize that, in practice, these phases are not perfectly discrete. For example, planning continues to take place during the postwriting stage, and revising, to at least a limited extent, takes place during the drafting stage. Nevertheless, an initial focus on the stages of writing does provide a process-type approach, which can assist students in thinking about what they are to do (Thomas, Englert, & Gregg, 1987).

Assessment

Even though writing produces a permanent product to aid teachers in assessment, a number of problems complicate such evaluation (Polloway et al., 1983). Of particular concern are the relative paucity of formal tools available and the emphasis of existing tests on contrived formats (e.g., multiple-choice items) that assess only the mechanical aspects of writing (Hogan & Mishler, 1979). This latter problem is particularly common in achievement-oriented tests with written language subtests, such as the California Achievement Test (Tiegs & Clark, 1970). Several formal diagnostic tools can provide a more comprehensive analysis of written language abilities.

☐ The Picture Story Language Test (PSLT) (Myklebust, 1965) is a tool for evaluating the abilities of children aged 7 to 17 in terms of productivity, syntax, and abstract/concrete thoughts expressed. The student is shown a picture and then is asked to write a story about it. The test can be administered to individuals or groups. Questions raised about its validity have led some to suggest restricting usage primarily to informal assessment (see Wallace & Larsen, 1978).

☐ The Test of Written Language (TOWL) (Hammill & Larsen, 1978, 1983) was developed to assess the adequacy of abilities in handwriting, spelling, and the various other components of written expression. The revised edition of the test includes scales for vocabulary, thematic maturity, word usage, and style. Both spontaneous and contrived formats provide a basis for assessment, with primary emphasis on evaluating an actual writing sample. This is the most well-designed, diagnostically useful formal tool available for analyzing the writing of students with handicaps (Polloway, 1985).

Because formal tools cannot fully evaluate the total scope of written expression, informal assessment approaches should receive primary attention. In the model presented by Polloway et al. (1983), each aspect of evaluation can become the basis for specific questions concerning students' writing samples. The techniques described in Table 11.3 facilitate analysis of a number of these aspects.

The key to using any of the procedures listed in Table 11.3 is to analyze students' writing samples. Frequent opportunities to communicate must be part of the weekly experiences of all students possessing basic skills in the area. Teachers should plan a sequence of skills that will be evaluated on an ongoing basis and should resist the temptation to provide corrective feedback for all types of errors simultaneously. Error analysis should thus focus on an individual skill deficit as a basis for remediation. For students with limited written language ability, assessing samples is relatively simple and straightforward. For students with more advanced skills requiring more complex analysis, Cartwright (1969), Moran (1983), Polloway and Smith (1982), and Wallace and Larsen (1978) can provide additional information.

Instruction

Prewriting Instruction taking place during the planning stage should reflect the reality of how students present themselves for instruction. In particular, assumptions should not be made that pupils with handicaps have had the necessary experiential prerequisites to develop ideation, that they have a desire to communicate via written means, or that they understand their purpose in writing and the nature of their intended audience. Each of these factors should be addressed by instruction.

The first concern at this stage is stimulation. Teachers should strive to provide opportunities to expose students to varied experiences through listening and reading; provide them with a chance to discuss and

clarify ideas on a given topic, thus encouraging active thinking about the task at hand; and establish a conducive, supportive classroom atmosphere. Concerned teachers working with learners with special needs must stimulate students before giving them a chance to write. Research, however (as summarized by Phelps-Gunn & Phelps-Terasaki, 1982), does not indicate an automatic effect of significant change in written performance, as measured in terms of syntax, vocabulary, and ideation. These findings simply show that stimulation alone does not promote basic skills. Rather, it provides for conceptualization and offers an organizational picture; it starts writers thinking clearly.

The second concern at this stage is motivation, which is particularly critical for adolescents with disabilities. A substantial amount of research focused on the writing of nonhandicapped students argues that motivation must come from within; teachers can stimulate students, but they cannot actually motivate them. According to this logic, if students have something meaningful and/or interesting to think about, their writing will flow (Tway, 1975). That premise in remedial and special education, however, presents some difficulty because writing just does not happen much of the time. Teachers of special students should consider remediating motivation, finding ways to incorporate external reward systems to complement internal motivation of reluctant writers.

Alley and Deshler (1979) provide several apt observations that summarize the motivational area. Identifying attitude toward writing as a key concern, they suggest the following strategies: encourage students to focus initially on ideation rather than mechanical skills so that they feel comfortable with writing before trying to achieve perfection (thus, sensing failure); expose students to a variety of experiences to build their

TABLE 11.3
Informal procedures for assessing written expression

Technique	Description	Methodology	Example	Comment
Type-token ratio	Measure of the variety of words used (types) in relation to overall number of words used (tokens)	$\dfrac{\text{Different words used}}{\text{Total words used}}$	type = 28 token = 50 ratio = $\dfrac{28}{50}$ = .56	Greater diversity of usage implies a more mature writing style.
Index of diversification	Measure of diversity of word usage	$\dfrac{\text{Total number of words used}}{\text{Number of occurrences of the most frequently used word}}$	total words = 72 number of times word *the* appeared = 12 index = 6	An increase in the index value implies a broader vocabulary base.
Average sentence length	Measure of sentence usage (number of words per sentence)	$\dfrac{\text{Total number of words used}}{\text{Total number of sentences}}$	total words = 54 total sentences = 9 words per sentence = 6	Longer length of sentences implies more mature writing ability.
Error analysis	Measure of word and sentence usage	Compare errors found in a writing sample with list of common errors		Teacher can determine error patterns and can prioritize concerns.
T-unit length (Hunt, 1965)	Measure of writing maturity	1. Determine the number of discrete thought units (T-units) 2. Determine average length of T-unit: $\dfrac{\text{Total words}}{\text{Total number of T-units}}$ 3. Analyze quantitative variables: a. no. of sentences used b. no. of T-units c. no. of words per T-unit 4. Analyze qualitative nature of sentences	"The summer was almost over and the children were ready to go back to school." *Quantitative* (1; 2; 5 + 10) *Qualitative:* 1. compound sentence 2. adverbs: of degree—"almost" of place—"back" 3. adjective—"ready" 4. infinitive—"to go" 5. prepositional phrase adverbial of place—"to school"	This technique gives the teacher information in relation to productivity and maturity of writing skills.

Source: From "Written Language for Mildly Handicapped Students" by E. A. Polloway, J. R. Patton, and S. B. Cohen, in *Promising Practices for Exceptional Children: Curriculum Implications* (pp. 300–301) by E. L. Meyen, G. A. Vergason, and R. J. Whelan (Eds.), 1983, Denver: Love. Copyright 1983 by Love Publishing Company. Reprinted by permission.

knowledge base for writing; use tape re-corders as a way to record thoughts, followed by subsequent efforts to transcribe and revise these thoughts; and have students write daily or weekly journals without corrective feedback.

The third aspect of planning is that of setting the purpose. The writer must have a clear understanding of who the audience is and, thus, what the purpose is. Expressive and functional writing have different intents and thus require different formats.

Writing The writing or drafting stage is the broadest of the three components. Consequently, it is of little surprise that problems and deficits in this phase are common in students who are handicapped. The educator's key concern is to determine how skills are most effectively learned and most effectively taught. With this focus, it is useful to consider the distinctions made by Smith (1982) and discussed by Isaacson (1987). Two roles can be seen as inherent in the writing process: the author role and the secretarial role. Whereas the author role is concerned with the formulation and organization of ideas and the selection of words and phrases to express those ideas, the secretarial role emphasizes the physical and mechanical concerns of writing, such as legibility, spelling, punctuation, and grammatical rules. Obviously, both roles are critical to a writer's success, and both have influenced instructional practice.

Sink (1975) distinguishes between a focus on teach-write and on write-teach. The former corresponds reasonably well with the secretarial role of writing; it emphasizes formal grammar instruction, structure, skills exercises, perhaps the diagramming of sentences, and often a reliance on worksheets and workbook pages. Even though this approach is extremely common in classrooms, its traditional and common contemporary usage is not indicative of proven effective-

ness. For example, Sherwin's (1964) extensive review of the literature on this topic found little evidence of the effectiveness of this approach with nonhandicapped learners. There is even less reason to believe that the teach-write approach is effective with learners with special needs. A major concern is that the instructional activities required can be completed without opportunity for actual writing. At the same time they can damage motivation to write by usurping a major block of time, something that special education writing programs have in only limited supply (Silverman, Zigmond, Zimmerman, & Vallecorsa, 1981; Zigmond, Vallecorsa, & Leinhardt, 1980). Thus, although skills are important, they may not be truly learned—that is, applied—in this fashion.

The alternative is the write-teach focus, with initial stress on the primacy of the author role, on ideation over form, with structure emphasized later. The write-teach approach capitalizes on the desire to write without stifling that effort. Structure can then be taught within the context of actual writing opportunities (Polloway & Decker, 1988).

Graves (1985) succinctly states the case for a write-teach approach.

Most teaching of writing is pointed toward the eradication of error, the mastery of minute, meaningless components that make little sense to the child. Small wonder. Most language arts texts, workbooks, computer software, and reams of behavioral objectives are directed toward the "easy" control of components that will show more specific growth. Although some growth may be evident on components, rarely does it result in the child's use of writing as a tool for learning and enjoyment. Make no mistake, component skills are important; if children do not learn to spell or use a pencil to get words on paper, they won't use writing for learning any more than the other children drilled on component skills. The writing-processing approach simply stresses meaning first, and then skills in the context of meaning. (p. 43)

If this option is adopted, there are a number of clear implications for instruction. Most significant is that for writing to improve, students need to write regularly. Graves (1985) recommends that students write at least 4 days per week and indicates that irregular instruction merely reminds students of their inability to write. Journal writing is an approach that has been used effectively for this purpose (see Fader & McNeill, 1968). A positive, supportive atmosphere is a logical supplement.

Once the opportunity to write is confirmed, the development of structural skills can best be handled through selective feedback, which focuses on a limited number of skills at a given point in time. Selective feedback is a preferred alternative to both extremes of inordinate corrections or meaningless comments about "good work." One way to accomplish selective feedback is through teacher conferencing (Barenbaum, 1983). With this technique the teacher proofreads written assignments and provides feedback directly to students, most often in an oral conference. Such an approach provides an opportunity to introduce and reinforce specific skills and conventions.

Experience, rather than empirical data, serves as the support for the write-teach approach. Therefore, it would be presumptuous to embrace the approach unquestioningly. One should not simplistically assume that the more students write, the better their writing will become. Unfortunately, that is often not the case. The teaching of individual skills must be tied to the opportunity to use them.

Vocabulary Development A major instructional concern is vocabulary building, which encourages students to use a variety of words. Because oral vocabulary is larger than written vocabulary in most cases, teachers should look for ways to facilitate transition from oral vocabulary to writing. The language experience approach (LEA) offers a natural lead-in by combining attention to listening, speaking, reading, and writing. With LEA, students dictate stories that teachers transcribe for subsequent reading. Students then revise the stories, establishing the link between oral and written expression.

Within the context of specific writing tasks, several strategies may promote vocabulary development. Students can generate specific words that might be needed in a writing assignment, and the teacher can write them on the chalkboard for illustration and later reference. A list of words can also be kept on a bulletin board for students to copy and place in a notebook for later use. This is especially helpful with high-frequency words that are also spelling demons. Having the accurate spellings of words that are likely to be used minimizes interruptions in the conceptualization process (Wallace et al., 1987). Instructional activities should also focus on the development of descriptive language. Students might brainstorm alternative words to use in a specific instance and then systematically substitute them in their own written compositions. This exercise can target synonyms as well as a variety of adjectives and adverbs to increase the descriptiveness of individual writing (see Bailey, 1975, for additional suggestions).

Vocabulary building can also be facilitated by various reward systems, as research on applied behavior analysis has clearly pointed out. A variety of contingency arrangements has been reported; collectively, they indicate that reinforcement for specific targets, such as use of unusual words, not only produces gains in that area but often produces generalization to related skills (see Polloway et al., 1983). A cautionary word comes from Cohen and Plaskon (1980), who note that it is preferable to develop a smaller, accurately used vocabulary than a larger, perhaps superficially impressive one. Certainly, fluency should not be sacrificed for improvements in overall lexicon. For some students, especially those who are lower functioning and have limited writing abilities, the most appropriate goal is the acquisition and correct use of a limited number of functional words.

Sentence Development Another significant aspect of writing instruction is sentence development. The sentence is the nucleus of structural work with students and the basis for teaching about appropriate syntax. Often, the poor writer's efforts are characterized by either safe, repetitive, short sentences or rambling prose without any structure. It is important to balance an emphasis on "real writing" with focused instruction on patterned sentence guides and structures (Isaacson, 1987). With such guides students can enhance their efforts to communicate effectively. The simplest form of patterned guide presents a picture for which students must write a sentence, following a set pattern. One such pattern might be "The (dog) is (running)."

Several other instructional alternatives are also available. The Fitzgerald Key (Fitzgerald, 1966) was developed for hearing-impaired children based on the assumption that written language would help them improve in oral language. Essentially, it analyzes sentences into a series of *Wh* questions (who, what, when, and where) instead of labeling nouns, verbs, adjectives, adverbs, and prepositions. This alternative is promising for students with handicaps, because it avoids the density of instruction in parts of speech. It keeps instruction meaningful and more relevant by focusing on things that students can deal with directly. The Fitzgerald Key has been modi-

fied in the Phelps Sentence Guide (Phelps-Terasaki & Phelps, 1980), which involves a structured sequence for generating, elaborating, and ordering sentences based on various stimuli and a series of questions posed to students. Students learn to expand from simple phrases to more complex sentences. Figure 11.5 provides an example of the Phelps Sentence Guide as it is presented in the program manual.

This model can be used in two ways. One approach is to take a sentence from a text or other available material and analyze it according to specific word categories, thus outlining the specific parts of a sentence. The second option is to have students generate a series of words or phrases to fit in each of these columns; at that point a sentence or series of sentences can be synthesized. Both exercises emphasize a direct relationship between words and sentences and facilitate sentence sense. Either approach enables students to appreciate how lexical items can vary sentence usage, sentence sense, and sentence generation. Further information on sentence development is available in the program of Phelps-Gunn and Phelps-Terasaki (1982).

A further step in sentence development is sentence combining, which expands simple sentences into more complex ones. Research has indicated that sentence combining is an effective way to increase syntactic maturity and improve the overall quality of writing (Isaacson, 1987; Scarmadalia & Bereiter, 1986). Among the most commonly used programs of sentence combining is one developed by Strong (1973, 1983), which asks students to combine clusters of sentences; they are informed that this can be accomplished in a variety of ways and that no specific response is indicated. A sample cluster from Strong's (1973) initial program is shown here.

1. Most of us remember Groper.
2. We remember from our high school days.

THE PHELPS SENTENCE GUIDE: SAMPLE STAGE 1 SENTENCES

First? Second? Next? Then? Last? At Last? Later?	Which? How many? What kind of?	Who? What?	How Much? Which? How many? What kind of?	Doing? (is, are, was, were, am, have, had, did, does)	What?	For what? To what? To whom? For whom?	When?	Where?	How? Why? If? So? Because? So that? Since?
	The fat	boy		is eating	cake				because it is his birthday.
		The man	in the long scarf	is driving	a sports car.				
		The rocket		is flying				to the moon.	
	The funny	clown		is juggling	bottles.				
		The boy	in the raincoat	is riding	his bike				
		The man	in the boots	is riding	the horse		at night.		
	The two	girls		are giving	the dog	a bath.		in the street.	
		The ghost		is scaring	the boy.				
	The pretty	lady		is wearing	a long dress.				
		The pitcher		is throwing	the ball	to the catcher.			
		The bird		is building	a nest			in the tree.	

FIGURE 11.5

Phelps Sentence Guide sample (From *Teaching Written Expression: The Phelps Sentence Guide Program* [pp. 16–17] by D. Phelps-Terasaki and T. Phelps, 1980, Novato, CA: Academic Therapy. Copyright 1980 by Academic Therapy Publications. Reprinted by permission.)

3. He was angular.
4. He was muscled.
5. He had huge hands.
6. The quarterback would send him down.
7. The quarterback would send him out into the flat.
8. And then the football would come.
9. It looped in an arc.
10. The arc spiraled.
11. Groper would go up.
12. He would scramble with the defense.
13. The defense clawed at his jersey.
14. He was always in the right place.
15. He was always there at the right time.
16. Now we all wonder.
17. We wonder about Groper.
18. He just hangs around town.
19. He does odd jobs.
20. You can see him in the evenings.
21. He watches the team.
22. The team practices. (p. 38)

Even though Strong's program does not begin with true writing, it does encourage students to expand and develop their own creation. Individual tasks finish with an invitation to finish the story.

Strong's (1983) program provides a positive prototype for instruction in this area. However, it has clear limitations for students with handicaps; most notably, the lessons are not extensive enough to provide the necessary amount of practice. Therefore, teachers would need to supplement the program with their own clusters. To this end, Reutzel (1986) illustrates a variety of sentence-combining techniques that students with writing difficulties would find useful.

Paragraph Development   Just as sentences are the transition from words to organized thoughts, paragraphs represent the transition from sentences to a unified composition. Instruction in paragraphing provides training in organization. Otto and colleagues (1973) note that students need to learn that paragraphs are simply a matter of making assertions and elaborating on those assertions; they have an introductory sentence that asks why, followed by two or three sentences that give the "because" (Buchan, 1979). To begin, teachers can identify a topical sentence, and students can provide elaboration. Then students can generate the first sentence, and the teacher can monitor their efforts. Later, teachers can have students support their topic sentences with three follow-up sentences and one clincher sentence.

To give some meaning to paragraph writing, teachers can assign functional tasks for initial instruction, because their purpose is often more apparent. One example is a one-paragraph letter ordering a particular item from a catalogue.

A helpful technique to assist in the building of paragraphs, as well as a useful skill for writing in general, is paraphrasing. One example of a paraphrasing strategy, developed by the University of Kansas Institute for Research on Learning Disabilities (Schumaker, Denton, & Deshler, 1984, cited in Ellis & Sabornie, 1986), is identified as RAP. The acronym comes from *r*ead a paragraph, *a*sk yourself what the main ideas and details in the paragraph were, and *p*ut the main idea and details into your own words.

Postwriting   The general goal of writing instruction is to enable students to communicate effectively with others while achieving personal satisfaction in the process. To achieve this goal, the revision stage must become a routine and integral part of the writing process. Students must be sold on the concept of the working draft as simply the initial effort to get on paper the information to be shared. The revision stage must acquire a positive association for students, removed from any connection with punitive action.

Postwriting requires the active involvement of the writer in the careful review and revision of what has been previously written. Consequently, instruction must be more specific than "Proofread your paper." Initially, students must have the opportunity to establish the concept and activate the skills. Training can begin with anonymous papers and direct instructions to identify correct and incorrect sentences, find three spelling errors, find all capitalization errors, and/or correct all punctuation errors on a given page. After reaching an acceptable criterion, students can shift to their own work.

Focusing on the full spectrum of proofreading is an overwhelming task for any student with difficulties in writing. Therefore, only one or two skills should be stressed at any time. A helpful approach for the organization of proofreading activities is the error-monitoring strategy indicated by the acronym COPS. Schumaker and colleagues (1981) encourage its use in monitoring these areas of concern.

- [ ] *Capitalization:* Have I capitalized the first word and proper nouns?
- [ ] *Overall appearance:* Have I made any handwriting, margin, messy, or spacing errors?
- [ ] *Punctuation:* Have I used end punctuation, commas, and semicolons correctly?
- [ ] *Spelling:* Do the words look like they are spelled right, can I sound them out, or should I use the dictionary?

The COPS process is intended to be introduced one step at a time. Students should first learn a particular skill and then the process of proofreading for that skill. After they have been trained to proofread for each of the components separately, they can be directed to use all four at the same time.

There is far more to the process of proofreading than checking for capitalization, overall appearance, punctuation, and spelling, however. If students acquire these skills, instruction should then focus on the higher levels of editing, with special attention to content and organization. As abilities progress, more specific guidelines can be provided. Krause (1983, p. 30) developed the following checklists:

Sentence Revision Checklist

1. Is my subject specific enough?
2. Do I need adjectives or other modifiers to create a better image?
3. Do I need adverbs or phrases to tell how, when, or where?
4. Have I used capital letters and punctuation marks correctly?
5. Do my subjects and verbs agree?

Paragraph Revision Checklist

1. Where is my most important sentence? Does it stand out?
2. Do all of my other sentences tell about the important sentence?
3. Can I combine some short sentences to make them sound better?
4. Are all of my pronouns clear?
5. Do all of the verbs refer to the same time?
6. Is the first line indented? Does every sentence use proper capitalization and punctuation?

General Strategies The list that follows summarizes some key strategies for teachers to consider in planning for the instruction of written expression. Specific activities to assist in implementing programs are provided later in the chapter.

1. Importance should be placed on functional writing (i.e., writing with meaning for the pupil's life). Through functional writing students see that their paragraphs, notes, or letters must have clear, precise meaning, or they may be misunderstood. Such an emphasis should not ignore the expressive element in writing, however.
2. Teachers should attempt to increase the variety of words known to students. This can be accomplished by introducing

them to objects and experiences outside their daily lives and assisting them in writing about these events.

3. Students should learn the basic rules of grammar so that they know how to write what they want to write. Overemphasis on mechanics should be avoided, however, because the goal is for students to gain skills to enable them to adapt to their life situations.

4. Constant application of the skills developed in written language should be actively encouraged. When students develop specific written language skills, teachers must give students many chances to use these skills.

5. Teachers should provide students with models that exhibit the desired behavior. Numerous methods can accomplish this: (a) the teacher can model the desired behavior by writing short stories, paragraphs, or essays that students copy; or (b) students who are approaching or have reached the desired outcome can exhibit their work for other pupils to view, thereby demonstrating correct behavior from a student perspective.

6. Students should be assisted in deriving the personal satisfaction from writing that comes from looking at it as a process rather than as a polished product. Attention should be paid to the importance of reviewing and editing written work.

7. When provided with an opportunity for creative writing, students need to be stimulated by topics of personal interest. Teachers should generate a collection of possible themes to use as general assignments. Table 11.4 (p. 276) presents some examples that have proven effective in various class settings.

ACTIVITIES

Within the various areas differentiation is not made between younger and older students because it is difficult to estimate how far written language has progressed. Specific activities that are particularly relevant for older students are so noted, however. Teachers should select activities based on both interest and functioning level, of course. The section on readiness includes a variety of ideas for developing the fine motor skills necessary for successful handwriting.

Readiness

1. To develop and coordinate fine eye/hand skills, have pupils put beads on a string.
2. Once pupils are able to get beads on a string in a facile manner, make the task more complex by having them copy simple designs with different colors, shapes, and/or numbers of beads.
3. Have the children trace shapes, which you make first, in sand, clay, or sawdust, using the finger or some pointed object such as a stick or stylus.
4. Make large designs or diagrams on a sheet of paper. Instruct pupils to trace the figures using first clear acetate and then onionskin paper. Finally, have the children copy the figures on a sheet of regular paper without the use of any type of overlay.

TABLE 11.4
Sample composition
topics

Topics for Writing Assignments
I knew something was wrong when I heard that sound . . .
My favorite television show is . . .
When I was a baby . . .
The day I became a . . . (name an animal)
My favorite pet
An interesting person I know
The day at the circus
A TV character I would like to be
What I plan to do after I graduate from high school
My favorite movie
My summer vacation
My favorite sports hero
Outer space
The secret clubhouse
My trip aboard a Martian aircraft
The Western character I would most like to be
If I could be anybody in the world for one day, I would most like to be . . .
I wish I could spend my summer vacation in . . .
My best friend is . . . because . . .
Why colors remind me of moods
The most disgusting TV commercial I've ever seen
Spending the day with my favorite rock group
Summer camp
Going steady
If I could change one thing in my past, I would change . . .
My hobbies
What I look for in a friend
My first job
My summer job
The senior class trip
The day I got my license to drive
The first thing I want to do when I turn 18 is . . . because . . .
My blind date
If I were a millionaire, I would . . .

5. Make a stick man on a sheet of paper. Have children draw a line from the stick man to some object the stick man is trying to reach.

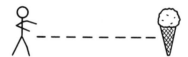

6. Have pupils connect two or more dots with a piece of crayon or a primary pencil.

7. Draw dots on a sheet of paper in a straight line; increase the distances from one dot to the next as students learn to draw straight lines between the dots.
8. Show two figures with a part missing on the second figure; have the children find the missing part and copy it on the second figure.
9. Ask pupils to pick out a shape or letter in a series that matches the shape or letter at the beginning of the series.
10. Have children cut out pictures that gradually get smaller.
11. Have children put together jigsaw puzzles that are gradually more difficult.
12. Tell each pupil to match a set of pictures by drawing a line up or down from one picture to the other.
13. Show pupils how to draw a line through two other lines (a tunnel), and then have them draw lines through tunnels that become progressively narrower.
14. Have the children connect dots in a circle. Place an arrow at the beginning to show where to start and which way to go.
15. Let the children color geometric shapes while stressing that they stay inside the lines.
16. Reinforce concepts of left and right by playing games in which the children must point to or touch some object on the left or right. The same type of activity can be used for other polar opposites, such as up/down, front/back, and so on.
17. While students paint, have them make circles and straight lines.
18. Play games in which students must make a circle or a straight line to complete a picture drawn on a sheet of paper.

19. Give students 36 thumb tacks and a yardstick. Instruct them to press a tack into each inch mark (Kimmell, 1968).
20. Games like jacks are excellent for improving motor control and eye/hand coordination.
21. Make simple dot-to-dot pictures using directional arrows after each dot. Students take turns rolling dice and drawing lines to connect as many dots as the total of the dice indicates. The first player to complete a picture wins.

Manuscript Writing

1. Make name tags for all students, and have them copy their names.
2. Write students' names at the top of a sheet of primary writing paper, and have them copy their names.
3. Make dot letters and have pupils form the letters by connecting the dots.
4. After a series or group of letters have been learned, have the children write the letters on primary writing paper.

5. Bring children to the board who are having problems making a certain letter, and help them make the problem letter on the chalkboard. This is a good early morning activity.

6. Make letters on the chalkboard, and let pupils add or take away some part of the letter to make another letter.

7. Dictate letters for students to write that they have previously learned, and check for formation, shape, size, and so on.

8. Let students take turns using their fingers to "write" a letter on a partner's back. Have the partner guess what the letter is.

9. Use flashcards with lowercase letters on them, and instruct students to write the uppercase form of each letter shown.

10. Have students fold a piece of paper into three columns and label the columns Tall Letters, Short Letters, and Letters with Tails. Guide students in correctly categorizing the letters of the alphabet.

11. Have students look at maps and find geographical locations that begin with given letters.

12. Give groups of students large sheets of chart paper, and have them use fine-point markers to make lists of given topics (e.g., animals, foods, popular music groups).

13. As pupils learn more letters of the alphabet, have them combine the letters to form words. The words chosen can be copied from a chart of words already in the students' vocabulary.

14. Have the class dictate several sentences about some event that has previously occurred, and then have students copy the sentences that you have written on the board or chart paper.

15. Play a game of "Something Is Wrong" by putting lowercase letters at the beginning of sentences and incorrect punctuation at the end of sentences. Have pupils find the errors and correct them.

16. Draw several rows of parallel dots. Show the children how to play Dots, a game in which the person who connects the last side of a dot box wins the box. The child who has the most boxes marked with his or her initials wins the game.

Cursive Writing

1. Make dot cursive letters and have students form the letters by connecting the dots.

2. Play Concentration using cards with manuscript or cursive letters copied on them. Students must match the cursive and manuscript forms of a letter.

3. Using an overhead projector, let students take turns writing on transparencies or tracing letters projected on the chalkboard.

4. Make lists of words to be written alphabetically in cursive.

5. Have students open a textbook to a given page and copy every fifth word in cursive.

6. Dictate for students to copy all letters that they have previously learned, and check for formation.

7. A good readiness activity for beginning cursive writing is to have pupils

draw looped lines from a starting point on a sheet of paper to an airplane placed near the bottom of the paper.

8. Let students collect samples of cursive writing to share and compare. Signatures from staff members, parents, or other community members can be interesting.

Spelling

1. Have each child spell different words by changing the initial or the final sounds.
2. Have younger children trace words in different media.
3. Have pupils keep in a box words that they can spell so that these words can be reviewed periodically. They can also be used for spelling games, alphabetizing, homework assignments, or creative writing.
4. Spelling can be combined with chip-trading activities. The teacher gives each child a word to spell and a certain color chip if the word is correctly spelled. As children collect chips, they can trade up for the next value chip (3, 5, 10). At the end of the game, children can count and compare their chip totals.
5. Students can keep their own dictionaries of words that they are learning to spell. A notebook with a page for each letter of the alphabet can be used for recording weekly words, words written incorrectly on assignments, or words that required teacher assistance. The notebooks can then be used for reference and studying.
6. The Dolch and other word lists can be grouped into different sets of words (e.g., nouns, adjectives). Have pupils pick out words that they do not know how to spell. Use these words to make spelling lists and lessons.
7. Older pupils can be taught to use the dictionary to help check their spelling. Picture dictionaries are extremely helpful in developing dictionary as well as spelling skills.
8. Show the children that there is some linguistic regularity to our language by giving them a word or stem and having them form other words (e.g., *-ad: had, dad, mad; -amp: damp, lamp, stamp; -oe: hoe, foe, toe*).
9. Give children groups of letters and ask them to spell as many words as they can, using only those letters (e.g., *lliks: skill, kills, ill, sill*).
10. Write words on the board or on a sheet of paper with a letter missing, and have pupils fill in the missing letters.
11. Give students a list of spelling words that they can pronounce. Have them take turns using a tape recorder to perform this sequence: read a word into the microphone, copy the word two times on paper, pro-

nounce the word again, and spell the word aloud. The next day, after studying the words, students can use the tapes as their own tutor. Later, the tapes can be used as a review to ensure mastery (Blau, 1968).

12. Two students work together. One student is blindfolded; the other student pronounces a spelling word and gives the blindfolded student a group of cut-out cardboard letters that spell the word. The blindfolded student puts the letters into the correct order as the other student traces each letter on the blindfolded student's back. After several practices the blindfolded student should be able to place the letters in the correct sequence without help. The students then change roles and spelling words (Blau, 1968).

13. After spelling words have been introduced to the class, prepare charts with the individual words written in a variety of different styles (e.g., *fat, fat, FAT, fat, fat*). Place the charts at key points in the room. This activity will help students with inconsistent form and those who lack the ability to retain letter sequence when the written style changes (Wulpe, 1968).

14. When students write each word "ten times," instruct the students to write with different writing forms, uppercase, lowercase, cursive, and so on (Wulpe, 1968).

15. Drill students on letter-sound recognition. Say letters in random order, and have students write just the letters. Next, say just the sounds, and have students write letters that represent the sounds.

16. Divide the class into two teams and list spelling words on the chalkboard in short columns. While students from each team stand with their backs to the board, pronounce a word. The students then turn and find the word on the board. The first person to find the word gets a point for the team.

17. Older students may enjoy opportunities to make, as well as solve, spelling puzzles. Students can make word searches by placing spelling words in different spaces on graph paper (diagonally, horizontally, vertically) and then filling in the other blocks with random letters. The puzzles can then be exchanged and solved by classmates.

18. Play spelling Wordo, similar to Bingo. Give each student a playing card. Instruct students to write a word from a current spelling list on each square of their cards. Collect and redistribute the cards. The game proceeds like Bingo, except the first student to cover the appropriate squares says "Wordo!"

19. Peck and Schultz (1969) suggest the use of a spelling "track meet." Rows of students correspond to relay teams. A leader is appointed in each row. On the command "Go," each leader pronounces the first word from a given list. The first student in each row rushes to the board and writes the word. If the student misspells it, the next student in the row corrects it. The leader must make sure that words are spelled correctly. The first team that completes its list of words correctly wins. To avoid copying, each leader is given a list of different words. Students should study before the game to prevent embarrassment.

20. Older students enjoy academic activities that have a sports flavor, such as spelling baseball. The class is divided into two teams. Batters must correctly pronounce and spell a given word. If they do, they move to

first base; the next batter does the same, and movement around the bases parallels regular baseball. The field can be specific areas in the classroom or can be drawn on the board so that students stay in their seats.

21. Pass out loose alphabet letters. Have students select the letters of their entire name and spell it out. Then they scramble the letters and spell as many words as possible, using only the letters of their name. Each word should be listed on a sheet of paper. Introduce anagrams with other words (Coleman, 1978).

22. Graham and Miller (1979) suggest proofreading activities useful in enhancing spelling skills: providing a short list of words that includes misspelled words to be located, providing a passage with errors ranging from easy ones to spelling demons, listing the total number of words purposely misspelled in a written composition and having students find them, and having students select the correctly spelled word from a series of alternatives.

Written Expression

1. Students can have fun making their own journals, using cardboard and scrap cloth material from home for a cover. At the beginning of the day, set aside a silent writing time for students to write in their journals. The aim of this activity is to foster enjoyment in writing; therefore, entries should not be evaluated. Make the journals a private venture; read them only with the students' permission.

2. Develop visual imagery as a prerequisite to writing. Students can imagine making an angel in the snow, flying a kite in March winds, eating ice cream on a hot summer day, burying a friend in a pile of leaves, floating down a river on a raft, riding a roller coaster, lying on a sandy beach, eating pizza. Initially, have students relax and think at their desks. Don't require them to write. Later, have students list adjectives associated with their images. Finally, direct students to write sentences or paragraphs.

3. Wiener (1981) suggests an activity called "boasts" that is particularly appropriate for adolescents. Assign students the task of writing four or five sentences about what makes them exceptional. It can be what they know, what they have done, or how they look.

4. One student can be chosen class secretary. This person can serve the class by writing letters to pupils who are ill, birthday notes, letters of invitation to guest speakers, letters of appreciation, and any other needed correspondence (Meredith & Landin, 1957).

5. Another student can be appointed TV guide for the class, responsible for posting weekly reports of shows of interest to the class. Special attention should be given to educational programs (Meredith & Landin, 1957).

6. Have students write one sentence from dictation and an original second sentence. McNeal (1979) lists more than 600 sentences as springboards for writing. Adolescents can progress to reading sentences and then writing original second sentences.

7. Direct adolescents to write responsible letters to local elected officials. Help students express their opinions on various political or social issues. These letters can be the foundation for a discussion on civic responsibility.

8. Have younger students keep a class diary. As a group, the class can discuss one topic as the teacher records comments on the board. Students then copy the writing in their notebooks, and after fifteen or so topics, the diaries can be sent home (Kline, 1987).

9. Brooke (1986) suggests having students develop family folklore scrapbooks. Students can write down and illustrate stories told to them by older relatives. Possible themes include good stories from hard times, practical jokes, stories of when others were young, and stories of things learned from older relatives.

10. Cohen and Plaskon (1980) suggest using films or slides to stimulate creative writing. Students can be asked to develop a script for a taped commercial, cartoon, or short story. The script can then be taped and presented to an audience.

11. Have older students write poems. Start by reading poetry aloud. Introduce unrhymed poetry before rhymed poetry. Print a booklet (complete with illustrations) of the students' poems for their parents and others in the school to read. Shel Silverstein's collection of poems *Where the Sidewalk Ends* is a good source of poetry to read aloud to older students (see Cheyney, 1979).

12. Progressive writing exercises are interesting activities. The object is to pick up where a classmate has left off and write for 2 or 3 minutes. The final writer should write a conclusion. One student can read the finished product. Later, improvements and corrections can be made.

13. Pretending to be an inanimate object, such as a rock on the road or grass in a park, students can write sentences containing gripes from the object's point of view (Wiener, 1981).

14. A class newspaper can help students improve their written expression. Assignments can be made according to ability and interest. Class, school, community, national, or international topics can be reported. Possible sections might be news, sports, jokes, riddles, a mystery person, book reports, poems, and store ads (Mann, Suiter, & McClung, 1979).

15. Use pictures to teach students topic sentence development. Start by describing the photograph, and then write sentences and paragraphs.

16. Guide students in writing a letter to the editor of a local paper. Their perspective on an issue might be greatly appreciated. Instruct them to keep the letter concise and to the point (Wiener, 1981).

17. A highly motivating activity that can include printing or writing, spelling, written expression, and reading is Contest Week. Many contests merely require students to place their name and address on a postcard and mail it to a company or radio station. Others require them to express ideas or opinions. Students can search through newspapers and magazines and be alert to contests advertised on the radio or television. The teacher can use the ads to devise a contest to be conducted by the class.

RESOURCES   Handwriting

Multisensory Capital Letters/Multisensory Lowercase Letters, Ideal School Supply. Multisensory letters provide an opportunity for discrimination and integration of kinesthetic, auditory, tactile, and visual abilities. The letters can be used to supplement instruction in basic letter recognition and formation.

Hoyle Gripper, R & D. These plastic three-sided tools fit over a writing utensil and assist the student experiencing difficulty with proper grip. They promote legibility by simplifying a potential problem area in visual/motor integration. Price is reasonable (approximately $.25 each with discounts for quantity orders).

Writing Our Language (Monroe), Scott, Foresman. These handwriting workbooks are part of a total language arts program. Overhead visuals accompany the teacher's manual; the visuals are used to help introduce new letters. A terminology chart at the back helps the teacher use consistent wording in reference to letters and their formation.

Penmanship Step by Step (Rosenhaus), Zaner-Bloser. This workbook features good aids for the teacher and the pupil. Teaching aids include explicit directions, suggested activities, and good drill practice for each letter.

D'Nealian Handwriting Program, Scott, Foresman. The purpose of the D'Nealian program is to reduce teaching/learning time by initially establishing the letter formations, rhythm, size, slant, and spacing that will be used for cursive writing. The program stresses continuous skill progression with transition from manuscript to cursive. Materials are available for readiness through eighth grade. The teacher's edition suggests ways to modify instruction for those experiencing motor coordination and other handwriting problems.

Spelling

Demon Spelling Words, Educational Activities. Contained on one record (cassette) are 105 hard-to-spell words at grade level 2.8. A record provides repetitions so that students can master words and saves the teacher from having to verbalize words over and over. This program is good for individual work (with headphones) and can be used with any age student.

The Magic World of Dr. Spello (Mollmeyer & Ware), Webster Division, McGraw-Hill. This book is designed for older students experiencing problems with basic spelling rules. It provides activities and drills for 20 spelling rules in workbook form.

Name Game, Media for Education. This is a series of six coloring books with words spelled out into the objects they describe.

Spelling, Behavioral Research Laboratories. This is a programmed spelling series designed to teach first-year spelling skills in conjunction with reading skills. Students learn to read the word, then spell it. This linguistic approach enables students to use the spelling program as they learn to read. After the sound-symbol relationships are learned, students use the known words as clues to sound out new words. Spelling words used in the series are also vocabulary words from the Sullivan Programmed Reading series. The series goes from Level 1 to Level 8.

Spelling Magic (Forte & Pangle), Incentive Publications. Activities, gimmicks, games, and unique ideas are included for use in spelling reinforcement.

Spelling Our Language (Monroe, Aaron, & Schiller), Scott, Foresman. These spelling workbooks are part of a total language arts program. The format is similar to that of many other spelling programs accompanying basals.

Spelling Word Power Laboratory, Science Research Associates (SRA). This is a personalized spelling program for use with students through Grade 7. The kit consists of a word wheel that teaches a specific spelling principle (changing *y* to *i,* adding suffixes, and so on). Students use a record book in conjunction with the word wheel and a check test card to determine whether they have mastered the principle well enough to go onto the next card. The record book allows practice of missed words and principles.

Systematic Speller (Casper), Educators Publishing Service. This book gives rules and examples for correct spelling in one complete source. Many examples are given of how a particular spelling rule works.

Boggle, Parker Brothers. This game is designed for persons from Grade 2 to adulthood. It can be used as stated in the directions, or the letter cubes can be used to enhance language skills. The game provides a fun, reinforcing practice activity.

Words to Spell Match-Ups, Playskool (Milton Bradley). Emphasis is on matching up letters in word activities using puzzle pieces and a tray frame. Designed for kindergarten to seventh grade, it can be used individually or in groups. It provides activities to promote readiness and initial reading skills.

Written Expression

How to Write Yourself Up, Frank E. Richards. This book is designed to give students practice in several areas, such as writing letters, filling out job applications, applying for credit, applying for Social Security, installment buying, and completing forms related to banking, mailing, and income tax. Much of the same material is covered in the Using Money Series and Getting Ready for Pay Day.

Report Writing Skills, Coronet. This package can be used as a supplement to a language arts program. The general aim of the program is to improve students' writing skills. Eight lessons provide the information that the student must use in workbook exercises. The lessons are on cassettes. Two pages in a student workbook are used with each cassette lesson.

Understanding English, Frank E. Richards. This is a comprehensive text for students ready to cover such topics as punctuation marks and parts of speech. It is designed to assist students with the mechanics of the English language and provides practice in everyday usage.

Basic Writing Skills, Educational Insights. This material enables students to practice and strengthen skills in the areas of thought organization, grammar, getting information, experience writing, and essays. The program consists of four workbooks, including Building Paragraphs, Constructing

Sentences, Letter Writing, and Beginning Essay Writing. The workbook sheets can be used as remediation material, introductory material, diagnostic testing, or practice activities.

Expressive Writing I, II (Engelmann & Silbert), Science Research Associates. This program teaches fundamental rules for translating observations into sentences, writing paragraphs that do not deviate from a topic, and editing others' as well as one's own work. It is designed for students who have not had previous instruction in expressive writing and who perform on the third-grade reading level. It also may be used effectively with older students who have not been taught basic expressive writing skills. It is thus appropriate for intermediate students and in some cases for high school students who are severely deficient in expressive skills.

12
Mathematics

The importance of mathematics in everyday living, although not always obvious, is great nonetheless. Many common activities involve mathematical concepts, with money handling being perhaps the most important (Bott, 1988). Many professionals in this area are suggesting that we rethink the math skills we teach to students with mild handicaps in light of their needs as adults (Cawley, Miller, & Carr, 1988; Sedlak & Fitzmaurice, 1981). Curricular decisions, and the instructional strategies to accomplish them, must be guided by the goal of successful adult outcomes (Patton & Polloway, 1988). A major emphasis of math instruction has to be functionality, leading to the acquisition of skills essential for coping with one's environment. The ability to deal minimally with the mathematical demands of community living requires skills at about a fourth to fifth grade level; functioning effectively requires skills at a significantly higher level.

Clarification of the terms *arithmetic* and *mathematics* is warranted. Although these terms are used somewhat interchangeably, they are different. *Mathematics* is best described as a "way of thinking" (Johnson & Rising, 1972) that involves quantities, their relationships, and ways of reasoning. Various branches of mathematics include arithmetic, geometry, algebra, and calculus, among others. *Arithmetic* refers to "the study of number, counting, notation, and operation with numbers" (Ballew, 1973, p. 460). It is the foundation of most elementary school mathematics programs; however, some other areas of mathematics such as algebra and geometry are also part of the elementary curriculum.

This chapter should aid teachers in their attempts to develop approaches to teaching mathematics to students with special needs. We share the perspective of Cawley and colleagues for accomplishing this task: "To provide these students with the best and most appropriate education in mathematics, teachers must break out of the 'traditional mold' from which they themselves were educated in math, and be willing to be innovative and creative" (1988, p. xx). We would add that teachers must also be guided by the principles of effective instructional practice.

GOALS OF MATHEMATICS INSTRUCTION

Most educators consider development of mathematic competence a high priority. Evidence of this can be seen in the amount of research conducted in this area (see Romberg & Carpenter, 1986). Currently, mathematics education is seen as more than mastery of basic computational skills; emphasis is being placed more on the application of these computational skills and the development of thinking and problem-solving abilities. Nonetheless, computational competence remains important for two valid reasons: (1) it is valuable for determining correct answers in problem-solving tasks, and (2) it helps a person to determine the reasonableness of responses in everyday situations (Cawley et al., 1988).

The National Council of Supervisors of Mathematics NCSM (1977) identifies 10 basic skill areas that need to be included in the curriculum.

1. problem solving
2. applying mathematics to everyday situations
3. alertness to the reasonableness of results
4. estimation and approximation
5. appropriate computational skills
6. geometry
7. measurement
8. reading, interpreting, and constructing tables, charts, and graphs
9. using mathematics to predict
10. computer literacy (p. 20)

Although these areas are postulated for regular mathematics education, they are appropriate for special populations, too. In fact, the first two items, which embody many of the other skills, are critically important for students with special needs, particularly as they prepare to exit high school.

Another way to identify important mathematical skills is to examine the minimal competency objectives required for graduation in many states. Even though there may be an inordinate emphasis placed on computational competence, as Smith (1978) points out, nearly all objectives involve the application of a math concept or principle, as illustrated by the 15 essential competencies required for graduation in Hawaii.

Basic Skills

Read and use printed materials from daily life. These include the newspaper, telephone book, road maps, charts and graphs commonly used in public media, and household product instructions.

Complete commonly used forms. These include personal checks, job applications, charge account applications, and other similar forms.

Demonstrate writing skills commonly used in daily life. These include writing directions, telephone messages, letters of inquiry or complaint, and personal correspondence.

Communicate orally in situations common to everyday life. These include giving simple directions and answering questions about directions or instructions, expressing personal opinions on a topic and responding to questions about the topic, and describing an object.

Use computational skills in situations common to everyday life. These include adding, subtracting, multiplying, and dividing whole numbers, adding and subtracting dollars and cents, and computing discount and simple interest.

Read and use scales on standard measuring devices. These include rulers, measuring cups and spoons, thermometers, and weight scales.

Interpret common visual symbols. These include traffic signs and road markings, directions to public facilities, and caution and warning labels and signs.

Other Life Skills

Reach reasoned solutions to commonly encountered problems. Reasoned solutions are those that incorporate the facts at hand, the constraints on the solution, the feasibility of carrying out the solution, and the values of those affected by the solution. Commonly encountered problems include decisions about family finance, career plans, physical health, and community issues.

Distinguish fact from opinion in TV and radio news broadcasts, advertising, newspaper and magazine articles, and public speeches.

Use resources for independent learning. These resources include the library, informed persons, and public and private agencies.

Identify the harmful effects of smoking, drinking, drug abuse, overeating, insufficient sleep, poor personal hygiene, and poor nutrition.

Identify the training, skill and background requirements of at least one occupation in which the student is interested.

Demonstrate knowledge of the basic structure and functions of national, state, and local governments.

Demonstrate knowledge of the citizen's opportunities to participate in political processes. These include voting, running for office, contacting elected representatives, and participating in election campaigns.

Demonstrate knowledge of important citizen rights and responsibilities. This includes the rights guaranteed by the Constitution and knowledge of traffic laws and major criminal offenses.

The primary focus on mathematical skills is readily apparent in the fifth and sixth competencies. But varying degrees of mathematical understanding—sometimes as basic as the use of a number system—are implicit in the successful demonstration of the other competencies as well.

If the ultimate goal in mathematics instruction of learners with special needs is to help them develop some consistent methods for solving number-related problems encountered in everyday situations, then teachers must be sensitive to those demands. Furthermore, students must receive systematic, direct instruction so that they will acquire a range of mathematical skills extending beyond computational competence. Concepts of money management, time, measurement, estimation, and geometry may eventually play greater roles in a person's life than computational skills (Sedlak & Fitzmaurice, 1981). Implicit within the goals of mathematics education for students with learning problems is the idea that those students must receive opportunities, encouragement, and instruction on using their fundamental skills to solve everyday problems.

Mathematics education for special populations is undergoing some major changes. An increasing amount of attention is being directed to this issue of functionality. In fact, subordinate importance of mathematics to reading is changing as well (Bartel, 1982). A number of recommendations about the future direction of mathematics education appear in *Agenda for Action: Recommendations for School Mathematics of the 1980s* (National Council of Teachers of Mathematics, 1980). Five of the eight recommendations offered are highlighted here because of their relevance to teaching students with mild handicaps.

☐ Recommendation: Problem solving must be the focus of school mathematics in the 1980s.
☐ Recommendation: The concept of basic skills in mathematics must encompass more than computational facility.
☐ Recommendation: Mathematics programs must take full advantage of the power of calculators and computers at all grade levels.

☐ Recommendation: The success of mathematics programs and student learning must be evaluated by a wider range of measures than conventional testing.
☐ Recommendation: More mathematics study must be required of all students, and a flexible curriculum with a greater range of options should be designed to accommodate the diverse needs of the student population. (p. 1)

These recommendations are commendable. They spell out the changing priorities of mathematics education, which teachers should incorporate into curricula for students with special needs.

To many people, mathematics conjures up recollections of unhappiness or discomfort. The phenomenon of math anxiety has received so much attention that math anxiety counselors, seminars, and self-help techniques have developed and prospered. Why do so many people loathe math? There are any number of plausible reasons, one of which is that we teach students to hate mathematics. Oberlin (1982) offers some examples.

How to Teach Children to Hate Mathematics[1]
1. Assign the same work to everyone in the class. This technique is effective with about two-thirds of the class. The bottom third of the class will become frustrated from trying to do the impossible while the top third will hate the boredom. WARNING: This may NOT be effective with the middle third of the students.
2. Go through the book, problem by problem, page by page. In time, the drudgery and monotony is bound to get to them.
3. Assign written work every day. Before long, just the word *mathematics* will remove every smile in the room.

[1]From "How to Teach Children to Hate Mathematics" by L. Oberlin, 1982, *School Science and Mathematics, 82,* p. 261. Copyright 1982 by School Science and Mathematics Association. Adapted by permission.

4. Be sure that each student has plenty of homework. This is especially important over weekends and vacation periods.

5. Never correlate mathematics with life situations. A student might find it useful and get to enjoy math.

6. Insist that there is ONLY one correct way to solve each problem. This is very important as some creative student might look for different ways to solve a problem. He could even grow to like math.

7. Assign mathematics as a punishment for misbehavior. The association works wonders. Soon math and punishment will take on the same meaning.

8. Be sure that ALL students complete ALL the review work in the front of the textbook. This ought to last until Thanksgiving or Christmas and is certain to kill off the interest of most students.

9. Use long drill-type assignments with many examples of the SAME type problem (for example, 30 long-column addition problems). This type of assignment requires little teacher time and keeps the student occupied a long time. The majority of the pupils are sure to dislike it.

10. Lastly, insist that EVERY problem worked incorrectly be reworked until it is correct. This procedure is most effective in promoting distaste for math, and if followed very carefully, the student may even learn to detest his teacher as well!

These examples are intended to get people thinking and are not meant as general indictment of mathematics instruction. Nevertheless, these situations do occur and often have a negative effect on students. Math instruction should be interesting, meaningful, and enjoyable; whether it is is largely a function of the teacher.

ASSESSMENT

Let us assume that Sheila responds to the following algorithm[2] as indicated:

[2]The term *algorithm* refers to the arrangement of numerals to enable one to solve a problem.

$2 + 4 =$ _____ . Is the response right or wrong? The teacher's decision may depend on any number of factors, such as knowledge of the student and/or the objectives that have been established for this activity. For instance, if Sheila frequently writes the numeral 6 this way, the teacher may accept her response as right—arithmetically. The important point is that teachers sometimes need to dig a little deeper to understand fully how a student is performing, and they need to remember what information they are evaluating.

Educational assessment is the systematic process whereby information about students is collected and used to make decisions about them. One educationally relevant question that should be asked and answered is, Which educational strengths and weaknesses does a student display? In other words, a major reason for assessing students is to obtain diagnostic information. Other motivations for assessing students may stem from a need to determine eligibility for services, to choose the most suitable placement option, or to evaluate student progress or program effectiveness. All of these reasons for assessing students occur daily in educational settings and are inexorably entwined with providing appropriate education. Nevertheless, the problems inherent in this process demand caution. If undertaken haphazardly, assessment can violate the rights of students and their families. (See chapter 3 for a full discussion of the assessment process.)

Typically, assessment is immediately associated with testing. Although testing is one way to answer some educationally relevant questions, it is not the only way. Information about students can and should be obtained through other techniques as well: direct observation of students' behaviors, interviewing, checklists and rating scales, examination of students' previous work, and inspection of cumulative folders. Assessment in mathematics should include all of these techniques but should not be limited solely to a demonstration of arithmetic skills. Affective dimensions (e.g., how students feel about math) are important, too.

Formal Measures of General Achievement

Achievement tests usually cover a range of skill domains (e.g., reading, spelling, mathematics) and result in a variety of derived scores. These norm-referenced instruments do nothing more than show how a student's score compares with those of other students on whom the test was standardized. From a planning perspective, such tests do provide some indication of the skill/subject areas in which students are strong or are having difficulty. However, these instruments are not intended to be diagnostic and therefore offer little information about where to start teaching.

There are two major types of achievement tests: individual and group. Individual tests have enjoyed a great deal of popularity in special education. Some of those more commonly used are presented in Table 12.1. Group achievement tests, such as the Stanford Achievement Test (Madden, Gardner, Rudman, Karlsen, & Merwin, 1973) and the Metropolitan Achievement Test Series (Balow, Farr, Hogan, & Prescott, 1979), are also used frequently in schools. These instruments have the advantage of possible administration to large numbers of students at one time. Both types of achievement tests are limited in giving only one or two different samples of any major skill area and in failing to show error patterns.

Formal Diagnostic Measures of Arithmetic Functioning

Instruments that assess specific functioning areas help teachers determine which particular problems students have and what their particular strengths are. For the most part, instruments in this category are attractive because of their diagnostic usefulness; they usually contain a number of mathematically related subtests. Some of the more frequently used instruments are discussed here.

KeyMath Diagnostic Arithmetic Test   One of the most popular math tests used today is the KeyMath (Connolly, Nachtman, & Pritchett, 1976). It is a standardized norm-referenced test, appropriate for students in Grades 1 to 9, and provides grade-reference information (e.g., a grade-equivalent score). In addition, it provides data on specific strengths and weaknesses (via a profile). Unlike general achievement tests, the KeyMath divides arithmetic into three major areas, which are further divided into 15 subtests.

1. Content: numeration, fractions, geometry, symbols
2. Operations: addition, subtraction, multiplication, division, mental computation, numerical reasoning
3. Applications: word problems, missing elements, money, measurement, time, metrics

The KeyMath may not be as diagnostic as teachers would like it to be; there are a limited number of behavioral samples for specific subskills within each subtest. Thus, to obtain the information necessary to plan instructional interventions, teachers must augment the KeyMath with informal, teacher-constructed measures. For example, if a student has difficulty with two items on the addition subtest (66 + 4 and 86 + 29), then it is advisable to explore this skill with additional problems (16 + 8, 19 + 15, 37 + 20, 66 + 44, 145 + 159, 390 + 148, 524 + 386).

Such an analysis provides a more detailed assessment of the pupil's ability to do

TABLE 12.1
Individual, norm-referenced general achievement tests with math subtests

Test	Age/Grade Appropriateness	Math Subtest(s)	Format	Types of Derived Scores	Remarks
Wide Range Achievement Test—Revised (Jastak & Wilkinson, 1984)	Ages 5–74	Arithmetic	Written responses	Standard scores Grade equivalents Percentiles	Basic computational problems only No word problems Two levels
Peabody Individual Achievement Test—Revised (Dunn & Markwardt, 1988)	Ages 5–adult	Mathematics	Forced choice responses No pencil and paper	Standard scores Grade/age equivalents Percentiles Normal curve equivalents (NCE)	New artwork New norms
Kauffman Test of Educational Achievement (Kaufman & Kaufman, 1985)	Grades 1–12	Computation Application	Written responses Verbal responses	Standard scores Grade equivalents Percentiles NCEs Stanines	Error analysis system Fall and spring norms Two forms
Diagnostic Achievement Battery (Newcomer & Curtis, 1984)	Ages 6–14	Math reasoning Math calculation	Motoric & verbal responses Uses picture book Written responses Can be group administered	Standard scores Percentiles Quotients	Profile

two- and three-digit addition problems that require carrying and handling a zero.

Two features of this test are worth noting. Although frequently used, it has questionable validity and reliability data. On a brighter note, there are behavioral objectives in the administration manual for each test item.

Stanford Diagnostic Mathematics Test (SDMT) Another device suitable for assessing specific math skills is the Stanford Diagnostic Mathematics Test (Beatty, Madden, Gardner, & Karlsen, 1978). The authors state that "the primary purpose of SDMT is to determine the specific areas in which each pupil is having difficulty" (p. 4). It has been suggested that the SDMT is better used as a general comparative test rather than one for highly specific instructional objectives (Taylor, 1984). The SDMT has four levels, each with three tests: Number Systems and Numeration, Computation, and Applications. Derived scores include grade equivalents, percentile ranks, and stanines. Validity and reliability data for the SDMT are good.

Diagnostic Test of Arithmetic Strategies (DTAS) The DTAS (Ginsburg & Mathews, 1984) is an individually administered diagnostic instrument designed to analyze the strategies that students use to perform arithmetic calculations in addition, subtraction, multiplication, and division. It is appropriate for students who are having difficulty in these computational areas. The test authors suggest that students should be able to understand the directions for the items, formulate some type of response, and display some facility with English. Each subtest is divided into four sections.

☐ Setting Up the Problem: Set up only, no calculations are performed.
☐ Number Facts: Students respond to basic problems presented to them visually.
☐ Calculation: Students work problems while verbalizing what they are doing.
☐ Informal Skills: Students work problems using pencil and paper while verbalizing what they are doing.

Test of Mathematical Abilities (TOMA) The TOMA (Brown & McEntire, 1984) is a diagnostic test designed for use with students in Grades 3 to 12. It includes five subtests: attitude, vocabulary, general cultural application, computation, and story problems. The first three of these are not typically found in formal instruments. Standard scores and percentiles can be obtained.

Brigance Diagnostic Inventories The Brigance instruments—Basic Skills (for Grades K to 6) and Essential Skills (for Grades 7 to 12)—are not norm-referenced devices although they are formal (i.e., they are commercially produced). The Diagnostic Inventory of Basic Skills includes subtests on computation, measurement, and geometry. The Diagnostic Inventory of Essential Skills includes computation, fractions, decimals, percents, and measurement.

Informal Techniques

The most instructionally useful methods of assessing mathematical performance and diagnosing math difficulties are measures based on the curriculum. This approach allows an in-depth probe of specific skills based on the types of problems encountered in everyday instructional situations. Other advantages of teacher-made tests are (1) items or problems assess a specific skill, (2) tests include enough problems to ensure knowledge or lack of knowledge regarding a specific skill, and (3) if the teacher has any doubts about the test results, similar problems can be constructed and given to the pupil, and those results can be checked against previous results. Some disadvantages of teacher-made tests are that (1) too much specificity (i.e., the teacher may overdo it by constructing too many problems); (2) if the problems are too easy, the student may get bored and make careless mistakes (conversely, if the problems are too difficult, the student may get discouraged and give up); (3) teachers sometimes mistakenly try to assess more than one concept or skill at a time; and (4) test construction can be very time-consuming.

Our earlier example shows how a teacher-constructed activity can expand on and/or subdivide concepts and skills found in formal instruments; other examples are available as well. For instance, a student might miss items on the WRAT designed to assess the concepts of "more and less" because of an inability to identify or recognize the numerals (or their value) or because of a lack of understanding of the concepts of more and less. (The specific WRAT assessment items are "Which is more: 9 or 6?" and "Which is more: 42 or 28?") In this case, to determine numerical identification and recognition, the teacher might present index cards to the student with one numeral on each card and have the student respond by naming each numeral. If the student hesitates or misses a particular numeral, the card should be presented again later to assess consistency. Another approach would be to present a group of numerals on a sheet of paper, pronounce a number, and ask the student to respond by pointing to that numeral. To determine whether numerical values are understood, the teacher might present an index card with a numeral on it

(a)	(b)	(c)	(d)
3 4	3 3	4 5	5 6
2̶5̶	2̶4̶0	3̶6̶3	4̶7̶0
−21	−205	−341	−443
13	130	112	120

FIGURE 12.1

and instruct the student to give the teacher the corresponding number of checkers. The task can be varied by instructing the student to select two checkers, five checkers, nine checkers, and so on.

By subdividing and expanding concepts and skills assessed in formal tests, teachers can begin to pinpoint precisely difficulty in acquiring specific arithmetic understanding, comprehension, and skills. The process of task analysis, as explained in chapter 3, should be incorporated to determine a hierarchical sequence. Sequencing becomes possible as teachers develop an understanding of arithmetic competencies.

Error Patterns If a teacher carefully examines the work samples of students, it is often possible to detect patterns in the types of errors they are making. Figure 12.1 illustrates a computational error pattern in the area of subtraction.

It is possible to classify computational errors into different categories. One possible system is outlined here.

☐ Random responding (RR). Students errors are without any recognizable reason.

$$\begin{array}{r} 24 \\ \times\ 2 \\ \hline 77 \end{array}$$

☐ Basic fact error (BF). Student performs the operation correctly but makes a simple error (addition, etc.).

$$\begin{array}{r} 20 \\ 4\overline{)84} \end{array}$$

☐ Wrong operation (WO). Student performs the wrong operation (e.g., adds instead of subtracting).

$$\begin{array}{r} 344 \\ -\ 192 \\ \hline 556 \end{array}$$

☐ Defective algorithm (DA). Student does not perform the operation appropriately; the steps involved are out of sequence or are performed improperly.

$$\begin{array}{r} 14 \\ \times\ 6 \\ \hline 34 \end{array}$$

☐ Place value problems (PV). To some extent this category is a subset of the previous category. Student knows the facts and the beginning stages of an operation but is deficient in some aspect of place value.

$$\begin{array}{r} 39 \\ +\ 42 \\ \hline 711 \end{array}$$

Whether teachers use this or another system, recognizing students' systematic errors is a diagnostic skill with great bearing on learning.

Other informal techniques exist as well. As suggested in chapter 3, diagnostic information may be obtained from checklists corresponding to thorough task analyses of specific computational operations. Table 12.2, which is presented later in the chapter, is an example of one such task analysis. This type of assessment data can help isolate specific problems.

GENERAL INSTRUCTIONAL CONSIDERATIONS

Some general concerns should guide programming in mathematics. Many of these issues are closely related and are as applicable to other subject areas as they are to mathematics. Nevertheless, they are of particular importance when teaching mathematical skills.

Curricular Decisions

Although a thorough discussion of this topic appears in chapter 8, a number of important points bear repeating here. At the elementary level the focus of the curriculum is developmental/remedial with the intent of establishing basic math skills that will be used later in applied ways. Teachers are advised to consult scope and sequence charts of math skill development. Some skills (e.g., decimals) may have to be taught earlier because of changes in mathematics instruction (e.g., the use of calculators). Others (Cawley et al., 1988) have even questioned the practice of teaching addition and subtraction before multiplication and division.

At the secondary level other pressing issues arise. Many special learners require a realistic examination of their subsequent environments. If postsecondary education is not likely, then the curriculum should reflect a strong orientation toward skills and knowledge needed to survive in the community, that is, a functional mathematics curriculum. On the other hand, some students should be encouraged to pursue a diploma and postsecondary education or training. School systems must remain sensitive to a range of student needs and commensurate educational goals.

Effective Teaching Practices

Mathematics instruction requires attention to all of the components of effective instruction depicted in Figure 2.2. Of the various precursors to teaching, a key factor is the scheduling of the math period. One way to schedule the class period was developed in the Missouri Mathematics Effectiveness Project, reported by Good and Grouws (1979). The major components include daily review, development, seat work, and homework assignments. Managing these components depends to a great extent on the nature of the class (i.e., the skill level of students). Many teachers have found daily timed test (about 2 or 3 minutes long) to be effective not only for reviewing and monitoring progress but also for organizing. Students tend to get on-task quickly when they know that they have only limited time to perform the tasks required.

Another useful antecedent factor is task analysis of various mathematical skills. For instance, computational operations can be analyzed sequentially to identify necessary intermediate steps. Table 12.2 gives an example of a task analysis. Especially in mathematics, teachers must be able to identify skills and break them down into their component parts.

TABLE 12.2
Task analysis of a
subtraction problem

Computational Task: $\begin{array}{r} 400 \\ -\,175 \\ \hline \end{array}$

Prerequisite Skills Required

1. Visually discriminate numbers
2. Write numerals
3. Follow written or oral directions
4. Name numerals
5. Match numerals with appropriate quantity
6. Identify the minus sign
7. Given the minus sign, state the concept of take-away
8. Compare basic subtraction facts
9. State the concept of regrouping or computing problems that require regrouping

Math Procedures Required

1. Identify the problem as subtraction
2. Identify the starting point
3. Recognize, state, refuse to compute 0 minus 5
4. Move to the tens column to regroup
5. Recognize, state, refuse to group 0 tens
6. Move to the hundreds column
7. Identify 4 hundreds as a number than can be regrouped
8. Regroup the hundreds
   a. Cross out 4
   b. Write 3 above 4
   c. Place 1 on tens column
9. Regroup tens
   a. Cross out 10
   b. Write 9 above 10 in tens column
   c. Write 1 on ones column
10. Subtract 10 minus 5
11. Write 5
12. Subtract 9 minus 7
13. Write 2
14. Subtract 3 minus 1
15. Write 2
16. Read the answer correctly (225)

Of particular importance among the teaching behaviors is ensuring that every student receives some teacher-directed instruction as part of the demonstration–guided practice–independent paradigm. Students with mild learning problems are not apt to acquire basic skills from workbooks or worksheets alone; they need to be taught these skills directly. Acquired skills can then be improved through practice. Unfortunately, many commercially available math materials do not provide enough practice, and few offer suggestions for presenting teacher-aided practice.

Foremost among follow-up activities is the need to give students feedback. For students who do not enjoy or see the relevance of mathematics, external systems may be required to provide motivational feedback. However, all students require informational feedback on their performance, particularly if their responses are incorrect. A recommended practice is to have students verbalize the procedures they used that resulted in errors; this process is similar to the analysis used in the Diagnostic Test of Arithmetic Strategies, discussed earlier. On completion of such an analysis, teaching strategies can be developed to address the specific problems.

Concept and Skill Development

Within the field of mathematics education for nondisabled students, there is some debate over two different instructional approaches: didactic and discovery. The didactic approach stresses initial instruction in basic skills development, followed by the application of these skills to problem solving. The discovery approach allows students to establish an understanding of the process needed to solve a problem prior to formal instruction in the basic skills. Advocates of a discovery approach believe that such an orientation enhances concept and skill development.

Teachers of special students must confront this dilemma as well. Recognizing that a discovery approach implies minimizing various prompts and teacher direction, Bartel (1982) warns that such an approach may not be warranted for students who need prompting.

Any discussion of skill development needs to address the question of generalization. Opportunities for applying basic skills to new situations may be programmed systematically. Teachers should give students many chances to apply their acquired skills and to incorporate math into other subject areas.

Diversity of Instruction

Even though drill and practice are essential to mastering certain math skills, learning need not be as tedious as it sometimes becomes. Variety in instructional techniques continues to be suggested (Bartel, 1982; Sternberg & Fair, 1983), yet it is often absent in classrooms.

A reality for many students with learning problems is a need for more practice than other students require. It is essential that teachers ensure fluency and mastery of specific math skills by developing novel practice activities (Bott, 1988). Many good teachers incorporate variety into their instruction as a matter of course; once identified, they can serve as good resources for ideas and assistance.

Another source of ideas for programming variety is a model developed by Cawley and his colleagues (1978). Their interactive unit model focuses on the interaction of teacher, students, and skill area but allows a great deal of instructional variation. The teacher can initiate instruction by

- [ ] manipulating something (e.g., physical action)
- [ ] displaying something to the students (e.g., materials or pictures)

- ☐ saying something
- ☐ writing something (e.g., on worksheet or chalkboard)

The student responds in one of four ways also

- ☐ by manipulating something (e.g., manipulative materials)
- ☐ by identifying something (e.g., pointing to or circling)
- ☐ by responding verbally
- ☐ by writing (i.e., graphically symbolizing)

The various combinations of teacher initiation and student response allow 16 ways to vary instruction. The virtue of this model is that it allows the teacher great flexibility when planning instruction for a diversity of student needs (Bartel, 1982). Figure 12.2 illustrates how this interactive idea can be used with three groups of students working on distinctly different skills: addition, geometry, and fractions. It also shows how the teacher-student interaction can be scheduled to provide direct teacher contact for all groups. This conceptual model provides the framework for a set of curricular materials called Project MATH, discussed later in this chapter.

Relevance

For those who have encountered much frustration with school to acquire skills they will need as adults, they must first find them relevant to their present as well as their future needs. This is particularly true of older students, who feel the greatest cumulative effect of frustration and disinterest. Sternberg and Sedlak (1978) relate this need for relevance to the idea of ecological meaning. They encourage applying target skills to students' real-life experiences. Patton (1983) strongly advocates infusing career education into the mathematics curriculum (see chapter 16 for a mathematical example of how this can be done.)

A useful tool for making math more acceptable to many students is the *Math Applications Kit* (Friebel & Gingrich, 1972), which is described at the end of this chapter. This resource can stimulate the development of other ideas, such as the sample activity depicted in Figure 12.3.

Related to the idea of making math instruction personally relevant is the notion of making students active learners. Torgesen (1982) suggests that many mildly handicapped students are only passively engaged in the tasks that are presented to them. Making instruction more relevant should improve the chances of actively engaging them.

Student interest is closely tied to relevance and to instructional diversity. Programming variety and career-relevant topics can make math exciting for both the students and the teacher. Teacher enthusiasm is something that students perceive and share, just as easily as they sense disinterest and drudgery.

Cautions

- ☐ *Language:* Be aware of students' language levels. Be careful not to confuse students initially by continually using different expressions to convey the same meaning (e.g., using terms like *less, take away* or *minus* interchangeably)
- ☐ *Boardwork.* Understand that some students experience a great deal of stress when they are at the chalkboard in front of the class. To them this activity can be terrifying.
- ☐ *Worksheets.* Be cognizant that worksheets can be overused.
- ☐ *Games.* Realize that games can be used instructionally, but there are potential problems associated with them. They can result in unproductive competition; they require gamesmanship skills; they may not be amusing to some students;

Group A: Geometry (8 students)	Group B: Fractions (10 students)	Group C: Addition (5 students)
Manipulate/Manipulate* *Input:* Teacher walks the perimeter of a geometric shape. *Output:* Learner does the same.	**Display/Write** *Input:* Write the fraction that names the shaded part. *Output:* Learner writes $\frac{1}{2}$	**Write/Write** *Input:* $\begin{array}{r} 3 \\ +2 \\ \hline \end{array}$ Write the answer. *Output:* Learner writes 5
Display/Identify *Input:* From the choices, mark the shape that is the same as the first shape. *Output:* Learner marks	**Manipulate/Say*** *Input:* Teacher removes portion of shape and asks learner to name the part. *Output:* Learner says, "One fourth"	**Display/Write** *Input:* Write the number there is in all. *Output:* Learner writes 5
Write/Identify *Input:* Circle Mark the shape that shows the word. *Output:* Learner marks	**Write/Write** *Input:* one half Write this word statement as a numeral. *Output:* Learner writes $\frac{1}{2}$	**Say/Say*** *Input:* Teacher says, "I am going to say some addition items. Six plus six. Tell me the answer." *Output:* Learner says, "Twelve"

15 minutes (each row)

*Teacher present in group

FIGURE 12.2

Interactive unit model (From *Developmental Teaching of Mathematics for the Learning Disabled* [p. 246] by J. F. Cawley (Ed.), 1984, Austin, Tx: Pro-Ed. Copyright 1984 by Pro-Ed, Inc. Reprinted by permission.)

SCIENCE

What makes a coconut weigh so much?

How much of the coconut's weight makes up
the husk, shell, meat, and milk?

You'll need...

1 coconut
1 hammer
1 screw driver
2 strong arms
4 large plastic containers
  (of the same weight)
1 spoon
1 scale
  data sheet
  pencil

Note: For safety reasons, ask your
teacher to have the coconut ready
for husking.

PROCEDURE

1. Label your containers 1, 2, 3, and 4.
2. Set the scale at 0 and make sure it is
   balanced for weighing.
3. Weigh the coconut and record the weight
   across the paper as shown on the data
   sheet.
4. Place one empty container on scale and
   set at 0 balance.
5. Peel the husk and place all the husk pieces
   into container 1.
6. Place shell into container 2 and crack open
   the shell using a hammer and/or screw
   driver.
7. Drain milk into container 2.
8. Scrape meat from the shell and place it
   into container 3.
9. Place empty shell into container 4.
10. Weigh each container and record the
    appropriate weight on the data sheet.
11. To find what fraction each part is to
    the whole coconut, divide the weight of each
    part by the weight of the coconut.

For example: Weight of husk = .2 oz.
              Weight of coconut = 1.6 oz.

Calculate: $\dfrac{.2}{1.6} = \dfrac{1}{8}$

Interpretation: The weight of the husk
                 is 1/8th the weight of
                 the coconut.

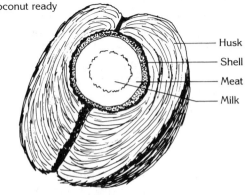

	Husk
	Shell
	Meat
	Milk

	Weight of husk	Weight of milk	Weight of meat	Weight of shell
Weight of coconut				

EXPLORING

Ways to recycle each part of
the coconut.

What are the related occupations?

How many coconuts would be
needed to fill a 5-pound bag
of shredded coconut flakes?

FIGURE 12.3
Math applications—Hawaiian style

and they may not really serve instructional objectives.

- ☐ *Homework.* Remember that acquisition learning should not be done as homework. Homework is ideal for proficiency-building and maintenance activities and should be assigned regularly in reasonable amounts.

APPROACHES TO TEACHING MATHEMATICS

With increasing attention being given to mathematics, new programs and materials appear on a regular basis. Some of the most recent materials are intriguing microcomputer software programs. This section presents major approaches to mathematics instruction that can be used with students who have problems in this area.

Basal Textbook Series

The most frequently employed approach to teaching math is the use of basal textbooks, which all major publishers have produced. It is important to remember that these textbooks are written primarily for students in regular math classes even though most of these series offer suggestions for addressing the needs of students with learning-related problems. Teachers of students who are experiencing difficulties in math must be prepared to augment and/or adapt these texts as necessary.

Although there are many commonalities across basal series, there are notable differences as well. Before selecting a specific series, teachers should evaluate thoroughly the instructional features of each. In particular, attention should be directed to the instructor's manual, the student textbook/workbook, and any supporting materials that accompany the series. A sample page from an instructor's manual is presented in Figure 12.4. The more effective series include specific suggestions for dealing with diverse needs and offer ways to augment lessons. A key variable is the amount of practice included to achieve mastery of the skill(s) being taught. Many commercially available textbooks now come with sets of supplementary hands-on materials as well, which must be evaluated in terms of students' needs.

There are advantages in using a textbook approach.

- ☐ Skill development is laid out in a comprehensive and sequential fashion.
- ☐ A number of primary and supplemental materials are provided: text, teacher's manual, student workbook, ditto masters, quizzes and placement tests, and record-keeping procedures.
- ☐ Some series are more oriented to real life.
- ☐ Some series provide a hands-on, activity-oriented approach.

There are also disadvantages.

- ☐ Teacher's manuals do not provide specific teaching strategies (acquisition stage).
- ☐ Not enough practice is provided (fluency/mastery stage).
- ☐ Movement from one skill/topic to another is too quick.
- ☐ Sometimes there is not enough review of previously acquired skills and knowledge (maintenance stage).
- ☐ Linguistic and conceptual complexity may inhibit student understanding.
- ☐ Types of activities have limited variety.
- ☐ The activities lack relevance to students.

Comprehensive Math Programs

Another approach to teaching mathematics is the use of multifaceted math programs, which are often published as kits or an as-

STUDENT OBJECTIVE
To interpret information from a mileage chart and relate the information to problem solving.

VOCABULARY
kilometer (km)

TEACHING SUGGESTIONS

Talk about distances between cities. (Materials: large map of the United States) Display the large map of the United States. Discuss the locations of many of the major cities listed on the mileage chart. It may be an interesting exercise to have the students estimate how far it is from one city to another. Their responses may be in miles. At this point, introduce the vocabulary word, *kilometer*, explaining that it is part of the metric system, which they will be learning more about as the year progresses.

READINESS

For students who need help reading charts.

Readiness for 60–61

Mileage Chart

City	Atlanta	Boston	Chicago	Dallas
Atlanta		1108	708	785
Boston	1108		1004	1753
Chicago	708	1004		921
Dallas	785	1753	921	

How many miles is it from

1. Atlanta to Boston? __1108__
2. Atlanta to Chicago? __708__
3. Boston to Chicago? __1004__
4. Chicago to Dallas? __921__
5. Dallas to Boston? __1753__
6. Dallas to Atlanta? __785__

Copymaster S82 or Duplicating Master S82

"Who can tell me what this chart is used for? Has anyone in your family used a chart like this to plan a trip? A mileage chart helps us plan trips by showing the distance between cities and towns. For example, to find the distance between Atlanta and Boston, place the index finger of your left hand on Atlanta and the index finger of your right hand on Boston. Move your left index finger straight across to the right and your right index finger straight down until your fingers touch. Did you touch on *1108*? That is about the number of miles between Atlanta and Boston."

Have the students find Chicago on the left and Chicago at the top. Ask why that box is blank. Assign the page.

Problem Solving / Interpreting a table

Many people work for airlines. Some fly the planes. Others work with passengers. Still others work on the planes.

Modern jets can fly long distances. The chart below shows the air distance in kilometers between certain cities of the world.

Air Distance in Kilometers between Cities

City	Chicago	Hong Kong	London	Montreal	Moscow	New York	Peking	San Francisco
Chicago		12,475	6,333	1,192	7,979	1,142	10,566	2,974
Hong Kong	12,475		9,584	12,378	7,099	12,896	1,947	11,048
London	6,333	9,584		5,206	2,502	5,550	8,118	8,587
Montreal	1,192	12,378	5,206		7,042	530	10,422	4,069
Moscow	7,979	7,099	2,502	7,042		7,493	5,771	9,416
New York	1,142	12,896	5,550	530	7,493		10,950	4,115
Peking	10,566	1,947	8,118	10,422	5,771	10,950		9,469
San Francisco	2,974	11,048	8,587	4,069	9,416	4,115	9,469	

USING THE PAGES

Explain the use of the distance chart on page 60.

To find the distance from New York to Hong Kong, the students should go down the left side of the chart until they find New York. They should move a finger across the row until they have located Hong Kong at the top of the chart. The number that coincides with New York and Hong Kong will tell them the distance in kilometers between these two cities. Do exercises 1–6 as a class.

To find the total distance between three or four cities, the students will have to record each separate distance and then find the sum. Do exercise 12 on the chalkboard. Have a student record the separate distances. Have another student add the numbers together.

CLASSWORK/HOMEWORK

Textbook Assignments	Basic	Average	Enriched
Exercises 1–17	✔	✔	✔
Keeping Skills Sharp	✔	✔	✔
Extra Problem Solving set 2 page 381	✔	✔	

Optional Materials	Basic	Average	Enriched
Readiness Worksheet	✔	✔	
Basic Worksheet	✔		
Enrichment Worksheet		✔	✔
Excursion Worksheet			✔
Calculator Worksheet	✔	✔	✔
Creative Problem Solving section 3	✔	✔	✔

FIGURE 12.4

Sample page from an instructor's manual (From *Heath Mathematics: Teacher's Edition* [p. 60] by W. E. Rucker, C. S. Dilley, and D. W. Lowry, 1987, Lexington, MA: D. C. Heath. Copyright 1987 by D. C. Heath and Company. Reprinted by permission.)

semblage of materials, usually containing teacher's manuals, student materials, and supplementary items or resources. One of the most useful programs, developed with special students in mind, is described here.

Project MATH Project MATH (Cawley et al., 1976) is a comprehensive developmental program that attempts to meet three major goals: (1) to provide students with a wide range of math experiences, (2) to minimize the effects of inadequately developed skills and abilities on mathematics performance, and (3) to use the qualities of mathematics and experiences that can be generated via mathematics to enhance the learner's affective and cognitive status. Project MATH has four levels: prekindergarten to Grade 1, Grades 1 and 2, Grades 2.5 through 4, and Grades 4 through 6. Each level contains directed activities in six strands of mathematics: geometry, sets, patterns, numbers, measurement, and fractions.

Project MATH incorporates the interactive unit (IU) model as the framework for a multiple-option curriculum; activities represent various combinations of teacher presentation formats and student responses. The activities have been developed with consideration for the requirements of learners with special needs.

The heart of the curriculum is the instructional guides. Each guide is in card form, is coded for easy access, and focuses on one particular concept. Included in each guide is information about instructor input and learner output as well as information on activities to be performed, materials needed, relevant supplemental activities, and a brief informal evaluation procedure to determine whether a student is ready to proceed to the next instructional task. Figure 12.5 presents one of the instructional guides from Project MATH.

The teacher considering Project MATH must also become familiar with the administrative guide, which presents the conceptual basis for the program as well as procedures for appropriate use. Of particular importance is the topical skill sequence, which relates the strand/area/concept being taught to a specific instructional guide. This feature is essential for identifying activities to be presented.

Other materials included in this curricular program are learner activity books, supplemental activity books, class and individual progress forms, and manipulative materials. An assessment tool, the Math Concept Inventory, is included for use either as a screening device to determine the proper placement of students in the Multiple Option Curriculum or as a curricular-based instrument to determine whether students have mastered a specific block of instruction.

The authors of Project MATH recognized the importance of problem-solving skills for special learners and included a verbal problem-solving component with the program. That portion of the Project MATH curriculum is discussed later in the chapter.

The authors suggest that the teacher first determine at which point to begin teaching by giving each student the Math Concept Inventory. After determining placement and grouping, the teacher can select the appropriate instructional guide, following the sequence of instructional activities outlined in the program to mix the six mathematical strands or selecting the strands they deem instructionally relevant. This program allows teachers to be creative also. With the interactive unit approach teachers should develop other suitable instructional activities to capitalize on the multiple input/output options.

Overall, Project MATH is a very useful instructional program. It covers a wide

FIGURE 12.5
An instructional guide
from Project MATH
(From *Project MATH*
by J. F. Cawley, H. A.
Goodstein, A. M.
Fitzmaurice, A.
Lepore, R. Sedlak,
and V. Althaus, 1976,
Tulsa, OK: Educational
Development.
Copyright 1976 by
Educational
Development
Corporation. Reprinted
by permission.)

LEVEL 2   **N137**

PROJECT MATH INSTRUCTIONAL GUIDE

STRAND	Numbers	INPUT	OUTPUT
AREA	Subtraction		
CONCEPT	Role of Zero		

	INSTRUCTOR	LEARNER
BEHAVIORAL OBJECTIVE	States subtraction number expressions.	Constructs representations of the number expressions.

ACTIVITIES

1. **Review.** Review with the learners the different types of subtraction problems. State a subtraction problem, and have a learner construct the answer. For example, say, "I had five books on my desk. Two belonged to Mrs. Jones, so I gave them back to her. Show me how many books I would still have on my desk." You may also state expressions such as, "Five take away three," and have a learner construct the remainder set.

Also review problems with a number other than the difference missing (e.g., _____ − 2 = 4, 6 − _____ = 4). Say, "I had some books. I gave two away. Now I have four. Show me how many I started with." Ask a learner to make the set of four and then to add to it the set of two books that were given away to find out how many books there were at the outset. Repeat the activity using other examples.

2. **Role of Zero.** Explain, "In subtraction problems, the number zero (Write "0" on the chalkboard.) plays an important part. When we subtract or take away zero from a number, the answer is always that number. The answer is identical to, or the same as, the number from which you subtract zero. For example, five blocks take away zero blocks is five blocks because nothing was taken away from the five blocks."

State different subtraction expressions in which 0 occurs. At the same time, give some blocks to a learner, and ask him to construct the sets in each expression. He should demonstrate his understanding by not taking any blocks away.

MATERIALS
Classroom objects, blocks or discs.

SUPPLEMENTAL ACTIVITIES   N137: a, b.

EVALUATION
Give the learner blocks or discs, and ask him to construct representations of four subtraction expressions such as the following:

$$3 - 2 \qquad 3 - 0 \qquad 5 - 1 \qquad 5 - 0$$

---

range of mathematical skill areas while allowing for differences in learning abilities and limitations.

Direct Instruction

A direct instruction approach to teaching mathematics is teacher-directed, structured, and reflective of the components of effective instruction presented in chapter 2. This section focuses on two specific commercial programs that adhere to the tenets of this orientation.

Direct Instruction Mathematics According to the authors of this program, "Direct instruction provides a comprehensive set of prescriptions for organizing instruction so that students acquire, retain, and generalize new learning in as humane, efficient, and effective a manner as possible" (Silbert, Carnine, & Stein, 1981, p. 2). Direct Instruction Mathematics is predicated on careful consideration of three major elements: (1) instructional design, (2) presentation techniques, and (3) organization of instruction. An underlying attitude that almost all students can learn mathematics is inherent in this program.

This program provides techniques for constructing effective lessons and developing specific instructional procedures. The authors suggest an eight-step sequence.

1. Specify objectives that are observable and measurable.
2. Devise problem-solving strategies, which can be useful across situations.
3. Determine necessary preskills and teach those first.
4. Sequence skills in an appropriate order.
5. Select a teaching procedure related to the three types of tasks required of students (motor, labeling, and strategy).
6. Design instructional formats, including the specifics of what the teacher does and says, correction procedures, and anticipated student responses (see Figure 12.6 for a sample instructional format).
7. Select examples based on what students are learning and what they have been taught previously.
8. Provide practice and review, including guided and independent practice.

Additional instructional suggestions address maintaining student attention, teaching to criterion, selecting various instructional materials, augmenting commercial materials, assessing students, and grouping for instruction.

Corrective Mathematics

Corrective Mathematics (Englemann & Carnine, 1981) is basically a remedial program developed for use with students in Grade 3 through a postsecondary level. Its primary focus is on four basic operations, referred to as modules. Each module contains certain strands: facts, computation operations, and story problems (the addition module also has a strand on reading and writing numbers). The program was developed for students who have not mastered addition. Students do need certain preskills to use this program, although advanced reading skills are not required. Poor readers can be placed in this program.

Corrective Mathematics is a systematic sequence of skill development. Each module contains a presentation book (i.e., teacher's guide), answer keys, and a student book. Each module also includes a placement test, a preskill test, and a series of mastery tests. Corrective Mathematics, like Direct Instruction Mathematics, is a structured and well-organized program. Using a teacher-directed approach, each presentation book provides specific instructional information for each of the many lessons. Each task within the lesson has a script telling exactly what the teacher should say and do as well as what the students should say and do. Each daily lesson involves some type of teacher-directed activity. Most lessons also require some independent student work.

An interesting feature of the program is the built-in point system by which students can accumulate points for successful performance with workbooks, in groups, in game situations, or on the mastery tests. Systems for awarding and monitoring points are programmed into the materials. A common theme in the Corrective Mathematics programs is the concept of teaching to criterion. The idea is that at the completion of any exercise, each student should be able to perform a given task without error.

Eclectic Orientation

An eclectic approach implies that a combination of techniques are utilized, which may prove helpful in maximizing the success of a

Day	Part A Structured Board Problems	Part B Structured Worksheet Problems	Part C Less Structured Worksheet Problems	Part D Supervised Practice Problems	Part E Independent Practice Problems
1-2	4				
3-4	2	6			
5-6		2	6		
7-8			2	6	
9-Until accurate				8	
Until fluent					8-12

PART A: Structured Board Presentation

TEACHER	STUDENTS

Write on board: $\frac{8}{12} = ($ $)$ —

1. "WE'RE GOING TO REDUCE THIS FRACTION. WE REDUCE BY PULLING OUT THE GREATEST COMMON FACTOR OF THE NUMERATOR AND DENOMINATOR. HOW DO WE REDUCE A FRACTION?"

"Pull out the greatest common factor of the numerator and denominator."

2. "WE WANT TO REDUCE 8/12. WHAT IS THE GREATEST COMMON FACTOR OF 8 AND 12?" Pause.

"4"

TO CORRECT: Tell correct answer. Explain why student's answer is incorrect.

3. "SO WE PULL OUT THE FRACTION 4/4. WHAT FRACTION DO WE PULL OUT OF 8/12?"

"4/4"

Write on board:
$$\frac{8}{12} = \left(\frac{4}{4}\right) —$$

4. "LET'S FIGURE OUT THE TOP NUMBER OF THE REDUCED FRACTION." Point to symbols as you read. "EIGHT EQUALS FOUR TIMES WHAT NUMBER?" Pause.
Write on board:
$$\frac{8}{12} = \left(\frac{4}{4}\right) \, 2$$

"2"

5. "LET'S FIGURE OUT THE BOTTOM NUMBER OF THE REDUCED FRACTION." Point to symbols as you read. "TWELVE EQUALS FOUR TIMES WHAT NUMBER?" Pause, signal.
Write on board:
$$\frac{8}{12} = \left(\frac{4}{4}\right) \frac{2}{3}$$

"3"

6. "THE FRACTION IN PARENTHESES EQUALS 1. WE DON'T CHANGE THE VALUE OF A FRACTION WHEN WE MULTIPLY BY 1. SO WE CAN CROSS OUT 4/4." Cross out. "WHEN WE PULL OUT THE FRACTION OF 1, THE REDUCED FRACTION IS 2/3. WHAT IS THE REDUCED FRACTION?"

"2/3"

FIGURE 12.6

Sample instructional format for reducing fractions in Direct Instruction Math (From *Direction Instruction Mathematics* [p. 326] by J. Silbert, O. Carnine, and M. Stein, 1981, Columbus, OH: Merrill. Copyright 1981 by Merrill Publishing Company. Reprinted by permission.)

math program. Our discussion focuses on the integration of different approaches with a basal textbook approach.

The reality of mathematics instruction is that most teachers use textbooks, even with their acknowledged limitations. One way to provide students with additional practice and to avoid the drudgery of using workbooks regularly is to supplement the textbook with materials from Project MATH. It is easy to cross-reference the topics in the text with the strands and related skills listed in the Project MATH administrative guide. Teachers can then use any of the following materials to augment the textbook: instructional guides, learner activity books, and supplemental activity books. Tindall (1985) developed a matrix that cross-references all of the skill areas in the Scott, Foresman *Math Around Us* textbook (Grade 3) with the Level Two component of Project MATH. Such a system offers a wealth of additional ways to ensure mastery and diversity.

To address the problem that many teacher's guides accompanying student texts do not provide specific instructional routines for acquisition learning, teachers may need to consult a resource like Direct Instruction Mathematics. With that supplement teachers can develop precise lesson formats that provide direct instruction on a particular topic. Some lesson formats already exist; others may have to be adapted. This combination is extremely useful for students who are having a difficult time grasping math concepts.

STRATEGIES FOR TEACHING SPECIFIC SKILLS

Computational Skills

In arithmetic computation students must possess certain competencies to learn new facts and operations or must develop them quickly to progress in mathematical learning.

Precomputational Skills

1. can discriminate among quantities, shapes, and sizes
2. understands one-to-one correspondence
3. can name symbols for numbers
4. can name symbols in order from 1 to 10
5. can recognize numerals from 0 through 9
6. can write numerals from 0 through 9

Although teachers generally think of addition as the first step in arithmetic, a pupil must have certain readiness or precomputation skills to be able to handle the process successfully. Bereiter and Englemann (1966) regard counting as the initial step or phase of arithmetic learning. Initially the pupil learns to count without meaning (by rote); next the pupil learns to count with meaning, that is, with numerals associated with sets of objects; and finally, the pupil learns to recognize different numerals and to write them.

During the same period students must learn to distinguish among quantities, shapes, and sizes of different common objects. Also at this time students learn to differentiate among numbers as well as letters. Other concepts that teachers need to foster at the precomputational level include big/little, long/short, few/many, more/less, and round/square. Because these words can be ordered into pairs, teaching them as polar opposites seems to be a good approach (Bereiter & Englemann, 1966).

One of the most important precomputational skills that a pupil needs to acquire is a knowledge of one-to-one correspondence, the idea that every one thing seen can be matched to one other thing that may or may not be seen. Teaching one-to-one correspondence begins by having a pupil match similar objects; later this task can be made more difficult by shifting the dimensions of the objects the pupil is to match. For example, a pupil may first be required to match a red chicken with a red chicken; later the teacher requires the pupil to match a chicken with a chicken, ignoring color or size.

Learning to write numerals from 1 through 10 is the activity that bridges the gap between precomputation and computation. As mentioned in chapter 11, writing of numerals should be coordinated with the learning of manuscript handwriting, but it is not totally dependent on mastery of handwriting.

Addition

1. can make combinations using at least two numbers from 1 to 10
2. can add at least two numbers less than 10 to yield a sum greater than 10
3. can count sequentially past 30
4. understands place value and understands concept of zero
5. can add two-place numbers to two-place numbers without carrying
6. can count sequentially to 100
7. can add sets of numbers using the process of carrying
8. can count sequentially past 200
9. can add sets of numbers yielding a sum greater than 100
10. can count sequentially past 1000
11. can add sets of numbers yielding a sum greater than 1000
12. can add numbers with decimals
13. can add fractional numbers

The skill area of addition forms the base of the arithmetic operational ladder. Many specific skills learned in addition are used over and over again as pupils climb the ladder through subtraction, multiplication, division, and arithmetic reasoning. Consequently, students who manifest deficits in basic addition skills are likely to have trouble in all other areas of computation as well. Nonetheless, Cawley and colleagues (1988) suggest that it is possible to teach any of the four basic operations in different sequences and that the strict requirement that addition and subtraction must precede multiplication and division may be misguided.

Initial instruction in addition should focus almost exclusively on the concrete, or enactive, representations of the arithmetic reality being taught. Traditional techniques have included the use of felt boards and pocket charts. Other easy materials to manipulate are counters and Cuisenaire rods, which can be used directly for counting. The abacus—the ancient Egyptian counter containing different-colored beads—is also a useful device for teaching addition.

As teachers move from the concrete, pupils may still need some visual help with computations. This help can be secured through the use of number lines. A short number line with numbers stopping at 10 should be used first. Later, as pupils progress to numbers past 10, a longer number line can be used.

Beginning Number Line

1 2 3 4 5 6 7 8 9 10

Advanced Number Line

1 2 3 4 5 6 7 8 9 10 11 12 13 14 15

These number lines can be taped to pupils' desks or made of heavy cardboard and kept inside the desks. For younger children number lines on the floor illustrate counting through movement. Familiarity with number lines will be useful later as pupils move into subtraction.

Throughout arithmetic instruction teachers should be careful to emphasize only one new concept at a time and should continue to teach this concept until students reach a predetermined mastery level. Continued instruction does not mean that students must learn arithmetic facts via boring repetition; short, intensive practice using a variety of ways to teach the same concept should be used to promote overlearning. Project MATH is an excellent resource for incorporating variety into the curriculum. As students learn more and more about one-to-one correspondence and can recognize numbers from 1 to

9, they should be given opportunities to make additive combinations using at least two numbers. While pupils master initial combinations, they will still rely on the concrete, but a gradual transition should be made to pictorial representations of the processes. The last step in this sequence is for pupils to be able to represent the process of addition exclusively with symbols and signs. The achievement of this last stage is enhanced by encouraging students to verbalize what they are doing rather than just having them respond to worksheets.

Teachers must keep in mind the need for a consistent repertoire of mathematical language throughout instruction. In one such study, Adachi (1981) found that many different expressions were used to suggest each of the fundamental operations. The term *plus* is viewed as a good way to introduce what happens during addition because this term can serve throughout all arithmetic instruction, whereas another term such as *and* may become confusing to pupils as they begin to work strictly with numbers (e.g., 2 plus 2 equals 4 is clearer than 2 and 2 makes 4). One of the ultimate teaching goals is maximum precision.

Some concepts that may not be directly involved in addition or computation must be learned at the same time that addition is being taught because they aid students in mastering all types of arithmetic problems. Such concepts include the words *before, after, between, more,* and *less* and an understanding that zero and its symbol do not have a value but that zero helps determine place value. Understanding these concepts leads directly to development of abilities in arithmetic reasoning. Therefore, the teacher must ensure that these concepts are learned and understood.

Subtraction

1. can subtract a one-place number from

another one-place number to yield values between 0 and 9
2. can subtract a one-place number from a two-place number less than 20
3. can subtract a set of numbers from another set of numbers without borrowing
4. can subtract a set of numbers from another set of numbers using the process of borrowing
5. can subtract numbers with decimals from each other
6. can subtract fractions from each other

Subtraction is the opposite of addition. In the process of addition, like objects or things are combined; in subtraction like objects or things are taken away from each other. Many of the skills learned during instruction in addition are used by students to solve subtraction problems. Likewise, most of the methods and procedures used for addition instruction can be used for subtraction instruction. Again, initial instruction should start in a concrete manner with gradual fading to the abstractions or number symbols.

The act of borrowing from one place to the next may be one of the most difficult parts of the subtraction process to grasp. Many students fail to understand why one cannot switch the 1 and 3 around when subtracting 23 from 41. It makes sense because we teach students that they can add in either direction (commutative property). Behind this confusion is a lack of understanding of place value. Getting pupils to perceive that the position a number occupies indicates something more about a number than just its name can be accomplished in several different ways. Initially, students need to see that regrouping numbers permits the lesser number to be subtracted from the greater number. For example, in subtracting 4 from 23, regrouping 23 into two tens (20) and three ones (3) and then changing this arrangement to one 10 and 13 ones makes it easy to subtract 4 from 13 and then add that number to the 10 not used to get an answer of 19. Students must understand that the 2 in 20 really stands for two tens. Another way to help students understand borrowing is to show the relationship of carrying in addition to borrowing in subtraction, using examples similar to the following:

$$
\begin{array}{cccccc}
22 & 13 & 33 & 26 & 60 & 44 \\
-9 & +9 & -7 & +7 & -16 & +16
\end{array}
$$

The first problem in each set shows the operation of borrowing, whereas the second problem shows the opposite operation of carrying. Once pupils understand the relationship, they can check their work by reversing the original operation.

Multiplication

1. can multiply a one-place number by a one-place number
2. can multiply a two-place number by a one-place number
3. can multiple a three- (or more) place number by a one-place number
4. can multiply a two-place number by a two-place number
5. can multiply a three- (or more) place number by a two- (or more) place number
6. can multiply a whole number by a decimal
7. can multiply a decimal by a decimal
8. can multiply a fraction by a whole number
9. can multiply a fraction by a fraction

Division

1. can divide a one-place number by a one-place number
2. can divide a two-place number by a one-place number
3. can divide a three- (or more) place number by a one-place number
4. can divide a two-place number by a two-place number
5. can divide a three- (or more) place number by a two- (or more) place number
6. can divide with numbers containing decimals
7. can divide with numbers containing fractions

Both multiplication and division require a great deal of rote memory, and neither process may be frequently used by persons with mild handicaps after they leave the formal learning environment. Yet with the potential benefits of these skills for independent functioning and with the emphasis and importance placed on mainstreaming, teachers must consider teaching multiplication and division if success in society and integration of students are to become feasible. Every attempt should be made to use practical examples to make multiplication and division relevant and varied ways of teaching the same content to reduce boredom. In addition, constantly requiring the student to verbalize various problem-solving operations enhances generalization and transfer of skills (see Project MATH). The importance of teaching students how to reason and problem solve cannot be overemphasized, yet traditional teaching of multiplication and division relies heavily on memorizing multiplication tables. Exceptional students may be drilled and taught to learn computational skills in such a rote fashion that the process itself interferes with learning problem-solving skills, or these students may learn rote computational skills but fail to learn how these skills are applied in practical situations, making the instructional time and effort expended impossible to justify. Because rote learning may be somewhat circumvented by teaching children how to use a calculator or a times table, it is recommended that teachers use teaching time to explain and clarify what multiplication and division processes are and to give examples of how the processes may be applied to the grocery store, gas station, or bank.

Multiplication can be thought of as a faster, more efficient way to add, and most students prefer a more facile method once they learn it. It is certainly faster and easier to multiply 7 times 10 than it is to first write 7 ten times and then add the 7s. There are other similarities between multiplication and addition: carrying from one place to another in multiplication is much the same as in addition. Also, the principle of reversibility (commutative property) applies to both, that is, the same answer results, regardless of the positions of particular numbers in the original combination.

Traditionally, teachers assist students in learning how to multiply by first using sets of objects and then by using tables showing multiplication combinations. These tables can be constructed in several different ways, two of which are shown here.

$1 \times 1 = 1$	$\times$	0	1	2	3	4	5
$1 \times 2 = 2$							
$1 \times 3 = 3$	0	0	0	0	0	0	0
$1 \times 4 = 4$	1	0	1	2	3	4	5
$1 \times 5 = 5$	2	0	2	4	6	8	10
	3	0	3	6	9	12	15
	4	0	4	8	12	16	20
	5	0	5	10	15	20	25

Instruction in multiplication must also focus initially on concrete examples. Later, the concrete examples can lead to practical examples that may vary in abstractness. When students come to multiplication, they may have a fairly good grasp of addition and subtraction facts. If so, they should be encouraged to begin checking answers to multiplication problems. This self-checking can be done in the same way that other arithmetic work is done, or students can be shown how to use a hand calculator for checking.

Division, the opposite of multiplication, requires many of the skills and manipula-

tions learned in multiplication. It is very important that teachers provide clear and systematic instruction in this area. If students are encountering problems in learning how to divide, we suggest consulting the Direct Instruction Mathematics material presented earlier. When beginning instruction in division, it is a good idea to require students to check all answers by multiplying the divisor by the quotient. For example, if the pupil divides 21 by 7 and gets the answer 3, the 7 should then be multiplied by the 3 to determine whether the product is actually 21. This process helps students develop a greater understanding of the relationship between multiplication and division.

Applied Math Skills: Measurement

Several different areas of arithmetic involve applications of the many skills learned in arithmetic computation and reasoning. These areas usually involve some type of measurement, such as time, money, length, weight, or volume. Although time and money may not generally be thought of as measurement, all measurement is based on relative comparisons. When defining time or the measurement of time, we are comparing a period between two events with a predetermined duration, usually called seconds, minutes, and so on. Likewise, money helps us compare the worth of objects, for example, something worth a quarter is more valuable than something worth a dime. Most children, including children with disabilities, enter school with some concept of measurement, especially of time and money. At this point, however, they are using these concepts in a gross manner; for example, time is seen as the difference between day and night or as the difference in the days of the week; money is viewed as an object that can be exchanged for items.

Time   One procedure to begin teaching

about time is an opening activity of the school day and requires a child to affix some symbol on a calendar showing the days of the week. Concepts of the days of the week and the months of the year are often presented when describing certain events during a particular time period, such as Monday being the first school day of the week or Christmas coming in the last month of the year.

However, if the concepts of days of the week and months are difficult for students to learn, this activity may not be advisable during opening exercises. These concepts may need to be considered on a more academic plane: they may be best presented in short, intense lessons each day using small groups. If math is taught every day using small groups, it may be advantageous to begin each session with a quick, clear, precise presentation of the days of the week, months, and year. This is an excellent example of a concept that is easy to present but may be exceedingly difficult for students to learn.

Learning to tell time on a clock is a difficult task for many children, and this difficulty may be confounded for students with learning problems. A prerequisite to telling time is an understanding of time itself. Concepts of today, tomorrow, yesterday, next week, and soon are basic to understanding time. Next, students need to understand that certain things happen at certain times, like lunch, recess, cleanup, and dismissal. The schedule of events greatly aids in teaching time. An extension of posting a daily schedule is to write in the approximate (if possible, exact) times that specific activities occur. Later, the teacher can use a clock face to show the different times that these familiar activities happen.

The precise telling of time, such as by minutes, requires knowledge of the difference between the concepts of before and after. One easy way to help pupils understand

is to make worksheets with clock facts on them but without the minute or hour hand showing, except in examples. In the example shown here, the student is required to determine before and after by drawing in the correct hand positions. Concepts of half-past, quarter till, and quarter after can also be taught in this manner.

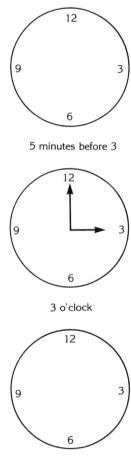

5 minutes before 3

3 o'clock

5 minutes after 3

Some authorities (Nibbelink & Witzenberg, 1981; Reisman & Kauffman, 1980) advocate abandoning the traditional way of teaching time. They suggest teaching the easier task of telling time by minutes first. Actually, the entire process of teaching temporal measurement must be evaluated in light of digital watches and clocks, which significantly modify the skills students need to be taught.

Money Children usually enter school with some knowledge about money and a fair amount of interest in obtaining it, especially at the junior high and high school levels. Students use money to buy lunch and go to school-sponsored activities. Teachers can easily take advantage of these activities to help pupils gain a more precise knowledge of money. A unit on different coins, up to a dollar, can be coordinated with instruction in addition and subtraction skills during the primary years.

One of the best ways to teach coin recognition and change making is to use real coins to make simulated purchases of various items; for example, a student may use two quarters to purchase a 30-cent candy bar and must then determine how much change should be received. With this approach the teacher does not have to worry about transfer of learning from play money to real money. Using real coins has the further advantage of providing concrete items for students to manipulate.

A workbook using pictures of real money, *Money Makes Sense* (Kahn & Hanna, 1960a) provides interesting practice opportunities. This workbook includes sections on recognizing coins, relative value of coins, deriving correct change from purchases of various items, and many others. An inexpensive change-making device in kit form, developed by Spellman (1972) and distributed by the Teach-Um Company, is appropriate for high school-aged students. The kit contains many examples of working with money. Some other companies, such as Janus and Quercus, have also produced materials useful for teaching these concepts and are appropriate for older students.

For older students topics covering paychecks, checking and savings accounts, and

home budgets are important items to cover. One of the easiest and most effective ways to deal with these topics on the high school level is to print up paychecks on ditto sheets and issue these checks to students at the end of the week. By explaining various types of withholding, students are forewarned that deductions are made from paychecks and they will actually receive less money than expected. Students can use numerous commercial materials in the exercise, but classroom instruction based on students' actual experiences with paychecks and yearly taxes is the most effective teaching technique. Students need to become familiar with various time schedules, reimbursements, deductions, taxes, and the corresponding calculations. The Real Life Math program described in the resource section at the end of this chapter can also help develop skills in these areas.

Home budgeting can be taught with ditto sheets of bills and statements for utilities, rent, food, and clothes. Basic bookkeeping skills can also be taught at this time. During the process students should be maintaining home records, filing receipts, and so on. Banking skills should also be taught directly. Students should learn how to deposit and withdraw money, write checks, and maintain a savings account, using both traditional methods and modern, electronic methods.

An alternative to workbooks or a simulated unit on money is a currency-based token economy in the classroom. Although token economies are usually developed to provide external motivation for students or to control disruptive behavior, a currency-based economy can also be used effectively to teach children many money-related concepts. It can enhance the teaching of counting, change-making, and the relative value of money; and it provides an environment that promotes decision making regarding the safekeeping of money, buying power, and many other concepts. At the vocational level students can be paid for coming to class on time, punching in and out, getting to work quickly without delay, and doing accurate work (correct number of questions answered, as in piecework).

As students become accustomed to the currency system, a bank can be developed, to introduce checking and savings accounts. Even more advanced is the development of a credit-card system. Also, students can set up their own proprietorships and sell things they make. If students do set up their own business, it might be interesting and educational to provide instruction in sales tax, sales skills, and advertising. *Living in the Classroom* by Payne, Polloway, Kauffman, and Scranton (1975) contains a detailed account of the development and implementation of such a system.

Volume and Weight Despite the common belief that there is a direct relationship between volume and weight, there is not even an indirect relationship between the two. Weight cannot be predicted from volume nor volume from weight. Weight is the heaviness of an object, whereas volume is the measured amount of a substance. Terms like *more* and *less* should be associated with volume.

Whenever children work with the volumes of substances as in cups, pints, quarts, liters, and so on—the initial instruction should be concrete—with the teacher actually demonstrating the change from a small measure to a larger one, and vice versa, by pouring a dry (e.g., sand or rice) or liquid (e.g., water) substance from one container to another. To learn about weight, pupils should be guided to compare two or more objects to determine which is heaviest. Students should begin the study of weight using pounds (kilograms) first (e.g., their own weight). Gradually, as several close weights are being compared, ounces (grams) can be used to determine which object is heaviest or lightest. Practical applications of using weight and volumetric measurement abound in science and should be pursued.

Linear Measurement One of the easier measurement ideas for pupils with mild handicaps to understand is linear, or distance, measurement. Measurement of feet (meters) and inches (centimeters) is similar to the use of number lines in learning to count and add. However, once linear measurement goes beyond the yards (meters) to miles (kilometers) or considers fractional parts of an inch, some students may run into trouble. Therefore, teachers should plan unit activities to reinforce learned concepts of inches and feet while moving pupils on to the more difficult areas of fractional inches and miles. In a practical sense students who have learning problems may not need to know how long a mile is, although knowing about fractional parts of inches probably helps in certain skill jobs such as carpentry or sewing. Looking over any school supply catalogue under the heading of measurement can provide ideas about teaching volume, weight, and linear measurement. Trundle wheels, gauges, calipers, capacity measures, scales, weights, protractors, thermometers, compasses, timers, and clocks will trigger numerous ideas, yet many of these teaching devices need not be purchased. The key in measurement is to keep instruction precise, simple, and practical.

Problem-Solving and Reasoning Skills

Problem solving has been targeted as one of the major areas of interest in the 1980s (NCTM, 1980). Unquestionably, many regular educators are devoting much attention to this important skill area, and special educators need to attend to this issue as well. Peterson (1982) suggests that teachers concern themselves with teaching students "process rather than rote learning" (p. 41). The implication here is clear: development of computational skills is necessary but not sufficient. Computation provides pupils with tools and a knowledge of how to use them. On the other hand, reasoning skills enable students to understand when they can use certain arithmetic tools.

Moses (1983) indicates that there are three major barriers to solving word problems: interest and motivation; deficiencies in basic skills, including areas such as reading; and lack of facility in cognitive skill areas. All three of these factors can be significant obstacles for students with special learning needs and must be taken into account when planning instruction. Students can perfect reasoning abilities in arithmetic in numerous ways. Techniques incorporating teacher-directed activities into a systematic program for skill acquisition, maintenance, and generalization provide the best opportunities for maximizing the probability of learning. In addition, four other factors must be considered: (1) the student's ability to understand the language of arithmetic; (2) instruction in finding significant words that indicate which operation to perform and discarding irrelevant, nonessential information; (3) verbalization of the problem; and (4) strategies to establish a procedure for working through a solution.

Although understanding arithmetic terms may seem quite simple, students who do not understand the terms involved are lost at the outset. Remediation of this problem depends on first determining exactly which terms are not understood and devising strategies to teach them. Often, students understand most of the terms they encounter daily but are confused when problems do not use terms exactly like those. Essentially, they lose the ability to decipher the clues to solve the problem. The following problems can illustrate that (1) Elwood has 55 cents.

He uses 15 cents to buy milk and 30 cents to buy a candy bar. How much money does Elwood have now? (2) Linda Sue bought a comic book for 75 cents. After reading the comic, she sold it for 40 cents, which she put with the 28 cents she already had. How much money did Linda Sue have originally? How much money does Linda Sue have now? Even though students may be able to read and understand the words in these two problems, neither gives obvious directions about the operations that will produce a solution.

With problems of this type, the teacher's job is to help students find the significant words that indicate which operation to perform and help them eliminate nonessential information. In the first problem the clue words are "has," "uses," and "to buy." "Has" tells the amount Elwood starts with, which is the amount to be added to or taken away from. "Uses" and "to buy" indicate that money is spent; therefore, subtraction should solve the problem. Teachers should have students ascertain the meanings of the clue words specifically within the context of the particular problem.

The second example poses a somewhat more complex dilemma. In this problem one must determine not only how much money Linda Sue presently has but how much she started with. It is in effect two problems, which brings us to the third strategy teachers can use to help pupils perfect reasoning skills—verbalizing the problem. In problems like this one, pupils must first find as many significant words as possible and then attempt to determine how these words contribute to answering the question at hand. Teachers should formulate and ask questions about the problem, causing the pupils to verbalize possible solutions. Then pupils can ask their own questions, which may not be as precise as the teachers' but which will lead to a solution if teachers encourage the verbal interchange. Once pupils have gone through several of these verbal exchanges, they are in a position to form a tentative solution. Teachers should employ strategies to cause students to talk through or verbally explain their solutions. The simplest way is to continue the interchange just mentioned. Another way is to have students write short explanations about the whole process or use drawings or diagrams.

A strategy found effective with older students uses a sequence of tasks to be performed each time a math problem is encountered.

1. Read (or listen) carefully.
2. Write a few words about the kind of answer needed (e.g., kilometers per hour).
3. Look for significant words and eliminate irrelevant information.
4. Highlight the numbers that are important.
5. Draw a diagram or sketch; this graphic does not have to be a work of art but should depict what the problem is describing.
6. Decide on the necessary calculations, and identify a math sentence for this situation.
7. Perform the calculations.
8. Evaluate the answer to determine its reasonableness.
9. Write the answer with the appropriate units.

Even though this strategy is straightforward, each step requires considerable instruction.

Project MATH provides problem-solving activities designed for special learners. Each level of this program contains a verbal problem-solving component composed of many different units. For example, Level 3 contains 175 different units. The problem situations provided in each unit give students a chance to apply their arithmetic skills in new contexts. The authors stress that students must be able to process information but need not possess highly developed reading skills. Thus, many students who encounter problems in reading may still be able to use these materials.

Crawley, Fitzmaurice, Shaw, Kahn, and Bates (1979) suggest the development of word problems that vary according to linguistic as well as mathematical complexity. These different problems can then be represented in a matrix format. The usefulness of matrix programming is that it provides teachers with a system for (1) addressing individual needs (e.g., controlling for limited reading ability while developing more advanced mathematical skills) and (2) systematically developing more sophisticated problem-solving abilities—both linguistically and mathematically.

Some students whose reading skills limit their ability to comprehend word problems encounter great difficulty dealing with the linguistic demands of math materials. For these students Cawley (1984) recommends using reading materials that the student can handle and infusing mathematic features into these passages. From this adapted material, word problems can be developed using language that the student understands. An example of this idea is provided in Figure 12.7.

Thus, the most effective ways to develop and enhance reasoning skills in arithmetic involve clearly defining the terms used, teaching strategies to identify significant clue words and to ignore nonessential information, using verbal mediation strategies to work through to the solution of a given problem, and providing procedures for systematically solving math problems.

Functional Math Skills

Functional math skills are those that are necessary to deal with everyday events in our lives. Also referred to as survival mathematics (Smith, 1981), functional math skills need to be a major part of the curriculum. In fact, the integration of survival math con-

FIGURE 12.7
Adapted reading passage (From *Developmental Teaching of Mathematics for the Learning Disabled* [pp. 83–84] by J. F. Cawley (Ed.), 1984, Austin, TX: Pro-Ed. Copyright 1984 by Pro-Ed, Inc. Reprinted by permission.)

Passage 1

Catching Fish

A big black bear is fishing in the lake. He is standing near the shore where the lake is not deep. The bear is smacking his lips. He is thinking how the fish will taste when he eats them.

The bear is catching more fish than he can eat. When he is full of fish, he will leave the rest on the shore. A fox or a mink will come and eat them.

Passage 2

Catching Fish

Two black bears are fishing in the lake. One bear is standing near the shore. This bear has already caught 5 fish. The other bear is sitting in the water, holding on to the 6 fish that she has caught.

Each bear is thinking about catching some more fish. Each bear is also thinking about eating the fish. After each bear caught 2 more fish, they went home.

cepts into the entire K–12 curriculum is warranted for all students (Smith, 1978). Even the few special students who are college-bound will need to succeed in the community when their formal schooling terminates. Learners with special needs must acquire math skills that will have practical value in their postsecondary lives.

We have separated functional math skills into three categories: vocational math skills, everyday math skills, and leisure math skills. These are arbitrary distinctions that are not mutually exclusive. For instance, what one may consider an everyday math skill (e.g., measurement in cooking) may be a vocational math skill for someone else. Leisure math skills, even though clearly part of daily living, have been isolated to emphasize the appropriate use of leisure time, an area that has always been problematic for many adults with disabilities. Some examples of the skills represented by these three areas appear here.

Vocational Math Skills

☐ filling in time cards
☐ keeping a driver's log
☐ taking orders
☐ understanding want ads
☐ measuring (e.g., woodworking, agriculture)

Everyday Math Skills

☐ maintaining a checking account
☐ using automated tellers
☐ paying bills
☐ living within a budget
☐ estimating expenses (e.g., on a date)
☐ purchasing goods and materials
☐ following cooking directions
☐ managing time
☐ using temperature settings

Leisure Math Skills

☐ finding radio stations
☐ keeping score (e.g., darts, ping pong, baseball)
☐ using tide charts for fishing
☐ measuring (e.g., crafts, gardening)
☐ recognizing coin value for coin collecting

Although some excellent resources are available for teaching functional math skills, students are the most valuable sources of information. Their life situations should direct instruction. For teachers who want additional ideas and suggestions for designing activities, the following materials may be useful: *Functional Mathematics* (Maryland State Department of Education, 1977) and the *Adult Performance Level Adaptation and Modification Project* (LaQuey, 1981).

For teachers interested in some recent mathematics teaching resources, the materials discussed in this chapter should prove valuable. Mathematics instruction can be interesting, relevant, and meaningful to students. But to achieve this goal, teachers must find it interesting as well and be willing to incorporate this enthusiasm in their teaching and share it with students.

ACTIVITIES

Precomputation

1. To develop the ability to count from 1 to 10, have pupils play rhyming games such as Buckle My Shoe.
2. Make different cutouts of three basic shapes (circles, triangles, rectangles); have pupils identify each shape. After pupils can identify each different shape, have them compare sizes of the different shapes to determine which is larger, smaller, and so on.
3. Pupils can learn the concepts of more and less by comparing groups of objects. Start with one object in one group and two or more objects in another group. Have the pupil identify which group has more and which has less. This activity could also be used to teach sameness.
4. Draw a line of objects, such as apples; have a pupil put an X on the number of objects designated by the numeral at the beginning of the line.
5. Have pupils match strings to kites, sails to boats, or stems to flowers to help develop an understanding of one-to-one correspondence.
6. Make up ditto sheets with similar but different-sized figures (e.g., animals, toys, buildings) in each of several boxes. Have pupils cross out the largest and/or smallest figure in each box.
7. Using a felt board or pocket chart, have pupils match a set of objects with a numeral. For example, they might match two apples with the numeral 2.
8. Using a felt board or pocket chart, have pupils match a number word with a set of objects. Next, have pupils match a numeral and a number word with a set of objects.
9. Group objects in sets from 1 to 10; place several numerals next to each set and instruct pupils to circle the correct numeral.
10. Instruction in writing numerals from 1 through 9 should be started at the same time that a pupil is learning to write in manuscript. Have pupils trace numerals to be learned, make the numerals by connecting dots, and finally write the numerals independently.
11. Have students complete dot-to-dot puzzles of simple designs (e.g., circle, square, triangle) and then of more complicated pictures (e.g., boats, animals, cars).
12. Spring-type clothespins can be used as counting devices. Attach cards with a numeral on each (1 to 10) to coat hangers; instruct youngsters to clip that number of clothespins to the hanger (Crescimbeni, 1965).
13. Cut numerals from old calendars and paste each on cardboard. Ask

pupils to arrange the numbers in proper sequence without using the calendar page (Crescimbeni, 1965).

14. Request students to count silently the number of times you bounce a ball or buzz a buzzer. Challenge a pupil to state the correct number; if correct, that student takes your role.

15. Make seasonal puzzles with numbers as cues (e.g., jack-o-lanterns with different numbers of teeth, turkeys with different numbers of tail feathers, Christmas trees with different numbers of decorations). The student must count the items, find the puzzle piece with the corresponding numeral, and fit the pieces together.

16. Make dittos with several different shapes on a page. At the top of the page, color code a sample of each shape. Instruct pupils to color each matching figure with the designated color (Lettau, 1975).

17. To aid in numeral recognition, make a ditto sheet with overlaid geometric patterns creating a design with numerous individual sections. In each section place a numeral, and color code each numeral at the top of the page. Instruct students to color all sections of the design to match the color code (Lettau, 1975).

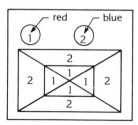

18. To give students practice matching numbers and numerals, make dittos with designs like those in Number 17, but this time place a different number of objects in each section of the design. Again, put numerals at the top of the page and color code each (Lettau, 1975).

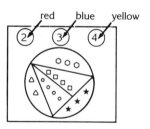

Computation

1. Have students make combinations of less than 10 by first counting real or pictured objects and then writing the correct number.

$$\triangle \triangle + \triangle = \underline{\hspace{1cm}}$$
$$\boxed{2} + \boxed{1} = \boxed{}$$

2. To ensure understanding of addition (or any other operation), introduce the concept of the missing element. This can be done in a way that is similar to the following example.

$$1 + 4 = \boxed{} \qquad 1 + \boxed{} = 5 \qquad \boxed{} - 4 = 5$$

3. An abacus is a good, concrete way to introduce students to the idea of place value. Show pupils that when they get to 10 beads in the same row on the abacus, a change is made to the next row. Let pupils make different combinations and then write the number indicated on the abacus.
4. Have students play counting games in which the counting changes direction every time a bell rings.
5. Strengthen concepts of before and after by having pupils find the missing number in a series.

before $\boxed{} \boxed{2} \boxed{3} \qquad \boxed{6} \boxed{7} \boxed{}$ after
$\boxed{} \boxed{4} \boxed{5} \qquad \boxed{5} \boxed{6} \boxed{}$

6. Help students learn to carry by covering all but the number column they are working with in a given problem.
7. Start work with fractional numbers by having students actually manipulate the fractional part to see that all parts are equal.
8. As students manipulate equal fractional parts, give them a chance to label them; for instance, if there are four parts, then each part should be labeled one-fourth or 1/4.
9. As students learn to count and write numerals, encourage them to make their own number line using tape or some other material.
10. Beginning instruction in subtraction should focus on actually taking away concrete objects, then crossing out pictures of objects, and finally working with pure abstraction.
11. Help students perceive the relationship of addition and subtraction by having them first add two sets of numbers and then subtract the two numbers from the derived sum.

$$\begin{array}{ccc} 28 & 60 & 60 \\ + 32 & - 32 & - 28 \\ \hline \end{array}$$

12. Since multiplication involves grouping of sets, show students an arrangement like the following, requesting that they make several similar sets.

$$\overset{\displaystyle \circ\circ}{2} \bigg| \overset{\displaystyle \circ\circ}{2} \bigg| \overset{\displaystyle \circ\circ}{2} = 6 \qquad\qquad 3 \times 2 = 6$$

13. Make a ditto sheet with objects in sets like those in Number 12. Have pupils write how many objects are in each set. Then instruct pupils to write the same statements, using only numbers.

14. To show the relationship between addition and multiplication, have students first add the same number several times and then multiply that number by the number of times it was added.

$$3 + 3 + 3 + 3 + 3 = 15 \qquad 3 \times 5 = 15$$
$$6 + 6 + 6 = 18 \qquad 6 \times 3 = 18$$

15. Concepts of more and less can be further developed by using multiplication facts. Require pupils to underline which is more or less.

more	*less*
2 threes or 5	3 fives or 18
3 twos or 7	4 twos or 10

16. A pupil with a short attention span can sometimes do as much work as another pupil if arithmetic work is broken into smaller segments. To achieve this goal, cut a worksheet into small parts (e.g., rows of problems) or make up arithmetic problems on three-by-five cards that the pupil picks up each time a problem is completed.

17. After students learn basic division facts, have them show how a given number is divided into several equal parts.

$$6 = \underline{\hspace{2cm}} \text{ twos} \qquad 6 = \underline{\hspace{2cm}} \text{ threes}$$
$$12 = \underline{\hspace{2cm}} \text{ sixes} \qquad 12 = \underline{\hspace{2cm}} \text{ threes}$$
$$12 = \underline{\hspace{2cm}} \text{ twos} \qquad 12 = \underline{\hspace{2cm}} \text{ fours}$$

18. A highly motivating type of worksheet is a shade-in math puzzle. Instruct the student to shade in the puzzle parts with numbers divisible by 2, shade in all multiples of 3, or shade in all problems with correct answers. The shaded puzzle parts form a picture. Prentice-Hall has two excellent books of math puzzles, one for primary students and one for older students—*Contemporary Math Shade-Ins/Primary* and *Contemporary Math Shade-Ins.*

For Older Students

1. Make a math center using index cards with basic computational skills of addition, subtraction, multiplication, or division on each card. Arrange the cards according to sequential skills (i.e., basic addition facts, carrying, and so on). Students can check their own answers with an answer sheet and record progress on their own recording sheets to

show individual growth. Commercially prepared activity cards, such as *Contemporary Math Facts Activity Cards* (Prentice-Hall Learning Systems), cover all math areas.

2. Lattices (i.e., crossed lines) can aid students with place value and position in long division.

Simple Lattice Approach to Mathematics Division (James & Pedrazzini, 1975) is an excellent book of individual lattice math sheets that are perforated and easy to reproduce in student booklets. The book begins with one-place quotient/one-place divisor and covers division skills sequentially.

3. Many of the electronic games recently developed can be used to teach or reinforce math skills. Students can check their work with them, too.

4. Simple calculators can be used to check work. In addition, these devices can be used for motivation: a student who finishes work on time or ahead of time can check it with the calculator.

5. More metric-related activities are needed to help handicapped students understand the different systems of measurement. To show the difference in liquid measurement, empty a liquid from a container with a known measure to a container showing the metric equivalent.

6. Play the game Greatest Sum Wins. Use poker chips and flashcards showing addition problems. Mix up the flashcards and place them face down. Each student picks up a card. The player with the greatest sum wins a chip. The player who has the most chips at the end of the game wins. Play the game with division, multiplication, and subtraction facts (Rucker & Dilley, 1981).

7. Discus the concept of symmetry through examples, such as a person's face or body. Ask the class to find as many examples of symmetry as they can in magazines and newspapers (Schminke & Dumas, 1981).

8. Using pictures of various items that can be bought in restaurants, direct students to make up menus and choose what they will eat. Have them write the name of the food and its price, and then add the prices to determine the total bill.

9. Give students practice reducing fractions to the lowest terms by making fraction cookies. Reduce all the fractions in the recipe and follow the directions as given.

Ingredients: $\frac{4}{2}$ cup of sugar
$\frac{2}{4}$ cup of milk
$\frac{3}{3}$ stick margarine
$\frac{4}{8}$ cup cocoa

Bring ingredients to a boil in a saucepan. Cool slightly.
Add $\frac{2}{2}$ cup peanut butter and $2\frac{2}{4}$ cup oatmeal. Drop on waxed paper.
Makes $1\frac{4}{4}$ dozen cookies.

10. Mercer (1979) suggests using money cards, like the ones illustrated here, to find correct change. Students mark out the amount of a purchase. The remaining amount is the correct change.

Purchase	$10.00 Money Card	Change
6.00	~~$~~ ~~$~~ ~~$~~ ~~$~~ ~~$~~ ~~$~~ $ $ $	3.00
.70	~~⑩~~ ~~⑩~~ ~~⑩~~ ~~⑩~~ ~~⑩~~ ~~⑩~~ ~~⑩~~ ⑩ ⑩	.20
.07	~~①~~ ~~①~~ ~~①~~ ~~①~~ ~~①~~ ~~①~~ ~~①~~ ① ① ①	.03
6.77		3.23

11. Let two students roll dice to practice addition facts. The object of the game is to be the first player to score 100 points from the totals on the dice rolled. The players take turns rolling the dice; each may continue to roll as long as neither die shows a one but may stop voluntarily at any point. When either die does show a one, the player gives up the turn and loses all points earned during that turn. If a one is rolled on both dice, the player gives up the turn, loses all points, and starts again at zero (Mercer, 1979).

12. Have three students play Divido. One player, the dealer, has a set of cards with division facts. The other two players have a set of answer cards. The dealer places a dealer's card (one with a division fact on it) on the table. The student putting the correct answer card down first wins the dealer's card and takes it. The player with the most cards at the end is the winner (Dumas, 1971).

13. Have each student draw a place-value chart like the one here. Draw a card from a deck of 10 with a digit (0 to 9) written on each. Direct students to record that digit in any column they wish. Continue drawing until five cards have been drawn. The student with the largest number wins. Require the winner to read the winning number correctly. Modify as appropriate.

Ten Thousands	Thousands	Hundreds	Tens	Ones

14. Cut a piece of tagboard into a circle as large as the center of a car tire. Tape the tagboard into the center of a tire. Write these directions on the tagboard: (a) measure the radius of the circle; (b) tell the diameter of the circle; (c) find the circumference of the circle. Use different types of tires and other circular items to vary this activity.

15. Wallace and Kauffman (1978) advise helping students decide whether fractions are greater than, less than, or equal to one whole by using fraction number lines.

RESOURCES   ## Instructional

Davidson, J. (1969). *Using Cuisenaire rods*. New Rochelle, NY: Cuisenaire. Grade range: K–6. Instructional aids with a discovery-based orientation; designed to teach conceptual knowledge. Consists of 291 rods of varying lengths and colors. Can be used to teach a host of mathematical skills (e.g., size, shape, color, counting, basic operations, fractions, metric length).

Englemann, S., & Carmine, D. W. (1975). *Distar arithmetic* (2nd ed.). Chicago: Science Research Associates. Grade range: K–3. A highly structured program for developing basic arithmetic skills. Uses intensive direct-instruction approach and places emphasis on reinforcement principles within small group structure. On three levels includes teacher manuals, teacher presentations books, student take-home booklets, and other miscellaneous materials associated with each level.

Friebel, A. C. & Gingrich, C. K. (1972). *Math applications kit*. Chicago: Science Research Associates. Grade range: 3/4–8. Relates math to the everyday real world and provides interest and variety without skill development. Activity oriented but will probably need modification for special learners. Includes 270 activity cards, 10 reference cards, and a world almanac. Has five content areas: (1) science, (2) social studies, (3) sports and games, (4) everyday things, and (5) occupations.

Schwartz, S. E. (1977). *Real-life math program*. Chicago: Hubbard. Grade range: high school for mildly handicapped students; intermediate school for nonhandicapped students. Presents basic arithmetic via role-playing activities and applications to real world. Uses money management and business transaction simulation. Includes 10 audio cassette tapes, 5 student skill books, a teacher's manual, spirit masters, posters, desk signs, mail box, and expendable materials.

Smith D., & Lovitt, T. (1982). *Computational arithmetic program*. Austin, TX: Pro-Ed. Grade range: 1–6. Data-based arithmetic program presenting basic computational skills (whole numbers) in sequenced instructional lessons accompanied by answer sheets. Includes teacher's manual, student folders, worksheet and answer-key pads, stickers and certificates of master, and optional timing tape. Covers addition, subtraction, multiplication, and division.

Sternberg, L., Sedlak, R., Cherkes, M., & Minick, B. (1978). *Essential math and language skills program*. Chicago: Hubbard. Grade range: premath. A developmental program following a meaning-to-skill approach (discovery). Includes four curriculum guides, tracking charts, and a teacher's guide. Covers six major areas: (1) sets and operations on sets, (2) numbers and operations on numbers, (3) patterns, (4) part-whole relations, (5) spatial relations, and (6) measurement.

Professional

Ashlock, R. B. (1986). *Error patterns in computation: A semi-programmed approach* (4th ed.). Columbus, OH: Merrill. Thoroughly examines the various computational errors students typically make. Presents many examples of these errors and suggests techniques for correcting them.

Bley, N. S., & Thornton, C. A. (1981). *Teaching mathematics to the learning disabled.* Rockville, MD: Aspen. Devoted in large part to activities for teaching a range of mathematical topics. Includes a chapter on upper grade topics such as ratio, proportion, percent, integers, and exponents, which may be a good source of ideas for teachers.

Burns, M. (1975). *The I hate mathematics book.* Boston: Little, Brown. A great source for some refreshing, interesting ideas.

Cawley, J. F. (Ed.). (1984). *Developmental teaching of mathematics for the learning disabled.* Austin, TX: Pro-Ed. Covers useful topics related to assessment, curricular sequences, instructional techniques, and management dimensions.

Coble, C. R., Hounshell, P. B., & Adams, A. H. (1977). *Mainstreaming science and mathematics: Special ideas and activities for the whole class.* Santa Monica, CA: Goodyear. Gives teachers a variety of math activities, organized to provide a different activity for each day of the school year.

Glennon, V. J. (1981). *The mathematical education of exceptional children and youth: An interdisciplinary approach.* Reston, VA: National Council of Teachers of Mathematics. For the most part devoted to strategies for students with specific disabling conditions.

Johnson, S. W. (1979). *Arithmetic and learning disabilities: Guidelines for identification and remediation.* Boston: Allyn & Bacon. Presents a system for categorizing specific arithmetic-learning disabilities. Suggests activities organized on a preschool, introductory, and postintroductory basis.

Peterson, D. L. (1973). *Functional mathematics for the mentally retarded.* Columbus, OH: Merrill. Focused on the needs of mentally retarded students. Covers a range of instructional topics organized on a school-cycle basis (e.g., early childhood, primary, and so on).

Reisman, F. K., & Kauffman, S. H. (1980). *Teaching mathematics to children with special needs.* Columbus, OH: Merrill. Divided into three major sections: a discussion of the factors that influence learning mathematics; strategies for teaching various topics; and information on interviewing, developing an individual mathematics program, and involving parents.

Schminke, C. W., & Dumas, E. (1981). *Math activities for child involvement* (3rd ed.). Boston: Allyn & Bacon. Contains a wealth of activities for teaching beginning number concepts, operations, geometry, fractions, and metric measurement. Also has a chapter of activities designed for special learners.

Silbert, J., Carnine, D., & Stein, M. (1981). *Direct instruction mathematics.* Columbus, OH: Merrill. Based on tenets of direct instruction; provides specific procedures for teaching math skills. Focuses on "efficient, effective, and humane instruction." Can be invaluable for teachers interested in seeing exactly how to teach certain skills.

Thornton, C. A., Tucker, B. F., Dossey, J. A., & Bazik, E. F. (1983). *Teaching mathematics to children with special needs.* Menlo Park, CA: Addison-Wesley. Contains basic information on teaching mathematics to special students as well as specific suggestions for teaching content.

13
Science and
Social Studies

Students are typically curious about their surroundings and about the people and things inhabiting them. As a result, they have a natural interest in seeking information about their environment. Teachers should take advantage of this curiosity by exposing students to science and social studies topics that capitalize on their interests.

Science and social studies often have a low priority in the educational curriculum for students with mild/moderate disabilities (Patton, Polloway, & Cronin, 1987, in press). Yet the importance of these two subject areas is reflected in the competencies required by many states for graduation from high school. In considering why these subject areas have been deemphasized, Price, Ness, and Stitt (1982) suggest that the overwhelming thrust in many programs for students with mild handicaps is on the development/remediation of basic skills. In addition, personnel-preparation programs have neglected these areas; few special education training programs require or even offer course work in these subjects. Patton and colleagues (1987, in press) found that a significant number of special education teachers reported that they had received no training of any type (i.e., preservice or in-service) in these areas. Not surprisingly, most special education personnel feel unprepared and uncomfortable teaching these subjects. However, many of them are assigned to teach in these areas, especially at the secondary level, and often find themselves teaching credit-generating science and social studies courses to students in diploma-track programs.

Regular educators also feel unprepared to work with special learners in these areas. Although increasing in frequency on a preservice level, instruction in how to accommodate the needs of students with mild handicaps in these subject areas has been lacking. Very few books written to help regular educators mainstream special learners

actually provide specific information in these curricular areas (cf., Schulz & Turnbull, 1983; Wood, 1989). Instructional suggestions for working with students with diverse learning needs have not usually been effectively conveyed to regular education personnel on an in-service basis either.

Two other important factors are administrative in nature. The first involves the inappropriate placement of students with learning problems in regular education science and social studies classes. In this situation these students are typically unable to read the textbooks or participate appropriately in class discussions and activities; the result is little learning, undesirable behaviors, and/or mere busywork. The other problem occurs when students receive special services (e.g., counseling, remedial reading) during periods when these subjects are being taught.

Science and social studies should be recognized as basic subjects and provided to all students. There are many reasons for doing so, including the following important benefits of good science and social studies programs.

☐ Firsthand experiences particularly help students become familiar with their surroundings (Jacobson & Bergman, 1980).

☐ Basic skills can be applied in meaningful contexts (Price et al., 1982).

☐ A rich experiential background can be developed to establish "knowledge frameworks into which students can integrate new ideas, relationships, and details" (Jenkins, Stein, & Osborn, 1981, p. 37).

☐ Students have the opportunity to develop critical thinking and problem-solving strategies.

☐ Information and skills necessary for adult living and useful for lifelong interests are acquired.

TEACHING SCIENCE TO SPECIAL LEARNERS

"Of all the subject areas taught to students, science may be one of the most intriguing as well as one of the most feared by many teachers" (Patton, 1988). The following example involves gifted students but illustrates both points.

> Not long ago, I was invited to go on a "reef walk" with a class of gifted third and fourth graders. It is very educational to do such a thing with this type of youngster. While we were wading in some shallow water, we came upon a familiar marine organism called a "feather duster." Being cognizant of being with a group of young students but forgetting that they were students with vocabularies which were well advanced of their nongifted age peers, I was about ready to say something like "Look how that thing hangs on the rock." Before I could get my highly descriptive statement out, Eddie, one of the students who always amazes us with his comments, offered the following: "Notice how securely anchored the organism is to the stationary coral." All I could say was "Yes, I do." (Patton, Payne, Kauffman, Brown, & Payne, 1987, p. 164)

How exciting to be out on a reef actually seeing, touching, and experiencing nature; but how threatening to realize that a student may know more about something than you do or that someone may ask you a question for which you do not have an immediate answer. Many teachers who do not have extensive science training express reservations about teaching anything connected with science. Nevertheless, by employing effective instructional techniques and by refusing to feel intimidated by the subject itself, teachers can provide dynamic science programs.

Teaching science can be exciting and rewarding. Few subject areas are as inherently interesting to teach, actively involve students as much, and can be made as relevant to students of varying backgrounds. Nonetheless, a teacher's attitude may be the most critical variable. And no matter how excited the teacher is about teaching science, not every student will share that enthusiasm. Even though many students are stimulated by an engaging science program, others do not respond in such fashion and require other motivational strategies.

Teachers harbor differing opinions about teaching science to special students. Cohen and Staley (1982) found that many teachers think science is neither meaningful nor appealing to students and is well beyond the capabilities of lower-achieving students. On the other hand, Jacobson and Bergman (1980) write that "science is an area suitable for involving the educable mentally handicapped . . . because of its concrete nature and the wide use of natural and physical materials" (p. 170).

Certain competencies are desirable in science teachers. The following list is not exhaustive; however, it can serve as a preliminary checklist.

- ☐ knowledge of basic content in the area of science
- ☐ familiarity with certain laboratory skills
- ☐ ability to follow a preestablished curriculum or to develop one
- ☐ knowledge of various approaches to and materials for teaching science to students with special learning needs
- ☐ ability to adapt materials and techniques for use with special learners
- ☐ skills needed to plan and carry out science investigations
- ☐ awareness of local and regional community resources
- ☐ ability to apply relevant science education research to the educational programs of special populations

Before examining the general approaches to and specific strategies for teaching science, some basic guidelines and suggestions are warranted. Boekel and Steele (1972) clarify what science is and what it is not.

Science is

☐ discovery
☐ solving of problems
☐ broadening of curiosity
☐ nurturing of interests
☐ finding answers to questions

Science is not

☐ hit-or-miss lessons
☐ pure memorization
☐ just substantive knowledge (p. 2)

Three major goals are woven throughout science education: the acquisition of relevant content and knowledge, the development of various inquiry-related skills, and the nurturing of a scientific attitude. Many of us have experienced science instruction that focused largely on content acquisition with little opportunity for hands-on activities. In recent years more emphasis has been given to the importance of skill acquisition, and attention is being directed toward the attitudinal/affective domain associated with science topics. All of these goals are important, and none should be emphasized to the detriment of the others. Saul and Newman (1986) illustrate this interrelationship by advocating the need to provide inquiry-oriented, hands-on experiences and develop student attitudes and interests but also pointing out the advantages of gaining factual information. They present six reasons why facts are important.

☐ They give form and precision to that which we understand.
☐ Information makes certain investigations possible.
☐ Facts are also intrinsically related to questions.
☐ Facts are closely related to language, and language is its own pleasure, its own power.
☐ Having facts in storage is convenient.
☐ Facts can help contextualize seemingly dry, quantitative information and make it interesting . . . [if teachers] make facts interesting, relevant, and provocative. (pp. 11–12)

Approaches to Teaching Science

Traditional elementary science programs have consisted primarily of a basic textbook and very few hands-on activities. As recent statistics show, many students have not found science engaging and have not chosen careers related to it. Fortunately, science educators are changing the way that science is taught. Unfortunately, these changes are not yet evidenced in a significant number of settings, particularly special education ones.

Textbook Approach This traditional approach continues to be used frequently today, especially at the upper elementary (Teters, Gabel, & Geary, 1984) and secondary levels. In their study of science education in special education settings, Patton and colleagues (in press) found that nearly 60% of the teachers who taught science used a regular education textbook in some fashion. Teachers can use commercially published textbooks in various ways. For some it is the primary vehicle of the science program, with students regularly reading and consulting it. Textbooks can also be used in a supplementary way, as part of a program that utilizes additional sources of science information and activities. In certain science programs textbooks are used only as occasional reference materials. Nearly all textbook series now include activities for students and an assortment of laboratory materials.

It is useful to examine the topics covered in a commercial textbook series. Although there is no generally accepted curricular sequence in science education, science programs typically include subject matter from three areas: **life science** (the study of living things); **physical science** (the study of nonliving things); and **earth science** (the study of such topics as astronomy, meteorology, and geology). Table 13.1 lists the K–6 scope and sequence of six major science textbook series currently available.

TABLE 13.1
Scope and sequence of commonly used textbook series (pp. 331–334)

Level	Addison-Wesley Science	Houghton Mifflin Science	Accent on Science (Merrill)	The New Exploring Science (Laidlaw)	Health Science	Silver Burdett Science
K	Health and Safety Animals Weather Our Senses Everyday Things Water Moving Things Earth Beneath Our Feet Plants Foods		Plants Animals The Senses: See, Feel, Smell, Taste The Seasons: Fall, Winter, Spring, Summer	Rocks and Sand Fun with Air Shapes, Colors, and Sizes of Blocks Fun with Food Fruits and Seeds Animals	Investigate the five senses, structures of the body, and foods necessary for good health Observe plants and animals and their environments Sort and classify objects by their properties Identify objects affected by a magnet Classify objects that sink and objects that float Measure, weigh, and quantify materials Observe changes in objects caused by heating Observe and describe seasonal changes Observe weather changes	Your Senses Your Body Seeds and Plants Animals Where Plants and Animals Live Matter Energy Our Earth The Weather The Sun and Moon
1	Animal Needs Plant Needs Pushes and Pulls Water and Ice Air Light Time Shells Growth	Exploring Observing Shapes Size Position Symmetry Making Changes Familiar Changes Changes Everywhere	You Observe You Group What Is Alive? Animals Around Us Water and Air Land Around Us Wild Animals Magnets Observe Plants	Water at Work Time Goes By Sorting Things Light and Shadows All About Animals All About Plants	Finding Out Living or Not Living? Animals Weather Air Water Plants Rocks and Soil	Learning About Our World Many Kinds of Plants Many Kinds of Animals Using Colors, Shapes, and Sizes

TABLE 13.1
(continued)

Level	Addison-Wesley Science	Houghton Mifflin Science	Accent on Science (Merrill)	The New Exploring Science (Laidlaw)	Health Science	Silver Burdett Science
	Your Body Space for Things Soil	Let's Find Out Properties	Plant Parts			Living and Not Living Moving Things Our Earth Looking at the Sky You and Weather Caring for Yourself
2	Seeds Living Things in Fall and Winter Standard Units Weather Food and Your Health Matter Particles Sound Work and Energy Traces of Living Things Living Things in Spring Energy from the Sun	Solids Liquids Gases Shapes of Objects Properties of Surfaces Measuring Surfaces Interaction Systems Interaction and Time Populations Population Properties	Animals Sound Around Us You Measure You Grow Heat Energy Light Energy Air and Weather Plants Changes on Earth	About Rocks and Soil Air All Around Working with Magnets Measuring Things Environments Food Chains	Seasons Sound Eating and Growing Light and Shadow Moving Night and Day Hot and Cold Magnets Plants and Animals on Land Plants and Animals in the Water Plants and Animals of Long Ago	Animals of Long Ago How Plants Grow Where Plants and Animals Live Things in Our World Fun with Magnets Heat and Light Our Earth's Air and Water Our Sun Our Weather Keeping Safe
3	Communities of Living Things Measurement—A Science Process Motion and Location Air—An Invisible Push Bones and Muscles Shadows and Light Sunlight on the Earth and Moon Heat and Temperature It All Depends!	Variation in Objects Variation in Matter Variation in Interaction Space Position Motion Interaction Energy Looking for Energy Interaction Within a Population Two Populations Interact	Seeds and Plants Work and Machines Matter and Its Changes Water Around Us Living Things Around Us Rocks in Our World Comparing Earth and Moon	About the Moon Water to Use Sounds All Around Working with Heat Behavior of Animals Plants with Seeds	Where Do Plants and Animals Live? Groups of Living Things A Community Water Cycle The Changing Land Stars Machines at Work Using Electricity What Do We Eat? How We Use What We Eat	Animals Animals Are Important Seed Plants Plants Are Important All About Matter Force, Work, and Energy Machines Sound The Changing Earth

TABLE 13.1
(continued)

Level	Addison-Wesley Science	Houghton Mifflin Science	Accent on Science (Merrill)	The New Exploring Science (Laidlaw)	Health Science	Silver Burdett Science
	Interdependence of Living Things		Patterns of Life Conserving Our Environment		Human Body Systems Making Choices About Your Body's Needs	Sources of Energy Changes in the Earth Cleaning Up the Earth Changes in the Weather Beyond the Solar System Support and Movement of the Body Transport Systems of the Body
6	Changing and Preserving Our Environment Water in the Air Images and Refraction Earth in Space Electric Charges and Currents Using Forces Changes in the Land Living Things—Continuity and Change Populations Energy and Energy Problems	More Than One Model The Small Particle Model Applying Models The Model World Models of Systems Using Models Observing Ecosystems Resources and Problems Using Energy Wisely Population Growth and Food Population Success Fuels for Population	Protists Interactions of Matter Earth Models Energy Resources Human Body Systems Exploring the Universe Understanding Ecology Electricity and Communication Patterns of Life Conserving Our Environment	Ecosystems Looking into Space Working with Matter Energy and You Life Cycles Reacting to Your Environment	Classifying Animals with Backbones Classifying Animals without Backbones Classifying Plants Life Cycles Elements and Compounds Electricity and Magnetism Sources of Energy Properties of Light Light and Vision Communications Climates of the World Energy for Living Things	Living Things Plant Growth and Response Animal Adaptations Climate and Life Matter and Atoms Chemical Changes in Matter Light Energy Using Electricity The Earth's Resources Changes in the Earth's Crust Forecasting the Weather Exploring Space Control Systems of the Body Growth and Development

Textbook use has both advantages and disadvantages.

Advantages
☐ excellent teacher aids
☐ utility for beginning teachers
☐ organized science program
☐ durability

Disadvantages
☐ readability problems
☐ potential to become the only source of information
☐ possible conflict with school system curricular guidelines
☐ tendency to become outdated

Student inability to read grade-level materials looms as the most significant barrier to using science texts with special populations. Certainly, teachers do not have the time to regularly rewrite textual material to meet the needs of their students, especially as grade levels progress. However, certain textbook series are worth considering because of their deemphasis on reading and their hands-on orientation. Two such texts are the Addison-Wesley and the Houghton Mifflin science programs.

Another problem related to reading ability is the need for certain reading skills for effective comprehension of information. Carnine and Silbert (1979) highlight some characteristics of content-area materials that can be problematic for students with restricted reading abilities.

☐ *Vocabulary.* It is usually more difficult than that used in narrative material.
☐ *Content.* Often the information presented is not familiar to students and can cause conceptual problems.
☐ *Style and organization.* There may be extensive use of headings/subheadings. Writing is very succinct and matter-of-fact.
☐ *Special features.* Graphics and illustra-

tions play an important part in presentation of information.

Carnine and Silbert also suggest ways to ameliorate some of these potential problems.

In an attempt to modify regular science materials for use with special learners, Lovitt, Rudsit, Jenkins, Pious, and Benedetti (1985, 1986) adapted a seventh-grade physical science textbook (Laidlaw Brothers' *Experiences in Physical Science*). Their energies focused on the development of two types of supplementary aids: structured outline formats and vocabulary practice sheets. Both adaptations were found to be effective in helping students acquire information.

Process-Oriented Approach Process-oriented approaches to science stress the use of process/inquiry skills more than the accumulation of substantive information. They underscore doing and discovery. For the most part these approaches require teachers to be facilitators of learning rather than distributors of information or fonts of knowledge. Not every teacher is comfortable with these curricula because of this facilitating role, but Kyle, Bonnstetter, McClosky, and Fults (1985) found that students preferred this type of science program to more traditional approaches.

Because such programs were initially developed for regular education students and require independent learning skills and self-direction, some question whether it is wise to use these approaches with students who are not as efficient in these skills. Boekel and Steele (1972) believe that many aspects of these materials can be used with students with disabilities, and others (Davies & Ball, 1978; Esler, Midgett, & Bird, 1977) have documented the use of process-oriented materials with special students.

Nonetheless even though inquiry-oriented programs can be used with mildly handicapped learners, a few concerns must be recognized. Some students require more structure and direction than is suggested in these programs. For instance, it may be necessary to prepare data collection sheets ahead of time to help students. Students may also require some teacher-directed instruction to understand certain concepts and facts. It is important that teachers become familiar with these programs and required roles before trying to use the materials.

> No matter how strong the support for the use of the inquiry process, it is unwise to undertake this approach unless teachers are well trained in its application, and administrators are prepared and able to commit the time and resources necessary to support teachers in this effort. (Price et al., 1982, p. 374)

Three of the most frequently used programs are presented here. Some of the materials described may be difficult to obtain because they are going out of print. However, these programs can usually be located in curriculum libraries of major teacher-training institutions.

☐ *Elementary Science Study* (ESS), originally published by McGraw-Hill, is intended for students in kindergarten through Grade 9. The 56 individual units can be used as a complete program or as supplementary materials at different grade levels. The units are interesting and can be tailored to the needs of special students. Reading is minimized, students are actively involved, and a special education teacher's guide (Ball, 1978) is available. The units cover physical, earth, and biological science and mathematics (see Table 13.2), and each unit has a teacher's

guide and requisite materials. Some units have supplementary materials, also.

☐ *Science Curriculum Improvement Study* (SCIIS)[1], published by Rand McNally, is intended for students in kindergarten through Grade 6. It is a complete science program with 13 sequential units (one unit for kindergarten and two units for each of the other grades). Emphasis is on the concept of interaction; the teaching strategy is referred to as exploration-invention-discovery. Reading is minimized. The two strands at each grade level focus on life/earth science and physical/earth science (see Table 13.3). The materials are presented in kit form, along with a teacher's guide and supplementary aids.

☐ *Science . . . A Process Approach II* (SAPA II)[2], published by Ginn and Company, is intended for students in kindergarten through Grade 6. It is a sequential modular program and must be used in this fashion. Each of 15 modules per grade level teaches one process skill. The program addresses 13 skill areas, and parts of the program may be used as supplements. Each module has a kit, and the program includes an instruction booklet and supplementary materials.

Programs Designed for Special Students
Although not plentiful, materials developed specifically for special populations are available. Three of the curricula—*Me Now, Me and My Environment,* and *Me in the Future*—were developed by the Biological Sciences Curriculum Study (BSCS). Boekel and Steele (1972) stress that these materials are not adaptations of exiting materials but are separate curricula. The final program pre-

---

[1]SCIIS (1978) is one of two revisions of the original 1962 SCIS program; it is very similar to the original program with certain modifications.

[2]SAPA II is a 1975 revision of the original 1961 SAPA program.

TABLE 13.2
Contents of ESS units

Physical Science	Life Science
Mobiles	Growing seeds
Spinning tables	Eggs and tadpoles
Sink or float	Brine shrimp
Clay boats	Bones
Drops, streams, and containers	Small things
Mystery powders	Earthworms
Ice cubes	Microgardening
Colored solutions	Behavior of mealworms
Batteries and bulbs	
Optics	*Math*
Pendulums	Match and measure
Water flow	Primary balancing
Heating and cooling	Pattern blocks
Balloons and gases	Geo blocks
Gases and airs	Tangrams
Kitchen physics	Attribute games and problems
	Peas and particles
Earth Science	Senior balancing
Rocks and charts	Mapping
Stream tables	
	General Skills
	Printing
	Structures
	Whistles and strings

sented here includes science activities adapted from the SCIS program.

☐ *Me Now,* published by Hubbard Scientific Company, is intended for students in the upper elementary grades (ages 10–13). This life science program is designed for educable mentally retarded students. It offers a 2-year sequence with a primary focus on systems of the human body. The program is both activity-oriented and inquiry-oriented.

It uses functional language and minimizes reading. The four units cover digestion and circulation; respiration and body waste; movement, support, and sensory processes; and growth and development. Program components include teacher's guides, multimedia supplementary materials, a supplies kit, student worksheets, and evaluation material.

☐ *Me and My Environment,* published by

TABLE 13.3
The SCIIS program

Level	Physical/Earth Science	Life/Earth Science
K	Beginnings	Beginnings
1	Material objects	Organisms
2	Interaction and systems	Life cycles
3	Subsystems and variables	Populations
4	Relative position and motion	Environments
5	Energy sources	Communities
6	Scientific theories	Ecosystems

Hubbard, is intended for junior high school students (ages 13–16). This environmental science program is designed for students with mild retardation. It offers a 3-year sequence and is activity-oriented as well as inquiry-oriented. Reading is minimized. The program is divided into five units: Exploring My Environment, Me as an Environment, Energy Relationships in My Environment, Transfer and Cycling of Materials in My Environment, and Water and Air in My Environment. Components include teacher's guides, multimedia supplementary materials (e.g., slides, games), a supplies kit, and student worksheets.

☐ *Me in the Future,* published by Biological Sciences Curriculum Study, is intended for high school students (ages 14 and above). This program is the culmination of the Hubbard programs and focuses on career education. It is activity-oriented and offers an adult interest level with a low readability level. The program's three major areas look at vocations, leisure, and daily living skills. Teacher's guides are included, in addition to multimedia supplementary materials and a supplies kit.

☐ *Science Enrichment for Learners with Physical Handicaps (SELPH),* published by the Center for Multisensory Learning (Lawrence Hall of Science), is intended for students in the upper elementary grades.[3] An adaptation of the *Science Activities for the Visually Impaired* (SAVI) program, this life and physical science program is designed for students with physical and learning problems. It is activity-oriented and multisensory and can be used in a range of settings. The

program's nine modules cover measurement, structures of life, scientific reasoning, communications, magnetism and electricity, mixtures and solutions, environments, kitchen interactions, and environmental energy. Program components include activity folios for each module, a training manual, and a materials kit.

Customized Approaches Many special education teachers have developed their own curricula. With this approach the content of the program needs careful consideration. If students are to be reintegrated into regular class settings, content should be similar to that of the regular education curriculum. For other students a more functional science program might better prepare them for young adulthood.

Another idea that is being implemented in some settings is integrative programming. Although this programming idea has been used most frequently with gifted students (e.g., Nakashima & Patton, in press), it can also be used with students with mild handicaps (Patton & Nakashima, 1987). The major principle of this type of programming is to integrate science and other subject and skill areas. Specific examples are provided later in this chapter.

Regardless of the specific content, however, a customized program must be sequenced appropriately with regard to concept development and teaching strategies (Price et al., 1982). Teachers interested in designing their own curricula should first consult other resources. One such resource is the scope and sequence chart of a commercial program, which shares information like that in Table 13.1. Another resource of note is an instructor's manual from any of the Hubbard materials (e.g., *Me and My Environment*); each includes a good discussion on developing science curricula.

---

[3]The SELPH program can be used effectively with special students in Grades 1–10.

Instructional Strategies

Science, like any other subject area, requires sound instructional practice that maximizes learning.

Classroom Management and Organization
Teachers must be able to control their classrooms. This objective can be achieved by establishing rules and procedures for specific tasks and appropriate functioning. This requirement is especially important for science activities that use potentially dangerous materials. It is helpful to establish systematic procedures for distributing and collecting materials before, during, and after an activity or class period. One method is to designate part of the room as the science area and to conduct most science instruction in this area. Within this area or wherever science instruction occurs, tables should be used as much as possible.

Safety is a primary concern. Teachers should anticipate and prepare for potential problems. All planned science activities should be performed ahead of time, and equipment should be checked to ensure that it is in proper working condition. Students' eyes should be protected, fire extinguishers should be readily available, and safety instructions should be demonstrated and practiced regularly. Dangerous, or potentially dangerous, materials should be secured and off-limits signs posted to protect students from injury and the teacher from liability. It is also advisable to consult the safety guidelines of the school district.

Inquiry Skills   One of the goals of science instruction is skill development. Many different abilities can be addressed, including organizational, basic academic, and social/behavioral skills. Other specific skills are not only extremely useful in science but also beneficial in other areas as well. These skills are commonly referred to as inquiry skills and are described here (as adapted from Cain & Evans, 1984, pp. 8–9).

- ☐ *Observation:* using the senses to find out about subjects and events
- ☐ *Classification:* grouping things according to similarities or differences
- ☐ *Measurement:* making quantitative observations
- ☐ *Communication:* using the written and spoken word, drawings, diagrams, or tables to transmit information and ideas to others.
- ☐ *Data collection, organization, and graphing:* making quantitative data sensible, primarily through graphic techniques
- ☐ *Inference:* explaining an observation or set of observations
- ☐ *Prediction:* making forecasts of future events or conditions, based on observations or inferences
- ☐ *Data interpretation:* finding patterns among sets of data that lead to the construction of inferences, predictions, or hypotheses
- ☐ *Formulation of hypotheses:* making educated guesses based on evidence that can be tested
- ☐ *Experimentation:* investigating, manipulating, and testing to determine a result

Attempts should be made to include these inquiry skills in science activities. Most activities require some of these skills; however, the goal is to get students to use as many of them as often as possible.

Elements of a Science Lesson   Effective instruction incorporates variety and systematic presentation of material. Some science lessons might be devoted to discussing a topic of current interest, watching educational television, reading science materials, listening to a guest speaker, going on a field trip, or carrying out activities in the classroom. However, all science lessons should be planned to accommodate individual differences and follow an organizational schema, which provides a certain structure that is helpful to teachers and helpful to students. The actual format of the instructional period depends to a great degree on the nature of the lesson. For most lessons the following components are appropriate (Cain & Evans, 1984).

Attention-getting and motivating techniques attempt to engage students in the lesson. They set the tone for the day's activities and should make clear to students what they are to do. The key is to activate student interest, get students to ask questions, and initiate discussion.

Data-gathering techniques typically involve actual hands-on activities. For many special learners some direct instruction may be needed. However, the emphasis is on students working individually or in small groups or dyads and performing tasks related to the topic under study. Students should record their observations and collect their data in logs or journals. Logs, which work best if they are in binders, can be supplemented by teacher-produced materials that help structure the assignment. Students should make entries into their logs regularly, and the logs should not be graded for handwriting, spelling, or syntactic correctness.

With data-processing techniques students try to make sense out of the data they have collected or the activity they have performed. They must organize the data in a way that helps explain the results. Data can be analyzed individually or pooled and examined on a classwide basis. This part of the lesson is an excellent time for discussion of observations, trends, and outcomes. Students can now begin to draw conclusions, make predictions, and suggest additional activities and experimentation.

Closure is important to ensure that students understand what they have been doing. This is a good time to review the day's activities, evaluate performance, emphasize major conclusions, and relate the lesson to the real world. This time might also be used to lead into the next day's activity or other future lessons.

Modifying Materials and Activities Many published science materials and suggested activities—some of them excellent—are not designed for special students and must be changed to be effective. Special education teachers must develop the ability to adapt materials proficiently and expeditiously, following some general guidelines.

- ☐ The fewer modifications required, the better.
- ☐ Modifications should not change the concept being addressed.
- ☐ After modification, activities should be uncomplicated, brief, sequentially presented, programmed for success and review, and relevant to students (Kolstoe, 1976).

Integration with Other Curricular Areas Science is an ideal subject for integration with other subject areas. Cohen and Staley (1982) recommend "using science topics, units, themes, or curricular materials as vehicles for bringing meaning to the study of other academic disciplines" (p. 565). The possibilities are exciting. Some schools have fashioned entire basic-skill programs around the themes of science or social studies. With reasonable effort science can be incorporated into all curricular areas.

Another perspective focuses on working other subjects and skill areas into science. The relationship of mathematics to science may be apparent, but other areas relate well, too. Many science topics involve art-related activities or can be followed up by art activities. For example, with the ESS unit entitled "Life of Beans and Peas," students should be expected to keep regular drawings of plant development. They also might use unsprouted beans in a decorative art project. With a unit entitled "Appliance Science," students might take apart and analyze telephones donated by the phone company. Students enjoy opening up phones and observing the amazing number of simple machines used inside. They also might be excited to make creative art projects using the variety of disassembled materials from inside the phones.

In addition, language arts can be worked into science very easily. In a unit on marine biology, students might be asked to produce various types of creative writing products (e.g., cinquains, haikus, acrostic poems, limericks), or they might give oral and written reports as an ongoing part of the program. Science eventually engages most students in research endeavors, which typically require reading, vocabulary development, note taking, and outlining.

In many circumstances music can also be integrated into science instruction. In Hawaii, for instance, it is not unusual to study cockroaches, because they are plentiful in the environment. The book *Beastly Neighbors* (Rights, 1981) has some great ideas for developing such a unit, and it certainly seems appropriate to acquaint students with the song "La Cucaracha." With the unit on marine biology, students might write lyrics to a "rap" song, which could be put to synthesized music and recorded.

Moreover, many career and life-skill topics should be worked into various subject areas. Science topics are quite appropriate. For instance, with the ESS unit entitled "Clay Boats," a number of careers (e.g., merchant marine, stevedore) and hobbies (e.g., sailing, fishing) can be explored. The science program *Me in the Future* was designed specifically to capitalize on this relationship between science and careers.

Use of Microcomputers   Microcomputers are increasingly more available and more utilized in special and regular education. As discussed in chapter 7 microcomputers have distinct advantages for use with special populations. Some examples of intriguing microcomputer usage in science are offered here.

☐   *Tutorials.* These programs can help students who need more time and different presentations of difficult concepts.
☐   *Simulations.* This type of software can substitute for certain dangerous situations (e.g., chemistry experiments) and can provide more experiences for students.
☐   *Databases.* Different types of databases are available. Some commercially produced software contain already-established databases on topics such as animals. Teachers can also create customized databases for their own particular needs. Table 13.4 is an example of a database created to help students organize information they collected on various marine organisms.
☐   *Probeware.* Hardware/software is now available that can be used as laboratory tools. Instruments that connect to the microcomputer can measure light intensity, temperature of liquids, and time. The measurements can be displayed on the monitor and recorded for future reference.

Field Trips   Field trips, for many teachers, conjure up unpleasant memories. However, appropriate use of this type of learning activity can enrich the world knowledge of many students with limited experiential backgrounds. Field trips do involve planning and preparation; instructional objectives should be identified, students should be told what to look for, and follow-up discussions should be scheduled. However, these trips need not involve colossal effort.

TABLE 13.4
Example of a customized database

Code #	Organism	Size	Color	Outstanding Feature	Dangerous?
1	Barracuda	Up to 10'	Variable	Widely separated dorsal fins	Y—murky water
2	Butterfly fish	4–8"	Variable	Tiny flexible teeth	N
3	Crab	Variable	Variable	Coconut crab able to climb trees	N
4	Eel	Up to 10'	Usually black	Dorsal fin	Sharp teeth
5	Jellyfish	1/2" to 6' diam.	Sky blue, yellow, or pink	Hard jelly body	Stinging cells
6	Lobster	Up to 3'6"	Red, blue, white, green	Claws	Claws & tail
7	Manta ray	5–6'(l), 20'(w)	Black or brown/white belly	Winglike fins	Y—strength
8	Opihi	Up to 1"	Dark brown, black	Spiral design on shell	N
9	Squid	Variable	Variable	Way prey is caught	Giant squid
10	Talapia	3–8"	Black, brown	Big eyes	N
11	Triggerfish	6" to 36"	Yellow, brown, black, red	The trigger	N

Code #	Locomotion	Habitat	Common Prey	Endangered?	Defense Mechanism
1	Caudal fin propels	Tropical waters	Plankton-eating fish	N	Teeth, speed
2	Swims	Reef	Invertebrates	N	Spines
3	Uses legs	Seashore	Fish	N	Pinchers
4	Swims	Rocks & coral	Small fish	N	Teeth
5	Jet propulsion	On/near water surface	Small fish	N	Stinging cells
6	Swimming & walking	Rock cave	Rock crabs	N	Claws & tail
7	Swims	Deep water near, +	Krill, plankton, sm fish	N	Strength
8	Feeler	Tidepools	Particles on rocks	N	Hard pointy shell
9	Jet propulsion	Coral, rock, seagrass	Fish	N	Squirts ink
10	Forward & sideward	Shallow water/rocks	Minnows & seaweed	N	Sharp teeth
11	Swims	Reefs	Sea urchins	N	Spikes on tail

For instance, a trip to the produce section of a grocery store can easily introduce a number of topics to develop.

Miscellaneous Suggestions   A list of common everyday materials useful in teaching elementary science concepts is presented in Table 13.5. Teachers can use science materials and ideas to give their classrooms a science flavor. Reynolds (1978) proposes that classrooms be more stimulating and actually function as a museum. She also presents a list of possible ideas. For those with unused space in their classrooms or with bulletin boards to dress, science themes can serve as excellent alternatives.

Careful consideration should also be given to animals in the classroom. Teachers should be aware of the responsibilities that come with this idea (e.g., daily care, costs, care during vacations, safety).

An extended list of resource materials is provided later in this chapter. Teachers who feel uncomfortable with science concepts should obtain resources that can give them background information (e.g., Howe, Joseph, & Victor, 1971). Student textbooks are also excellent sources of basic science information.

In addition, teachers should be aware of certain journals/periodicals that can be useful sources of current thinking and instructional ideas.

☐ *Science and Children*
☐ *Science Education*
☐ *School Science and Mathematics*
☐ *Journal of Research in Science Teaching*
☐ *Science Teacher*

There are also periodicals that are written for children.

☐ *3-2-1 Contact*
☐ *National Geographic World*
☐ *Your Big Backyard*
☐ *Current Science*

☐ *Ranger Rick*

ACTIVITIES

1. Have students build the lightest possible device capable of keeping a raw egg unharmed when dropped from a height of 10 to 20 feet.

2. Experiment with decomposition by burying various items in a container filled with soil. Mark the items with a stick and label. Add moisture periodically. After a few weeks examine the buried items, record what is found, and discuss the results (Cain & Evans, 1984).

3. Study anatomy by examining parts of a chicken. This is an easy animal to get, and it lends itself well to study because students are familiar with it.

4. Have pupils collect plant seeds or small plants; ask them to describe what they see when the seeds are planted or the plants are small. Have them make periodic written observations to demonstrate that plants do change. Have them place the plants under different conditions—no water, no sun, too much water—and observe the results.

5. So that pupils can better understand weather changes, have them keep weather charts that record temperature on different days, rain or snow accumulation, and other data students may want to collect. Questions to ask are, Does it rain when the sun shines? What happens to water when you freeze it? What does snow look like close up?

6. Science in the home provides a wealth of opportunities for a science unit: What makes an iron work? What causes cakes to rise? What causes bread to mildew?

7. Depending on students' ages and the

TABLE 13.5
Common materials for teaching science

Common Classroom Items

1. Cardboard
2. Paper clips
3. Popsicle sticks
4. Razor blades
5. Rubber bands
6. Ruler
7. Scissors
8. Straight pins
9. Tacks
10. Tape (masking and regular)

Science-Related Apparatuses

1. Aquariums
2. Balance, equal-arm
3. Beakers, polyethylene
4. Compass, magnetic
5. Cylinder, graduated
6. Dishes, petri
7. Droppers, medicine
8. Flasks (esp. 250-ml Erlenmeyer)
9. Funnels
10. Hatchery/incubator
11. Hot plate
12. Microscopes and slides
13. Models
14. Nets, insect
15. Pails
16. Pipets
17. Ring stand (with clamp and ring)
18. Rubber stoppers
19. Rubber tubing
20. Small animal cages
21. Test tubes
22. Thermometers
23. Tongs
24. Wire gauze

Hardware Equipment

1. Garden spade
2. Hammer
3. Pliers (needle-nose)
4. Screwdrivers (both types)

Materials from Home and Elsewhere

1. Dish pans, rubber
2. Film containers
3. Jars
4. Knives, forks, spoons
5. Milk cartons
6. Nails
7. Tin cans (#10)
8. Plastic pitcher (large)
9. Straws (paper and plastic)

Science-Related Materials

1. Batteries, dry cell (1.5 volts, 6 volts, and flashlight)
2. Battery holder for D battery
3. Bell wire (insulated)
4. Buzzer
5. Candles
6. Circuit switch
7. Corks
8. Filter paper (15 cm)
9. Goggles, safety
10. Light bulb recepticle
11. Litmus paper
12. Magnets (horseshoe and bar)
13. Magnifiers, hand
14. Prism

Chemicals

1. Alcohol, rubbing
2. Baking powder
3. Baking soda
4. Benedict's solution
5. Cornstarch
6. Flour
7. Formaldehyde
8. Gel
9. Iodine
10. Iron filings
11. Lemon juice
12. Limewater tablets
13. Plaster of Paris (calcium sulfate)
14. Salt
15. Sugar
16. Vinegar

area from which they originate, take students to farms where food is grown and/or animals are raised. Older pupils or pupils who live in farming regions can actually grow food products or raise farm animals.

8. Build small models of simple machines, such as a pulley, wheel and axle, wedge, screw and inclined plane. Use a spring scale to measure the amount of energy saved by using the machines to move and raise books or other heavy objects.

9. A study of different types of plants and flowers can be aided by keeping a log of the plants found for the project. The log can be most effective if the plants are sketched or pressed. (To press put the plant in a catalog with heavy objects on top and leave it for approximately 4 to 6 days.)

10. To aid students with the vocabulary that they encounter in science, have them make small books for each unit. They should take white paper and divide it into fourths. In each quarter they should write a vocabulary word, define it in their own words, illustrate it and explain their illustration. Then have them design a title page for the unit, cut out the pages, and staple the book together (Heukerott, 1987).

11. To aid students in memorizing information, first state the information for them in a sentence. Then have the students repeat the sentence to you and act out the meaning of the sentence motorically. To test their memory, cue the students with the main verb, and have them state the entire sentence (Freides & Messina, 1986).

12. Vocabulary usage and comprehension can be strengthened by having students participate in round-robin stories. After science vocabulary has been introduced, have the students sit in a circle. Choose a student to begin a story, following the rule that one of the words just introduced must be included. At some point tell the student to stop and have the story continued by the next student. Continue this pattern around the circle until all the words have been used. Be sure that the task of continuing the story rests with you once in a while (Kotting, 1987).

13. Science at work requires adolescents to identify basic elements of science that they encounter in their work settings. This activity can involve notebooks, essays, oral reports, or whatever the teacher decides is appropriate to students' abilities, work roles, industry or business, and understanding of science principles. For example, one student may demonstrate the sterilization of eating utensils at the school cafeteria, and another may report on the necessity of lubrication for machines.

14. Many students have trouble comprehending the concept of environment. Direct students to make note of their surroundings on an index card. Have them print their first and last names in the center of the card. In the upper-right corner they should write the average temperature of their environment; in the upper-left corner, the name of an animal that lives in their environment. Under their names have them write something they really like about their environment. In the lower-left corner they can give the name of something they think would improve their environment; in the lower-right corner, the name of a plant that lives in their environment (Richardson, Harris, & Sparks, 1979).

15. Examine different types of soil to see which holds water best. To make a sieve, punch holes in the bottom of a cup. Place a jar underneath the cup.

Ask students to bring in soil from a garden and around the school. Try to sample clay, sand, and humus. Fill the sieve with one type of soil, and use a watch to record how fast water runs through. Discuss why soil is important for plants to grow in the garden. Encourage students to create their own gardens (Sund, Tillery, & Trowbridge, 1970).

16. Make insect mounts. Direct students to collect insects around their home and near the school. Obtain carbon tetrachloride from the science department. To kill the insects, place a false bottom in a jar, place a cotton ball soaked in carbon tetrachloride under it, and place the insect on top of the false bottom. This will keep the insect from getting entangled in the cotton. Pin the insects to cardboard. Make labels for identification. Discuss insect behavior and the variety of insects.

17. Obtain a set of teeth from a dentist and place the set in a glass of soft drink. Have students make observations over several days. Place a tooth in plain water as a control. Discuss the effect of sugar on tooth decay. Invite a dental hygienist to speak to the class about dental care.

18. Aquariums and terrariums in the classroom give students an opportunity to observe the behavior of communities of organisms. Many books show how to construct these items.

19. To find out what color absorbs the sun's heat the most, take students outside and place an ice cube on various colors of construction paper. Which cube melts first? Would a white shirt be cooler than a brown shirt? Would a house with a white roof be cooler than a house with a dark roof? (Oak Ridge Associated Universities, 1978).

20. Arrange a field trip to a local zoo so that students can observe the behaviors of a variety of animals. Encourage students to take cameras and use their pictures as part of a bulletin board display. The purpose for the trip should be clearly stated, and a handout to guide observations at the zoo is helpful. Encourage students to ask questions of the zoo keepers.

21. Explore ways that machines transfer force and make work easier. The egg beater and bicycle are great examples. Have students note how gears change the direction of force. What turns the big wheel? the small wheel? Have the students count the number of turns the rear wheel makes for one turn of the pedal on a bicycle. Look at general merchandise catalogs for pictures of different kinds of machines. Demonstrate care and maintenance of bearings, gears, and so on (Blough & Schwartz, 1974).

22. Explore the composition, construction, and operation of a book of matches or a cigarette lighter. Talk about the three elements essential to fire: oxygen, heat, and fuel (the fire triangle). Discuss ways to extinguish fire by removing one of the three elements.

23. Discuss the effects of air temperature on the activity level of humans and insects. Collect a black cricket. Have students count the number of times it chirps in 14 seconds. Add 40 to that number to find the approximate air temperature. Compare the estimate with the actual thermometer reading. Discuss the reason for this relationship (Howe, Joseph, & Victor, 1971).

24. Find out whether bird seed is alive or dead. Ask students to suggest a way to find out. Make observations and measurements. Draw conclusions about

dormancy and its purpose. This is an excellent activity for introducing the scientific method, because it triggers curiosity (Baker, 1981).

25. Teens are increasingly called to make decisions about what to eat. Appearance is such an important factor in self-concept and social development that teachers are in a good position to help students understand calories and their effect on the body. Most secondary science textbooks have directions for making a calorimeter. Have students keep a record of foods they eat for 1 week. Discuss the importance of knowing caloric intake for appearance and health reasons (Karlin & Berger, 1969).

RESOURCES

Abruscato, J., & Hassard, J. (1977). *The whole cosmos: Catalog of science activities.* Santa Monica, CA: Goodyear. This book is loaded with activities, suggestions for obtaining resources, and information. It is a fun book to read, and it stimulates ideas.

Allison, L. (1975). *The reasons for seasons: The great cosmic megagalactic trip without moving from your chair.* Boston: Little, Brown. One of many selections from the Brown Paper School series, this book contains many intriguing activities organized according to the seasons of the year.

Allison, L. (1976). *Blood and guts: A working guide to your own insides.* Boston: Little Brown. This is an exciting book about how the human body works. Experiments related to various parts of the body are suggested. It is an excellent adjunct for units on this topic.

Cain, S. E., & Evans, J. M. (1984). *Sciencing: An involvement approach to elementary science methods* (2nd ed.). Columbus, OH: Merrill. This textbook is an excellent introduction to various approaches to teaching science, major curricular models, and teaching techniques.

Cobb, V. (1979). *More science experiments you can eat.* New York: J. B. Lippincott. Similar to Cobb's first book entitled *Science Experiments You Can Eat,* this book examines how science is related to foods, cooking, and other kitchen activities.

DeVito, A., & Krockover, G. H. (1976). *Creative sciencing: Ideas and activities for teachers and children.* Boston: Little, Brown. This is basically an activity book. It is loaded with engaging activities that can be easily incorporated into a science program. Authors have included a topical table of contents in which activities are organized by science skills and subject areas.

Goldstein-Jackson, K., Rudnick, N., & Hyman, R. (1978). *Experiments with everyday objects: Science activities for children, parents, and teachers.* Englewood Cliffs, NJ: Prentice-Hall. This book is appealing because it succinctly presents a vast number of easy-to-perform activities.

Hadary, D. E., & Cohen, S. H. (1978). *Laboratory science and art for blind, deaf, and emotionally disturbed children: A mainstreaming approach.* Austin, TX: Pro-Ed. This resource material provides examples of science and art activities, relating them together in a most interesting manner.

Harlan, J. (1980). *Science experiments for the early childhood years* (2nd ed.). Columbus: OH: Merrill. The major portion of this textbook contains thorough information for teaching various science concepts. This book is appropriate for use in elementary science as well.

Herbert, D. (1980). *Mr. Wizard's supermarket science.* New York: Random House. As the title implies, the book focuses on science themes related to supermarket topics. It contains more than 100 easy-to-perform activities.

Hone, E. B., Joseph, A., & Victor, E. (1971). *A sourcebook for elementary science* (2nd ed.). New York: Harcourt Brace Jovanovich. This is a comprehensive sourcebook of science concepts typically covered at the elementary level. For occasions requiring certain scientific information, this source usually suffices.

Jacobson, W. J., and Bergman, A. B. (1980). *Science for children: A book for teachers.* Englewood Cliffs, NJ: Prentice-Hall. This textbook provides information for teaching science and acts as a resource for science concepts and substantive knowledge.

Rights, M. (1981). *Beastly neighbors: All about wild things in the city, or why earwigs make good mothers.* Boston: Little, Brown. This is one of the most exciting resources a teacher can possess. It is primarily concerned with nature study and uses the local environment as the laboratory. The author provides many interesting activities and ideas.

Saul, W., & Newman, A. R. (1986). *Science fare: An illustrated guide and catalog of toys, books, and activities for kids.* New York: Harper & Row. This book is almost a catalog. It discusses the bases for teaching science and provides a multitude of resources and materials worth having. There is a very good chapter on science and children's literature.

Simon, S. (1975). *Pets in a jar: Collecting and caring for small wild animals.* New York: Penguin Books. This book, although written for students, can be a useful source of information for teachers who find themselves wondering how to keep those bugs in the mayonnaise jar alive.

Stein, S. (1979). *The science book.* New York: Workman. This book contains a wealth of ideas and activities that most students find very interesting. It is the type of book that gets one excited about teaching science.

Strongin, J. (1976). *Science on a shoestring.* Menlo Park, CA: Addison-Wesley. This book was written for those who teach science but do not have laboratories. It contains many activities that use everyday materials.

TEACHING SOCIAL STUDIES TO SPECIAL LEARNERS

More and more attention is being given to the community adjustment needs of special learners. As a result, preparing them to be contributing members of their communities has become a major goal of education. Social studies, perhaps as much as any other subject area, attempts to do this. At its very core

it is citizenship education. Moreover, social studies promotes informational skills and value development that contribute substantially to the concept of world knowledge.

Goals and Objectives

The specific goals of social studies are not generally agreed upon but can be extracted from various sources—professional organizations, state program objectives, competency requirements, and professional literature. Sorgman, Stout-Hensen, and Perry (1979) offer these goals:

☐ *full citizenship for every individual:* development of useful "socio-civic and personal behaviors" (p. 109)
☐ *truthful pictures of social reality:* the addressing of social problems and issues, particularly as they relate to students' immediate communities
☐ *tolerance of diversity:* students' need to be aware of and accept human variability
☐ *enhancement of self-concept:* dealing with students' "feelings, values, attitudes, and beliefs" (p. 109)

Another way of looking at the goals of social studies has been suggested by the National Council for the Social Studies (NCSS) (Osborn et al., 1979). Four major domains are identified as a basis for programs.

☐ *knowledge:* "knowledge about the real world and knowledge about the worthiness of personal and social judgments" (p. 262) obtained through the social sciences (e.g., history, sociology, geography)
☐ *abilities:* the development of skills that are required of citizens—(1) intellectual/thinking skills (ability to analyze, evaluate); (2) data processing skills (inter-

pretive skills, as with charts and maps); and (3) human relations skills (listening skills) (Ochoa & Shuster, 1980)

☐ *values:* related to the decision-making process, recognition of a personal values system

☐ *social participation:* opportunities to apply knowledge, skills, and values

The question arises of whether these goals apply to special students. Certain professionals (Curtis, 1974; Ochoa & Shuster, 1980) believe these goals are suitable for students with learning problems. If we want these students to be well-adjusted, contributing members of society, then these goals are well worth our attention. However, program planning must be guided by a realistic appraisal of student abilities and values.

Cautions

A significant number of learners with mild handicaps are not receiving social studies instruction (Patton, Polloway, & Cronin, 1987). In the Patton et al. study of special education classes for students with mild and moderate learning problems, they found that no social studies instruction was occurring in almost one-third of those classes where it should be taught. What could not be determined was the appropriateness of the social studies instruction that was occurring.

Social studies is a subject area that contains many complex topics, issues, and concepts. For instance, the concept of community is abstract, requiring certain cognitive and conceptual skills. The subject also favors students with rich experiential backgrounds, who find the topics more meaningful. In addition, most social studies classes demand proficiency in a variety of areas: for example, reading, writing, oral expression, study, and library skills.

Another concern related to social studies instruction is the training background of teachers, many of whom feel unprepared to teach social studies. Patton and colleagues (1987) found that 43% of the special education teachers they surveyed had had no training in how to teach this subject. Many secondary-level special education teachers, in particular, are unfamiliar with curriculum, teaching strategies, and appropriate materials in this area. Furthermore, they often face classes with students of varying needs and sometimes must teach more than one social studies program simultaneously.

Nonetheless, teachers must not be intimidated by this subject area and must realize that difficulties can be overcome.

Content

The content (i.e., scope and sequence) of any social studies program for special students depends on students' needs. A program that parallels the regular curriculum is indicated for some students; others, especially students at the secondary level, need a program that emphasizes life skills.

For the most part the K–12 curricular sequence in social studies is fairly standard in classrooms across the nation (Superka, Hawke, & Morrissett, 1980). The common themes by grade level are reflected in Table 13.6, which reveals two major patterns: a focus in Grades K to 6 on expanding environments, followed by recurrent attention (Grades 7 to 9 and 10 to 12) on contracting environments. This sequence represents social studies curricula in general, even though not all commercially available textbook series adhere to this schemata. The scope of the social studies curriculum at the high school level may vary considerably from one state to another; however, courses such as U.S. history and world history are typically required for graduation. In addition, particular states commonly require that students take units pertaining to their own state histories and cultures (e.g., 4th and 11th graders in Hawaii take a course entitled Hawaiiana).

Approaches to Teaching Social Studies

How social studies should be taught and what should be addressed have always been debatable topics. Yet certain emphases have been observed at various times. Birchell and Taylor (1986) report a shift toward a back-to-basics orientation in many elementary social studies programs. If the current infatuation with competency testing is any indication, then this trend is also present at the secondary level.

Of the various ways to present social studies content to students, the most frequently used in regular education is the textbook. This was the case in the 1970s (Turner, 1976) and is continuing in the 1980s (Woodward, Elliott, & Nagel, 1986). Furthermore, Patton and colleagues (1987) found that approximately 37% of the spe-

TABLE 13.6
Typical social studies themes by grade level

Grade Level	Theme
K	Self, school, community, home
1	Families
2	Neighborhoods
3	Communities
4	State history, geographic regions
5	United States history
6	World cultures, western hemisphere
7	World geography or history
8	American history
9	Civics or world cultures
10	World history
11	American history
12	American government

Source. From "The Current and Future Status of the Social Studies" by D. P. Superka, S. Hawke, and I. Morrissett. Reprinted from the *Social Education* (Vol. 44 No. 5, 1980, pp. 362–369) with permission of the National Council for the Social Studies.

cial education teachers who teach social studies use a textbook as the basis of their program. It is also likely that many of the teachers who indicated that they used a combination of approaches (an additional 40%) used textbooks in some substantial way.

Textbook/Lecturer/Discussion   Approach
Teachers familiar with textbook series in social studies know that the most significant problem is readability. Johnson and Vardian (1973) studied the readability of 68 texts and found that the reading levels of many of the texts were above the grade levels for which they were designed. Shepherd and Ragan (1982) corroborate this reality, suggesting that elementary social studies textbooks may have the highest readability levels of any textual material at a particular grade level. This factor remains problematic for at least two reasons. First, many special students are not reading at their grade level. Second, readability is compounded by what Lundstrum (1976) refers to as vocabulary loading and concept loading. These factors need to be considered in the selection of any material—textbook, supplement, or worksheet.

Most major publishers have developed a social studies series, and some of the series seem to accommodate individual differences better than others. Teachers should examine these series closely, looking for certain features in the student materials (e.g., controlled reading levels, organization, language demands, conceptual level) and in the teacher materials (e.g., guidelines for modifying instruction, additional activity-oriented ideas for covering the topic, supplemental materials). Ochoa and Shuster (1980) performed such an analysis on seven series published in the late 1970s.

Two commercial series have been adapted extensively for use with visually impaired students through Project MAVIS (Materials

Adaptations for Visually Impaired Students in the Social Studies), a federally funded project awarded to the Social Science Education Consortium. The two programs adapted were the Houghton Mifflin *Windows on Our World* and the *Silver Burdett Social Science* series. One very interesting conclusion derived from the project was that large-scale literal adaptation, although useful to teachers and students, is not feasible because of its expense and the tendency of materials to become dated too quickly (Singleton, 1982).

Easy-reading textbooks are also available. These are especially important for students at the secondary level, and most serve this population by matching topics that are covered at secondary levels. Memory and McGowan (1985) promote the use of these materials in regular education classes; however, such texts are equally appropriate for use in special classes. Many of these texts have been identified by Memory and McGowan and are listed in Table 13.7. Two additional publishers have produced texts that are written at low reading levels (second to third grade) and cover secondary-level topics. The contents of those texts are outlined in Table 13.8.

If a textbook series is to be used, instructional techniques should be selected to assist students in understanding the content (see Carnine & Silbert, 1979). Potter (1978) suggests using textbook inventories that ask students questions about the structure and organization of the textbook itself. She also recommends reading guides to assist students in comprehending the literal information of a reading passage. Another suggestion calls for activities that ask students to restate the material they have read using a cloze procedure. Lastly, Potter mentions that some students may need rewritten material, an admirable idea that is often impractical because of time constraints. Schneider and Brown (1980) suggest using

various types of study guides as well as an assortment of concept and vocabulary development activities. They offer many other suggestions, and their work should be more thoroughly investigated. Downey (1980) presents the interesting idea that pictures with historical relevance, often found in history texts, be used for instructional purposes. Such pictures "can add to the students' intellectual experience . . . [and] can be used to give students practice in critical thinking and in interpreting visual evidence" (p. 93). Another recommendation is that students be presented with recordings of textual material (Tyo, 1980).

Inquiry Approach This approach, also referred to as a process approach, puts a premium on skills used in solving problems or addressing issues. Kelly (1979) indicates that this approach is "conducive to development of initiative, judgment, and good study habits" (p. 130). Although attractive in many ways, this approach requires that students possess certain abilities and prerequisite skills. Teachers, too, need specific skills, and for this reason many find the approach unattractive (Jarolimek, 1981).

The use of a total inquiry-oriented approach for teaching social studies to special learners is questionable. As in science, the use of process approaches with special students is not prohibited, but a certain amount of structured instruction is probably necessary. Thus, it is important, first to assess whether students can effectively use inquiry skills and then to present at least some substantive information via a systematic teaching paradigm.

Interestingly, Curtis and Shaver (1980) report that a social studies program that is inquiry-oriented and focuses primarily on the study of contemporary problems can be employed effectively with special students. They contend that such a program is interesting to students because it deals with local community issues and helps develop decision-making skills. These authors also stress that special students "can engage in more sophisticated studies than those described in many social studies curriculum guides" (p. 307). Special learners are too infrequently afforded opportunities to experience innovative, dynamic programs. Such programs, many of which are inquiry-oriented, should be considered, but their ef-

TABLE 13.7
Easy-reading social studies materials for secondary students

American History

Highlights of American History, Janus (2^2)*
Famous Americans, Janus (2^2)
America's Story, Steck-Vaughn (2^2–3)
Foundations in History, Opportunities for Learning (4)
America's Early Years, Steck-Vaughn (4–5)
Twentieth Century America, Steck-Vaughn (4–5)
American Nation, Follett (4–7) (JHS)
New Exploring American History, Globe (5–6) (JHS)
The United States in the Making, Globe (5–6) (JHS)
Building the American Nation, Harcourt Brace Jovanovich (5–6) (JHS)
Foundations in American History, Globe (5–6)
Life and Liberty, Scott, Foresman (5–6) (HS)
American History, Follett (5–7)
Exploring Our Nation's History, Globe (6–7) (HS)
Building the United States, Harcourt Brace Jovanovich (7–8) (HS)

Geography and World Cultures

Culture Studies Program, Addison-Wesley (5)
Exploring a Changing World, Globe (5–6)
World Geography, Follett (6)
Scholastic World Cultures, Scholastic (6–8)

Civics and Government

Government in Action, Janus (2^2)
The Government and You, Follett (3^2)
The Law and You, Follett (3^2)
Citizens Today, Steck-Vaughn (3–4)
Government and Law, Level 1, McGraw-Hill Paperbacks (3–4)
United States Government, Bowmar/Noble (4–6)
Democracy in Action, Steck-Vaughn (5–6)
Exploring American Citizenship, Globe (5–6)
Civics: Citizens and Society, Webster/McGraw-Hill (5–6)
Civics, Follett (6–7)

World History

World History and You, Steck-Vaughn (4)
Building the Modern World, Harcourt Brace Jovanovich (5–6)
World History for a Global Age, Globe (5–6)
Exploring World History, Globe (5–6) (HS)
World History, Follett (6–8)
Scholastic World History Program, Scholastic

*The numbers and letters in parentheses are readability levels; the superscript 2 indicates the second half of the school year.

Source. From "Using Multilevel Textbooks in Social Studies Classes" by D. M. Memory and T. M. McGowan, 1985, The Social Studies, 76, p. 178. Copyright 1985 by The Social Studies. Reprinted by permission.

TABLE 13.8
Contents of two
easy-reading social
studies texts

Quercus Corporation	C. C. Publications*
American History	*American History*
To The New Land	The First Americans
In the Colonies	Explorers and Discoverers
Statehood, the West, and Civil War	Colonial Times
Industrial Giant	Revolution and Independence
The Americans Since 1914	Westward Expansion
American History Activities	Civil War and Reconstruction
	Industrial Revolution
Geography and World Cultures	Immigration
Geography I: The Earth and Its	World War I
Resources	Roaring Twenties and the
Geography II: The Earth and Its	Depression
People	World War II
	The Nuclear Age
Civics and Government	
Government Is News	*Geography and World Cultures*
Government Is News Activity Book	Geography
State and Local Government	
State and Local Government	
Activity Book	
World History	
World History I	
World History II	
World History III	
World History I, II, III Activities	

*Now published by Science Research Associates.

fectiveness should be evaluated.

Eclectic Approaches Many teachers have developed social studies programs that combine existing techniques/materials or are completely customized. For example, a program might use a textbook but also regularly include inquiry-type activities. Some programs have incorporated the use of a newspaper as a supplement to the text (Gregory, 1979); other programs have used a newspaper as the primary vehicle for instruction. Another eclectic approach uses Goldstein's (1975) Social Learning Curriculum as the basis for social development of special students.

Eclectic/customized programs can be engaging, relevant, and appropriate for special learners. However, teachers should consult available resources for assistance in developing such curricula. It may be important that the customized curriculum not deviate too much from the regular curriculum in terms of general content even though methodology and selected topics may be very different. Table 13.9 summarizes the highlights of each approach.

Instructional Strategies

We have little documented information on how to teach social studies to special learners (Curtis & Shaver, 1980). However, we do know that many of the instructional principles discussed in chapter 2 and in this chapter's section on science instruction are

TABLE 13.9
A summary of instructional approaches in social studies

Approach	Positive Features	Negative Features	Components
Textbook	Has been simplified in recent series (Birchell & Taylor, 1986) Includes good aesthetic features (e.g., illustrations) Includes good resource/reference materials Introduces content-related terms (Armstrong, 1984) Lessens teacher's workload (i.e., preparation time)	Presents readability problems Introduces language complexity Develops too many concepts too quickly Lacks sufficient organizational aids (e.g., headings and subheadings) (Adams, Carnine, & Gersten, 1982) Makes understanding difficult because of superficial and disconnected coverage of topics (Woodward, Elliott, & Nagel, 1986) Does not adequately accommodate special learners in teacher's guides Is typically used only in combination with discussion	Teacher's guide Student text Student workbook Supplemental materials (e.g., filmstrips)
Inquiry	Emphasizes organizational and problem-solving skills Is student-centered Capitalizes on student curiosity and interests	Requires organizational and problem-solving skills Demands self-directed behavior (i.e., independent learning) Requires the use of outside materials that may not be readable and/or available (e.g., in Braille or on tape) Requires special skills of the teacher	Tradebooks Reference materials Library work Field work Media Resource persons Student reports (oral or written) Microcomputers
Eclectic (customized)	Focuses on students and teacher Is relevant to students' interests and experiences Uses local context Can be student-generated Should be activity-oriented Can include a combination of instructional practices Can integrate curricular areas	Typically requires considerable teacher effort May be conceptually confusing Can result in too narrow a focus	Texts Trade books Media Role-playing Simulations Group work Microcomputers

equally relevant in this subject area. Other techniques are described here.

Modifying Materials and Activities Teaching social studies can involve many different instructional practices. WIthin the classroom setting teachers can employ discussions, demonstrations, and learning centers. Other intriguing techniques involve simulation activities, role-playing, or dramatic improvisation (Wagener, 1977). The efficient use of media is another way of making content interesting and instructionally relevant. A substantial number of films, filmstrips, and videotapes are available for instructional use. Karlin and Berger (1969) suggest periodic use of a total immersion technique. For example, if the topic under consideration is a particular foreign country and its culture, then students might be introduced to its food, dress, music, and any other identifiable characteristics.

Some additional techniques that teachers can utilize to enhance student performance are presented here according to instructional methodology (Patton & Andre, in press).

☐ *textual material:* prepare study/reading guides and vocabulary exercises, rewrite materials, preview reading selections, have students do something special after they read selections, use a language experience approach, develop graphic organizers
☐ *independent study:* teach study, library, and research skills
☐ *lectures:* use advanced organizers, check note-taking skills, follow prepared outlines, frame outlines
☐ *inquiry approaches:* emphasize cooperative learning, provide some teacher-directed learning

Outside the classroom, field trips to museums, historical sites, and community locations can be engaging. The local neighborhood can serve as a plentiful and primary source of information. Weitzman (1975) has capitalized on this idea in his excellent book *My Backyard History Book.* For instance, the history and culture associated with any local cemetery is bountiful but often overlooked. Another outside resource is people from the community who can easily augment and embellish most social studies programs.

It is also well worth the effort to obtain materials such as maps, globes, charts, diagrams, and graphs. In addition, teachers should maintain an awareness of the microcomputer software being developed today.

Integration with Other Curricular Areas Social studies, like science, relates easily to other subject and skill areas. One successful example involves a unit on ecology. The unit starts off with the old Marvin Gaye song "Mercy, Mercy, Me . . . the Ecology." It then explores topics such as government regulation and historical examples of the effect of pollution on the environment. Another example has been demonstrated by Oyama (1986), who took a commonly used basal reading series by Ginn and developed social studies topics for each story (see Table 8.2).

A comprehensive example of how skill areas can be integrated with social studies is demonstrated in Table 13.10. Andre (1982) has suggested the listed activities for a unit on the Rocky Mountain states from the fifth-grade textbook *The Americas* of the Follett series *Exploring Our World.*

Music is a great way to demonstrate how other subject areas can be worked into social studies. Much popular music can be easily integrated for this purpose. For instance, songs like Madonna's "Papa, Don't Preach," the Pretenders' "My City Was Gone," and Billy Joel's "You're Only Human" all address topics relevant to social studies.

Computer Applications Certain applica-

TABLE 13.10
Example of an integrated curriculum for a social studies unit, Exploring the Rocky Mountain States

Skill Area	Activity
Art	Do a sand painting using an Indian design. Design a cattle brand.
Listening skills	Tell the story of the Mormon church, and have students listen to the Mormon Tabernacle Choir.
Math	Make up a ditto for which the answers to computations are guidelines to help a miner get to his gold mine.
Oral expression	Talk about ghost towns and mining towns. Discuss national parks and geysers. Discuss dust storms and their causes.
Spelling	Learn how to spell these words correctly: *Indian, Mormon, mountain, plains,* and *Rocky.*
Vocational	Study careers available in farming and ranching.
Written expression	Write a story using Indian symbols.

tions of microcomputers are well suited for use in social studies. Even though much software is limited graphically, better products are being developed regularly. One of the most exciting uses of microcomputers in this subject area is in conjunction with interactive video systems. Other applications include

☐ simulations (e.g., *Oregon Trail*)

☐ word processing/desktop publishing: school newspapers
☐ databases: data on community resources, information on legislators, city council, or another government body
☐ spreadsheets: economic trends
☐ graphics: demographic information
☐ communications: electronic field trips, on-line databases

ACTIVITIES

1. Obtain pictures of different people in the community, show one picture, and have students discuss what that person does, how the person is important to the community, and what would happen if this person did not do the job. Students need to be aware of sources of help in the community. Examples can include police officers, postal workers, doctors, and rescue squads.
2. To develop awareness of societal values, discuss the Declaration of Independence and the Bill of Rights of the Constitution. List specific values, rights, and responsibilities on the chalkboard. Discuss applications to the school setting.
3. Nickell and Kennedy (1987) provide numerous games that teach social concepts and provide motor activity, which is needed by all students.
4. Let students be responsible for some of the classroom decisions that affect them: seating arrangements, selection of daily helpers, and the rules of the room. This is a good way to introduce many social concepts that are used in daily living (Hurst, 1986).
5. When discussing current events, use popular music as a vehicle for

raising some of the issues on people's minds.

6. To add interest to the study of foreign cultures, have students try to collect the stamps of these cultures. Outside sources can offer help (see Abruscato & Hassard, 1978).

7. An often-overlooked treasure of information is grandparents. A great way to investigate history is to ask them about past events. Students might also request autobiographical information from them.

8. For additional work on map skills, have students make maps of their neighborhoods. If cameras are available, have students take pictures of various significant sites.

9. Develop a unit on tools. Other subject-area content can be easily incorporated into it (e.g., science, career education). Have students study the tools used by workers in different vocations today and in times past.

10. Take a field trip to a cemetery. A wealth of historical information can be drawn from such a visit. Have students do some rubbings of the gravestones. Abruscato and Hassard (1978) and Weitzman (1975) present additional ideas.

11. Acquire an old Sears, Roebuck & Co. catalog (e.g., 1902). Have students compare consumer interest and tendencies of that time with those of today (Abruscato & Hassard, 1978).

12. Another neighborhood-based activity to assist students in refining their map and directional skills is a walk rally—similar in format to a road rally. Give students directions (e.g., written prompts, pictures) that they must use to follow a preplanned course. They are to answer questions along the way and ultimately reach a designated destination.

13. Have students construct family histories, using many sources of information. Weitzman (1975) offers a number of related ideas.

14. Every region of the country has established folklore (e.g., legends, ghost stories, superstitions). Have students investigate and report on legends in the community. See Bogojavlensky, Grossman, Topham, and Meyer (1977) for more information.

15. To assist students with map work and learning the location and capitals of the 50 states, enlarge a map to fit on a bulletin board. Then make cards that have a state's name on one side and the capital on the other, within an outline of the shape of the state. Have students match the outline of the state on the map with the name on the card and then identify the capital. They can self-check themselves.

16. To help students remember the great amount of information found in a social studies curriculum, mnemonic strategies are great aids. For example, if memorizing the capitals of the 50 states, sayings like the following can help: Charles Ton lives west of his friend, the Rich Man (Charleston, West Virginia, and Richmond, Virginia).

17. Study cards can help special needs learners prepare for exams. On one side of an index card, print the important event, name, or place covered in the chapter. On the back make a mark of any sort to use as a key. On another card print information that explains, defines, or identifies the word printed on the first card. Place the same symbol on the back of this second card. Students can then study at school or at home by reading the study cards and matching them. The cards are self-checking, provide instant reinforcement, and let students work on infor-

mation in small, manageable pieces.

18. Combine practice of written expression and reference skills by having your class make a travel brochure for a state or region of study. Have students use library sources to gather interesting information about a specific area, tourist attraction, or culture found within this region. Then have them prepare a paragraph that highlights the facts and sparks interest in visiting that spot. They can also find pictures that add meaning to their writing. Both pictures and paragraphs can be cut, pasted, and copied to make the class's work a brochure for all to read.

19. A number of law-related activities may be appropriate for many special learners. Bogojavlensky and colleagues (1977) suggest activities related to a variety of topics, such as FBI wanted posters, children's rights, and shoplifting.

20. Have students conduct opinion polls on any number of topics. This exercise requires students to use various data-gathering and interpretative skills.

21. To develop more ethnic awareness, have students conduct a community survey, focusing on different ethnic groups in the area (King, 1980).

22. Have students use graphing skills as often as possible. Activities requiring graphing can be found in almost any area. For example, students can graph the number of brothers and sisters they have.

23. As you begin to study a particular time period or event, read aloud to the students from a book that tells about that period. The book should be one that interests them and pulls them into the time (De Lin, DuBois & McIntosh, 1986). Book bibliographies can be found in social studies periodicals (e.g., *Social Education*, April/May 1987, pp. 290–300).

24. To combine written expression and thoughts on social issues, have students write. Place a topic on the board and allow them to write about it for 5 minutes. Let the students know that their work will be evaluated on quantity, not quality. This approach encourages them to write freely and helps special needs students learn to express their thoughts fluently (Tamura & Harstad, 1987).

RESOURCES

Abruscato, J., & Hassard, J. (1978). *The earthpeople activity book: People, places, pleasures & other delights*. Santa Monical, CA: Goodyear. This book is full of ideas and activities related to a variety of social studies topics. It is most appropriate for older students, but some of the ideas can be modified for younger students.

Adams, A. H., Coble, C. R., & Hounshell, P. B. (1977). *Mainstreaming language arts and social studies: Special ideas and activities for the whole class*. Santa Monica, CA: Goodyear. Organized on a 36-week basis, this book has many activities for both language arts and social studies.

Bogojavlensky, A. R., Grossman, D. R., Topham, C. S., & Meyer, S. M., III. (1977). *The great learning book*. Menlo Park, CA: Addison-Wesley. Designed for students at the upper-elementary level and beyond, this book is a great resource for stimulating ideas. Although the book has activities applicable to many curricular areas, many of the suggestions work well in social studies curricula.

Forte, I., & Mackenzie, J. (1976). *Kids' stuff social studies.* Nashville: Incentive. This book is also activity-oriented and is designed to augment ongoing elementary-level social studies programs. The three major areas addressed are Close to Home, Outward Bound, and the World and Beyond.

Jantzen, S. L. (1977). *Winning ideas in the social studies: 25 creative lessons that really work.* New York: Teachers College Press. This book presents 25 lessons designed for high school students. Each lesson is interesting, although some may not be appropriate for special learners because of the nature of the skills required.

King, E. W. (1980). *Teaching ethnic awareness: Methods and materials for the elementary school.* Santa Monica, CA: Goodyear. This book offers teachers useful information and activities for addressing cultural diversity.

McLoone-Basta, M., & Siegel, A. (1985). *The kid's world almanac of records and facts.* New York: World Almanac Publications. This book is exactly what it claims to be: a book containing much factual information, written with students in mind. There are 23 major topics and a variety of related subtopics.

Ryan, F. L. (1980). *The social studies sourcebook: Ideas for teaching in the elementary and middle schools.* Boston: Allyn & Bacon. This is an exhaustive source of activities—479 of them. It is organized around four major domains: skills, concepts, topics of study, and affective/evaluative concerns.

Short, J. R., & Dickerson, B. (1980). *The newspaper: An alternative textbook.* Belmont, CA: Pitman Learning. This book provides many ideas for using the newspaper to tie in with social studies objectives.

Skeel, D. J. (1979). *The challenge of teaching social studies in the elementary school* (3rd ed.). Santa Monica, CA: Goodyear. This book examines the nature of social studies as well as some of the approaches to teaching it. It is an excellent resource for suggestions on methods and materials.

Smith, J. A. (1979). *Creative teaching of the social studies in the elementary school* (2nd ed.). Boston: Allyn & Bacon. This book is a valuable methods textbook. It provides much information on teaching social studies creatively, and the ideas are suitable for special settings.

Weitzman, D. (1975). *My backyard history book.* Boston: Little, Brown. This book, like others of the Brown Paper School series, is a remarkable resource. It presents a number of very creative ideas, using home-based activities that can be relevant to students.

14
Study Skills

JOHN J. HOOVER
University of Texas at Tyler

Study skills are essential for all students at all grade levels. Although the appropriate use of study skills is particularly essential at the secondary level, acquisition of study skills should begin early in the educational process. Programs should then develop, refine, and maintain these skills throughout a student's educational career.

Only recently has the topic of study skills been emphasized with regard to learners with handicaps (Brown, 1984). Current literature suggests the need for increased study skill development in these learners. Gearheart and Weishahn (1984) write that some students with learning problems do not possess adequate study skills for success in regular classrooms. Unfortunately, adolescent students with learning disabilities generally have not been taught study skills during elementary education (Alley & Deshler, 1979). Carlson and Alley (1981) note deficiencies in the listening, note-taking, test-taking, and scanning abilities of secondary students who are disabled. Link (1980) also reports that secondary students with learning disabilities exhibit problems associated with note taking and skimming. Saski, Swicegood, and Carter (1983) write that adolescents with learning disabilities often experience problems with the organization of information. Deficient test-taking skills in students who are mildly handicapped are noted by Scruggs and Mastropieri (1986). Thus, evidence suggests the need for an increased emphasis on effective study skills for students with special learning needs at both the elementary and secondary levels of education.

Study skills include "those competencies associated with acquiring, recording, organizing, synthesizing, remembering, and using information and ideas found in school" (Devine, 1987, p. 5). Such skills assist students in confronting the educational tasks associated with the learning process. Thus,

study skills facilitate mastery of learning components, several of which are listed and defined here. For a more detailed discussion the reader is referred to Hoover (1988).

☐ *acquisition:* the crucial first step involved in learning, the first experiences encountered by learners

☐ *recording:* any activity in the classroom that requires the learner to record responses, answers, or ideas, including both written and verbal forms of communication

☐ *location:* seeking out and finding information

☐ *organization:* arranging and managing learning activities effectively

☐ *synthesis:* integrating elements or parts to form a whole, creating something that was not clearly evident prior to synthesis

☐ *memorization:* remembering learned material, storing and recalling or retrieving information

TYPES OF STUDY SKILLS

Various study skills exist, including reading at different rates, listening, note taking/ outlining, report writing, making oral presentations, using graphic aids, test taking, using the library, using reference materials, managing time, and managing behavior. Table 14.1 briefly identifies the importance of each of these skills. For more comprehensive coverage of the various study skills, the reader is referred to Devine (1987), Hoover (1988), and Wallace and Kauffman (1986).

Reading at Different Rates

The ability to use different reading rates is an important study skill (Rubin, 1983; Santeusanio, 1983) that is most evident as students progress through the grades

TABLE 14.1
Study skills for
effective and efficient
learning

Study Skill	Significance for Learning
Reading at different rates	Reading rates should vary with type and length of reading assignments.
Listening	Listening skills are necessary to complete most educational tasks or requirements.
Note taking/outlining	Effective note-taking/outlining skills allow students to document key points of topics for future study.
Report writing	Report writing is a widely used method of documenting information and expressing ideas.
Making oral presentations	Oral presentations provide students an alternative method to express themselves and report information.
Using graphic aids	Graphic aids may visually depict complex or cumbersome material in a meaningful format.
Test taking	Effective test-taking abilities help to ensure more accurate assessment of student abilities.
Using the library	Library usage skills facilitate easy access to much information.
Using reference materials	Independent learning may be greatly improved through effective use of reference materials and dictionaries.
Managing time	Time management assists in reducing the number of unfinished assignments and facilitates more effective use of time.
Managing behavior	Self-management assists students to assume responsibility for their own behaviors.

Source. From *Teaching Handicapped Students Study Skills* (2nd ed.) by J. J. Hoover, 1988, Lindale, TX: Hamilton. Copyright 1988 by Hamilton Publications. Adapted by permission.

(Heilman, Blair, & Rupley, 1981). Teachers at the secondary level must often teach their students how to develop reading rate skills (Mercer, 1987). Although various terms are used to describe the different rates, reading rates include skimming, scanning, rapid reading, normal reading, and careful, or study-type, reading.

Skimming refers to a fast-paced reading rate used to grasp the general idea of material. As students quickly skim material, dif-ferent sections may be glossed over purposely. Scanning is also a fast-paced reading rate, used to identify specific items or pieces of information. Students might scan material to search for a name or a telephone number. Rapid reading is used to review familiar material or grasp main ideas. In rapid reading, some details may be identified, especially if the reader requires only temporary use of the information.

Normal rate is used when students must

identify details or relationships, solve a problem, or find answers to specific questions. Careful, or study-type, reading is a slow rate used to master details, retain or evaluate information, follow directions, or perform other similar tasks (Harris & Sipay, 1980; Santeusanio, 1983).

The nature of the material being read helps to determine the need for varied reading rates (Evans, Evans, & Mercer, 1986); different activities also require different reading rates. In many reading situations two or more rates must be employed. For example, a student may scan several pages to locate a name and then use normal or study-type reading to learn the details surrounding that name. Varied reading rates, when used appropriately, can be highly effective and important study skills for students with handicaps.

Listening

Listening also is involved in many different activities. Gearheart and Weishahn (1984) estimate that listening-related activities comprise approximately 66% of a student's school day. Similarly, Devine (1987) writes that much instruction in elementary and secondary school relies heavily on the listening abilities of students. Listening includes both hearing and comprehending a spoken message (Lerner, 1985). As was noted earlier in this text, listening involves the ability to receive information, apply meaning, and provide evidence of understanding what was heard. Effective listening is required in formal presentations, conversations, exposure to auditory environmental stimuli, and attending to various audio and audiovisual materials (Gearheart & Weishahn, 1984). Devine (1987) and Lerner (1985) suggest that listening skills can be improved through teaching and practice.

Teachers must ensure that classroom conditions facilitate effective listening.

Note Taking/Outlining

Note taking/outlining requires students to document major ideas and relevant topics for later use (Cheek & Cheek, 1983), to classify (Ekwall & Shanker, 1985), and to synthesize information (Estes & Vaughan, 1985). Note taking becomes less difficult once outlining skills have been acquired (Ekwall & Shanker, 1985). Furthermore, study skills associated with reading, listening, thinking, and using vocabulary may improve significantly as students develop effective note-taking abilities (Devine, 1987). With note-taking/outlining skills students are able to summarize ideas and organize information into a useful format for future use. Instruction in this study skill area "is particularly appropriate for learning disabled students, who often have difficulties organizing academic information" (Saski, Swicegood, & Carter, 1983, p. 270). With sufficient practice and systematic instruction, these students are capable of acquiring note-taking/outlining skills, even though they tend to exhibit some difficulty in the process (Gearheart & Weishahn, 1984).

Report Writing

Report writing involves the various skills necessary to organize and present ideas on paper in a meaningful and appropriate way (Devine, 1987). Included are topic selection, note taking, organization of ideas, outlining, spelling and punctuation, and sentence structure (Wallace & Kauffman, 1986). Teachers of students with handicaps must provide direction in each area associated with written reports to ensure satisfactory growth and progress.

Making Oral Presentations

Many skills necessary for report writing are also important in oral presentations of various types—interviews, debates, group discussions, and individual or group presentations (Devine, 1987). Caution should be used to ensure that oral presentations occur in a nonthreatening environment to minimize student anxiety. Devine (1987) also suggests that the oral presentation task be clearly defined and that students be provided with preparation time, guidance, and structure in planning their oral presentations. Oral reporting can be an effective supplement or substitute for written assignments on occasion.

Using Graphic Aids

The use of graphic aids—materials such as charts, graphs, maps, models, pictures, or photographs—can be another effective tool to facilitate learning. Wallace and Kauffman (1986) cite Carder, Coy, and Rickert (1979) in explaining that graphic aids (1) may assist students in more easily comprehending complex material; (2) may facilitate the presentation of large abstractions in small, more manageable pieces; and (3) may assist students in ascertaining similarities within and differences between cultural, geographic, and economic situations. Thus, numerous important concepts or events can be addressed through visual material (Devine, 1987). Students with disabilities can benefit from graphic aids if they are taught what to look for and attend to while reading and interpreting visual material.

Test Taking

Students are subjected frequently to various forms of assessment and evaluation. Even though tests are one of the primary means of assessing students in school, many students do not possess sufficient test-taking skills (Rubin, 1982). Test-taking skills are those abilities necessary to "apply systematic procedures in studying for and taking exams" (Cheek & Cheek, 1983, p. 95). They are important to ensure that tests accurately measure students' knowledge rather than their poor test-taking abilities. Test-taking skills include reading and following directions, thinking through questions prior to recording responses, and proofreading and checking answers (Estes & Vaughan, 1985). Students who are handicapped may lack these abilities, which can be learned through instruction and practice (Scruggs & Mastropieri, 1986).

Using the Library

Library activities are periodically required of students at any grade level. Dallmann, Rouch, Char, and DeBoer (1982) indicate that library usage requires skill in locating library materials and using the card catalog; locating films, filmstrips, resource guides, and curriculum materials; and understanding the general layout and organization of the library. Knowledge of the important role of the media specialist is also important. Although library usage becomes especially important at the secondary level of education, it should be taught gradually and systematically throughout a student's schooling.

Using Reference Materials

Other study skills become important when students locate materials within the classroom or school library. Students must be knowledgeable about the uses and functions of dictionaries and various other reference materials and must be familiar with various aspects of their design. They must be able to use a table of contents and an index; to alphabetize and use chapter headings; and to understand how content is arranged in dictionaries, encyclopedias, and other reference books (Dallmann et al., 1982). Again, students with handicaps are capable of acquiring these skills if they receive guided instruction and practice (Lerner, 1985).

Managing Time

Time management involves the effective use of time to complete daily assignments and carry out responsibilities. It includes allocating time and organizing the environment to effectively study, complete projects, and balance various aspects of individual schedules (Kerr, Nelson, & Lambert, 1987). Alley and Deshler (1979) write that some students with special needs lack awareness of time. Lewis and Doorlag (1987) hold that some students have difficulty with the organization and management of time, which may lead to incorrect or unfinished assignments. As students enter secondary schools and work loads increase, effective time management becomes increasingly important. Teachers of learners with handicaps must structure learning situations to encourage students to manage their time responsibly throughout their elementary and secondary education.

Managing Behavior

Another important tool necessary for learning is the ability to manage one's own behavior, especially during independent work time. Inappropriate behaviors can seriously interfere with task completion. Brown (1986) writes that students learn to assume responsibility for their own behaviors when educational programs emphasize self-management and control of behavior. As Schloss (1987) indicates, a student "with

strong self-management skills is able to identify and alter potentially disruptive social behavior independently" (p. 40). In addition, Reiter, Mabee, and McLaughlin (1985) found self-monitoring to be effective in increasing time on-task and reducing time required to complete tasks. Self-monitoring also reduces the demands on teachers for data collection (Lewis & Doorlag, 1987). Several programs concerned with self-control and self-management currently exist (Fagen, Long, & Stevens, 1975; Workman, 1982), and the reader is also referred to chapter 5 for more comprehensive coverage of this topic.

ASSESSMENT OF STUDY SKILLS

Numerous instruments exist for assessing study skills; they include norm-referenced, criterion-referenced, and standardized devices as well as informal and teacher-made checklists. Table 14.2 identifies a variety of such devices. The appropriate use of the various types of instruments is discussed here; selected devices are presented to familiarize the reader with existing instruments, not to provide evaluative judgments. The reader should consult each instrument's manual or cited references for additional information and evaluative reviews. Table 14.3 summarizes additional information about selected norm- and criterion-referenced instruments. It is based on information provided by Cheek and Cheek (1983); Ekwall and Shanker (1985); Evans, Evans, and Mercer (1986); Harris and Sipay (1980); McLoughlin and Lewis (1986); Rubin (1982); and Salvia and Ysseldyke (1985).

Norm-Referenced Instruments

Although norm-referenced general achievement tests are used in most schools, "these measures tend to produce a low estimate of handicapped students' performance"

TABLE 14.2
Study skill assessment instruments

Norm-Referenced General Achievement Tests

California Achievement Tests (CTB/McGraw-Hill)
Comprehensive Tests of Basic Skills (CTB/McGraw-Hill)
Iowa Silent Reading Tests (Harcourt Brace Jovanovich)
Iowa Tests of Basic Skills (Riverside)
Sequential Tests of Educational Progress (STEP) (Addison-Wesley)
SRA Achievement Series—Reading (Science Research Associates)
Tests of Achievement and Proficiency (Riverside)

Criterion-Referenced Instruments

Analysis of Skills: Reading (Scholastic Testing Service)
BRIGANCE Diagnostic Inventories (Curriculum Associates)
Diagnosis: An Instructional Aid: Reading (Science Research Associates)
Fountain Valley Reading Skills Tests (Zweig Associates)
Individual Pupil Monitoring System—Reading (Riverside)
System for Objective-Based Assessment—Reading (Science Research Associates)
System FORE (Foreworks Publications)
Wisconsin Tests for Reading Skill Development (NCS/Educational Systems)

Standardized Study Skill Instruments

Study Habits Checklist (Science Research Associates)
Study Skills Counseling Evaluation (Western Psychological Services)

Informal and Teacher-Made Checklists

Checklist of Reading Abilities (Maier, 1980)
Reading Difficulty Checklist (Ekwall, 1985)
Study Habits Inventory (Devine, 1987)
Study Skills Checklist (Estes & Vaughan, 1985)

Source. From *Teaching Handicapped Students Study Skills* (2nd ed.) by J. J. Hoover, 1988, Lindale, TX: Hamilton. Copyright 1988 by Hamilton Publications. Reprinted by permission.

(McLoughlin & Lewis, 1986, p. 126). In addition, this type of test may pose particular problems to students who are handicapped because such instruments are often timed and require students to record their own answers. Such tests assume that students have sufficient independent work habits to monitor their own time and behavior and to sustain attention to the various tasks presented by the tests (McLoughlin & Lewis, 1986). Furthermore, Wallace and Kauffman (1986) note that these tests frequently include only a small number of items to assess study skills and thus may not adequately assess student abilities. Nonetheless, group tests are often appropriate as screening devices to identify students requiring additional assistance (McLoughlin & Lewis, 1986). When study-skill assessment does include use of group-administered, norm-referenced general achievement tests, results must be interpreted carefully.

Criterion-Referenced Instruments

Salvia and Ysseldyke (1985) write that "criterion-referenced tests measure a person's development of particular skills in terms of absolute levels of mastery" (p. 30). They suggest that criterion-referenced tests be used to assist classroom teachers in program planning. The criterion-referenced

TABLE 14.3
Norm- (NR) and criterion-referenced (CR) assessment devices

Test	Type	Subtest	Grade Level
Analysis of Skills: Reading	CR	Study Skills	1–8
Brigance Diagnostic Inventories	CR	Reference Skills/ Graphs and Maps	K–12
California Achievement Tests	NR	Reference Skills	3.6–12.9
Comprehensive Test of Basic Skills (CTBS)	NR	Reference Skills	2.5–12
Diagnosis: An Instructional Aid: Reading	CR	Study Skills	1–6
Fountain Valley Reading Skills Test	CR	Study Skills	1–6, Secondary
Individual Pupil Monitoring System	CR	Discrimination/ Study Skills	1–6
Iowa Silent Reading Tests	NR	Directed Reading	6–14
Iowa Tests of Basic Skills	NR	Reference Materials	1.7–9
Sequential Tests of Educational Progress (STEP)	NR	Study Skills	3–12
System for Objective-Based Assessment—Reading	CR	Study Skills	K–9
System FORE	CR	Study Skills	K–12
Tests of Achievement and Proficiency	NR	Sources of Information	7–12
Wisconsin Tests for Reading Skill Development	CR	Study/Reference Skills	K–6

tests listed in Table 14.3 may assist in identifying specific study skills that students have and have not mastered.

Standardized Devices

Standardized devices designed to specifically assess study skills also exist. The Study Habits Checklist (Preston & Botel, 1967) is designed for students in Grades 9 to 14 and assesses a variety of study-skill areas, providing scores for 37 study skills and habits (Estes & Vaughan, 1985; Harris & Sipay, 1980). The Study Skills Counseling Evaluation (Demos, 1976) is another instrument normed with secondary and postsecondary students. This instrument contains 50 items within several study-skill areas, including study-time distribution, test taking, study conditions, and note taking (McLoughlin & Lewis, 1986).

Informal Devices

Several informal inventories and teacher-made checklists for assessing study skills also exist. The Reading Difficulty Checklist (Ekwall, 1985) contains several study-skill items, including reading rate and dictionary usage. The Study Skills Checklist (Estes & Vaughan, 1985) assesses several areas, including test taking, use of graphic aids, note taking, and outlining skills. The Checklist of Reading Abilities (Maier, 1980) assesses reading rate, use of graphic aids, reference material/dictionary usage, library usage, and note taking/outlining. And the Study Habits Inventory (Devine, 1987) assesses time management, note taking and outlining, use of graphic aids, reading rates, library usage, reference material/dictionary usage, and report writing.

Despite the availability of these instruments, many teachers find themselves needing to develop their own informal checklists to assess study skills. Teacher-made devices can assess study skills in a quick and efficient manner as areas requiring further assistance are identified (McLoughlin & Lewis, 1986). Estes and Vaughan (1985) write that "informal analysis of students' study skills may be the easiest aspect of diagnosis for . . . helping students improve their learning abilities" (p. 120), and they identify several steps that should be followed in informal assessment of study skills.

1. Identify study skills necessary to complete various tasks or courses.
2. Construct a teacher checklist based on the items identified in Step 1.
3. Construct a student self-analysis checklist similar to the teacher checklist.
4. Develop and implement evaluative activities requiring the student to employ desired study skills.
5. Observe the student during these activities, record results, and have the student complete the self-analysis form.

6. Compare teacher and student checklist results, and design a study-skills program to address areas requiring further assistance.

If commercial study-skill devices are inappropriate for a particular situation or student, teachers may want to develop an inventory like the one provided in Figure 14.1.

STUDY STRATEGIES

Student application of study skills may be improved through the use of various study-skill strategies. Study strategies are "self-directed procedures" employed by students to complete learning activities (Cheek & Cheek, 1983, p. 182). Several such strategies are presented here; none are appropriate for all students with special learning needs. Individual needs and abilities must be considered. Some of these strategies are part of a learning-strategies model, which presents "a problem-solving approach that is not restricted to applications specific to the context in which the strategy is taught" (Ritter & Idol-Maestas, 1986). However, each strategy discussed here is presented relative to specific study skills. For additional information, the reader is referred to the specific sources cited for each strategy.

SQ3R

SQ3R, the "oldest and most commonly used study strategy" (Cheek & Cheek, 1983, p. 177) follows five procedural steps (Cheek & Cheek, 1983; Wallace & Kauffman, 1986).

☐ *Survey.* Students initially survey an introductory statement, various headings, and summaries in an attempt to grasp the main idea of the reading material. Specific attention is paid to graphic aids.

☐ *Question.* Students formulate questions about the material to identify purpose

Name: _____

Date (pre): _____   Date (post): _____

Rating scale: 1 = not mastered; 2 = partial mastery/needs improvement; 3 = mastered.

Study Skills	Pre	Post
Reading Rates		
Scanning		
Skimming		
Normal rate		
Rapid reading		
Careful reading		
Listening		
Attends to listening tasks		
Applies meaning to verbal messages		
Filters out auditory distractions		
Note Taking/Outlining		
Appropriate use of headings		
Brief and clear notes		
Records important information		
Uses for report writing		
Uses during lectures		

Study Skills	Pre	Post
Test Taking		
Organizes answers		
Proofreads		
Reads and understands directions		
Identifies clue words		
Properly records responses		
Answers difficult questions last		
Narrows possible correct answers		
Corrects previous test-taking errors		
Library Usage		
Use of card catalog		
Ability to locate materials		
Organization of library		
Role of media specialist		
Reference/Dictionary Usage		
Identifies components		

Well-organized outlines		
Note card format organized		
Report Writing		
Organizes thoughts		
Proper punctuation		
Proper spelling		
Proper grammar		
Oral Presentations		
Participates freely		
Organizes presentation		
Uses gestures		
Speaks clearly		
Use of Graphic Aids		
Attends to relevant elements		
Understands purposes		
Incorporates in presentations		
Develops own visuals		
Uses guide words		
Understands uses of each		
Uses for written assignments		
Identifies different reference materials		
Time Management		
Organizes daily activities		
Completes tasks on time		
Organizes weekly/monthly schedules		
Understands time management		
Reorganizes time when necessary		
Prioritizes activities		
Self-Management of Behavior		
Monitors own behavior		
Changes own behavior		
Thinks before acting		
Responsible for own behavior		

FIGURE 14.1
Study-skills inventory (From *Teaching Handicapped Students Study Skills* (2nd ed.) by J. J. Hoover, 1988, Lindale, TX: Hamilton. Copyright 1988 by Hamilton Publications. Adapted by permission.)

for reading the selection. Questions related to who, what, where, when, why, and how are considered.

☐ *Read.* Students read the material, attending specifically to the questions generated.

☐ *Recite.* After reading the material, students attempt to answer the questions without direct reference to the selection or to notes compiled.

☐ *Review.* Students verify answers to the questions through review of the reading material and notes compiled during the reading.

In reference to special learners, Mercer and Mercer (1985) write that this strategy may provide a systematic approach to improve study skills. Alley and Deshler (1979) suggest that the SQ3R method be individualized for students. It requires practice and is best used with specific content material (Wallace & Kauffman, 1986).

PARS

PARS is recommended for use with younger students and those who have limited experience in the use of study strategies (Cheek & Cheek, 1983; Smith & Elliot, 1979). The PARS procedure follows four steps (Cheek & Cheek, 1983).

☐ *Preview.* Preview the material.
☐ *Ask questions.* Formulate questions the teacher wishes to emphasize.
☐ *Read.* Read the material with these questions in mind.
☐ *Summarize.* Summarize the material and verify responses to the questions.

PQ4R

PQ4R, another variation of the SQ3R method, may assist students in becoming more discriminating and systematic readers (Cheek & Cheek, 1983). The PQ4R process

is to preview, question, read, reflect, recite, and review. During reflection the student rereads various parts of the reading material that were initially unclear. This helps students organize their thoughts as answers to questions are sought (Cheek & Cheek, 1983; Thomas & Robinson, 1972).

PANORAMA

PANORAMA was devised by Edwards (1973) and includes three stages (Cheek & Cheek, 1983; Wallace & Kauffman, 1986).

☐ *Stage I (Preparatory stage).* The student determines the purpose for reading the material and the most appropriate reading rate and formulates questions about the selection based on the headings.

☐ *Stage II (Intermediate stage).* The student surveys the material to determine its organization, reads the material, and takes notes relative to the formulated questions.

☐ *Stage III (Concluding stage).* The student learns the material with the aid of outlines, summaries, and an evaluation component to determine retention of content.

ReQuest

ReQuest, developed by Manzo (1969), helps to relate previous knowledge with new learning (Estes & Vaughan, 1985). *ReQuest* refers to reciprocal questioning and focuses on (1) encouraging learners to question prior to reading and (2) having students base their reading on anticipated questions. With this approach, both teacher and students ask questions about the initial sentence(s) in a passage. The teacher's questions should help students realize what knowledge they already possess about the topic and should serve as a model of appropriate types of questions that might be asked. The teacher's questions are answered without reference to the selection, and this process continues through the first few paragraphs until students are capable of projecting answers to questions such as "What do you think you will find out in the rest of the selection?" (Estes & Vaughan, 1985, p. 149). These same authors write that ReQuest provides students with an opportunity for feedback and modeling of questions, as well as an emphasis on strategies for questioning.

RARE

Discussed by Gearheart, DeRuiter, and Sileo (1986), this reading comprehension strategy includes four steps.

1. *Review* each question located at the end of the passage.
2. *Answer* all questions already known.
3. *Read* the selection.
4. *Express* answers to the remaining questions, which students were unable to answer initially.

RARE emphasizes reading for a specific purpose. With this method students read material carefully to obtain answers to questions they are unable to answer prior to a careful reading of the selection.

TQLR

Developed by Tonjes and Zintz (1981), this strategy assists students with listening. TQLR refers to turning in, questioning, listening, and reviewing. This strategy suggests that students must be ready for the verbal message, should identify the position the speaker may take, and should listen for the actual position taken. The listener should generate questions about the topic during the verbal communication, and mental review should occur after the talk to ensure that important points are retained

(Wallace & Kauffman, 1986).

GLP

The Guided Lecture Procedure (GLP) is a strategy used to facilitate effective note taking during lectures (Kelly & Holmes, 1979). Several procedural steps are followed. Initially, students are told the lecture's purposes and objectives, which they write down on paper. Students are then instructed to listen closely and not to take notes during the initial part of the lecture. About midway through the lecture, the lecturer stops and instructs students to write in brief form all information they can recall from the lecture. The lecture is then completed, and students discuss the entire lecture in small groups with teacher guidance. Students take notes as information is shared and thus develop the actual lecture notes during this group work. After the small group activity students reflect on the lecture content and the GLP process. They then summarize in narrative form the major points of the lecture without using their lecture notes. Cheek and Cheek (1983) suggest that the GLP strategy actively involves students in the lecture process and thus helps to motivate them.

COPS and TOWER

COPS, discussed earlier in chapter 11, is an error-monitoring method (Schumaker, Deshler, Nolan, Clark, Alley, & Warner, 1981) used to assist with written assignments. This strategy addresses four areas that pertain to written assignments:

- ☐ capitalization (C),
- ☐ overall appearance (O),
- ☐ punctuation (P), and
- ☐ spelling (S) (Schumaker et al., 1981).

TOWER is a strategy that provides a structured approach to written reports; it is employed prior to and during the actual writing assignment. The TOWER process is to think, order ideas, write, edit, and rewrite. The strategies of COPS and TOWER may be used together to complete a report and to monitor errors as writing is generated (Mercer & Mercer, 1985).

SCORER

SCORER is a test-taking strategy designed to assist students in focusing on effective test-taking skills (Carman & Adams, 1972). Mercer and Mercer (1985) outline the steps involved.

☐ *Schedule* your time for all parts of the test and the process prior to beginning the test.

☐ *Look* for *clue* words within different items.

☐ *Omit* difficult questions until last.

☐ *Read* each item and the directions carefully.

☐ *Estimate* answers for problems requiring calculation before you select the final answers, to eliminate obviously wrong answers.

☐ *Review* your work before turning in your test.

SCORER has been found to be effective with students with poor reading comprehension (Ritter & Idol-Maestas, 1986).

SQRQCQ

SQRQCQ was developed by Fay (1965) to assist students with math word problems. It involves six steps (Cheek & Cheek, 1983).

☐ *Survey* the word problem.

☐ Determine the *question* being asked.

☐ *Read* the problem more carefully.

☐ *Question* the processes needed to obtain the answer.

☐ *Compute* the answer.

☐ *Question* again to ascertain whether the problem was answered correctly and logically.

SSCD Approach

This four-step approach is effective in assisting upper elementary and secondary level students with unfamiliar vocabulary that they encounter in reading material (Devine, 1987). Devine (1987) also suggests that SSCD is appropriate for learning unfamiliar math terms.

1. *Sound clues:* emphasizing that unfamiliar words in print may not be unfamiliar when heard
2. *Structure clues:* emphasizing that unfamiliar words can be analyzed by examining word parts (e.g., prefixes, roots, suffixes)
3. *Context clues:* emphasizing the study of a word in context
4. *Dictionary:* emphasizing the dictionary as a necessary reference for words that a student is unable to understand through sound, structure, or context clues

The SSCD approach should be reviewed on a regular basis to be effective. This strategy reminds learners "that vocabulary is important, that it can be developed, and that it needs to be attacked from several angles" (Devine, 1987, p. 49).

IMPLEMENTING A STUDY-SKILLS PROGRAM

A study-skills program should introduce simple variations of study skills in the lower elementary grades and should gradually increase in complexity as students progress through the grades (Jarolimek & Foster, 1985). The age, ability, and individual needs of special learners must determine that complexity; however, early efforts may prove beneficial throughout entire educational programs. Devine (1987) outlines several guidelines for teachers to follow in developing and/or improving their study-skills programs. Although the guidelines can be applied to all students, they are of particular significance for teachers of students with special learning needs.

1. Establish and define specific goals for your study-skills program.
2. Know the individual strengths and abilities of your students, and select and modify study strategies accordingly.
3. Know what motivates your students, and relate use of study-skill strategies to that motivation.
4. Explain and demonstrate to your students the proper use of study-skill strategies.
5. Provide opportunities for continued practice and guided instruction in the use of study-skill strategies.

Students at any grade level and especially students with disabilities require direct teacher guidance in study-skill areas. In addition to the general guidelines just presented, teachers may find more specific instructional strategies useful in implementing a study-skills program.

Reading Rates

1. Ensure that proper reading rates are used for different reading activities.
2. Establish clear purposes for each reading assignment.
3. Ensure that each student is familiar with each type of reading rate.
4. Provide opportunities for the appropriate use of each reading rate.

Listening Skills

1. Minimize distractions and deal quickly with classroom disruptions (Conaway, 1982).

2. Encourage each student to speak loudly enough so that all can hear.
3. Repeat and emphasize important items in the verbal message (Wallace & Kauffman, 1986).
4. Begin each lecture at a point that is familiar to all students, and gradually bridge to new material (Conaway, 1982).
5. Summarize the verbal message at strategic points in the lecture.
6. Support oral presentations with visual material (Conaway, 1982).

Note Taking / Outlining

1. Encourage students to follow a consistent note-taking/outlining format.
2. Teach students to identify and focus on key topics and ideas.
3. Discuss with students the uses and advantages of making outlines and taking notes.
4. Model different note-taking/outlining formats for students.
5. Begin with simple note-taking/outlining activities, and gradually introduce more complex types of activities.

Report Writing

1. Clarify the purpose for each writing assignment, and assist students in organizing their ideas.
2. Begin writing activities with simple, less complex written assignments, and gradually introduce more difficult types of written reports.
3. Insist that students use a dictionary and other reference materials when necessary and that they proofread their written work.
4. Work with students as they complete different stages of writing assignments.
5. Provide periodic review and encouragement to students as they complete written reports.

Oral Presentations

1. Allow sufficient time for students to prepare for oral presentations (Devine, 1987).
2. Conduct oral presentations in a non-threatening environment to minimize peer criticism (Wallace & Kauffman, 1986).
3. Provide different situations for oral presentations (e.g., with students seated in or standing by their desks, standing in front of a small group, addressing the whole class) (Devine, 1987).
4. Ensure that students know and understand the purposes for oral presentations (Devine, 1987).

Use of Graphic Aids

1. Allow students to use graphic aids in conjunction with or as alternatives to oral and written reports.
2. Ensure that students know why specific material is presented in graphic form (Wallace & Kauffman, 1986).
3. Incorporate visual material into oral presentations.
4. Assist students in focusing on important aspects of graphic aids.
5. Provide sufficient time for students to read and interpret graphic aids presented during lectures.

Test Taking

1. Discuss with students the purposes of tests, and show them how to complete different types of tests (Devine, 1987).
2. Explain the different methods of study necessary to prepare for objective and essay tests (Rubin, 1983).
3. Review test-taking errors with students (Wallace & Kauffman, 1986).
4. Ensure that students know the time allotted for completion of each test (Mercer & Mercer, 1985).
5. Explore test-making procedures with students to ensure that they are familiar with different types of test questions (Devine, 1987).

Library Usage

1. Review the uses and importance of a library, and familiarize students with the organizational layout of a library.
2. Structure assignments so that students must use a library to complete them.
3. Be sure that students know the purpose of using the library in any library activity.
4. Teach students to consult media specialists and other library personnel as necessary.

Reference Material Usage

1. Ensure that dictionaries are readily available to all students.
2. Structure various assignments to require students to use reference materials.
3. Be sure that each student possesses sufficient skills to successfully use general reference and dictionary materials when these are required.
4. Create situations that help students understand the uses of reference materials.
5. Familiarize students with the different components of general reference materials and dictionaries prior to requiring their use in assignments.

Time Management

1. Reward effective use of time (Alley & Deshler, 1979).
2. Structure classroom activities so that students are required to budget their own time periodically.
3. Praise on-task behaviors, especially during independent work times.
4. Ensure that students know the allotted amount of time for completion of each activity.
5. Provide sufficient time and opportunity for students to manage their own time and to complete assigned tasks.

Self-Management of Behavior

1. Be sure that students know specific behavioral expectations.
2. Establish student self-management programs and monitor associated progress.
3. Assist students in setting realistic and attainable goals in a self-management program.
4. Be consistent in enforcing behavioral expectations of students.
5. Allow sufficient time for a self-management program to be implemented before the effects of the program are tested.

RESOURCES

Algier, A. S., & Algier, K. W. (Eds.). (1982). *Improving reading and study skills.* San Francisco: Jossey-Bass. This book consists of 10 chapters that deal with methods of enhancing student learning. Research results, along with specific ideas for study-skill development, are presented.

Devine, T. G. (1987). *Teaching study skills: A guide for teachers* (2nd ed.). Boston: Allyn & Bacon. This book provides comprehensive coverage of specific study methods to help students succeed in school. Numerous study skills are presented, along with hundreds of activities and strategies to facilitate study-skill development and usage.

Hoover, J. J. (1988) *Teaching handicapped students study skills* (2nd ed.). Lindale, TX: Hamilton Publications. This book represents one of the first books addressing study-skills education for students with handicaps. Eleven major study-skill areas, 21 study-skills assessment devices, 17 study strategies, and more than 140 teaching activities and suggestions are discussed.

Wallace, G., & Kauffman, J. M. (1986). *Teaching students with learning and behavior problems* (3rd ed.). Columbus, OH: Merrill. Chapter 12 of this text covers the topic of study skills. Several study-skill strategies, numerous teaching activities, and commercial materials for teaching study skills are presented.

15
Personal and
Social Skills

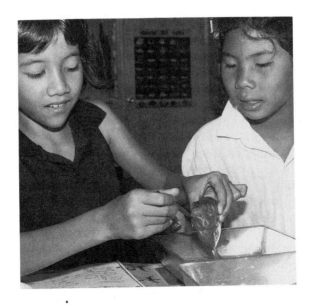

Personal and social skills are of crucial importance to all who have special needs. The resolution of adjustment problems affects academic skill development and remains a preeminent concern throughout the life span of all persons who are handicapped. Unfortunately, instructional attention has historically been limited by the predominant emphasis on remediation of basic skill deficits. Bartlett (1979) attributes this trend to the growth in the area of learning disabilities and the concomitant focus on academic skills. He cautions that "the mentally retarded child has academic needs . . . but because of the wide sector of society with which he must come in contact, education for him becomes more than academics" (p. 3). Similar perceptions from the fields of learning disabilities and behavior disorders have spawned curricular development in social areas to complement academic instruction (e.g., McGinnis, Goldstein, Sprafkin, & Gershaw, 1984; Zigmond & Brownlee, 1980).

Social adjustment concerns should receive major curricular attention for virtually all students who are mentally retarded or emotionally disturbed and for many individuals with learning disabilities. This emphasis should blend with attention to other critical domains of learning—especially academic and career and life skills—and should emphasize how each can contribute to the others in producing effective, affective, and relevant educational programs.

Teachers can assume that exceptional students experience a variety of adjustment problems and may display varied inappropriate and/or unacceptable behaviors that interfere with their total development. The literature is replete with attention to the presence of such problems in students who are mildly or moderately handicapped (e.g., Balthazar & Stevens, 1975; Beier, 1964; Cullinan & Epstein, 1984; Epstein, Bursuck, & Cullinan, 1985; Matson, Epstein, & Cullinan, 1984; Polloway, Epstein, & Cullinan,

1985; Reiss, Levitan, & McNally, 1982). Instructional efforts must respond to these students' educational needs. Personal/social variables are major determinants of success in special education settings and in integrated environments in both school and postschool settings. Polloway and Patton (1986) highlight the importance of social integration.

> As professionals there may be nothing that we can agree on more than the need for successful integration into society of those persons we purport to represent. It is the one goal that we can all champion, the one vision, though nebulous, to which we can all commit. . . .
>
> If we can agree that social integration in its broad connotations is in fact central to virtually all that professionally concerns us, then we can shift our attention from goal to process. While the former seems universally lauded, the latter begins to produce schisms in [the field]. . . . Yet we must tackle process first else the goal becomes simply a platitudinous gesture. (p. 1)

Students with handicaps need to acquire specific social skills and grow affectively. Although skills development lends itself to instructional methodologies comparable to those in other curricular areas, affective development requires a focus on feelings, values, and attitudes as well as techniques that promote change in this area (e.g., simulations, role-playing, and interactive games).

This chapter discusses key facets within the development of personal and social skills. Attention to assessment and instructional approaches that are appropriate for common problem areas is followed by an overview of counseling approaches relevant to learners with special needs. The chapter concludes with a discussion of sex education, an integral aspect of personal and social development that makes special demands on the teacher.

ASSESSMENT

Despite the broad, subjective nature of the personal/social domain, a variety of tools can assist in bringing a reasonable degree of clarity to the process of assessing student characteristics. The available methods of evaluation can be divided into four groups: adaptive behavior scales, self-report techniques, sociometric techniques, and direct observation strategies. One or more of these methods may be appropriate in particular problem areas. For example, Gresham (1983) points to the use of naturalistic observations and sociometric ratings along with teacher evaluations in making decisions concerning the possible mainstreaming of students with handicaps.

Adaptive Behavior Scales

In response to the increasing orientation toward social competence found in the American Association on Mental Retardation's (AAMR) definition of mental retardation (Grossman, 1973, 1977, 1983; Heber, 1959, 1961), developmental work on adaptive behavior scales has increased dramatically in the past 25 years. A number of alternatives are currently available.

Before the mid-1960s the most commonly used scale was the Vineland Social Maturity Scale (Doll, 1953). Unfortunately, because of its standardization on nonhandicapped persons, its lack of attention to maladaptation, and its questionable value in program planning, the Vineland had limited diagnostic value to educators. However, the recently revised Vineland (Sparrow, Balla, & Cicchetti, 1984), retitled the *Vineland Adaptive Behavior Scales,* has resulted in several distinct changes. Key problems with the standardization sample have been rectified, an optional maladaptive scale has been added, and three versions of the scale have

been developed, including a classroom scale typically filled in by the teacher.

In addition to the Vineland scales, several other alternatives are available; the most commonly used are discussed here. In addition, Table 15.1 provides a summary of a number of the scales derived from the *Index to Adaptive Behavior Scales* (North Carolina Department of Public Instruction, n.d.), which provides an excellent review of the various instruments available.

To fill the void that existed when adaptive behavior was included in the definition of mental retardation, the American Association on Mental Retardation (Nihira, Foster, Shellhaas, & Leland, 1969, 1974) published its own scales. By providing for easy administration, including a maladaptive section, and relating to program planning, the AAMR Adaptive Behavior Scales made a significant contribution to the assessment of personal and social adjustment. However, because the scales were normed on an institutional population, their applicability to public school students was limited. A public school version of the scales (Lambert, Windmiller, Cole, & Figueroa, 1974) was developed, and their value to educators was increased by including normative data on students with mild and moderate retardation, students identified as educationally handicapped (LD/ED), and nonhandicapped students. The AAMR scales consist of adaptive and maladaptive sections covering a variety of domains, which are listed in Table 15.2.

Even though the school edition of the AAMR scales (Lambert, Windmiller, Tharinger, & Cole, 1981) has further improved the tool's suitability for school usage, it remains a modification of the original scales rather than an instrument geared primarily to those variables that are central to individuals in school and the community. Despite the tool's apparent advantages in administration and interpretation, it is limited in its

TABLE 15.1
Adaptive behavior scales

Scale	Behavioral Focus		Population				Purpose		Age Levels
	In School	Out of School	EMR	TMR	S/PH	LD	Eligibility	Programming	
AAMR-ABS:									
1974 edition	X	X		X	X			X	3 to 69
School edition (rev.)		X	X	X		X	X	X	3 to 16
Vineland Social Maturity Scale		X	X	X	X		X		0 to 30
Vineland Adaptive Behavior Scales	X	X	X	X	X	X	X	X	0 to 30
Children's Adaptive Behavior Scale		X	X				X		5 to 10.11
Adaptive Behavior Inventory for Children		X	X	X			X		5 to 11
Weller-Strawser Scale	X					X		X	6 to 18
Balthazar Scales	X	X			X			X	NA
Cain-Levine Social Competency Scale	X	X		X	X			X	5 to 13
Fairview Self-Help		X		X	X			X	0 to 12 (developmental)
Camelot Behavioral Checklist	X	X	X	X	X		X	X	NA

Source. From *Index of Adaptive Behavior Scales* (p. 2), n.d., Raleigh, NC: North Carolina Department of Public Instruction. Adapted by permission.

Code: EMR = educable mental retardation; TMR = trainable mental retardation; S/PH = severe/profound handicap; LD = learning disability.

TABLE 15.2
Domains of the AAMR adaptive behavior scales

Part One	Part Two
Independent functioning	Violent and destructive behavior
Physical development	Antisocial behavior
Economic activity	Rebellious behavior
Language development	Untrustworthy behavior
Numbers and time	Withdrawal
Domestic activity	Stereotyped behavior and odd mannerisms
Vocational activity	Inappropriate interpersonal manners
Self-direction	Unacceptable vocal habits
Responsibility	Unacceptable or eccentric habits
Socialization	Self-abusive behavior
	Hyperactive tendencies
	Sexually aberrant behavior
	Psychological disturbances
	Use of medications

usefulness for eligibility judgments and program planning for students who are mildly and moderately handicapped.

Questions concerning the applicability of existent scales to students with mild and moderate handicaps have led to the publication of a number of other instruments. The Adaptive Behavior Inventory for Children (ABIC) (Mercer & Lewis, 1977), developed as a form of the System of Multi-cultural Pluralistic Assessment (SOMPA), focuses on the concept of adaptive behavior in community settings and attempts to provide a measure of how well a student adapts to social roles in the home and community. The inventory's primary use is in determining eligibility for services; it does not offer significant benefits for program planning and must be considered within the limited out-of-school context of adaptive behavior (see Polloway & Smith, 1983, and Reschly, 1982, for further discussion of this issue).

Another recent addition to the options for adaptive behavior assessment is the Children's Adaptive Behavior Scale (Richmond & Kicklighter, 1980), which, like the ABIC, is useful with students who are mildly handicapped. This instrument can afford the user a relatively quick method of measuring de-

velopment, which can be helpful in determining placement and establishing tentative instructional objectives. Another tool, the Weller-Strawser Scales of Adaptive Behavior (Weller & Strawser, 1981), was developed primarily for use with students who are learning disabled, to complement assessment focused on academic performance.

Several other scales are available for use with individuals with severe handicaps. The Balthazar scales (Balthazar, 1971, 1973) contain excellent sections on adaptive and maladaptive social behaviors, facilitating the utilization assessment of results in training programs. The Cain-Levine Social Competency Scale (Cain, Levine, & Elzey, 1963) includes subscales on self-help, imitativeness, social skills, and communication. The scale was developed for and standardized on students in classes for the trainable mentally retarded. Both the Balthazar and Cain-Levine scales have sections applicable to populations other than those represented by the norm group. The major strength of these instruments lies in their detailed behavioral analysis, which can lead to specific instructional programs and can assist in the evaluation of intervention efforts. Based on assessment information, teachers can analyze and measure specific components of a behavior and plan and implement strategies to modify it.

Self-Report Techniques

Self-report techniques allow students to evaluate their own personal and social behaviors. Because the information comes directly from students, its validity depends on their ability to understand and perform the task involved as well as their willingness to report the information requested. Lister (1969) notes three ways to interpret self-report data. First, one can assume the information is objectively accurate—an assumption demanding caution. Second, the reported data can be analyzed for what it can predict about behavior. Third, the report can be viewed inferentially, with the teacher attempting to form impressions based on the information volunteered. In all three cases the teacher is entering the realm of subjectivity to make use of this self-reported information and is encouraged to consult a counselor or psychologist.

Several sources provide formats for self-report techniques. Formal tests, such as the SRA Junior Inventory (Remmers & Shimberg, 1957) and the California Test of Personality (Thorpe, Clark, & Tiegs, 1953), attempt to measure personality characteristics or identify adjustment problems. The Bower-Lambert screening scales (Bower & Lambert, 1962) contain three self-report vehicles for students at various chronological levels. For students in kindergarten through Grade 3 the Picture Game presents simple illustrations with a series of statements that students must relate to their own interests; for Grades 7 to 12 the Student Survey asks students to select statements most or least like them. The Piers-Harris Self-Concept Scale (Piers & Harris, 1969) can be used in Grades 3 through 12 and consists of a series of statements (e.g., "I am lucky") to which

students must respond with a yes or no, identifying whether they think the statement accurately describes them.

Several self-report formats can be adapted for use in an informal fashion. Autobiographies give students a chance to tell about their lives, thus revealing self-concepts and related concerns. For students with difficulty in expressive writing, recorded oral presentations can be incorporated. Interviews can be used to obtain specific information from students or to permit them to express their feelings and opinions. This approach requires significant interpersonal skills, sensitivity, and judgment to obtain a true picture of how students feel about themselves and others (Kauffman, 1985). Questionnaires and checklists are easy to administer and can give teachers insight into how students view themselves and others.

Self-report data should be viewed as a complement to other forms of assessment. Such data can be particularly useful in identifying less apparent problems and/or concerns in order to select intervention targets. For example, a student may indicate a personal concern about an inability to deal with stressful situations. With more complete information the teacher may then artificially produce stressful situations that provide opportunities to monitor existing behavior. The student might participate in competitive games, problem-solving activities, or simulated situations; feedback might come via video- or audiotape or peer appraisal.

Sociometric Techniques

Sociometric techniques enable teachers to assess how classmates view other students. The information obtained can be helpful in identifying specific interpersonal relationships, ascertaining student's status within the classroom, and creating a sociological map of the structure of groups (Brown,

1987). The classic research of Johnson (1950) illustrates how sociometrics can determine whether students are stars, isolates, or outcasts within the classroom.

Sociometric tools promote an ecological assessment of individual students. As Wallace and Larsen (1978) state, "The professional who conducts an ecological assessment attempts to view the child and his or her own environment . . . in its totality rather than as discrete and separately functioning entities" (p. 98). Wallace and Larsen's text contains a full discussion of the rationale of ecological assessment and the role that sociometrics can play within the overall scheme.

Two common approaches are used in sociometric evaluation: the sociometric test and the opinion test or peer nomination (Lister, 1969). The former elicits students' preferences for work and play partners; the latter can determine which pupils fit various behavioral descriptions, such as quiet, funny, popular, and leading the way.

Sociometric data can be used to construct a classroom sociogram. Construction can be based on test questions such as, Who would you most like to work with? or Who would you most like to sit with? A simple sociogram is presented in Table 15.3.

Assessment may reveal that a student is socially rejected by classmates. Further assessment may indicate specific causes for the rejection. Based on such an assessment, the teacher must then determine whether to approach the problem by attempting to change the rejectee's behavior or the peers' attitudes. The former might be accomplished by manipulating antecedent and subsequent events, whereas counseling and discussion might be effective in modifying the latter.

Sociometric techniques have been prone to criticism from educators who see them as visible illustrations of student popularity. However, emphasizing positive rather than negative responses and minimizing the discussion of test procedures and results should help alleviate some of these concerns.

Direct Observation

Observational approaches range from a teacher's general awareness of interactions within the classroom to specific daily behavioral measurement during a particular activity or over a specified time. The latter is often referred to as target behavior assessment. One obvious advantage of direct observation is that the behaviors to be assessed need not be preselected (Coleman, 1986).

Target behavior assessment can be viewed as a two-step procedure. First, the teacher must determine which of a student's behaviors appears to be causing problems. Selection might consider a behavior's effect on (1) the teacher, (2) the student's aca-

TABLE 15.3
A sample sociogram

Selector	Peers Chosen					
	Tom	JoAnn	Virginia	Richard	Greg	Betty
Tom		X			X	
JoAnn	X					X
Virginia					X	X
Richard					X	X
Greg			X			X
Betty		X			X	

demic performance, (3) peers' ability to work or interact in the classroom, and (4) peers' opinions toward the student. In addition, the behavior's importance as a skill for personal and social adjustment must be considered.

The second step is to measure the behavior. A variety of direct observational tools are available, depending on the specific type of behavior to be assessed and the availability of support personnel. Event or frequency recording tallies discrete occurrences of a given behavior during a given period. Duration recording summarizes the total amount of time during which the student is engaged in the specific behavior. Interval recording measures whether a student exhibits the target behavior at specified intervals. Planned Activity Check (PLA-Check) (Doke & Risley, 1972) is a measure of group behavior based on the number of children participating in a group activity divided by the number physically present in the area.

Because event recording is a relatively simple tool, it is chosen when the behavior in question can be meaningfully measured as a frequency. Examples include talking out of turn, swearing, raising one's hand in class, and responding to questions. For behaviors such as self-stimulation (e.g., finger twirling) and being out of one's seat or on/off task, frequency figures are misleading. In these cases duration measures are appropriate for teachers to use on their own, perhaps with a stop watch, and interval recording is appropriate when an aide or volunteer is available to collect the data.

Observational information can be used to compare students' behavior with that of their peers but more importantly to evaluate change in behavior after an intervention strategy has been implemented. In target behavior assessment teachers pinpoint the behaviors that need to be increased, decreased, maintained, or eliminated. Among the many articles and books written on tar-

get behavior assessment and applied behavior analysis, three excellent resources are Cooper (1981), Alberto and Troutman (1986), and Cooper, Heron, and Heward (1987).

Assessment in Perspective

The assessment approaches discussed here should provide information that is useful in developing instructional programs for students with personal/social deficits. However, confidence in personal/social assessment information is linked to one's perception of the primary focus of intervention in this domain. The traditional debate in special education between humanists and behaviorists has emphasized the rigid characterizations of the former as child-centered, feeling-oriented, somewhat unstructured, perhaps permissive and the latter as rigidly adhering to a mechanistic system of environmental events and consequences. This dichotomy has clouded the focus on what works best for a given teacher with a given student at a given point in time. Fortunately, as Morse (1974) notes, "Practice has always been more eclectic than theory" (p. 205).

Nevertheless, if teachers are change agents (Worell & Nelson, 1974), it is crucial to determine that change has indeed taken place. From an affective or more humanistic perspective, the goal of change in self-concept and attitude (e.g., toward school, peers, adults) is a primary concern and, when improved, should be reflected in behavioral change. From a behavioral perspective an increase or decrease in overt actions is generally the goal, with the underlying assumption that such change will yield an improved self-concept. Regardless of primary theoretical or practical focus, for evaluation and accountability the use of direct observational tools is essential to demonstrate that the changes deemed most important within the intervention program have occurred.

INSTRUCTION

This section presents suggestions for dealing with specific problems within six areas of the personal/social domain: self-concept, independent functioning, interpersonal relationships, disruptive classroom behaviors, attitudes toward school and relationships with adults, and stress management. These subsections are not intended as all-inclusive discussions of the areas but should be viewed as complementary to the previous discussions on teaching and learning, classroom management and organization, behavior management, and curriculum. The personal and social skills and/or problems exhibited by students are frequently a reflection of the structure and climate of the learning situation established by the teacher. Obviously, many students may not exhibit these specific adjustment problems. However, some will, and teachers would do well to become familiar with the activities listed with each of the problem areas.

Self-Concept

The development of a positive self-image in each student is a subjective goal of all teachers. Because of past failures, however, especially in academic domains, exceptional learners often have very poor self-concepts. Special education services, by their very nature, produce essentially negative labels that segregate students from a normalized environment, encouraging them to question their status. Relative to this concern, the efficacy studies conducted in the 1950s, 1960s, and 1970s attempted to determine the effects of special class placement on the self-concept of students with mild retardation, but mixed findings were reported (e.g., Meyerowitz, 1962; Welch, 1966). Likewise, the effects of programs for other students identified as mildly handicapped have never been clearly determined. Regardless of the program in which students are enrolled, the classroom environment must be reinforcing to promote the development of healthy self-concepts.

Several behaviors may indicate poor self-concept or distorted self-image. The most easily observed are stereotyped behaviors that entail constant repetition, such as pencil twirling, hair twirling, and other self-stimulatory activities. Withdrawn, overly anxious, and immature behaviors do not catch an observer's eye as quickly but limit a student's interaction nevertheless. Closely related to these behavioral clusters is a lack of self-confidence in academic work. Academic failure must be considered a key causal agent in the poor self-concepts of many learners with special needs.

Despite these behavioral inadequacies, this area should not be viewed as appropriate only for remediation of deficits. There is a need to address developmental concerns with all children. Young children need to develop a sense of self-importance, which can be fostered by active involvement in various classroom activities as well as by successful learning experiences. Older students should be encouraged to balance their failure set with an appreciation of their specific talents and abilities. Ultimately, students should be shown how they can become, in DeCharms's (1976) terms, origins rather than pawns; that is, responsible for events in their lives rather than viewing themselves as aimless, powerless, and subject to others' whims.

The following activities may assist students in increasing their self-awareness, improving their self-concept, and becoming more actively involved in controlling their own life events.

1. Trace around each child's body on butcher paper. Have each child cut out the figure, draw in features and colors,

and hang it up in the room. These pictures can be hung up with pictures of persons the children like and respect.

2. Record the pupils' voices on tape and play them back.

3. Keep individual or class charts showing each child's height, weight, address, and birthday. Schedule morning or weekly activities around these facts.

4. Have students write autobiographies and illustrate them with pictures. Show the students how to emphasize positive aspects with items such as "I like. . . ."

5. To increase body awareness, have students complete puzzles of people with each major body part represented by a puzzle piece. Children can also cut out large pictures and label body parts.

6. Encourage withdrawn students to work in groups or with a partner, especially with more popular, outgoing members of the class. This interaction can come initially in pairs, as in tutoring situations, and can build up to group projects. During recess or physical education periods, this interaction can develop from contact with a partner on a seesaw or with a group of students on a climbing frame or jungle gym (Bijou, 1966) and through team sports. This participation should be reinforced socially with praise and touching.

7. Use stories during oral reading periods that require students to consider their values and decide how they would respond in given situations. The Pal Paperback series (Xerox Press) lends itself especially well to this approach.

8. Discuss different behaviors and their consequences so that students can know what to expect if they perform these behaviors.

9. Have students verbally identify the positive things that have happened to them during the past day (or week). Encourage other students to respond with enthusiastic comments (e.g., "Great!" or "That's neat"). Students should then name one action or behavior that they think they will be able to accomplish during the next day (or week). The class or instructor should again respond with reassuring support. This exercise can be conducted with an individual or a group.

10. When a child initiates a self-stimulatory behavior (e.g., pencil twirling), issue a soft reprimand ("Stop that"). Avoid giving students any positive attention at such a time; catch them *not* doing it at a later time and praise them then (Wallace & Kauffman, 1986). Use this method when a glance, other verbal stimuli, and proximity control have not proven effective.

11. For students who unconsciously engage in stereotyped or immature behaviors (e.g., thumbsucking), develop a mutual signal that you can use to remind the child to stop the behavior. Calling the student's name with a particular voice inflection reserved for these occasions draws minimal attention from the rest of the class.

12. Simulations and role-playing activities can offer a variety of benefits to students. Adolescents often respond to a well-conceived lesson built on real-life situations.

13. Collins and Collins (1975) suggest involving the whole class in self-concept development. Give each student a copy of the class roll, and ask each to write one descriptive, complimentary adjective next to every name. Allow time to discuss complimentary adjectives in the beginning and the results at the end.

14. Use bulletin boards to enhance self-concept by displaying baby pictures and comparing them to recent photos. Get students to write captions for the

pictures. On tagboard print descriptions of students, including their characteristics, interests, and desires (Borba & Borba, 1978).

15. Hoagland (1972) and Cianciolo (1965) advocate bibliotherapy as a means of developing self-concept. Bibliotherapy should involve initial reading, retelling the story, identifying with characters, discussing the consequences of specific behaviors, and considering the desirability of alternative actions.

16. Have students interview the person sitting at the desk beside them, and introduce that person to the class (Wiener, 1981).

17. Have students list several things they love. Then direct them to find appropriate pictures in magazines to develop a collage illustrating these things (Simon & O'Rourke, 1977).

18. Family and friends communicate many emotional messages. List sample messages and discuss their effect: (a) "You have a good head for math, just like your father," (b) "You're as graceful as a bull in a china shop," (c) "You are not as smart as your sister." Brainstorm good messages to send (DeSpelder & Prettyman, 1980).

19. Photographs can be used in many different ways to help enhance self-images. Individual pictures can be taken at the beginning of the year to display with student work. Students can be encouraged to prepare for these "portraits" by wearing favorite outfits or carrying a favorite toy. Scrapbooks can be kept of class events and activities. Double prints should be made so that children have pictures to take home also.

20. Computers can have social-emotional as well as academic benefits. High-interest programs can be individually geared to ensure success. Students who master computer usage acquire a skill valued by teachers and peers. They receive praise for their accomplishments and consequently begin to view themselves more positively.

21. Students with learning disabilities need to have an understanding of that concept. In particular, they need to know what LD refers to (e.g., it is not short for learning dummies or other negative referents) (Gerber, 1986).

Independent Functioning

This term is used to refer to personal skills that may be viewed as extensions of the basic self-care concerns associated with students who are quite young and/or more seriously handicapped. The vast majority of children with mild and moderate handicaps come to school with at least marginal toilet, dressing, and eating skills (see Snell, 1987; Wehman & McLaughlin, 1981; Wehman, Renzaglia, & Bates, 1985, for further information on self-care instruction). However, a number of other key skills related to independent functioning are among the educational goals of special education programs for many students. Balla and Zigler (1979) underscore the importance of this area for individuals who are retarded: "The shift from dependence to independence is the single most important factor that would enable retarded persons to become self-sustaining members of society" (pp. 145–146).

Among the topics included under this heading, cleanliness and grooming are often noted as deficit areas. Development of skills in this area may be an important determinant of the ability to obtain and hold employment and thus may be crucial to postschool adjustment. Teaching personal hygiene, however, may be complicated by the fact that some students come from homes without facilities that promote cleanliness, such as indoor plumbing. Teachers must learn about the significant variables that may interfere with cleanliness and/or good personal appearance; they must be sensitive to specific situations and may wish to consult a visiting teacher, social worker, or counselor for help. Nonetheless, the teacher's responsibility includes teaching basic hygiene skills and differentiation between appropriate and inappropriate appearance. The teaching approach must be selected on the basis of what the problem is and why it exists. In some cases group instruction is appropriate, whereas in others a problem should be handled individually, with tact and delicacy.

Responsibility, self-direction, and initiative also fall within the area of personal skills and are crucial to the ability to function independently in society. Because teaching an understanding of responsibility, self-direction, and initiative requires interaction among students, teachers must be prepared to guide, monitor, and encourage attention to these important abstract concepts. For instance, students must learn not only what initiative means but also how it is expressed, as in reporting to work a little before starting time, doing a little bit extra for someone else, volunteering when asked, "Would you mind. . . ?" In addition, because students with various learning problems have frequently been viewed as having an external locus of control (e.g., Achenbach & Zigler, 1968; Grimes, 1981; Pearl, Bryan, & Donahue, 1980; Turnure & Zigler, 1964), a major task for teachers is to promote greater self-reliance among students.

1. Establish a daily routine for putting toys and learning tools and utensils away.
2. Develop instructional units, as discussed in chapter 4, on the importance of appropriate dress.
3. Promote personal concern for health and appearance by having guests from the community come in to speak to the class. Speakers might include doctors, dentists, nurses, barbers, hairdressers, and cosmetologists.
4. Have each student construct a grooming card for attention to concerns in this area (Brolin & Kokaska, 1979).
5. To develop initiative, allow adolescents choices in activities, as in arts and crafts and prevocational and vocational projects. Suggest options and reinforce those who choose a project and follow it through to completion.
6. Assign daily tasks that children are responsible for remembering to complete during a particular time. If necessary and appropriate, build in rewards for children as they gradually develop independence in these skills.
7. Make specific academic assignments that a student can definitely do independently. Praise the child for completion as well as for the ability to do the task without assistance.
8. Train students to care for specific pieces of audiovisual equipment. Praise prompt and proper set up and use of equipment. The goal should be to have students competent enough that the teacher need only request that the equipment be set up.
9. Help students develop goal-setting behavior. Tell them that they spend 5 or 6 hours a day in the classroom and ask what they want to accomplish in that time that is particularly important to them. Students can compile lists of individual or group goals. Subsequent planning for the achievement of those goals is important (Epstein, 1979).
10. Students often limit their alternatives in a given situation. Ask them to choose the best alternative for each of the following: (a) ways to say no to friends who want you to do something that may get you into trouble, (b) ways to make

money, (c) ways to prevent pregnancy, (d) ways to end a relationship, and (e) ways to handle rejection (DeSpelder & Prettyman, 1980).

11. Talk about the importance of doing things for or giving to others for personal, emotional, and mental health. List volunteer services in which students can become involved. Have them develop a volunteer service for other students in the school.

12. Plot the location of various recreational facilities on a local map. Visit some of them. Talk about the importance of recreation and productive use of leisure time for mental health.

Interpersonal Relationships

The ability to socialize and get along with peers is also an important skill for persons who are handicapped to develop. Goals must include increasing appropriate interpersonal contacts and decreasing antisocial behaviors. The data on peer relationships indicate that special class settings may be associated with higher levels of peer acceptance (Goodman, Gottlieb, & Harrison, 1972; Gottlieb & Budoff, 1973; Johnson, 1950). Factors behind a lack of acceptance in regular classes range from antisocial behavior (Baldwin, 1958) to academic incompetence (Gottlieb, 1974). It may be that students with special needs have been unprepared or poorly prepared for integration. The current proliferation of research and curricular development in this area underscores this concern (e.g., *Exceptional Education Quarterly*, 1981; Goldstein, Sprafkin, Gershaw, & Klein, 1980; Gresham, 1982).

Gresham (1982) identifies three faulty assumptions of the practice of mainstreaming: (1) regular class placement alone will result in increased social interaction among children with handicaps and their nonhandicapped peers, (2) such placement will in-

crease social acceptance, and (3) students with handicaps will model their regular class peers simply with exposure. Gresham contends that without social skills training students with disabilities are not likely to succeed in the regular classroom. He concludes, "If the child's level of social skill does not suggest that he or she would function successfully in a mainstreamed setting, then he or she should be placed in a more structured setting until the required social skill level has been obtained" (p. 430).

Common difficulties found in this area include failure to cooperate, lack of consideration for others, and overly aggressive or violent behavior, all of which can hinder the ability to develop healthy peer relationships. Lack of cooperation or consideration may indicate a need to learn some appropriate social skills for interaction. Aggressiveness is one of the most salient adjustment problems of students, regardless of sex, age, or classification (Epstein, Cullinan, & Polloway, 1986), and requires modification of current behavior.

A variety of activities can enhance interpersonal relationships.

1. Noncompetitive games, including noncompetitive versions of competitive games, can be used to help foster cooperation among children. Nonelimination musical chairs, for example, might encourage children to sit together to keep everyone in the game.

2. Use the technique of sociodrama to probe interpersonal relationships. The five aspects are to identify a relevant social problem; explore the problem to determine circumstances and people involved; dramatize the encounter with role-playing; evaluate the sociodrama, considering alternative solutions to the problem; and search for the hidden motivation behind what is being communicated (Kolstoe, 1976).

3. Start a to-be-a-friend folder at the beginning of the school year requiring students to identify characteristics they want in a friend and qualities they have to offer as a friend to someone else. At regular intervals students review, change, or add to the two lists, including a written or verbal discussion of each change. The folder provides a long-term account of students' sensitivity to their own needs and corresponding attempts to establish peer friendships.

4. Organize daily class meetings. Give students an opportunity to evaluate the performance of each of their peers. This technique is particularly appropriate for adolescents.

5. Encourage students to undertake group projects to develop cooperative skills. Especially good are problem-solving activities that require children to think together to reach a solution. These activities can tap performance skills through puzzles and verbal skills through something like the moon game, which gives students a list of equipment and survival items and has them rank-order their importance for someone stranded on the moon.

6. Choose physical education activities that require cooperation and teamwork. Chapter 18 lists many such activities.

7. Knowledge and assumptions about peers can determine how individuals relate to them. Therefore, attention should be given to the accuracy of the knowledge and assumptions. Assumptions are hazardous because they can originate in the subjective; knowledge is safer because it is objective. Help students understand the effect of these two factors on peer relationships by listing and discussing the inadequacy of assumptions.

8. Prejudice can be an upsetting problem. To help students get along with their peers, use bulletin boards, films, displays, field trips, guest speakers, or taped interviews with ethnic community members (Collins & Collins, 1975) to emphasize the positive contributions of particular ethnic groups.

9. Have students list the things they like in other people (e.g., for people in general, of the same sex, or of the opposite sex). Discuss how these things affect what one looks for in a companion or date.

10. Students can create masks with distinct expressions, such as angry or happy. When a student displays a mask, have the other students tell what they think the mask looks like and then try to make faces similar to the mask. Have students think of events that would cause a person to make a particular face.

11. Have students draw pictures of their best friend and then look through magazines for pictures of things they do together. Collages can be created.

Disruptive Classroom Behaviors

Because of their effects on instruction, disturbing behaviors often become the primary concern of teachers seeking to remediate adjustment problems. Control of conduct disorders is a prerequisite for successful academic instruction. In most cases appropriate arrangement of antecedents and manipulation of consequences (as discussed in chapter 5) are the key. Worell and Nelson (1974, pp. 50–51) list the following objective and subjective criteria for deciding whether to intervene:

1. Is the behavior interfering with the freedom or personal comfort of another individual (e.g., tantrums, yelling)?

2. Is the behavior harming other people or property (e.g., kicking, tearing books)?

3. Does the behavior interfere with academic progress (e.g., out of seat, persistent talking)?

4. Does the child's behavior negatively affect the classroom teacher (e.g., time wasted, personal discomfort)?

5. Does the behavior negatively influence peer acceptance?

Most frequently disturbing to teachers and disruptive to the classroom are excessive talking out and out-of-seat behaviors. A wide variety of positive and negative consequences can be used to modify these behaviors (see chapter 5 for behavior management principles). Distractibility and hyperactivity are two other behaviors that teachers may need to confront. Behaviors falling within these general clusters are commonly found among students who are handicapped.

Stealing, lying, and cheating are a triad of behaviors often linked because they are similar and are frequently committed by the same individual. Similar techniques are used to control these and the other disturbing behaviors in this area.

The following activities suggest ways to deal effectively with specific disruptive and disturbing classroom behaviors.

1. Establish a class government with the power to hear charges of rule infractions and then assess penalties according to a preordained fine system.

2. To control stealing, institute overcorrection procedures (Azrin & Wesolowski, 1974). Any student who commits a theft must return the stolen item(s) to the victim plus additional items of equal value.

3. To help hyperactive students learn to decrease their motor activity, use a stopwatch to time how long they can remain perfectly still. Build in reinforcement for gradually increasing amounts

of time (e.g., 5, 10, . . . 30 seconds) (Madsen & Madsen, 1983).

4. Position a red light in front of the class. Whenever talk-outs become too frequent or loud, turn it on as a signal to stop (Lobitz, 1974). If the stimulus cue alone fails to control the behavior, count the number of times it is used to determine the resulting consequences of the behavior.

5. Play the good behavior game. Put children on teams and count each inappropriate behavior against the team. Total tallies can determine which privileges are gained/lost by the team (Barrish, Saunders, & Wolf, 1969).

6. To minimize cheating, avoid giving too-difficult assignments. All independent work should be maintenance rather than acquisition activities.

7. To teach students that there are times to talk and not to talk, post signs in front of the room that announce TALKING or NO TALKING. Another approach is to have a traffic light (electric or cardboard) in front of the class with green indicating that talking is allowed; red, no talking; and amber, prepare to stop talking.

8. Design the classroom to include talking and no-talking areas.

9. Give students a check mark for every morning and afternoon that they refrain from fighting. Let them use the checks to obtain toys, letters of commendation sent to parents, and time spent with the counselor (Kirschner & Levin, 1975).

10. If one child hits another, isolate the aggressor and give minimal attention. Attend only to the needs of the victim (Pinkston, Reese, LeBlanc, & Baer, 1973).

11. If aggression occurs frequently, make special activities contingent on nonhitting or nonaggressive behavior. Madsen

and Madsen (1983) suggest allowing the child 5 minutes to talk with the principal for successfully making it through a period without aggressive acts.

School Attitudes and Relationships with Adults

Do students view school as a pleasurable place? Is it a place to avoid or from which to escape? Do they challenge the teachers' and the principal's authority? Can they adjust to the rules established for the school's smooth operation? A healthy attitude toward school and school personnel promotes students' adjustment and perhaps their academic performance. School should be a stimulating place that provides positive reinforcement.

School absenteeism is a common problem in special education programs and may reflect a wide range of factors, from a weak physical constitution to parents' disinterest in their children's education. Two types of problems appear regularly—truancy and school phobia. Truant adolescents indicate that they have better things to do than to go to school; they must either be coerced to attend or, preferably, convinced that school has something to offer. The school-phobic child is afraid to attend and may need to be desensitized before coming to and participating in school activities.

Students who respond negatively to authority figures and are frequently involved in confrontational situations include those who are quarrelsome, defiant, and assaultive. Bias in selection procedures has traditionally resulted in a preponderance of such students in special classes. A common school response to their behavior has been suspension or expulsion. Interestingly, however, recent research (Vandever, 1983) has found no significant differences in the numbers of suspensions for students with mild retardation and for nonretarded children.

This finding may reflect special educators' reluctance to recommend such a response to behavioral problems or administrators' reluctance to defy recent legal caveats against such practices (Lichtenstein, 1980). Clearly, in-school educational treatment programs must be developed for such students.

A variety of methods can be used with students who react negatively to school and school authority figures.

1. Develop a buddy system for truant students that pairs them with an older student or peer whom they like and who has regular attendance. The buddy, if possible, should go by the home of the truant student each morning to walk to school with the student, or the buddy may call the truant student and plan to meet at school at a certain time to do something enjoyable together.
2. Make special activities or awards contingent on consistent school attendance. These might include certificates of perfect attendance, special class topics, classroom privileges, or extra snacks.
3. Extinguish arguing with the teacher by ignoring all responses of this type and reinforcing desirable verbalizations with praise and attention (Hall et al., 1971).
4. Students may be truant because they do not feel successful in school. It may help to have these students keep a notebook of their daily successes. A few minutes each day can be set aside to discuss with the counselor or teacher some of the successful activities that were completed. New tasks can be added each day, and as the list grows, the student can be encouraged to discuss past happenings and plan for the future.
5. Desensitization of chronic school phobia has been successful with a step-by-step procedure. Over several days and

weeks these steps might include walking to the school without going inside, briefly visiting the school and classroom, then an hour in the room, a half day, and finally a full day (Lazarus, Davison, & Polefka, 1965, in Ross, 1972).

6. For recent, acute cases of school phobia, take immediate action to overcome the problem. Parents should insist that their child go back to school the next day and should then ignore all complaints or discussion of the issue. At the end of the next school day, the child should be positively reinforced for attendance with a special meal or activity (see Kennedy, 1975, or Madsen & Madsen, 1983, for a full report on this approach).

7. To reduce negative reactions to authority figures, respected community members might be invited to assist in school functions, give testimonials about some of the problems and successes they experienced while they attended school, or sponsor children in a type of big brother/big sister program. Respected community members may include retired citizens, ministers, business professionals, civic leaders, local athletes, and so on.

8. To assist students in understanding some of the problems that authority figures themselves face, instructional units might be developed around questions like: Is there a generation gap in my family? What is my role at school? Am I prejudiced? What is my role as a citizen? Specific ideas and materials may be found in *Making Value Judgments* (listed in the resources section).

9. Sharing experiences with converted exconvicts, persons who at one time experienced problems with the law, lawyers, police officers, and so on often leaves children and adolescents with positive, influential impressions.

10. Set up a brainstorming session. Ask students to think of all the things that might occur without rules in the classroom, school, home, neighborhood, community, state, nation, or world.

11. Activities to get feedback on teaching can encourage expression of opinion. House and Lapan (1978) suggest providing a receptacle in which students can place their written comments about what they like or don't like in the class. Anonymity can be advantageous.

12. Set up an arrangement for potentially disruptive or defiant students to voluntarily withdraw, without penalty, to avoid a confrontation. Assistance from a counselor would be an additional benefit (Lichtenstein, 1980).

Stress Management

Life in contemporary society has often been characterized as stressful. Although the effects of stress on adults have received considerable attention (see Kutash & Schlesinger, 1980), the effects on children are less well known. However, stress may be responsible for some childhood disabilities (Elkind, 1983).

Stress can be conceptualized as those factors (e.g., events or demands) that tax a person's abilities to function effectively and can lead to various emotional, psychological, and/or biological reactions. According to Elkind (1983), stress is "the wear and tear on the body that is attributable to living, and all facets of living, both positive and negative, are potentially stressful" (p. 72). The impact of life events/demands depends, to a great extent, on how they are perceived. In other words, certain situations may provoke no stress in some individuals but may be very stressful to others. Airline travel serves as a good example.

It is not practical or possible to list all stressful situations that might have a bearing on school performance. However, some examples are helpful in focusing attention on this area.

- ☐ going to the blackboard
- ☐ participating in a spelling bee
- ☐ having an after-school appointment with the dentist
- ☐ anticipating unsatisfactory grades on report cards
- ☐ being called on during an oral, round-robin reading session
- ☐ breaking off a relationship with a steady partner
- ☐ being sent to the principal's office for disciplinary reasons
- ☐ having to give a class presentation
- ☐ moving to a new classroom or school with unfamiliar peers
- ☐ fearing other students who are bothersome or physically threatening
- ☐ fearing that a quiz will be given, particularly when the student is unprepared.
- ☐ taking college examination tests
- ☐ expecting to be the last one chosen for team activities in physical education class

Students react to stressful situations in a variety of ways—some positive and adaptive, others negative, inappropriate, and sometimes unhealthy. One fact is typically characteristic: a student's way of reacting reflects what has been successful in the past (Schultz & Heuchert, 1983). Adaptive reactions to stressors imply that students are able to recognize the situation and take some action to correct it. In the "going to the blackboard" example, for instance, a student might approach the teacher and explain the apprehension associated with such a demand. Inappropriate reactions, although they may have positive short-term benefits, imply that students lack effective long-term coping techniques. In the previous example the student going to the blackboard might feign sickness or actually become ill. Elkind (1983) provides three im-

portant reasons for an examination of stress in children.

1. It focuses upon the child's difficulty in the context of his or her overall adaptive capacity in relation to the young person's total life situation. . . .
2. It requires not only an assessment of the environmental stressors . . . but also some understanding of how the child perceives the stressful situation or events. . . .
3. It forces us to take account of the social dimension of all learning situations. (pp. 75–77)

Perhaps the best way to assess stress in children is to establish a good relationship with them and then talk with them individually, inquiring about the concerns they have. Stress scales have been designed for use with children (see Schultz & Heuchert, 1983), but teachers should carefully evaluate the reliability, validity, and utility of such instruments. Ultimately, regardless of the technique used, it will be important to obtain information about student needs, feelings, and perceptions relative to family, school, and general life situations.

Students should be shown how to recognize and manage stressful situations. It is never possible to avoid all stressful events in life; however, students can be taught to avoid some unnecessary ones. Some general suggestions and activities are presented here.

1. Allow time for individual and group counseling, and create mechanisms for students to identify and share stressful situations.
2. Provide relaxation training to students.
3. Refer students to other professionals for more in-depth assistance when needed.
4. Create a classroom environment that is supportive, friendly, and optimistic.
5. Accommodate differential reactions to stress-provoking school situations.

6. Teach students how to utilize resources (e.g., other people, time management sheets) to minimize stressful events.

7. Remember that some stressful situations are temporary, but others are likely to continue until some action is taken.

8. Avoid letting teacher stress and maladaptive reactions to it affect students.

9. Role-play socially stressful situations; reenact them to explore possible options.

10. Provide an opportunity at least occasionally for every student to act as the leader of an activity. Be sure that all students understand what is expected of both leaders and followers. Involving students in leadership opportunities can lead to a reduction in anxiety.

11. Older students who are beginning to date often experience stress in communicating with members of the opposite sex. Several strategies may assist in building skills and minimizing stress. Role-play dating situations, such as ordering from a menu at a restaurant, talking about problems in a relationship, introducing a date to one's parents, and meeting someone at a party. Ask students to identify conflicts, alternative responses to a given situation, and the consequences of various actions; then ask them to describe what choice they would make and why (De-Spelder & Prettyman, 1980).

Curricular Units

When a broad-based social skills program is warranted, an effective curriculum must be based on a comprehensive view. Many of the resources listed at the end of the chapter (e.g., *Social Learning Curriculum, Developing Understanding of Self and Others*) attempt to incorporate varied topics into a sequence of instructional lessons. Teachers should orga-

nize instruction around topics relevant to student needs. The following topics represent a sampling of areas that lend themselves well to a unit plan of instruction, as discussed in chapter 4.

- ☐ appreciating self-worth
- ☐ dealing with emotions
- ☐ family roles and responsibilities
- ☐ making friends
- ☐ learning how to get along with others
- ☐ determining what is best for me
- ☐ working together
- ☐ appropriate social behavior
- ☐ responsibilities of being an adolescent

The organizational framework of a representative program within this domain is shown in Table 15.4 which outlines the components of the prosocial skills taught in *Skillstreaming the Elementary School Child* (McGinnis, Goldstein, Sprafkin, & Gershaw, 1984).

COUNSELING[1]

In order for students to make wise decisions concerning the future, they must receive good advice about many personal and career concerns. Often this advice comes from school personnel who have had little or no formal training in the area of counseling. For example, a student may seek advice from a trusted teacher or from the teacher-coach of a team on which the student plays. Hence, it is important for teachers to be acquainted with counseling techniques that may help them to provide sound advice to students for whom professional counseling is not necessary or available.

---

[1]This section is adapted from *Teaching Exceptional Adolescents* by J. E. Smith and J. S. Payne, 1980, Columbus, OH: Merrill, and is used by permission. The authors acknowledge the assistance of Ken West of Lynchburg College in preparing the material for inclusion in this text.

A Definition of Counseling

The concept of counseling can be defined in numerous ways. According to Blocher (1987),

"Counseling" is simply a generic name given to a model of help-giving that involves an expert, professional worker dispensing some kind of specialized assistance face-to-face to a client who seeks that help. In a broad sense,

TABLE 15.4
A program of prosocial skills

Classroom Survival Skills

Listening
Asking for help
Saying thank you
Bringing materials to class
Following instructions
Completing assignments
Contributing to discussions
Offering help to an adult
Asking a question
Ignoring distractions
Making corrections
Deciding on something to do
Setting a goal

Friendship-Making Skills

Introducing yourself
Beginning a conversation
Ending a conversation
Joining in
Playing a game
Asking a favor
Offering help to a classmate
Giving a compliment
Accepting a compliment
Suggesting an activity
Sharing
Apologizing

Skills for Dealing with Feelings

Knowing your feelings
Expressing your feelings
Recognizing another's feelings
Showing understanding of another's
    feelings
Expressing concern for another
Dealing with your anger
Dealing with another's anger
Expressing affection
Dealing with fear
Rewarding yourself

Skill Alternatives to Aggression

Using self-control
Asking permission
Responding to teasing
Avoiding trouble
Staying out of fights
Problem solving
Accepting consequences
Dealing with an accusation
Negotiating

Skills for Dealing with Stress

Dealing with boredom
Deciding what caused a problem
Making a complaint
Answering a complaint
Dealing with losing
Showing sportsmanship
Dealing with being left out
Dealing with embarrassment
Reacting to failure
Accepting no
Saying no
Relaxing
Dealing with group pressure
Dealing with wanting something
    that isn't mine
Making a decision
Being honest

Source. Reprinted by permission from McGinnis, E., & Goldstein, A. P. (1984). *Skillstreaming the Elementary School Child: A Guide for Teaching Prosocial Skills* (pp. 108–109). Champaign, IL: Research Press.

counseling covers much of the assistance given to individuals by ministers, physicians, lawyers, or even financial advisors. . . . [It stresses] rational planning, problem solving, decision making, and stress management in practical situations. It is generally focused on helping "normal" people with problems and concerns arising from everyday life. Often it is seen as preventive rather than remedial, in the sense that it offers help with problems and difficulties before they reach proportions that may trigger complete breakdowns in functioning. (p. 8)

Corsini (1984) posits that all counseling theories have in common the fact that they each represent methods of learning.

All psychotherapies are intended to change people: to make them think differently (cognition), to make them feel differently (affection), and to make them act differently (behavior). Psychotherapy is learning: one may be learning something new or relearning something one has forgotten, it may be learning how to learn, it may be unlearning, and paradoxically, it may even be learning what one already knows. (pp. 4–5)

These definitions bring a number of general thoughts to the fore: (1) a major goal of the counseling process is to help the client become more independent (the counselor assists the client in seeing that the environment can be controlled in many instances); (2) one specific role of the counselor is to help the individual develop and explore alternative means for dealing with problems or conflicts; (3) another role of the counselor is to help the client overcome obstacles that impede progress; (4) the client is helped to overcome these heretofore undefined obstacles through an information-gathering and -sorting process; and (5) as a result of information derived from the counseling process, the client is better able to make decisions that will lead to a resolution of present uncertainties and conflicts. Ultimately, the individual who comes to the counseling environment is responsible for solving personal problems or conflicts. The counselor only facilitates the client's efforts.

Personal Counseling

Learners with special needs experience a number of difficulties, which often become more complex during the secondary school years. Although the required counseling services are often provided by school counselors or school psychologists, teachers often supplement these services, especially in the area of personal and social concerns.

When a student comes to the counseling situation, the counselor must perform certain tasks to help the student progress smoothly and reorganize the behaviors that occasioned the counseling. Cottle and Downie (1970) indicate that in the first meeting of the counselor and the student, the immediate counseling needs of the student should be identified, and the structure within which counseling will take place should be described. The counselor should then move to more specific tasks that will hopefully help to resolve the problem. These specific tasks are listening, examining, specifying alternatives, drawing conclusions, and developing new behaviors. This approach does not center on specific forms of counseling, such as rational-emotive therapy (Ellis, 1973), behavioral counseling (Krasner & Ullman, 1965; Wilson, 1984), or person-centered counseling (Rogers, 1951, 1980); instead, it is an eclectic approach.

Listening When a student begins to talk to the counselor, the counselor should attempt to gain a complete view of the problem through active listening. Premature advice is to be avoided. The primary goal at this point is to achieve a match between what the client says is the problem and what the counselor hears the client say is the problem.

Examining After the counselor and the student mutually agree on the specifics of the student's problems, the process of examining contributing behaviors and actions should begin. Often the counselor may ask the student exactly which behaviors cause the conflict or prohibit the resolution of the conflict. In some cases an individual cannot avoid conflict; indeed, in certain instances conflict helps to motivate needed action.

Specifying Alternatives Once the student can describe specifically what the problem is and can identify the factors that contribute to the permanence of the conflict, the next step is to jointly devise alternative behaviors or actions that may lead to a solution. At the beginning of the planning stage, it is not imperative that all of the alternatives be realistic or especially good. What is important is the realization that there is at least one method available to resolve the problem. Poppen and Thompson (1974) recommend that after several alternatives have been articulated, the student should write them down to avoid rediscovering known alternatives.

Drawing Conclusions After a list of alternatives has been formulated by the student, the next step is to narrow the list to the most reasonable alternatives. The counselor can often help the student reduce the possibilities by asking questions, such as "What will happen if you do this?" or "How will this action change the present situation?" The counselor should examine the student's answers in order to understand their implications. In some cases the student may draw conclusions that are reasonable but appear less likely to succeed. During this part of the process the counselor must show restraint and not impose personal conclusions.

Developing New Behaviors The last step in the counseling process calls for the stu-

dent to adopt a certain alternative or solution and adhere to it until the problem is resolved or the particular alternative proves inappropriate. The counselor should support the student by using reinforcement and encouragement. Obviously, finding the solution to one problem does not solve other problems. The student and the counselor may have to repeat this sequence of steps to solve other problems that arise.

Counselors use various techniques to facilitate a student's movement through the steps just described.

Role-Playing With this technique the student practices a role. The counselor may ask the student to assume the role of the teacher, parent, or administrator with whom there is a conflict. The counselor then assumes the student's role, and a common situation is acted out. One purpose of this exercise is to have the student understand what the other person feels like in the conflicting situation or to have the student learn to predict some of the actions and reactions of this other person. If the student understands that some of the other person's behavior is predictable, the student may be able to modify certain personal behaviors to lessen the other person's negative behaviors. Role-playing can also provide an opportunity to rehearse appropriate behaviors that challenge previously established irrational behaviors (Rotatori, Sexton, & Fox, 1986). Students can practice new responses that may prove more effective than their old ones.

Behavioral Counting This is another technique frequently used to specify which behaviors are maintaining a conflict. Behavioral counting requires the student (or someone else) to record specific behaviors. For example, a student might believe that talking out in class is causing problems with fellow students and the teacher. The student could relate this belief to the counselor, who could then come to the classroom, observe, and record certain predetermined behaviors of the student.

Negative Behaviors

1. talking out in class without raising a hand or waiting for a turn
2. chewing gum or eating food during a work period
3. arriving late for class

Positive Behaviors

1. raising a hand to signal a desire to talk or waiting for a turn to talk
2. completing class work during a work period
3. arriving on time for class

If a counting procedure is followed for several successive days, it should be possible to specify which negative behaviors are causing the student's problems in the classroom. Instead of using an outside observer/recorder, the student could also self-record behavior by checking a card of punching out holes on a card every time a certain behavior occurs.

Rehearsal This technique involves practicing or rehearsing a selected alternative before putting it into effect. Sports teams go through a similar procedure when preparing a new play or planning to execute a special play, such as the onside kick in football. The purpose of the rehearsal procedure is to familiarize the student with probable reactions once the new strategy is put into effect.

Counseling Strategies for Teachers

Even though many teachers have no formal training in the area of counseling, all teachers can help students with special needs in a number of ways. Teachers can serve as good role models, can actively listen to students' problems, can assist students in identifying

potential solutions to problems, and can accept students' chosen alternatives as long as they violate no standards of conduct. Teachers can also help students develop skills for controlling emotions (Litton, 1986).

The following strategies and activities should prove helpful to teachers in dealing with students' personal and social adjustment problems.

1. Ask students to write a short autobiographical sketch, emphasizing the positive aspects of their lives. This type of activity promotes a healthy self-concept and self-awareness.
2. Make highly desired activities (such as leaving school early or coming late) contingent on students' avoiding a troublesome behavior (Premack, 1959).
3. Make students aware of the clues that others give through facial and gestural expressions. Present pictures showing different emotions and expressions, such as love, pain, anger, or surprise.
4. Use class discussion periods to find out what problems students are having and what they perceive as solutions to those problems.
5. When appropriate, help students understand the meaning of the disability with which they have been labeled. This is particularly important for students with learning disabilities (Gerber, 1986).
6. Some students may not see their behavior as a problem, perhaps because they blame others. Such children may require initial efforts to build more positive self-images and to develop an internal locus of control before they can successfully participate in behavior change strategies (Raiche, Fox, & Rotatori, 1986).

It can be said that teachers are trained to teach and counselors are trained to counsel. However, both share the common goal of seeing that all students continue to acquire and refine educational, social, emotional, and career-related skills. Teachers must continue their primary role as providers of direct instruction while they work with trained counselors to assist students in dealing with significant personal and social problems.

SEX EDUCATION

Attention to sex education is included in this chapter because of its acceptance as an important, often crucial component in the social development of individuals with handicaps. This topic is separated from the rest of the discussion on social adjustment only for organizational convenience; in practice it must be considered an integral part of personal-social development.

Sex education should be viewed as a much broader concept than sex instruction per se. The resource guide developed by the Sex Information and Education Council of the United States (SIECUS) (1971) notes this distinction:

> Sex education begins with concepts and attitudes toward masculinity and femininity that are developed subtly from earliest infancy—and which are affected by every aspect of and activity in one's life. (p. 6)

Sex education is education about human sexuality; that is, it defines sex as something people are rather than something they do (Gendel, 1968).

Developing and implementing a sex education program requires teachers to first examine personal attitudes on the subject to determine whether effective instruction is possible. Attitudes about sex that are conveyed to students are more crucial than the content covered. Edmonson (1980), summarizing the discussion by Kempton and Forman (1976) on this topic, notes a need for stability, flexibility, and resourcefulness in conjunction with honest communication and lack of embarrassment concerning sexual topics and language.

Gendel (1968) lists two unhealthy types of motivation for initiating a sex education program. First, if the motivation is directed toward controlling sexual behavior, the tone may be punitive. Second, if the motivation is to develop a panacea for sociosexual ills, the program scope may be narrow, and its expectations may be unrealistic and misleading. Sex education programs should be broad-based, comprehensive, continuous, and aware of developmental considerations.

Considerations for Persons with Handicaps

Research has disproven common assumptions about the interest of persons who are handicapped in sexual matters. Only extremely low-functioning individuals may be considered beyond the need for accurate information for sociosexual development. Nevertheless, ". . . ignorance, confusion, and misunderstanding abound with respect to sex" (Edmonson, 1980, p. 70). Edmonson and Wish's (1975) research illustrates the gap between the social aspirations and the degree of preparation of persons with moderate retardation. Edmonson, McCombs, and Wish (1979) state that the sexual stimuli available through media and acquaintances have made virtually all persons at least somewhat knowledgeable; thus, any inclination to preserve a state of naiveté among persons with handicaps is not reasonable. Edmonson et al. (1979) conclude that educators must provide instruction in sexual outlooks and practices to help students function responsibly. The successful learning and generalization demonstrated in programs for students who are severely handicapped (e.g., Hamre-Nietupski & Williams, 1977) further illustrates the potential gains that can be made in this area. The following considerations are provided by SIECUS (1971, p. 12) as a basis for developing programs for students who are retarded. They have broader applicability as well.

1. Children with retardation, particularly those who are mildly retarded, share the concerns of their nonhandicapped peers about similar topics at about the same chronological ages.
2. Intellectual limitations of children restrict the use of many instructional materials that have been prepared for and used by nonhandicapped students.
3. All materials should be examined before use and should be modified, if necessary, to fit the needs of special children. It is particularly important that films and other audiovisual materials be examined before use.
4. Many children come from backgrounds quite different from those of teachers. Their values may be different; their lifestyles may be different. Teachers must refrain from passing judgment.
5. Teachers must be good listeners as well as skillful dispensers of information.
6. Teachers should not rely on abstract teaching approaches, such as lecturing.
7. Teachers should be constantly alert for indications of personal concerns on the part of individual pupils.

To summarize the developmental concerns of students with handicaps relative to sexual development, Table 15.5 outlines their needs, typical questions asked, and appropriate responses. It is based on an original model developed by Block (1972) and adapted by Steward (1975). It has been updated to reflect the sexual awareness that often comes earlier to children and adolescents in the 1980s, possibly because of media influence. Age ranges are intended only as general predictors of interest level.

Clearly, children and adolescents have a need to know, and this information can be best provided by someone who can accurately respond to their questions.

Assessment and Instruction

Assessment in this domain focuses primarily on interest and current knowledge base. Formal testing should not be considered a necessity, although instruments for evaluating attitudes toward sexual practices and understanding of central concepts and facts are available (e.g., *Socio-Sexual Knowledge and Attitudes Test,* Wish, McCombs, & Edmonson, 1979). Interest inventories provide a valuable source of information and can be geared to specific populations; the example in Table 15.6 was designed for adolescent girls with handicaps.

In considering a sex education curriculum, teachers should keep in mind the various constituencies that may be interested in implementation of such a program. Bass (1972) provides a detailed description of how community acceptance can be obtained for such an effort by overcoming potential obstacles. The recommendations provided by SIECUS (1971) should be observed in the development of a comprehensive multiclass program.

1. Select an advisory committee that includes various key constituencies from both the school and the community.
2. Keep parents informed and involved as much as possible in program development.
3. Obtain the school administration's support for both internal assistance and external, public relations purposes.
4. Establish curriculum objectives for individuals at different functioning levels, consistent with the views of committee members.
5. Determine curriculum content.

TABLE 15.5
Development of human sexuality*

Stages	Sexual Needs	Bases for Questions	Responses	Common Concerns
Early awareness (ages 4–9)	Family patterns for people and animals	Curiosity, simple interest, and limited attention span; making sense of their world	Simple, direct, and to the point	How do dogs have puppies? Where do kittens grow before they're born? Why am I a girl?
Increased awareness (ages 9–14)	Security in attitudes toward developing sexuality; need for factual information to clarify numerous concerns	Tremendous desire to learn about all facets	Direct and accurate responses to aspects of anatomy, physiology, and sociology	How do girls go to the bathroom? What is normal penis size? What does "getting laid" mean? Why haven't I begun to have periods? What is VD?
Active involvement (ages 13–19)	Active sexual experimentation of various types; knowledge and understanding of personal feelings and other's perceptions	Inquisitiveness and impatience for information; making decisions	Honest, nonjudgmental responses; incorporation into curricular units of study	Is it important to be a virgin? Everyone else is doing it; should I? How does it feel to have a baby? I think I have herpes—what should I do? Is it wrong to be gay?

*The authors acknowledge the assistance of Kathy Steward in the development of this table.

6. Provide in-service education to staff who will be involved in the program.
7. Conduct a pilot program with several classes.

The major role of the teacher is, of course, to develop and implement the curriculum. Several basic issues should be considered.

1. *What to teach.* Accurate, developmentally appropriate information is the key to content. The resource guides developed by Fischer, Krajicek, and Borthick (1974); SIECUS (1971); and Kempton and Forman (1976) can be helpful. Table 15.7 provides an example of some accurate data that might be shared.

2. *When to teach.* Instruction should begin before problems arise—that is, prepuberty. This can probably be handled best

TABLE 15.6
Interest Inventory

Which Questions Would You Like to Know More About?
1. Do all girls start their periods at the same age?
2. What are wet dreams? Do girls get wet dreams?
3. Why are my periods irregular?
4. Is it wrong to masturbate?
5. Does it hurt to have a baby?
6. How old will I be when my periods quit?
7. If boys get excited, do they have to have sex?
8. Is it wrong to have sex before you are married?
9. Can a woman have sex when she is on her period?
10. How do you know what true love is?
11. What is the safest form of birth control?
12. Do all Kotex machines work the same? Can I learn how to use all machines?
13. Can I go swimming when I have my period? Can I work in the garden? Can I take a bath or a shower?
14. What does the inside of a men's bathroom look like?
15. Is it easy to be a good mother?
16. Is it bad to fight with someone you love?
17. Can a woman who is a virgin use Tampax?
18. How can I find the women's room? What other words besides *Ladies* and *Girls* are used?
19. When will I stop growing?
20. How can I find out if I'm pregnant?
21. What do babies look like before they are born?
22. If I'm pregnant, do I have to have the baby?
23. What happens when you get a PAP smear?
24. How do I check for breast cancer?

by integrating information into the curriculum as well as by taking advantage of spontaneous situations.

3. *Where to teach.* Other than for specific anatomical details and body functions that are best discussed in the bathroom, the classroom is the most appropriate place for instruction.

4. *How to teach.* The key is to give direct, honest, short answers that provide specific information in response to questions.

5. *What resources to use.* The teacher should identify community organizations that sponsor counseling and discussion groups related to sexuality. Representatives from such organizations could be invited to talk to the class about the services available and the characteristics to their discussion groups. Thus, students could identify possible resources for information or counseling that might not be available in the public schools. Other resources are listed at the end of the chapter.

The following list of study units provides a general guide for developing specific curricular objectives.

1. awareness of self
   a. sexual identification
   b. knowledge of body parts

TABLE 15.7
Data regarding the effectiveness of contraceptive methods

Method	Theoretical Effectiveness (Effectiveness if used perfectly, consistently all the time)*	Use Effectiveness (Effectiveness based on surveys of actual couples who use the method)**
Pills (combined estrogen and progestin)	99.66%	90%–96%
Mini-pills (progestin only)	98.5%–99%	90%–95%
Condoms and foam (together)	99 + %	95%
IUD	97%–99%	95%
Condoms (rubbers)	97%	90%
Fertility awareness method (with abstinence)	97%	84%–92.5%
Diaphragm	97%	83%
Foam	97%	78%
Withdrawal (pulling out)	91%	75%–80%
Rhythm (calendar)	87%	79%

*These percentages represent 100 fertile couples using a method for the first year. "97% effective" means that 97 out of 100 couples using the method for 1 year **will not** have an unplanned pregnancy.

**The best method of birth control is often the one that makes a couple feel most natural and most comfortable and that the couple will use consistently and correctly.

Source. From "Facts About Methods of Contraception" (5th rev.) by M. S. Y. Whang, 1988, Honolulu: Hawaii State Department of Health, Office of Family Planning. Copyright 1982 by Hawaii State Department of Health. Reprinted by permission.

2. understanding maturity and puberty
   a. development of genitalia and secondary sex characteristics
   b. menstruation
   c. emotional factors
3. interpersonal relationships
   a. dating, boyfriends, and girlfriends
   b. sex roles
   c. peer pressures
4. sexual responsibilities and relationships
   a. intercourse
   b. pregnancy
   c. birth
   d. masturbation
   e. sexual varieties and alternative lifestyles
5. sex and marriage
   a. understanding a spouse's feelings
   b. frequency of sexual relations
   c. responsibilities with the relationship
   d. common problem areas
6. childbearing and child rearing
7. venereal disease
   a. syphilis
   b. gonorrhea
   c. herpes virus
   d. acquired immune deficiency syndrome

Concern for the sexual development and education of students with handicaps must be a part of special education's role. Effective instruction and some external direction may ultimately lead to students' ability to accept responsibility for and exercise control of their sexuality.

ACTIVITIES   ## Sex Education

Sex education should not become an amalgam of marginally related activities and lessons. An effective program must present sequential units of study relevant and important to the student while capitalizing on life events. The list that follows provides some suggestions for individual activities that can be integrated into such a sequence. Numerous activities to develop self-concept and appropriate peer relationships can also aid various facets of sexual development.

1. Have students discuss the definition of *love* when applied to parents, siblings, teachers, friends of the same and opposite sex (SIECUS, 1971).
2. Discuss the bodily changes that children experience as they enter puberty. Help students understand that such changes occur at different times for different people.
3. Have students identify what they see as acceptable patterns of social interaction in their school, at their age level. Discussion might include walking home together, dancing, dating, holding hands, kissing, and petting. Ask students to discuss how they themselves, their peers, parents, and school officials perceive these activities.
4. If your school system is willing, invite a member of the health department or a physician to speak to the class about topics relevant to your program (e.g., human sexual anatomy and development, contraceptives, family planning, and venereal disease).
5. Burt and Brower (1970) advise the use of a question box. Before a unit on sex education, have students write questions anonymously on index cards. Nonwriters can share their questions privately with you.
6. Have students interview a married couple invited as guests then discuss the many benefits and problems of marriage.
7. DeSpelder and Prettyman (1980) offer many helpful classroom activities on parenthood and family living. One readiness activity they suggest is to have students make a list of the food, clothing, shelter, and health needs of a newborn baby and estimate the cost of supporting a child through the first 6 years of life. Have students use newspapers or catalogs to price furniture, food, and clothing. Advanced groups could also consider rent and the cost of day care, babysitters, and recreation. Have students compare living costs for single persons, married couples, and couples with a child.
8. Have students cut out advertisements in newspapers and magazines and look for TV ads that use sex to sell products. Point out the motivation for and the implications of these kinds of ads. Discuss how they affect our perceptions of sexuality.
9. Use the telephone directory to identify various family planning and social service organizations in your area. Discuss their locations and the types of services provided.
10. Assign students short reports on each month of prenatal growth. Encourage students to make illustrations to present to the class. The

illustrations could be combined for a bulletin board (Burt & Brower, 1970).

11. Help students develop sexual responsibility by discussing such questions as, Should there be mutual consent to have sex? What commitment must people have to a relationship? How do my parents' views on sexual behavior affect me? Have I discussed the topic of sex with my parents? How is sex used as a weapon or a bribe? What are effective contraceptive methods? How does one know if one is prepared to handle the emotional factors associated with sexual behavior? (DeSpelder & Prettyman, 1980).

12. Shiller (1977) recommends setting up a problem situation for discussion. Students can be given facts and reports by experts and professionals in advance. Students might be asked how they would advise a pregnant 17-year-old girl who planned to try adoption. Realistic situations will be of most benefit to students.

RESOURCES

Social Skills

ACCEPTS Social Skills Curriculum, Pro-Ed. The ACCEPTS (A Curriculum for Children's Effective Peer and Teacher Skills) program prepares children with special needs to function in the least restrictive environment and provides an instructional program to teach skills to enhance classroom adjustment and peer acceptance. It is intended for children with mild and moderate handicaps in kindergarten through sixth grade who are deficient in classroom social and behavioral competencies. The program includes instruction in classroom skills, basic interaction, getting along, making friends, and coping.

Developing Understanding of Self and Others (DUSO), American Guidance Services. The DUSO program is available in two kits: D-1 for use with kindergarten and first-grade level and D-2 for use with upper-primary and fourth-grade level. Both are organized around eight themes, with manual, storybooks, records, posters, and puppets provided.

Kids Don't Learn from People They Don't Like, Human Resource Development Press. This excellent guide helps reassess what teachers do in the classroom to aid in developing personal relationships.

Little Twirps Understanding People Books and *Little Twirps Creative Thinking Workbooks,* Silbert & Bress Publications. This series of easy-reading, high-interest stories and workbooks depicting humorous adventures in growing up is lighthearted but provides excellent springboards for class discussions in the area of social skills and self-concept.

Making Value Judgments: Decisions for Today, Merrill. This book can be read by or to students. It encourages discussion and thinking on values and issues such as smoking, drinking, the law, prejudice, and decision making. A teacher's manual accompanies the selections.

My Friends and Me, American Guidance Services. This personal and social development program focuses on identity, social skills, and understanding. The kit includes cassette tapes, puppets, game board, instructional activities, and magnetic board with objects.

100 Ways to Enhance Self-Concept in the Classroom, Prentice-Hall. This book is written for teachers to use in the classroom to build a positive, healthy environment. All activities are concisely described. It is an excellent tool for special education teachers interested in developing personal growth activities.

Pal Paperbacks, Xerox Education Publications. The Pal series includes stories on many topics of interest. Many of the stories present situations that lend themselves to class discussions on values and decision making.

Peace, Harmony, Awareness, Learning Concepts. This package is a relaxation program for children and includes an instructional manual and a series of tapes for students to listen to. Units provide attention to self-concept, behavior problems, stress, and creativity.

People Need Each Other, Incentive Publications. This highly motivating collection of activities emphasizes social awareness in the context of career education.

School Survival Skills Curriculum, University of Pittsburgh Development of Special Education. The Schools Survival Skills Curriculum emphasizes exploring and developing school coping skills for adolescent students with disabilities. The curriculum is contained in a notebook that outlines the behaviors and study skills necessary to achieve success in school. The manual gives specific activities to facilitate teaching each skill.

The Skills of Teaching Interpersonal Skills, Human Resources Development Press. This is good text to guide teachers in teaching interpersonal skills to students of all ages.

Skillstreaming the Adolescent, Research Press. This excellent program for developing social skills in handicapped adolescents focuses on what specific behaviors need to be taught to students with social deficits. Modeling, role-playing, feedback, and transfer of training are included.

Skillstreaming the Elementary School Child, Research Press. This book advocates the teaching of prosocial behaviors to children through planned and systematic applied psychoeducational techniques.

Social Learning Curriculum, Merrill. The Social Learning Curriculum was designed for use on the primary level with special children. The kit contains 10 units on social and emotional adjustment along with supplementary charts, pictures, and duplicating books.

Strategies for Planning and Facilitating the Reintegration of Students with Behavioral Disorders, Iowa Department of Public Instruction. This excellent manual provides step-by-step procedures for successful mainstreaming efforts. The monograph was developed by Maureen White for BD students but does have broader applicability.

Toward Affective Development (TAD), American Guidance Services. The TAD kit was designed for use with ages 8 to 12 or Grades 3 to 6. It is organized into five general sections with individual subunits in each. The kit includes the manual, pictures, posters, a cassette, duplicating masters, and career folders.

Sex Education

PROFESSIONAL

Bass, M. S. (1972). *Developing community acceptance of sex education for the mentally retarded.* New York: SIECUS/Human Services Press.

Comfort, A. (1972). *The joy of sex.* New York: Crown.

Craft, A., & Craft, M. (1979). *Handicapped married couples.* Boston: Routledge & Kegan Paul.

de la Cruz, F. F., & LaVeck, G. D. (1973). *Human sexuality and the mentally retarded.* New York: Brunner/Mazel.

Edmonson, B. (1980). Sociosexual education for the handicapped. *Exceptional Education Quarterly, 1* (2), 67–76.

Greengross, W. (n.d.). *Sex and the handicapped child.* Rugby, England: National Marriage Guidance Council.

McKee, L., & Blacklidge, V. (1981). *An easy guide for caring parents: A book for parents of people with handicaps.* Walnut Creek, CA: Planned Parenthood of Contra Costa.

Reuben, D. (1970). *Everything you always wanted to know about sex—but were afraid to ask.* New York: David McKay.

Sheffield, M., & Bewley, S. (1973). *Where do babies come from?* New York: Alfred A. Knopf.

Stewart, W. F. R. (1979). *The sexual side of handicap: A guide for caring professionals.* Cambridge, England: Woodhead-Faulkner.

To grow up now: An instructional guide for teachers. (1977). Neenah, WI: Kimberly Clark.

Tymchak, A., & Baladerina, N. (1986). *Answers to questions adolescents have about sex.* Portland, OR: Ednick Communications.

INSTRUCTIONAL

Clarity Collective. (1986) *Taught not caught.* Portland, OR: Ednick Communications.

Edwards, J., & Wapnick, S. (1985). *Being me: A social/sexual training guide for those who work with the developmentally disabled.* Portland, OR: Ednick Communications.

Fischer, H. L., Krajicek, M. K., & Borthick, W. A. (1974). *Sex education for the developmentally disabled: A guide for parents, teachers, and professionals.* Austin, TX: Pro-Ed.

McKee, L., Kempton, W., & Stiggal, L. (1980). *An easy guide to loving carefully for men and women.* Walnut Creek, CA: Planned Parenthood of Contra Costa.

Throckmorton, T. (1980). *Becoming me: A personal adjustment guide for secondary students.* Grand Rapids, MI: Grand Rapids Public Schools.

16
Career Development, Transition Planning, and Life Skills Preparation

A major goal of education is to prepare individuals to function as responsible, competent community members, operating effectively in a number of roles. Most learners with special needs must be introduced to postsecondary realities in a systematic, programmed way. Traditionally, any preparation for "life after high school" has focused on vocational needs, certainly an important consideration. Most adolescents with learning problems are fully capable of moving into the work force, and should be appropriately trained. Many students with mild handicaps who are in strictly academic curricula (i.e., diploma-track) also need this training.

However, vocational concerns are not the only ones that need to be addressed. Students also need to acquire the skills to be competent family members, consumers, users of leisure time, and resourceful community members. Unfortunately, until recently, very few comprehensive career development and transition programs were in operation.

This chapter examines the school-based preparation of students for careers. It is divided into four major sections: career development; transition planning; life skills preparation; and job development, training, and placement.

CAREER DEVELOPMENT

Career development suggests that individuals should be presented with information that is "relevant and practical to community living and working needs required in the real world" (Brolin, 1982a, p. 1). The term *career* can be misleading because it is often viewed solely from an occupational perspective. However, the broader notion of career includes various adult roles (e.g., in the home and community).

> Career education is not simply preparation for a job. It is also preparation for other productive work roles that comprise one's total career functioning. This includes the work of a

homemaker and family member, the participation as a citizen and volunteer, and the engagement in productive leisure and recreational pursuits that are of benefit to oneself and others. (Brolin, 1986, p. vii)

Program Goals

According to Smith and Payne (1980), one of the first steps in developing a sound career development program is forming a set of program objectives or goals. It is important to consider career development as a lifelong process that can begin at the preschool level and continue past retirement. Clark (1979) suggests some objectives that should be included in an elementary-level career-education program.

☐ Provide instruction and guidance for developing positive habits, attitudes, and values toward work and daily living.

☐ Provide instruction and guidance for establishing and maintaining positive human relationships at home, school, and at work.

☐ Provide instruction and guidance for developing awareness of occupational alternatives.

☐ Provide instruction for an orientation to the realities of the world of work, as a producer and as a consumer.

☐ Provide instruction for acquiring actual job and daily living skills. (p. 13)

These objectives are critical to a systematic career development program that *should* begin in the primary grades. The crucial ingredient for implementing Clark's suggestions is preparing teachers to undertake such a venture. Accentuating the importance of career education, demonstrating its educational relevance, and providing techniques for incorporating it into the existing curriculum will assist in its successful implementation.

We suggest that additional goals be added to Clark's list to highlight other roles that become important as individuals enter young adulthood.

☐ Explore the variety of leisure activities, including hobbies and recreational activities.

☐ Discuss what is expected of a contributing member of the community.

☐ Examine the responsibilities of maintaining a house or an apartment, assuming both an owner's and a renter's perspective.

As the need for specific occupational preparation becomes more urgent, other program goals arise.

☐ Enhance the occupational awareness and aspirations of students through career counseling.

☐ Conduct an assessment of each student's vocational interests and skills.

☐ Integrate the assessment information into each student's IEP and ultimately into daily lesson planning.

☐ Provide each student with community-based training opportunities.

☐ Ensure the development of entry-level job skills.

☐ Provide job placement for and support to students as needed.

Curricular Models

Within recent years various career education curricular models have emerged that are appropriate for students with special needs. Clark (1979) presents a school-based career education model that emphasizes work careers but addresses other life careers as well. His model directs instruction to four principal areas: (1) values, attitudes, and habits; (2) human relationships; (3) occupational information; and (4) acquisition of job and daily living skills. These domains provide a foundation for a number of career/

vocational options later in school and life. A more detailed description of the model as well as teaching strategies and suggestions for obtaining materials can be found in Clark's text, *Career Education for the Handicapped Child in the Elementary Classroom.*

Another curricular model with which teachers should be familiar is the Life-Centered Career Education (LCCE) Model developed by Brolin (1978, 1986) and his colleagues. Interest in this curriculum has continued to grow since its publication, resulting in its adoption by many school districts in various regions of the country. The LCCE curriculum identifies 22 major competencies that are necessary to function effectively in school, family, and community roles. These competencies can be categorized into three major domains: daily living, personal/social, and occupational. Figure 16.1 shows the major functional areas, the accompanying competencies, and related subcompetencies. This curriculum affords school personnel a competency-based system for providing career education throughout a student's schooling.

Apparent in both of these models is the concept of career education as more than occupational education. It is essential that students be introduced to topics such as family relations, child rearing, and use of leisure/recreational time.

Instructional Considerations

As students move from the elementary to the secondary level of schooling, curricular emphases become important to their futures. All too often an academic orientation predominates; but for students whose formal school careers will soon end, such an approach is not appropriate. In many school systems the secondary-level curriculum takes a more vocational orientation. Even though this focus seems appropriate because students will soon be moving toward the world

FIGURE 16.1
Life-Centered Career Education Model (From *Life-Centered Career Education: A Competency-Based Approach* [rev. ed.] by D. E. Brolin, 1986, Reston, VA: Council for Exceptional Children.)

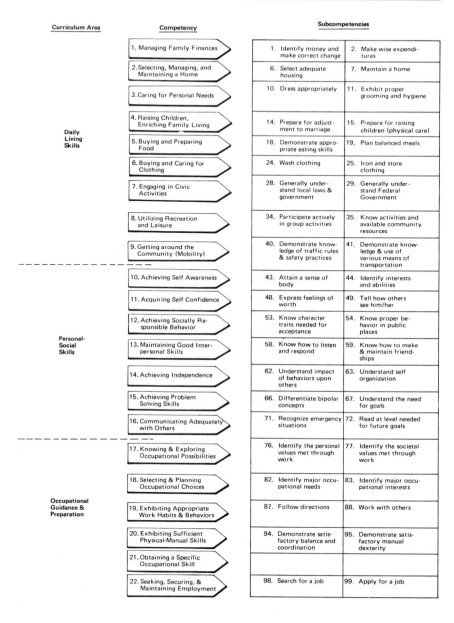

of work, this late exposure does not promote a realistic view of work or life in general. Students are rarely exposed to real work situations until they near the end of their formal schooling. The obvious answer to this dilemma is to begin to promote career awareness as early as possible in the primary grades and to increase this awareness with more career-related skills in later years.

Unfortunately, relatively little instruction in career education occurs at the elementary level. A major reason for this situation is the small number of teachers—regular or special—who receive training in providing career education. Related topics and in-

FIGURE 16.1
continued

3. Obtain and use bank and credit facilities	4. Keep basic financial records	5. Calculate and pay taxes		
8. Use basic appliances and tools	9. Maintain home exterior			
12. Demonstrate knowledge of physical fitness, nutrition, & weight control	13. Demonstrate knowledge of common illness prevention and treatment			
16. Prepare for raising children (psychological care)	17. Practice family safety in the home			
20. Purchase food	21. Prepare meals	22. Clean food preparation areas	23. Store food	
26. Perform simple mending	27. Purchase clothing			
30. Understand citizenship rights and responsibilities	31. Understand registration and voting procedures	32. Understand Selective Service procedures	33. Understand civil rights & responsibilities when questioned by the law	
36. Understand recreational values	37. Use recreational facilities in the community	38. Plan and choose activities wisely	39. Plan vacations	
42. Drive a car				
45. Identify emotions	46. Identify needs	47. Understand the physical self		
50. Accept praise	51. Accept criticism	52. Develop confidence in self		
55. Develop respect for the rights and properties of others	56. Recognize authority and follow instructions	57. Recognize personal roles		
60. Establish appropriate heterosexual relationships	61. Know how to establish close relationships			
64. Develop goal seeking behavior	65. Strive toward self actualization			
68. Look at alternatives	69. Anticipate consequences	70. Know where to find good advice		
73. Write at the level needed for future goals	74. Speak adequately for understanding	75. Understand the subtleties of communication		
78. Identify the remunerative aspects of work	79. Understand classification of jobs into different occupational systems	80. Identify occupational opportunities available locally	81. Identify sources of occupational information	
84. Identify occupational aptitudes	85. Identify requirements of appropriate and available jobs	86. Make realistic occupational choices.		
89. Work at a satisfactory rate	90. Accept supervision	91. Recognize the importance of attendance and punctuality	92. Meet demands for quality work	93. Demonstrate occupational safety
96. Demonstrate satisfactory stamina and endurance	97. Demonstrate satisfactory sensory discrimination			
100. Interview for a job	101. Adjust to competitive standards	102. Maintain postschool occupational adjustment		

structional applications should become an integral part of preservice and in-service training programs. Another major factor is the perception that career education is one more subject area that must be added to an already-demanding daily schedule. In reality, career education can be effectively integrated into a regular curriculum.

Making Academic Subject Areas Career-Relevant One approach to career education is to infuse its objectives into regular academic subject areas. Although championed by a number of educators (Brolin, 1982b; Brolin & Kokaska, 1979; Gillet, 1981), this approach has not been widely instituted. However, making academic areas career-relevant can aid teachers in making them more meaningful and interesting. And adding career education to the academic curriculum need not require excessive amounts of time, although some effort is required. Teachers who want to make their instruction career-relevant need to (1) be motivated to do so; (2) examine their curricula in some detail; (3) be willing to augment these curricula; and (4) incorporate career and life-skill aspects into their instruction (Patton, 1983). The results are worth it. An exercise on volumetric measurement taken from the third-level text of the math series *Mathematics Around Us* (Scott, Foresman) is reproduced in Figure 16.2 and provides a good example of the potential for career relevance.

Most teachers using the textbook illustrated in Figure 16.2 would assign that particular page for the mathematical objectives implicit in the activity but would overlook

its career development possibilities. However, it does not require too much effort to go beyond the mathematics and explore various aspects of the chef's job, extend this to the career cluster area of hospitality and recreation (see Table 16.1), or suggest the realities of cooking in the context of everyday living. A systematic way to plan for this type of infusion activity is to use a form like that presented in Figure 16.3, keeping in mind that career development topics include occupational as well as nonoccupational roles.

Unit Teaching   Another approach that has been used with elementary students is unit teaching. Although this technique can be effective, Suhor (1979) suggests caution.

> Generating a limited repertoire of career-oriented units within traditional disciplines is another poor strategy, because it supports the

FIGURE 16.2
Sample page from a mathematics workbook (From *Mathematics Around Us: Skills and Applications* (p. 327) by L. C. Bolster et al., 1978, Glenview, IL: Scott, Foresman. Copyright 1978 by Scott, Foresman and Company. Reprinted by permission.)

TABLE 16.1
Occupational clusters identified by the U.S. Office of Education

Career Groups	
Agriculture agri-business	Hospitality & recreation
Business & office	Manufacturing
Communication & media	Marine science
Construction	Marketing & distribution
Consumer education & home economics	Natural resources & environment
	Personal Services
Fine arts & humanities	Public service
Health	Transportation

notion that career education is after all a series of artifices grafted onto "real" subject-area content. (p. 215)

Career education should not be restricted to a selected number of units about career topics, nor should it be perceived as an add-on subject area. The unit approach has appeal but should be used in an integrated context in which career education is infused into instructional units related to academic subject areas.

Developing a Work Personality

U.S. culture is results-oriented. Many of the results that are usually accorded positive treatment in our society are work-related (i.e., those who hold a job are held in higher esteem than those who fail to hold a job). The individual with a results- or work-oriented personality is in a better position to obtain a job than the individual who is negative or naive about work. Clearly then, education should assist students in developing strong positive work personalities with habits and attitudes that will ultimately lead them to become what they are interested in and capable of becoming.

During the preschool stage, youngsters observe the daily living and working habits of those around them. Their observations, as well as interactions with older persons in their environment, begin to form the perceptions of life that will ultimately cause these individuals to develop a particular type of work personality. It is readily apparent that the family has a tremendous influence on the child. Families who are consistent in meeting family member needs or who are work-oriented tend to produce persons who behave in the same fashion, whereas families who are not consistent in meeting family member needs or who are not work-oriented tend to produce individuals who exhibit these same types of behaviors. Certainly, there are exceptions to this generalization, but it depicts the tremendous importance of the family to the preschool child.

During the elementary school stage, students form a clearer, more precise perception of the world and their immediate surroundings. Parks (1976) reports that stereotyping of career roles can occur even at this age. She further states that evidence supports the finding that children at this level are developing their own values, interests, and concerns about work. As students engage in academic and nonacademic endeavors, teachers need to be aware of the importance of their developing behaviors that will lead to positive work habits and positive work personalities—for example, starting a task on time, cooperating with others, being neat, or cleaning up and putting things away. As children get older and can accept more responsibilities, they should be given more important jobs in

Curricular Reference Point	Career Development Idea(s)/Topic(s)	Occupational Cluster Area	Miscellaneous Notes

FIGURE 16.3
Career development infusion worksheet

school. Students should also be given tasks that require them to express their ideas and understanding about different vocations; for example, pupils might be asked to write a composition or tell a story about a certain job, such as being a carpenter, or students might role-play the actions of different persons, such as a park ranger, magician, or bricklayer.

A further activity that is appropriate for elementary or middle school students is the development of job awareness notebooks containing articles and advertisements relative to one or more of the 15 career cluster areas presented in Table 16.1 Students should acquire information to answer some of the following questions: What occupations are included in the cluster? Who works in these occupations? What is the life-style of the workers? Who do they work with? Where are their jobs? How do the workers accomplish their jobs? Activities such as these not only expose students to the different roles of different workers but also aid students in clarifying alternatives for future study and consideration.

The secondary school period is a crucial stage in the life of the potential worker. Most adolescents with learning problems require a comprehensive curriculum that is responsive to their current needs and consistent with their transitional needs across the life span. Initially, formal career counseling should be instituted if it has not already begun, and a realistic appraisal should be made of each student's postsecondary environment. For students with mild learning problems, further educational possibilities can be considered.

In the postsecondary stage individuals usually obtain a job and begin to assume their roles in the community and/or within their families. However, changes often occur in jobs (e.g., layoffs, promotions) and in families (e.g., offspring, divorce), requiring a reeducation process for many people.

TRANSITION PLANNING

Transition implies change. Transition within the field of special education refers to the movement from one educational environment to another. According to Polloway (1987), many transitions occur throughout the school careers of all students. However, the one particular transition that has received the most attention is the movement from school to community.

The initial focus on transition, spearheaded by the Office of Special Education and Rehabilitative Services (OSERS) (Will, 1984), was largely a response to the alarming data on the high dropout rates of students and the high rates of unemployment and underemployment of adults with disabilities. Major efforts to provide an appropriate education for students with disabilities were not paying off. The model of transition espoused by OSERS centered primarily on the school-to-work linkage; a more comprehensive model was proposed later by Halpern (1985). Unquestionably, these models have provided the backdrop for much subsequent work in this area.

A universally recognized and clearly defined definition of this transition from school to community does not exist (Martin, 1986), yet certain elements are obvious. Clearly, the "concept of transition links the two themes of adolescence and adulthood" (Patton, Payne, Kauffman, Brown, & Payne, 1987, p. 228). Key components of the process include

☐ school-related issues at the secondary level (e.g., curricula)
☐ transitional management issues (e.g., linkage between school and postsecondary services)
☐ community issues (e.g., postsecondary options)

Articulating a set of goals for transition planning is just as challenging as trying to define the concept. Nevertheless, three general objectives can be identified (Hawaii Transition Project, 1987).

□ Arrange for opportunities and services that will support quality adult living.

□ Prevent the interruption of needed services.

□ Maximize the community participation, independence, and productivity of adolescents with disabilities who are entering young adulthood.

Principles of Transition Planning

Effective transitional planning should follow principles that adhere to the goals of transition while respecting variances in the organizational structures and procedures of different localities. Patton and Browder (1988) suggest these five principles: (1) families should be involved; (2) planning should be comprehensive; (3) secondary-level curricula should reflect adult outcomes and the availability of services and opportunities; (4) planning should involve interagency cooperation and collaboration; (5) and planning should be flexible, responsive to changes in values, goals, and experiences.

Of these five principles, none is more important than the first. It is critical that families become active participants in the transitional process because it is likely, especially for students with mild handicaps, that no one else will offer assistance; parents may have to become both advocates and case coordinators. The stark reality for many young adults with mild disabilities is that adult services are not mandated and may be fragmented; no one entity is assigned to coordinate services; and various agencies have differing requirements for eligibility and participation (Hawaii Transition Project, 1987). Consequently, transition planning should be conducted *with* parents, not *for* them, so that they become intimately involved in the process (Patton & Browder, 1988). Parents need to learn as much as they can about the transition process and the realistic probabilities of life af-

ter high school for their sons and daughters. Certain factors—such as cultural values, family values, and family resources—can significantly affect efforts to involve families, and service providers must evaluate and be sensitive to these variables.

Key Areas of Transition

Transitional planning can be broken down into two general domains (life and support), which can then be further subdivided as shown in Figure 16.4. The major life domains represent how most people organize their lives: (1) the world of work or education/training in preparation for work; (2) home and family (including religious involvement); (3) leisure time and recreational pursuits; and (4) community involvement. The support domains represent those areas related to food, shelter, and clothing as well as to personal health needs; these dimensions must be addressed before individuals can participate adequately in the major life domains. Thus, secondary-level curricula and postsecondary services should reflect concern for all six of the areas represented in Figure 16.4.

Transition Planning Process

A crucial dimension in effective transition planning is a systematic time line of critical events. Historically, one of the major problems in appropriately preparing students for adulthood has been the lateness of the attention. It is essential that parents, school personnel, and adult service providers recognize that early and sequential planning increases the likelihood of successful transition. Table 16.2 gives a cursory outline of certain events that should be performed during the high school years as well as suggestions for who has the major responsibility for each specific activity. Parents should be encouraged to become active participants in

FIGURE 16.4
Transition planning
areas (From Hawaii
Transition Project,
1987, Honolulu:
University of Hawaii,
Department of Special
Education. Reprinted
by permission.)

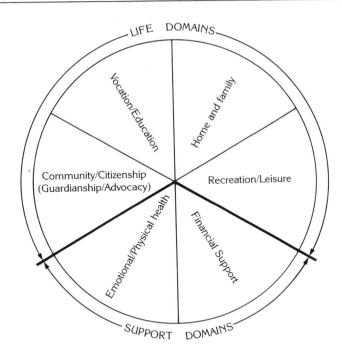

these events even if they are not listed as the principal agents of responsibility.

The primary vehicle that specifically documents this transitional planning is the individual transition plan (ITP). The ITP may or may not be incorporated into the IEP, depending on local circumstances. However, the ITP differs substantively from the IEP in that it is a plan for services rather than a plan for skill/knowledge acquisition, and it should reflect the individual's as well as the family's values, plans, and needs. Like IEPs, ITPs have no set format; unlike IEPs, ITPs do not have required elements. Typically, ITPs are organized around the key areas in the transition model adopted by the local school system. One example of an ITP format is offered in Figure 16.5.

Another tool with great utility for students, parents, school personnel, and adult service providers is the career planning packet, which contains a vast amount of important information about students and their specific transitional plans. The con-

tents of one such packet developed by the Hawaii Transition Project (1987) are summarized in Table 16.3 (p. 426). Most of the eight components can be completed while students are still in school, although some relevant information will be added at later dates.

Community Linkages

Someone within a secondary school setting must assume the role of coordinator of the transitional process. In many locations teachers have been trained as transition specialists to undertake these duties. Such specialists must not only be knowledgeable about the school component of this process but must also be aware of the postsecondary arena. The business community represents an important linkage for two reasons: it is a source of training sites, and it contains a large number of potential employers. Job placements must be found, developed, and maintained.

TABLE 16.2

Timeline for transition planning

High School Level	Transition Activity	Responsibility
First year	*Initial transition planning:* Identify potential postsecondary services and placements in the nine transition areas	School representatives, parents, student
	Begin to match the needs of the student with available local community resources	School representatives
	Appropriate communication: Provide information to community agencies regarding the transition needs of the student	School representatives
Middle years	*Active transition planning:* Conduct formal vocational assessment	School representatives
	Determine appropriateness of referrals to specific community agencies	Transition team
	Begin appropriate enrollment (e.g., SSI, waitlists, etc.)	Parents/guardians, student
	Review programming implications for the school	School representatives
	Initiate IEP planning to support transition plan	Transition team
Last year	*Facilitation of transition to the community:* Arrange cooperative programming	School representatives
	Identify responsibility for continuing transition coordination	School representatives, parents, adult service providers
	Finalize enrollment in postsecondary education or employment	Parents/guardians, student, school representatives, adult service providers
	Assist families to enroll students in service programs as needed	School representatives

Source. From Hawaii Transition Project, 1987, Honolulu: University of Hawaii, Department of Special Education. Reprinted by permission.

Another important linkage should be established and maintained with the state vocational rehabilitation agency, whose primary function is to provide services to persons at or near an employable age who are having or are apt to have employment problems. Until recently, state rehabilitation agencies hesitated to accept as clients persons still in school. However, many school systems and vocational rehabilitation agencies have now entered into cooperative agreements whereby the rehabilitation agencies do provide services for students of school age with disabilities. Only recently have vocational rehabilitation offices been directed to provide services to learning disabled populations as well (Gerber, 1981). Currently, state vocational rehabilitation agencies continue to provide services as needed after students graduate. Among some of the services provided are testing and evaluation to determine job potential and skills, training, placement in temporary or permanent jobs, follow-up and adjustment counseling, and evaluation.

Other community organizations that should be considered in the development of comprehensive transitional networks include community colleges, trade schools, private/nonprofit organizations that provide services/assistance, rehabilitation centers, mental health centers, military services, recreational programs, and governmental offices that provide services to persons with disabilities.

Employers

Of the many different elements that contribute to the vocational success of individuals with disabilities, the employer is the element most often taken for granted or, in some cases, forgotten entirely. Those who have worked in adult services know how important it is to find and nurture employers who are willing to hire workers who have disabilities. It is vitally important to let such employers know how much their actions are appreciated and to recognize them as much as possible. In addition, it is important not to abuse cooperative employers by overloading them with clients or by failing to provide support services to them.

A close look at community employers reveals that they can provide a variety of services, including (1) general dissemination of career and vocational information, (2) specific skill training and client evaluation, and (3) employment. The first level of participation is the dissemination of information. During this phase employers may explain the operation of their businesses to a class or provide group tours of plants or shops. This service allows potential workers to observe employers and employees; equally important, it permits community business persons to observe prospective workers and become familiar with a school's vocational training program.

The second phase of employer participation involves providing a placement site for clients, where they can receive some specific skill training. Up to this point clients have probably been acquiring and perfecting many general work-related skills. At this time, however, they are introduced to the reality of work through a community placement. While on the job, clients' work skills are evaluated by a supervisor or the employer, and the results are communicated to the agency responsible for vocational preparation. It may be necessary for the agency or school personnel to provide continued on-site training.

The last phase for the employer is providing actual full-time employment for clients. Some employers are willing to absorb these workers into their work force. Other employers retain clients as full-time employees if certain support services remain available.

Individualized Transition Plan

Student _____ School _____ Grade _____
Student # _____ Date of birth _____ Date of expected graduation _____

Transition Service Areas	Person Responsible	Time Line
Vocational/educational service goal: _____ Plan for this year*: Residency/work documents: _____ Social Security _____ Health certificate _____ Work permit _____ State ID _____ Green card _____ Bus pass Transportation/mobility:		
Community service goal: _____ Plan for this year: Transportation/mobility:		
Recreation/leisure service goal: _____ Plan for this year: Transportation/mobility:		

FIGURE 16.5
A sample format for an individual transition plan (From Hawaii Transition Project, 1987, Honolulu: University of Hawaii, Department of Special Education. Reprinted by permission.)

Regardless of how this phase is accomplished, these employers must not be forgotten, overlooked, or taken for granted.

Establishing and Maintaining Employer Relations To establish good working relationships, employers must first develop an interest in the vocational preparation program (i.e., invest in it) so that they see themselves as members of a team and not just as someone saddled with a task that no one else wants. In other words, the employer needs to be program-oriented, not just product-oriented. A program-oriented employer can experience a certain amount of

failure with a client without thinking that the program has completely failed. However, if the employer is product-oriented and the client experiences failure, the employer perceives total failure. Disabled workers do experience various degrees of failure, just as other workers do, and employers need to be aware that vocational training programs are broader than the experience of any single client.

An effective technique for helping workers with disabilities adjust to and succeed at their jobs is referred to as supportive employment. With this approach an employment specialist (job coach) who is on-site with the worker assists the individual in

Transition Service Areas	Person Responsible	Time Line
Home and family service goal: _____ Plan for this year: Transportation/mobility:		
Financial support service goal: _____ Plan for this year: Transportation/mobility:		
Health service goal: _____ Plan for this year: Transportation/mobility:		
*Place a check mark by all plans that will be addressed in the student's IEP. Date of ITP meeting _____ ITP coordinator _____ Persons agreeing to ITP (signatures) _____ _____ _____ _____ _____ _____		

FIGURE 16.5
continued

learning how to perform the job. This technique requires the employment specialist to learn the job as well so that particular job-related tasks can be taught to the client. Even though this supportive arrangement is only temporary (the employment specialist gradually withdraws), employers like this setup because on-the-job resources ensure success.

Good employer relationships can be maintained in several ways. The agency seeking to place workers with disabilities with a certain employer should begin with a winner, that is, a worker who appears to have a good chance of succeeding on the job site. Thereafter and throughout the program, employers should be reminded of how important their role is. Often this task can be accomplished by reporting positive changes observed in client's behavior since

coming to work for this employer; for example, "Curtis has learned to get to work on time," or "Doreen is cleaning up her work area every day after work."

Another means of maintaining good employer relationships is to assist employers in developing training skills. With an explanation of the principles derived from behavioral research, employers can be shown how to systematically observe employee behaviors. When certain behaviors need modification, employers can be helped to (1) identify a definable objective, (2) select some way to measure this objective, (3) implement a change procedure, and (4) determine whether the original objective has been met. Employers may find these training skills transferable to other situations.

Employer conferences are also an effective means of keeping employers actively in-

TABLE 16.3
Career planning packet

Component	Description	Person(s) Responsible	Time Line
Vital information	Demographic and medical information	Parent or guardian	Last semester in high school
Career log	All volunteer, training, and employment experiences	Student or vocational studies coordinator	End of each semester
Assessment results	All formal assessments (when and where conducted)	Counselor	As assessments are conducted or annually and year end
Employability skills checklist	Career development skills mastered	Teacher of record or IEP coordinator	Annually at IEP-ITP meeting
Employability skills summary	Summary of the skills acquired and work behaviors learned	Student (as self-assessment) or work supervisor	After each vocational training experience
Transition plan/IEP/ IWRP	Outline of plans for service and/or skill training	Transition plan: ITP team IEP: IEP team IWRP: vocational rehabilitation counselor	Annually at IEP-ITP meeting
Job application	Sample for completing other job application forms	Student	Once
Job references	List of employment and personal references	Student with guidance of vocational instructor or parents	Annually at year end or after each work experience

Source. From Hawaii Transition Project, 1987, Honolulu: University of Hawaii, Department of Special Education. Reprinted by permission.

volved in a vocational preparation program. Such conferences are good for several reasons: (1) different employers have a chance to talk to each other about their successes; (2) employers can also talk about particular problems that they have been experiencing; (3) through discussions new teaching and training suggestions can be formulated; and (4) conferences can lead to improved client evaluation.

LIFE SKILLS PREPARATION

Functioning in community settings requires many varied skills. Unfortunately, the myth that students automatically adjust to community living after successfully progressing through school is not completely true. Too many students and their families suddenly realize during the last year of high school that they have to make some important choices about life. Table 16.4 delineates many of the demands of young adulthood that are often ignored by secondary-level programs. This list is not exhaustive but does suggest the types of life skills needed.

There is a growing need to provide comprehensive life skills curricula to students with special needs. As detailed in chapter 8, such curricula must be responsive to stu-

dents' present and future needs. The need for curricular innovation has been documented by Halpern and Benz (1987) in their study of secondary level teachers.

Life skills preparation involves different things for different students. For example, students for whom higher education is a possibility should be in academically oriented programs. Other students, for whom

TABLE 16.4
Life problems of U.S. adults, aged 18 to 30

Vocation and Career	*Home and Family Living*	*Personal Development*
Exploring career options	Courting	Improving your reading ability
Choosing a career line	Selecting a mate	Improving your writing ability
Getting a job	Preparing for marriage	Improving your speaking ability
Being interviewed	Family planning	Improving your listening ability
Learning job skills	Preparing for children	Continuing your general education
Getting along at work	Raising children	Developing your religious faith
Getting ahead at work	Understanding children	Improving problem-solving skills
Getting job protection of military service	Preparing children for school	Making better decisions
Getting vocational counseling	Helping children in school	Getting along with people
Changing jobs	Solving marital problems	Understanding yourself
	Using family counseling	Finding your identity
Health	Managing a home	Discovering your aptitudes
Keeping fit	Financial planning	Clarifying your values
Planning diets	Managing money	Understanding other people
Finding and using health services	Buying goods and services	Learning to be self-directing
Preventing accidents	Making home repairs	Improving personal appearance
Using first aid	Gardening	Establishing intimate relations
Understanding children's diseases		Dealing with conflict
Understanding how the human body functions	*Community Living*	Making use of personal counseling
Buying and using drugs and medicines	Relating to school and teachers	
Developing a healthy life-style	Learning about community resources	*Enjoyment of Leisure*
Recognizing the symptoms of physical and mental illness	Learning how to get help	Choosing hobbies
	Learning how to exert influence	Finding new friends
	Preparing to vote	Joining organizations
	Developing leadership skills	Planning your time
	Keeping up with the world	Buying equipment
	Taking action in the community	Planning family recreation
	Organizing community activities for children and youth	Leading recreational activities

Source. From *The Adult Learner: A Neglected Species* (2nd ed., pp. 146–147) by M. Knowles, 1978, Houston: Gulf. Copyright 1978 by Gulf Publishing Company. Adapted by permission.

high school may be the termination of formal schooling, require a different course of studies. The major features that should characterize innovative programming for most students with learning-related problems include the following:

☐ *Adult-referenced.* The content of the program should be based on a top-down strategy, reflecting considerations down from the objective of successful community adjustment rather than up from an elementary-oriented focus.

☐ *Comprehensive.* Curricula offered to students should include a broad range of topics—generally, a combination of academics, vocational training, social skill development, and life skills preparation.

☐ *Relevant.* Students at the secondary level need meaningful programs. As Cronin (1988) points out, "A student who can relate academic concepts to his or her own experiences is more apt to understand the concept and be able to apply it" (p. xx).

☐ *Empirically and socially valid.* Students must acquire skills that are valuable to them personally, appropriate for the communities in which they live, and meaningful to other members of that community.

☐ *Flexible.* Curricula must be flexible enough to accommodate a wide variety of diverse student needs as well as the idiosyncrasies of different community settings.

☐ *Community-based.* Much of the training should occur out of the classroom and in actual community settings to increase the probability that skills will generalize across settings and conditions.

A Curricular Example: The Adult Performance Level Adaptation and Modification Project (APLAMP)

The Adult Performance Level (APL) model was developed by the University of Texas at Austin as an adult basic education program stressing the acquisition of functional competencies and skills necessary for survival in typical day-to-day situations. This program was subsequently modified for use in secondary-level special education settings by LaQuey (1981) and her colleagues.

Functional competence, as addressed in this curriculum, is conceptualized as two dimensional, major skill areas are integrated into general content/knowledge domains. Table 16.5 provides an illustration of this relationship. The major skills that are deemed requisite for success are reading, writing, speaking/listening/viewing, problem solving, interpersonal relations, and computation. These skills are infused into the topical domains of consumer economics (three levels), occupational knowledge, health (two levels), community resources, and government/law. This interaction between major skill areas and content domains produces 42 life skills on which instruction is based (see table 16.6).

The APLAMP materials represent a program of studies to help students in their subsequent environments. One outstanding feature of the APLAMP program is that it can be used, with school system approval, as a diploma-generating curriculum. LaQuey (1981) describes how this particular program can be designed to meet graduation requirements.

This type of curriculum is worth further examination. However, it is not a program that can be obtained and immediately implemented at a particular school. Cronin (1988) points out that APLAMP should be used as a core guide that can be modified to

TABLE 16.5
Examples of tasks in APL model of functional competency

	Consumer Economics	Occupational Knowledge	Health	Community Resources	Government and Law
Reading	Read an ad for a sale	Read a job description	Read first aid directions	Read a movie schedule	Read about rights after arrest
Writing	Fill in income tax form	Complete a job application	Write a menu	Complete an application for community service	Write your congressman
Speaking, Listening, Viewing	Ask question to IRS	Listen to an employer talk about a job	Listen to a doctor's directions	Use the telephone	Describe an accident
Problem solving	Decide which house to rent	Decide which job suits you	Decide when to call a doctor	Use stamp machines in the post office	Decide which candidate to vote for
Interpersonal relations	Relate to a sales clerk	Be successful in a job interview	Interact with hospital personnel	Ask directions	Interact with police successfully
Computation	Compute sales tax	Calculate paycheck deductions	Decide how many times a day to take a pill	Calculate the time it takes to travel a distance	Calculate the cost of a speeding ticket

Source. From *APL Model of Functional Competency*, 1981, Austin: University of Texas. Reprinted by permission.

meet the needs of a specific school. Furthermore, the program needs augmentation, especially in the areas of vocational training and social skill development. Nevertheless, innovative programs like this one need to be developed and implemented in secondary-level settings.

RELATED CONCERNS

Counseling Services

As students move to the upper elementary grades, and certainly by the time of junior high school, personnel in the counseling area should attempt to increase alternatives for vocational consideration. Students should be able to engage in many vocational experiences during their school years without the fear of losing a job or money.

An It's-Who-You-Know resource file can be a valuable tool for students seeking future employment and can be added easily to the career planning packet. Each entry should include valuable information on people to contact at various agencies in the

TABLE 16.6

Life skills of the Adult Performance Level Model

Consumer Economics

1. Counting and converting
2. Consumer fraud
3. Money management
4. Income tax
5. Care/upkeep of personal possessions
6. Comparison shopping
7. Catalog ordering
8. Advertising techniques
9. Ordering food
10. Housing/utilities
11. Car buying/maintenance
12. Insurance
13. Using credit
14. World resources
15. Banking services
16. Measuring and metrics

Community Resources

17. Public assistance program
18. Recreation
19. Information and aid
20. Mass media/public opinion
21. Driving
22. Transportation

Health

23. Safety measures/emergencies and first aid
24. Preventive care and health maintenance
25. Drug control/drug abuse
26. The adolescent
27. Self
28. Marriage and the family
29. Parenting and family planning
30. Pregnancy and childbirth
31. Child rearing
32. Nutrition/food preparation

Occupational Knowledge

33. Job selection and satisfaction
34. Sources of employment
35. Job applications and interviews
36. Employment agencies
37. Effective job behavior
38. Financial and legal aspects of employment

Government and Law

39. Government structure and function
40. Citizen rights and duties
41. Criminal and civil law
42. Legal documents

community for assistance in gaining and maintaining employment. Students should actually practice contacting these people through personal visits, telephone calls, and letters to develop familiarity with forms and procedures.

In preparing students with mild handicaps for some type of vocation, school counselors must keep several factors in mind. First of all, these students, like all other students, have their own goals, beliefs, and capabilities. They should be counseled invidually and not treated as a monolithic, homogeneous group. In a related sense, one program for vocational development does not work for all students,

just as one math program does not work for all students. All school systems need to develop a general program for career development that extends from preschool to the secondary level and perhaps beyond, but schools must remain aware that career programs must change as people, jobs, and communities change.

The specific roles and functions of a counselor include providing personal and career counseling. Personal counseling helps individuals to specifically identify personal problems, develop alternative ways and means of solving those problems, and set realistic short- and long-term goals. Activities to achieve these objectives can range from assigning autobiographical sketches, to using rap sessions for identifying student problems, to encouraging aggressive youths' participation in martial arts programs. Career counseling should also assess career and vocational potential.

Assessment

School programs are responsible for the assessment of aptitudes, interests, and competencies that relate to career development. Unfortunately, the amount of career/vocational information that is accumulated for students with mild learning problems is generally negligible. Even more tragic is that, when it does exist, such information is rarely used to develop individual program plans or daily lesson plans (Meehan & Hodell, 1986). Career-related assessment can be very valuable, particularly situational assessment of students.

Various tools that have been frequently used to evaluate aptitude and interest include The Differential Aptitude Test (Bennett, Seashore, & Wesman, 1969) and the Reading-Free Interest Inventory (Becker, 1975). One instrument, the Occupational Aptitude Survey and Interest Schedule (OASIS) (Parker, 1983), is particularly relevant.[1]

The OASIS Aptitude Survey is a standardized measure designed to assess the strengths and weaknesses of students in Grades 8 through 12 in several aptitude areas related to the work world. The subtests of the survey are based on verbal, numerical, spatial, perceptual, manual dexterity, and general ability factors derived from extensive analyses of existing aptitude tests. The content, item format, and administration procedures for each subtest are described here.

---

[1]The authors acknowledge the assistance of Ginger Blalock in providing these analyses of the OASIS and TPK.

1. *Vocabulary.* To measure verbal ability, every item presents a list of four words, two of which are either antonyms or synonyms. Examinees read and select the appropriate pair for each of 40 items.
2. *Computation.* To assess numerical ability, 30 arithmetic and algebra problems are posed in a multiple-choice format offering five alternative answers.
3. *Spatial relations.* To measure spatial aptitude, inspection of a two-dimensional figure is required, and a subsequent choice of the three-dimensional figure that can be constructed from the initial drawing.
4. *Word comparison.* To determine a general perceptual level, each item demands that subjects judge whether two sets of words, numbers, or nonsense syllables are the same or different. This is one of two speed subtests in the OASIS-AS and features 95 items to be completed within 5 minutes.
5. *Making marks.* To assess manual dexterity, this subtest also involves speed and requires subjects to draw three lines in the form of an asterisk in individual boxes as rapidly as possible.

The OASIS Interest Schedule is a standardized tool to assist junior and senior high school students in exploring their vocational interests via a comprehensive, understandable, nonsexist, and concise format. The interest schedule was designed to accompany the OASIS Aptitude Survey so that career investigation and planning might be undertaken in as informed a manner as possible. The 12 scales of the interest schedule are based on the major occupational categories derived from analyzing all major occupational research to date, as described in the manual. Each scale consists of 20 items, half of which are job or career titles and half of which are job activities, for which subjects identify their degree of fondness. The 12 areas are these:

- ☐ artistic
- ☐ scientific
- ☐ nature (e.g., outdoor work)
- ☐ protective (e.g., law enforcement)
- ☐ mechanical
- ☐ industrial
- ☐ business detail
- ☐ selling
- ☐ accommodating (e.g., hair care)
- ☐ humanitarian
- ☐ leading/influencing
- ☐ physical performing

It is also possible to assess students' knowledge and skills for functioning in everyday life via the Test of Practical Knowledge (TPK) (Wiederholt & Larsen, 1983). The TPK is a standardized measure developed to assess acquired knowledge about everyday life situations in Grades 8 through 12. It is based on the assumption that the measurement of functional competency differs from achievement, intelligence, occupational, and affective assessment by focusing solely on the knowledge, skills, and/or applications required in adult daily life, all of which are learned. Two examples from each section of the TPK are presented in Table 16.7.

Computerized systems of assessing career interest are also being used in many areas of the country. Regardless of the method used, ultimately the teacher or counselor should assist students in eliminating certain alternatives as well as developing short- and long-term career goals.

ACTIVITIES

1. Some occupations or vocations can be sampled or explored on field trips to various businesses. In addition, class visits by guest speakers from construction, retail and wholesale sales, food preparation, and education can be arranged. Speakers should provide students with information about specific skills required for the job, the activities of a typical day, and specific places of employment.
2. Retzlaff (1973) reports on a school system that used videotaping for career education. Workers and workplaces were taped for students to study and explore.
3. Use bulletin boards to illustrate various jobs in which students might be interested. Set aside one bulletin board to portray a different vocation every month. Statistics and job descriptions are available in occupational handbooks. See your local guidance office for help.
4. Have students practice completing job applications, which can be secured from various local businesses and the chamber of commerce.
5. Meyer (1973) developed an activity based on the TV program "What's My Line?" for middle school handicapped children. Students prepare to be guests by reading, watching films, and listening to tapes of the careers they represent. They are encouraged to bring recordings of career sounds. Each career is labeled as product- or service-oriented. Then members of the class ask the guests questions and receive a yes or no response. The teacher or a student can be the moderator. Videotape the game to show to other classes.
6. Start a vocations club or special-interest club including vocations appropriate for handicapped students. Have businesspersons and crafts people sponsor various activities and volunteer as guest speakers. Get

TABLE 16.7

Examples from the Test of Practical Knowledge

Personal Knowledge

1. You are frying a hamburger for lunch. The oil catches fire. Which of the following should you do first?
   A. throw water on the fire
   B. call the fire department
   C. move the pan off the stove until it stops burning
   D. run from the house
   E. put baking soda on the fire

2. A house is advertised with a $12,500 "assumption." This means that
   A. $12,500 will buy the house
   B. $12,500 must be borrowed to buy the house
   C. a person can move into the house and pay $12,500 later
   D. a new loan must be taken out to buy the house
   E. none of the above

Social Knowledge

3. Lee is scheduled to be at a meeting in Tucson at 4:00 P.M. He plans to fly to Tucson, which will take 1 hour and 20 minutes. Once he lands in Tucson, it will take 15 minutes to go from the airport to the meeting. Planes leave at 8:00 A.M., 1:30 P.M., and 3:30 P.M. The latest plane Lee can take without being late for the meeting is

   A. 8:00 A.M.
   B. 1:00 P.M.
   C. 1:30 P.M.
   D. 3:00 P.M.
   E. 3:05 P.M.

4. Ginny and Hal are thinking of getting married. On a visit to her doctor, Ginny is advised that she should receive genetic counseling before marriage. One thing genetic counseling could tell Ginny is whether

   A. she should have children
   B. Hal would make a good husband
   C. she should be married in the near future
   D. she and Hal have enough money to be married
   E. she needs to have psychiatric care

Occupational Knowledge

5. Which of the following refers only to jobs that females hold?
   A. secretary
   B. counselor
   C. librarian
   D. usherette
   E. telephone operator

6. June makes $5.00 an hour and works 40 hours per week. She is told that she is going to receive an 8% raise in her pay. How much more money will June make per week?
   A. $16.00
   B. $30.00
   C. $20.00
   D. $14.00
   E. $15.00

Source. From the *Test of Practical Knowledge* by J. L. Wiederholt and S. C. Larsen, 1983, Austin, TX: Pro-Ed. Copyright 1983 by Pro-Ed. Reprinted by permission.

recent graduates of special education classes to act as big brothers and sisters and to speak of their vocational experiences.

7. Set up a weekly lunch offered to school personnel for a reasonable price and prepared by your students. Have the students plan a balanced meal, go to the store and purchase the items necessary, read recipes, cook the food, serve the "customers," collect money and make change, bus the tables, and clean up the dishes. Each student can be assigned a different job weekly on a rotating basis. By observing the students' work behaviors and skills, you will have concrete information to use as a guide for future employment opportunities.

8. Encourage students to try such self-employment activities as babysitting, mowing lawns, delivering papers, cutting wood, and landscaping. Such jobs enhance the ability to work steadily and to sustain routine, complete work on time, achieve self-awareness, run a business, maintain work quality, and handle money.

9. The ability to get along with others and to communicate is an important vocational skill that can be fostered through volunteering. Volunteer work is available through local government agencies, schools, civic groups, and churches.

10. A visit and tour of the local employment commission will inform students of the many services this organization provides. Students should learn about unemployment insurance and the proper handling of a layoff.

11. Students can take turns role-playing a job interview situation. Provide students with questions they might be asked during an interview.

12. Plot the location of various health-care facilities on a local map. Talk about the services they provide. Practice setting up a doctor's appointment. Visit some of these facilities.

13. Telephone directories can show students how to find consumer information, such as the best buy on a record, without driving all around town. Practice procedures for requesting information over the telephone. Discuss telephone manners. McGee (1979) has developed a worksheet for telephone directory activities.

14. Assist students in making choices for leisure time by allowing them time during the school day to self-initiate an activity. Set up a system in which students choose between two or more activities for which they already possess the skills necessary for participation. Then monitor the amount of time that they stay involved with their choice. Provide reinforcement and prompts to keep them actively involved and interested in developing their individual leisure abilities (Nietupski & Hamre-Nietupski, 1986).

15. Memorizing locker combinations, vocational procedures, and proper social skills can be aided by teaching students verbal or visual elaboration. This process has students add something to what they are trying to learn to make it more memorable. For example, one might assign the numbers of a locker combination to the figure of a man. The first number could be visualized with the man's head, the second with his hand, and the last with his foot. Further suggestions and illustrations can be found in Scruggs and Laufenberg's article (1986).

RESOURCES

Application Forms, Frank E. Richards. The student has many opportunities to fill out different application forms.

The Be-Informed Series, New Readers Press. This consumer-information series is written on a third- to seventh-grade reading level. Topics covered in the series include buying a house, paying taxes, and applying for credit.

Career Education for Children with Learning Disabilities (Gillet), Academic Therapy Publications. This material (in binder form) contains many suggestions for creating activities as well as a thorough listing of resources.

Career Education for Handicapped Children and Youth (Brolin & Kokaska), Merrill. This book takes a comprehensive look at the concept of career education. The volume clearly delineates exceptionality and career education.

Career Education for the Handicapped Child in the Elementary Classroom (Clark), Love. This book presents a school-based career education model, focusing primarily on the kindergarten to sixth-grade level.

Comics Career Awareness Program, King Features Syndicate. Fifteen different career areas are covered in this program. All materials are in comic-book format that should be of high interest to adolescents.

Education and Rehabilitation Techniques (Payne, Mercer, & Epstein), Behavioral Publications. Techniques for helping handicapped persons secure gainful employment are discussed in detail.

A High School Work-Study Program for Mentally Subnormal Students (Kolstoe & Frey), Southern Illinois University Press. Many high school work-study programs throughout the nation are based on the model advocated in this book. Topics ranging from curricular needs, to a proposed academic program, to the sheltered workshop are included.

Job Application Skill Test, Special Service Supply. Thirty-six different job application forms are found in this booklet. Some applications contain problems to be solved.

Life-Centered Career Education: A Competency-Based Approach (Brolin), Council for Exceptional Children. This book looks at career education from a total life perspective.

Modern Consumer Education (Mosenfelder, Crowell, Crowell, Tushman), Grolier Educational Corporation. Topic modules cover separate areas of consumerism for individualized instruction at various levels. The self-contained modules need not be presented in a specified order.

Of Work and Worth: Career Education for the Handicapped (Gillet), Olympus. This book covers a range of topics pertinent to career education for handicapped students. Of particular interest is a chapter entitled "Relating Academic Subjects to Career Education."

Pacemaker Vocational Readers (Glasner & Typin), Fearon Pitman. This series includes 10 books depicting realistic situations in the world of work for students with limited abilities. It is an excellent series and a helpful addition to a secondary special education program.

Tips for Infusing Career Education in the Classroom (Taylor), Social Science Education Consortium. This publication presents a rationale and practical suggestions for infusing career education into the social studies area. (This material is also listed in *Resources in Education.*)

Vocational Preparation of Retarded Citizens (Brolin), Merrill. This book provides a comprehensive, informative look at the total process of vocational preparation. Specific techniques for vocational preparation and adjustment are included. Program models and evaluation processes are also discussed.

17
Creative Arts: Art, Music, and Drama

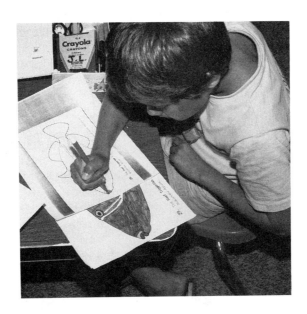

To the casual as well as the careful observer of self-contained or resource programs serving students with various handicapping conditions, it is apparent that the most common curricular emphasis is on the development of basic skills and the remediation of specific deficits. Although the need to develop basic language arts competencies and mathematical skills is not in question, the omission of other subject areas from the curriculum is. This chapter focuses on one domain that is often the victim of such omission—the creative arts.

Starms (1979) highlights the contribution of music, art, dance, drama, and literature to what she calls a humane curriculum. Eisner (1987) expands on the role of the arts: "Since humans experience and give expression to their most deeply held values, beliefs, and images through the arts, there can be no adequate form of general education that does not include them" (pp. 38–39). Similarly, Peotter (1979) asserts that "the arts have, in fact, been called the hub of all learning: other subjects are the spokes" (p. iv). Whether this analogy is appropriate for special populations is debatable. However, subject areas such as art, music, and drama should be considered essential to the comprehensive education of all students. In their classic early text on teaching methods in special education, Kirk and Johnson (1951) also argue for the role of the arts within the curriculum. The arts have

> no confining limits with reference to age, abilities, or capabilities and as such become an integral part of our daily activities. The fine arts, correlated with the other subjects in the curriculum, render an incalculable service in clarifying ideas the children are attempting to visualize and express. Consequently, children should be given opportunities and encouragement to use the arts as a means of expression. (p. 300)

Instruction in the creative arts presents a unique paradox. On the one hand, these subject areas are often the first within which special students are mainstreamed because they require less reading and other related skills. Yet few special students receive instruction in these areas. Nocera (1979) indicates that "only about two million handicapped children (out of eight million) are currently receiving *any kind of arts education*" (p. 4). The precision of this figure may be debatable, but its message is not: many special students do not receive adequate arts education.

Under the full-service provisions of PL 94–142, educational programs available to regular education students should likewise be available to special education students. According to Duerksen (1981), special arts education is an extension of regular arts education. Therefore, although arts education is not specifically mandated by PL 94–142, its provision is implied. Art and music therapy are specified in PL 94–142 as related services.

Why then are so few special students exposed to art, music, and drama instruction? Aside from the second-class status of these subjects, there are a number of possible explanations. In most school settings the resource room arrangement focuses on basic skills development. Typically, students served by this arrangement are expected to receive arts instruction in regular class settings (although this may not always occur because of scheduling conflicts). Another major reason that arts education is omitted is that annual goals and short-term objectives for art and music are rarely included in students' IEPs. And if they are not included, they will probably not be taught. Finally, many special education teachers do not feel competent to provide instruction in these areas, probably because of the lack of attention these subjects receive within many teacher training programs.

The purpose of this chapter is to introduce techniques for teaching art, music, and dramatic arts to special students. Special educators need to become comfortable with and skillful in teaching these subjects, because they can be exciting to teach and, more importantly, because some students who encounter school problems will find these subjects interesting and rewarding, an experience that is all too infrequent. In addition, these areas represent significant potential for leisure activities outside the school setting and should be taught in connection with the rest of the curriculum.

> The arts should not be taught merely for the sake of teaching music or drawing in its various forms or solely for the sake of introducing the children to the various forms of art and art materials. They should rather be taught and used in relation to other activities, making them both meaningful and pleasurable to the child. Gradually the child should develop an understanding of and an insight into their functions in the out-of-school world. (Kirk & Johnson, 1951, p. 301)

ART EDUCATION FOR LEARNERS WITH SPECIAL NEEDS

For many years art and its frequent companion, crafts, played a significant role in special education curricula for students with handicaps, often to the detriment of academic and vocational instruction in the classroom. In the 1970s and 1980s instruction has moved away from this arts and crafts orientation and has become much more academically oriented.

Nonetheless, regardless of whether former or current curricula are examined, art education for students with special needs has been very narrowly conceptualized. Many people believe art education is inappropriate in special education. Rubin (1975) remarks, "Unfortunately negative expectations are not at all uncommon, as can be seen with a quick glance at the literature on

art for the handicapped" (p. 8). The long-standing problem of special education teachers without skills in art education and regular art teachers without information about the needs of special students maintains this air of confusion.

Components of Art Education

If art education can be perceived as the creative and expressive use of art within or outside the classroom (Frith & Mitchell, 1983; May, 1976), then other uses of art can be put into perspective as well. Teachers need to expand their conception of art and art education and consider art's aesthetic qualities rather than just the mechanics. Furthermore, art instruction needs to extend to lower-functioning students. Rubin (1975) captures the essence of this idea.

> It may also be necessary to expand one's notion of what "art" is, so that it can encompass the manipulation of collage materials with feet by an armless child, or the rhythmic repetitive swabbing of paint by a psychotic boy. In a way, such manipulative and making activities are to art as babbling and jargon are to speech. They are a preparation for formal expression, and constitute as legitimate a part of "art" with the handicapped as "reading readiness" for the average learner. (pp. 8–9)

Art education includes more than just crafts, or applied art, and is more than a functional and enjoyable adjunct to academics. Art instruction also differs significantly from art therapy. Unquestionably, art has been recognized for its therapeutic value, as Osdol (1972) notes, "The use of creative art as therapy has an important place in the special education curriculum" (p. 51). Much can be learned about special students from their artwork. What students observe, perceive, and recall is reflected in their creative activities. Thus, art for exceptional learners can be therapeutic because they can effectively speak about themselves through art (Osdol, 1972). Yet the teacher must remember that the ultimate objective of art therapy is nonartistic.

Rationale for Art Instruction

Art can help meet several general needs of students. Skills development in this area can help students see the positive results of creative ideas and work efforts, thus promoting a feeling of confidence and achievement. Art can also be blended with other interests and units of study. It gives rise to communication, providing other means of expression as well as a relief from tension. Through art, students can further develop skills in social, emotional, motor, sensory, and cognitive areas (Aach, 1981). In addition, May (1976) points out that art can help develop perception and imagination. Art has no limits: it can be enjoyed by young and old and can move from simple to complex. As Harcum (1972) notes, "When life can hold so many failures and frustrations, teachers must capitalize on every experience which can lead to potential achievement" (p. 40).

Several basic reasons can thus be seen for including art in the curricula of students with special needs. Art permits every pupil to experience success in some way. It is not necessary to compare work or expect students to achieve a certain proficiency. Instead, students can be rewarded for whatever they do accomplish and thus can achieve success. This is especially important for students with mild handicaps because of their lack of achievement and frequent failure in other academic areas. In reviewing the literature on art education for students who are handicapped, Frith and Mitchell (1983) summarize some of the most frequently cited reasons in its support. Art can serve as

☐   a potential vocation
☐   a leisure-time activity
☐   reinforcement for learning academic skills
☐   an asset in establishing contact with one's environment
☐   a contributor to independent living
☐   an aid in color discrimination as a necessity for safety and recognition of danger (p. 138)

Art can also help develop aesthetic awareness and expressive capacities, which are just as important to persons with handicaps as they are to nonhandicapped persons. If self-definition and independent functioning are critical dimensions of art education, as Rubin (1975) suggests, then a curriculum setting these elements as major goals is well-warranted.

It appears safe to conclude that art education can play an important role in exceptional learners' development. The traditional principles derived from Kirk and Johnson (1951) continue to have validity and provide some general guidance to teachers as they move from accepting the importance of the arts to planning instructional programs (p. 303).

☐   Techniques and skills should be taught in purposeful and functional situations.
☐   Art should be used as a method of expression in correlation with other class activities, such as those in academic areas or within communication domains.
☐   The choice of a specific focus of a project should originate with the child.
☐   Students should derive personal satisfaction from a successfully completed task.
☐   The instructional program should be developed in such a way that it improves attitudes toward school, peers, and learning.

Instructional Techniques

Lovano-Kerr and Savage (1976) surveyed special educators in Indiana and found that few actually used or followed an art curriculum. Indeed, in many classrooms art instruction was unsequenced and haphazard. Turnbull and Schulz (1979) sensed this problem as well.

> Art education is often provided in elementary and junior high schools in a random rather than systematic fashion. Much instruction in art can be characterized as a series of unconnected activities rather than as a developmental process. This random approach to art instruction can penalize handicapped as well as nonhandicapped students in developing artistic interests, abilities, and talents. In order for handicapped students to progress maximally in artistic concept development, systematic instruction is a basic requirement. (p. 297)

Thus, students with special needs require a planned program to prosper from art education.

Some special students may also require modified content and procedures. Adaptations of many art activities are obvious for students who lack gross or fine motor skills. Similarly, asking poor readers to illustrate a story may be an impossible task without alternatives to reading. Reality has forced competent special education teachers to become adept at modifying curriculum and adapting teaching techniques. Certain art educators (Aach, 1981; Gister, 1981) have recognized the value of task analysis.

> Painting or drawing common things like trees must be translated into large, simple movements—up, down, or across. Once straight lines are understood, the level of difficulty in the task can be increased and circular movements are added to the lines to make new objects. (Gister, 1981, p. 25)

Teachers need to be flexible in adapting their instruction to the individual learning needs of their students.

Rubin (1975) presents the notion that students need a certain amount of structure within their art programs while at the same time requiring an opportunity to explore and choose for themselves. Rubin's concept of "freedom within structure" is worth adopting. It simultaneously allows for creative expression, a key element of art education, and for the systematic approach to instruction that students with special needs so desperately need.

When actually teaching an art lesson, teachers might find it helpful to consider the suggestions of Wiggin (1961, cited by Lovano-Kerr & Savage, 1972). Tempered by student ages and ability levels, art instruction should

- ☐ be a structured activity starting with shape
- ☐ have display possibilities
- ☐ lead to discovery of some new purpose
- ☐ be familiar
- ☐ make use of materials larger than the hand
- ☐ be three dimensional

Kolstoe (1976) offers additional suggestions. He believes that art education for students who are handicapped should systematically concentrate on the basic elements of expression: line, color, shape, balance, space, texture, and light. Appropriate instruction in these areas can assist in developing the ability to convey feelings and ideas through art and an appreciation for art in general.

A rather different idea (e.g., Anderson, 1975; Anderson & Barnfield, 1974) is the concept of the total curriculum being art centered. In other words, art is used as a way to teach all skill areas. With this design art becomes the core of the special education curriculum, reflecting Peotter's (1979) theory of the arts as the hub of all learning. Although some imaginative, effective programs may subscribe to this approach, such an orientation may not work with special learners.

The range of possible art activities is vast. Some excellent ideas can be found in the materials listed in the resource section later in this chapter. In addition, Battaglini and Wert (1981) discuss a number of creative activities that teachers should consider.

- ☐ drawing and painting
- ☐ sculpture: modeling, casting, carving, constructing
- ☐ fibers/fabrics: weaving, fabric collage, rugs, batik, stitchery
- ☐ media
- ☐ printmaking: relief prints, stencil prints, intaglio, lithography

St. John (1986) suggests that some students are not ready for the demands of a regular art curriculum that requires students to benefit from outside stimulation through observation and attention, cooperate with peers, transfer learning, accept criticism, and deal with frustration. For these individuals, pre-art in the form of art therapy or therapeutic art can assist in developing a readiness for regular instruction. Paletta (1979, cited by St. John, 1986) sees a therapeutic art program as having the following goals:

1. develop manual dexterity
2. develop patterns of movement
3. develop social communicability
4. master environment through control of materials and tools
5. encourage observation
6. discriminate color, shape, and texture
7. stimulate imagination
8. encourage self-identification, creativity, and meaningful experiences (p. 15)

Teachers should consult specialists in the areas of art therapy and therapeutic art if such services are deemed necessary and potentially beneficial for individual students.

Incorporating Art into Other Curricular Areas

As noted earlier, emphasis should be placed on incorporating art-related activities into other academic subjects. In other words, art can be used to supplement or enhance these other subject areas. Lindsay provides a good example.

> Theories now indicate that an inability to understand spatial relationships plays a significant part in creative learning difficulties with the three Rs, regardless of IQ. . . . It would seem that an art curriculum directed toward developing the responses to tactual experiences, with a clearer definition of movement, direction, rhythm and spatial relationships, could help to supplement other areas of learning. (pp. 42–43)

Several examples demonstrate how art can be an integral part of selected academic areas.

- ☐ *Reading.* When using language experience activities, it is common practice to have students visually represent stories they have developed.
- ☐ *Social studies.* Studying history or other cultures of the world typically requires students to become familiar with various forms of art.
- ☐ *Science.* Students who maintain science journals can include drawings related to the science activities being presented.

Some professionals have noted a connection between art activities and job training in later life, because skills in both areas demand fine motor skills. Lindsay (1972) acknowledges this connection: "Since so many factory occupations will demand such skills as matching and assembling objects, much valuable practice through creative activity can be given by encouraging the child to attempt to place a variety of materials in different positions" (p. 45).

The important points here are that art can be incorporated into other subject areas effectively and can thus add to the variety of instructional repertoires. An excellent discussion of the trend toward integration of the arts into other subjects can be found in *Art Education* (November, 1985, *38*:6). Specific attention is given to the infusion of art into reading, writing, and science. In this text, a number of integrative lessons are included in the activities list at the end of this first part of the chapter.

Recommendations

Photography   If possible, teachers should consider this form of art. It is exciting to most students and can give them a chance to be creative. As Bildman (1982) notes in reference to students with learning disabilities, photography can bring students into greater touch with the environment, can enhance a sense of sequence in events along with a perception of time and space, can assist in developing a sense of environmental order, and can improve self-esteem. These capabilities are particularly evident when Polaroid cameras are used.

Photography can be easily integrated into other subject areas. Helpful resources include *Classroom Projects Using Photography (Part 1: For the Elementary School Level; Part II: For the Secondary School Level)* (Eastman Kodak); *Teaching Your Children Photography* (Cyr, 1977); and *Doing the Media* (Laybourne & Cianciolo, 1978). The reader may also wish to consult the May, 1987, issue of *Arts and Activities* (*101*:4) for a special focus on the use of photography in an art program.

Storage and Organization   All art materi-

als should be organized systematically so that they can be stored efficiently and monitored for availability. Materials should be stored so that they do not distract students.

Materials and Equipment   The need for art materials and equipment depends directly on the nature of the art education curriculum. Many common household items can be used effectively (cf. Wirtenberg, 1968, in the resource section that follows). Teachers may also want to obtain certain basic items. Gallagher (1979) suggests that teachers in self-contained classes for students with behavior disorders should have the following minimum supplies: oil and finger paints; colored chalk; pencils; pens; crayons; paint brushes; construction, drawing, and finger paint paper (in a variety of colors and sizes ranging from 9″ × 12″ to 24″ × 26″); posterboard; oaktag; clay; popsicle sticks; yarn; and burlap (p. 39).

Clearly, more extensive supplies are needed if the teacher serves as the primary art instructor. Anderson (1978) compiled what she calls the art survival kit, which includes the materials and equipment needed to teach art to a primary-level class of 12 students for an entire year (see Table 17.1).

ACTIVITIES

The following art activities can be altered to suit the skill and developmental level of each child, the goals the teacher has for each student, and the current units of study.

For Younger Students

1. Have students mold numbers or letters (such as the letters in their names) from clay (such as play dough). Let them dry and then have students paint them with water colors or tempera paint. This ac-

TABLE 17.1
The art survival kit purchase list

Item*	Amount	Comment	Source
Brushes	16, ¹/₂ inch (c. 1 cm), flat with short handles; 4, ¹/₄ inch (c. ¹/₂ cm) wide; No. 6 watercolor can also be used. All should have short handles.	There is no need to invest in expensive brushes. They wear out too quickly. Handles can be cut off if too long. Hold back some for later in the year.	Local discount stores
Clay	25 pounds (c. 11 kg) of water base (earth) clay (or) 10 pounds (c. 4.5 kg) flour and 10 pounds (c. 4.5 kg) salt	Check school for kiln. If using kiln, need to order 4 pints (c. 1840 g) of glaze. Check with art supervisor on recommended type. Water base clay can be ordered and mixed by class. Cheaper but more time-consuming. Cannot be used for making wind chimes or liquid-holding containers.	School district central warehouse may stock, or mail-order house. School kitchen may provide, or local grocery store.
Construction paper	8 packages of 50 sheets each, assorted colors, 12 by 18 inches (c. 30 by 45 cm)	Can be cut in half for smaller sheets. If paper cutter available, can order in larger sizes and save some money. Cheapest source will probably be central warehouse or mail-order house.	School district central warehouse or mail-order house or local variety and/or art store
Crayons	1 box per child in boxes of 8 assorted colors, plus 4 extra boxes for refills	Older children can use thinner crayons. Some classes may bring their own.	Same as above
Drawing paper	12 packages, 50 sheets each, 12 by 18 inches (c. 30 by 45 cm); cream manila or white paper, 60 pound (c. 27 kg) weight	Can be cut in half for smaller projects. If paper cutter available, order in larger sizes and save money. Drawing paper is also used for painting. Cheapest source will probably be central warehouse or mail-order house.	Same as above

Item	Quantity/Description	Notes	Source
Glue	1/2 gallon (c. 2 l) white, nontoxic (or) 12, 1 3/4 oz. (c. 350g) containers for the children, and 3 larger 16 oz. (c. 145 g) containers	Can share with another teacher and buy 1 gallon of glue (c. 4 l). Smaller containers can be refilled from larger ones.	Same. Local hardware stores also supply white glue.
Markers	12 sets of 8 assorted colors	Best to have 1 set per child. May order 2 or 3 larger sets and share.	Local discount store or school district central warehouse or mail-order supplier
Masking tape	3 rolls, 3/4 inch (c. 1.5 cm) wide, 60 yard (60 m) rolls	Needed for displaying art work, taping papers to work surface, etc.	Local discount stores often cheapest. School districts may provide as part of office supplies.
Newsprint	500 sheets of 12 by 18 inch (c. 30 by 45 cm)	Local newspaper may donate. Computer printout paper can be substituted. Local firms will donate used printout paper. Newsprint used for many drawing and some printing activities.	School district central warehouse or mail-order house or local art store
Scissors	12 pairs, 4 inch (c. 10 cm), blunt; 2 pairs pointed; 1 pair large desk type	May need to order some left-handed pairs. May need 4-holed training scissors. Some children provide their own.	School district central warehouse or mail-order house or local variety or discount store
Tempera paint	Dry 1 pound (450 g) cans—4 each: red, blue, yellow; 2 each: black, white, orange, green, violet (purple), brown	Dry paint is cheaper but must be mixed and stored. (Mix with liquid soap for easier cleaning.) If ordering liquid, increase amount of each color by 1 unit.	School district central warehouse or mail order house Local discount stores may have in smaller amounts. Local art stores may carry.
Wrapping paper	1 roll, 36 inches (c. 1m) wide	Can share with other classes. Often front office has wrapping paper. Scrap cardboard can be substituted in many of the activities. Makes a good large painting surface. White is more expensive than brown.	School district central warehouse or mail-order house

Source. From *Art for All the Children: A Creative Sourcebook for the Impaired Child* (pp. 250–257) by F. E. Anderson, 1978, Springfield, IL: Charles C Thomas. Copyright 1978 by Charles C Thomas, Publisher. Reprinted by permission.

*It is crucial that all art materials be nontoxic. Materials should have their nontoxicity stated on the label. If there is no such statement, check with the manufacturer.

tivity can help to teach children both visual and tactual recognition of numbers and letters.

2. Write students' names or other letters of the alphabet in very large letters (36 inches tall) on large paper (can be obtained from newspaper printers). Have students fill in the letters with paints (tempera). This teaches alphabet recognition and gives children a feel for the letters.

3. Let students mold clay to form animals, foods, people, and objects, and have them tell you what they are making. Rolling pins and cookie cutters can be used. This stimulates creativity and imagination, develops hand coordination, and encourages speech.

4. Mathematical concepts such as fractions, addition, and subtraction can be demonstrated as children count clay balls and tear clay into more than one part.

5. Have children lie down on a very large sheet of paper (obtained from newspaper printers). Draw around them individually and let them color in eyes, nose, mouth, and other facial details. Have children color in clothes they are wearing and cut the figures out. This helps to develop self-concept and idea of body image. Cutting develops eye-hand coordination.

6. Put a bit of paint on a sheet of paper. Have pupils blow through a straw to spread the paint. This encourages creativity and is a good easy success activity (children can make a beautiful painting with little skill).

7. Have pupils paint large macaroni (use water color or tempera). When dry, have children string the macaroni into a necklace (use kite string or shoelaces). Painting encourages creativity. Stringing develops hand coordination. The children feel proud that they can make something useful.

8. Have students paint half of the outside bottom of an egg carton, adding eyes and pipe cleaner antennae to make a caterpillar. Draw a butterfly outline on paper and have the children decorate it and cut it out. Then glue it onto a pinch clothespin. Coordinate this idea with the concept of caterpillars changing into butterflies. Painting and decorating encourage creativity; cutting develops eye-hand coordination. In addition, this project illustrates a scientific concept.

9. Take a walk or have a scavenger hunt to collect flowers, leaves, nuts, and seeds. Have students glue these to a sheet of paper to make a picture or put them in between sheets of waxed paper, iron the sheets together (low setting), and make a place mat. Coordinate this with a discussion about changing seasons (fall or spring). Talk about things found in the woods or coordinate with a unit on ecology. This activity encourages creativity, allows the children to create something useful, and illustrates a scientific concept.

10. Have pupils collect leaves in the fall and bring them to class. Using white or brown paper, place different sized leaves under different pieces of paper. Then have students rub crayons over the top of the paper. After outlines of the leaves are formed on the paper, have students cut the leaves out. These cutouts can be put on a bulletin board or made into student scrapbooks.

11. Have students make tissue-paper collages using colored tissue paper, mat board, diluted glue, scissors, brushes, and pen and ink for accenting. Students can create different colors by overlapping different colors of tissue paper (Alkema, 1973).

12. Obtain scrap wallpaper from paint stores. Let students develop appreciation for shape by making wallpaper collages.

13. Lessons that integrate several of the fine arts are particularly valuable additions to the curriculum. For example, Hester (1987) describes an instructional activity in which students learn about and then apply theatrical makeup and sing a related song (i.e., "Put on a Happy Face").

14. Art and science can make an excellent combination within an instructional lesson. For example, students can be taken on a brief nature walk and asked to select and hug a tree. Then they are prompted with a series of questions (e.g., What do you see? feel?) and are encouraged to consider texture, color, size, function, and emotional features. This walk can be followed up with a drawing activity in the classroom (Swift, 1986).

15. Taunton (1983) suggests that young children must talk about art with others to learn how to respond to it. Teachers should be aware of the types of questions that can be asked to enhance these discussions. Children can be asked what they see, what relationships exist between parts of a work, what the main idea or theme is, and what type of evaluative judgments can be made.

16. Try Styrofoam sculptures. Scrap Styrofoam can be obtained from electronic supply houses, hardware stores, and florist shops. Items that can be used for decorating include pipe cleaners, wire strips, thread, straws, beads, toothpicks, ribbon, yarn, and feathers (Cherry, 1972).

For Older Students

1. Science fiction movies (e.g., the *Star Wars* trilogy, the *Star Trek* series, *E.T., Close Encounters of the Third Kind,* and *Batteries not Included*) are very popular with adolescents. Ask pupils to create a three-dimensional object from a science fiction movie or television show they have seen.

2. As students get older, they often want to assume some responsibility for instructional activities in the classroom. Have students who have shown some interest and ability in art activities develop different thematic bulletin board displays that reflect self-expression.

3. Secondary school classes frequently do skits and plays for their school assemblies. Members of an art class might help in such endeavors by designing and building the sets for these skits and plays.

4. Have students make paper, plastic, and wooden lanterns that can be used as decorations for school dances or other social events.

5. Very Special Arts Festivals are developing throughout the country, characterized by the motivation and personal rewards that have made the Special Olympics successful in terms of students' physical development and enjoyment. Teachers can encourage students to participate in the full range of art through class projects or individual works. These celebrations have further value in providing a link for the continuation of art into the students' adult years. Further information about local and statewide festivals should be available through state departments of education.

6. Secondary students often enjoy one or more of the following general arts and crafts activities: jewelry making, gem craft, metal working, woodworking, plastic craft, silkscreening, leather craft, papier mâché, weaving, shell crafts, and ceramics. Books on these topics are available in most libraries and bookstores.

7. Macrame is the art of knot tying. Students can make plant hangers, belts, bracelets, or wall hangings. This kind of

activity is also good for building listening skills.

8. Students enjoy making wall hangings by weaving natural objects such as bark, reeds, dried flowers, feathers, grasses, and sticks onto a warp made of string. Heavy cardboard can support the warp. Rolled newspaper can be used to adjust tension (Linderman, 1976).

9. Have students paint designs on glass. Materials required include pieces of glass, heavy cardboard, construction paper, scissors, tempera, tape, and picture holders. After the designs are painted, use construction paper as a background and cardboard as a backing for the glass design. Fasten a picture holder onto the cardboard (MacDonald, 1964).

10. Students can make wastebaskets from large ice cream tubs or 5-gallon metal cans and paint, wallpaper, magazine pictures, clear shellac, and yarn. They should wash and dry the containers; apply wallpaper, pictures, and so on; and cover with shellac (MacDonald, 1964).

11. To help students discover a variety of surfaces in the environment, lead them outside to make texture rubbings. Have them do these on white paper, using different colored crayons. They can cut out the shapes and glue them onto construction paper.

12. Murals are an excellent art project for students at virtually all age levels. Discussing possible themes beforehand, as well as specific features and materials that can be used (e.g., colored paper, yarn, buttons, crayons, foil, tissue) helps students plan their project. Themes might include the beach, the city, the Olympics, a garden, or vacation time. For inner-city schools a visit to several building murals might help to develop motivation (Bercsi, 1986).

13. Art and reading can be combined in book review collages. Students should select a book they have completed and then cut out words and pictures from magazines and newspapers to illustrate the idea of the book (Crisculo, 1985).

14. James (1983) suggests the following as features that older students prefer: using heavier materials such as clay or wood; using tools and materials that cost more money; creating products as gifts; using tools such as those needed in sculpture or ceramic work; and creating three-dimensional rather than flat, two-dimensional projects.

15. Hold a kids-teach-kids contest. Have students choose an art project that they think would be appropriate for younger children. The students must then prepare plans to teach the younger students how to make the project. Winners of the contest might act as art teachers for a group of children (Walker-Taylor, 1986).

RESOURCES

Alkema, C. J. (1971). *Art for the exceptional.* Boulder, CO: Pruett. This book presents a number of art experiences that can be used effectively with special populations. Chapters are organized categorically with most content devoted to students who are mentally retarded.

Anderson, F. E. (1978). *Art for all the children: A creative sourcebook for the impaired child.* Springfield, IL: Charles C Thomas. This textbook covers a number of topics ranging from evaluation/assessment to techniques for integrating art into other subject areas. The last chapter, covering necessary art materials and sources for acquiring them, is extremely useful.

Art and the exceptional student. (1980). Northbrook, IL: Hubbard. This booklet is one module of the Project STRETCH program. It presents six major objectives of teaching art to special students. Useful information and activities are also included.

Barker, P. C. (1983). *Art on a budget: 62 complete projects*. Portland, ME: J. Weston Walch. As the title suggests, this book contains many project ideas. It also includes suggestions for material attainment and management.

James, P. (1983). *Teaching art to special students*. Portland, ME: J. Weston Walch. This book contains project ideas for teaching art to children with various handicaps. It also includes general guidelines for teaching art to special students and for planning individualized instruction.

Taylor, F. D., Artuso, A. A. & Hewett, F. M. (1970). *Creative art tasks for children: Implications for use with the exceptional child*. Denver: Love. This book presents 146 art activities that are easy to perform and do not require elaborate materials or facilities.

Uhlin, D. M., & Chiara, E. D. (1984). *Art for exceptional children* (3rd ed.). Dubuque, IA: Wm. C. Brown. The majority of this book is given to case studies of children with various handicapping conditions relative to their art projects. A chapter on the "Development of the Normal Child in Art" and a chapter on "Art Activities and Procedures" are particularly useful.

Wankelman, W. G., Wigg, P., & Wigg, M. (1968). *A handbook of arts & crafts* (3rd ed.). Dubuque, IA: Wm. C. Brown. This book is a comprehensive sourcebook of many different arts and crafts activities. It is organized by different types of media and/or techniques.

Winsor, M. T. (1972). *Arts and crafts for special education*. Belmont, CA: Fearon. Following a monthly sequence, this book suggests 70 seasonal arts and crafts activities that are easy, even for nonartistic teachers.

Wirtenberg, P. Z. (1968). *All-around-the house art and craft book*. Boston: Houghton Mifflin. This is a very interesting book emphasizing that creative works of art can be produced inexpensively from materials found in the kitchen, laundry, attic, garage, or yard.

MUSIC

Music is an unavoidable part of everyday life. Think how many times music enters our lives each day and how it affects us.

> Music plays a major role in the every day and special day lives of most people. It has frequent applications ranging from simple sounds for improving the environment to complex, integrated, artistic works forming the core of life's important ceremonies. . . . Music is used whenever humanity wishes to transcend, when humans want to mark the most important ceremonies of transition in life, when events are to be made memorable, when it is important to unify groups, and to achieve physical sedation or stimulation. (Duerksen, 1981, p. 1)

Music is an integral part of our lives and should be a significant component of students' educational programs. Starm's (1979) comments are particularly noteworthy: "Music is an interdisciplinary and interdependent way of living and learning for people. It is part of all of us. Music for children should be spontaneous, and filled with exploration and enjoyment" (p. 70). Music can and should be exciting for all involved. Bruscia (1981) extends this idea by indicating that music instruction "is essentially a process of exploring and developing the musical potential that lies within each child" (p. 101).

Music is just as important to individuals with disabilities, and its potential for complementing an instructional program in special education should not be overlooked. Reichard and Gregoire (1984) make a compelling case for attention to music within the curriculum.

> Music reaches all children. It is as much a part of them as the rhythm of their heartbeat. Severely retarded children have been observed responding motorically to music when other stimuli failed to elicit observable responses. Autistic children have responded physically, and in some cases verbally, to music when other methods of reaching them were exhausted. Preschoolers have been observed reciting the alphabet with little or no difficulty when it was taught rhythmically. All students

can learn something from the use of music in the classroom; therefore, music should be used (by all teachers) in the mainstream of education as an instructional technique. One need only watch "Sesame Street" or "The Electric Company" for affirmation that music reaches, teaches, and reinforces in a variety of ways. (p. 288)

Music Education for Special Learners

The goals of music education for students with special needs should not differ from those for regular students. However, Thompson (1982) notes that music education for special students has typically emphasized "the development of motor skills, perceptual skills, social skills, and other nonmusical behaviors" (p. 26). Thus, it lacks an aesthetic orientation.

Teachers must become aware of what music education is, knowledgeable about how it can be taught, and skillful at teaching it. Peotter (1979) has pointed out that special education teachers are not often musically inclined and may hesitate to include music education objectives in their instructional plans. However, teachers who enjoy music should be able to incorporate it into their daily schedules. Music can be used to promote mental health, assist in social development and adjustment, teach language concepts, and develop motor coordination. Music can be an effective organizing influence for students who experience disorganization; the repetitive, definable rhythms can provide an organized element to which they can relate (Bildman, 1982). Music can be incorporated into games, finger plays, group singing and listening, and use of rhythm instruments. Learning a counting song may help students learn certain math concepts; a song that teaches the concepts of on, over, in, and out may assist in language development; and the beating of a drum or pounding of rhythm sticks may develop some large and small muscles. But probably the most important contribution of music is that it promotes various types of learning through activities that can be very enjoyable.

The use of music with special students can be categorized according to three major orientations (Duerksen, 1981).

- ☐ *Special music education.* This orientation closely resembles regular music education in that it focuses on the development of musical skills and knowledge as well as on students' participation in musical activities and their aesthetic interaction with music.
- ☐ *Music therapy.* This orientation, which has goals quite different from those of music education (Thompson, 1982), is concerned with music as a means of enhancing personal development. Its main goals are nonmusical. The use of music in therapeutical ways also includes adjunctive uses, such as mood control or motivation.
- ☐ *To teach other subjects.* Music has been used very successfully to provide variety to the teaching of other subject areas.

Teachers interested in detailed suggestions for sequencing a music education program should consult state curriculum guidelines and should contact state-level music specialists. Another resource that may be useful is Gordon's (1980) text, *Learning Sequences in Music.* Teachers interested in developing programs for adolescents who are moderately retarded should see the music curriculum described by Beal and Gilbert (1982). Ideas for incorporating music into the programs of students with severe handicaps are offered by Lathom and Eagle (1982).

Instructional Techniques

Music instruction can be modified to accommodate students' individual needs and learning styles. Graham and Beer (1980) provide some general suggestions for working with students with mild retardation who have been integrated into regular class settings. Their instructional hints are relevant for special settings as well.

1. Begin the music-education program at the earliest possible age; a preschool music-education program is highly advisable.
2. Provide a good singing model for the child at an early age and encourage the child to, first, copy the singing model and, second, sing along with the singing model.
3. Demonstrate the posture and other behaviors associated with good listening habits. Reinforce approximations of these behaviors whenever they occur at early ages.
4. Encourage the child to experiment with the singing voice and with other sound sources within the context of the regular music class. Special singing and instrumental activities will have to be developed by the music educator to facilitate such activities.
5. Make certain that every "reading song" has been thoroughly learned by rote before any attempt is made to read the song from the printed page.
6. Provide opportunities for the mentally retarded child to exhibit his music skills frequently in the regular music class setting.
7. Permit the child to have some leadership experience in the areas of his personal music strength.
8. Even when slow cognitive development prevents high levels of music functioning, arrange music experiences which will permit group participation by the handicapped child (e.g., singing simplified parts in vocal ensembles, playing one rather than a variety of classroom instruments, thus permitting the development of at least one reliable skill).
9. Encourage the child to practice weak areas at home under the direction of the parents or other interested persons with at least some rudimentary knowledge of the music skills being practiced.

10. Never base progress in music solely on the basis of acquisition of one skill or another (particularly not upon music-reading skills). Music is by nature multifaceted and permits progress of the individual in many ways. (pp. 56–57)

The question of assessment warrants special attention. Because few special educators receive a thorough preparation for teaching music, they may be unaware of the means for determining students' music abilities. Standardized tests are available (see Bruscia, 1981, for a listing); these instruments usually must be modified for use with students with special needs. Another technique for establishing levels of music ability is the use of a rating scale that lists skills (Thompson, 1980).

The musical content that needs to be taught may vary from program to program, but three areas are very important.

☐ *musical knowledge*—concept of rhythm; awareness of musical diversity
☐ *musical skills*—ability to match pitches, listen intently, sing, and play instruments
☐ *musical attitude*—appreciation of music

Skill Areas

Like any curricular activity, music should begin simply and expand as students' musical abilities and talents increase. Musical experiences need to be repeated often in a variety of different ways. Music can be learned and enjoyed through the use of games and play.

Listening   One of the best ways to develop listening skills in music is to give students an opportunity to listen to their own voices. Recording students' songs may begin with selections that the children like and that have immediate appeal. Children, especially of primary age, need not stay seated to listen to music; they can be encouraged to move to the rhythm, clap, or tap to the beat of the song. As students get older, they may become interested in folk music and dances. It is also appropriate to read stories to the children about band instruments.

When selecting records or cassettes to be used in the class, teachers should select music with lasting and instructional value, not just current popular music. Also, children can be encouraged to bring records from home. Filmstrips used with records/cassettes further enhance attention.

In addition, teachers may wish to discuss types of music heard in church, on the radio, and on television. One interesting activity is to have a member from the school band give a short explanation and demonstration of an instrument. Another excellent listening activity that capitalizes on current interest is taping commercials (radio or television) with musical jingles, which can be used instructionally in a number of ways.

Singing In theory, singing can be divided into four different categories: melody, harmony, lyrics, and rhythm (Peotter, 1979). All four of these aspects can be addressed in a music program. When presenting a song for the first time, teachers should tell the students what the song is about and explain unfamiliar or difficult words. Background information is beneficial and necessary, but should be kept brief.

Songs should be chosen wisely. They should contain lyrics to which students can relate and should be age-appropriate. Peotter (1979) points out four basic types of songs: happy, thoughtful, poetic, and socially relevant. Each category serves a particular purpose; for example, the last category can be used creatively to teach social studies.

After a brief introduction to a new song, the teacher may sing the song or play a recording of it. If sung by the teacher, the song should be enunciated clearly. Expression may establish the mood, and eye contact can hold interest and attention. To learn a song, students must hear as well as sing it a number of times. After listening to the song several times, students should be encouraged to sing along with the parts they remember. Of course, longer and more difficult songs should be broken down into smaller teaching units. The use of rebuses may help students learn the words.

When pupils have difficulty with tone patterns, teachers may use up-and-down hand movements or draw line notations in relative positions on the chalkboard (_–_–) to help explain tone patterns. If rhythm is a problem, line notations may be used, with short lines representing short notes and longer lines representing notes that are held longer. Clapping and tapping also assist in understanding rhythm.

Most importantly, teachers should remain enthusiastic and present music in an enjoyable manner. When students' enthusiasm begins to wane on new and unfamiliar songs, teachers should move to a different activity and/or song and return to the new song later.

Playing Instruments Peotter (1979) states that "instrumental music provides an excellent opportunity in musical expression" (p. 33). He discusses the advantages and disadvantages of selected instruments, such as strings, wood instruments, autoharps, drums, cymbals, and resonator bells. Careful consideration must be given to selecting instruments for use with special groups. Teachers can consult this resource for further information.

Developing a sense of rhythm and learning how to use rhythm instruments are important to music appreciation and enjoyable to do. Rhythm can be taught by teaching students to walk, march, skip, clap, and stomp to records with a strong beat. After the children learn the pattern, the teacher can vary the kinds of rhythm—fast, slow, quiet, and loud.

Many different kinds of rhythm instruments can be purchased or made inexpensively. Many books on rhythm activities include sections on making rhythm instruments. It may be advisable to use only two or three different instruments per song.

Using Music in Other Subject Areas Creative teaching has always been distinguished by innovation and diversity. Incorporating music into other curricular areas is one way to offer variety and maximize student interest. Duerksen (1981) suggests five strategies for using music to accomplish the instructional objectives of other subject areas.

☐ *Music as setting.* With this approach music is used to learn actual content. For instance, many students learn the alphabet this way.

☐ *Music as background.* Some teachers have found that music can establish a mood. It can also set a tempo for classroom activity.

☐ *Music as content.* With this strategy actual musical content is used as the springboard for instruction. Songs with historical information or contemporary social commentary are superb ways of using music as a basis for discussion.

☐ *Music as physical structure.* This technique is most often employed to work on students' physical coordination. Music in this application sets a rhythm useful for task performance.

☐ *Music as reinforcement.* This strategy should *not* be the only way students receive music in their school day; however, music can be used as a reinforcer activity. This concept has also been used in structured classroom settings in which students may earn points to "buy" listening time.

Recommendations

In music, as in other curricular areas, hearing or reading about personal experiences can be very helpful to both new and established teachers. The following hints should enhance the teaching of music.

1. Obtain an adequate collection of inexpensive musical instruments. Some teachers prefer commercially produced instruments, as do many students, but inexpensive, homemade ones can suffice. Figures 17.1 and 17.2 show examples of easy-to-make instruments; for more ideas see Mandell and Wood (1974).

2. If you use audio recordings in your class, cassettes can serve most purposes. They are easier to use and less prone to damage. If you are hoping to play a particular song repeatedly, however, a record may be more efficient.

3. Try to avoid bringing personal records and tapes to school. We suggest making copies.

4. The ability to play the piano is a real asset if you have access to one. If you cannot play the piano, elicit the help of someone who can and tape various selections.

5. Teachers should use music more frequently as background. Music can help set a relaxing, comforting mood.

6. Special educators should try to learn as much as they can about teaching music to special students (i.e., attend workshops, enroll in classes).

7. Teachers should include relevant music goals and objectives in students' IEPs. This inclusion is most appropriate for students in self-contained programs.

8. Computers have recently provided an additional vehicle for music instruction. Teachers who wish to develop a music program that incorporates technology should consult the special issue on computers and music education in the *Music Educators Journal* (December, 1986, 73[4]).

FIGURE 17.1
Easy-to-make musical
instruments

Rhythm blocks

Use a cross-cut saw and make scraps of wood into two blocks of the same size; sand them smooth. Nail spools or narrow blocks of wood on the backs as handles.

Minstrel bones

Remove the meat from short ribs of beef, wash the bones with soap and water, and dry them in the sun. Play the bones by cupping one in the hand and hitting it across the top with the other bone.

Maracas

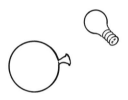

Apply papier mâché around a light bulb or small balloon. After it dries, break the light bulb or pop the balloon and fill the cavity with rice and dried beans. The open end can be filled with plaster of paris.

Brass tube triangle

Use a 12-inch length of brass tubing (¼-inch thick) for the triangle and a 6-inch brass rod for the striker. Drill holes so that it can be threaded with string and hung up.

Coat hanger triangle

Use an unpainted coat hanger, hold it by the hook, and tap it with a heavy nail.

Cap tinkles

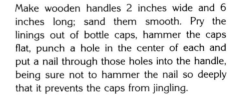

Make wooden handles 2 inches wide and 6 inches long; sand them smooth. Pry the linings out of bottle caps, hammer the caps flat, punch a hole in the center of each and put a nail through those holes into the handle, being sure not to hammer the nail so deeply that it prevents the caps from jingling.

Flowerpot bells

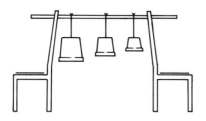

Attach a string to the bottoms of earthenware flowerpots. Suspend the pots upside down from a wooden rod so that they hang freely and are in descending order of size (and tone). Place the rod over the backs of two chairs. Strike the pots with a wooden stick or toy hammer.

Kettle drums

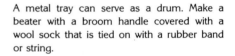

A metal tray can serve as a drum. Make a beater with a broom handle covered with a wool sock that is tied on with a rubber band or string.

Pot cover gong and cymbal

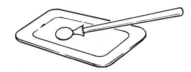

Hold a pot cover by its handle and strike the edge with a stick. Hold two pot covers of the same size by their handles and strike them together like cymbals.

Drums

Make drumsticks from unsharpened pencils with eraser tops, or glue large wooden beads on small paintbrush handles. Strike the bottoms of empty oatmeal or shortening containers.

FIGURE 17.2
More easy-to-make musical instruments

ACTIVITIES

Activities For Younger Students

1. Have children act out popular nursery rhymes such as "Jack and Jill" or "Little Miss Muffett" to the accompaniment of music.
2. Large and small groups of children can be taught seasonal songs, such as "Frosty the Snow Man," to be sung at school functions. Although Christmas is a popular time for such an activity, May Day can provide a similar opportunity; children can sing about the advent of spring and summer.
3. Another way to use the suggestion in the preceding activity is to have children who sing reasonably well and who know the words to a song sing solos. One child might sing an entire song, or several children might sing solo parts of a song.
4. Many popular children's songs can be related to a theme connected with social studies. For example, as children are learning about our country, they could also learn the song "This Land Is Your Land"; or when studying transportation, the could learn such songs as "City of New Orleans."
5. Many electronic musical toys are available. Children who have such toys can learn to play certain notes or songs in much the same way that rhythm instruments are played.
6. Create rhythm instruments out of materials available in the home, school shop, and local lumber yard. Students can play the instruments to accompany recorded music or group singing. The Association for Childhood Education International publishes a bulletin entitled "Children Can Make It" with detailed instructions for making sandblocks, cymbals, jingle sticks, jingle bells, rattles, drums, tambourines, castanets, one-string instruments, and xylophones.
7. Use music as a cue for rest periods, as a calming influence before or after lunch, and/or as reinforcement for appropriate classroom behavior (Reichard & Gregoire, 1984).
8. Encourage children to respond to music by moving in various ways. Children might walk at different heights and different speeds, might imitate animals or characters presented in the music, or might respond to the rhythm by skipping, galloping, or jumping (Graham & Beer, 1980).

Activities For Older Students

1. Because one goal for adolescents with disabilities is to develop satisfying social relationships, music and dance activities can be sponsored to enable these young persons to learn some of the new popular dances.
2. "The Music Corner" can be a weekly or monthly period in the curriculum that brings students into direct contact with musicians, disc jockeys, dance instructors—people who have a career in music. Students should be exposed to all forms of music and instruments (from bluegrass to classical), dance (from ballroom to the latest craze), and locations (from auditorium to night club.)
3. History topics can be made more enjoyable and perhaps more understandable by using songs as discussion points. For example, "The Battle of New Orleans" can be used as a focal point in discussing the War of 1812. Similarly, "The Night They Drove Ol' Dixie Down" and "Sinking of the Bismark" can serve as centers of discussion for the Civil War and World War II, respectively.
4. All adolescents like to feel that they are an integral part of the school society. One way of increasing the sociability of students with handicaps is to teach

them school-related songs, such as the alma mater or school fight song.

5. These same songs can provide many pleasurable moments for students on bus trips, hiking experiences, and camping expeditions.

6. To reinforce the ability to recognize rhythmic pattern and melody, have students play Name That Tune. Use a tape recorder to play prominent phrases of songs. Ask students to listen to excerpts and guess the song (Moore, 1973).

7. Guide students in taping a program of various forms of music. Students can make it entertaining and informative by putting in short segments about groups, musicians, and singers along with the music. Assign the different tasks in making the program (e.g., reading, writing, recording) according to student abilities and interests. The finished tape can be played during informal listening times.

8. Provide students with the various art supplies needed to make a record jacket or album cover. Have students create a cover to advertise their favorite song, music, singer, or group. One side might be artistic and the other informational (Athey & Hotchkiss, 1975).

9. Combine music and art by directing students to listen to various kinds of music and draw lines to express their emotional responses. Tell them that curved lines are associated with graceful and delicate music. Angular lines are connected with excitement or confusion. Horizontal lines are linked with rest and calm, vertical lines with dignity and poise, and diagonal lines with speed or motion. Students might draw white chalk lines on black construction paper for a distinctive effect or might use any combination of chalk colors.

10. Holt and Thompson (1980) suggest brief, informal listening times for stu-dents to become acquainted with all forms of music. These times can be scheduled when students first arrive in the morning, during homeroom, between classes, immediately before and after lunch, and/or at the end of the day.

11. Schedule a regular time for listening to music from varying times in history, different genres, or different countries. For example, a series of instructional periods might be devoted to country music, big band sounds, or Mexican music (Reichard & Gregoire, 1984). Relate applicable music to social studies themes.

12. A variety of software programs have been developed recently to provide specific instruction in rhythm. Coffman and Smallwood (1986) present a detailed review of 14 such programs.

13. Expose students to various types of ethnic music, especially when studying different cultures in social studies. Miller and Brand (1983) suggest studying ethnic music to promote understanding and appreciation of other cultures. They recommend the Bowmar record and filmstrip series (Bellwin-Mills Publishing Company), which introduce music from Latin American, Arabic, Oriental, African, and Jewish cultures.

RESOURCES

Graham, R. M., & Beer, A. S. (1980). *Teaching music to the exceptional child: A handbook for mainstreaming.* Englewood Cliffs, NJ: Prentice-Hall. This textbook is designed to offer suggestions to teachers. It includes chapters on the development of IEPs in music, the particular needs of special students, and techniques for teaching. A very attractive feature is the inclusion of annual goals and short-term objectives in the chapters on singing, playing, and moving.

Hardesty, K. W. (1979). *Silver Burdett music for special education.* Morristown, NJ: Silver Burdett. This book provides various musical activities for students through middle school ages. Included in the book are records that complement the musical activities. The overview that introduces the book is helpful for programming music instruction.

Nocera, S. D. (1979). *Reaching the special learner through music.* Morristown, NJ: Silver Burdett. This comprehensive book includes general teaching information, activities for developing music skills, and a number of actual songs, poems, and stories.

Peotter, J. (1979). *Teaching music to special students.* Portland, ME: J. Weston Walch. This valuable resource includes a range of information. The chapters on singing and playing are particularly helpful.

CREATIVE DRAMATICS

Like art and music, drama has been much neglected in the curricula of most students, with or without handicaps. Unfortunately, there is little published literature on teaching creative dramatics to special populations; and the unpublished materials (e.g., theses, dissertations, project reports), which might be useful, cannot be easily located or obtained. Interestingly, in examining the literature on creative dramatics and students with handicaps, Siegmund (1985) found more documentation of programs involving creative dramatics with individuals with severe handicaps than with individuals with mild handicaps. Nevertheless, she was able to find 17 studies that are relevant to the use of creative dramatics with students with mild handicaps and remedial needs. Illustrative examples of these studies are identified in Table 17.2.

The benefits of the arts in the curriculum have already been highlighted. Additionally, some students who experience significant difficulties with tasks such as reading or written expression may excel in creative drama. A good example is the student who is frustrated by an inability to write well, which affects both in-school and homework

performance. However, at her parents' weekend party, her engaging magic show is the center of attraction and entertains all who watch. Predictably, school focuses on her writing problems without acknowledging this area of strength. Unfortunately, drama skills are seldom assessed, either formally or informally, and are often not a regular part of the school experience. Creative dramatics favors students who learn best by **doing.** In some cultures, such as that in Polynesia, doing is the primary method of learning; fishing, for example, is learned by watching and imitating others, not by attending to lectures and worksheets. The potential outcome of utilizing creative dramatics in the curriculum includes skill development (e.g., sensorimotor, linguistic, social) as well as personal and artistic development. Bloomquist and Rickert (1988) suggest that creative dramatics provides students with opportunities to express themselves individually or cooperatively with other students in noncompetitive, success-oriented situations.

Creative dramatics can be defined in a number of different ways, but always involves the process of expression, whether through movement or vocalization. In the process, students are guided through various experiential activities by a leader (usually their teacher), and the process is valued as the focal learning experience. This emphasis is distinctly different from that of (1) **theater,** which is concerned with product (i.e., performance) and the communication between actors and audience; (2) **therapy,** which strives to achieve certain treatment goals; and (3) **physical education,** which includes acquisition of specific physical and motor skills. Finer distinctions exist with regard to other areas, such as creative movement (a part of creative dramatics) as opposed to formal types of dance, which require technical skills (e.g., ballet, folk dancing).

TABLE 17.2
Research on the use of creative dramatics

Study	Population	Procedure	Measured Behavior
McIntyre (1957, cited in McIntyre, 1963)	Children aged 10 to 14 with speech disorders	Creative activities including creative dramatics	Articulated skills
O'Connell (1966)	1st and 2nd graders	Creative dramatics	Creative reading
Martin (1977)	Brain-damaged children aged 4 to 15 with specific learning disabilities	Creative dramatics	School skills and personal development
Berrol (1978)	1st graders with learning and perceptual-motor problems	Dance/movement therapy, tactile stimulation	Perceptual-motor ability, academic achievement, and behavior
Reber and Sherrill (1981)	Hearing impaired children aged 9 to 14	Dance/movement lessons	Creative thinking and dance movement skills
Schmais and Orleans (1981, cited in Ochroch 1981)	Students with specific learning disabilities	Dance/movement therapy	Range of movement, body image, social skills
Iverson (1982)	Young children	Free play	Problem solving, on-task behavior

Instructional Techniques

In most classrooms a systematic creative dramatics curriculum does not exist; there really is not a step-by-step program to follow. However, some general considerations are worth noting and may be helpful in incorporating creative dramatics into the overall curriculum.

☐ Teachers should serve as the leaders of and participants in the planned activities.
☐ It is best to begin with simple activities that are known to the students.
☐ It is advisable to start with individual activities and then move on to small group activities before attempting a large group format.

☐ When trying to get students involved in activities, teachers should select topics in which students are interested.
☐ Behavior management needs to be addressed. For the most part, students will behave appropriately; but when certain students behave inappropriately, some type of management system is required. Jennings (1973) has found that the use of hand cues can work effectively. However, the cues must be understood by all of the students and must indicate certain consequences.

A variety of activities can be developed within the general domain of creative dramatics.

☐ *individual activities:* improvisation, puppetry, pantomime

- □ *small group activities:* re-creation of fact (e.g., historical event) or fiction (e.g., folktale)
- □ *large group activities:* class play

Bloomquist and Rickert (1988) provide an example of how to begin with simple activities and move to more complex while integrating individual expression into small group activity. The following sequence depicts an activity they refer to as the elephant exercise.

Technique	*Student Activity*
1. Define a basic movement.	Line up as elephants.
2. Add improvisation.	Explore the environment; avoid quicksand; hiccup.
3. Form small groups.	Move together; discover one another's differences.
4. Introduce a problem.	Help each other through quicksand.
5. Combine the groups.	All elephants work together.
6. Add conflict.	A hunter is looking for elephants.
7. Introduce vocalization.	Make elephant sounds, separating ages and types.
8. Develop a complete improvisation.	Seek protection from the hunter, confront his arrival, and resolve his conflict. (pp. 8–9)

This example can provide a frame of reference for developing other drama experiences, and it highlights how creative dramatics can be used to embellish a science or social studies topic.

Another example, recounted for one of the authors by a supervising teacher, illustrates how creative dramatics can be used within an integrated curriculum, also to augment subject matter.[1] During the study of how the Hawaiian islands were created, a class was divided into three groups, and each was given the task of creatively dramatizing the different theoretical views on formation. Students had to research the topic, design their dramatization, and express their findings through movement and narrative. At a later time students were involved in recreating the voyage of the Hokule'a, a replica of an earlier Polynesian sailing vessel. In this activity students out in a large field represented various land forms in the Pacific Ocean, and one student representing the Hokule'a retraced the voyage of rediscovery, which simulated the navigational feats of the first visitors to the Hawaiian Islands.

Thistle (1987) describes ways to enrich common folktales. She employs visualization, pantomime, and actual dramatization in engaging ways and also uses some clever techniques to get students involved. She identifies the following folktales as excellent because of their action and characters: "Little Red Riding Hood," "Hansel and Gretel," "The Three Billy Goats Gruff," and "Rumpelstiltskin."

If a school play is to be attempted, the following suggestions should be considered (Grabow & O'Neal, 1986, pp. 56–57):

- □ *play selection:* consider student abilities and interests as well as the characteristics of the play
- □ *location:* can be anywhere; does not have to be in the auditorium
- □ *set design:* keep it simple; use some props

---

[1]Integrated curricula are discussed in chapter 8. Readers interested in further information about this and other related examples can contact Joy Kataoka, ASSETS School, P.O. Box 106, Pearl Harbor, HI 96860.

- ☐ *costume design:* keep it simple; request assistance from parents
- ☐ *role assignments:* accommodate individual strengths and weaknesses
- ☐ *evaluation:* focus on student pleasure and satisfaction

The resources presented at the end of the chapter offer more detailed information about this area. Siegmund (1985) notes that two factors largely determine whether teachers incorporate creative dramatics into their instructional regimens: (1) their own exposure to creative activities as students; and (2) the nature of the teacher preparation program that they experienced. Many teachers feel unprepared for and uncomfortable with teaching drama. However, by focusing on personal expression rather than on a polished product, creative dramatics should make it possible for teachers without theatrical backgrounds to utilize this important subject area.

ACTIVITIES

The following activities are appropriate for use with children and adolescents with various handicapping conditions. Included here are suggestions adapted from the work of the Alliance for Drama Education (1983).

1. Have students use their bodies, faces, rhythm, and space to express feelings, embody ideas and images, or respond to music.
2. Have students practice verbal exchanges in pairs or in small groups to replicate real or imaginary human encounters.
3. Pantomime can help students learn to communicate their ideas and feelings without using words.
4. Have students use the five senses to become more aware of inner sensations and the ways that they can feed the imagination.
5. Provide opportunities for students to try out various acting parts or life roles (waitress or waiter, astronaut, parent, policewoman or policeman).
6. Develop audience manners by teaching students how to be a generous and receptive audience for the efforts of their peers.
7. Have students practice moving and/or speaking so that their stage partners can feel secure and all can work as a team. This activity also reinforces responsibility to others.
8. Have students work in small groups to shape and highlight the sounds of interesting poems with vocal inflection, coloring, and orchestration.

RESOURCES

Behr, M. W., Snyder, M. A., & Clopton, M. A. (1979). *Drama integrates basic skills: Lesson plans for the learning disabled.* Springfield, IL: Charles C Thomas. This book, best suited to instruction of elementary-aged children, provides a step-by-step method of teaching basic skills through the mode of drama. Each lesson contains the method, materials, setting, and skills to be taught.

Cottrell, J. (1987). *Creative drama in the classroom grades 1–3: Teacher's resource book for the theater arts.* Lincolnwood, IL: National Textbook Company. This book contains ideas, sample lesson plans, and ways to evaluate students' progress relative to the use of drama in the classroom. The author includes many helpful appendixes, including additional resources and stories to dramatize.

Cottrell, J. (1987). *Creative drama in the classroom grades 4–6: Teacher's resource book for the theater arts.* Lincolnwood, IL: National Textbook Company. This book is a companion volume to the previous resource and presents a parallel format. It offers six appendixes with helpful materials appropriate to Grades 4 to 6.

McCaslin, N. (1980). *Creative drama in the classroom* (3rd ed.). New York: Longman. This book discusses various activities related to movement, pantomime, and improvisation. Also included are suggestions for using simple stories and poetry for dramatic presentations.

Rosenberg, H. S. (1987). *Creative drama and imagination: Transforming ideas into action.* New York: CBS College Publishing. This book includes activities to be conducted for young people in Grades K through 12. The book focuses on theory as well as exercises and activities. Guidelines for evaluation/assessment are also included.

Tomlinson, R. (1982). *Disability, theatre and education.* Bloomington: Indiana University Press. This book was designed to assist the individual who wishes to involve persons with handicaps in performing a play or dramatic presentation.

18
Motor Skills and
Physical Education

The academic and social difficulties commonly experienced by individuals with handicaps have perhaps led special educators to downplay the area of motor development, except when clear evidence of significant delay is present. This chapter draws attention to the error of such inattention and encourages the development of effective intervention programs within this vital domain. It also addresses the important role of special education teachers in teaching physical education to their students (Roice, 1981).

Motor activities present the potential for providing essential success experiences to students with special needs. Therefore, complacency in program development is not warranted, even in the absence of apparent motor delay. A physical education program should be as systematic in its presentation of goals, objectives, activities, and materials as other facets of the curriculum if motor learning and physical development are to be maximized.

PHYSICAL EDUCATION IN THE CURRICULUM

Physical education should play a central role in the curriculum. Within the psychomotor domain the objectives of the physical education program include developing or increasing coordination, strength, speed, dexterity, balance, locomotion, and posture. Coordination refers to the ability to manipulate one's body and objects smoothly. Strength is the capacity for exertion or endurance. The objective of increasing speed is to help a student move faster. Dexterity is closely related to coordination; it refers to the learner's ability to grasp, hold, and release large and small objects fluidly or precisely. To attain balance and locomotion a child first needs to coordinate body movements and then to explore the environment and begin

to procure objects beyond immediate reach. Increasing this locomotion requires more speed and dexterity. Posture indicates the positioning of the body to decrease tiring effects. Good posture implies normal sitting, standing, and running positions. An effective program must be concerned with blending these related skills.

The benefits of a program of physical development are not limited to the psychomotor domain. Affective gains can be achieved in the form of enhanced self-concept and increased opportunities for social interaction (Moon & Renzaglia, 1982; Odom, 1981; Roswal & Frith, 1980). Successful participation in physical activities can also contribute to increased academic performance and language learning (Moon & Renzaglia, 1982; Roice, 1981) and to a greater degree of self-reliance and risk taking (Roswal & Frith, 1980), thus leading to increased independence in school tasks. In addition, employability—and hence, postschool adjustment—have been found to correlate with motor performance (Kolstoe, 1976). Chapter 4 discusses the scheduling of physical education or movement periods. When schedule flexibility is possible, such a period can provide an excellent complement to key academic sessions by shifting the emphasis of instruction. And finally, physical education is simply fun (Litton, 1978) if one can succeed in the activities.

A basic appreciation of normal motor development is a prerequisite for understanding the needs of all children in this domain. Gross motor skills develop initially in a cephalocaudal direction (i.e., proceeding from the upper to the lower portions of the body), which explains why an infant usually moves the head first and other body parts later. As a child nears school age, the focus shifts to developing fine motor skills at the periphery of the body, following the proximaldistal gradient (i.e., proceeding from the midline to the periphery). Research has indicated that motor development is generally uniform in sequence although variable in rate (Ersing, Loovis, & Ryan, 1982).

Bunker (1978) broadly outlines this hierarchical progression (see Figure 18.1). In her outline, body management abilities refer to dealing with one's body in relationship to the environment, including awareness, posture, and basic levels of physical fitness; fundamental movement skills include the areas of fine motor and gross motor development; and movement applications refer to a host of activities in which an individual is involved. Students who are handicapped may experience difficulties on any of these levels.

The focus of this chapter is primarily on the development of gross motor skills and related benefits through the implementation of a systematic physical education pro-

gram.[1] Fine motor skills certainly cannot be overlooked, especially in their relevance to functional writing and various instructional activities (Bender & Valletutti, 1976). However, the discussion of fine motor skills within this chapter is intended simply to complement their inclusion in chapter 11.

Physical Education and Special Education

Advancements in programming for learners with handicaps have come as a direct result of the Education for All Handicapped Chil-

---

[1] In discussions of motor development and physical education, it is helpful to distinguish between the terms *motor fitness* and *physical fitness*. The former refers to coordinated muscle movements related to task performance, whereas physical fitness demands less skilled performance that does not require refined neuromotor integration (Crowe, Auxler, & Pyfer, 1981).

FIGURE 18.1
Development of movement skills (From "Motor Skills," by L. Bunker, in *Systematic Instruction of the Moderately and Severely Handicapped* [p. 181] by M. E. Snell [Ed.], 1978, Columbus, Oh: Merrill. Copyright 1978 by Merrill Publishing Company. Reprinted by permission.)

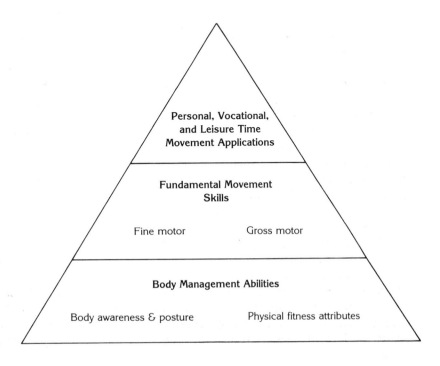

Personal, Vocational, and Leisure Time Movement Applications

Fundamental Movement Skills

Fine motor   Gross motor

Body Management Abilities

Body awareness & posture   Physical fitness attributes

dren Act of 1975. PL 94–142 has helped to redirect traditional concepts of special education away from a strictly academic focus and toward a broader interpretation that includes physical education. As stated in the PL 94–142 definition of special education that is used in the *Federal Register,*

> Special education means specifically designed instruction, at no cost to the parents, to meet the unique needs of a handicapped child, including classroom instruction, **instruction in physical education,** and instruction in hospitals and institutions.

Over the past decade many improvements have been made in the education of persons who are handicapped. However, progress in the area of physical education has not come as rapidly as advancements in the remediation of academic deficits. Speaking specifically of adapted physical education, Churton (1987) notes,

> Physical education, although cited within the definition of special education, has not grown to the same degree relative to the number of teachers trained and children served. Financial assistance from the federal government helped develop adapted physical education programs, but it has not been adequate to meet the needs.

Churton (1987) believes that much improvement in this area is needed, even though the Office of Special Education has made available more than $12 million since 1975. These allotted monies represent 8% of the overall funding in special education.

Adapted Versus Regular Programming

The question of appropriate placement is particularly significant in physical education because that class period most frequently integrates students who are mildly and moderately handicapped. The criteria for appropriate placement are clearly discussed by

Pyfer (1982). Some controversy has surrounded the debate between integrated and specialized physical education programming. The existence of a special body of knowledge for the physical education of most groups of children who are handicapped has been disputed because the goals, activities, sequences, and developmental progressions are similar to those of regular programs (Stein, 1977). However, the key concern of a specialized approach is necessary modifications and adaptations. Summarizing the guidelines developed by the American Alliance for Health, Physical Education, and Recreation[2] (AAHPER) (1973), Stein (1977) identifies the following elements of special programs:

- ☐ corrective features to deal with postural and orthopedic difficulties
- ☐ therapeutic movement activities
- ☐ remedial exercises to change or improve function
- ☐ adaptation of sports and games
- ☐ developmental motor ability training
- ☐ special emphasis on the specific needs of persons who are disabled

In many cases a full range of adapted physical education[3] activities is not available to students. However, special provisions should be available for any student who is unable "to safely or successfully participate in unrestricted activities of general and regular programs" (Stein, 1977, p. 4) or to derive personal satisfaction from regular programs. Furthermore, such services should be based on individual need rather than on

---

[2]The organization changed its name to the American Alliance for Health, Physical Education, Recreation, and Dance (AAHPERD) in 1979.

[3]Adapted physical education can be defined as "a comprehensive service delivery system designed to meet the unique needs of children with problems in the psychomotor domain" (Sherrill, 1982, p. 1). It refers to both a body of knowledge and an area of service to individuals with specific needs.

unwarranted assumptions associated with designated handicap categories.

Special education teachers frequently need to play three key roles in ensuring appropriate programming for students with handicaps. First, these teachers should advocate adapted programs when needed, whether available or not. Second, they should work toward integrated activities for each student who can derive benefit from them. Third, they should participate actively in implementing programs in conjunction with regular class and physical education teachers or, if necessary, on their own. Students must be evaluated individually and continually to determine whether their total social and physical needs are best met through special, integrated, or combined programs.

A variety of legal debates surround physical education programming for students who are handicapped. Geddes (1981) provides an excellent question-and-answer review of specific concerns that may facilitate administrative decisions about these services.

ASSESSMENT

Evaluation of motor skills should be sufficiently comprehensive to accomplish four objectives: (1) to facilitate correct placement of a child in an adapted, regular, or combined physical education program; (2) to provide diagnostic information on the individual's specific strengths, deficits, and motor learning needs; (3) to direct the design of appropriate physical education programs and the selection of specific exercises and activities; and (4) to evaluate the degree of progress of individual students.

The following motor competencies might be included in a checklist for assessment and subsequent program planning. These competencies include some that many students achieve prior to school enrollment; nevertheless, they should not be overlooked.

Gross motor competencies include some basic body management areas that are requisite to successful locomotion. In most cases they can be subdivided into several objectives for students experiencing difficulty.

1. identifies various body parts receptively and expressively
2. demonstrates basic concepts of directionality
3. demonstrates appropriate bilateral body movements
4. exhibits appropriate posture in a sitting position
5. exhibits appropriate posture in a standing position
6. maintains balance in various body positions (e.g., kneeling, standing on one foot)
7. maintains balance while walking forward
8. walks without falling (sideways, backwards)
9. successfully ascends and descends stairs
10. runs without falling
11. jumps with both feet
12. hops on one foot
13. gallops by skipping with one foot always forward
14. skips, using alternate feet
15. grasps, holds, and releases large objects
16. rolls a ball in a straight line
17. throws objects (over increasingly greater distances)
18. kicks stationary and moving objects
19. catches thrown objects (from increasingly greater distances)
20. applies basic gross motor skills to various games, activities, and leisure pursuits (e.g., bicycle riding, kickball, running races, bowling)

Fine motor competencies include the following:

1. grasps, holds, and releases small objects
2. stacks small objects in a tower
3. strings beads (or the equivalent)

4. successfully uses buttons, zippers, and other fasteners (of increasing difficulty)
5. traces objects and forms
6. copies objects and forms
7. draws objects with a brush or a large pencil
8. copies letters and words
9. writes letters and small words from memory
10. laces shoes and ties shoelaces
11. holds and uses appropriate eating utensils
12. cuts straight and curved lines with appropriate instruments
13. applies basic skills to advanced written language demands
14. applies basic skills to various recreational activities (e.g., pinball machines, video games)
15. applies basic skills to specific vocational tasks

Depending on students' particular characteristics, teachers can add to these competencies.

Assessing specific motor skills acquisition can be done both informally and formally. Checklists provide a structured format for informal assessment. Teacher observation can provide the data from various activities demanding motor skills, such as free play in the class, playground games, academic tasks, and lunch.

Formal Assessment

A great variety of diagnostic tools can be used to assess motor skills and physical development. These tools are periodically reviewed by AAHPERD. The following discussion highlights several of the most commonly used assessment devices.

The Purdue Perceptual-Motor Survey (Roach & Kephart, 1966) provides a series of 11 subtests that enable the teacher to assess perceptual-motor skills of children between the ages of 6 and 10. The survey includes sections on walking, board balance, jumping, identification of body parts, movement imitation, angels-in-the-snow, chalkboard exercises, rhythmic writing, and ocular pursuit. The instrument can be used in its entirety, or specific subtests can be selected in key areas of concern. The test items are closely correlated with the activities outlined in Kephart's *The Slow Learner in the Classroom* (1971), discussed later in this chapter.

The Bruininks-Oseretsky Test of Motor Proficiency (Bruininks, 1977), a revision of the Lincoln-Oseretsky Motor Development Scale, provides a measure of motor skills in children between the ages of 4 and 18. It includes items that assess skills in strength, agility, balance, coordination, and response speed.

Both of these tools, as well as other tests used in the schools (e.g., Denver Developmental Screening Test [Frankenberg & Dodds, 1967]; and Cratty Perceptual Motor Battery [Cratty, 1970]), are of value primarily with children for whom some assumption of motor deficit exists. However, because most students who are mildly handicapped do not exhibit significant delays or specific disabilities, teachers should not consider these tools mandatory or even recommended with the majority of such students.

A more significant problem for individual students may be physical fitness. The basic fitness assessment tool in use in many schools is the AAHPER Youth Fitness Test (AAHPER, 1967), which has been revised. It includes seven subtests covering various facets of this area. A modified form, the AAHPER-Kennedy Foundation Special Fitness Test for the Mentally Retarded (AAHPER, 1968, 1976) is also available and is appropriate for ages 8 to 18. Included in the Special Fitness Test are seven subtests: flexed arm hang, sit-ups, shuttle run, standing broad jump, 50-yard dash, softball throw, 300-yard run/walk. The flexed arm hang is similar to the pull-up subtest on the Youth Fitness Test. The 300-yard run/walk subtest is a shortened version of the 600-yard run/walk subtest of the Youth Fitness Test. These tests are good screening devices for detecting significant fitness problems. Results may be combined with those of the informal checklist mentioned earlier to direct a fitness program for each child.

An awards program for students with mild retardation was originally a companion to the Special Fitness Test; that program can be modified for use with lower-functioning students (see Litton, 1978). Another alternative for these students is the Motor Fitness Test for the Moderately Mentally Retarded (Johnson & Londeree, 1976).

One other assessment system should be considered because of its comprehensive approach to evaluating a variety of motor abilities and applications. The Geddes Psychomotor Inventory (GPI) (Geddes, 1981) was developed to assess the physical skills of students who are handicapped from infancy to young adulthood. It is accompanied by the Geddes Psychomotor Development Program (Geddes, 1981), which provides an individualized educational program based on assessment data. Part I of the GPI is concerned with normal psychomotor development and focuses on evaluating the acquisition of basic skills, such as sitting, standing, walking, and running. Chronological age ranges are provided for each motor behavior. Long and short forms are available, with the former being highly specific. A profile from the Early Childhood Level of the GPI is presented in Figure 18.2. Part II of the GPI provides descriptions of specific deviations from normal development that are common to various handicapping conditions. Checklists are organized according to mild-moderate subaverage intellectual function, severe-profound subaverage intellectual function, learning and behavioral

disabilities, and autistic-like conditions.

INSTRUCTIONAL PROGRAMMING

Following informal or formal assessment, intervention programs should be planned and implemented to remediate specific motor deficits and/or to develop skills needed to derive maximum benefits from physical education. Special educators may have responsibility for providing these programs directly to their students. Obviously, in a totally integrated arrangement, the primary role of the special education classroom teacher is to monitor the success of students in the regular program and consult with the physical education teacher about specific adaptations that may be needed. When specialized—or at least segregated—programs are utilized, the teacher's involvement in curricular design is often more significant and may include direct responsibility for implementation.

Table 18.1 provides an estimate of the relative time to be spent in various activities within an adapted physical education program. The most significant feature is the primary emphasis placed on movement exploration at the preschool level and the increasing attention to games and dance at subsequent grade levels. This shift should continue at middle school and high school levels with increasing attention given to activities that have social value within the context of the school and community, personal interest for the individual student, and potential for incorporation into leisure pursuits after high school.

Competition and Cooperation

An important question in the design of programs is the degree of competition to be built into instructional activities. Although educators may consciously attempt to avoid competitive games and sports, such a focus

AGE RANGE	Specific Balance	Walks	Runs	Climbs	Body Mechanics	Jumps	Hops	Gallops	Skips	Spatial Orientation	Identify Body Parts	Hand, Eye, Foot Preference	Grasp and Release	Builds Tower	Writing and Drawing	Manipulates Objects	Places Cubes in Cup	Places Forms	Rides Tricycle, Bicycle	Throws	Catches	Kicks	Strikes
5-6																							
4-5																							
3-4																							
2-3																							

Column groups: BALANCE & POSTURAL MAINTENANCE (Specific Balance); LOCOMOTION & BASIC MOVEMENT (Walks, Runs, Climbs, Body Mechanics, Jumps, Hops, Gallops, Skips); BODY AWARENESS (Spatial Orientation, Identify Body Parts); EYE-BODY COORDINATION (Hand, Eye, Foot Preference, Grasp and Release, Builds Tower, Writing and Drawing); MANIPULATION (Manipulates Objects, Places Cubes in Cup, Places Forms); PERFORMS ON APPARATUS (Rides Tricycle, Bicycle); BALL HANDLING (Throws, Catches, Kicks, Strikes)

Directions: Enter scores (using code) that best represent the performance levels identified on the Geddes Psychomotor Inventory (GPI). Use different colors to record the following on the chart:

_____ Pretest _____ Interim _____ Posttest
(date)   (date)   (date)

Code: [•] Functions within this age range   [X] Not testable/no performance

[?] Assumed level of function

Name: _____ Birthdate: ___/___/___
         (Last)   (First)   (Middle)   mo. day yr.

C.A.: _____ Pretest _____ Interim _____ Posttest   Class/Group: _____

Type of Handicapping Condition: _____

Checklist(s) Summary: _____

Other Assessment Items or Batteries—Summary: _____

FIGURE 18.2
Geddes Psychomotor Inventory profile (From *Psychomotor Individualized Educational Programs for Intellectual, Learning and Behavioral Disabilities* [p. 47] by D. Geddes, 1981, Boston: Allyn & Bacon. Copyright 1981 by Allyn & Bacon, Inc. Reprinted by permission.)

TABLE 18.1
Recommended percentages of time for activities in adapted physical education

Type of Activity	Percentage of Time per Grade Level		
	Preschool	1–3	4–6
Movement Exploration	90	70	50
Self-testing			
Gymnastics			
Track			
Ball handling			
Water play and/or swimming			
Rhythmical activities			
Games	5	15	25
Low organized			
Lead-up			
Relays			
Lifetime sports			
Dance	5	15	25
Singing games			
Creative			
Folk			
Square			
Ballroom			

Source. From Sherrill, Claudine, ADAPTED PHYSICAL EDUCATION AND RECREATION: A MULTIDISCIPLINARY APPROACH. © 1977 Wm. C. Brown Publishers, Dubuque, Iowa. All rights reserved. Reprinted by permission.

is a necessary part of the adjustment of every individual. Sherrill (1976) and Stein and Klappholz (1972) outline developmental sequences for competition that include competition against self, individual and dual competition, and team competition. The specific stages identified by Stein and Klappholz (1972, p. iv) and modified by Sherrill (1976) are these:

1. Compete with oneself to improve one's own performance as one tries to do more sit-ups or push-ups, jump rope longer, or throw a ball higher into the air and catch it.

2. Compete with oneself against one's own best performances as one tries to run the 50-yard dash or swim the 25-yard freestyle faster, jump higher or further, or throw a softball further.

3. Try to attain specific goals to receive a medal, certificate, patch, ribbon, points, other recognition, or the personal satisfaction that comes from success.

4. Cooperate with others to achieve a mutual goal such as winning a relay, simple game, or lead-up activity.

5. Compete with a partner or one opponent in individual sports like bowling, golf, and tennis. Compete against other also in trying to make the best score in fitness, track, and self-testing activities.

6. Compete in dual sports like doubles in tennis, badminton, and table tennis. Cooperate with one's partner in doubles tennis, with one's team in bowling, and in other situations demanding a limited number of interactions.

7. Compete with others to win a position on a team or a place in a group in which only a

certain number can participate, and/or compete against other teams or groups. (p. 56)

Competition can provide a positive means to increase participation and encourage a sense of achievement. At the same time, it represents a more normal approach to activity, as distinct from the "normalized" opportunities (i.e., noncompetitive) to which individuals with handicaps are often limited (Levine & Langness, 1983).

Cooperative games, on the other hand, are based on acceptance, success, and mutual reliance and are designed to develop strong self-concepts (Orlick, 1978), which many learners with handicaps greatly need. Weak self-concepts tend to discourage participation in any activities. Orlick (1978) cites the following benefits of cooperative games (pp. 6–7).

☐ **Cooperation** is directly related to communication, cohesiveness, trust, and the development of positive social interaction skills. The players must help one another by working together as a unit, with each player a necessary and contributing part of that unit.

☐ **Acceptance** is directly related to heightened self-esteem and overall happiness. In cooperative games each individual has a meaningful role to play in the game.

☐ **Involvement** is directly related to a feeling of belonging, a sense of contribution, and satisfaction with the activity.

☐ **Fun** is the end result and the primary reason that children play games.

According to Sobel (1983), many individuals eliminate themselves from participation in activities that require physical involvement because they have been turned off by too much competition. A program that overemphasizes competition in physical education frequently results in elimination and

failure for individuals who are not motorically advanced.

Students with special needs must be exposed to and encouraged to participate in a variety of activities that permit them both to enjoy competition and to learn cooperation. A balance between these two compatible goals should be sought.

Instructional Presentations

An effective physical education program requires a well-conceived presentation of various interesting activities. Unlike recess, which may be time for unstructured play and fun, physical education is another instructional period. Thus, it must be organized like any other lesson with introductory activities, activities to accomplish the objectives for the period, and closing activities. The best way to increase motor skills is through systematic presentation of stimuli and activities. Chambless, Anderson, and Poole (1981) encourage incorporation of cues, participation, reinforcement, and feedback to make maximum use of students' senses. In all physical education programs learners produce some motoric actions usually on a verbal command or signal from the teacher. Presented here are techniques to increase students' chances of producing the desired actions and thereby accomplishing the goals and objectives of the physical education lesson.

1. Keep directions and explanations as short as possible.
2. Keep rules simple and easy to understand.
3. Demonstrate action.
4. Be sure that directions and demonstrations are consistent over time.
5. Use varied stimuli to teach basic movement skills.
6. Reinforce correct behavior.
7. Prevent incorrect behavior.

8. Don't allow an activity to become tiresome.
9. Vary activities.
10. Keep the element of fun in activities.

By keeping directions and explanations as short as possible, the instructor can hold student attention and can jump right into the participation phase of the lesson. Most students are ready to do something and do not want to listen to a lecture. Rules should also be kept simple so that it is easy to understand what is to be accomplished and how. If students have any doubt about which actions to perform, the simplest technique is to demonstrate. Thereafter, students should be queried to determine whether they now understand. At this juncture the teacher should help students move through the task. Later, they can be required to perform the task by themselves. Allowing students to practice and rehearse mastered skills builds confidence as well as ability.

Closely linked to these suggestions is the need to keep directions and demonstrations consistent over time. The teacher should tell and show the same things from one day to the next. Any variation of an already-known activity should be explained.

When specific skills are difficult to acquire, varied teaching stimuli should be used. The following are recommended by AAHPER (Physical Activities, 1976, p. 6):

☐ *Manual manipulation.* This physical prompting guides body parts through desired movements to result in a proper response. This technique gives participants the feel of the action and can do much to alleviate the initial fear of a new skill or activity.

☐ *Coaction.* General or specific movement patterns are felt by placing the learner's hands on parts of the body of an individual, mannequin, or doll going through desired movement patterns.

☐ *Tactile.* Touch to relate more effectively what part of the body is to be used. This is an effective means of reinforcing other stimuli.

☐ *Visual.* Use of visual aids (e.g., slides, diagrams, demonstrations, pictures, films, mirrors) can be combined with other stimuli. Caution should be exercised in the use of mirrors with left and right concepts because of the reversed reflection.

☐ *Verbal.* Oral instructions depend on an awareness of students' language understanding levels. Sometimes a concept is understood but is eclipsed by unfamiliar terminology.

☐ *Abstract.* Signals, signs, and words can be used that students must receive and interpret prior to reaction.

This text has consistently stressed that teachers should reinforce correct behavior and prevent incorrect behavior. Reinforcing correct behavior in the physical domain may consist simply of praising students (e.g., "Good hit," "Good catch," "That was a fine run you made") or actually touching them if they are nearby. Of course, any of these reinforcing actions can occur in isolation or in combination and can be paired with some tangible reinforcer. The point is to let students know when their actions are correct.

Physical educators and movement specialists prefer learning on a trial-by-success rather than a trial-by-error basis. To prevent incorrect behavior, the teacher can arrange the environment so that incorrect behavior cannot occur. For example, if balls are not to be thrown or bounced before the teacher finishes explaining an upcoming activity, then the balls should be kept away from the students until the proper time.

As students learn more games and activities, they will naturally come to prefer some over others. The teacher may use these preferred games and activities many times but should not allow an activity to become tiresome by its overuse. Based on the Premack principle (1959), one method is to schedule preferred games or activities less frequently (i.e., make the preferred games or activities contingent on playing a less preferred activity). Even a reinforcing activity should be stopped short of satiation to ensure that the desired activity retains its positive value. Good activities are abundant once students develop the necessary prerequisite skills.

Sometimes students indicate little or no preference for a game or activity—that is, they follow directions but remain emotionally neutral—yet later in the program or period, these same students show a strong dislike for this same activity. These students are telling the teacher to vary activities to prevent inappropriate behavior. Variation means that several different activities should be used to foster the same goal, to alleviate problems such as boredom, inattention, and negative reactions.

Even though physical education should be considered an instructional area, elements of play need not be eliminated from the program. Students will often perform actions that they might otherwise avoid if these activities are made pleasurable. The teacher should always attempt to keep the element of fun in physical education activities. Effective instructional procedures should allow both teacher and students to achieve their goals.

Core Curricula

Although the majority of physical education programs for students with handicaps include a variety of activities that the teacher sequences, the teacher can take several approaches to core curricula.

Physical Fitness Research has traditionally indicated that deficits in physical fitness may be more common in students who are mildly handicapped, especially in those identified as mentally retarded, than in their non-handicapped peers (Dunn, 1973; Francis & Rarick, 1959; Rarick & McQuillian, 1977). Additionally, there are clear benefits for all persons who participate in organized fitness programs, ranging from improvement in health to change in behavior (Jansma & Combs, in press).

A program that has been used with success in special education programs is the **Royal Canadian Air Force Exercise Plans for Physical Fitness.** This program contains two similar plans, one for females and one for males, both of which have been effective in developing physical fitness. Each plan takes about 12 minutes a day. Regardless of physical condition, individuals start at the beginning of the program and systematically proceed through each step; those in good condition progress through the program faster than their less physically fit peers. This program can be easily structured to fit the needs of students with special needs because of its simplicity and efficiency and because it provides an opportunity for initial success and charting of subsequent improvements. It can be used in the classroom because it does not require specific equipment, and it fits conveniently into any daily schedule. One disadvantage is that its primary focus is on muscle endurance; it should therefore be supplemented with activities designed to develop flexibility.

Another program, designed by Smoot (1985) for students with mild physical handicaps, can be adapted for use in a variety of situations. The program is intended to be coordinated by a physical education teacher, but it provides some guidance to a classroom teacher involved in programming. Smoot describes the various steps of setting up the program (p. 264).

☐ *Step 1.* Research begins by checking the student's records and talking to the student's other teachers. If the child receives physical therapy services, the therapist may have suggestions.

- □ *Step 2.* Write the program:
  - □ assess current level of functioning with regard to range of motion, strength, posture, height, weight, and other important factors
  - □ choose appropriate exercises
  - □ start with success
  - □ use numbers on exercise chart that represent the number of repetitions, number of sets, or length of time in a position
- □ *Step 3.* Make the arrangements:
  - □ select a convenient time for sessions
  - □ select a peer-trainer (to help with recording and encouragement)
  - □ get the program underway (monitor how exercises are being done and how effective trainers are)
- □ *Step 4.* Periodically re-evaluate:
  - □ review the program after 10 sessions/ 2 weeks
  - □ change exercises?
  - □ change helpers?

According to Smoot (1985), the benefits of this program include improved self-image and the development of more realistic and optimistic goals. A program such as this can help meet the individual physical, social, and emotional needs of learners with special needs within the framework of physical education.

One other alternative worthy of note, especially for older students, is participation in regular aerobic exercise programs, widely available in most communities. In addition to the fitness benefits, these programs involve students in recreational activity that carries over to life after school. Participation of 30 minutes several days a week is the recommended minimum to take advantage of the benefits of such a program.

Perceptual/Motor Training A variety of programs have been instituted over the last several decades that purport to train perceptual/motor skills both as the basis for motor development and for their benefits in academic areas. Because efficacy data on these programs is generally lacking, the teacher should consider their usage carefully, monitor their direct benefits regularly, and avoid assuming that such benefits transfer to other domains. Several research reviews and discussion articles are available and should be consulted before adopting such a program as a core curriculum (e.g., Hallahan & Cruickshank, 1973; Hammill & Bartel, 1982; Mann, 1970, 1979).

Perhaps the most widely used perceptual/ motor training program was developed by Kephart (1971) and is summarized in his text, *The Slow Learner in the Classroom.* The program is based on Kephart's contention that motor learning is requisite to developing perceptions and concepts, and thus, the program encourages a systematic approach to developing motor skills and subsequently improving cognitive abilities.

A variety of exercises form the basis for Kephart's training program. Walking boards or balance beams are used to develop directionality, laterality, balance, and posture. Ocular pursuit exercises train eye/motor coordination. Chalkboard exercises are specifically geared to improving directionality. Form perception is trained via various object- and picture-matching activities. Because of the scarce efficacy data, however, the teacher should consider using the program only as a resource for activities that can be matched to an individual child's specific motor needs.

A number of other perceptual/motor training programs are also used in various geographical areas and may supplement special education classes. Examples include Movigenics (Barsch, 1967), Sensory-Integrative Therapy (Ayres, 1973, 1978), and the visuomotor training model of Getman (1965). Again program effectiveness should be proven before the teacher considers the adoption of any of these programs.

Psychomotor Training The terms *psychomotor* and *perceptual/motor* overlap for purposes of training efforts. As used here, however, the former refers to programs that are more localized within the motor domain and are free from presumptions about direct cognitive benefits. One recently developed program of this type is the Geddes Psychomotor Development Program (GPDP) (Geddes, 1981). It provides a sequence of activities that can be tied to the GPI profile discussed earlier in the chapter. An extensive list of suggested lessons is provided for primary, intermediate, and young adult levels; and the program is carefully coded to the GPI. Teachers are encouraged to emphasize primarily activities that correspond to areas needing improvement and to place less emphasis on areas needing only maintenance.

The GPDP incorporates a variety of interesting and beneficial instructional activities into a conceptually sound sequence. It can be viewed favorably for two reasons: it affords a structure that can be adapted to the needs of an individual student and/or class, and it provides a useful resource for motor learning exercises that the teacher can use even if the total program is not implemented.

Another program, Project I CAN, has generated a series of adaptive physical education programs that present objective-based systems for developing individualized instruction for learners with special needs. The Primary Skills program provides methods to help students acquire basic motor skills and cognitive concepts related to daily living, fitness, and recreation. It includes four modules: fundamental skills, body management, health and fitness, and aquatics. The Sports, Leisure, and Recreation Skills program emphasizes the basic physical skills necessary for participating in various leisure activities. It includes the following modules: team sports, dance, and individual sports (e.g., bowling); backyard and neighborhood activities; and outdoor activities. Both programs were developed and field-tested in conjunction with a federal grant awarded for that purpose.

Special Olympics

One organized activity closely associated with the physical development of persons with mental retardation is the Special Olympics. The Olympics were begun in 1968 after a survey in the mid-1960s indicated that fewer than 25% of school children who were retarded receiving physical education instruction. This information prompted the Joseph P. Kennedy Foundation to initiate the program to make such opportunities more widely available (Sherrill, 1976). The stated purpose of the Olympics is "to contribute to the physical, social, and psychological development of the mentally retarded . . . and help them gain confidence and self-mastery and start to build a self-image associated with success rather than failure" (*Facts*, 1977, p. 1).

Without question, the Special Olympics have provided an opportunity for many persons to succeed in an area in which they once could only fail. As Orelove, Wehman, and Wood (1982) note, the program has a number of key positive aspects: participation and competition at one's own ability level, favorable and supportive contact with other members of the community, training prior to the competition, parent involvement, and spin-off benefits to other aspects of local special education programs. In addition, specific activities within the program may have particular benefits. For example, Wright and Cowden (1986) conclude that participation in the swimming training program results in a significant increase in both self-concept and cardiovascular endurance in persons who are mildly or moderately retarded.

Despite the apparent benefits of the Special Olympics, teachers should keep in mind several concerns when planning such events for their students.

> The potential problem of the Special Olympics closely parallels their very essence. In an era when legislators and professionals are proclaiming the merits of integrating the handicapped into society, the Olympics stand somewhat symbolically as evidence of the traditionally purported "difference" between retarded and [nonretarded] children. (Polloway & Smith, 1978, p. 432)

Polloway and Smith (1978) cite two specific concerns about participation in the Olympics: the possibility of alternative, integrated programming within the community and the possible stigma associated with the Olympics by media coverage. Polloway and Smith encourage more careful assessment of opportunities for participation in regular athletic programs (e.g., intramural and interscholastic) in response to the first concern.

Another potential problem with the Special Olympics is the amount of time that may be spent in training (Orelove et al., 1982). As Miller (in press) notes, training should not become a substitute for physical education or for academic and basic skills instruction. Attending to this concern would necessitate training after school hours.

Teachers must carefully balance the benefits and limitations of participation in the Special Olympics. Although the Olympics can provide contacts with caring people and the many benefits of training, a closer evaluation of purpose must be sought, specifically as to who profits most from the Olympics. The spirit central to the eligibility regulations should suffice: participation should be limited to, and encouraged for, those persons who are handicapped and who would not otherwise be able to fully participate successfully in integrated athletic programs (Polloway & Smith, 1978).

No exact guidelines can govern the participation of a given group of students who are mildly or moderately handicapped. Decisions must be made individually. However, given the population changes in the 1970s and 1980s in programs for students with educable retardation (see MacMillan & Borthwick, 1980; Polloway & Smith, 1983, in press), a larger percentage of students in such classes may now be prime candidates for involvement.

ACTIVITIES

The following lists provide examples of activities that can help promote motor skill development and complement a physical education curriculum. Chapter 11 contains additional suggestions in the fine motor domain.

Fine Motor Activities for Younger Students

1. Painting with large brushes can help students refine eye-hand motor skills. Finger painting can be done prior to starting with a brush if the teacher suspects that the pupil will have trouble using a brush.
2. Stringing objects such as beads or bolts is a fascinating activity for many children. Games can be played in which students match another set of objects already on a string or place certain objects on a string by command.
3. Many of the same items used in the preceding activity can be dropped into precut holes in a piece of wood. Holes can be cut so that only a

certain shape will pass through (e.g., a square bolt through a square hole).

4. Using small blocks similar to the ones found in many kindergarten classes, have students make any designs they wish. As they become adept at this task, request that they copy designs previously drawn on a card.

5. Sorting small objects into different trays or boxes is well suited for developing fine motor skills. This task can be made more or less difficult by adding or removing dimensions from the primary sorting task (e.g., the student may be required to sort objects according to shape as well as color).

6. Tracing shapes or figures in several different media—such as sand, sawdust, or clay—not only improves finger dexterity but also provides much sensory input concerning the way each medium feels and looks.

7. After students have learned to grasp and hold a brush and pencil, they may need some help in forming straight and curved lines. Draw tunnels (two parallel lines) and tell students to go through the tunnels without touching the sides. Frostig, Lefever, and Whittlesey (1964) include many similar activities that may help in remediating motor skill deficits.

8. Going a step beyond the previous activity, construct differently shaped mazes on a ditto sheet, and have pupils draw lines through the mazes without touching the walls, having to turn back, or erasing a line that went to a dead end.

9. Most elementary classrooms have puzzles to take apart and put back together again. To aid a student in moving from less complex to more complex puzzles, first place puzzles with large segments in student play areas. As different pupils begin to assemble puzzles with large pieces easily, move these pupils to another area and let them play with more intricate and challenging puzzles.

10. Filling in dots and playing dot games can be pleasurable for children and easy for the teacher. The teacher can make ditto sheets with several dot pictures or simply construct a sheet with dots only and let children make their own drawing, picture, or dot game.

11. Draw different geometric shapes on a sheet of paper, and have students color these shapes. Be sure that students stay within the lines as much as possible.

12. Encourage pupils to use scissors in certain activities, such as in cutting and pasting during the arts and crafts period. Shapes to be cut should be large initially with a gradual reduction to smaller shapes.

13. During different holiday seasons throughout the year, children notice animals and objects associated with that particular season (e.g., turkeys with Thanksgiving or rabbits with Easter). Have the children draw one of these animals on a large paper bag and cut it out to make two cutouts of the animal. The student can then sew the cutouts together with needle and thread to make a stuffed animal. As children develop more skill in this activity, cloth can be substituted for paper in making the stuffed animals.

14. Some children exhibit difficulty in learning to tie their shoes. Large cutouts can be used to teach this necessary fine motor skill. The shoe cutout can be made from strong cardboard with holes punched in it for

the shoelaces. Have pupils practice lacing up the cutout shoe. Large, commercially made shoe models are also available and are helpful in practicing this skill.

15. Fastening buttons on clothes or zipping zippers can be taught in a manner similar to that for tying shoes.

Fine Motor Activities for Older Students

1. Older pupils with deficiencies in the fine motor area can improve these skills by constructing model planes or cars. They should first attempt larger objects and gradually move to smaller ones.

2. Fine motor skills can be developed during craft activities focusing on making objects out of paper. Paper crafts can range from simple glider airplanes, to folded fans, to intricate Japanese-style lanterns.

3. Pottery or clay sculpturing is a good technique to remediate problems in the fine motor area. Pupils can be shown how to shape objects from clay and how to use a potter's wheel. After these demonstrations, pupils can begin individual projects.

4. Activities using weaving can be used to develop fine motor skills and to raise funds. Students should begin this task with small looms or weaving frames and move on to larger looms. Making colorful potholders is a fun way to start this kind of activity.

5. Kits like erector sets provide pupils with a purposeful need to screw on screws and fasten bolts. As students develop skills in using these materials, they can be taught to make simple machines that really work.

6. The teacher and class can contribute to their own record book that includes such things as accounts of daily exercise, weekly achievements in particular events, and the leading record holders in each category of motor skills, physical education, and leisure activities. The intent is to encourage students to explore a wide variety of activities and value their progressive development in each endeavor. Particular emphasis should be placed on activities that students can continue in their adult years.

7. Give older students classroom jobs that involve fine motor skills, such as using scissors in constructing bulletin boards, stapling handouts, filing papers, cutting paper, and applying reinforcements to loose-leaf paper.

8. Fine motor skills can be improved in arts and crafts activities: jewelry making, woodworking, leather craft, papier mâché, and weaving. Other recommended activities include cooking, furniture repair, sewing, and card games (dealing and shuffling).

9. One table in the classroom can be set aside for students to manipulate old clocks, household appliances, lawn mower engines, automobile parts, cameras, door locks, motors, stereos, or bicycles. Students can be given time to break down and rebuild these times, perhaps as a part of a contingency contracting program.

10. Students can improve their hand coordination by tying neckties. Make the activity interesting by using out-of-fashion neckties and neckcloths. Model the process. Use a handout that illustrates important moves.

This is also an appropriate activity for developing listening skills and helping students follow directions.

11. Haughton (1974) explains how to make abacus wrist counters, which can also be used for behavioral self-monitoring activities. Materials needed include tanned leather, pipe cleaners, beads, leather thongs, and rulers.

Gross Motor Activities for Younger Students

1. Put water or some other liquid into a container so that it reaches the top of the container. Ask a student to pick up the container and bring it to some specified point without spilling any water. This activity helps the student who does not walk correctly to modify walking habits.

2. Line students up on the playground and play a game of walking through the maze. This is done by walking along and describing objects that must be walked around, over, or under. Stress to the students that this is a walking game and that running is not allowed.

3. Play a variation of Simon Says by having children imitate certain motor movements, such as "people walk," "dogs walk," "horses walk."

4. Because marching is actually rhythmic walking, many marching activities can be used to aid students in perfecting walking skills. A good example is marching to the song "This Old Man" while singing the different verses.

5. Many relay or tag games are well suited to developing running abilities. For example, Twenty is a tag game in which a leader counts to 20 and points to each person while counting. The person who is 20 is "it" and must tag other players. Players who are tagged help the original person to tag the remaining players. When all players are tagged, a new game may begin.

6. Divide the class into two teams with an equal number of players on each team. Give the leaders of the teams an eraser and have them race to a point about 50 feet away. As soon as they touch the spot, they are to turn around, return to the starting point, and give the eraser to the next person on the team, who then runs to that same distant point and returns. The team that finishes first wins.

7. Punchball is a good activity to develop running skills and coordination, especially if playing space is limited. The only equipment needed is a large ball such as a soccer ball or kickball. Rules for punchball are similar to those for regular baseball, except that stealing bases is not allowed and only one strike or two fouls are allowed for each batter. Also, a batter may be tagged out or actually hit with the ball while running the bases.

8. An all-time favorite running game of many children is Dodge Ball. There are many variations of this game, but basically runners are grouped inside a prescribed area and two or more players at the end of the playing area attempt to put other players out of the game by hitting them with a large ball.

9. For many children, playing one of the team sports such as baseball, basketball, football, or soccer offers many opportunities to engage in running activities and to develop gross motor skills.

10. Kraft (1981) suggests the use of the game Minefield to enhance perceptual/motor skills. Mines (beanbags) are scattered on the floor. Students are divided into pairs, with one member of each pair blindfolded. Children give specific verbal commands to guide their partners across the classroom without stepping on a mine.

11. Provide practice in pretending, body awareness, and control of movement by blindfolding students and having them pretend that they are made of a substance that melts in the sun (i.e., snowmen, chocolate bars, ice cream cones, etc.). Have them melt slowly, demonstrating control over their body movements (Eastman & Safran, 1986).

12. Increase awareness of left and right by having the students line up one in front of the other. Present the first child with a ball and have him twist to the right to pass the ball to the person behind him. The next student twists left and so on. Only their shoulders and trunk should move as they twist (Eastman & Safran, 1986).

Gross Motor Activities for Older Students

1. Mallet games such as croquet provide good gross motor activities while providing a great deal of fun. This type of game has the potential to improve eye-hand coordination, increase use of large and small muscles, and help students learn to wait for their turn.

2. Shuffleboard games can be used in much the same way and for the same reasons as croquet.

3. Because running is currently receiving a lot of public attention, activities related to running can be effectively used to promote gross motor skills. For example, pupils can be shown that doing certain warm-up exercises increases flexibility. Many of these warm-up activities can also be used with other sports.

4. For older pupils, playing one of the team sports such as baseball, basketball, football, or soccer offers many opportunities to engage in running activities. In these games the teacher needs to be sure that teams or individuals are matched in skill and interest levels.

5. Rope pulls and relay races are activities that can be used to develop gross motor skills as well as to build team spirit and the ability to cooperate.

6. Recreational activities for gross motor skill development include camping, hiking, rowing, and rappelling. Elium and Evans (1982) emphasize the benefits that can be derived from a variety of activities related to camping.

7. The class can bowl at the local bowling alley. Many lanes are open during school hours.

8. Many schools have auxiliary gyms that special education teachers can make use of to supplement regular physical education activities. Auxiliary gym activities include dancing, gymnastics and tumbling exercises, aerobic exercises, relay games, table tennis, badminton, dart games, weight lifting, and jumping rope.

9. Use nerf balls for indoor football and basketball activities without fear of damaging lights, etc. Frisbees can also be used inside gyms as part of organized activities.

10. If aquatic facilities are available, swimming and aquatic activities can be used to improve gross motor ability and to provide critical skill development for students. An occasional or regular visit to a local college or community swimming pool might be arranged.

11. Daniels and Davies (1975) suggest a focus on individual sports for students with handicaps. Although they may enjoy team sports, they may become frustrated because of their disabilities. Bait casting and golf are two recommended individual sports.

12. Teachers should be alert to the types of sports and games that are particular favorites in the school and/or community. An opportunity to develop skills in a valued area carries social as well as motor benefits for students both during school years and after completion of school.

13. Jones (1981) recommends setting unusual world records to add enjoyment to a physical education program. Suggested records include world's tallest paper cup tower, consecutive catches of a tennis ball in a fish net, human domino chains, and tallest inner-tube sandwich (tubes and people stacked alternately).

14. Physical education activities that can be related to other school subjects are particularly relevant additions to the curriculum. The reader may wish to consult Cratty (1971) for further information on the teaching of academic skills through motor activities.

15. To assist students with attention to and performance of motor activities, peer tutors can be used. These peers provide one-on-one attention, praise, and assistance with the skills needed to participate in individual or group activities (Webster, 1987).

RESOURCES

The materials listed below represent a variety of resources to assist in designing motor learning and physical education programs. A more inclusive list of available curricular materials can be obtained by contacting the American Alliance for Health, Physical Education, Recreation, and Dance (AAHPERD). This organization has also published a series of activities books that provide examples of how to vary instructional lessons to meet the specific needs of a given group of students.

AAHPER-Kennedy Foundation Special Fitness Test Manual for the Mentally Retarded, AAHPERD. This manual details how the AAHPER youth fitness tests were restructured to assess the physical fitness skills of persons who are mentally retarded. Percentiles are provided to compare a child's score with those of other children.

AAHPER Youth Fitness Test Manual, AAHPERD. This manual gives the rationale for developing youth fitness tests and explains how to administer and score each test. Tables are provided for comparing students' scores with their peers.

Active Learning: Games to Enhance Academic Abilities, Prentice-Hall. Games and activities in this book are aimed directly at academic skills in such areas as reading, math, and spelling. However, the last chapter of the book is devoted to problems of coordination and can be helpful in developing motor skills.

"Activities to Develop Your Students' Motor Skills" (Eastman & Safran,

1986), *Teaching Exceptional Children, 19*(1). This short article suggests six teacher-directed activities designed to serve children with mild handicaps and motor difficulties.

Cooperative Sports and Games Book, Pantheon Books. Many cooperative games are included for children aged 3 through 12. Also included are suggestions for adapting games for adult use.

Everybody Wins: Noncompetitive Games for Young Children, Walker. This book offers many activity ideas for young children in nursery school through age 12. Each game is labeled with the appropriate age for the game and the materials needed.

"Exercise Programs for Mainstreamed Handicapped Students" (Smoot, 1985), *Teaching Exceptional Children, 17*(3). This short article suggests four steps to develop an individual physical education program for improvement of motor movements. Ideas for recording data are also included.

A Guide for Programs in Recreation and Physical Education for the Mentally Retarded, AAHPERD. This guide describes how to establish and maintain a comprehensive recreation and physical education program for persons who are retarded. Suggestions are offered for developing activities, assessing individual progress, and securing facilities, equipment, and supplies.

I Can: Physical Education Program, Hubbard. A complete motor curriculum is presented in this program, including performance and enabling objectives, teaching/learning activities, game activities, and a developmental inventory.

Physical Activities for the Mentally Retarded: Ideas for Instruction, AAHPERD. Instructional ideas in this book are organized within several areas: suggested teaching techniques, activities, and sample units. Physical activities are divided into four different levels, beginning with basic movements and extending to individual participation in specific sports, games, and highly organized activities. Many illustrations show how to perform an activity or game.

Portage Guide to Early Education, Cooperative Educational Agency #12, Portage, WI. The Portage Guide includes card files for five curricular domains, including motor development. The motor activities range from basic body control to skipping and somersaults.

Recreation and Physical Activity for the Mentally Retarded, CEC, AAHPERD. This short but informative book gives a brief overview of the fields of recreation and mental retardation. Descriptions of objectives, outcomes, and principles of organization are also provided. The activities section of the book includes numerous recreational activities for use with pupils with mental retardation.

Royal Canadian Air Force Exercise Plans for Physical Fitness, Simon & Schuster. This program was originally developed for men and women in the Royal Canadian Air Force but has been extended for use by persons outside the military. Two plans for physical fitness are reviewed in this manual: plan XBX is a daily physical fitness program for females, and plan 5BX is a daily fitness program for males.

The Slow Learner in the Classroom, Merrill. Activities to remediate problems in the motor and perceptual area are included in this now-classic volume.

Parts I and II of the book are mainly concerned with development, achievement, and Kephart's perceptual survey rating scale. Part III names and explains different activities to remediate motor deficits.

Appendix:
Publishers' Addresses

Abingdon Press
    201 Eighth Avenue, S
    Nashville, TN 37202

Academic Therapy Publications
    20 Commercial Boulevard
    Novato, CA 94947

Acropolis Books
    2400 17th Street, NW
    Washington, DC 20009

Allyn & Bacon, Inc.
    7 Wells Avenue
    Newton, MA 02159

Behavioral Publications/Human Sciences Press
    72 Fifth Avenue
    New York, NY 10011

Belwin Mills Publishers
    25 Deshon Drive
    Melville, NY 11747

Bobbs-Merrill Company, Inc.
    866 Third Avenue
    New York, NY 10022

Wm. C. Brown Company Publishers
    2460 Kemper Boulevard
    Dubuque, IA 52001

Citation Press
    730 Broadway
    New York, NY 10003

Consulting Psychologists Press
    577 College Avenue
    Palo Alto, CA 94306

Crown Publishers
    225 Park Avenue, S
    New York, NY 10003

Educational Activities, Inc.
    1937 Grand Avenue
    Baldwin, NY 11520

EMC Corporation
    300 York Avenue
    St. Paul, MN 55101

Ginn & Company
    191 Spring Street
    Lexington, MA 02173

Harcourt Brace Jovanovich, Inc.
    1250 Sixth Avenue
    San Diego, CA 92101

Harper & Row Publishers, Inc.
    10 East 53rd Street
    New York, NY 10022

Holt, Rinehart & Winston, Inc.
    383 Madison Avenue
    New York, NY 10017

Houghton Mifflin Company
    One Beacon Street
    Boston, MA 02107

Human Policy Press
    P.O. Box 127
    Syracuse, NY 13210

Human Resource Development Press
    22 Amherst Road
    Amherst, MA 01002

Humanics Press
    P.O. Box 7447
    Atlanta, GA 30309

Incentive Publications
    3835 Cleghorn Avenue
    Nashville, TN 37215

Interstate Printers & Publishers, Inc.
    19–27 North Jackson Street
    Danville, IL 61832

Alfred A. Knopf
    201 E. 50th Street
    New York, NY 10022

Lea & Febiger Publishing
    600 S. Washington Square
    Philadelphia, PA 19106

Love Publishing Company
    1777 S. Bellaire Street
    Denver, CO 80222

Macmillan Company
    866 Third Avenue
    New York, NY 10022

McGraw-Hill Book Company
    1221 Avenue of the Americas
    New York, NY 10020

David McKay Company
    2 Park Avenue
    New York, NY 10016

Merrill Publishing Company
    1300 Alum Creek Drive
    Columbus, OH 43216

Milton Bradley Company
433 Shaker Road, E
Longmeadow, MA 01028

C. V. Mosby Company
11830 Westline Industrial Drive
St. Louis, MO 63146

NEA Publications & Sales
1210 16th Street, NW
Washington, DC 20036

New Readers Press
1320 Jamesville Avenue
Box 131
Syracuse, NY 13210

Northwestern University Press
1735 Benson Avenue
Evanston, IL 60201

Oxford University Press, Inc.
200 Madison Avenue
New York, NY 10016

Parker Publishing Company
Sylvan Avenue
Englewood Cliffs, NJ 07632

Pro-Ed
5341 Industrial Oaks Boulevard
Austin, TX 78735

Psychological Corporation
1250 Sixth Avenue
San Diego, CA 92101

Psychological Dimensions
10 W. 66th Street, Suite 4H
New York, NY 10023

Reader's Digest Services
Educational Division
Pleasantville, NY 10570

Research Press
P.O. Box 31771
Champaign, IL 61820

Scott, Foresman & Company
1900 East Lake Avenue
Glenview, IL 60025

Silbert & Bress Publications
P.O. Box 68
Mahopac, NY 10541

Southern Illinois University Press
P.O. Box 3697
Carbondale, IL 62901

Southern Regional Educational Board
1340 Spring Street, NW
Atlanta, GA 30309

Syracuse University Press
1600 Jamesville Avenue
Syracuse, NY 13244

Charles C Thomas Publisher
2600 S. First Street
Springfield, IL 62794

United States Department of Health and Human
Services
200 Independence Avenue, SW
Washington, DC 20201

University of Chicago Press
5801 Ellis Avenue
Chicago, IL 60637

University of Illinois Press
54 E. Gregory Drive
Champaign, IL 61820

University of Wisconsin Press
114 N. Murray Street
Madison, WI 53715

Wadsworth Publishing Company
10 Davis Drive
Belmont, CA 94002

George Wahr Publishing Company
$304\frac{1}{2}$ S. State Street
Ann Arbor, MI 48104

Western Psychological Services
12031 Wilshire Boulevard
Los Angeles, CA 90025

John Wiley & Sons
605 Third Avenue
New York, NY 10158

Zaner-Bloser Company
2300 W. Fifth Avenue
P.O. Box 16764
Columbus, OH 43216

References

Aach, S. (1981). Art and the IEP. In L. N. Kearns et al. (Eds.), *Readings: Developing arts programs for handicapped students*. Harrisburg: Pennsylvania State Department of Education.

AAHPER. (1967). *Youth fitness test manual*. Washington, DC: President's Council on Physical Fitness.

AAHPER. (1968, 1976). *AAHPER-Kennedy Foundation Special Fitness Test*. Washington, DC: Author.

Abrahamsen, A., Cavallo, M., & McCluer, A. (1985). Is the sign advantage a robust phenomenon? From gesture to language in two modalities. *Merrill-Palmer Quarterly, 31,* 177–209.

Abruscato, J., & Hassard, J. (1978). *The earthpeople activity book: People, places, pleasures & other delights*. Santa Monica, CA: Goodyear.

Achenbach, T., & Zigler, E. (1968). Cue-learning and problem-learning strategies in normal and retarded children. *Child Development, 39,* 827–848.

Acredalo, L. & Goodwyn, S. (1985). Symbolic gesturing in language development: A case study. *Human Development, 28,* 40–49.

Adachi, M. (1981). *The language for the four fundamental operations in elementary school mathematics in Hawaii*. Honolulu: University of Hawaii.

Adams, A., Carnine, D., & Gersten, R. (1982). Instructional strategies for studying content area texts in the intermediate grades. *Reading Research Quarterly, 18,* 27–55.

Alabiso, F. (1972). Inhibitory functions of attention in reducing hyperactive behavior. *American Journal of Mental Deficiency, 77,* 259–282.

Alberto, P. A., & Troutman, A. C. (1982, 1986). *Applied behavior analysis for teachers*. Columbus: Merrill.

Algozzine, B., & Korinek, L. (1985). Where is special education for students with high prevalence handicaps going? *Exceptional Children, 51,* 388–394.

Algozzine, B., Mirkin, P., Thurlow, M., & Graden, J. (1981, October). *Opportunity to learn as a function of what your teacher thinks of you— Practice, practice, practice: An update on the work of the Minnesota Research Institute*. Paper presented at the Third Annual Conference of the Council for Learning Disabilities, Houston, TX.

Alkema, C. (1973). *Tissue paper creations*. New York: Sterling.

Allen, R. V., & Halvorsen, G. C. (1961). The language experience approach to reading instruction. *Contributions in Reading*. Boston: Ginn.

Alley, G. R., & Deshler, D. D. (1979). *Teaching the learning disabled adolescent: Strategies and methods*. Denver: Love.

Alliance for Drama Education. (1983). *An overview to getting dramatic*. (Available from the Alliance for Drama Education, 45–305 Makalani Street, Kaneohe, HI 96744)

Anderson, F. E. (1975). Mainstreaming art as well as children. *Art Education, 28,* (8), 26–27.

Anderson, F. E. (1978). *Art for all the children: A creative sourcebook for the impaired child*. Springfield, IL: Charles C Thomas.

Anderson, F. E., & Barnfield, L. S. (1974). Art especially for the exceptional. *Art Education, 27* (4/5), 13–15.

Andre, K. (1982). *An adapted social studies outline for fifth grade learning disabled students*. Unpublished manuscript, University of Hawaii at Manoa.

Armstrong, D. G. (1984). Helping youngsters grapple with textbook terminology. *The Social Studies, 75,* 216–219.

Arnold, A. J. (1983, February). What's new? *Learning, 27.*

Ashlock, H. R. (1986). *Error patterns in computation: A semi-programmed approach* (4th ed.). Columbus, OH: Merrill.

Athey, M., & Hotchkiss, G. (1975). *A galaxy of games for the music class*. West Nyack, NY: Parker.

Atkinson, R. C., & Shiffrin, R. M. (1968). Human memory: A proposed system and its control processes. In K. W. Spence & J. T. Spence (Eds.). *The psychology of learning and motivation* (Vol. 2, pp. 89–195). New York: Academic Press.

Aukerman, R. C. (1971). *Approaches to beginning reading*. New York: John Wiley & Sons.

Aullis, M. (1978). *Developmental and remedial reading in the middle grades*. Boston: Allyn & Bacon.

Axelrod, S. (1983). *Behavior modification for the*

classroom teacher (2nd ed.). New York: McGraw-Hill.

Axelrod, S., Hall, R. V., & Tams, A. (1979). Comparison of two common classroom seating arrangements. *Academic Therapy, 15,* 29–36.

Ayres, A. J. (1973). *Sensory integration and learning disorders.* Los Angeles: Western Psychological Services.

Ayres, A. J. (1978). Learning disabilities and the vestibular system. *Journal of Learning Disabilities, 11,* 18–29.

Azrin, N. H., & Powers, M. A. (1975). Eliminating classroom disturbances of emotionally disturbed children by positive practice. *Behavior Therapy, 6,* 525–534.

Azrin, N. H., & Wesolowski, M. D. (1974). Theft reversal: An overcorrection procedure for eliminating stealing by retarded persons. *Journal of Applied Behavior Analysis, 7,* 577–581.

Bailey, E. J. (1975). *Academic activities for adolescents with learning disabilities.* Evergreen, CO: Learning Pathways.

Baker, M. (1981). *Focus on life science.* Columbus, OH: Merrill.

Baldwin, D. W. (1958). The educable mentally retarded child in the regular grades. *Exceptional Children, 25,* 106–108, 112.

Ball, D. W. (1978). *ESS/special education teacher's guide.* St. Louis: Webster/McGraw-Hill.

Balla, D., & Zigler, E. (1979). Personality development in retarded persons. In N. R. Ellis (Ed.), *Handbook of mental deficiency: Psychological theory and research* (2nd ed., pp. 143–168). Hillsdale, NJ: Lawrence Erlbaum.

Ballew, H. (1973). *Teaching children mathematics.* Columbus, OH: Merrill.

Balow, I. H., Farr, R., Hogan, T. P., & Prescott, G. A. (1979). *Metropolitan Achievement Tests.* New York: Psychological Corporation.

Balthazar, E. E. (1971). *Balthazar Scales of Adaptive Behavior for the Profoundly and Severely Mentally Retarded: Section 1. Scales of Functional Independence.* Champaign, IL: Research Press.

Balthazar, E. E. (1973). *Balthazar Scales of Adaptive Behavior II: Scales of Social Adaptation.* Palo Alto, CA: Consulting Psychologists Press.

Balthazar, E. E., & Stevens, H. A. (1975). *The emotionally disturbed, mentally retarded: A historical and contemporary perspective.* Englewood Cliffs, NJ: Prentice-Hall.

Bangs, T. E. (1975). *Vocabulary Comprehension Scale.* Boston: Teaching Resources.

Barbe, W. B., Milone, M. N., & Wasylyk, T. M. (1983). Manuscript is the "write" start. *Academic Therapy, 18,* 397–405.

Barenbaum, E. M. (1983). Writing in the special class. *Topics in Learning and Learning Disabilities, 3*(3), 12–20.

Barhydt, F. (1987). Have you interrupted a good book lately? *Instructor, 96,* 70.

Baroni, D. (1987). Have primary children draw to expand vocabulary. *The Reading Teacher, 40,* 819–820.

Barrish, H. H., Saunders, M., & Wolf, M. M. (1969). Good behavior game: Effects of individual contingencies for group consequences on disruptive behavior in a classroom. *Journal of Applied Behavior Analysis, 2,* 119–124.

Barsch, R. H. (1967). A visual-spatial concept of spelling. *Academic Therapy, 3,* 5–8.

Bartel, N. R. (1982). Problems in mathematics achievement. In D. D. Hammill & N. R. Bartel (Eds.), *Teaching children with learning and behavior problems* (3rd ed.). Boston: Allyn & Bacon.

Bartlett, R. H. (1979). Mental retardation—Where does the future lie? *Education and Training of the Mentally Retarded, 14,* 3–4.

Barton, L. E., Brulle, A. R., & Repp, A. C. (1983). Aversive techniques and the doctrine of least restrictive alternative. *Exceptional Education Quarterly, 3*(4), 1–8.

Bass, M. S. (1972). *Developing communication acceptance of sex education for the mentally retarded.* New York: Human Sciences Press.

Bateman, B. D. (1971). *The essentials of teaching.* Sioux Falls, SD: Dimensions.

Bateman, B. D. (1982) Legal and ethical dilemmas of special educators. *Exceptional Education Quarterly, 2*(4), 57–67.

Battaglini, C., & Wert, N. (1981). Art: Many options for creative activity. In L. N. Kearns et al. (Eds.), *Readings: Developing arts programs for handicapped students.* Harrisburg: Pennsylvania State Department of Education.

Baumeister, A. A., & Brooks, P. H. (1981). Cognitive deficits in mental retardation. In J. M.

Kauffman & D. P. Hallahan (Eds.), *Handbook of special education*. Englewood Cliffs, NJ: Prentice-Hall.

Baumeister, A. A., Smith, T., & Rose, J. (1965). The effects of stimulus complexity and retention interval upon short term memory. *American Journal of Mental Deficiency, 70*, 129–134.

Beal, M. R., & Gilbert, J. P. (1982). Music curriculum for the handicapped. *Music Educators Journal, 68*(8), 52–55.

Bean, T., & Peterson, J. (1981). Reasoning guides: Fostering readiness in the content areas. *Reading Horizons, 21*, 196–199.

Beatty, L. S., Madden, R., Gardner, E. F., & Karlsen, B. (1978). *Stanford Diagnostic Mathematics Test*. New York: Psychological Corporation.

Becker, R. L. (1975). *AAMD-Becker Reading-Free Interest Inventory*. Washington, DC: AAMD.

Becker, W. C. (1977). Teaching reading and language to the disadvantaged: What have we learned from field research? *Harvard Educational Review, 47*, 518–543.

Becker, W. (1984). Corrective reading program evaluated with secondary students in San Diego. *Association for Direct Instruction News, 3*(3), 1, 23.

Becker, W. C., & Carnine, D. W. (1980). Direct instruction. In B. B. Lahey & A. E. Kazdin (Eds.), *Advances in clinical child psychology* (Vol. 3, pp. 429–473). New York: Plenum.

Becker, W. C., & Carnine, D. W. (1981). Direct instruction: A behavior theory model for comprehensive educational intervention with the disadvantaged. In S. W. Bijou & R. Ruiz (Eds.), *Behavior modification: Contributions to education* (pp. 145–210). Hillsdale, NJ: Lawrence Erlbaum.

Becker, W. C., Englemann, S., & Thomas, D. R. (1971). *Teaching: A course in applied psychology*. Chicago: Science Research Associates.

Beier, D. C. (1964). Behavioral disturbances in the mentally retarded. In H. Stevens & R. Heber (Eds.), *Mental retardation: A review of research* (pp. 453–487). Chicago: University of Chicago Press.

Belmont, J. M. (1966). Long-term memory in mental retardation. In N. R. Ellis (Ed.), *International review of research in mental retardation* (Vol 1). New York: Academic Press.

Bender, M., & Valletutti, P. (1976). *Teaching the moderately and severely handicapped*. Austin, TX: Pro-Ed.

Bennett, H., Seashore, G., & Wesman, A. G. (1969). *Differential Aptitude Tests*. New York: Psychological Corporation.

Bennett, R. (1982). Applications of microcomputer technology to special education. *Exceptional Children, 49*, 102–105.

Bercsi, C. (1986). Mural magic. *Arts and Activities, 100*(3), 64–65.

Bereiter, C., & Englemann, S. (1966). *Teaching disadvantaged children in the preschool*. Englewood Cliffs, NJ: Prentice-Hall.

Berrol, C. E. (1978). The effects of two movement remediation programs on selected measures of perceptual-motor ability, academic achievement, and behavior on first grade children manifesting learning and perceptual-motor problems. *Dissertation Abstracts International, 38*, 5443A–5444A.

Biberdorf, J. R., & Pear, J. J. (1977). Two-to-one versus one-to-one student-teacher ratios in the operant verbal training of retarded children. *Journal of Applied Behavior Analysis, 10*, 506.

Bijou, S. W. (1966). Implications of behavioral science for counseling and guidance. In J. Krumboltz (Ed.), *Revolution in counseling*. Boston: Houghton Mifflin.

Bildman, J. L. (1982). Creative arts. In E. Siegel & R. F. Gold (Eds.), *Educating the learning disabled* (pp. 274–294). New York: Macmillan.

Birch, J. W., & Reynolds, M. C. (1982). Special education as a profession. *Exceptional Education Quarterly, 2*(4), 1–13.

Birchell, G. R., & Taylor, B. L. (1986). Is the elementary social studies curriculum headed "back-to-basics"? *The Social Studies, 77*, 80–82.

Blackhurst, E. (1983). *Designing computer-assisted instruction programs*. Unpublished manuscript, University of Kentucky, Lexington.

Blalock, V. E. (1984). *Factors influencing the effectiveness of paraprofessionals with disabled populations*. Unpublished doctoral dissertation, University of Texas at Austin.

Blanchard, K., & Johnson, S. (1982). *The one-minute manager: The quickest way to increase your own prosperity*. New York: Morrow.

Blatt, B. (1987). *The conquest of mental retardation.* Austin, TX: Pro-Ed.

Blau, H. (1968). Unusual measures for the spelling invalid. In J. I. Arena (Ed.), *Building spelling skills in dyslexic children.* San Rafael, CA: Academic Therapy.

Blocher, D. H. (1987). *The professional counselor.* New York: Macmillan.

Block, W. A. (1972). *What your child really wants to know about sex and why.* Englewood Cliffs, NJ: Prentice-Hall.

Bloom, L., & Lahey, M. (1978). *Language development and language disorders.* New York: John Wiley & Sons.

Bloomquist, J., & Rickert, W. (1988). Creative dramatics. In G. Robinson, J. R. Patton, E. A. Polloway, & L. R. Sargent (Eds.), *Best practices in mental disabilities* (Vol. 2). Des Moines: State Department of Education.

Blosser, P. E. (1986). What research says: Improving science education. *School Science and Mathematics, 86,* 597–612.

Blough, G., & Schwartz, J. (1974). *Teaching elementary science.* New York: Holt, Rinehart & Winston.

Boehm, A. E. (1980). *Boehm Test of Basic Concepts.* New York: Psychological Corporation.

Boekel, N., & Steele, J. M. (1972). Science education for the exceptional child. *Focus on Exceptional Children, 4*(4), 1–15.

Bogojavlensky, A. R., Grossman, D. R., Topham, C. S., & Meyer, S. M., III. (1977). *The great learning book.* Menlow Park, CA: Addison-Wesley.

Bolmeier, E. C. (1976). *Legality of student disciplinary practices.* Charlottesville, VA: Michie.

Boomer, L. W. (1981). Meeting common goals through effective teacher-paraprofessional interaction. *Teaching Exceptional Children, 13,* 51–53.

Borba, M., & Borba, C. (1978). *Self-esteem: A classroom affair.* Oak Grove, MN: Winston Press.

Borkowski, J. G., & Cavanaugh, J. C. (1979). Maintenance and generalization of skills and strategies by the retarded. In N. B. Ellis (Ed.), *Handbook of mental deficiency: Psychological theory and research.* Hillsdale, NJ: Lawrence Erlbaum.

Borus, J. F., Greenfield, S., Spiegel, B., & Daniels, G. (1973). Establishing imitative speech employing operant techniques in a group setting. *Journal of Speech and Hearing Disorders, 38,* 533–541.

Bos, C. S. (1982). Getting past decoding: Assisted and repeated readings as remedial methods for learning disabled students. *Topics in Learning and Learning Disabilities, 1*(4), 51–57.

Bott, D. A. (1988). Mathematics. In J. Wood, *Mainstreaming: A practical guide for teachers.* Columbus, OH: Merrill.

Bower, E. M., & Lambert, N. M. (1962). *A process for in-school screening of children with emotional handicaps.* Princeton, NJ: Educational Testing Service.

Bransford, J., Stein, B., Delclos, V., & Littlefield, J. (1986). Computers and problem solving. In C. Kinzer, R. Sherwood, & J. Bransford (Eds.), *Computer strategies for education* (pp. 147–180). Columbus, OH: Merrill.

Bray, N. W. (1979). Strategy production in the retarded. In N. R. Ellis (Ed.), *Handbook of mental deficiency: Psychological theory and research* (2nd ed., pp. 699–737). Hillsdale, NJ: Lawrence Erlbaum.

Brigance, A. H. (1980). *Brigance Diagnostic Inventory of Essential Skills.* N. Billerica, MA: Curriculum Associates.

Brigance, A. H. (1983). *Brigance Diagnostic Inventory of Basic Skills.* N. Billerica, NA: Curriculum Associates.

Brizzi, E. (1982). *Developing a partnership: A resource guide for working with paraprofessionals.* Downey, CA: Los Angeles County Superintendent of Schools.

Brody, S. (1984). *Patterning: Reading becomes easy.* Milford, NH: Brody Books.

Brody, S. (1986, March). *The Brody reading method.* Paper presented at the 23rd Annual Meeting of the Association of Children and Adults with Learning Disabilities, New York.

Brolin, D. E. (Ed.). (1978). *Life-centered career education: A competency-based approach.* Reston, VA: Council for Exceptional Children.

Brolin, D. E. (1982a). Life-centered career education for exceptional children. *Focus on Exceptional Children, 14*(7), 1–15.

Brolin, D. E. (1982b). *Vocational preparation of retarded citizens.* Columbus, OH: Merrill.

Brolin, D. E. (1986). *Life-centered career educa-tion: A competency-based approach* (rev. ed.). Reston, VA: Council for Exceptional Children.

Brolin, D. E., & Kokaska, C. (1979, 1984). *Career education for handicapped children and youth.* Columbus, OH: Merrill.

Brooke, P. (1986). Exploring family folklore. *In-structor, 96,* 114–120.

Brophy, J. E. (1979). Teacher behavior and its ef-fects. *Journal of Teacher Education, 71,* 733–750.

Brophy, J., & Good, T. L. (1986). Teacher behav-ior and student achievement. In M. C. Wit-trock (Ed.), *Handbook of research on teaching* (3rd ed.). New York: Macmillan.

Brown, A. L., & Palinscar, A. (1982). Inducing strategic learning from texts by means of in-formed, self-control training. *Topics in Learn-ing and Learning Disabilities, 2*(1), 1–17.

Brown, L. (1986). Evaluating and managing classroom behavior. In D. D. Hammill & N. R. Bartel (Eds.), *Teaching students with learning and behavior problems* (pp. 225–293). Austin, TX: Pro-Ed.

Brown, L. (1987). Assessing socioemotional de-velopment. In D. D. Hammill (Ed.), *Assessing the abilities and instructional needs of students* (pp. 505–609). Austin, TX: Pro-Ed.

• Brown, L., Hermanson, J., Klemme, H., Han-brich, P., & Ora, J. P. (1970). Using behavior modification principles to teach sight vocabu-lary. *Teaching Exceptional Children, 2,* 120–128.

Brown, V. L. (1984). Focus on the four Ms: Methods-materials-management-measurement. *Remedial and Special Education, 5*(2), 61.

Brown, V. L., & McEntire, E. (1984). *Test of Math-ematical Abilities.* Austin, TX: Pro-Ed.

Brueckner, L. J., & Bond, G. L. (1967). *Diagnosis and treatment of learning difficulties.* In E. C. Frierson & W. B. Barbe (Eds.), *Educating chil-dren with learning disabilities.* New York: Appleton-Century-Crofts.

Bruininks, H. (1977). *Bruininks-Oseretsky test of motor proficiency.* Circle Pines, MN: American Guidance Service.

Bruscia, K. (1981). The musical characteristics of mildly and moderately retarded children. In L. N. Kearns et al. (Eds.), *Readings: Develop-ing arts programs for handicapped students.*

Harrisburg: Pennsylvania State Department of Education.

Bryan, T. (1983, October). *The hidden curriculum: Social and communication skills.* Paper pre-sented at Lynchburg College, Lynchburg, VA.

Bryan, T., Pearl, R., Donahue, M., Bryan, J., & Pflaum, S. (1983). The Chicago Institute for the Study of Learning Disabilities. *Exceptional Education Quarterly, 4,* 1–22.

Bryen, D., & Joyce, D. (1985). Language inter-vention with the severely handicapped: A dec-ade of research. *Journal of Special Education, 19,* 7–36.

Buchan, V. (1979, September-October). By using the why and because method. *Today's Educa-tion, 32–34.*

Budoff, M., Thormann, J., & Gras, A. (1984). *Mi-crocomputers in special education.* Cambridge, MA: Brookline Books.

Bunker, L. K. (1978). Motor skills. In M. E. Snell (Ed.), *Systematic instruction of the moderately and severely handicapped* (pp. 180–226). Co-lumbus, OH: Merrill.

Burnette, J. (1987). *Adapting instructional materi-als for mainstreamed students.* Reston, VA: Council for Exceptional Children.

Burt, J., & Brower, L. (1970). *Education for sexu-ality: Concepts and programs for teaching.* Philadelphia: W. B. Saunders.

Busching, B. (1981). Reader's theatre: An educa-tion for language and life. *Language Arts, 58,* 330–338.

Bush, C. S. (1979). *Language remediation and ex-pansion: 100 skill-building reference lists.* Tuc-son: Communication Skill Builders.

Caccamo, J., & Watkins, R. (1982, January). Computer saves time in writing IEPs. *Missouri Schools,* 20–22.

Cain, L. E., Levine, S., & Elzey, F. F. (1963). *Man-ual for the Cain-Levine Social Competency Scale.* Palo Alto, CA: Consulting Psycholo-gists Press.

Cain, S. E., & Evans, J. M. (1984). *Sciencing: An involvement approach to elementary science methods* (2nd ed.). Columbus, OH: Merrill.

• Carbo, M. L. (1978). A word imprinting tech-nique for children with severe memory disor-ders. *Teaching Exceptional Children, 11,* 3–5.

Carlson, S. A., & Alley, G. R. (1981). *Performance and competence of learning disabled and high-achieving high school students on essential cognitive skills.* Lawrence: University of Kansas Institute for Research in Learning Disabilities.

Carman, R. A., & Adams, W. R. (1972). *Study skills: A student's guide for survival.* New York: John Wiley & Sons.

Carnine, D. (1983). Direct instruction: In search of instructional solutions for educational problems. In *Interdisciplinary voices in learning disabilities and remedial education* (pp. 1–60). Austin, TX: Pro-Ed.

Carnine, D., & Silbert, J. (1979). *Direct instruction reading.* Columbus, OH: Merrill.

Carpenter, D. (1985). Grading handicapped pupils: Review and position statement. *Remedial and Special Education, 6*(4), 54–59.

Cartledge, G., & Milburn, J. F. (1986). *Teaching social skills to children: Innovative approaches.* New York: Pergamon Press.

Cartwright, G. P. (1969). Written expression and spelling. In R. M. Smith (Ed.), *Teacher diagnosis of educational difficulties.* Columbus, OH: Merrill.

Caskey, H. J. (1970). Guidelines for teaching comprehension. *The Reading Teacher, 23,* 649–654.

Cassidy, V. M., & Stanton, J. E. (1959). *An investigation of factors involved in the educational placement of mentally retarded children.* Columbus: Ohio State University.

Cavallaro, C. (1983). Language interventions in natural settings. *Teaching Exceptional Children, 16,* 65–70.

Cavallaro, C., & Poulson, C. (1987). Teaching language to handicapped children in natural settings. *Education and Treatment of Children, 8*(1), 1–24.

Cawley, J. F. (Ed.). (1984). *Developmental teaching of mathematics for the learning disabled.* Austin, TX: Pro-Ed.

Cawley, J. F., Fitzmaurice, A. M., Shaw, R. A., Kahn, H., & Bates, H. (1978). Mathematics and learning disabled youth: The upper grade levels. *Learning Disability Quarterly, 1,* 37–52.

Cawley, J. F., Fitzmaurice, A. M., Shaw, R. A., Kahn, H., & Bates, H. (1979). Math word problems: Suggestions for LD students. *Learning Disability Quarterly, 2*(2), 25–41.

Cawley, J. F., Goodstein, H. A., Fitzmaurice, A. M., Lepore, A., Sedlak, R., & Althaus, V. (1976). *Project MATH.* Tulsa: Educational Progress.

Cawley, J. F., Miller, D., & Carr, S. (1988). Mathematics. In G. Robinson, J. R. Patton, E. A. Polloway, & L. R. Sargent (Eds.), *Best practices in mental disabilities* (Vol. 2). Des Moines: Iowa Department of Education, Bureau of Special Education.

Cegelka, P. T. (1977). Exemplary projects and programs for the career development of retarded individuals. *Education and Training of the Mentally Retarded, 12,* 161–162.

Cegelka, W. J. (1971). *Policy statements on the education of mentally retarded children.* Arlington, TX: National Association for Retarded Citizens.

Cegelka, W. J. (1978). Educational materials: Curriculum guides for the mentally retarded: An analysis and recommendations. *Education and Training of the Mentally Retarded, 13,* 187–188.

Chalfant, J. C., Pysh, M. V., & Moultrie, R. (1979). Teacher assistance teams: A model for within-building problem solving. *Learning Disability Quarterly, 2*(3), 85–96.

Chambless, J. R., Anderson, E., & Poole, J. H. (1981). IEPs and mastery learning applied to psychomotor activities. In G. R. Roice (Ed.), *Teaching handicapped students physical education* (pp. 20–22). Washington, DC: National Education Association.

Cheek, E. H., Jr., & Cheek, M. C. (1983). *Reading instruction through content teaching.* Columbus, OH: Merrill.

Cherry, C. (1972). *Creative art for the developing child.* Belmont, CA: Fearon.

Cheyney, A. (1979). *The writing corner.* Santa Monica, CA: Goodyear.

Churton, M. W. (1987). Impact of the Education of the Handicapped Act on adapted physical education: A ten-year overview. *Adaptive Physical Activity Quarterly, 4,* 1–8.

Cianciolo, J. (1965). Children's literature can affect coping behavior. *Personnel and Guidance Journal, 43,* 897–903.

Clark, G. M. (1979). *Career education for the handicapped child in the elementary classroom.* Denver: Love.

Clark, R. (1983). Reconsidering research on learning from media. *Review of Educational Research, 53,* 445–459.

Cluver, L. (March, 1987). *Cooperation between special and regular education: Using Virginia standards of learning.* Paper presented at the annual meeting of the Speech and Hearing Association of Virginia.

Coffman, D. D., & Smallwood, D. (1986). Some software cures for rhythm blues. *Music Educators Journal, 73*(4), 40–43.

Cohen, H., & Staley, F. (1982). Integrating with science: One way to bring science back into the elementary day. *School Science and Mathematics, 82,* 565–572.

Cohen, R. (1983). Self-generated questions as an aid to reading comprehension. *The Reading Teacher, 36,* 770–775.

Cohen, S., & deBettencourt, L. (1983). Teaching children to be independent learners: A step-by-step strategy. *Focus on Exceptional Children, 16*(3), 1–12.

Cohen, S. B., Perkins, V. L., & Newmark, S. (1985). Written feedback strategies used by special education teachers. *Teacher Education and Special Education, 8,* 183–187.

Cohen, S. B., & Plaskon, S. P. (1980). *Language arts for the mildly handicapped.* Columbus, OH: Merrill.

Cohen, S. B., Safran, J., & Polloway, E. A. (1980). Minimum competency testing and its implications for retarded students. *Education and Training for the Mentally Retarded, 15,* 250–255.

Cole, M., & Cole, J. (1980). *Effective intervention with the language impaired.* Rockville, MD: Aspen Systems.

Coleman, J. (1978). Using name anagrams. *Teaching Exceptional Children, 11,* 41–42.

Coleman, M. C. (1986). *Behavior disorders: Theory and practice.* Englewood Cliffs, NJ: Prentice-Hall.

Collins, M., & Collins, D. (1975). *Survival kits for teachers and parents.* Pacific Palisades, CA: Goodyear.

Collins, P. J., & Cunningham, G. W. (1978). *Vocabulary instructional programs.* Tigard, OR: C. C. Publications.

Combs, W. E. (1975). Sentence-combining practice aids reading comprehension. *Journal of Reading, 21,* 18–24.

Comfort, A. (1972). *The joy of sex.* New York: Crown.

Compton, C. (1984). *A guide to 65 tests for special education.* Belmont, CA: Fearon.

Conant, S., & Budoff, M. (1986). Speech samples: A clinical check on validity. *Journal of Childhood Communication Disorders, 9,* 169–181.

Conaway, M. S. (1982). Listening: Learning tool and retention agent. In A. S. Algier & K. W. Algier (Eds.), *Improving reading and study skills* (pp. 51–63). San Francisco: Jossey-Bass.

Cone, T. E., & Wilson, L. R. (1981). Quantifying a severe discrepancy: A critical analysis. *Learning Disability Quarterly, 4,* 359–371.

Connis, R. T. (1979). The effects of sequential pictorial cues, self-recording, and praise on the job-task sequencing of retarded adults. *Journal of Applied Behavior Analysis, 12,* 355–361.

Connolly, A. J., Nachtman, W., & Pritchett, E. M. (1976). *KeyMath Diagnostic Arithmetic Test.* Circle Pines, MN: American Guidance Service.

Cooke, N. L., Heron, T. E., & Heward, W. L. (1983). *Peer tutoring: Implementing classwide programs in the primary grades.* Columbus, OH: Special Press.

Cooper, J. O. (1981). *Measuring behavior* (2nd ed.). Columbus, OH: Merrill.

Cooper, J. O., Heron, T. E., & Heward, W. L. (1987). *Applied behavior analysis.* Columbus, OH: Merrill.

Corsini, J. (Ed.). (1984). *Current psychotherapies* (3rd ed.). Itasca, IL: F. E. Peacock.

Cottle, W. C., & Downie, N. M. (1970). *Preparation for counseling.* Englewood Cliffs, NJ: Prentice-Hall.

Cratty, B. J. (1970). *Perceptual and motor development in infants and children.* New York: Macmillan.

Cratty, B. J. (1971). *Active learning.* Englewood Cliffs, NJ: Prentice-Hall.

Crescimbeni, J. (1965). *Arithmetic enrichment activities for elementary school children.* West Nyack, NY: Parker.

Criasculo, N. P. (1985). Creative approaches to teaching reading through art. *Art Education, 38*(6), 13–16.

Cronin, M. E. (1988). Adult performance outcomes/life skills. In G. Robinson, J. R. Patton, E. A. Polloway, & L. R. Sargent (Eds.), *Best practices in mental disabilities* (Vol. 2). Des Moines: Iowa Department of Education, Bureau of Special Education.

Cronin, M. E., & Gerber, P. J. (1982). Preparing the learning disabled adolescent for adulthood. *Topics in Learning and Learning Disabilities, 2*(3), 55–68.

Crowe, W. C., Auxler, D., & Pyfer, J. (1981). *Principles and methods of adapted physical education and recreation* (4th ed.). St. Louis: C. V. Mosby.

Culhane, J. W. (1970). Cloze procedures and comprehension. *The Reading Teacher, 23,* 410–413.

Cullinan, D., & Epstein, M. H. (1984). Patterns of maladjustment of behaviorally disordered male students. *Behavioral Disorders, 9,* 175–181.

Cullinan, D., Epstein, M. H., & Lloyd, J. W. (1983). *Behavior disorders of children and adolescents.* Englewood Cliffs, NJ: Prentice-Hall.

Curtis, C. K. (1974). Social studies for the slow learner. *The Clearing House, 48,* 456–460.

Curtis, C. K., & Shaver, J. P. (1980). Slow learners and the study of contemporary problems. *Social Education, 44,* 302–309.

Cyr, D. (1977). *Teaching your children photography: A step-by-step guide.* Garden City, NY: American Photographic Book.

Dallmann, M., Rouch, R. L., Char, L. Y. C., & DeBoer, J. J. (1982). *The teaching of reading.* New York: Holt, Rinehart & Winston.

Daniels, A., & Davies, E. (1975). *Adapted physical education.* New York: Harper & Row.

Davies, J. M., & Ball, D. W. (1978). Utilization of the Elementary Science Study with mentally retarded students. *Journal of Research in Science Teaching, 15,* 281–286.

DeCharms, R. (1976). *Enhancing motivation: Change in the classroom.* New York: Irvington.

Deitz, D. E. D., & Repp, A. C. (1983). Reducing behavior through reinforcement. *Exceptional Education Quarterly, 3*(4), 34–46.

Deitz, S. M., Repp, A. C., & Deitz, D. E. D. (1976). Reducing inappropriate classroom behavior of retarded students through three procedures of differential reinforcement. *Journal of Mental Deficiency Research, 20,* 155–170.

de la Cruz, F. E., & LaVeck, G. D. (1973). *Human sexuality and the mentally retarded.* New York: Brunner/Mazel.

De Lin Du Bois, B., & McIntosh, M. E. (1986). Reading aloud to students in secondary history classes. *The Social Studies, 77,* 256–259.

Demos, G. (1976). *The study skills counseling evaluation.* Los Angeles: Western Psychological Services.

Denham, C., & Lieberman, A. (1980). *Time to learn.* Washington, DC: National Institute of Education.

Deno, E. (1970). Special education as developmental capital. *Exceptional Children, 37,* 229–237.

Deno, S. L. (1985). Curriculum-based measurement: The emerging alternative. *Exceptional Children, 52,* 219–232.

Deno, S. L., & Fuchs, L. S. (1987). Developing curriculum-based measurement systems for data-based special education problem solving. *Focus on Exceptional Children, 19*(6), 1–16.

Deshler, D. D., Alley, G. R., Warner, M. M., & Schumaker, J. B. (1981). Instructional practices for promoting skill acquisition and generalization in severely learning disabled adolescents. *Learning Disability Quarterly, 4,* 415–421.

Deshler, D. D., & Schumaker, J. B. (1986). Learning strategies: An instructional alternative for low-achieving adolescents. *Exceptional Children, 52,* 583–589.

Deshler, D. D., Schumaker, J. B., Lenz, B. K. & Ellis, E. (1984). Academic and cognitive interventions for LD adolescents: Part II. *Journal of Learning Disabilities, 17,* 170–179.

DeSpelder, L., & Prettyman, N. (1980). *A guidebook for teaching family living.* Boston: Allyn & Bacon.

Devine, T. G. (1987). *Teaching study skills: A guide for teachers* (2nd ed). Boston: Allyn & Bacon.

Dinkmeyer, D. D. (1972). *Developing understanding of self and others.* Circle Pines, MN: American Guidance Service.

Doke, L. A., & Risley, T. R. (1972). The organization of day-care environments: Required vs.

optional activities. *Journal of Applied Behavior Analysis, 5,* 405–420.

Doll, E. A. (1953). *The Vineland Social Maturity Scale.* Vineland, NJ: The Training School.

Dollaghan, C., & Kaston, N. (1986). A comprehension monitoring program for learning-impaired children. *Journal of Speech and Hearing Disorders, 51,* 264–271.

Dorry, G. W., & Zeaman, D. (1975). Teaching a simple reading vocabulary to retarded children: Effectiveness of fading and nonfading procedures. *American Journal of Mental Deficiency, 79,* 711–716.

Dougherty, E. H., & Dougherty, A. (1977). The daily report card: A simplified and flexible package for classroom behavior management. *Psychology in the Schools, 14,* 191–195.

Downey, M. T. (1980). Pictures as teaching aids: Using the pictures in history textbooks. *Social Education, 44,* 93–99.

Doyle, W. (1986). Classroom organization and management. In M. C. Wittrock (Ed.), *Handbook of research on teaching* (3rd ed., pp. 392–431). New York: Macmillan.

Dreikurs, R., Grunwald, B. B., & Pepper, F. C. (1982). *Maintaining sanity in the classroom: Classroom management techniques* (2nd ed.). Philadelphia: Harper & Row.

Dudley-Marling, C., & Rhodes, L. (1987). Pragmatics and literacy. *Language, Speech, and Hearing Services in the Schools, 18,* 41–52.

Duerksen, G. L. (1981). Music for exceptional students. *Focus on Exceptional Children, 14*(4), 1–11.

Dumas, E. (1971). *Math activities for child involvement.* Boston: Allyn & Bacon.

Duncan, J., & Perozzi, J. (1987). Concurrent validity of a pragmatic protocol. *Language, Speech, and Hearing Services in the Schools, 18,* 80–85.

Duncan, J. R., Schofer, R. C., & Veberle, J. (1982). *Comprehensive system of personnel development: Inservice considerations.* Columbia: University of Missouri Department of Special Education.

Dunlap, G., Koegel, R. L., & Burke, J. C. (1981). Educational implications of stimulus overselectivity in autistic children. *Exceptional Education Quarterly, 2*(3), 37–50.

Dunn, L. M. (1965, 1980). *Peabody Picture Vocabulary Test.* Circle Pines, MN: American Guidance Service.

Dunn, L. M. (1968). Special education for the mildly retarded—Is much of it justifiable? *Exceptional Children, 35,* 5–22.

Dunn, L. M. (1973). Children with mild general learning disabilities. In L. M. Dunn (Ed.), *Exceptional children in the schools: Special education in transition.* New York: Holt, Rinehart & Winston.

Dunn, L. M., & Dunn, L. M. (1981). *Peabody Picture Vocabulary Test* (rev.). Circle Pines, MN: American Guidance Service.

Dunn, L. M., Horton, K. B., & Smith, J. O. (1967, revised 1982). *Peabody language development kits.* Circle Pines, MN: American Guidance Service.

Dunn, L. M., & Markwardt, F. C. (1970). *Peabody Individual Achievement Test.* Circle Pines, MN: American Guidance Service.

Dunn, L. M., & Markwardt, F. C. (1988). *Peabody Individual Achievement Test—Revised.* Circle Pines, MN: American Guidance Service.

Dunn, L. M., & Smith, J. O. (1966). *Peabody language development kits levels 1, 2, & 3.* Minneapolis: American Guidance Service.

Durkin, D. (1978–79). What classroom observations reveal about reading comprehension instruction. *Reading Research Quarterly, 14,* 481–533.

Durost, G. H., Bixler, N. L., Wrightstone, M. E., Prescott, G., & Bow, B. (1978). *Metropolitan Achievement Test.* New York: Harcourt, Brace & World.

Durrell, D. D., & Catterson, J. (1980). *Durrell analysis of reading difficulty.* New York: Harcourt, Brace & World.

Eanet, M. G., & Manzo, A. V. (1976). REAP—A strategy for improving reading/writing/study skills. *Journal of Reading, 19,* 647–652.

Early, G. H., Nelson, D. A., Kleber, D. J., Treegoob, M., Huffman, E., & Cass, C. (1976). Cursive handwriting, reading, and spelling achievement. *Academic Therapy, 12*(1), 67–74.

Eastman, M. K., & Safran, J. S. (1986). Activities to develop your students' motor skills. *Teaching Exceptional Children, 19*(1), 24–27.

Edelsky, C. (1978). Teaching oral language. *Language Arts, 55*, 291–296.

Edgar, E. (1987). Secondary programs in special education: Are many of them justifiable? *Exceptional Children, 53*(6), 555–561.

Edgington, R. (1968). "But he spelled them right this morning." In J. I. Arena (Ed.), *Building spelling skills in dyslexic children* (pp. 23–24). Belmont, CA: Academic Therapy.

Edmark Associates. (1982). *Edmark reading program.* Bellevue, WA: Author.

Edmonson, B. (1980). Sociosexual education for the handicapped. *Exceptional Education Quarterly, 1*(2), 67–76.

Edmonson, B., McCombs, K., & Wish, J. (1979). What retarded adults believe about sex. *American Journal of Mental Deficiency, 84*(1), 11–18.

Edmonson, B., & Wish, J. (1975). Sex knowledge and attitudes of moderately retarded males. *American Journal of Mental Deficiency, 80*, 172–179.

Edwards, P. (1973). Panorama: A study technique. *Journal of Reading, 17*, 132–135.

Eisner, E. W. (1987). Educating the whole person: Arts in the curriculum. *Music Educators Journal, 73*(8), 37–41.

Ekwall, E. E. (1985). *Locating and correcting reading difficulties.* Columbus, OH: Merrill.

Ekwall, E. E. (1986). *Ekwall Reading Inventory* (2nd ed.). Boston: Allyn & Bacon.

Ekwall, E. E., & Shanker, J. L. (1983). *Diagnosis and remediation of the disabled reader.* Boston: Allyn & Bacon.

Ekwall, E. E. & Shanker, J. L. (1985). *Teaching reading in the elementary school.* Columbus, OH: Merrill.

Elium, M. D., & Evans, B. (1982). A model camping program for college students and handicapped learners. *Education and Training of the Mentally Retarded, 17*(3), 241–246.

Elium, M. D., & McCarver, R. B. (1980). *Group vs. individual training on a self-help skill with the profoundly retarded.* (ERIC Document Reproduction Service No. ED 223 060).

Elkind, D. (1983). Stress and learning disabilities. In *Interdisciplinary voices in learning disabilities and remedial education* (pp. 67–81). Austin, TX: Pro-Ed.

Ellis, A. (1973). The no cop-out therapy. *Psychology Today, 7*, 56–62.

Ellis, A. (1982). *Rational-emotive therapy and cognitive behavior therapy.* New York: Springer.

Ellis, E. S., Lenz, K., & Sabornie, E. J. (1987a). Generalization and adaptation of learning strategies to natural environments: Part 1. Critical Agents. *Remedial and Special Education, 8*(1), 6–20.

Ellis, E. S., Lenz, K., & Sabornie, E. J. (1987b). Generalization and adaptation of learning strategies to natural environments: Part 2. Research into practice. *Remedial and Special Education, 8*(2), 6–23.

Ellis, E. S., & Sabornie, E. J. (1986). Teaching learning strategies to learning disabled students in post-secondary settings. Unpublished manuscript, University of South Carolina, Columbia.

Ellis, N. R. (1963). The stimulus trace and behavioral inadequacy. In N. R. Ellis (Ed.), *Handbook of mental deficiency.* New York: McGraw-Hill.

Ellis, N. R. (1970). Memory processes in retardates and normals. In N. R. Ellis (Ed.), *International review of research in mental retardation* (Vol. 4). New York: Academic Press.

Emmer, E. T., Evertson, C. M., Sanford, J. P., Clements, B. S., & Worsham, M. E. (1984). *Classroom management for secondary teachers.* Englewood Cliffs, NJ: Prentice-Hall.

Engelmann, S., Becker, W. C., Hanner, S., & Johnson, G. (1980). *Corrective reading program.* Chicago: Science Research Associates.

Engelmann, S., & Bruner, E. (1974, 1975). *DISTAR reading.* Chicago: Science Research Associates.

Engelmann, S., & Carnine, D. (1981). *Corrective mathematics.* Chicago: Science Research Associates.

Engelmann, S., & Osborn, J. (1971, 1972, 1976). *DISTAR language.* Chicago: Science Research Associates.

Englert, C. S. (1983). Measuring special education teacher effectiveness. *Exceptional Children, 50*, 247–254.

Epstein, C. (1979). *Classroom management and teaching: Persistent problems and rational solutions.* Reston, VA: Reston.

Epstein, M. H., Bursuck, W., & Cullinan, D. (1985). Patterns of behavior problems among the learning disabled: II. Boys aged 12–18, girls aged 6–11, girls aged 12–18. *Learning Disability Quarterly, 8,* 123–131.

Epstein, M. H., Cullinan, D., & Polloway, E. A. (1986). Patterns of maladjustment among mentally retarded children and youth. *American Journal of Mental Deficiency, 91,* 127–134.

Epstein, M. H., Polloway, E. A., & Patton, J. R. (in press). Academic achievement probes: Reliability of measures for students with mild retardation. *Special Services in the Schools.*

Epstein, M. H., Polloway, E. A., Patton, J. R., & Foley, R. (in press). Mild retardation: Student characteristics and services. *Education and Training in Mental Retardation.*

Ersing, W., Loovis, M., & Ryan, T. (1982). On the nature of motor development in special populations. *Exceptional Education Quarterly, 3*(1), 64–71.

Esler, W. K., Midgett, J., & Bird, R. C. (1977). Elementary science materials and the exceptional child. *Science Education, 61,* 181–184.

Estes, T. H., & Vaughan, J. L., Jr. (1985). *Reading and learning in the content classroom: Diagnostic and instructional strategies.* Boston: Allyn & Bacon.

Estes, W. K. (1970). *Learning theory and mental development.* New York: Academic Press.

Evans, S. S., Evans, W. H., & Mercer, C. D. (1986). *Assessment for instruction.* Boston: Allyn & Bacon.

Evertson, C. M., Emmer, E. T., Clements, B. S., Sanford, J. P., & Worsham, M. E. (1984). *Classroom management for elementary teachers.* Englewood Cliffs, NJ: Prentice-Hall.

Facts on Special Olympics. (1977). Washington, DC: Joseph P. Kennedy Foundation.

Fader, D. N., & McNeill, E. B. (1968). *Hooked on books: Program and proof.* New York: Berkeley.

Fagen, S., Long, N. J., & Stevens, D. (1975). *Teaching children self-control.* Columbus, OH: Merrill.

Favell, J. E., Favell, J. E., & McGimsey, J. F. (1978). Relative effectiveness and efficiency of group vs. individual training of severely retarded persons. *American Journal of Mental Deficiency, 83,* 104–109.

Fay, L. (1965). Reading study skills: Math and science. In J. A. Figural (Ed.), *Reading and inquiry* (pp. 93–94). Newark, DE: International Reading Association.

Fernald, G. M. (1943). *Remedial techniques in basic school subjects.* New York: McGraw-Hill.

Feuerstein, R. (1979). *The dynamic assessment of retarded performers.* Austin, TX: Pro-Ed.

Fiehler, G. (1977). *Auditory memory for sounds.* St. Louis: Milliken.

Finch-Williams, A. (1984). The developmental relationship between cognition and communication: Implications for assessment. *Topics in Language Disorders, 5*(1), 1–13.

Fink, W. T., & Sandall, S. R. (1978). One-to-one vs. group academic instruction with handicapped and nonhandicapped preschool children. *Mental Retardation, 16,* 236–240.

Fink, W. T., & Sandall, S. R. (1980). A comparison of one-to-one and small group instructional strategies with developmentally disabled preschoolers. *Mental Retardation, 18,* 73–84.

Fischer, H. L., Krajicek, M. J., & Borthick, W. A. (1974). *Sex education for the developmentally disabled: A guide for parents, teachers, and professionals.* Austin, TX: Pro-Ed.

Fisher, L. (1970). Attention deficit in brain damaged children. *American Journal of Mental Deficiency, 74,* 502–508.

Fitzgerald, E. (1966). *Straight language for the deaf.* Washington, DC: Volta Bureau.

Fitzgerald, J. (1951). *The teaching of spelling.* Milwaukee: Bruce.

Flavell, J. H., Beach, D. R., & Chinsky, J. M. (1966). Spontaneous verbal rehearsal in a memory task as a function of age. *Child Development, 37,* 283–299.

Fokes, J. (1976). *Fokes Sentence Builders.* New York: Teaching Resources.

Forness, S. R. (1985). Effects of public policy at the state level: California's impact on MR, LD, and ED categories. *Remedial and Special Education, 6*(3), 36–43.

Fowler, G. L. (1982). Developing comprehension skills in primary students through the use of story frames. *The Reading Teacher, 36,* 176–180.

Fowler, G. L., & Davis, M. (1986). The story frame approach: A tool for improving reading comprehension for EMR children. *Teaching Exceptional Children, 17,* 296–298.

Foxx, R. M., & Azrin, N. H. (1972). Restitution: A method of eliminating aggressive-disruptive behavior of retarded and brain-damaged patients. *Behavior Research and Therapy, 10,* 15–27.

Foxx, R. M., & Azrin, N. H. (1973). The elimination of autistic self-stimulatory behavior by over-correction. *Journal of Applied Behavior Analysis, 6,* 1–14.

Francis, R. J., & Rarick, G. L. (1959). Motor characteristics of the mentally retarded. *American Journal of Mental Deficiency, 63,* 792–811.

Frankenberg, W. K., & Dodds, J. B. (1967). *Denver Developmental Screening Test.* Denver: LADOCA Project and Publishing Foundation.

Freides, D., & Messina, C. A. (1986). Memory improvement via motor encoding in learning disabled children. *Journal of Learning Disabilities, 19,* 113–115.

Friebel, A. C., & Gingrich, C. K. (1972). *Math applications kit.* Chicago: Science Research Associates.

Frith, G. H., & Mims, A. (1985). Burnout among special education paraprofessionals. *Teaching Exceptional Children, 17,* 225–227.

Frith, G. H., & Mitchell, J. W. (1983). Art education for mildly retarded students: A significant component of the special education curriculum. *Education and Training of the Mentally Retarded, 18,* 138–141.

Frostig, M., Lefever, W., & Whittlesey, J. R. (1964). *Marianne Frostig Developmental Test of Visual Perception.* Palo Alto, CA: Consulting Psychologists Press.

Fuchs, L., Deno, S., & Mirkin, P. (1984). The effects of frequent curriculum-based measurement and evaluation on pedagogy, student achievement, and student awareness of learning. *American Educational Research Journal, 21,* 449–460.

Fuchs, L. S., & Fuchs, D. (1986). Effects of systematic formative evaluation: A meta-analysis. *Exceptional Children, 53*(3), 199–208.

Fuchs, L., Fuchs, D., Hamlett, C., & Hasselbring, T. (1987). Using computers with curriculum-based monitoring: Effects on teacher efficiency and satisfaction. *Journal of Special Education Technology, 8*(4), 14–27.

Gall, M. D. (1981). *Handbook for evaluating and selecting curriculum materials.* Boston: Allyn & Bacon.

Gallagher, P. A. (1979). *Teaching students with behavior disorders: Techniques for classroom instruction.* Denver: Love.

Gardner, W. I. (1977). *Learning and behavior characteristics of exceptional children and youth.* Boston: Allyn & Bacon.

Garner, R. (1987). *Metacognition and reading comprehension.* Norwood, NJ: Ablex.

Gartner, A., Jackson, V. C., & Riessman, F. (Eds.). (1977). *Paraprofessionals in education today.* New York: Human Sciences Press.

Gast, D. L., & Nelson, C. M. (1977). Legal and ethical considerations for the use of time-out procedures in special education settings. *Journal of Special Education, 11,* 457–467.

Gates, A. I., & McKillop, A. S. (1962). *Gates-McKillop Reading Diagnostic Test.* Los Angeles: Western Psychological Service.

Gates, A. I., & Russell, D. (1940). *Gates-Russell Spelling Diagnostic Test.* New York: Columbia University Press.

Gearheart, B. R. (1985). *Learning disabilities: Educational strategies.* Columbus, OH: Merrill.

Gearheart, B. R., DeRuiter, J. A., & Sileo, T. W. (1986). *Teaching mildly and moderately handicapped students.* Englewood Cliffs, NJ: Prentice-Hall.

Gearheart, B. R., & Weishahn, M. W. (1984). *The exceptional student in the regular classroom.* Columbus, OH: Merrill.

Geddes, D. (1982). *Psychomotor individualized educational programs for intellectual, learning and behavioral disabilities.* Boston: Allyn & Bacon.

Gendel, E. S. (1968). *Sex education of the mentally retarded child in the home.* Arlington, TX: Association for Retarded Citizens.

Gerber, M. M. (1985). The Department of Education's sixth annual report to Congress on PL 94–142: Is Congress getting the full story? *Exceptional Children, 51,* 209–224.

Gerber, P. J. (1981). Learning disabilities and eligibility for vocational rehabilitation services: A chronology of events. *Learning Disability Quarterly, 4,* 422–425.

Gerber, P. J. (1986). Counseling the learning disabled. In A. F. Rotatori, P. J. Gerber, F. W. Litton, & R. A. Fox (Eds.), *Counseling exceptional students* (pp. 99–122). New York: Human Sciences Press.

Gerlach, K., & Patton, J. R. (1988). *Time management for teachers.* Honolulu: University of Hawaii, Project Ho'okoho.

Getman, G. N. (1965). The visuomotor complex in the acquisition of learning skills. In J. Hellmuth (Ed.), *Learning disorders* (Vol. 1). Seattle: Special Child Publications.

Gickling, E. E., & Thompson, V. P. (1985). A personal view of curriculum-based assessment. *Exceptional Children, 52,* 205–218.

❛ Gillet, P. (1981). Its elementary! Career education activities for mildly handicapped students. *Teaching Exceptional Children, 15,* 199–205.

Gillingham, A., & Stillman, B. (1960). *Remedial teaching for children with specific disability in reading, spelling, and penmanship.* Cambridge, MA: Educators Publishing Service.

Ginsburg, H. P., & Mathews, S. C. (1984). *Diagnostic Test of Arithmetic Strategies.* Austin, TX: Pro-Ed.

Gister, C. A. (1981). Art for children with very special needs. *School Arts, 80*(8), 24–25.

Glass, E. W., & Glass, G. G. (1978). *Glass analysis for decoding only.* New York: Easier to Learn.

Glazzard, P. H. (1978). Visual motivation in the classroom. *Teaching Exceptional Children, 10*(4), 106–109.

Glazzard, P. (1982). *Learning activities and teaching ideas for the special child in the regular classroom.* Englewood Cliffs, NJ: Prentice-Hall.

Glisan, E. M. (1984). *Record keeping for individualized junior-senior high school special education programs.* Freeport, IL: Peekan.

Goldenberg, E. (1979). *Special technology for special children.* Austin, TX: Pro-Ed.

Goldenberg, E., Russell, S., & Carter, C. (1984). *Computers, education and special needs.* Reading, MA: Addison-Wesley.

Goldman, R., Fristoe, M., & Woodcock, R. (1970). *The Goldman-Fristoe-Woodcock Test of Auditory Discrimination.* Circle Pines, MN: American Guidance Service.

Goldman, R., Fristoe, M., & Woodcock, R. W. (1974). *G-F-W Diagnostic Auditory Discrimination Test.* Circle Pines, MN: American Guid-

ance Service.

Goldstein, A. P., Sprafkin, R. P., Gershaw, N. J., & Klein, P. (1980). *Skill-streaming the adolescent: A structured learning approach to teaching prosocial skills.* Champaign, IL: Research Press.

Goldstein, H. (1975). *The social learning curriculum.* Columbus, OH: Merrill.

Goldstein, M., Harberle, E. J., & McBride, W. (1971). *The sex book.* New York: Barron's Educational Series.

Gonzales, E. (1981). Issues in the assessment of minorities. In H. Lee Swanson & Billy L. Watson (Eds.), *Educational and psychological assessment of exceptional children: Theories, strategies, and applications* (pp. 375–392). Columbus, OH: Merrill.

Good, T. L. (1983). Classroom research: A decade of progress. *Educational Psychologist, 18,* 127–144.

Good, T. L., & Grouws, D. A. (1979). The Missouri mathematics effectiveness project: An experimental study in fourth-grade classrooms. *Journal of Educational Psychology, 71,* 355–362.

Goodman, H., Gottlieb, J., & Harrison, R. H. (1972). Social acceptance of EMRs integrated into a nongraded elementary school. *American Journal of Mental Deficiency, 76,* 412–417.

Gordon, E. E. (1980). *Learning sequences in music.* Chicago: G.I.A.

Gottlieb, J. (1974). Attitudes toward retarded children: Effects of labeling and academic performance. *American Journal of Mental Deficiency, 79,* 268–273.

Gottlieb, J., & Budoff, M. (1973). Social acceptability of retarded children in nongraded schools differing in architecture. *American Journal of Mental Deficiency, 78,* 15–19.

Gottlieb, J., & Leyser, Y. (1981). Facilitating the social mainstreaming of retarded children. *Exceptional Education Quarterly, 1*(4), 57–69.

Grabow, G., & O'Neal, A. (1986). 10 steps to successful school play production. *Arts and Activities, 100*(2), 56–57.

Graden, J., Thurlow, M. L., & Ysseldyke, J. E. (1982). *Academic engaged time and its relationship to learning: A review of the literature* (Monograph No. 17). Minneapolis: University of Minnesota Institute for Research on Learning Disabilities.

Graham, R. M., & Beer, A. S. (1980). *Teaching music to the exceptional child: A handbook for mainstreaming.* Englewood Cliffs, NJ: Prentice-Hall.

Graham, S. (1983a). The effects of self-instructional procedures on LD students' handwriting performance. *Learning Disabilities Quarterly, 6,* 231–234.

Graham, S. (1983b). Measurement of handwriting skills: A critical review. *Diagnostique, 8,* 32–42.

Graham, S., & Miller, L. (1979). Spelling research and practice: A unified approach. *Focus on Exceptional Children, 12*(2), 1–16.

Graham, S., & Miller, L. (1980). Handwriting research and practice: A unified approach. *Focus on Exceptional Children, 13*(2), 1–16.

Graves, D. H. (1985). All children can write. *Learning Disabilities Focus, 1*(1), 36–43.

Gregory, G. P. (1979). Using the newspaper in the mainstreamed classroom. *Social Education, 43,* 140–143.

Gregory, R. P., Hackney, C., & Gregory, N. M. (1982). Corrective reading programme: An evaluation. *British Journal of Educational Psychology, 52,* 33–50.

Gresham, F. M. (1982). Misguided mainstreaming: The case for social skills training with handicapped children. *Exceptional Children, 48,* 422–433.

Gresham, F. M. (1983). Social skills assessment as a component of mainstreaming placement decisions. *Exceptional Children, 49,* 331–386.

Grimes, L. (1981). Learned helplessness and attribution theory: Redefining children's learning problems. *Learning Disability Quarterly, 4*(1), 91–100.

Grobman, H. (1972). Accountability for what? *Nations Schools.*

Grossman, H. J. (Ed.). (1973). *Manual on terminology and classification in mental retardation* (rev. ed.). Washington, DC: American Association on Mental Deficiency.

Grossman, H. J. (Ed.). (1977). *Manual on terminology and classification in mental retardation.* Washington, DC: American Association on Mental Retardation.

Grossman, H. J. (Ed.). (1983). *Classification in mental retardation.* Washington, DC: American Association on Mental Deficiency.

Guerin, G. R., & Maier, A. S. (1983). *Informal assessment in education.* Palo Alto, CA: Mayfield.

Hagen, D. (1984). *Microcomputer resource book for special education.* Reston, VA: Reston.

Hagen, J. W., & Huntsman, N. J. (1971). Selective attention in mental retardates. *Developmental Psychology, 5,* 151–160.

Hagen, J. W., & Kail, R. V. (1975). The role of attention in perceptual and cognitive development. In W. M. Cruickshank & D. P. Hallahan (Eds.), *Perceptual and learning disabilities in children: Vol. 2. Research and theory.* Syracuse: University Press.

Halderman v. Pennhurst (1977). C.A. no. 74-1345 (E.B. Pa. Dec. 23).

Haley-James, S., & Hobson, C. (1980). Interviewing: A menas of encouraging the drive to communicate. *Language Arts, 57,* 497–502.

Hall, J. K. (1981). *Evaluating and improving written expression: A practical guide for teachers.* Boston: Allyn & Bacon.

Hall, R. V., Fox, R., Willard, D., Goldsmith, L., Emerson, M., Owen, M., Davis, F., & Porcia, E. (1971). The teacher as an observer and experimenter in the modification of disputing and talking-out behaviors. *Journal of Applied Behavior Analysis, 4,* 141–149.

Hallahan, D. P., & Cruickshank, W. M. (1973). *Psychoeducational foundations of learning disabilities.* Englewood Cliffs, NJ: Prentice-Hall.

Hallahan, D. P., & Kauffman, J. M. (1977). Labels, categories, behaviors: ED, LD, and EMR reconsidered. *Journal of Special Education, 11,* 129–149.

Hallahan, D. P., Kauffman, J. M., & Lloyd, J. W. (1985). *Introduction to learning disabilities* (2nd ed.). Englewood Cliffs, NJ: Prentice-Hall.

Hallahan, D. P., Lloyd, J., Kosiewicz, M. M., Kauffman, J. M., & Graves, A. W. (1979). Self-monitoring of attention as a treatment for a learning disabled boy's off-task behavior. *Learning Disability Quarterly, 2,* 24–32.

Hallahan, D. P., Lloyd, J. W., & Stoller, L. (1982). *Improving attention with self-monitoring: A manual for teachers.* Charlottesville, VA: University of Virginia Learning Disabilities Research Institute.

Hallahan, D. P., Marshall, K. J., & Lloyd, J. W. (1981). Self-recording during group instruction: Effects on attention-to-task. *Learning Disability Quarterly, 4,* 407–413.

Hallahan, D. P., Stainback, S., Ball, D. W., & Kauffman, J. M. (1973). Selective attention in cerebral palsied and normal children. *Journal of Abnormal Child Psychology, 1,* 280–291.

Hallahan, D. P., Tarver, S. G., Kauffman, J. M., & Graybeal, N. L. (1978). A comparison of the effects of reinforcement and response cost on the selective attention of learning disabled children. *Journal of Learning Disabilities, 11,* 430–438.

Halpern, A. S. (1985). Transition: A look at the foundation. *Exceptional Children, 51,* 479–486.

Halpern, A. S., & Benz, M. R. (1987). A statewide examination of secondary special education for students with mild disabilities: Implications for the high school curriculum. *Exceptional Children, 54,* 122–129.

Hamilton, C., Miller, A., & Wood, P. (1987). Group books. *Teaching Exceptional Children, 19*(3), 46–47.

Hammill, D. D. (1971). Evaluating children for instructional purposes. *Academic Therapy, 16,* 341–353.

Hammill, D. D. (1985). *Detroit Tests of Learning Aptitude.* Austin, TX: Pro-Ed.

Hammill, D. D. (1986). Handwriting. In D. D. Hammill & N. E. Bartel (Eds.), *Teaching children with learning and behavior problems* (4th ed.). Boston: Allyn & Bacon.

Hammill, D. D., & Bartel, N. R. (1982). *Teaching children with learning and behavior problems* (3rd ed.). Boston: Allyn & Bacon.

Hammill, D. D., Brown, V. L., Larsen, S. C., & Wiederholt, J. L. (1987). *Test of Adolescent Language—2.* Austin, TX: Pro-Ed.

Hammill, D. D., & Larsen, S. C. (1978, 1983). *Test of Written Language.* Austin, TX: Pro-Ed.

Hammill, D. D., & Newcomer, P. L. (1982a). *Test of Language Development—Intermediate.* Austin, TX: Pro-Ed.

Hammill, D. D., & Newcomer, P. L. (1982b). *Test of Language Development—Primary.* Austin, TX: Pro-Ed.

Hamre-Nietupski, S., & Williams, W. (1977). Implementation of selected sex education and social skills to severely handicapped students. *Education and Training of the Mentally Retarded, 12*(4), 364–372.

Handleman, J. S., & Harris, S. L. (1983). A comparison of one-to-one versus couplet instruction with autistic children. *Behavioral Disorders, 9,* 22–26.

Harcum, P. M. (1972). Using clay bodies in multidimensional teaching of the retarded. *Education and Training of the Mentally Retarded, 7,* 39–45.

Harden, L. (1987). Reading to remember. *The Reading Teacher, 40*(6), 580–581.

Hargis, C. H. (1982). Word recognition development. *Focus on Exceptional Children, 14*(9), 1–8.

Haring, N. G. (1974). In J. M. Kauffman & C. D. Lewis (Eds.), *Teaching children with behavior disorders: Personal perspectives.* Columbus, OH: Merrill.

Harris, A. J., & Sipay, E. R. (1980). *How to increase reading ability.* New York: Longman.

Harris, K. R. (1985). Definitional, parametric, and procedural considerations in timeout interventions and research. *Exceptional Children, 51,* 279–288.

Hasselbring, T. S. (1986). Toward the development of expert assessment systems. *Special Services in the Schools, 2*(2/3), 43–56.

Hasselbring, T., & Crossland, C. (1982). Application of microcomputer technology to spelling assessment of learning disabled students. *Learning Disability Quarterly, 5,* 80–82.

Hasselbring, T. S., Goin, L. I., & Bransford, J. D. (1987, April). *Assessing and developing math automaticity in learning disabled students: The role of microcomputer technology.* Paper presented at the annual meeting of the American Educational Research Association, Washington, D.C.

Hasselbring, T., & Hamlett, C. (1984a). AIMSTAR [computer program]. Distributed by ASIEP Education Company, P.O. Box 12147, Portland, OR 97212.

Hasselbring, T., & Hamlett, C. (1984b). Planning and managing instruction: Computer-based decision making. *Teaching Exceptional Children, 16,* 248–252.

Haughton, E. (1974). Myriad counter: Or beads that aren't for worrying. *Teaching Exceptional*

Children, 7, 203–209.

Hawaii Transition Project. (1987). [Transition resources]. Honolulu: University of Hawaii, Department of Special Education.

Heber, R. (1959). *A manual on terminology and classification in mental retardation.* Willimantic, CT: American Association on Mental Deficiency.

Heber, R. (1961). Modifications in the manual on terminology and classification in mental retardation. *American Journal of Mental Deficiency, 65*(4), 499–500.

Hegge, T. G., Kirk, S. A., & Kirk, W. D. (1955). *Remedial reading skills.* Ann Arbor, MI: George Wahr.

Heilman, A., Blair, T., & Rupley, W. (1981). *Principles and practices of teaching reading.* Columbus, OH: Merrill.

Heimlich. J. E., & Pittelman, S. D. (1986). *Semantic mapping: Classroom applications.* Newark, DE: International Reading Association.

Heins, E. D. (1980). *Training learning disabled children's self-control: Cued and non-cued self-recording in the classroom.* Unpublished doctoral dissertation, University of Virginia.

Heller, H. W. (1982). Professional standards for preparing special educators: Status and prospects. *Exceptional Education Quarterly, 2*(4), 77–86.

Henk, W. A., Helfeldt, J. P., & Platt, J. M. (1986). Developing reading fluency in learning disabled students. *Teaching Exceptional Children, 18,* 202–206.

Hermelin, B., & O'Connor, N. (1964). Short-term memory in normal and subnormal children. *American Journal of Mental Deficiency, 69,* 121–125.

Heron, T. (1978). Punishment: A review of the literature with implications for the teacher of mainstreamed children. *Journal of Special Education, 12,* 243–252.

Heron, T. E. (1987a). Overcorrection. In J. O. Cooper, T. E. Heron, & W. E. Heward (Eds.), *Applied behavior analysis* (pp. 427–438). Columbus, OH: Merrill.

Heron, T. E. (1987b). Response cost. In J. O. Cooper, T. E. Heron, & W. E. Heward (Eds.), *Applied behavior analysis* (pp. 454–464). Columbus, OH: Merrill.

Heron, T. E., & Harris, K. C. (1982). *The educational consultant: Helping professionals, parents, and mainstreamed students.* Boston: Allyn & Bacon.

Hersch, E. D. (1987). *Cultural literacy: What every American needs to know.* Boston: Houghton Mifflin.

Hester, S. M. (1987). Put on a happy face. *Arts and Activities, 101*(5), 34.

Heukerott, P. B. (1987) "Little books" for content areas vocabulary. *The Reading Teacher, 40,* 489.

Heward, W. L., Dardig, J. C., & Rossett, A. (1979). *Working with parents of handicapped children.* Columbus, OH: Merrill.

Hewett, F. M. (1968). *The emotionally disturbed child in the classroom.* Boston: Allyn & Bacon.

Hoagland, J. (1972). Bibliotherapy: Aiding children in personality development. *Elementary English, 49,* 390–394.

Hodges, R. E. (1966). The case for teaching sound-to-letter correspondences in spelling. *The Elementary School Journal, 66,* 327–336.

Hofmeister, A. M. (1983). *Microcomputer applications in the classroom.* New York: Holt, Rinehart & Winston.

Hofmeister, A. M. (1984). The special educator in the information age. *Peabody Journal of Education, 62*(1), 5–21.

Hogan, T. P., & Mishler, C. J. (1979). Judging the quality of students' writing: Where and how. *The Elementary School Journal, 79,* 142–146.

Holt, D., & Thompson, K. (1980). *Developing competencies to teach music in the elementary classroom.* Columbus, OH: Merrill.

Homme, L. (1969). *How to use contingency contracting in the classroom.* Champaign, IL: Research Press.

Hoover, J. J. (1986, 1988). *Teaching handicapped students study skills.* Lindale, TX: Hamilton.

Horn, E. (1954). *Teaching spelling.* Washington, DC: American Educational Research Association.

Houck, C. K. (1984). *Learning disabilities: Understanding concepts, characteristics, and issues.* Englewood Cliffs, NJ: Prentice-Hall.

Houk, C., & McKenzie, R. G. (1985). *ASSIST: Aides serving students: An individual system of training.* Bowling Green: Western Kentucky University College of Education.

House, E., & Lapan, S. (1978). *Survival in the*

classroom: Negotiating with kids, colleagues, and bosses. Boston: Allyn & Bacon.

Howe, E., Joseph, A., & Victor, E. (1971). *A source book for elementary science.* New York: Harcourt Brace Jovanovich.

Howell, K. W., Kaplan, J. S., & O'Connel, C. Y. (1979). *Evaluating exceptional children: A task analysis approach.* Columbus, OH: Merrill.

Howell, K. W., & Morehead, M. K. (1987). *Curriculum-based evaluation for special and remedial education.* Columbus, OH: Merrill.

Howell, K. W., Rueda, R., & Rutherford, R. B. (1983). A procedure for teaching self-recording to moderately retarded students. *Psychology in the Schools, 20,* 202–209.

Hunt, K. W. (1965). *Grammatical structures written at three grade levels* (Research Report No. 3). Champaign, IL: National Council of Teachers of English.

Hurst, J. B. (1986). A skills-in-living perspective rather than trivial pursuit. *The Social Studies, 77*(2), 69–73.

Hurvitz, J. A., Pickert, S. M., & Rilla, D. C. (1987). Promoting children's language interaction. *Teaching Exceptional Children, 19*(3), 12–15.

Idol, L., Nevin, A., & Paolucci-Whitcomb, P. (1986). *Models of curriculum-based assessment.* Rockville, MD: Aspen.

Idol, L., Paolucci-Whitcomb, P., & Nevin, S. (1986). *Collaborative consultation.* Rockville, MD: Aspen.

Idol-Maestas, L. (1983). *Special educator's consultation handbook.* Rockville, MD: Aspen.

Ingalls, R. P. (1978). *Mental retardation: The changing outlook.* New York: John Wiley & sons.

Inhelder, B. (1968). *The diagnosis of reasoning in the mentally retarded.* New York: John Day.

Isaacson, S. L. (1987). Effective instruction in written language. *Focus on Exceptional Children, 19*(6), 1–12.

Iverson, B. (1982). Play, creativity, and schools today. *Phi Delta Kappan, 63,* 693–694.

Jackson, N. F., Jackson, D. A., & Monroe, C. (1983). *Program guide: Getting along with others.* Champaign, IL: Research Press.

Jacobson, W. J., & Bergman, A. B. (1980). *Science for children: A book for teachers.* Englewood Cliffs, NJ: Prentice-Hall.

James, P. (1983). *Teaching art to special students.* Portland, OR: J. Weston Welch.

James, S., & Pedrazzini, L. (1975). *Simple lattice approach to mathematics.* Englewood Cliffs, NJ: Prentice-Hall Learning Systems.

Jamison, P. J., & Shevitz, L. A. (1985). RATE: A reason to read. *Teaching Exceptional Children, 18*(1), 46–50.

Jansma, P., & Combs, C. S. (in press). The effects of fitness training on maladapted behaviors of institutionalized mentally retarded/emotionally disturbed adults. *Education and Training in Mental Retardation.*

Jaquish, C., & Stella, M. A. (1986). Helping special needs students move from elementary to secondary school. *Counterpoint, 7*(1), 1.

Jarolimek, J. (1981). The social studies: An overview. In H. D. Mehlinger & O. I. Davis (Eds.). *The social studies: Eightieth Yearbook of the National Society for the Study of Education* (pp. 3–18). Chicago: University of Chicago Press.

Jarolimek, J., & Foster, C. D. (1985). *Teaching and learning in the elementary school.* New York: Macmillan.

Jastak, J. F., & Jastak, S. R. (1965, 1978). *The Wide Range Achievement Test.* Wilmington, DE: Guidance Associates.

Jastak, J. F., & Wilkinson, F. (1984). *The Wide Range Achievement Test—Revised.* Wilmington, DE: Jastak Associates.

Jenkins, J. R., Mayhall, W. F., Peschka, C. M., & Jenkins, J. M. (1974). Comparing small group and tutorial instruction in resource rooms. *Exceptional Children, 40,* 245–251.

Jenkins, J. R., Stein, M. L., & Osborn, J. R. (1981). What next after decoding? Instruction and research in reading comprehension. *Exceptional Education Quarterly, 2*(1), 27–39.

Jennings, S. (1973). *Remedial drama.* New York: Theatre Arts Books.

Jens, K. G., Belmore, K., & Belmore, J. (1976). Language programming for the severely handicapped. *Focus on Exceptional Children, 8,* 1–15.

Johnson, D., & Johnson, R. (1984). Classroom

learning structure and attitudes toward handicapped students in mainstream settings: A theoretical model and research evidence. In R. Jones (Ed.), *Attitudes and attitude change in special education* (pp. 118–142). Reston, VA: Council for Exceptional Children.

Johnson, D. A., & Rising, G. R. (1972). *Guidelines for teaching mathematics.* Belmont, CA: Wadsworth.

Johnson, G. O. (1950). A study of the social position of mentally handicapped children in the regular grades. *American Journal of Mental Deficiency, 55,* 60–89.

Johnson, J. L., Flanagan, K., Burge, M. E., Kaufman-Debriere, S., & Spellman, C. R. (1980). Interactive individualized instruction with small groups of severely handicapped students. *Education and Training of the Mentally Retarded, 15,* 230–237.

Johnson, L. E., & Londeree, B. R. (1976). *Motor fitness testing manual for moderately mentally retarded.* Washington, DC: American Alliance for Health, Physical Education, and Recreation.

Johnson, R., & Vardian, E. R. (1973). Reading readability and the social studies. *The Reading Teacher, 26,* 483–488.

Johnston, E. B., Weinrich, B. D., & Johnson, A. R. (1984). *A sourcebook of pragmatic activities.* Tucson, AZ: Communication Skill Builders.

Joiner, L., Silverstein, B., & Ross, J. (1980). Insights from a microcomputer center in a rural school district. *Educational Technology, 20*(5), 36–40.

Jones, R. (1981). Shared victory: A collection of unusual world records. In G. R. Roice (Ed.), *Teaching handicapped students physical education* (pp. 13–14). Washington, DC: National Education Association.

Kahn, C. H., & Hanna, J. B. (1960, 1979). *Money makes sense.* Palo Alto, CA: Fearon.

Kaluger, G., & Kolson, C. J. (1969). *Reading and learning disabilities.* Columbus, OH: Merrill.

Karlin, M. S., & Berger, R. (1969). *Successful methods for teaching the slow learner.* West Nyack, NY: Parker.

Karnes, M. B. (1968). *Helping young children develop language skills.* Arlington, VA: Council for Exceptional Children.

Karnes, M. B. (1972). *Game-oriented activities for learning.* Springfield, MA: Milton Bradley.

Karnes, M. B. (1978). *Learning language at home.* Reston, VA: Council for Exceptional Children.

Kauffman, J. M. (1985). *Characteristics of children's behavior disorders* (3rd ed.). Columbus, OH: Merrill.

Kauffman, J. M., & Hallahan, D. P. (1974). The medical model and the science of special education. *Exceptional Children, 41,* 97–102.

Kaufman, A. S., & Kaufman, N. L. (1985). *Kaufman Test of Educational Achievement.* Circle Pines, MN: American Guidance Service.

Kazdin, A. E. (1972). *Token economies: An annotated bibliography* (Journal Supplement Abstract Service Catalog of Selected Documents in Psychology). Washington, DC: American Psychological Association.

Kazdin, A. E. (1977). *The token economy: A review and evaluation.* New York: Plenum Press.

Kazdin, A. E., & Bootzin, R. R. (1972). The token economy: An evaluative review. *Journal of Applied Behavior Analysis, 5,* 343–372.

Kazdin, A. E., & Erickson, L. M. (1975). Developing responsiveness to instructions in severely and profoundly retarded residents. *Journal of Behavior Therapy and Experimental Psychiatry, 6,* 17–21.

Kean, M. H., Summers, A. A., Raivetz, M. J., & Farber, I. J. (1979, May). *What works in reading? Summary of a joint school district/Federal Reserve Bank empirical study in Philadelphia* (ERIC Document Reproduction Service No. ED 176 216).

Kelly, B. W., & Holmes, J. (1979). The guided lecture procedure. *Journal of Reading, 22,* 602–604.

Kelly, E. J. (1979). *Elementary school social studies instruction: A basic approach.* Denver: Love.

Kempton, W., & Forman, R. (1976). *Guidelines for training in sexuality and the mentally handicapped.* Philadelphia: Planned Parenthood Association of Southeast Pennsylvania.

Kennedy, W. A. (1975). School phobia: Rapid treatment of fifty cases. *Journal of Abnormal Psychology, 70,* 285–289.

Kephart, N. C. (1971). *The slow learner in the*

classroom (2nd ed.). Columbus, OH: Merrill.

Kerr, M. M., & Nelson, C. M. (1983). *Strategies for managing behavior problems in the classroom.* Columbus, OH: Merrill.

Kerr, M. M., Nelson, C. M., & Lambert, D. L. (1987). *Helping adolescents with learning and behavior problems.* Columbus, OH: Merrill.

Kimmell, G. M. (1968). Teaching spelling on a splash of color. In J. J. Arena (Ed.). *Building spelling skills in dyslexic children.* San Rafael, CA: Academic Therapy.

King, E. W. (1980). *Teaching ethnic awareness: Methods and materials for the elementary school.* Santa Monica, CA: Goodyear.

Kirk, S. A., & Chalfant, J. C. (1984). *Academic and developmental learning disabilities.* Denver: Love.

Kirk, S. A., & Johnson, G. O. (1951). *Educating the retarded child.* Cambridge, MA: Houghton Mifflin.

Kirk, S., Kirk, W., & Minskoff, E. (1986). *Phonic remedial reading lessons.* Novato, CA: Academic Therapy.

Kirk, S. A., Kliebhan, J. M., & Lerner, J. (1978). *Teaching reading to slow and disabled learners.* Boston: Houghton Mifflin.

Kirk, S. A., & Monroe, M. (1940). *Teaching reading to slow-learning children.* Boston: Houghton Mifflin.

Kirschner, N. M., & Levin, L. (1975). A direct school intervention program for the modification of aggressive behavior. *Psychology in the Schools, 12,* 202–208.

Klausmeier, H. J., Feldhusen, J., & Check, J. (1959). *An analysis of learning efficiency in arithmetic of mentally retarded children in comparison with children of average and high intelligence.* Madison: University of Wisconsin Press.

Klein, M. (1979). Designing a talk environment for the classroom. *Language Arts, 56,* 647–656.

Klein, N. K., Pasch, M., & Frew, T. W. (1979). *Curriculum analysis and design for retarded learners.* Columbus, OH: Merrill.

Kline, S. (1987). Dear diary . . . I couldn't teach without you! *Instructor, 96,* 80–81.

Kneedler, R. D., & Hallahan, D. P. (1981). Self-monitoring of on-task behavior with learning disabled children: Current studies and directions. *Exceptional Education Quarterly, 2*(3),

73–82.

Knoblock, P. (1975). Open education for emotionally disturbed children. In H. Dupont (Ed.), *Educating emotionally disturbed children.* New York: Holt, Rinehart & Winston.

Knowles, M. (1978). *The adult learner: A neglected species* (2nd ed.). Houston: Gulf.

Koegel, R. L., & Rincover, A. (1974). Treatment of psychotic children in a classroom environment: I. Learning in a large group. *Journal of Applied Behavior Analysis, 7,* 45–59.

Kohl, F. L., Wilcox, B. L., & Karlan, G. R. (1978). Effects of training conditions on the generalization of manual signs with moderately handicapped students. *Education and Training of the Mentally Retarded, 13,* 327–335.

Kolstoe, O. P. (1972). *Mental retardation: An educational viewpoint.* New York: Holt, Rinehart & Winston.

Kolstoe, O. P. (1976). *Teaching educable mentally retarded children* (2nd ed.). New York: Holt, Rinehart & Winston.

Kolstoe, O. P., & Frey, R. M. (1965). *A high school work-study program for mentally subnormal students.* Carbondale: Southern Illinois University Press.

Konczak, L. J., & Johnson, C. M. (1983). Reducing inappropriate verbalizations in a sheltered workshop through differential reinforcement of other behavior. *Education and Training of the Mentally Retarded, 18,* 120–124.

Kosiewicz, M. M., Hallahan, D. P., Lloyd, J., & Graves, A. W. (1982). Effects of self-instruction and self-correction procedures on handwriting performance. *Learning Disability Quarterly, 5,* 71–78.

Kotting, D. (1987). Round robin vocabulary. *The Reading Teacher, 40,* 711–712.

Kounin, J. (1970). *Discipline and group management in classrooms.* New York: Holt, Rinehart & Winston.

Kozol, J. (1986). *Illiterate America.* New York: Doubleday.

Kraft, R. E. (1981). Perceptual-motor activities for children with learning disabilities. In G. R. Roice (Ed.). *Teaching handicapped students physical education* (pp. 27–29). Washington, DC: National Education Association.

Kramer, J. J., Nagle, R. J., & Engle, R. W. (1980). Recent advances in mnemonic strategy training with mentally retarded persons: Implications for educational practice. *American Journal of Mental Deficiency, 85,* 306–314.

Krasner, L., & Ullman, L. (1965). *Research in behavior modification.* New York: Holt, Rinehart & Winston.

Krause, L. A. (1983). Teaching the second "R." *The Directive Teacher, 5*(1), 30.

Krueger, K., & Fox, H. (1984). *Techniques for teacher-aide communication.* Paper presented at in-service training workshop, Albuquerque Public Schools Special Education Department.

Krupski, A. (1981). An interactional approach to the study of attention problems in children with learning handicaps. *Exceptional Education Quarterly, 2,* 1–11.

Kutash, I. L., & Schlesinger, L. B. (Eds.). (1980). *Handbook of stress and anxiety.* San Francisco: Jossey-Bass.

Kyle, W. C., Bonnstetter, R. J., McClosky, S., & Fults, B. A. (1985). Science through discovery: Students love it. *Science and Children, 23* (2), 39–41.

Lake, J. C. (1987). Calling all letters. *The Reading Teacher, 40,* 815.

Lamb, P. (1967). *Guiding children's language learning.* Dubuque, IA: Wm. C. Brown.

Lambert, N., Windmiller, M., Cole, L., & Figueroa, R. (1974). *AAMD Adaptive Behavior Scale: Public school version.* Washington, DC: American Association on Mental Deficiency.

Lambert, N., Windmiller, M., Tharinger, D., & Cole, L. (1981), *AAMD-ABS school edition: Administration and instructional planning manual.* Washington, DC: AAMD.

Lambie, R. A. (1980). A systematic approach for changing materials, instruction, and assignments to meet individual needs. *Focus on Exceptional Children, 12*(1), 1–12.

LaQuey, A. (1981). *Adult performance level adaptation and modification project.* Austin, TX: Educational Service Center, Region XIII.

Larsen, S. C., & Hammill, D. D. (1976). *Test of Written Spelling.* Austin, TX: Empire Press.

Lasley, T. J., & Walker, R. (1986). Time-on-task: How teachers can use class time more effectively. *National Association of Secondary School Principals Bulletin, 70,* 59–64.

Lathom, W., & Eagle, C. T. (1982). Music for the severely handicapped. *Music Educators Journal, 68*(8), 30–31.

Lawrence, E. A., & Winschel, J. F. (1975). Locus of control: Implications for special education. *Exceptional Children, 41,* 483–490.

Laybourne, K., & Cianciolo, P. (1978). *Doing the media: A portfolio of activities, ideas, and resources* (rev. ed.). New York: McGraw-Hill.

Leone, J., Moore, N. R., Kalan, N. T., & Diaz, V. T. (1980). *A model for the teacher/paraprofessional instructional team.* Broward County, FL: School Board, Bilingual Exceptional Student Education Demonstration Project.

Lerner, J. W. (1985). *Learning disabilities: Theories, diagnosis, and teaching strategies* (4th ed.). Boston: Houghton Mifflin.

Lesgold, A. M. (1983). A rationale for computer-based reading instruction. In A. C. Wilkenson (Ed.), *Classroom computers and cognitive science* (pp. 165–181). New York: Academic Press.

Lettau, J. H. (1975). *3-R math readiness.* Englewood Cliffs, NJ: Prentice-Hall Learning Systems.

Leverentz, F., & Garman, D. (1987). What was that you said? *Instructor, 96,* 66–77.

Levine, H. G., & Langness, L. L. (1983). Context, ability, and performance: Comparison of competitive athletics among mildly mentally retarded and nonretarded adults. *American Journal of Mental Deficiency, 87*(5), 528–538.

Lewis, R. B., & Doorlag, D. H. (1987). *Teaching special students in the mainstream.* Columbus, OH: Merrill.

Lichtenstein, E. (1980). Suspension, expulsion, and the special education student. *Phi Delta Kappan,* 459–461.

Lillie, D. (1980). *A microcomputer-assisted IEP.* Paper presented at the Seventh Annual Conference of the Association of Severely Handicapped, Los Angeles.

Linderman, E. (1976). *Teaching secondary art.* Dubuque, IA: Wm. C. Brown.

Lindsay, Z. (1972). *Art and the handicapped child.* New York: Van Nostrand Reinhold.

Lindsley, O. R. (1964). Direct measurement and prosthesis of retarded behavior. *Journal of Education, 147,* 62–81.

Link, D. P. (1980). *Essential learning skills and the*

low achieving student at the secondary level: A rating of 24 academic abilities. Unpublished master's thesis, University of Kansas.

Lister, J. L. (1969). Personal-emotional-social skills. In R. M. Smith (Ed.), *Teacher diagnosis of educational difficulties*. Columbus, OH: Merrill.

Litton, F. W. (1978). *Education of the trainable mentally retarded: Curriculum, methods, materials*. St. Louis: C. V. Mosby.

Litton, F. W. (1986). Counseling the mentally retarded child. In A. F. Rotatori, P. J. Gerber, F. W. Litton, & R. A. Fox (Eds.), *Counseling exceptional students* (pp. 78–98). New York: Human Sciences Press.

Lloyd, J. W. (1980). Academic instruction and cognitive behavior modification: The need for attack strategy training. *Exceptional Education Quarterly, 1*(1), 53–63.

Lloyd, J. W., & deBettencourt, L. J. U. (1982). *Academic strategy training: A manual for teachers*. Charlottesville, VA: University of Virginia Learning Disabilities Research Institute.

Lloyd, J. W., Hallahan, D. P., Kosiewicz, M. M., & Kneedler, R. D. (1982). Reactive effects of self-assessment and self-recording on attention to task and academic productivity. *Learning Disability Quarterly, 5*, 216–227.

Lobitz, W. C. (1974). A simple stimulus cue for controlling disruptive classroom behavior. *Journal of Abnormal Child Psychology, 2*, 143–152.

Lock, C. (1981). *Study skills*. West Lafayette, IN: Kappa Delta Pi.

Logan, D. R., & Rose, E. (1982). Characteristics of the mildly mentally retarded. In P. T. Cegelka & H. J. Prehm (Eds.), *Mental retardation: From categories to people*. Columbus, OH: Merrill.

Lorenz, L., & Yockell, E. (1979). Using the neurological impress method with learning disabled readers. *Journal of Learning Disabilities, 12*, 67–69.

Lovaas, O. J., Schreibman, L., & Koegel, R. L. (1974). A behavioral modification approach to the treatment of autistic children. *Journal of Autism and Childhood Schizophrenia, 4*, 111–129.

Lovano-Kerr, J., & Savage, S. (1972). Incremental act curriculum model for the mentally retarded. *Exceptional Children, 39*, 193–199.

Lovano-Kerr, J., & Savage, S. L. (1976). Survey of art programs and art experiences for the mentally retarded in Indiana. *Education and Training of the Mentally Retarded, 11*, 200–211.

Lovitt, T. C. (1975). Applied behavior analysis and learning disabilities: Part 2. *Journal of Learning Disabilities, 8*, 504–518.

Lovitt, T., Rudsit, J., Jenkins, J., Pious, C., & Benedetti, D. (1985). Two methods of adapting science materials for learning disabled and regular seventh graders. *Learning Disability Quarterly, 8*, 275–285.

Lovitt, T., Rudsit, J., Jenkins, J., Pious, C., & Benedetti, D. (1986). Adapting science materials for regular and learning disabled seventh graders. *Remedial and Special Education, 7*(1), 31–39.

Lund, K. A., Schnaps, L., & Bijou, S. W. (1983). Let's take another look at record keeping. *Teaching Exceptional Children, 15*, 155–159.

Lundstrum, J. P. (1976). Reading in the social studies: A preliminary analysis of recent research. *Social Education, 40*, 10–17.

Maccoby, E. E., & Hagen, J. W. (1965). Effects of distraction upon central versus incidental recall: Developmental trends. *Journal of Experimental Child Psychology, 2*, 280–289.

MacDonald, E. (1964). *A curriculum guide in arts and crafts for the educable mentally retarded*. Augusta, ME: State Department of Education.

MacDonald, J., & Horstmeier, D. (1978). *Environmental language intervention program*. Columbus, OH: Merrill.

Machart, N. C. (1987). Creating an opportunity for student-teacher reading conferences. *The Reading Teacher, 40*, 488–489.

MacMillan, D. L. (1982). *Mental retardation in school and society* (2nd ed.). Boston: Little, Brown.

MacMillan, D. L., & Borthwick, S. (1980). The new educable mentally retarded population: Can they be mainstreamed? *Mental Retardation, 18*, 155–158.

MacMillan, D. L., Forness, S., & Trumbull, J. (1973). The role of punishment in the classroom. *Exceptional Children, 40*, 85–96.

Madden, R., Gardner, E. F., Rudman, H. C., Karlsen, B., & Merwin, J. C. (1973). *Stanford*

Achievement Test. New York: Psychological Corporation.

Maddux, C. D. (1984). Using microcomputers with the learning disabled: Will the potential be realized? *Educational Computer,* 31–32.

Madsen, C. H., Jr., & Madsen, C. K. (1983). *Teaching/discipline: A positive approach for educational development.* Raleigh, NC: Contemporary Publishing.

Mager, R. F. (1975). *Preparing instructional objectives.* Belmont, CA: Fearon.

Maier, A. S. (1980). Checklist of reading abilities. In G. R. Guerin & A. S. Maier, *Informal assessment in education* (pp. 248–251). Palo Alto, CA: Mayfield.

Mandell, M., & Wood, R. (1974). *Make your own instruments.* New York: Sterling.

Mann, L. (1970). Perceptual training: Misdirections and redirections. *American Journal of Orthopsychiatry, 40*(1), 30–38.

Mann, L. (1979). *On the trail of process: A historical perspective on cognitive processes and their training.* New York: Grune & Stratton.

Mann, P., Sulter, P., & McClung, R. (1979). *Handbook in diagnostic-prescriptive teaching.* Boston: Allyn & Bacon.

Mansdorf, I. J. (1977). Rapid token training of an institution ward using modeling. *Mental Retardation, 15*(2), 37–38.

Manzo, A. V. (1969). ReQuest procedure. *Journal of Reading, 13,* 123–126.

Marquis, M. A. (1985). *Pragmatic-language trivia: A game for promoting effective communication in older children and adolescents.* Tucson, AZ: Communication Skill Builders.

Marston, D., & Magnusson, D. (1985). Implementing curriculum-based measurement in special and regular education settings. *Exceptional Children, 52,* 266–276.

Martin, B. (1983). *Brown bear, brown bear, what do you see?* New York: Scholastic.

Martin, E. W. (1986). Some thoughts on transition: A current appraisal. In L. G. Perlman & G. F. Austin (Eds.), *The transition to work and independence for youth with disabilities* (pp. 107–117). Alexandria, VA: National Rehabilitation Association.

Martin, G., & Pear, J. (1983). *Behavior modification: What it is and how to do it.* Englewood Cliffs, NJ: Prentice-Hall.

Maryland State Department of Education. (1977). *Functional mathematics.* Baltimore: Maryland State Department of Education, Division of Instruction.

Mason, G. E. (1983). The computer in the reading clinic. *The Reading Teacher, 36,* 504–507.

Matson, J. L., DiLorenzo, T. M., & Esveldt-Dawson, K. (1981). Independence training as a method of enhancing self-help skills acquisition of the mentally retarded. *Behavior Research and Therapy, 19,* 399–405.

Matson, J. L., Epstein, M. H., & Cullinan, D. (1984). A factor analytic study of the Quay-Peterson scale with mentally retarded adolescents. *Education and Training of the Mentally Retarded, 19,* 150–154.

May, D. C. (1976). Integration of art education into special education programs. *Art Education, 29*(4), 16–20.

May, J. (1979). Encouraging children's creative oral responses through non-narrative films. *Language Arts, 56,* 244–250.

McBride, J. W., & Forgnone, C. (1985). Emphasis of instruction provided LD, EH, and EMR students in categorical and cross-categorical programming. *Journal of Research and Development in Education, 18*(4), 50–54.

McClure, A. A. (1985). Predictable books: Another way to teach reading to learning disabled children. *Teaching Exceptional Children, 17,* 267–273.

McGee, D. (1979). Using the telephone directory as a learning tool. *Teaching Exceptional Children, 12,* 34–36.

McGinnis, E., Goldstein, A. P., Sprafkin, R. P., & Gershaw, N. J. (1984). *Skill-streaming the elementary school child: A guide for teaching prosocial skills.* Champaign, IL: Research Press.

McIntyre, B. M. (1963). *Informal dramatics: A language arts activity for the special pupil.* Pittsburgh: Stanwix House.

McLaughlin, T. F., Krappman, V. F., & Welsh, J. M. (1985). The effects of self-recording for on-task behavior of behaviorally disordered special education students. *Remedial and Special Education, 6*(4), 42–45.

McLoone, B. B., Scruggs, T. E., Mastropieri, M. A., & Zucker, S. F. (1986). Memory strategy instruction and training with learning disabled adolescents. *Learning Disabilities Re-*

search, 2, 45–53.

McLoughlin, J. A., & Lewis, R. B. (1986). *Assessing special students* (2nd ed.). Columbus, OH: Merrill.

McNeal, B. (1979). *Springboards for writing.* Novato, CA: Academic Therapy.

McNinch, G. H. (1981). A method for teaching sight words to disabled readers. *The Reading Teacher, 34,* 269–272.

McNutt, G., & Mandlebaum, L. H. (1980). General assessment competencies for special education teachers. *Exceptional Education Quarterly, 1*(3), 21–29.

Mecham, M. (1971). *Verbal language development scale.* Circle Pines, MN: American Guidance Service.

Medland, M. B., & Stachnik, T. J. (1972). Good behavior game: A replication and systematic analysis. *Journal of Applied Behavior Analysis, 5,* 45–51.

Meehan, K. A., & Hodell, S. (1986). Measuring the impact of vocational assessment activities upon program decisions. *Career Development for Exceptional Individuals, 9,* 106–112.

Meichenbaum, D. (1980). Cognitive behavior modification with exceptional children: A promise yet unfulfilled. *Exceptional Education Quarterly, 1*(1), 83–88.

Meichenbaum, D. (1983). Teaching thinking: A cognitive-behavioral approach. In *Interdisciplinary voices in learning disabilities and remedial education.* Austin, TX: Pro-Ed.

Memory, D. M., & McGowan, T. M. (1985). Using multilevel textbooks in social studies classes. *The Social Studies, 76,* 174–179.

Merbler, J. B. (1978). A simple method for estimating instructional time. *Education and Training of the Mentally Retarded, 13,* 397–399.

Mercer, C. D. (1979). *Students with learning disabilities* (2nd ed.). Columbus, OH: Merrill.

Mercer, C. D. (1987). *Students with learning disabilities* (3rd ed.). Columbus, OH: Merrill.

Mercer, C. D., Hughes, C., & Mercer, A. R. (1985). Learning disabilities definitions used by state education departments. *Learning Disability Quarterly, 8,* 45–55.

Mercer, C. D., & Mercer, A. R. (1985). *Teaching students with learning problems* (2nd ed.). Columbus, OH: Merrill.

Mercer, C. D., & Payne, J. S. (1975). Learning theories and their implications. In J. M. Kauffman & J. S. Payne (Eds.), *Mental retardation: Introduction and personal perspectives.* Columbus, OH: Merrill.

Mercer, C. D., & Snell, M. E. (1977). *Learning theory in mental retardation: Implications for teaching.* Columbus, OH: Merrill.

Mercer, J. R., & Lewis, J. P. (1977). *System of multicultural pluralistic assessment: Parent interview manual.* New York: Psychological Corporation.

Meredith, P., & Landin, L. (1957). *100 activities for gifted children.* Palo Alto, CA: Fearon.

Merlin, S. B., & Rogers, S. F. (1981). Direct teaching strategies. *The Reading Teacher, 35,* 292–297.

Merrill, P. (1982). The case against Pilot: The pros and cons of computer-assisted instruction languages and authoring systems. *Creative Computing, 8*(7), 70–77.

Meyen, E. L. (1976). *Instructional based appraisal systems (IBAS).* Bellevue, WA: Edmark.

Meyen, E. L., & Lehr, D. H. (1980). Evolving practices in assessment and intervention for mildly handicapped adolescents: The case for intensive instruction. *Exceptional Education Quarterly, 1*(2), 19–26.

Meyen, E. L., Vergason, G. A., & Whelan, R. J. (Eds.). (1983). *Promising practices for exceptional children: Curriculum implications.* Denver: Love.

Meyer, J. A. (1973). Career education game: What's my line? *Teaching Exceptional Children, 6,* 129–130.

Meyerowitz, J. H. (1962). Self-derogations in young retardates and special class placement. *Child Development, 33,* 443–451.

Miccinati, J. (1979). The Fernald technique: Modifications to increase the probability of success. *Journal of Learning Disabilities, 12,* 6–9.

Miller, S. D., & Brand, M. (1983). Music in other cultures in the classroom. *The Social Studies, 74,* 62–64.

Miller, S. E. (in press). Training personnel and procedures for Special Olympics athletes. *Education and Training in Mental Retardation.*

Modolfsky, P. B. (1983). Teaching students to determine the central story problem: A practical application of schema theory. *The Reading Teacher, 36,* 740–745.

Monroe, M. (1973). *Writing our language.* Glenview, IL: Scott, Foresman.

Montgomery, M. D. (1978). The special educator as consultant: Some strategies. *Teaching Exceptional Children, 10,* 110–112.

Mocn, M. S., & Renzaglia, A. (1982). Physical fitness and the mentally retarded: A critical review of the literature. *Journal of Special Education, 16,* 269–287.

Moore, K. (1973). *Note: Suggested activities to motivate the teacher of music.* Culpeper, VA: American Instructional Materials Service.

Moos, R. (1976). *The human context: Environmental determinants of behavior.* New York: John Wiley & Sons.

Moran, M. R. (1983). Analytical evaluation of formal written language skills as a diagnostic procedure. *Diagnostique, 8,* 17–31.

Morgan, S. R. (1986). Locus of control in children labeled learning disabled, behaviorally disordered, and learning disabled/behaviorally disordered. *Learning Disabilities Research, 2,* 10–13.

Morley, J. (1972). *Improving aural comprehension.* Ann Arbor: University of Michigan Press.

Morocco, C., & Neuman, S. (1987). *Teachers, children, and the magical writing machine* (Final Report). Newton, MA: Education Development Center.

Morse, W. C. (1974). In J. M. Kauffman & C. D. Lewis (Eds.), *Teaching children with behavior disorders: Personal perspectives* (pp. 198–216). Columbus, OH: Merrill.

Moses, B. (1983). Individual differences in problem solving. *Arithmetic Teacher, 30*(4), 10–14.

Moyer, S. P. (1982). Repeated reading. *Journal of Learning Disabilities, 15,* 619–623.

Mullins, J., Joseph, F., Turner, C., Zawadski, R., & Saltzman, L. (1972). A handwriting model for children with learning disabilities. *Journal of Learning Disabilities, 5,* 306–311.

Musselwhite, C. R. (1986). Using signs as gestural cues for children with communication impairments. *Teaching Exceptional Children, 18,* 32–35.

Myklebust, H. (1965). *Picture Story Language Test.* Los Angeles: Western Psychological Services.

Nakashima, J. C., & Patton, J. R. (in press). An integrated approach to teaching exceptional learners. *Science and Children.*

National Commission on Excellence in Education. (1983). *A nation at risk.* Washington, DC: U.S. Department of Education.

National Council of Supervisors of Mathematics. (1977). Position paper on basic mathematical skills. *The Arithmetic Teacher, 25,* 19–22.

National Council of Teachers of Mathematics. (1980). *An agenda for action: Recommendations for school mathematics of the 1980's.* Reston, VA: Author.

Nelson, C. M., & Rutherford, R. B. (1983). Timeout revisited: Guidelines for its use in special education. *Exceptional Education Quarterly, 3*(4), 56–67.

Nelson, R. O., Lipinski, D. P., & Boykin, R. A. (1978). The effects of self-recorders' training and the obtrusiveness of the self-recording device on the accuracy and reactivity of self-monitoring. *Behavior Therapy, 9,* 200–208.

Neuman, S., & Morocco, C. (1986). *Two hands is hard for me: Keyboarding and learning disabled children.* Newton, MA: University of Lowell, Education Development Center.

Neville, D. D., & Hoffman, R. R. (1981). The effect of personalized stories on the cloze comprehension of seventh grade retarded readers. *Journal of Reading, 24,* 475–478.

Newcomer, P. L., & Curtis, D. (1984). *Diagnostic Achievement Battery.* Austin, TX: Pro-Ed.

Nibbelink, W. H., & Witzenberg, H. G. (1981). A comparison of two methods for teaching younger children to tell time. *School Science and Mathematics, 81,* 429–435.

Nickell, P., & Kennedy, M. (1987). How to do it: Global perspectives through children's games. *Social Education, 51*(3), 1–8.

Nietupski, J., & Hamre-Nietupski, S. (1986). Self-initiated and sustained leisure activity participation by students with moderate/severe handicaps. *Education and Training of the Mentally Retarded, 21,* 259–264.

Nihira, K., Foster, R., Shellhaas, M., & Leland, H. (1969). *Adaptive behavior scales: Manual.* Washington, DC: American Association on Mental Deficiency.

Nihira, K., Foster, R., Shellhaas, M., & Leland, H. (1974). *AAMD Adaptive Behavior Scale man-*

ual (rev. ed.). Washington, DC: American Association on Mental Deficiency.

Nocera, S. D. (1979). *Reaching the special learner through music.* Morristown, NJ: Silver Burdett.

North Carolina Department of Public Instruction. (n.d.). *Index to adaptive behavior scales.* Raleigh, NC: Author.

Norton, D. E. (1980). *The effective teaching of language arts.* Columbus, OH: Merrill.

Oak Ridge Associated Universities. (1978). *Solar energy* [A packet of science activities]. Oak Ridge, TN: U.S. Department of Energy.

Oakland, T. (1980). Nonbiased assessment of minority group children. *Exceptional Education Quarterly, 1*(3), 31–46.

Oberlin, L. (1982). How to teach children to hate mathematics. *School Science & Mathematics, 82,* 261.

Ochoa, A. S., & Shuster, S. K. (1980). *Social studies in the mainstreamed classroom, K–6.* Boulder, CO: Social Science Education Consortium.

Ochroch, R. (Ed.). (1981). *The diagnosis and treatment of minimal brain dysfunction in children.* New York: Human Sciences Press.

O'Connell, L. (1966). *A study of the influence of creative dramatics on creative reading in the primary grades.* Unpublished master's thesis, University of Hawaii.

Odom, S. L. (1981). The relationship of play to developmental level in mentally retarded children. *Education and Training of the Mentally Retarded, 16,* 136–141.

Okada, K. K. (1987). *Grading special students: Issues, practices, and recommendations.* Unpublished master's paper, University of Hawaii.

O'Leary, K. D., & Drabman, R. (1971). Token reinforcement programs in the classrooms: A review. *Psychological Bulletin, 75,* 379–398.

Oliva, P. F., & Henson, K. T. (1980). What are the essential generic teaching competencies? *Theory into Practice, 19*(2), 117–121.

Oliver, P. R. (1983). Effects of teaching different tasks in group versus individual training formats with severely handicapped individuals. *Journal of the Association for the Severely Handicapped, 8,* 79–91.

Oliver, P. R., & Scott, T. L. (1981). Group versus individual training in establishing generaliza-

tion of language skills with severely handicapped individuals. *Mental Retardation, 19,* 285–289.

Orelove, F. P. (1982). Acquisition of incidental learning in moderately and severely handicapped adults. *Education and Training of the Mentally Retarded, 17,* 131–136.

Orelove, F. P., Wehman, P., & Wood, J. (1982). An evaluative review of Special Olympics: Implications for community integration. *Education and Training for the Mentally Retarded, 17*(4), 325–329.

Orlick, T. (1978). *The cooperative sports and games book.* New York: Pantheon Books.

Orton, J. L. (1964). *A guide to teaching phonics.* Winston-Salem, NC: Orton Reading Center.

Osborn, A. (1963). *Applied imagination: Principles and procedures of creative problem solving.* New York: Charles Scribner's Sons.

Osborn, R., Curlin, L., & Hill, G. (1979). Revision of the NCSS social studies curriculum guidelines. *Social Education, 43,* 261–273.

Osdol, B. M. (1972). Art education for the mentally retarded. *Mental Retardation, 5,* 51–53.

Otto, W., McMenemy, R. A., and Smith, R. J. (1973). *Corrective and remedial teaching.* Boston: Houghton Mifflin.

Owens, S., Fox, B., & Hasselbring, T. (1983). The microcomputer: An investigation of its effectiveness for diagnosing spelling errors. *Diagnostique 8*(3), 170–178.

Oyama, E. (1986). *Curricular integration through a basal reading series.* Unpublished master's paper, University of Hawaii.

Paratore, J. R., & Indrisano, R. (1987). Intervention assessment of reading comprehension. *The Reading Teacher, 40,* 778–783.

Parker, R. M. (1983). *Occupational Aptitude Survey & Interest Schedule.* Austin, TX: Pro-Ed.

Parks, B. J. (1976). Career development—How early? *Elementary School Journal, 76,* 468–474.

Patton, J. R. (1983, October). *Strategies for making academic subject areas career-relevant.* Paper presented at the Fifth International Conference of the Council for Learning Disabilities, San Francisco.

Patton, J. R. (1985). The buzzword is transition. *AAMD Education Division Newsletter, 1*(1), 2.

Patton, J. R. (1988). Science. In G. Robinson, J. R. Patton, E. A. Polloway, & L. R. Sargent (Eds.), *Best practices in mental disabilities* (Vol. 2). Des Moines, IA: Iowa Department of Education, Bureau of Special Education.

Patton, J. R., & Andre, K. E. (1989). Individualization for science and social studies. In J. Wood, *Mainstreaming: A practical approach for teachers.* Columbus, OH: Merrill.

Patton, J. R., & Browder, P. (1988). Transitions into the future. In B. Ludlow, R. Luckasson, & A. Turnbull (Eds.), *Transitions to adult life for persons with mental retardation: Principles and practices.* Baltimore: Paul H. Brookes.

Patton, J. R., & Nakashima, J. K. (1987, April). *Integrated programming for mildly handicapped students.* Paper presented at the 65th Annual Conference of the Council for Exceptional Children, Chicago.

Patton, J. R., Payne, J. S., & Beirne-Smith, M. (1986). *Mental retardation* (2nd ed.). Columbus, OH: Merrill.

Patton, J. R., Payne, J. S., Kauffman, J. M., Brown, G., & Payne, R. A. (1987). *Exceptional children in focus* (4th ed.). Columbus, OH: Merrill.

Patton, J. R., & Polloway, E. P. (1988). Curricular orientations for students with mental disabilities. In G. Robinson, J. R. Patton, E. A. Polloway, & L. R. Sargent (Eds.), *Best practices in mental disabilities* (Vol. 2). Des Moines, IA: Bureau of Special Education, Department of Education, State of Iowa.

Patton, J. R., Polloway, E. A., & Cronin, M. E. (1987). Social studies instruction for handicapped students: A review of current practices. *The Social Studies, 71,* 131–135.

Patton, J. R., Polloway, E. A., & Cronin, M. E. (in press). Science education for mildly handicapped students: A status report. *Science Education.*

Payne, J. S. (1972). Teaching teachers and teaching mind readers. *Phi Delta Kappan, 53,* 375–376.

Payne, J. S., Mercer, C. D., Payne, R. A., & Davison, R. G. (1973). *Head start: A tragicomedy with epilogue.* New York: Behavioral Publications.

Payne, J. S., Polloway, E. A., Kauffman, J. M., & Scranton, T. R. (1975). *Living in the classroom: The currency-based token economy.* New York: Human Sciences Press.

Pearl, R., Bryan, T., & Donahue, M. (1980). Learning disabled children's attributions for success and failure. *Learning Disability Quarterly, 3*(1), 3–9.

Pearson, V. L. (1987). Vocabulary building: Old word retirement. *Teaching Exceptional Children, 19*(2), 77.

Peck, M., & Schultz, M. (1969). *Teaching ideas that make learning fun.* West Nyack, NY: Parker.

Pelham, W. E. (1981). Attention deficits in hyperactive and learning disabled children. *Exceptional Education Quarterly, 2,* 13–23.

Peotter, J. (1979). *Teaching music to special students.* Portland, ME: J. Weston Walch.

Personkee, C., & Yee, A. H. (1966). A model for the analysis of spelling behavior. *Elementary English, 43,* 278–284.

Personkee, C., & Yee, A. H. (1968). The situational choice and the spelling program. *Elementary English, 45,* 32–37, 40.

Peterson, D. L. (1972). *Functional mathematics for the mentally retarded.* Columbus, OH: Merrill.

Phelps-Gunn, T., & Phelps-Terasaki, D. (1982). *Written language instruction: Theory and remediation.* Rockville, MD: Aspen Systems.

Phelps-Terasaki, D., & Phelps, T. (1980). *Teaching written expression: The Phelps sentence guide program.* Norato, CA: Academic Therapy.

Physical activities for impaired, disabled, and handicapped individuals. (1976). Washington, DC: American Alliance for Health, Physical Education, and Recreation.

Pickett, A. L. (1986). *A training program to prepare teachers to supervise and work more effectively with paraprofessional personnel.* New York: City University of New York, National Resource Center for Paraprofessionals.

Piers, E., & Harris, D. (1969). *The Piers-Harris Self-Concept Scale.* Nashville: Counselor Recordings and Tests.

Pinkston, E. M., Reese, N. M., LeBlanc, J. M., & Baer, D. M. (1973). Independent control of a preschool child's aggression and peer interaction by contingent teacher attention. *Journal of Applied Behavior Analysis, 6,* 115–124.

Polloway, C. H., & Polloway, E. A. (1978). Expanding reading skills through syllabication. *Academic Therapy, 13,* 455–462.

Polloway, E. A. (1984). The integration of mildly retarded students in the schools: An historical review. *Exceptional Education Quarterly, 5,* (4), 18–28.

Polloway, E. A. (1985). [Review of *Test of Written Language*]. In J. V. Mitchell (Ed.), *Ninth mental measurements yearbook.* Lincoln, NB: Buros Institute of Mental Measurements.

Polloway, E. A. (1987). Early age transition services for mildly mentally retarded individuals. In R. Stodden & R. Ianacone (Eds.), *Transitional issues and directions for individuals who are mentally retarded* (pp. 11–24). Reston, VA: Council for Exceptional Children, Division on Mental Retardation.

Polloway, E. A., Cronin, M. E., & Patton, J. R. (1986). The efficacy of group instruction v. one-to-one instruction: A review. *Remedial and Special Education, 7*(1), 22–30.

Polloway, E. A., & Decker, T. W. (1988). Written language. In G. Robinson, J. R. Patton, E. A. Polloway, & L. R. Sargent (Eds.), *Best practices in mental disabilities* (Vol. 2). Des Moines: Iowa Department of Education.

Polloway, E. A., Epstein, M. H., & Cullinan, D. (1985). Prevalence of behavior problems among educable mentally retarded students. *Education and Training of the Mentally Retarded, 20,* 3–13.

Polloway, E. A., Epstein, M. H., Polloway, C., Patton, J. R., & Ball, D. W. (1986). Corrective reading program: An analysis of effectiveness with learning disabled and mentally retarded students. *Remedial and Special Education, 7*(4), 41–47.

Polloway, E. A., & Patton, J. R. (1986). Social integration: The goal and the process. *AAMD Education Division Newsletter, 2*(1), 1–2.

Polloway, E. A., & Patton, J. R. (in press). Conceptualizing the identification of learning disabilities: A decision-making model. *Education and Treatment of Children.*

Polloway, E. A., Patton, J. R., & Cohen, S. B. (1981). Written language for the mildly handicapped. *Focus on Exceptional Children, 14*(3), 1–16.

Polloway, E. A., Patton, J. R., & Cohen, S. B. (1983). Written language. In E. L. Meyen,

G. A. Vergason, & R. J. Whelan (Eds.), *Promising practices for exceptional children: Curriculum implications* (pp. 285–320). Denver, CO: Love.

Polloway, E. A., & Polloway, C. H. (1979). Auctions: Vitalizing the token economy. *Journal for Special Educators, 15,* 121–123.

Polloway, E. A., & Polloway, C. H. (1980). Remediating reversals through stimulus fading. *Academic Therapy, 15,* 539–543.

Polloway, E. A., & Polloway, C. H. (1981). Survival words for disabled readers. *Academic Therapy, 16,* 443–448.

Polloway, E. A., & Smith, J. D. (1978). Special Olympics: A second look. *Education and Training of the Mentally Retarded, 13,* 432–433.

Polloway, E. A., & Smith, J. D. (1980a). PL 94-142 and educational placement decisions. *Journal for Special Educators.*

Polloway, E. A., & Smith, J. D. (1980b). Remediation revisited: Response to Chaplin. *Kappa Delta Pi Record, 16,* 127.

Polloway, E. A., & Smith, J. D. (1983). Changes in mild mental retardation: Population, programs, and perspectives. *Exceptional Children, 50,* 149–159.

Polloway, E. A., & Smith, J. D. (in press). Current status of the mild mental retardation construct: Identification, placement, and programs. In M. C. Wang, M. C. Reynolds, & H. J. Walberg (Eds.), *The handbook of special education: Research and practice.* Oxford, England: Pergamon Press.

Polloway, E. A., & Smith, J. E. (1982). *Teaching language skills to exceptional learners.* Denver: Love.

Pope, L. (1970). *Guidelines to teaching remedial reading* (rev. ed.). Brooklyn, NY: Faculty Press.

Poppen, W. A., & Thompson, C. L. (1974). *School counseling: Theories and concepts.* Lincoln, NE: Professional Educators.

Potter, S. (1978). Social studies for students with reading difficulties. *The Social Studies, 69,* 56–64.

Premack, D. (1959). Toward empirical behavior laws: I. Positive reinforcement. *Psychological Review, 66,* 219–233.

Preston, R. C., & Botel, M. (1967). *Study habits checklist.* Chicago: Science Research Associates.

Price, M., & Goodman, L. (1980). Individualized education programs: A cost study. *Exceptional Children, 46*, 446–454.

Price, M., Ness, J., & Stitt, M. (1982). Beyond the three R's: Science and social studies instruction for the mildly handicapped. In T. L. Miller & E. E. Davis (Eds.), *The mildly handicapped student*. New York: Grune & Stratton.

Prutting, C., & Kirchner, D. (1983). Applied pragmatics. In T. M. Gallagher & C. A. Prutting (Eds.), *Pragmatic assessment and intervention issues in language* (pp. 29–64). San Diego: College-Hill Press.

Pyfer, J. (1982). Criteria for placement in physical education experiences. *Exceptional Education Quarterly, 3*(1), 10–16.

Quay, H. C. (1966). *Empirical-experimental approach to the nature and remediation of conduct disorders of children* (ERIC Document Reproduction Service No. ED 021 896).

Ragan, W. B., & Shepherd, G. D. (1971). *Modern elementary curriculum*. New York: Holt, Rinehart & Winston.

Raiche, B. M., Fox, R., & Rotatori, A. F. (1986). Counseling the mildly behaviorally disordered child. In A. F. Rotatori, P. J. Gerber, F. W. Litton, & R. A. Fox (Eds.), *Counseling exceptional students* (pp. 123–143). New York: Human Sciences Press.

Ranieri, L., Ford, A., Vincent, L., & Brown, L. (1984). 1:1 versus 1:3 instruction of severely multihandicapped students. *Remedial and Special Education, 5*(5), 23–28.

Rarick, G. L., & McQuillian, J. P. (1977). *The factor structure of motor abilities of trainable mentally retarded children: Implications for curriculum development*. Berkeley: University of California.

Reber, R., & Sherrill, C. (1981). Creative thinking and dance/movement skills of hearing-impaired youth: An experimental study. *American Annals of the Deaf, 126*, 1004–1009.

Reichard, C., & Gregoire, M. (1984). Music and the exceptional child. In C. V. Morsink (Ed.), *Teaching special needs students · in regular classrooms* (pp. 228–300). Boston: Little, Brown.

Reid, D. K., & Hresko, W. P. (1981). *A cognitive approach to learning disabilities*. New York: McGraw-Hill.

Reisman, F. K., & Kauffman, S. H. (1980). *Teaching mathematics to children with special needs*. Columbus, OH: Merrill.

Reiss, S., Levitan, G. W., & McNally, R. J. (1982). Emotionally disturbed mentally retarded people: An underserved population. *American Psychologist, 37*, 361–367.

Reiter, S. M., Mabee, W. S., & McLaughlin, T. F. (1985). Self-monitoring: Effects for on-task and time to complete assignments. *Remedial and Special Education, 6*(1), 50–51.

Remmers, H. H., & Shimberg, B. (1957). *SRA Junior Inventory: Form S*. Chicago: Science Research Associates.

Repp, A. C. (1983). *Teaching the mentally retarded*. Englewood Cliffs, NJ: Prentice-Hall.

Reschly, D. J. (1982). Assessing mild retardation: The influence of adaptive behavior, sociocultural status, and prospects for nonbiased assessment. In C. R. Reynolds & T. B. Gutkin (Eds.), *A handbook for school psychology*. New York: John Wiley & Sons.

Retzlaff, W. (1973). Career education in practice. *Teaching Exceptional Children, 6*, 134–137.

Reutzel, D. R. (1986). The reading basal: A sentence-combining composing book. *The Reading Teacher, 39*, 194–199.

Reynolds, K. E. (1978). Science space. *California Science Teachers Journal, 8*(4), 8–9.

Richardson, J., Harris, A., & Sparks, O. (1979). *Life science*. Morristown, NJ: Silver Burdett.

Richmond, B. O., & Kicklighter, R. H. (1980). *Children's Adaptive Behavior Scale*. Atlanta: Humanics Press.

Rights, M. (1981). *Beastly neighbors: All about wild things in the city, or why earwigs make good mothers*. Boston: Little, Brown.

Rincover, A., & Koegel, R. L. (1977). Classroom treatment of autistic children: II. Individualized instruction in a group. *Journal of Abnormal Child Psychology, 5*, 113–126.

Ritter, S., & Idol-Maestas, L. (1986). Teaching middle school students to use a test-taking strategy. *Journal of Educational Research, 79*(6), 350–357.

Roach, C., & Kephart, N. (1966). *The Purdue Perceptual-Motor Survey Test*. Columbus, OH:

Merrill.

Robech, M., & Wilson, J. A. (1974). *Psychology of reading: Foundations of instruction.* New York: John Wiley & Sons.

Robinson, N. M., & Robinson, H. B. (1976). *The mentally retarded child* (2nd ed.). New York: McGraw-Hill.

Rogan, L. L., Dadouch, J., & Wennberg, J. (1980). *Cove School reading program.* Allen, TX: Developmental Learning Materials.

Rogers, C. (1951). *Client-centered therapy: Its current practice, implications, and theory.* Cambridge, MA: Riverside Press.

Rogers, C. R. (1980). *A way of being.* Boston: Houghton Mifflin.

Roice, G. R. (Ed.). (1981). *Teaching handicapped students physical education.* Washington, DC: National Education Association (NEA).

Romberg, T. A., & Carpenter, T. P. (1986). In M. C. Wittrock (Ed.), *Handbook of research on teaching* (3rd ed., pp. 850–873). New York: Macmillan.

Rooney, K. (1987). *Learning strategies.* Richmond, VA: Learning Resource Center.

Rooney, K. J., Hallahan, D. P., & Lloyd, J. W. (1984). Self-recording of attention by learning disabled students in the regular classroom. *Journal of Learning Disabilities, 17,* 360–364.

Rooney, K., Polloway, E. A., & Hallahan, D. P. (1985). The use of self-monitoring procedures with low-IQ learning disabled students. *Journal of Learning Disabilities, 18,* 384–390.

Rose, T. L. (1983). A survey of corporal punishment of mildly handicapped students. *Exceptional Education Quarterly, 3*(4), 9–19.

Rosenshine, B., & Stevens, R. (1986). Teaching functions. In M. C. Wittrock (Ed.), *Handbook of research on teaching* (3rd ed., pp. 376–391). New York: Macmillan.

Ross, A. O. (1972). Behavior therapy. In H. C. Quay & J. S. Werry (Eds.), *Psychopathological disorders of childhood.* New York: John Wiley & Sons.

Roswal, G., & Frith, G. H. (1980). The children's developmental play program: Physical activity designed to facilitate the growth and development of mildly handicapped children. *Education and Training of the Mentally Retarded, 15*(4), 322–324.

Rotatori, A. F., Sexton, D., & Fox, R. (1986).

Strategies for changing behaviors. In A. F. Rotatori, P. J. Gerber, F. W. Litton, & R. A. Fox (Eds.), *Counseling exceptional students* (pp. 55–77). New York: Human Sciences Press.

Rothstein, J. H. (1971). *Mental retardation: Readings and resources* (2nd ed.). New York: Holt, Rinehart & Winston.

Rubin, D. (1982). *Diagnosis and correction in reading instruction.* New York: Holt, Rinehart & Winston.

Rubin, D. (1983). *Teaching reading and study skills in content areas.* New York: Holt, Rinehart & Winston.

Rubin, J. A. (1975). Art is for all human beings, especially the handicapped. *Art Education, 28*(8), 5–10.

Rucker, W., & Dilley, C. (1981). *Heath mathematics.* Lexington, MA: Allyn & Bacon.

Rucker, W. E., Dilley, C. A., & Lowry, D. W. (1987). *Heath mathematics: Teacher's edition.* Lexington, MA: D. C. Heath.

Runge, A., Walker, J., & Shea, T. (1975). A passport to positive parent-teacher communications. *Teaching Exceptional Children, 7*(3), 91–92.

Rupley, W. H., & Blair, T. R. (1979). *Reading diagnosis and remediation.* Chicago: Rand McNally.

Russell, S. J. (1986). But what are they learning? The dilemma of using microcomputers in special education. *Learning Disability Quarterly, 9*(2), 100–104.

St. John, P. A. (1986). Art education, therapeutic art, and art therapy: Some relationships. *Art Education, 39*(1), 14–16.

Salend, S. J., Esquivel, L., & Pine, P. B. (1984). Regular and special education teachers' estimates of use of aversive consequences. *Behavioral Disorders, 9,* 89–94.

Salvia, J., & Ysseldyke, J. E. (1985, 1988). *Assessment in special and remedial education.* Boston: Houghton Mifflin.

Samuels, S. J. (1979). The method of repeated readings. *The Reading Teacher, 32,* 403–408.

Santeusanio, R. P. (1983). *A practical approach to content area reading.* Reading, MA: Addison-Wesley.

Saski, J., Swicegood, P., & Carter, J. (1983). Note-taking formats for learning disabled adolescents. *Learning Disability Quarterly, 6*(3), 265–272.

Saul, W., & Newman, A. R. (1986). *Science fare: An illustrated guide & catalog of toys, books, & activities for kids.* New York: Harper & Row.

Savage, J. F., & Mooney, J. F. (1979). *Teaching reading to children with special needs.* Boston: Allyn & Bacon.

Scarmadalia, M., & Bereiter, C. (1986). Research on written composition. In M. C. Wittrock (Ed.), *Handbook of research on teaching* (3rd ed., pp. 778–803). New York: Macmillan.

Schewel, R. H., & Waddell, J. G. (1986). Metacognitive skills: Practical strategies. *Academic Therapy, 22*(1), 19–25.

Schiffman, G., Tobin, D., & Buchanan, B. (1982). Microcomputer instruction for the learning disabled. *Journal of Learning Disabilities, 15,* 557–559.

Schilit, J., & Caldwell, M. L. (1980). A word list of essential career/vocational words for mentally retarded students. *Education and Training of the Mentally Retarded, 15,* 113–117.

Schilling, D., & Cuvo, A. J. (1983). The effects of a contingency-based lottery on the behavior of a special education class. *Education and Training of the Mentally Retarded, 18*(1), 52–58.

Schloss, P. J. (1987). Self-management strategies for adolescents entering the work force. *Teaching Exceptional Children, 19*(4), 39–43.

Schloss, P. J., & Sedlak, R. A. (1986). *Instructional methods for students with learning and behavior problems.* Boston: Allyn & Bacon.

Schminke, C., & Dumas, E. (1981). *Math activities for child involvement.* Boston: Allyn & Bacon.

Schneider, D. O., & Brown, M. J. (1980). Helping students study and comprehend their social studies textbooks. *Social Education, 44,* 105–112.

Schniedewind, N., & Salend, S. (1987). Cooperative learning works. *Teaching Exceptional Children, 19*(2), 22–25.

Schoolfield, L. D., & Timberlake, J. B. (1974). *Phonovisual method book.* Rockville, MD: Phonovisual Products.

Schultz, E. W., & Heuchert, C. M. (1983). *Child stress and the school experience.* New York: Human Services Press.

Schulz, J. B., & Turnbull, A. P. (1983). *Mainstreaming handicapped students* (2nd ed.). Boston: Allyn & Bacon.

Schumaker, J. B., Deshler, D. D., Alley, G. R., & Denton, P. H. (1982). Multipass: A learning strategy for improving comprehension. *Learning Disability Quarterly, 5,* 295–304.

Schumaker, J. B., Deshler, D. D., Nolan, S., Clark, F. L., Alley, G. R., & Warner, M. M. (1981). Error monitoring: A learning strategy for improving academic performance of LD adolescents (Research Report No. 32). Lawrence: University of Kansas Institute for Research on Learning Disabilities.

Scott, K. G., & Scott, M. S. (1968). Research and theory in short-term memory. In N. R. Ellis (Ed.), *International review of research in mental retardation* (Vol. 3). New York: Academic Press.

Scruggs, T. E., & Laufenberg, R. (1986). Transformational mnemonic strategies for retarded learners. *Education and Training of the Mentally Retarded, 21,* 165–173.

Scruggs, T. E., & Mastropieri, M. A. (1986). Improving the test-taking skills of behaviorally disordered and learning disabled children. *Exceptional Children, 53,* 63–68.

Sedlak, R. A., & Fitzmaurice, A. M. (1981). Teaching arithmetic. In J. M. Kauffman & D. P. Hallahan (Eds.), *Handbook of special education.* Englewood Cliffs, NJ: Prentice-Hall.

Seligman, M. E. P. (1975). *Helplessness: On depression, development, and death.* San Francisco: W. H. Freeman.

Semmel, M. I., & Cheney, C. O. (1979). Social acceptance and self-concept of handicapped pupils in mainstreamed environments. *Education Unlimited, 1*(2), 65–68.

Semrau, B. L., LeMay, D. C., Tucker, M. B., Woods, J. N., & Hurtado, T. K. (1979). *The teacher aide is special: A training course for the special education teacher aide.* Jonesboro, AR: Focus.

Sendak, M. (1962). *Chicken soup with rice.* New York: Harper & Row.

Sex Information and Education Council of the United States (SIECUS). (1971). *A resource guide in sex education for the mentally retarded.* Washington, DC: AAHPER.

Shafer, R. E., Staab, C., & Smith, K. (1983). *Language functions and school success.* Glenview,

IL: Scott, Foresman.

Shavelson, R. (1973). What is the basic teaching skill? *Journal of Teacher Education, 24,* 144–151.

Shavelson, R. (1976). Teacher's decision making. In N. L. Gage (Ed.), *The psychology of teaching methods* [Yearbook of the National Society for the Study of Education]. Chicago: University of Chicago Press.

Shepherd, G. D., & Ragan, W. B. (1982). *Modern elementary curriculum* (6th ed.). New York: Holt, Rinehart & Winston.

Sherrill, C. (1976). *Adapted physical education and recreation: A multidisciplinary approach.* Dubuque, IA: Wm. C. Brown.

Sherrill, C. (1982). Adapted physical education: Its role, meaning, and future. *Exceptional Education Quarterly, 3*(1), 1–9.

Sherwin, J. S. (1964). *Four problems in teaching English: A critique of research.* Scranton, PA: International Textbook (for National Council of Teachers of English).

Shiller, P. (1977). *Creative approach to sex education and counseling.* Chicago: Follett.

Siegmund, P. A. (1985). *The role of creative dramatics with the learning disabled student.* Unpublished master's thesis, University of Hawaii.

Silbert, J., Carnine, D., & Stein, M. (1981). *Direct instruction mathematics.* Columbus, OH: Merrill.

Silvaroli, N. J. (1986). *Classroom Reading Inventory.* Dubuque, IA: Wm. C. Brown.

Silverman, R., Zigmond, N., Zimmerman, J. M., & Vallecorsa, A. (1981). Improving written expression in learning disabled students. *Topics in Language Disorders, 1*(2), 91–99.

Simon, S., & O'Rourke, R. (1977). *Developing values with exceptional children.* Englewood Cliffs, NJ: Prentice-Hall.

Singleton, L. R. (1982). Personal communication.

Sink, D. M. (1975). Teach-write/Write-teach. *Elementary English, 52,* 175–177.

Skinner, B. F. (1968). *The technology of teaching.* New York: Appleton-Century-Crofts.

Slavin, R. E. (1980). Cooperative learning. *Review of Educational Research, 50,* 315–342.

Slavin, R. E. (1983). *Cooperative learning.* New York: Longman.

Slavin, R. E. (1984). Team-assisted individualiza-

tion: Cooperative learning and individualized instruction in the mainstreamed classroom. *Remedial and Special Education, 5*(6), 33–42.

Slavin, R., Leavey, M., & Madden, N. (1984). Combining cooperative learning and individualized instruction. *Elementary School Journal, 84,* 410–422.

Slavin, R. E., Madden, N. A., & Leavey, M. (1984). Effects of cooperative learning and individualized instruction on mainstreamed students. *Exceptional Children, 50,* 434–443.

Slingerland, B. H. (1962). *Screening tests for identifying children with specific language disability.* Cambridge, MA: Educators Publishing Services.

Slosson, R. L. (1975). *Slosson Intelligence Test for Children and Adults.* East Aurora, NY: Slosson Educational Publications.

Smith, C. B., & Elliot, P. G. (1979). *Reading activities for middle and secondary schools.* New York: Holt, Rinehart & Winston.

Smith, D. D. (1981). *Teaching the learning disabled.* Englewood Cliffs, NJ: Prentice-Hall.

Smith, F. (1975). The role of prediction in reading. *Elementary English, 52,* 305–311.

Smith, F. (1979). *Reading without nonsense.* New York: Teachers College Press.

Smith, F. (1982). *Writing and the writer.* New York: Holt, Rinehart & Winston.

Smith, J. D., & Dexter, B. L. (1980). The basics movement: What does it mean for the education of mentally retarded students? *Education and Training of the Mentally Retarded, 15,* 72–79.

Smith, J. D., Polloway, E. A., & West, K. G. (1979). Corporal punishment and its implications for exceptional children. *Exceptional Children, 45,* 264–268.

Smith, J. E., & Payne, J. S. (1980). *Teaching exceptional adolescents.* Columbus, OH: Merrill.

Smith, M., & Meyers, A. (1979). Telephone skills training for retarded adults: Group and individual demonstrations with and without verbal instruction. *American Journal of Mental Deficiency, 83,* 581–587.

Smith, R. M. (1974). *Clinical teaching: Methods of instruction for the retarded.* New York: McGraw-Hill.

Smith, R. M., & Neisworth, J. T. (1969). Fundamentals of informal educational assessment.

In R. M. Smith, *Teacher diagnosis of educational difficulties.* Columbus, OH: Merrill.

Smith, W. D. (1978). Minimal competencies: A position paper. *The Arithmetic Teacher, 26*(3), 25–26.

Smoot, S. L. (1985). Exercise programs for mainstreamed handicapped students. *Teaching Exceptional Children, 17*(3), 262–266.

Snell, M. E. (1987). *Systematic instruction of persons with severe handicaps* (3rd ed.). Columbus, OH: Merrill.

Snell, M. E. (n.d.). *The active-response in-service training method.* Unpublished manuscript, Charlottesville, VA.

Snell, M., Thompson, M. S., & Taylor, K. G. (1979). Providing in-service to educators of the severely handicapped: The active-response in-service training model. *Education and Training of the Mentally Retarded, 14,* 25–33.

Snider, V. (1987). Use of self-monitoring of attention with LD students: Research and application. *Learning Disability Quarterly, 10,* 139–151.

Sobel, J. (1983). *Everybody wins: Noncompetitive games for young children.* New York: Walker.

Sorgman, M., Stout-Hensen, S., & Perry, M. L. (1979). "The least restrictive environment": Social studies goals and practices. *The Social Studies, 70,* 108–111.

Sowards, G. W. (1969). The Florida State University model program for the preparation of elementary school teachers. *Journal of Research and Development in Education, 2*(3).

Spache, E. B., & Spache, G. D. (1973). *Reading in the elementary school.* Boston: Allyn & Bacon.

Sparrow, S. S., Balla, D. A., & Cicchetti, D. V. (1984). *Vineland Adaptive Behavior Scales.* Circle Pines, MN: American Guidance Service.

Special fitness test manual for the mentally retarded. (1968). Washington, DC: American Association for Health, Physical Education, and Recreation.

Spekman, N. J., & Roth, F. P. (1984). Intervention strategies for learning disabled children with oral communication disorders. *Learning Disabilities Quarterly, 7,* 7–18.

Spellman, A. (1972). *Change-making kit.* Overland Park, KS: Teach-Um.

Spitz, H. H. (1973). The channel capacity of educable mental retardates. In D. K. Routh (Ed.), *The experimental psychology of mental retardation* (pp. 133–156). Chicago: Aldine.

Spitz, H. H. (1980). [A review of *Cognitive psychology and information processing* by R. Lachman, J. L. Lachman, & E. C. Butterfield], *American Journal of Mental Deficiency, 84,* 641.

Spradlin, J. (1967). Procedures for evaluating processes associated with receptive and expressive language. In R. Schiefelbusch, R. Copeland, & J. O. Smith (Eds.), *Language and mental retardation.* New York: Holt, Rinehart & Winston.

Staats, A. W. (1971). *Child learning, intelligence, and personality.* New York: Harper & Row.

Staats, A. W. (1975). *Social behaviorism.* Homewood, IL: Dorsey Press.

Stainback, W. C., Payne, J. S., Stainback, S. B., & Payne, R. A. (1973). *Establishing a token economy in the classroom.* Columbus, OH: Merrill.

Stainback, W., & Stainback, S. (1984). A rationale for the merger of special and regular education. *Exceptional Children, 51,* 102–111.

Stainback, W., Stainback, S., Courtnage, L., & Jaben, T. (1985). Facilitating mainstreaming by modifying the mainstream. *Exceptional Children, 52,* 144–152.

Stanton, J. E., & Cassidy, V. M. (1964). Effectiveness of special classes for educable mentally retarded. *Mental Retardation, 2*(1), 8–13.

Starms, F. B. (1979). Music is interwoven with life. In *The interdisciplinary use of art, music and literature in habilitation of the young handicapped child.* Madison: Wisconsin State Department of Public Instruction.

Stebbins, L. B., St. Pierre, R. G., Proper, E. C., Anderson, R. B., & Cerva, T. R. (1977). *Education as experimentation: A planned variation model* (Vol. 4-A). Cambridge, MA: Abt Associates.

Stein, J. U. (1977). Physical education, recreation, and sports for special populations. *Education and Training of the Mentally Retarded, 12*(1), 4–13.

Stein, J. U., & Klappholz, L. A. (1972). *Special Olympics instructional manual: From beginners to champions.* Washington, DC: American Alliance for Health, Physical Education, and Recreation.

Stephens, T. M. (1970). *Directive teaching of children with learning and behavioral problems.* Columbus, OH: Merrill.

Sternberg, L., & Fair, G. W. (1983). Mathematics programs and materials. In T. O. Miller & E. E. Davis (Eds.), *The mildly handicapped student.* Austin, TX: Pro-Ed.

Sternberg, L., & Sedlak, R. (1978). Mathematical programming for problem adolescents. In D. Sabatino & A. Mauser (Eds.), *Intervention strategies for specialized secondary education.* Boston: Allyn & Bacon.

Stevens, R., & Rosenshine, B. (1981). Advances in research on teaching. *Exceptional Education Quarterly, 2*(1), 1–9.

Stevenson, H. W. (1972). *Children's learning.* Englewood Cliffs, NJ: Prentice-Hall.

Stevenson, H. W., & Zigler, E. (1958). Probability learning in children. *Journal of Experimental Psychology, 56,* 185–192.

Steward, K. L. (1975). *Three stages of sexuality.* Unpublished manuscript, University of Virginia, Charlottesville.

Stewart, C. A., & Sirgh, N. B. (1986). Overcorrection of spelling deficits in moderately mentally retarded children. *Behavior Modification, 10,* 355–363.

Stodden, R. A., & Boone, R. (1987). Assessing transition services for handicapped youth: A cooperative interagency approach. *Exceptional Children, 53,* 537–545.

Storm, R. H., & Willis, J. H. (1978). Small group training as an alternative to individual programs for profoundly retarded persons. *American Journal of Mental Deficiency, 83,* 283–288.

Strong, W. (1973). *Sentence combining: A composing book.* New York: Random House.

Strong, W. (1983). *Sentence combining: A composing book* (2nd ed.). New York: Random House.

Suhor, C. (1979). Goals of career education and goals of subject-area instruction: A model. *Journal of Career Education, 5,* 215–219.

Sund, R., Tillery, B., & Trowbridge, L. (1970). *Elementary science discovery lessons: The earth sciences.* Boston: Allyn & Bacon.

Superka, D. P., Hawke, S., & Morrissett, I. (1980).

The current and future status of the social studies. *Social Education, 44,* 362–369.

Swanson, H. L. (1982). Strategies and constraints—A commentary. *Topics in Learning and Learning Disabilities, 2,* 79–81.

Swanson, H. L., & Watson, B. L. (1982). *Educational and psychological assessment of exceptional children: Theories, strategies, and applications.* Columbus, OH: Merrill.

Swift, J. L. (1986). Did your students ever hug a tree? *Arts and Activities, 100*(2), 54–55.

Tamura, E. H., & Harstad, J. R. (1987). Freewriting in the social studies classroom. *Social Education, 51,* 256–259.

Tarver, S. G. (1981). Underselective attention in learning disabled children: Some reconceptualizations of old hypotheses. *Exceptional Education Quarterly, 2*(3), 25–36.

Taunton, M. (1983). Questioning strategies to encourage children to talk about art. *Art Education, 36,* 40–43.

Taylor, F., Artuso, A. A., Hewett, F. M., Johnson, A., Kramer, G., & Clark, K. (1972). *Individualized reading instruction: Games and activities.* Denver, CO: Love.

Taylor, R. L. (1984). *Assessment of exceptional students: Educational and psychological procedures.* Englewood Cliffs, NJ: Prentice-Hall.

Teters, P., Gabel, D., & Geary, P. (1984). Elementary teachers' perspectives on improving science education. *Science and Children, 22*(3), 41–43.

Thistle, L. (1987). Make a story come alive: Dramatize. *Arts and Activities, 101*(5), 24–28.

Thomas, C. C., Englert, C. S., & Gregg, S. (1987). An analysis of errors and strategies in the expository writing of learning disabled students. *Remedial and Special Education, 8*(1), 21–30.

Thomas, E. L., & Robinson, H. A. (1972). *Improving reading in every class.* Boston: Allyn & Bacon.

Thompson, D. G. (1977). *Writing long-term and short-term objectives: A painless approach.* Champaign, IL: Research Press.

Thompson, K. (1982). Music for every child: Education of handicapped learners. *Music Educators Journal, 68*(8), 25–28.

Thompson, K. P., et al., (Eds.). (1980). *In tune with PL 94-142: A guide for training teachers responsible for music education of handicapped learners.* Reston, VA: Music Educators National Conference.

Thorne, M. T. (1978). "Payment for reading": The use of the "corrective reading scheme" with junior maladjusted boys. *Remedial Education, 13,*(2), 87–90.

Thorpe, L. P., Clark, W. W., & Tiegs, E. W. (1953). *California Test of Personality.* Monterey, CA: California Test Bureau.

Thurber, D. N., & Jordan, D. R. (1978). *D'Nealian handwriting.* Glenview, IL: Scott, Foresman.

Thurlow, M. L., Ysseldyke, J. E., Graden, J. L., & Algozzine, B. (1983). What's "special" about special education resource rooms for learning disabled students? *Learning Disability Quarterly, 6,* 283–288.

Tiedt, S., & Tiedt, I. (1978). *Language arts activities for the classroom.* Boston: Allyn & Bacon.

Tiegs, E. W., & Clark, W. W. (1970). *California Achievement Test.* Monterey, CA: CTB/McGraw-Hill.

Tikunoff, W. J. (1982). *An emerging description of successful bilingual instruction: An executive summary of Part I of SBIF descriptive study* (Contract No. 400-80-0026). Washington, DC: National Institute of Education.

Tindall, S. K. (1985). *Adaptation of a basic math text for special learners.* Unpublished master's paper, University of Hawaii.

Tonjes, M. J., & Zintz, M. V. (1981). *Teaching reading/thinking/study skills in content classrooms.* Dubuque, IA: Wm. C. Brown.

Torgesen, J. K. (1982). The learning disabled child as an inactive learner: Educational implications. *Topics in Learning and Learning Disabilities, 2*(1), 45–51.

Torgesen, J. K. (1984). Instructional uses of microcomputers with elementary-aged mildly handicapped children. *Specialized Services in the Schools, 1*(1), 37–48.

Torgesen, J. (1986). Computer-assisted instruction with learning disabled children. In J. Torgesen & B. Wong (Eds.), *Psychological and educational perspectives on learning disabilities* (pp. 417–435). Orlando, FL: Academic Press.

Torgesen, J. K., & Greenstein, J. J. (1982). Why do some learning disabled children have problems remembering? Does it make a difference? *Topics in Learning and Learning Disabilities, 2,* 54–61.

Tunn, S., & Van Kleeck, A. (1986). The quality of a language sample as a function of its placement in an assessment battery. *Journal of Childhood Communication Disorders, 9,* 125–132.

Turla, P. A., & Hawkins, K. L. (1983). *Time management made easy.* New York: E. P. Dutton.

Turnbull, A. (1988, January). *Accepting the challenge of providing comprehensive support to families.* Paper presented at CEC-MR conference, Honolulu.

Turnbull, A. P., & Schulz, J. B. (1979). *Mainstreaming handicapped students: A guide for the classroom teacher.* Boston: Allyn & Bacon.

Turnbull, A. P., & Turnbull, H. R. (1986). *Families, professionals, and exceptionality.* Columbus, OH: Merrill.

Turner, T. N. (1976). Making the social studies textbook a more effective tool for less able readers. *Social Education, 40,* 38–41.

Turnure, J., & Zigler, E. (1964). Outer-directedness in the problem solving of normal and retarded children. *Journal of Abnormal and Social Psychology, 69,* 427–436.

Tway, E. (1975). Creative writing: From gimmick to goal. *Elementary English, 52,* 173–174.

Tyler, R. (1950). *Basic principles of curriculum and instruction.* Chicago: University of Chicago Press.

Tyo, J. (1980). An alternative for poor readers in social science. *Social Education, 44,* 309–310.

United States Department of Education. (1986). *The reading report card.* Washington, DC: Author.

Vacc, N. (1987). Word processor versus handwriting: A comparative study of writing samples produced by mildly mentally handicapped students. *Exceptional Children, 54*(2), 156–165.

Vandever, T. R. (1983). Comparison of suspensions of EMR and nonretarded students. *American Journal of Mental Deficiency, 87*(4), 430–434.

VanJura, W. J. (1982). The role of questioning in developing reading comprehension in the social studies. *Journal of Reading, 26*, 214–216.

Vasa, S. F., Steckelberg, A. L., & Ronning, L. (1983). *Guide for effective utilization of paraprofessionals in special education.* Lincoln: University of Nebraska at Lincoln.

Vergason, G. A. (1983). Curriculum content. In E. L. Meyen, G. A. Vergason, & R. J. Whelan (Eds.), *Promising practices for exceptional children: Curriculum implications.* Denver: Love.

Verriour, P. (1984). The reflective power of drama. *Language Arts, 61*, 125–130.

Wagener, E. H. (1977). Drama: Key to history for the visually impaired child. *Education of the Visually Handicapped, 9*, 45–47.

Walker, H. M. (1983). Applications of response cost in school settings: Outcomes, issues, and recommendations. *Exceptional Education Quarterly, 3*(4), 47–55.

Walker, H. M., McConnel, S., Holmes, D., Todis, B., Walker, J., & Golden, N. (1983). *The Walker social skills curriculum: The ACCEPTS program.* Austin, TX: Pro-Ed.

Walker, J. E., & Shea, T. M. (1984). *Behavior management: A practical approach for educators* (3rd ed.). Columbus, OH: Merrill.

Walker-Taylor, S. (1986). Kids teach kids. *Arts and Activities, 99*, 56–57.

Wallace, G., Cohen, S. B., & Polloway, E. A. (1987). *Language arts: Teaching exceptional students.* Austin, TX: Pro-Ed.

Wallace, G., & Kauffman, J. M. (1973, 1978, 1986). *Teaching children with learning problems.* Columbus, OH: Merrill.

Wallace, G., & Larsen, S. C. (1978). *Educational assessment of learning problems.: Testing for teaching.* Boston: Allyn & Bacon.

Walsh, B. F., & Lamberts, F. (1979). Errorless discrimination and picture fading as techniques for teaching sight words to TMR students. *American Journal of Mental Deficiency, 83*, 473–479.

Walton, W. (1986). Educators' responses to methods of collecting, storing, and analyzing behavioral data. *Journal of Special Education Technology, 7*(1), 50–55.

Wang, M. C. (1980). Adaptive instruction: Building on diversity. *Theory into Practice, 19*, 122–128.

Wang, M., & Birch, J. (1984). Comparison of full-time mainstreaming program and a resource room approach. *Exceptional Children, 51*, 33–40.

Webber, M. (1981). *Communication skills for exceptional learners.* Rockville, MD: Aspen.

Webster, G. E. (1987). Influence of peer tutors upon academic learning time—Physical education of mentally handicapped students. *Journal of Teaching in Physical Education, 6*, 393–403.

Wehman, P., & McLaughlin, P. J. (1981). *Program development in special education.* New York: McGraw-Hill.

Wehman, P., Renzaglia, A., & Bates, P. (1985). *Functional living skills for moderately and severely handicapped individuals.* Austin, TX: Pro-Ed.

Weinrich, B., Glaser, J., & Johnston, E. (1986). *A sourcebook of adolescent pragmatic activities.* Tucson, AZ: Communication Skill Builders.

Weinstein, R. S. (1983). Student perceptions of schooling. *Elementary School Journal, 83*, 287–312.

Weinstein, R. S., & Mayer, B. (1986). Learning strategies. In M. C. Wittrock (Ed.), *Handbook of research in teaching* (3rd ed.). New York: Macmillan.

Weir, S., Russell, S. J., & Valente, J. (1982). LOGO: An approach to educating disabled children. *Byte, 7*(9), 342–360.

Weir, S., & Watt, D. (1981). LOGO: A computer environment for learning disabled students. *Computing Teacher, 8*(5), 11–17.

Weisenfeld, R. B. (1986). The IEPs of Down syndrome children: A content analysis. *Education and Training of the Mentally Retarded, 21*, 211–219.

Weitzman, D. (1975). *My backyard history book.* Boston: Little, Brown.

Welch, E. A. (1966). The effects of segregated and partially integrated school programs on self-concept and academic achievement of educable mental retardates. *Dissertation Abstracts, 26*, 5533–5534.

Weller, C., & Strawser, S. (1981). *Weller-Strawser Scales of Adaptive Behavior.* Novato, CA: Academic Therapy Press.

Wepman, J. M. (1973). *Auditory Discrimination*

Test. Chicago: Language Research.

Wepman, J. M., & Morency, A. (1973a). *Auditory memory span.* Chicago: Language Research.

Wepman, J. M., & Morency, A. (1973b). *Auditory Sequential Memory Test.* Chicago: Language Research.

Wesson, C., King, R., & Deno, S. (1984). Facilitating the efficiency of ongoing curriculum-based measurement. *Teacher Education and Special Education, 9,* 166–172.

West, G. K. (1986). *Parenting without guilt.* Springfield, IL: Charles C Thomas.

West, R., Young, R., & Johnson, J. (1984). *Using microcomputers to summarize and analyze outcome-based education.* Unpublished manuscript, Utah State University.

Westling, D. L., Ferrell, K., & Swenson, K. (1982). Intraclassroom comparison of two arrangements for teaching profoundly mentally retarded children. *American Journal of Mental Deficiency, 86,* 601–608.

Westling, D. L, & Koorland, M. A. (1979). Some considerations and tactics for improving discrimination learning. *Teaching Exceptional Children, 11*(3), 97–100.

White, R. M. (1975). *Hi there, young lady: A handbook for parents and teachers of trainable girls.* Pittsburgh, PA: Allegheny Intermediate Unit 3.

Wiederholt, J. L., & Bryant, B. (1986). *Gray Oral Reading Test.* Austin, TX: Pro-Ed.

Wiederholt, J. L., Hammill, D. D., & Brown, V. L. (1983). *The resource teacher: A guide to effective practices* (2nd ed.). Austin, TX: Pro-Ed.

Wiederholt, J. L., & Larsen, S. C. (1983). *Test of Practical Knowledge.* Austin, TX: Pro-Ed.

Wiederholt, J. L., & McNutt, G. (1979). Assessment and instructional planning: A conceptual framework. In D. Cullinan & M. H. Epstein (Eds.), *Special education for adolescents: Issues and perspectives* (pp. 63–87). Columbus, OH: Merrill.

Wielkiewitcz, R. M. (1986). *Behavior management in the schools: Principles and practices.* New York: Pergamon Press.

Wiener, H. (1981). *The writing room.* New York: Oxford University Press.

Wiig, E. H., & Semel, E. M. (1980). *Clinical evaluation of language functions.* New York: Psychological Corporation.

Will, M. (1984). *OSERS programming for the transition of youth with disabilities: Bridges from school to working life.* Washington, DC: Office of Special Education and Rehabilitative Services.

Williams, R. M., & Rooney, K. J. (1986). *A handbook of cognitive behavior modification procedures for teachers.* Charlottesville, VA: University of Virginia Institute for Research on Learning Disabilities.

Wilson, C. R. (1983). Teaching reading comprehension by connecting the known to the new. *The Reading Teacher, 36,* 382–390.

Wilson, G. T. (1984). Behavior therapy in counseling psychotherapies. In R. Corsini (Ed.), *Current psychotherapies.* Itasca, IL: F. E. Peacock.

Winton, P. (1986). Effective strategies for involving families in intervention efforts. *Focus on Exceptional Children, 19* (2), 1–10.

Winschel, J. F., & Ensher, G. L. (1978). Educability revisited: Curricular implications for the mentally retarded. *Education and Training of the Mentally Retarded, 13,* 131–138.

Wish, J. R., McCombs, K. F., & Edmonson, B. (1980). *The Socio-Sexual Knowledge and Attitude Test.* Chicago: Stoelting.

Witt, B., & Boose, J. (1986). *TOTAL: Teacher-organized training for acquisition of language.* Tucson, AZ: Communication Skill Builders.

Wong, B. Y. L. (1982). Understanding learning disabled students' reading problems: Contributions from cognitive psychology. *Topics in Learning and Learning Disabilities, 1*(4), 43–50.

Wong, B. L., & Jones, W. (1982). Increasing metacomprehension in learning disabled and normally achieving students through self-questioning training. *Learning Disability Quarterly, 5,* 228–240.

Wood, J. (1989). *Mainstreaming: A practical approach for teachers.* Columbus, OH: Merrill.

Wood, K. D., & Mateja, J. A. (1983). Adapting secondary level strategies for use in elementary school. *The Reading Teacher, 36,* 492–496.

Wood, N. F. (1969). *Verbal learning.* San Rafael, CA: Dimensions.

Woodcock, R. W. (1986). *Woodcock Reading Mastery Test.* Circle Pines, MN: American Guidance Service.

Woodward, A., Elliott, D. L., & Nagel, K. C.

(1986). Beyond textbooks in elementary social studies. *Social Education, 50,* 50–53.

Woodward, J., Carnine, D., & Collins, M. T. (1986). *Closing the performance gap in secondary education.* Unpublished manuscript, University of Oregon.

Worell, J., & Nelson, C. M. (1974). *Managing instructional problems: A case study workbook.* New York: McGraw-Hill.

Workman, A. E. (1982). *Teaching behavioral self-control to students.* Austin, TX: Pro-Ed.

Wright, J., & Cowden, J. E. (1986). Changes in self-concept and cardiovascular endurance of mentally retarded youths in a Special Olympics swim training program. *Adaptive Physical Activity Quarterly, 3,* 177–183.

Wulpe, W. W. (1968). A form constancy technique for spelling proficiency. In J. I. Arena (Ed.), *Building spelling skills in dyslexic children.* San Rafael, CA: Academic Therapy.

Ysseldyke, J. E., & Christenson, S. L. (1986). *The Instructional Environment Scale.* Austin, TX: Pro-Ed.

Ysseldyke, J. E., & Christenson, S. L. (1987). Evaluating students' instructional environments. *Remedial and Special Education, 8*(3), 17–24.

Zeaman, D., & House, B. J. (1963). The role of attention in retarded discrimination learning. In N. R. Ellis (Ed.), *Handbook of mental deficiency.* New York: McGraw-Hill.

Zentall, S. (1983). Learning environments: A review of physical and temporal factors. *Exceptional Education Quarterly, 4*(2), 90–109.

Zigler, E. (1966). Research on personality structure in the retardate. In N. R. Ellis (Ed.), *International review of mental retardation* (Vol. 1). New York: Academic Press.

Zigler, E. (1973). The retarded child as a whole person. In D. K. Routh (Ed.), *The experimental psychology of mental retardation.* Chicago: Aldine.

Zigmond, N., & Brownlee, J. (1980). Social skills training for adolescents with learning disabilities. *Exceptional Education Quarterly, 1*(2), 77–84.

Zigmond, N., & Sansone, J. (1986). Designing a program for the learning disabled adolescent. *Remedial and Special Education, 7*(5), 13–17.

Zigmond, N., Vallecorsa, A., & Leinhardt, G. (1980). Reading instruction for students with learning disabilities. *Topics in Language Disorders, 1*(1), 89–98.

Zigmond, N., Vallecorsa, A., & Silverman, R. (1983). *Assessment for instructional planning in special education.* Englewood Cliffs, NJ: Prentice-Hall.

Zimmerman, I. L, Steiner, V. G., & Evatt, R. L. (1979). *Preschool Language Scale* (2nd ed.). Columbus, OH: Merrill.

AUTHOR
INDEX

SUBJECT INDEX

WE VALUE YOUR OPINION—PLEASE SHARE IT WITH US

Merrill Publishing and our authors are most interested in your reactions to this textbook. Did it serve you well in the course? If it did, what aspects of the text were most helpful? If not, what didn't you like about it? Your comments will help us to write and develop better textbooks. We value your opinions and thank you for your help.

Text Title _____ Edition _____

Author(s) _____

Your Name (optional) _____

Address _____

City _____ State _____ Zip _____

School _____

Course Title _____

Instructor's Name _____

Your Major _____

Your Class Rank _____ Freshman _____ Sophomore _____ Junior _____ Senior

_____ Graduate Student

Were you required to take this course? _____ Required _____ Elective

Length of Course? _____ Quarter _____ Semester

1. Overall, how does this text compare to other texts you've used?

    _____ Superior _____ Better Than Most _____ Average _____ Poor

2. Please rate the text in the following areas:

	Superior	Better Than Most	Average	Poor
Author's Writing Style	_____	_____	_____	_____
Readability	_____	_____	_____	_____
Organization	_____	_____	_____	_____
Accuracy	_____	_____	_____	_____
Layout and Design	_____	_____	_____	_____
Illustrations/Photos/Tables	_____	_____	_____	_____
Examples	_____	_____	_____	_____
Problems/Exercises	_____	_____	_____	_____
Topic Selection	_____	_____	_____	_____
Currentness of Coverage	_____	_____	_____	_____
Explanation of Difficult Concepts	_____	_____	_____	_____
Match-up with Course Coverage	_____	_____	_____	_____
Applications to Real Life	_____	_____	_____	_____

3. Circle those chapters you especially liked:

1   2   3   4   5   6   7   8   9   10   11   12   13   14   15   16   17   18   19   20

What was your favorite chapter? _____

Comments:

4. Circle those chapters you liked least:

1   2   3   4   5   6   7   8   9   10   11   12   13   14   15   16   17   18   19   20

What was your least favorite chapter? _____

Comments:

5. List any chapters your instructor did not assign. _____

6. What topics did your instructor discuss that were not covered in the text?_____

_____

7. Were you required to buy this book? _____ Yes _____ No

Did you buy this book new or used? _____ New _____ Used

If used, how much did you pay? _____

Do you plan to keep or sell this book? _____ Keep _____ Sell

If you plan to sell the book, how much do you expect to receive? _____

Should the instructor continue to assign this book? _____ Yes _____ No

8. Please list any other learning materials you purchased to help you in this course (e.g., study guide, lab manual).

_____

9. What did you like most about this text? _____

_____

10. What did you like least about this text? _____

_____

11. General comments:

May we quote you in our advertising? _____ Yes _____ No

Please mail to: Boyd Lane
                  College Division, Research Department
                  Box 508
                  1300 Alum Creek Drive
                  Columbus, Ohio 43216

Thank you!